Introduction to 3D Game Programming with DirectX® 10

Introduction to 3D Game Programming with DirectX® 10

Frank D. Luna

Wordware Publishing, Inc.

Library of Congress Cataloging-in-Publication Data

Luna, Frank D.
  Introduction to 3D game programming with DirectX 10 / by Frank D. Luna.
    p. cm.
  Includes bibliographical references and index.
  ISBN-13: 978-1-59822-053-7 (pbk.)
  ISBN-10: 1-59822-053-5 (pbk.)
  1. Computer games—Programming. 2. DirectX. 3. Three-dimensional display systems.
  I. Title.
  QA76.76.C672L834 2008
  794.8'1536—dc22   2008025034

1100 Summit Avenue, Suite 102
Plano, Texas 75074

ISBN-13: 978-1-59822-053-7
ISBN-10: 1-59822-053-5

10 9 8 7 6 5 4 3 2 1
0806

All inquiries for volume purchases of this book should be addressed to Wordware Publishing, Inc., at the above address. Telephone inquiries may be made by calling:

(972) 423-0090

To my parents, Frank and Kathryn

Contents

Part I — Mathematical Prerequisites

Contents

Part II — Direct3D Foundations

Part III — Direct3D Topics

Appendices

Acknowledgments

I would like to thank Rod Lopez, Jim Leiterman, Hanley Leung, Rick Falck, Tybon Wu, Tuomas Sandroos, and Eric Sandegren for putting in the time to review this book for both accuracy and improvements. I want to thank Tyler Drinkard for building some of the 3D models and textures used in the demo programs of this book. I also want to thank Dale E. La Force, Adam Hault, Gary Simmons, James Lambers, and William Chin for their assistance. Lastly, I want to thank the staff at Wordware Publishing, in particular, Tim McEvoy, Beth Kohler, Martha McCuller, and Denise McEvoy, and cover designer Alan McCuller.

Introduction

This book presents an introduction to programming interactive computer graphics, with an emphasis on game development, using Direct3D 10. It teaches the fundamentals of Direct3D and shader programming, after which the reader will be prepared to go on and learn more advanced techniques. The book is divided into three main parts. Part I explains the mathematical tools that will be used throughout this book. Part II shows how to implement fundamental tasks in Direct3D, such as initialization, defining 3D geometry, setting up cameras, creating vertex, pixel, and geometry shaders, lighting, texturing, blending, and stenciling. Part III is largely about applying Direct3D to implement a variety of interesting techniques and special effects, such as working with meshes, terrain rendering, picking, particle systems, environment mapping, normal mapping, shadows, and rendering to textures.

For the beginner, this book is best read front to back. The chapters have been organized so that the difficulty increases progressively with each chapter. In this way, there are no sudden jumps in complexity that leave the reader lost. In general, for a particular chapter, we will use the techniques and concepts previously developed. Therefore, it is important that you have mastered the material of a chapter before continuing. Experienced programmers can pick the chapters of interest.

Finally, you may be wondering what kinds of games you can create after reading this book. The answer to that question is best obtained by skimming through this book and seeing the types of applications that are developed. From that you should be able to visualize the types of games that can be developed based on the techniques taught in this book and some of your own ingenuity.

Intended Audience

This book was designed with the following three audiences in mind:

- Intermediate level C++ programmers who would like an introduction to 3D programming using the latest iteration of Direct3D.
- 3D programmers experienced with an API other than DirectX (e.g., OpenGL) who would like an introduction to Direct3D 10.
- Experienced Direct3D 9 programmers wishing to learn the latest iteration of Direct3D.

Prerequisites

It should be emphasized that this is an introduction to Direct3D 10, shader programming, and game programming; it is *not* an introduction to general computer programming. The reader should satisfy the following prerequisites:

- An understanding of high school mathematics: algebra, trigonometry, and (mathematical) functions, for example.
- Competency with Visual Studio: should know how to create projects, add files, and specify external libraries to link, for example.
- Intermediate C++ and data structure skills: comfortable with pointers, arrays, operator overloading, linked lists, inheritance, and polymorphism, for example.
- Familiarity with Windows programming with the Win32 API is helpful, but not required; we provide a Win32 primer in Appendix A.

Required Development Tools and Hardware

To program Direct3D 10 applications, you will need the DirectX 10 SDK; the latest version can be downloaded from http://msdn2.microsoft.com/en-us/xna/aa937788.aspx. Once downloaded, follow the instructions given by the installation wizard.

As of the March 2008 DirectX SDK release, the SDK will only officially support versions of Visual Studio 2005 and Visual Studio 2008.

Direct3D 10 requires Direct3D 10-capable hardware. The demos in this book were tested on a GeForce 8800 GTS.

 Online: Step-by-step instructions for setting up a Direct3D 10 project in Visual Studio .NET 2005 and Visual Studio .NET 2008 are provided on this book's website (www.d3dcoder.net) and the publisher's website (www.wordware.com/files/0535dx10).

Use of the D3DX Library

Since version 7.0, DirectX has shipped with the D3DX (Direct3D Extension) library. This library provides a set of functions, classes, and interfaces that simplify common 3D graphics-related operations, such as math operations, texture and image operations, mesh operations, and shader operations (e.g., compiling and assembling). That is to say, D3DX contains many features that would be a chore to implement on your own.

We use the D3DX library throughout this book because it allows us to focus on more interesting material. For instance, we would rather not spend pages explaining how to load various image formats (such as BMPs and JPEGs) into a Direct3D texture interface when we can do it in a single call to the D3DX function D3DX10CreateTextureFromFile. In other words, D3DX makes us more productive and lets us focus more on actual content rather than spending time reinventing the wheel.

Other reasons to use D3DX:

- D3DX is general and can be used with a wide range of different types of 3D applications.
- D3DX is fast, at least as fast as general functionality can be.
- Other developers use D3DX; therefore, you will most likely encounter code that uses D3DX. Consequently, whether you choose to use D3DX or not, you should become familiar with it so that you can read code that uses it.
- D3DX already exists and has been thoroughly tested. Furthermore, it becomes more improved and feature rich with each iteration of DirectX.

Using the DirectX SDK Documentation and SDK Samples

Direct3D is a huge API and we cannot hope to cover all of its details in this one book. Therefore, to obtain extended information it is imperative that you learn how to use the DirectX SDK documentation. You can launch the C++ DirectX online documentation by executing the *directx_sdk.chm* file in the *DirectX SDK\Documentation\DirectX10* directory, where *DirectX SDK* is the directory to which you installed DirectX. In particular, you will want to navigate to the Direct3D 10 section (see Figure 1).

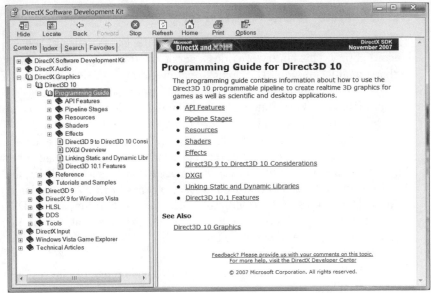

Figure 1: The Direct3D Programming Guide in the DirectX documentation.

The DirectX documentation covers just about every part of the DirectX API; therefore it is very useful as a reference, but because the documentation doesn't go into much depth, or assumes some previous knowledge, it isn't the best learning tool. However, it does get better and better with every new DirectX version released.

As said, the documentation is primarily useful as a reference. Suppose you come across a DirectX-related type or function, such as the function D3DXMatrixInverse, for which you would like more information. You simply do a search in the documentation index and you get a description of the object type or, in this case, function, as shown in Figure 2.

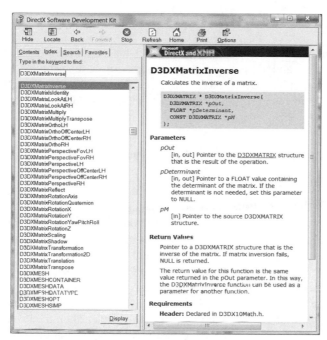

Figure 2:
Index of the DirectX
documentation.

Note: In this book we may direct you to the documentation for
further details from time to time.

The SDK documentation also contains some introductory tutorials at the
URL */directx_sdk.chm::/d3d10_graphics_tutorials.htm* (or just type "tutorial"
in the index search). These tutorials roughly correspond to some of the topics in the first part of this book. We recommend that you study these
tutorials at the same time you read through the first part of this book so
that you can get alternative explanations and examples.

We would also like to point out the available Direct3D sample programs
that ship with the DirectX SDK. The C++ Direct3D samples are located in
the *DirectX SDK\Samples\C++\Direct3D10* directory. Each sample illustrates how to implement a particular effect in Direct3D. These samples are
fairly advanced for a beginning graphics programmer, but by the end of this
book you should be ready to study them. Examination of the samples is a
good "next step" after finishing this book.

Clarity

We want to emphasize that the program samples for this book were written with clarity in mind and not performance. Thus, many of the samples may be implemented inefficiently. Keep this in mind if you are using any of the sample code in your own projects, as you may wish to rework it for better efficiency.

Sample Programs and Online Supplements

The website for this book (www.d3dcoder.net) plays an integral part in getting the most out of this book. On the website you will find the complete source code and project files for every sample in this book. In many cases, DirectX programs are too large to fully embed in a textbook; therefore, we only embed relevant code fragments based on the ideas being shown. It is highly recommended that the reader study the corresponding demo code to see the program in its entirety. (We have aimed to make the demos small and focused for easy study.) As a general rule, the reader should be able to implement a chapter's demo(s) on his or her own after reading the chapter and spending some time studying the demo code. In fact, a good exercise is trying to implement the samples on your own using the book and sample code as a reference.

In addition to sample programs, the website also contains a message board. We encourage readers to communicate with each other and post questions on topics they do not understand or need clarification on. In many cases, getting alternative perspectives and explanations to a concept shortens the time it takes to comprehend it.

And lastly, additional program samples and tutorials may be added to the website on topics that we could not fit into this book for one reason or another.

Part I

Mathematical Prerequisites

Video games attempt to simulate a virtual world; however, computers, by their very nature, crunch numbers. Thus the problem of how to convey a world to a computer arises. The answer is to describe our worlds, and the interactions therein, completely mathematically. Consequently, mathematics plays a fundamental role in video game development.

In this prerequisites part, we introduce the mathematical tools that will be used throughout this book. The emphasis is on vectors, coordinate systems, matrices, and transformations, as these tools are used in just about every sample program of this book. In addition to the mathematical explanations, a survey and demonstration of the relevant classes and functions from the D3DX math library are provided.

Note that the topics covered here are only those essential to understanding the rest of this book; it is by no means a comprehensive treatment of video game mathematics, as entire books are devoted to this topic. For readers desiring a more complete reference to video game mathematics, we recommend [Verth04] and [Lengyel02].

Chapter 1, "Vector Algebra"

Vectors are, perhaps, the most fundamental mathematical objects used in computer games. We use vectors to represent positions, displacements, directions, velocities, and forces, for example. In this chapter, we study vectors and the operations used to manipulate them.

1

Chapter 2, "Matrix Algebra"

Matrices provide an efficient and compact way of representing transformations. In this chapter, we become familiar with matrices and the operations defined on them.

Chapter 3, "Transformations"

This chapter examines three fundamental geometric transformations: scaling, rotation, and translation. We use these transformations to manipulate 3D objects in space. In addition, we explain change of coordinate transformations, which are used to transform coordinates representing geometry from one coordinate system into another.

Chapter 1

Vector Algebra

Vectors play a crucial role in computer graphics, collision detection, and physical simulation, all of which are common components in modern video games. Our approach here is informal and practical; for a book dedicated to 3D game/graphics math, we recommend [Verth04]. We emphasize the importance of vectors by noting that they are used in just about every demo program in this book.

Objectives:

- To learn how vectors are represented geometrically and numerically.
- To discover the operations defined on vectors and their geometric applications.
- To become familiar with the D3DX library's vector math functions and classes.

1.1 Vectors

A *vector* refers to a quantity that possesses both magnitude and direction. Quantities that possess both magnitude and direction are called *vector-valued quantities*. Examples of vector-valued quantities are forces (a force is applied in a particular direction with a certain strength — magnitude), displacements (the net direction and distance a particle moved), and velocities (speed and direction). Thus, vectors are used to represent forces, displacements, and velocities. We also use vectors to specify pure directions, such as the direction the player is looking in a 3D game, the direction a polygon is facing, the direction in which a ray of light travels, or the direction in which a ray of light reflects off a surface.

A first step in characterizing a vector mathematically is geometrically: We graphically specify a vector by a directed line segment (see Figure 1.1), where the length denotes the magnitude of the vector and the aim denotes the direction of the vector. We note that the location in which we draw a vector is immaterial because changing the location does not change the magnitude or direction (the two properties a vector possesses). That is, we say two vectors are equal if and only if they have the same length and they point in the same direction. Thus, the vectors **u** and **v** drawn in Figure 1.1a are actually equal because they have the same length and point in the same direction. In fact, because location is unimportant for vectors, we can always translate a vector without changing its meaning (since a translation changes neither length nor direction). Observe that we could translate **u** such that it completely overlaps with **v** (and conversely), thereby making them indistinguishable — hence their equality. As a physical example, the vectors **u** and **v** in Figure 1.1b both tell the ants at two different points, *A* and *B*, to move north ten meters from their current location. Again we have that **u** = **v**. The vectors themselves are independent of position; they simply instruct the ants how to move from where they are. In this example, they tell the ants to move north (direction) ten meters (length).

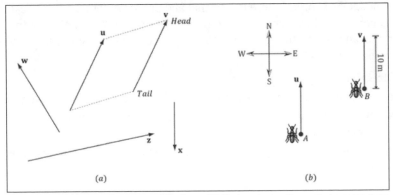

Figure 1.1: (a) Vectors drawn on a 2D plane. (b) Vectors instructing ants to move ten meters north.

1.1.1 Vectors and Coordinate Systems

We could now define useful geometric operations on vectors, which can then be used to solve problems involving vector-valued quantities. However, since the computer cannot work with vectors geometrically, we need to find a way of specifying vectors numerically instead. So what we do is introduce a 3D coordinate system in space, and translate all the vectors so that their tails coincide with the origin (Figure 1.2). Then we can identify a vector by specifying the coordinates of its head, and write $\mathbf{v} = (x, y, z)$ as shown in Figure 1.3. Now we can represent a vector with three `float`s in a computer program.

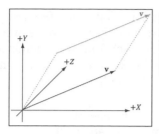

Figure 1.2: We translate **v** so that its tail coincides with the origin of the coordinate system. When a vector's tail coincides with the origin, we say that it is in _standard position_.

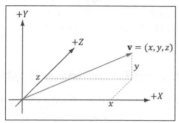

Figure 1.3: A vector specified by coordinates relative to a coordinate system.

Consider Figure 1.4, which shows a vector **v** and two frames in space. (Note that we use the terms _frame, frame of reference, space,_ and _coordinate system_ to mean the same thing in this book.) We can translate **v** so that it is in standard position in either of the two frames. Observe, however, that the coordinates of the vector **v** relative to frame A are different from the coordinates of the vector **v** relative to frame B. In other words, the _same_ vector has a different coordinate representation for distinct frames.

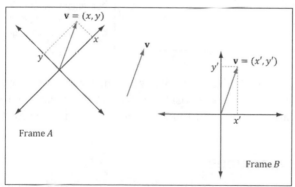

Figure 1.4: The _same_ vector **v** has different coordinates when described relative to different frames.

The idea is analogous to, say, temperature. Water boils at 100° Celsius or 212° Fahrenheit. The physical temperature of boiling water is the _same_ no matter the scale (i.e., we can't lower the boiling point by picking a different scale), but we assign a different scalar number to the temperature based on the scale we use. Similarly, for a vector, its direction and magnitude, which are embedded in the directed line segment, does not change; only the coordinates of it change based on the frame of reference we use to describe it. This is important because it means whenever we identify a vector by coordinates, those coordinates are relative to some frame of reference. Often in 3D computer graphics we will utilize more than one frame of reference and, therefore, will need to keep track of which frame the coordinates of a vector are described relative to; additionally, we will need to know how to convert vector coordinates from one frame to another.

Note: We see that both vectors and points can be described by coordinates (x, y, z) relative to a frame. However, they are not the same; a point represents a location in 3-space, whereas a vector represents a magnitude and direction. Points are discussed further in §1.5.

1.1.2 **Left-Handed Versus Right-Handed Coordinate Systems**

Direct3D uses a so-called left-handed coordinate system. If you take your left hand and aim your fingers down the positive x-axis, and then curl your fingers toward the positive y-axis, your thumb points roughly in the direction of the positive z-axis. Figure 1.5 illustrates the differences between a left-handed and right-handed coordinate system.

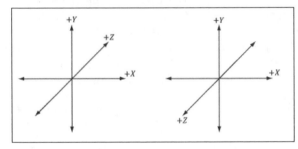

Figure 1.5: On the left we have a left-handed coordinate system. Observe that the positive z-axis goes into the page. On the right we have a right-handed coordinate system. Observe that the positive z-axis comes out of the page.

Observe that for the right-handed coordinate system, if you take your right hand and aim your fingers down the positive x-axis, and then curl your fingers toward the positive y-axis, your thumb points roughly in the direction of the positive z-axis.

1.1.3 **Basic Vector Operations**

We now define equality, addition, scalar multiplication, and subtraction on vectors using the coordinate representation.

- Two vectors are equal if and only if their corresponding components are equal. Let $\mathbf{u} = (u_x, u_y, u_z)$ and $\mathbf{v} = (v_x, v_y, v_z)$. Then $\mathbf{u} = \mathbf{v}$ if and only if $u_x = v_x$, $u_y = v_y$, and $u_z = v_z$.
- We add vectors componentwise; as such, it only makes sense to add vectors of the same dimension. Let $\mathbf{u} = (u_x, u_y, u_z)$ and $\mathbf{v} = (v_x, v_y, v_z)$. Then $\mathbf{u} + \mathbf{v} = (u_x + v_x, u_y + v_y, u_z + v_z)$.

■ We can multiply a scalar (i.e., a real number) and a vector, and the result is a vector. Let k be a scalar, and let $\mathbf{u} = (u_x, u_y, u_z)$, then
$k\mathbf{u} = (ku_x, ku_y, ku_z)$. This is called scalar multiplication.

■ We define subtraction in terms of vector addition and scalar multiplication. That is, $\mathbf{u} - \mathbf{v} = \mathbf{u} + (-1 \cdot \mathbf{v}) = \mathbf{u} + (-\mathbf{v}) = (u_x - v_x, u_y - v_y, u_z - v_z)$.

Example 1.1

Let $\mathbf{u} = (1,2,3)$, $\mathbf{v} = (1,2,3)$, $\mathbf{w} = (3,0,-2)$, and $k = 2$. Then,

■ $\mathbf{u} + \mathbf{w} = (1, 2, 3) + (3, 0, -2) = (4, 2, 1)$;

■ $\mathbf{u} = \mathbf{v}$;

■ $\mathbf{u} - \mathbf{v} = \mathbf{u} + (-\mathbf{v}) = (1,2,3) + (-1,-2,-3) = (0,0,0) = \mathbf{0}$;

■ $k\mathbf{w} = 2(3,0,-2) = (6,0,-4)$.

The difference in the third line illustrates a special vector, called the *zero-vector*, which has zeros for all of its components and is denoted by $\mathbf{0}$.

Example 1.2

We'll illustrate this example with 2D vectors to make the drawings simpler. The ideas are the same as in 3D; we just work with one less component in 2D.

■ Let $\mathbf{v} = (2,1)$. How do $\mathbf{v}$ and $-1/2\mathbf{v}$ compare geometrically? We note $-1/2\mathbf{v} = (-1,-1/2)$. Graphing both $\mathbf{v}$ and $\;\;1/2\mathbf{v}$ (Figure 1.6a), we notice that $-1/2\mathbf{v}$ is in the direction directly opposite of $\mathbf{v}$ and its length is 1/2 that of $\mathbf{v}$. Thus, geometrically, negating a vector can be thought of as "flipping" its direction, and scalar multiplication can be thought of as scaling the length of the vector.

■ Let $\mathbf{u} = (2,1/2)$ and $\mathbf{v} = (1,2)$. Then $\mathbf{v} + \mathbf{u} = (3,5/2)$. Figure 1.6b shows what vector addition means geometrically: We parallel translate $\mathbf{u}$ so that its *tail* coincides with the *head* of $\mathbf{v}$. Then, the sum is the vector originating at the tail of $\mathbf{v}$ and ending at the head of $\mathbf{u}$. (We get the same result if we keep $\mathbf{u}$ fixed and translate $\mathbf{v}$ so that its tail coincides with the head of $\mathbf{u}$. In this case, $\mathbf{u} + \mathbf{v}$ would be the vector originating at the tail of $\mathbf{u}$ and ending at the head of the translated $\mathbf{v}$.) Observe also that our rules of vector addition agree with what we would intuitively expect to happen physically when we add forces together to produce a net force: If we add two forces (vectors) in the same direction, we get another stronger force (longer vector) in that direction. If we add two forces (vectors) in opposition to each other, then we get a weaker net force (shorter vector). Figure 1.7 illustrates these ideas.

■ Let $\mathbf{u} = (2,1/2)$ and $\mathbf{v} = (1,2)$. Then $\mathbf{v} - \mathbf{u} = (-1,3/2)$. Figure 1.6c shows what vector subtraction means geometrically. Essentially, the difference $\mathbf{v} - \mathbf{u}$ gives us a vector aimed from the head of $\mathbf{u}$ to the head of $\mathbf{v}$. If we instead interpret $\mathbf{u}$ and $\mathbf{v}$ as points, then $\mathbf{v} - \mathbf{u}$ gives us a vector aimed from the point **u** to the point **v**; this interpretation is important as we will often want the vector aimed from one point to another. Observe also that the length of **v** − **u** is the distance from **u** to **v**, when thinking of **u** and **v** as points.

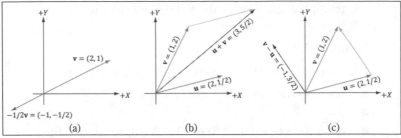

Figure 1.6: (a) The geometric interpretation of scalar multiplication. (b) The geometric interpretation of vector addition. (c) The geometric interpretation of vector subtraction.

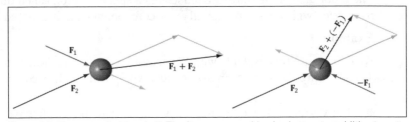

Figure 1.7: Forces applied to a ball. The forces are combined using vector addition to get a net force.

1.2 **Length and Unit Vectors**

Geometrically, the magnitude of a vector is the length of the directed line segment. We denote the magnitude of a vector by double vertical bars (e.g., $\|\mathbf{u}\|$ denotes the magnitude of **u**). Now, given a vector $\mathbf{v} = (x, y, z)$, we wish to compute its magnitude algebraically. The magnitude of a 3D vector can be computed by applying the Pythagorean theorem twice; see Figure 1.8.

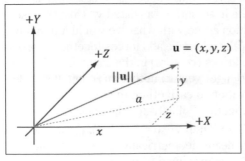

Figure 1.8: The 3D length of a vector can be computed by applying the Pythagorean theorem twice.

First, we look at the triangle in the xz-plane with sides x, z, and hypotenuse a. From the Pythagorean theorem, we have $a = \sqrt{x^2 + z^2}$. Now look at the triangle with sides a, y, and hypotenuse $\|\mathbf{u}\|$. From the Pythagorean theorem again, we arrive at the following magnitude formula:

$$\|\mathbf{u}\| = \sqrt{y^2 + a^2} = \sqrt{y^2 + \left(\sqrt{x^2 + z^2}\right)^2} = \sqrt{x^2 + y^2 + z^2} \tag{1.1}$$

For some applications, we do not care about the length of a vector because we want to use the vector to represent a pure direction. For such direction-only vectors, we want the length of the vector to be exactly one. When we make a vector unit length, we say that we are _normalizing_ the vector. We can normalize a vector by dividing each of its components by its magnitude:

$$\hat{\mathbf{u}} = \frac{\mathbf{u}}{\|\mathbf{u}\|} = \left(\frac{x}{\|\mathbf{u}\|}, \frac{y}{\|\mathbf{u}\|}, \frac{z}{\|\mathbf{u}\|}\right) \tag{1.2}$$

To verify that this formula is correct, we can compute the length of $\hat{\mathbf{u}}$:

$$\|\hat{\mathbf{u}}\| = \sqrt{\left(\frac{x}{\|\mathbf{u}\|}\right)^2 + \left(\frac{y}{\|\mathbf{u}\|}\right)^2 + \left(\frac{z}{\|\mathbf{u}\|}\right)^2} = \frac{\sqrt{x^2 + y^2 + z^2}}{\sqrt{\|\mathbf{u}\|^2}} = \frac{\|\mathbf{u}\|}{\|\mathbf{u}\|} = 1$$

So $\hat{\mathbf{u}}$ is indeed a unit vector.

Example 1.3

Normalize the vector $\mathbf{v} = (-1, 3, 4)$. We have $\|\mathbf{v}\| = \sqrt{(-1)^2 + 3^2 + 4^2} = \sqrt{26}$. Thus,

$$\hat{\mathbf{v}} = \frac{\mathbf{v}}{\|\mathbf{v}\|} = \left(-\frac{1}{\sqrt{26}}, \frac{3}{\sqrt{26}}, \frac{4}{\sqrt{26}}\right)$$

To verify that $\|\hat{\mathbf{v}}\|$ is indeed a unit vector, we compute its length:

$$\|\hat{\mathbf{v}}\| = \sqrt{\left(-\frac{1}{\sqrt{26}}\right)^2 + \left(\frac{3}{\sqrt{26}}\right)^2 + \left(\frac{4}{\sqrt{26}}\right)^2} = \sqrt{\frac{1}{26} + \frac{9}{26} + \frac{16}{26}} = \sqrt{1} = 1$$

1.3 The Dot Product

The dot product is a form of vector multiplication that results in a scalar value; for this reason, it is sometimes referred to as the scalar product. Let $\mathbf{u} = (u_x, u_y, u_z)$ and $\mathbf{v} = (v_x, v_y, v_z)$; then the dot product is defined as follows:

$$\mathbf{u} \cdot \mathbf{v} = u_x v_x + u_y v_y + u_z v_z \tag{1.3}$$

In words, the dot product is the sum of the products of the corresponding components.

The dot product definition does not present an obvious geometric meaning. Using the law of cosines, we can find the relationship,

$$\mathbf{u} \cdot \mathbf{v} = \|\mathbf{u}\|\|\mathbf{v}\|\cos\theta \qquad (1.4)$$

where θ is the angle between the vectors $\mathbf{u}$ and $\mathbf{v}$ such that $0 \leq \theta \leq \pi$ (see Figure 1.9). So, Equation 1.4 says that the dot product between two vectors is the cosine of the angle between them scaled by the vectors' magnitudes. In particular, if both $\mathbf{u}$ and $\mathbf{v}$ are unit vectors, then $\mathbf{u} \cdot \mathbf{v}$ is the cosine of the angle between them (i.e., $\mathbf{u} \cdot \mathbf{v} = \cos\theta$).

Equation 1.4 provides us with some useful geometric properties of the dot product:

■ If $\mathbf{u} \cdot \mathbf{v} = 0$, then $\mathbf{u} \perp \mathbf{v}$ (i.e., the vectors are orthogonal).

■ If $\mathbf{u} \cdot \mathbf{v} > 0$, then the angle θ between the two vectors is less than 90° (i.e., the vectors make an acute angle).

■ If $\mathbf{u} \cdot \mathbf{v} < 0$, then the angle θ between the two vectors is greater than 90° (i.e., the vectors make an obtuse angle).

Note: The word "orthogonal" can be used as a synonym for "perpendicular."

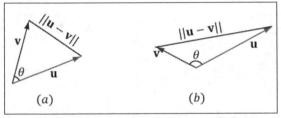

Figure 1.9: On the left, the angle θ between **u** and **v** is an acute angle. On the right, the angle θ between **u** and **v** is an obtuse angle. When we refer to the angle between two vectors, we always mean the smallest angle, that is, the angle θ such that $0 \leq \theta \leq \pi$.

Example 1.4

Let $\mathbf{u} = (1, 2, 3)$ and $\mathbf{v} = (-4, 0, -1)$. Find the angle between $\mathbf{u}$ and $\mathbf{v}$. First we make the following computations:

$$\mathbf{u} \cdot \mathbf{v} = (1, 2, 3) \cdot (-4, 0, -1) = -4 - 3 = -7$$

$$\|\mathbf{u}\| = \sqrt{1^2 + 2^2 + 3^2} = \sqrt{14}$$

$$\|\mathbf{v}\| = \sqrt{(-4)^2 + 0^2 + (-1)^2} = \sqrt{17}$$

Now, applying Equation 1.4 and solving for theta, we get:

$$\cos\theta = \frac{\mathbf{u}\cdot\mathbf{v}}{\|\mathbf{u}\|\|\mathbf{v}\|} = \frac{-7}{\sqrt{14}\sqrt{17}}$$

$$\theta = \cos^{-1}\left(\frac{-7}{\sqrt{14}\sqrt{17}}\right) \approx 117°$$

Example 1.5

Consider Figure 1.10. Given $\mathbf{v}$ and the _unit_ vector $\mathbf{n}$, find a formula for $\mathbf{p}$ using the dot product.

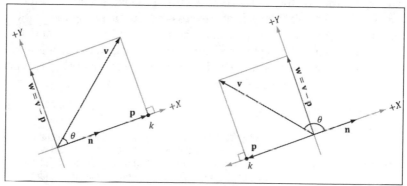

Figure 1.10: The orthogonal projection of **v** on **n**

First, observe from the figure that there exists a scalar k such that $\mathbf{p}=k\mathbf{n}$; moreover, since we assumed $\|\mathbf{n}\|=1$, we have $\|\mathbf{p}\|=\|k\mathbf{n}\|=|k|\|\mathbf{n}\|=|k|$. (Note that k may be negative if and only if $\mathbf{p}$ and $\mathbf{n}$ aim in opposite directions.) Using trigonometry, we have that $k=\|\mathbf{v}\|\cos\theta$; therefore, $\mathbf{p}=k\mathbf{n}=(\|\mathbf{v}\|\cos\theta)\mathbf{n}$. However, because $\mathbf{n}$ is a unit vector, we can say this in another way:

$$\mathbf{p}=(\|\mathbf{v}\|\cos\theta)\mathbf{n}=(\|\mathbf{v}\|\cdot 1\cos\theta)\mathbf{n}=(\|\mathbf{v}\|\|\mathbf{n}\|\cos\theta)\mathbf{n}=(\mathbf{v}\cdot\mathbf{n})\mathbf{n}$$

In particular, this shows $k=\mathbf{v}\cdot\mathbf{n}$, and this illustrates the geometric interpretation of $\mathbf{v}\cdot\mathbf{n}$ when $\mathbf{n}$ is a unit vector. We call $\mathbf{p}$ the _orthogonal projection_ of $\mathbf{v}$ on $\mathbf{n}$, and it is commonly denoted by

$$\mathbf{p}= proj_{\mathbf{n}}(\mathbf{v})$$

If we interpret $\mathbf{v}$ as a force, $\mathbf{p}$ can be thought of as the portion of the force $\mathbf{v}$ that acts in the direction $\mathbf{n}$. Likewise, the vector $\mathbf{w}=\mathbf{v}-\mathbf{p}$ is the portion of the force $\mathbf{v}$ that acts orthogonal to the direction $\mathbf{n}$. Observe that $\mathbf{v}=\mathbf{p}+\mathbf{w}$, which is to say we have decomposed the vector $\mathbf{v}$ into the sum of two orthogonal vectors $\mathbf{p}$ and $\mathbf{w}$.

If **n** is not of unit length, we can always normalize it first to make it unit length. Replacing **n** by the unit vector $\frac{\mathbf{n}}{\|\mathbf{n}\|}$ gives us the more general projection formula:

$$\mathbf{p} = proj_{\mathbf{n}}(\mathbf{v}) = \left(\mathbf{v} \cdot \frac{\mathbf{n}}{\|\mathbf{n}\|} \right) \frac{\mathbf{n}}{\|\mathbf{n}\|} = \frac{(\mathbf{v} \cdot \mathbf{n})}{\|\mathbf{n}\|^2} \mathbf{n}$$

1.4 **The Cross Product**

The second form of multiplication vector math defines is the cross product. Unlike the dot product, which evaluates to a scalar, the cross product evaluates to another vector; moreover, the cross product is only defined for 3D vectors (in particular, there is no 2D cross product). Taking the cross product of two 3D vectors **u** and **v** yields another vector, **w** that is mutually orthogonal to **u** and **v**. By that we mean **w** is orthogonal to **u**, and **w** is orthogonal to **v** (see Figure 1.11). If $\mathbf{u}=(u_x, u_y, u_z)$ and $\mathbf{v}=(v_x, v_y, v_z)$, then the cross product is computed like so:

$$\mathbf{w} = \mathbf{u} \times \mathbf{v} = (u_y v_z - u_z v_y, u_z v_x - u_x v_z, u_x v_y - u_y v_x) \tag{1.5}$$

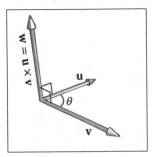

Figure 1.11: The cross product of two 3D vectors, **u** and **v**, yields another vector, **w**, that is mutually orthogonal to **u** and **v**. If you take your left hand and aim the fingers in the direction of the first vector **u**, and then curl your fingers toward **v** along an angle $0 \leq \theta \leq \pi$, then your thumb roughly points in the direction of **w** =**u**× **v**; this is called the *left-hand-thumb rule*.

Example 1.6

Let **u** = (2, 1, 3) and **v** = (2, 0, 0). Compute **w**= **u** × **v** and **z**= **v**× **u**, and then verify that **w** is orthogonal to **u** and that **w** is orthogonal to **v**. Applying Equation 1.5 we have,

$$\mathbf{w} = \mathbf{u} \times \mathbf{v}$$
$$= (2, 1, 3) \times (2, 0, 0)$$
$$= (1 \cdot 0 - 3 \cdot 0, 3 \cdot 2 - 2 \cdot 0, 2 \cdot 0 - 1 \cdot 2)$$
$$= (0, 6, -2)$$

and

$$\mathbf{z} = \mathbf{v} \times \mathbf{u}$$
$$= (2, 0, 0) \times (2, 1, 3)$$
$$= (0 \cdot 3 - 0 \cdot 1, 0 \cdot 2 - 2 \cdot 3, 2 \cdot 1 - 0 \cdot 2)$$
$$= (0, -6, 2)$$

This result makes one thing clear, generally speaking: $\mathbf{u} \times \mathbf{v} \neq \mathbf{v} \times \mathbf{u}$. Therefore, we say that the cross product is *anti-commutative*. In fact, it can be shown that $\mathbf{u} \times \mathbf{v} = -\mathbf{v} \times \mathbf{u}$. You can determine the vector returned by the cross product by the *left-hand-thumb rule*. If you curve the fingers of your left hand from the direction of the first vector toward the second vector (always take the path with the smallest angle), your thumb points in the direction of the returned vector, as shown in Figure 1.11.

To show that $\mathbf{w}$ is orthogonal to $\mathbf{u}$ and that $\mathbf{w}$ is orthogonal to $\mathbf{v}$, we recall from §1.3 that if $\mathbf{u} \cdot \mathbf{v} = 0$, then $\mathbf{u} \perp \mathbf{v}$ (i.e., the vectors are orthogonal). Because

$$\mathbf{w} \cdot \mathbf{u} = (0, 6, -2) \cdot (2, 1, 3) = 0 \cdot 2 + 6 \cdot 1 + (-2) \cdot 3 = 0$$

and

$$\mathbf{w} \cdot \mathbf{v} = (0, 6, -2) \cdot (2, 0, 0) = 0 \cdot 2 + 6 \cdot 0 + (-2) \cdot 0 = 0$$

we conclude that $\mathbf{w}$ is orthogonal to $\mathbf{u}$ and that $\mathbf{w}$ is orthogonal to $\mathbf{v}$.

1.5 Points

So far we have been discussing vectors, which do not describe positions. However, we will also need to specify positions in our 3D programs; for example, the position of 3D geometry and the position of the 3D virtual camera. Relative to a coordinate system, we can use a vector in standard position (see Figure 1.12) to represent a 3D position in space; we call this a *position vector*. In this case, the location of the tip of the vector is the characteristic of interest, not the direction or magnitude. We will use the terms "position vector" and "point" interchangeably since a position vector is enough to identify a point.

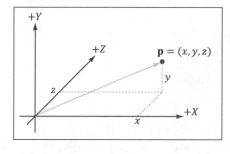

Figure 1.12: The position vector, which extends from the origin to the point, fully describes the location of the point relative to the coordinate system.

One side effect of using vectors to represent points, especially in code, is that we can do vector operations that do not make sense for points; for instance, geometrically, what should the sum of two points mean? On the other hand, some operations can be extended to points. For example, we define the difference of two points $\mathbf{q} - \mathbf{p}$ to be the vector from $\mathbf{p}$ to $\mathbf{q}$. Also, we define a point $\mathbf{p}$ plus a vector $\mathbf{v}$ to be the point $\mathbf{q}$ obtained by displacing $\mathbf{p}$

by the vector **v**. Conveniently, because we are using vectors to represent points relative to a coordinate system, no extra work needs to be done for the point operations just discussed as the vector algebra framework already takes care of them (see Figure 1.13).

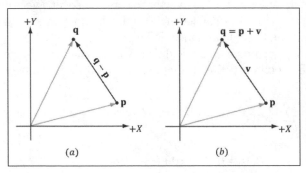

Figure 1.13: (a) The difference **q** − **p** between two points is defined as the vector from **p** to **q**. (b) A point **p** plus the vector **v** is defined to be the point **q** obtained by displacing **p** by the vector **v**.

Note: Actually there is a geometrically meaningful way to define a special sum of points, called an *affine combination*, which is like a weighted average of points. However, we do not use this concept in this book.

1.6 **D3DX Vectors**

In this section, we spend some time becoming familiar with the D3DXVECTOR3 class, which is the class we often use to store the coordinates of both points and vectors in code relative to some coordinate system. Its class definition is:

```
typedef struct D3DXVECTOR3 : public D3DVECTOR
{
public:
    D3DXVECTOR3() {};
    D3DXVECTOR3( CONST FLOAT * );
    D3DXVECTOR3( CONST D3DVECTOR& );
    D3DXVECTOR3( CONST D3DXFLOAT16 * );
    D3DXVECTOR3( FLOAT x, FLOAT y, FLOAT z );

    // casting
    operator FLOAT* ();
    operator CONST FLOAT* () const;

    // assignment operators
    D3DXVECTOR3& operator += ( CONST D3DXVECTOR3& );
    D3DXVECTOR3& operator -= ( CONST D3DXVECTOR3& );
    D3DXVECTOR3& operator *= ( FLOAT );
    D3DXVECTOR3& operator /= ( FLOAT );

    // unary operators
    D3DXVECTOR3 operator + () const;
```

```
        D3DXVECTOR3 operator - () const;

        // binary operators
        D3DXVECTOR3 operator + ( CONST D3DXVECTOR3& ) const;
        D3DXVECTOR3 operator - ( CONST D3DXVECTOR3& ) const;
        D3DXVECTOR3 operator * ( FLOAT ) const;
        D3DXVECTOR3 operator / ( FLOAT ) const;

        friend D3DXVECTOR3 operator * (FLOAT, CONST struct
                                       D3DXVECTOR3& );

        BOOL operator == ( CONST D3DXVECTOR3& ) const;
        BOOL operator != ( CONST D3DXVECTOR3& ) const;

    } D3DXVECTOR3, *LPD3DXVECTOR3;
```

Note that D3DXVECTOR3 inherits its coordinate data from D3DVECTOR, which is defined as:

```
typedef struct _D3DVECTOR {
    float x;
    float y;
    float z;
} D3DVECTOR;
```

Also observe that the D3DXVECTOR3 overloads the arithmetic operators to do vector addition, subtraction, and scalar multiplication.

In addition to the above class, the D3DX library includes the following useful vector-related functions:

■ FLOAT D3DXVec3Length(// Returns $\|\mathbf{v}\|$
        CONST D3DXVECTOR3 *pV);   // Input $\mathbf{v}$

■ FLOAT D3DXVec3LengthSq(// Returns $\|\mathbf{v}\|^2$
        CONST D3DXVECTOR3 *pV);   // Input $\mathbf{v}$

■ FLOAT D3DXVec3Dot(// Returns $\mathbf{v}_1 \cdot \mathbf{v}_2$
        CONST D3DXVECTOR3 *pV1,   // Input $\mathbf{v}_1$
        CONST D3DXVECTOR3 *pV2); // Input $\mathbf{v}_2$

■ D3DXVECTOR3 *D3DXVec3Cross(
        D3DXVECTOR3 *pOut,   // Returns $\mathbf{v}_1 \times \mathbf{v}_2$
        CONST D3DXVECTOR3 *pV1,   // Input $\mathbf{v}_1$
        CONST D3DXVECTOR3 *pV2); // Input $\mathbf{v}_2$

■ D3DXVECTOR3 *WINAPI D3DXVec3Normalize(
        D3DXVECTOR3 *pOut,   // Returns $\mathbf{v} / \|\mathbf{v}\|$
        CONST D3DXVECTOR3 *pV,   // Input $\mathbf{v}$
```
```

Note: Remember to link the *d3dx10.lib* (or *d3dx10d.lib* for debug builds) library file with your application to use any D3DX code; moreover, you will also need to `#include <d3dx10.h>`.

The following short code provides some examples on how to use the D3DXVECTOR3 class and four of the five functions listed above.

```cpp
#include <d3dx10.h>
#include <iostream>
using namespace std;

// Overload the  "<<" operators so that we can use cout to
// output D3DXVECTOR3 objects.

ostream& operator<<(ostream& os, D3DXVECTOR3& v)
{
    os << "(" << v.x << ", " << v.y << ", " << v.z << ")";
    return os;
}

int main()
{
    // Using constructor, D3DXVECTOR3(FLOAT x, FLOAT y, FLOAT z);
    D3DXVECTOR3 u(1.0f, 2.0f, 3.0f);

    // Using constructor, D3DXVECTOR3(CONST FLOAT *);
    float x[3] = {-2.0f, 1.0f, -3.0f};
    D3DXVECTOR3 v(x);

    // Using constructor, D3DXVECTOR3() {};
    D3DXVECTOR3 a, b, c, d, e;

    // Vector addition: D3DXVECTOR3 operator +
    a = u + v;

    // Vector subtraction: D3DXVECTOR3 operator -
    b = u - v;

    // Scalar multiplication: D3DXVECTOR3 operator *
    c = u * 10;

    // ||u||
    float L = D3DXVec3Length(&u);

    // d = u / ||u||
    D3DXVec3Normalize(&d, &u);

    // s = u dot v
    float s = D3DXVec3Dot(&u, &v);

    // e = u x v
    D3DXVec3Cross(&e, &u, &v);
```

```
        cout << "u              = " << u << endl;
        cout << "v              = " << v << endl;
        cout << "a = u + v       = " << a << endl;
        cout << "b = u - v       = " << b << endl;
        cout << "c = u * 10      = " << c << endl;
        cout << "d = u / ||u||   = " << d << endl;
        cout << "e = u x v       = " << e << endl;
        cout << "L = ||u||       = " << L << endl;
        cout << "s = u.v         = " << s << endl;

        return 0;
}
```

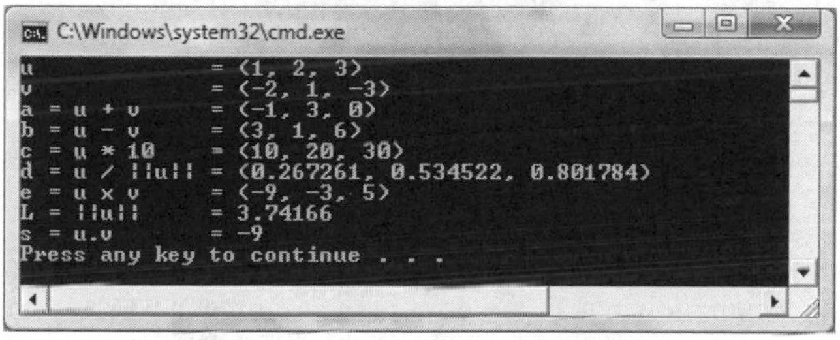

Figure 1.14: Output for the above program.

While we're on the subject of working with vectors on a computer, we should be aware of the following. When comparing floating-point numbers, care must be taken due to floating-point imprecision. Two floating-point numbers that we expect to be equal may differ slightly. For example, mathematically, we'd expect a normalized vector to have a length of 1, but in a computer program, the length will only be approximately 1. Moreover, mathematically, $1^p = 1$ for any real number p, but when we only have a numerical approximation for 1, we see that the approximation raised to the pth power increases the error; thus, numerical error also accumulates. The following short program illustrates these ideas:

```
#include <iostream>
#include <d3dx10.h>
using namespace std;

int main()
{
        cout.precision(8);

        D3DXVECTOR3 u(1.0f, 1.0f, 1.0f);
        D3DXVec3Normalize(&u, &u);

        float LU = D3DXVec3Length(&u);

        // Mathematically, the length should be 1. Is it numerically?
```

```
        cout << LU << endl;
        if( LU == 1.0f )
                cout << "Length 1" << endl;
        else
                cout << "Length not 1" << endl;

        // Raising 1 to any power should still be 1. Is it?
        float powLU = powf(LU, 1.0e6f);
        cout << "LU^(10^6) = " << powLU << endl;
}
```

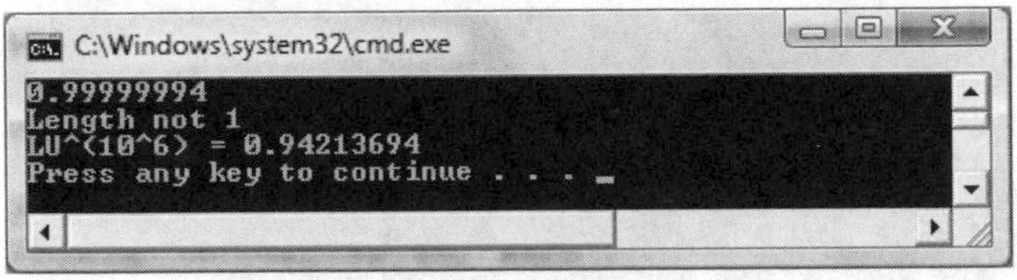

Figure 1.15: Output for the above program.

To compensate for floating-point imprecision, we test if two floating-point numbers are approximately equal. We do this by defining an EPSILON constant, which is a very small value we use as a "buffer." We say two values are approximately equal if their distance is less than EPSILON. In other words, EPSILON gives us some tolerance for floating-point imprecision. The following function illustrates how EPSILON can be used to test if two floating-point values are equal:

```
const float EPSILON = 0.001f;
bool Equals(float lhs, float rhs)
{
        // Is the distance between lhs and rhs less than EPSILON?
        return fabs(lhs - rhs) < EPSILON ? true : false; }
```

1.7 **Summary**

- Vectors are used to model physical quantities that possess both magnitude and direction. Geometrically, we represent a vector with a directed line segment. A vector is in standard position when it is translated parallel to itself so that its tail coincides with the origin of the coordinate system. A vector in standard position can be described numerically by specifying the coordinates of its head relative to a coordinate system.

- If $\mathbf{u} = (u_x, u_y, u_z)$ and $\mathbf{v} = (v_x, v_y, v_z)$, then we have the following vector operations:

   Addition: $\mathbf{u} + \mathbf{v} = (u_x + v_x, u_y + v_y, u_z + v_z)$

   Subtraction: $\mathbf{u} - \mathbf{v} = (u_x - v_x, u_y - v_y, u_z - v_z)$

   Scalar multiplication: $k\mathbf{u} = (ku_x, ku_y, ku_z)$

Length: $\|\mathbf{u}\| = \sqrt{x^2 + y^2 + z^2}$

Normalization: $\hat{\mathbf{u}} = \frac{\mathbf{u}}{\|\mathbf{u}\|} = \left(\frac{x}{\|\mathbf{u}\|}, \frac{y}{\|\mathbf{u}\|}, \frac{z}{\|\mathbf{u}\|} \right)$

Dot product: $\mathbf{u} \cdot \mathbf{v} = \|\mathbf{u}\|\|\mathbf{v}\|\cos\theta = u_x v_x + u_y v_y + u_z v_z$

Cross product: $\mathbf{u} \times \mathbf{v} = (u_y v_z - u_z v_y, \; u_z v_x - u_x v_z, \; u_x v_y - u_y v_x)$

- The D3DXVECTOR3 class is used to describe a 3D vector in code. This class contains three float data members for representing the x-, y-, and z-coordinates of a vector relative to some coordinate system. The D3DXVECTOR3 class overloads the arithmetic operators to do vector addition, subtraction, and scalar multiplication. Moreover, the D3DX library provides the following useful functions for computing the length of a vector, the squared length of a vector, the dot product of two vectors, the cross product of two vectors, and normalizing a vector:

```
FLOAT D3DXVec3Length(CONST D3DXVECTOR3 *pV);
FLOAT D3DXVec3LengthSq(CONST D3DXVECTOR3 *pV);
FLOAT D3DXVec3Dot(CONST D3DXVECTOR3 *pV1, CONST D3DXVECTOR3 *pV2);
D3DXVECTOR3* D3DXVec3Cross(D3DXVECTOR3 *pOut,
    CONST D3DXVECTOR3 *pV1, CONST D3DXVECTOR3 *pV2);
D3DXVECTOR3* WINAPI D3DXVec3Normalize(D3DXVECTOR3 *pOut,
    CONST D3DXVECTOR3 *pV);
```

1.8 Exercises

1. Let $\mathbf{u} = (1,2)$ and $\mathbf{v} = (3,-4)$. Perform the following computations and draw the vectors relative to a 2D coordinate system:

   a. $\mathbf{u} + \mathbf{v}$

   b. $\mathbf{u} - \mathbf{v}$

   c. $2\mathbf{u} + 1/2\mathbf{v}$

   d. $-2\mathbf{u} + \mathbf{v}$

2. Let $\mathbf{u} = (-1, 3, 2)$ and $\mathbf{v} = (3, -4, 1)$. Perform the following computations:

   a. $\mathbf{u} + \mathbf{v}$

   b. $\mathbf{u} - \mathbf{v}$

   c. $3\mathbf{u} + 2\mathbf{v}$

   d. $-2\mathbf{u} + \mathbf{v}$

3. This exercise shows that vector algebra shares many of the nice properties of real numbers (this is not an exhaustive list). Assume $\mathbf{u} = (u_x, u_y, u_z)$, $\mathbf{v} = (v_x, v_y, v_z)$, and $\mathbf{w} = (w_x, w_y, w_z)$. Also assume that c and k are scalars. Prove the following vector properties:

   a. $\mathbf{u} + \mathbf{v} = \mathbf{v} + \mathbf{u}$ (Commutative property of addition)

   b. $\mathbf{u} + (\mathbf{v} + \mathbf{w}) = (\mathbf{u} + \mathbf{v}) + \mathbf{w}$ (Associative property of addition)

c. $(ck)\mathbf{u} = c(k\mathbf{u})$ (Associative property of scalar multiplication)

d. $k(\mathbf{u}+\mathbf{v}) = k\mathbf{u} + k\mathbf{v}$ (Distributive property 1)

e. $\mathbf{u}(k+c) = k\mathbf{u} + c\mathbf{u}$ (Distributive property 2)

Hint: Just use the definition of the vector operations and the properties of real numbers. For example,

$$(ck)\mathbf{u} = (ck)(u_x, u_y, u_z)$$
$$= ((ck)u_x, (ck)u_y, (ck)u_z)$$
$$= (c(ku_x), c(ku_y), c(ku_z))$$
$$= c(ku_x, ku_y, ku_z)$$
$$= c(k\mathbf{u})$$

4. Solve the equation $2((1, 2, 3) - \mathbf{x}) - (-2, 0, 4) = -2(1, 2, 3)$ for $\mathbf{x}$.

5. Let $\mathbf{u} = (-1, 3, 2)$ and $\mathbf{v} = (3, -4, 1)$. Normalize $\mathbf{u}$ and $\mathbf{v}$.

6. Let k be a scalar and let $\mathbf{u} = (u_x, u_y, u_z)$. Prove that $\|k\mathbf{u}\| = |k|\|\mathbf{u}\|$.

7. Is the angle between $\mathbf{u}$ and $\mathbf{v}$ orthogonal, acute, or obtuse?

   a. $\mathbf{u} = (1, 1, 1), \mathbf{v} = (2, 3, 4)$

   b. $\mathbf{u} = (1, 1, 0), \mathbf{v} = (-2, 2, 0)$

   c. $\mathbf{u} = (-1, -1, -1), \mathbf{v} = (3, 1, 0)$

8. Let $\mathbf{u} = (-1, 3, 2)$ and $\mathbf{v} = (3, -4, 1)$. Find the angle θ between $\mathbf{u}$ and $\mathbf{v}$.

9. Let $\mathbf{u} = (u_x, u_y, u_z)$, $\mathbf{v} = (v_x, v_y, v_z)$, and $\mathbf{w} = (w_x, w_y, w_z)$. Also let c and k be scalars. Prove the following dot properties:

   a. $\mathbf{u} \cdot \mathbf{v} = \mathbf{v} \cdot \mathbf{u}$

   b. $\mathbf{u} \cdot (\mathbf{v} + \mathbf{w}) = \mathbf{u} \cdot \mathbf{v} + \mathbf{u} \cdot \mathbf{w}$

   c. $k(\mathbf{u} \cdot \mathbf{v}) = (k\mathbf{u}) \cdot \mathbf{v} = \mathbf{u} \cdot (k\mathbf{v})$

   d. $\mathbf{v} \cdot \mathbf{v} = \|\mathbf{v}\|^2$

   e. $\mathbf{0} \cdot \mathbf{v} = 0$

Hint: Just use the definition, for example,

$$\mathbf{v} \cdot \mathbf{v} = v_x v_x + v_y v_y + v_z v_z$$
$$= v_x^2 + v_y^2 + v_z^2$$
$$= \left(\sqrt{v_x^2 + v_y^2 + v_z^2}\right)^2$$
$$= (\|\mathbf{v}\|)^2$$

10. Use the law of cosines ($c^2 = a^2 + b^2 = 2ab \cos\theta$, where a, b, and c are the lengths of the sides of a triangle and θ is the angle between sides a and b) to show:

$$u_x v_x + u_y v_y + u_z v_z = \|\mathbf{u}\|\|\mathbf{v}\| \cos\theta.$$

    Hint: Consider Figure 1.9 and set $c^2 = \|\mathbf{u} - \mathbf{v}\|$, $a^2 = \|\mathbf{u}\|^2$, and $b^2 = \|\mathbf{v}\|^2$, and use the dot product properties from the previous exercise.

11. Let $\mathbf{n} = (-2, 1)$. Decompose the vector $\mathbf{g} = (0, -9.8)$ into the sum of two orthogonal vectors, one parallel to $\mathbf{n}$ and the other orthogonal to $\mathbf{n}$. Also, draw the vectors relative to a 2D coordinate system.

12. Let $\mathbf{u} = (-2, 1, 4)$ and $\mathbf{v} = (3, -4, 1)$. Find $\mathbf{w} = \mathbf{u} \times \mathbf{v}$, and show $\mathbf{w} \cdot \mathbf{u} = 0$ and $\mathbf{w} \cdot \mathbf{v} = 0$.

13. Let the following points define a triangle relative to some coordinate system: $\mathbf{A} = (0, 0, 0)$, $\mathbf{B} = (0, 1, 3)$, and $\mathbf{C} = (5, 1, 0)$. Find a vector orthogonal to this triangle.

    Hint: Find two vectors on two of the triangle's edges and use the cross product.

14. Prove that $\|\mathbf{u} \times \mathbf{v}\| = \|\mathbf{u}\|\|\mathbf{v}\|\sin\theta$. *Hint*: Start with $\|\mathbf{u}\|\|\mathbf{v}\|\sin\theta$ and use the trigonometric identity $\cos^2\theta + \sin^2\theta = 1 \Rightarrow \sin\theta = \sqrt{1 - \cos^2\theta}$; then apply Equation 1.4.

15. Prove that $\|\mathbf{u} \times \mathbf{v}\|$ gives the area of the parallelogram spanned by $\mathbf{u}$ and $\mathbf{v}$ (see Figure 1.16).

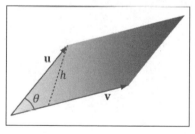

Figure 1.16: Parallelogram spanned by two 3D vectors $\mathbf{u}$ and $\mathbf{v}$; the parallelogram has base $\|\mathbf{v}\|$ and height h.

16. Give an example of 3D vectors $\mathbf{u}$, $\mathbf{v}$, and $\mathbf{w}$ such that $\mathbf{u} \times (\mathbf{v} \times \mathbf{w}) \neq (\mathbf{u} \times \mathbf{v}) \times \mathbf{w}$. This shows the cross product is generally not associative. *Hint*: Consider combinations of the simple vectors $\mathbf{i} = (1, 0, 0)$, $\mathbf{j} = (0, 1, 0)$, and $\mathbf{k} = (0, 0, 1)$.

17. Prove that the cross product of two nonzero parallel vectors results in the null vector; that is, $\mathbf{u} \times k\mathbf{u} = 0$. *Hint*: Just use the cross product definition.

18. The D3DX library also provides the D3DXVECTOR2 and D3DXVECTOR4 classes for working with 2D and 4D vectors. We will later use 2D vectors to describe 2D points on texture maps. The purpose of 4D vectors will make more sense after reading the next chapter when we discuss homogeneous coordinates. Rewrite the program in §1.6 twice, once using 2D vectors (D3DXVECTOR2) and a second time using 4D vectors (D3DXVECTOR4). Note that there is no 2D cross product function, so you can skip that. (*Hint*: Search the index for these keywords in the DirectX SDK documentation: D3DXVECTOR2, D3DXVECTOR4, D3DXVec2, and D3DXVec4.)

Chapter 2

Matrix Algebra

In 3D computer graphics, we use matrices to compactly describe geometric transformations such as scaling, rotation, and translation, and also to change the coordinates of a point or vector from one frame to another. This chapter explores the mathematics of matrices.

Objectives:

- To obtain an understanding of matrices and the operations defined on them.
- To discover how a vector-matrix multiplication can be viewed as a linear combination.
- To learn what the identity matrix is, and what the transpose and inverse of a matrix are.
- To become familiar with the subset of classes and functions provided by the D3DX library used for matrix mathematics.

2.1 Definition

An $m \times n$ *matrix* $\mathbf{M}$ is a rectangular array of real numbers with m rows and n columns. The product of the number of rows and columns gives the dimensions of the matrix. The numbers in a matrix are called *elements* or *entries*. We identify a matrix element by specifying the row and column of the element using a double subscript notation M_{ij}, where the first subscript identifies the row and the second subscript identifies the column.

Example 2.1

Consider the following matrices:

$$
\mathbf{A} = \begin{bmatrix} 3.5 & 0 & 0 & 0 \\ 0 & 1 & 0 & 0 \\ 0 & 0 & 0.5 & 0 \\ 2 & -5 & \sqrt{2} & 1 \end{bmatrix}
\quad
\mathbf{B} = \begin{bmatrix} B_{11} & B_{12} \\ B_{21} & B_{22} \\ B_{31} & B_{32} \end{bmatrix}
\quad
\mathbf{u} = \begin{bmatrix} u_1, u_2, u_3 \end{bmatrix}
\quad
\mathbf{v} = \begin{bmatrix} 1 \\ 2 \\ \sqrt{3} \\ \pi \end{bmatrix}
$$

- Matrix **A** is a 4×4 matrix; matrix **B** is a 3×2 matrix; matrix **u** is a 1×3 matrix; and matrix **v** is a 4×1 matrix.

- We identify the element in the fourth row and second column of matrix **A** by $A_{42} = -5$. We identify the element in the second row and first column of matrix **B** by B_{21}.

- Matrices **u** and **v** are special matrices in the sense that they contain a single row or column, respectively. We sometimes call these kinds of matrices *row vectors* or *column vectors* because they are used to represent a vector in matrix form (e.g., we can freely interchange the vector notations (x, y, z) and $[x, y, z]$). Observe that for row and column vectors, it is unnecessary to use a double subscript to denote the elements of the matrix — we only need one subscript.

Occasionally we like to think of the rows of a matrix as vectors. For example, we might write:

$$
\begin{bmatrix} A_{11} & A_{12} & A_{13} \\ A_{21} & A_{22} & A_{23} \\ A_{31} & A_{32} & A_{33} \end{bmatrix} = \begin{bmatrix} \leftarrow \mathbf{A}_{1,*} \rightarrow \\ \leftarrow \mathbf{A}_{2,*} \rightarrow \\ \leftarrow \mathbf{A}_{3,*} \rightarrow \end{bmatrix}
$$

where $\mathbf{A}_{1,*} = [A_{11}, A_{12}, A_{13}]$, $\mathbf{A}_{2,*} = [A_{21}, A_{22}, A_{23}]$, and $\mathbf{A}_{3,*} = [A_{31}, A_{32}, A_{33}]$. In this notation, the first index specifies the row, and we put an asterisk (*) in the second index to indicate that we are referring to the entire row vector. Likewise, we can do the same thing for the columns:

$$
\begin{bmatrix} A_{11} & A_{12} & A_{13} \\ A_{21} & A_{22} & A_{23} \\ A_{31} & A_{32} & A_{33} \end{bmatrix} = \begin{bmatrix} \uparrow & \uparrow & \uparrow \\ \mathbf{A}_{*,1} & \mathbf{A}_{*,2} & \mathbf{A}_{*,3} \\ \downarrow & \downarrow & \downarrow \end{bmatrix}
$$

where

$$
\mathbf{A}_{*,1} = \begin{bmatrix} A_{11} \\ A_{21} \\ A_{31} \end{bmatrix}, \quad \mathbf{A}_{*,2} = \begin{bmatrix} A_{12} \\ A_{22} \\ A_{32} \end{bmatrix}, \text{ and } \mathbf{A}_{*,3} = \begin{bmatrix} A_{13} \\ A_{23} \\ A_{33} \end{bmatrix}
$$

In this notation, the second index specifies the column, and we put an asterisk (*) in the first index to indicate that we are referring to the entire column vector.

We now define equality, addition, scalar multiplication, and subtraction on matrices:

- Two matrices are equal if and only if their corresponding elements are equal; as such, two matrices must have the same number of rows and columns in order to be compared.

- We add two matrices by adding their corresponding elements; as such, it only makes sense to add matrices that have the same number of rows and columns.

- We multiply a scalar and a matrix by multiplying the scalar with every element in the matrix.

- We define subtraction in terms of matrix addition and scalar multiplication. That is, $\mathbf{A} - \mathbf{B} = \mathbf{A} + (-1 \cdot \mathbf{B}) = \mathbf{A} + (-\mathbf{B})$.

Example 2.2

Let

$$\mathbf{A} = \begin{bmatrix} 1 & 5 \\ -2 & 3 \end{bmatrix}, \mathbf{B} = \begin{bmatrix} 6 & 2 \\ 5 & -8 \end{bmatrix}, \mathbf{C} = \begin{bmatrix} 1 & 5 \\ -2 & 3 \end{bmatrix}, \text{ and } \mathbf{D} = \begin{bmatrix} 2 & 1 & -3 \\ -6 & 3 & 0 \end{bmatrix}$$

Then,

$$\mathbf{A} + \mathbf{B} = \begin{bmatrix} 1 & 5 \\ -2 & 3 \end{bmatrix} + \begin{bmatrix} 6 & 2 \\ 5 & -8 \end{bmatrix} = \begin{bmatrix} 1+6 & 5+2 \\ -2+5 & 3+(-8) \end{bmatrix} = \begin{bmatrix} 7 & 7 \\ 3 & -5 \end{bmatrix}$$

$$\mathbf{A} = \mathbf{C}$$

$$3\mathbf{D} = 3\begin{bmatrix} 2 & 1 & -3 \\ -6 & 3 & 0 \end{bmatrix} = \begin{bmatrix} 3(2) & 3(1) & 3(-3) \\ 3(-6) & 3(3) & 3(0) \end{bmatrix} = \begin{bmatrix} 6 & 3 & -9 \\ -18 & 9 & 0 \end{bmatrix}$$

$$\mathbf{A} - \mathbf{B} = \begin{bmatrix} 1 & 5 \\ -2 & 3 \end{bmatrix} - \begin{bmatrix} 6 & 2 \\ 5 & -8 \end{bmatrix} = \begin{bmatrix} 1-6 & 5-2 \\ -2-5 & 3-(-8) \end{bmatrix} = \begin{bmatrix} -5 & 3 \\ -7 & 11 \end{bmatrix}$$

2.2 **Matrix Multiplication**

The next section defines how to multiply two matrices together. We will see in Chapter 3 that matrix multiplication is used to transform points and vectors and to concatenate transformations.

2.2.1 **Definition**

If $\mathbf{A}$ is an $m \times n$ matrix and $\mathbf{B}$ is an $n \times p$ matrix, then the product $\mathbf{AB}$ is defined and is an $m \times p$ matrix $\mathbf{C}$, where the ijth entry of the product $\mathbf{C}$ is given by taking the dot product of the ith row vector in $\mathbf{A}$ with the jth column vector in $\mathbf{B}$, that is,

$$C_{ij} = \mathbf{A}_{i,*} \cdot \mathbf{B}_{*,j} \tag{2.1}$$

So note that in order for the matrix product $\mathbf{AB}$ to be defined, we require that the number of columns in $\mathbf{A}$ be equal to the number of rows in $\mathbf{B}$, which is to say, we require that the dimension of the row vectors in $\mathbf{A}$ equal the dimension of the column vectors in $\mathbf{B}$. If these dimensions did not match, then the dot product in Equation 2.1 would not make sense.

Example 2.3

Let

$$\mathbf{A} = \begin{bmatrix} 1 & 5 \\ -2 & 3 \end{bmatrix} \text{ and } \mathbf{B} = \begin{bmatrix} 2 & -6 \\ 1 & 3 \\ -3 & 0 \end{bmatrix}$$

The product $\mathbf{AB}$ is not defined since the row vectors in $\mathbf{A}$ have a dimension of 2 and the column vectors in $\mathbf{B}$ have a dimension of 3. In particular, we cannot take the dot product of the first row vector in $\mathbf{A}$ with the first column vector in $\mathbf{B}$ because we cannot take the dot product of a 2D vector with a 3D vector.

Example 2.4

Let

$$\mathbf{A} = \begin{bmatrix} -1 & 5 & -4 \\ 3 & 2 & 1 \end{bmatrix} \text{ and } \mathbf{B} = \begin{bmatrix} 2 & 1 & 0 \\ 0 & -2 & 1 \\ -1 & 2 & 3 \end{bmatrix}$$

We first point out that the product $\mathbf{AB}$ is defined (and is a 2×3 matrix) because the number of columns of $\mathbf{A}$ equals the number of rows of $\mathbf{B}$. Applying Equation 2.1 yields:

$$\mathbf{AB} = \begin{bmatrix} -1 & 5 & -4 \\ 3 & 2 & 1 \end{bmatrix} \begin{bmatrix} 2 & 1 & 0 \\ 0 & -2 & 1 \\ -1 & 2 & 3 \end{bmatrix}$$

$$= \begin{bmatrix} (-1,5,-4)\cdot(2,0,-1) & (-1,5,-4)\cdot(1,-2,2) & (-1,5,-4)\cdot(0,1,3) \\ (3,2,1)\cdot(2,0,-1) & (3,2,1)\cdot(1,-2,2) & (3,2,1)\cdot(0,1,3) \end{bmatrix}$$

$$= \begin{bmatrix} 2 & -19 & -7 \\ 5 & 1 & 5 \end{bmatrix}$$

Observe that the product $\mathbf{BA}$ is not defined because the number of columns in $\mathbf{B}$ does *not* equal the number of rows in $\mathbf{A}$. This demonstrates that, in general, matrix multiplication is not commutative; that is, $\mathbf{AB} \neq \mathbf{BA}$.

2.2.2 **Vector-Matrix Multiplication**

Consider the following vector-matrix multiplication:

$$\mathbf{u}\mathbf{A} = [x, y, z] \begin{bmatrix} A_{11} & A_{12} & A_{13} \\ A_{21} & A_{22} & A_{23} \\ A_{31} & A_{32} & A_{33} \end{bmatrix} = [x, y, z] \begin{bmatrix} \uparrow & \uparrow & \uparrow \\ \mathbf{A}_{*,1} & \mathbf{A}_{*,2} & \mathbf{A}_{*,3} \\ \downarrow & \downarrow & \downarrow \end{bmatrix}$$

Observe that $\mathbf{u}\mathbf{A}$ evaluates to a 1×3 row vector in this case. Now, applying Equation 2.1 gives:

$$\begin{aligned} \mathbf{u}\mathbf{A} &= \begin{bmatrix} \mathbf{u} \cdot \mathbf{A}_{*,1}, & \mathbf{u} \cdot \mathbf{A}_{*,2}, & \mathbf{u} \cdot \mathbf{A}_{*,3} \end{bmatrix} \\ &= \begin{bmatrix} xA_{11} + yA_{21} + zA_{31}, & xA_{12} + yA_{22} + zA_{32}, & xA_{13} + yA_{23} + zA_{33} \end{bmatrix} \\ &= \begin{bmatrix} xA_{11}, xA_{12}, xA_{13} \end{bmatrix} + \begin{bmatrix} yA_{21}, yA_{22}, yA_{23} \end{bmatrix} + \begin{bmatrix} zA_{31}, zA_{32}, zA_{33} \end{bmatrix} \\ &= x \begin{bmatrix} A_{11}, A_{12}, A_{13} \end{bmatrix} + y \begin{bmatrix} A_{21}, A_{22}, A_{23} \end{bmatrix} + z \begin{bmatrix} A_{31}, A_{32}, A_{33} \end{bmatrix} \\ &= x\mathbf{A}_{1,*} + y\mathbf{A}_{2,*} + z\mathbf{A}_{3,*} \end{aligned}$$

Thus,

$$\mathbf{u}\mathbf{A} = x\mathbf{A}_{1,*} + y\mathbf{A}_{2,*} + z\mathbf{A}_{3,*} \tag{2.2}$$

Equation 2.2 is an example of a *linear combination*, and it says that the vector-matrix product $\mathbf{u}\mathbf{A}$ is equivalent to a linear combination of the row vectors of the matrix $\mathbf{A}$ with scalar coefficients $x, y,$ and z given by the vector $\mathbf{u}$. Note that, although we show this for a 1×3 row vector and a 3×3 matrix, the result is true in general. That is, for a $1 \times n$ row vector $\mathbf{u}$ and an $n \times m$ matrix $\mathbf{A}$, we have that $\mathbf{u}\mathbf{A}$ is a linear combination of the row vectors in $\mathbf{A}$ with scalar coefficients given by $\mathbf{u}$:

$$[u_1, \ldots, u_n] \begin{bmatrix} A_{11} & \cdots & A_{1m} \\ \vdots & \ddots & \vdots \\ A_{n1} & \cdots & A_{nm} \end{bmatrix} = u_1 \mathbf{A}_{1,*} + \cdots + u_n \mathbf{A}_{n,*} \tag{2.3}$$

2.2.3 **Associativity**

Matrix multiplication has some nice algebraic properties. For example, matrix multiplication distributes over addition: $\mathbf{A}(\mathbf{B} + \mathbf{C}) = \mathbf{A}\mathbf{B} + \mathbf{A}\mathbf{C}$. In particular, however, we will use the associative law of matrix multiplication from time to time, which allows us to choose the order in which we multiply matrices:

$$(\mathbf{AB})\mathbf{C} = \mathbf{A}(\mathbf{BC})$$

2.3 **The Transpose of a Matrix**

The *transpose* of a matrix is found by interchanging the rows and columns of the matrix. Thus the transpose of an $m \times n$ matrix is an $n \times m$ matrix. We denote the transpose of a matrix $\mathbf{M}$ as $\mathbf{M}^T$.

Example 2.5

Find the transpose for the following three matrices:

$$\mathbf{A} = \begin{bmatrix} 2 & -1 & 8 \\ 3 & 6 & -4 \end{bmatrix} \quad \mathbf{B} = \begin{bmatrix} a & b & c \\ d & e & f \\ g & h & i \end{bmatrix} \quad \mathbf{C} = \begin{bmatrix} 1 \\ 2 \\ 3 \\ 4 \end{bmatrix}$$

The transposes are found by interchanging the rows and columns, thus

$$\mathbf{A}^T = \begin{bmatrix} 2 & 3 \\ -1 & 6 \\ 8 & -4 \end{bmatrix} \quad \mathbf{B}^T = \begin{bmatrix} a & d & g \\ b & e & h \\ c & f & i \end{bmatrix} \quad \mathbf{C}^T = \begin{bmatrix} 1 & 2 & 3 & 4 \end{bmatrix}$$

2.4 **The Identity Matrix**

There is a special matrix called the *identity matrix*. The identity matrix is a square matrix that has zeros for all elements except along the main diagonal; the elements along the main diagonal are all ones.

For example, below are 2×2, 3×3, and 4×4 identity matrices.

$$\begin{bmatrix} 1 & 0 \\ 0 & 1 \end{bmatrix} \quad \begin{bmatrix} 1 & 0 & 0 \\ 0 & 1 & 0 \\ 0 & 0 & 1 \end{bmatrix} \quad \begin{bmatrix} 1 & 0 & 0 & 0 \\ 0 & 1 & 0 & 0 \\ 0 & 0 & 1 & 0 \\ 0 & 0 & 0 & 1 \end{bmatrix}$$

The identity matrix acts as a multiplicative identity; that is, if $\mathbf{A}$ is an $m \times n$ matrix, $\mathbf{B}$ is an $n \times p$ matrix, and $\mathbf{I}$ is the $n \times n$ identity matrix, then

$$\mathbf{AI} = \mathbf{A} \text{ and } \mathbf{IB} = \mathbf{B}$$

In other words, multiplying a matrix by the identity matrix does not change the matrix. The identity matrix can be thought of as the number 1 for matrices. In particular, if $\mathbf{M}$ is a square matrix, then multiplication with the identity matrix is commutative:

$$\mathbf{MI} = \mathbf{IM} = \mathbf{M}$$

Example 2.6

Let $\mathbf{M} = \begin{bmatrix} 1 & 2 \\ 0 & 4 \end{bmatrix}$ and let $\mathbf{I} = \begin{bmatrix} 1 & 0 \\ 0 & 1 \end{bmatrix}$. Verify that $\mathbf{MI} = \mathbf{IM} = \mathbf{M}$.

Applying Equation 2.1 yields:

$$\mathbf{MI} = \begin{bmatrix} 1 & 2 \\ 0 & 4 \end{bmatrix}\begin{bmatrix} 1 & 0 \\ 0 & 1 \end{bmatrix} = \begin{bmatrix} (1,2)\cdot(1,0) & (1,2)\cdot(0,1) \\ (0,4)\cdot(1,0) & (0,4)\cdot(0,1) \end{bmatrix} = \begin{bmatrix} 1 & 2 \\ 0 & 4 \end{bmatrix}$$

and

$$\mathbf{IM} = \begin{bmatrix} 1 & 0 \\ 0 & 1 \end{bmatrix}\begin{bmatrix} 1 & 2 \\ 0 & 4 \end{bmatrix} = \begin{bmatrix} (1,0)\cdot(1,0) & (1,0)\cdot(2,4) \\ (0,1)\cdot(1,0) & (0,1)\cdot(2,4) \end{bmatrix} = \begin{bmatrix} 1 & 2 \\ 0 & 4 \end{bmatrix}$$

Thus it is true that $\mathbf{MI} = \mathbf{IM} = \mathbf{M}$.

Example 2.7

Let $\mathbf{u} = [-1, 2]$ and let $\mathbf{I} = \begin{bmatrix} 1 & 0 \\ 0 & 1 \end{bmatrix}$. Verify that $\mathbf{uI} = \mathbf{u}$.

Applying Equation 2.1 yields:

$$\mathbf{uI} = [-1,2]\begin{bmatrix} 1 & 0 \\ 0 & 1 \end{bmatrix} = \left[(-1,2)\cdot(1,0), \quad (-1,2)\cdot(0,1) \right] = [-1,2]$$

Note that we cannot take the product $\mathbf{Iu}$ because the matrix multiplication is not defined.

2.5 The Inverse of a Matrix

Matrix algebra does not define a division operation, but it does define a multiplicative inverse operation. The following list summarizes the important information about inverses:

- Only square matrices have inverses; therefore, when we speak of matrix inverses we assume we are dealing with a square matrix.
- The inverse of an $n \times n$ matrix $\mathbf{M}$ is an $n \times n$ matrix denoted as $\mathbf{M}^{-1}$.
- Not every square matrix has an inverse. A matrix that does have an inverse is said to be *invertible*, and a matrix that does not have an inverse is said to be *singular*.
- The inverse is unique when it exists.
- Multiplying a matrix with its inverse results in the identity matrix: $\mathbf{MM}^{-1} = \mathbf{M}^{-1}\mathbf{M} = \mathbf{I}$. Note that multiplying a matrix with its own inverse is a case when matrix multiplication is commutative.

Matrix inverses are useful for solving for other matrices in a matrix equation. For example, suppose that we are given the matrix equation $\mathbf{p}' = \mathbf{pM}$. Further suppose that we are given $\mathbf{p}'$ and $\mathbf{M}$, and want to solve for $\mathbf{p}$. Assuming that $\mathbf{M}$ is invertible (i.e., $\mathbf{M}^{-1}$ exists), we can solve for $\mathbf{p}$ like so:

$$\mathbf{p}' = \mathbf{pM}$$
$$\mathbf{p}'\mathbf{M}^{-1} = \mathbf{pMM}^{-1} \qquad \text{Multiply both sides of the equation by } \mathbf{M}^{-1}.$$
$$\mathbf{p}'\mathbf{M}^{-1} = \mathbf{pI} \qquad \mathbf{MM}^{-1} = \mathbf{I}, \text{ by definition of inverse.}$$
$$\mathbf{p}'\mathbf{M}^{-1} = \mathbf{p} \qquad \mathbf{pI} = \mathbf{p}, \text{ by definition of the identity matrix.}$$

Techniques for finding inverses are beyond the scope of this book, but they are described in any linear algebra textbook (it is not difficult; it is just not worth digressing into the procedure here). In §2.6 we will learn about a D3DX function that will find the inverse of a matrix for us, and in the next chapter we will simply give the inverses of the important types of matrices that we will work with in this book.

To conclude this section on inverses, we present the following useful algebraic property for the inverse of a product:

$$(\mathbf{AB})^{-1} = \mathbf{B}^{-1}\mathbf{A}^{-1}$$

This property assumes both $\mathbf{A}$ and $\mathbf{B}$ are invertible and that they are both square matrices of the same dimension. To prove that $\mathbf{B}^{-1}\mathbf{A}^{-1}$ is the inverse of $\mathbf{AB}$, we must show $(\mathbf{AB})(\mathbf{B}^{-1}\mathbf{A}^{-1}) = \mathbf{I}$ and $(\mathbf{B}^{-1}\mathbf{A}^{-1})(\mathbf{AB}) = \mathbf{I}$. This is done as follows:

$$(\mathbf{AB})(\mathbf{B}^{-1}\mathbf{A}^{-1}) = \mathbf{A}(\mathbf{BB}^{-1})\mathbf{A}^{-1} = \mathbf{AIA}^{-1} = \mathbf{AA}^{-1} = \mathbf{I}$$

$$(\mathbf{B}^{-1}\mathbf{A}^{-1})(\mathbf{AB}) = \mathbf{B}^{-1}(\mathbf{A}^{-1}\mathbf{A})\mathbf{B} = \mathbf{B}^{-1}\mathbf{IB} = \mathbf{B}^{-1}\mathbf{B} = \mathbf{I}$$

2.6 **D3DX Matrices**

For transforming points and vectors, we use 1×4 row vectors and 4×4 matrices. The reason for this will be explained in the next chapter. For now, we just concentrate on the D3DX class used to represent 4×4 matrices.

To represent 4×4 matrices in D3DX, we use the D3DXMATRIX class, which is defined as follows:

```
typedef struct D3DXMATRIX : public D3DMATRIX
{
public:
    D3DXMATRIX() {};
    D3DXMATRIX( CONST FLOAT * );
    D3DXMATRIX( CONST D3DMATRIX& );
    D3DXMATRIX( CONST D3DXFLOAT16 * );
    D3DXMATRIX(FLOAT _11, FLOAT _12, FLOAT _13, FLOAT _14,
               FLOAT _21, FLOAT _22, FLOAT _23, FLOAT _24,
               FLOAT _31, FLOAT _32, FLOAT _33, FLOAT _34,
```

```
            FLOAT _41, FLOAT _42, FLOAT _43, FLOAT _44);

    // access grants
    FLOAT& operator () ( UINT Row, UINT Col );
    FLOAT  operator () ( UINT Row, UINT Col ) const;

    // casting operators
    operator FLOAT* ();
    operator CONST FLOAT* () const;

    // assignment operators
    D3DXMATRIX& operator *= ( CONST D3DXMATRIX& );
    D3DXMATRIX& operator += ( CONST D3DXMATRIX& );
    D3DXMATRIX& operator -= ( CONST D3DXMATRIX& );
    D3DXMATRIX& operator *= ( FLOAT );
    D3DXMATRIX& operator /= ( FLOAT );

    // unary operators
    D3DXMATRIX operator + () const;
    D3DXMATRIX operator - () const;

    // binary operators
    D3DXMATRIX operator * ( CONST D3DXMATRIX& ) const;
    D3DXMATRIX operator + ( CONST D3DXMATRIX& ) const;
    D3DXMATRIX operator - ( CONST D3DXMATRIX& ) const;
    D3DXMATRIX operator * ( FLOAT ) const;
    D3DXMATRIX operator / ( FLOAT ) const;

    friend D3DXMATRIX operator*(FLOAT, CONST D3DXMATRIX& );

    BOOL operator == ( CONST D3DXMATRIX& ) const;
    BOOL operator != ( CONST D3DXMATRIX& ) const;

} D3DXMATRIX, *LPD3DXMATRIX;
```

Observe that D3DXMATRIX inherits its data members from D3DMATRIX, which is defined as:

```
typedef struct _D3DMATRIX {
    union {
        struct {
            float       _11, _12, _13, _14;
            float       _21, _22, _23, _24;
            float       _31, _32, _33, _34;
            float       _41, _42, _43, _44;
        };
        float m[4][4];
    };
} D3DMATRIX;
```

The D3DXMATRIX class has a myriad of useful operators, such as testing for equality, and adding, subtracting, and multiplying matrices. In addition, the overloaded parenthesis operator provides a convenient syntax for accessing the elements in a D3DMATRIX by specifying its row and column (using zero-based indices).

In addition to the above class, the D3DX library includes the following four useful functions for obtaining the 4×4 identity matrix, computing the transpose of a matrix, computing the inverse of a matrix, and a few different functions for multiplying vectors and matrices.

■ D3DXMATRIX *D3DXMatrixIdentity(
    D3DXMATRIX *pOut);   // Makes input the identity matrix.

■ D3DXMATRIX *D3DXMatrixTranspose(
    D3DXMATRIX *pOut,   // Output $\mathbf{M}^T$
    CONST D3DXMATRIX *pM); // Input $\mathbf{M}$

■ D3DXMATRIX *D3DXMatrixInverse(
    D3DXMATRIX *pOut,   // Output $\mathbf{M}^{-1}$
    FLOAT *pDeterminant,   // Not needed, specify zero
    CONST D3DXMATRIX *pM); // Input $\mathbf{M}$

■ D3DXVECTOR4 *D3DXVec4Transform(
    D3DXVECTOR4 *pOut,   // Output $\mathbf{vM}$
    CONST D3DXVECTOR4 *pV, // Input $\mathbf{v}$
    CONST D3DXMATRIX *pM); // Input $\mathbf{M}$

The following code provides some examples on how to use the D3DXMATRIX class and the four functions listed above.

```cpp
#include <d3dx10.h>
#include <iostream>
using namespace std;

// Overload the "<<" operators so that we can use cout to
// output D3DXVECTOR4 and D3DXMATRIX objects.

ostream& operator<<(ostream& os, D3DXVECTOR4& v)
{
    os << "(" << v.x << ", " << v.y << ", "
        << v.z << ", " << v.w << ")";
    return os;
}

ostream& operator<<(ostream& os, D3DXMATRIX& m)
{
    for(int i = 0; i < 4; ++i)
    {
        for(int j = 0; j < 4; ++j)
            os << m(i, j) << " ";
        os << endl;
    }
    return os;
```

```
    }

int main()
{
    D3DXMATRIX A(1.0f, 0.0f, 0.0f, 0.0f,
                 0.0f, 2.0f, 0.0f, 0.0f,
                 0.0f, 0.0f, 4.0f, 0.0f,
                 1.0f, 2.0f, 3.0f, 1.0f);

    D3DXMATRIX B;
    D3DXMatrixIdentity(&B);

    // matrix-matrix multiplication
    D3DXMATRIX C = A*B;

    D3DXMATRIX D, E, F;

    D3DXMatrixTranspose(&D, &A);

    D3DXMatrixInverse(&E, 0, &A);

    F = A * E;

    D3DXVECTOR4 P(2.0f, 2.0f, 2.0f, 1.0f);
    D3DXVECTOR4 Q(2.0f, 2.0f, 2.0f, 0.0f);
    D3DXVECTOR4 R, S;
    D3DXVec4Transform(&R, &P, &A);
    D3DXVec4Transform(&S, &Q, &A);

    cout << "A = "                 << endl << A << endl;
    cout << "B = "                 << endl << B << endl;
    cout << "C = A*B = "           << endl << C << endl;
    cout << "D = transpose(A)= "   << endl << D << endl;
    cout << "E = inverse(A) = "    << endl << E << endl;
    cout << "F = A*E = "           << endl << F << endl;
    cout << "P = "                 << P << endl;
    cout << "Q = "                 << Q << endl;
    cout << "R = P*A = "           << R << endl;
    cout << "S = Q*A = "           << S << endl;

    return 0;
}
```

Note: Remember to link the _d3dx10.lib_ (or _d3dx10d.lib_ for debug builds) library file with your application to use any D3DX code; moreover, you will also need to `#include` `<d3dx10.h>`.

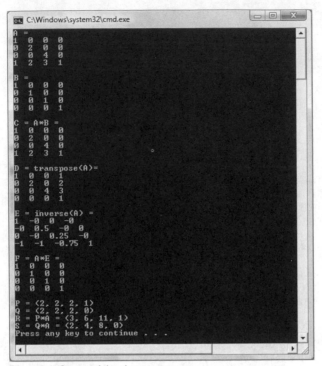

Figure 2.1: Output of the above program.

2.7 **Summary**

- An $m \times n$ matrix **M** is a rectangular array of real numbers with m rows and n columns. Two matrices of the same dimensions are equal if and only if their corresponding components are equal. We add two matrices of the same dimension by adding their corresponding elements. We multiply a scalar and a matrix by multiplying the scalar with every element in the matrix.

- If **A** is an $m \times n$ matrix and **B** is an $n \times p$ matrix, then the product **AB** is defined and is an $m \times p$ matrix **C**, where the ijth entry of the product **C** is given by taking the dot product of the ith row vector in **A** with the jth column vector in **B**; that is, $C_{ij} = \mathbf{A}_{i,*} \cdot \mathbf{B}_{*,j}$.

- Matrix multiplication is not commutative (i.e., $\mathbf{AB} \neq \mathbf{BA}$, in general). Matrix multiplication is associative: $(\mathbf{AB})\mathbf{C} = \mathbf{A}(\mathbf{BC})$.

- The *transpose* of a matrix is found by interchanging the rows and columns of the matrix. Thus the transpose of an $m \times n$ matrix is an $n \times m$ matrix. We denote the transpose of a matrix **M** as $\mathbf{M}^T$.

- The identity matrix is a square matrix that has zeros for all elements except along the main diagonal, and the elements along the main diagonal are all ones.
- Multiplying a matrix with its inverse results in the identity matrix: $\mathbf{MM}^{-1} = \mathbf{M}^{-1}\mathbf{M} = \mathbf{I}$. The inverse of a matrix, if it exists, is unique. Only square matrices have inverses and even then, a square matrix may not be invertible.

2.8 **Exercises**

1. Solve the following matrix equation for : $\mathbf{X}$.

$$3\left(\begin{bmatrix} -2 & 0 \\ 1 & 3 \end{bmatrix} - 2\mathbf{X}\right) = 2\begin{bmatrix} -2 & 0 \\ 1 & 3 \end{bmatrix}$$

2. Compute the following matrix products:

   a. $\begin{bmatrix} -2 & 0 & 3 \\ 4 & 1 & -1 \end{bmatrix}\begin{bmatrix} 2 & -1 \\ 0 & 6 \\ 2 & -3 \end{bmatrix}$

   b. $\begin{bmatrix} 1 & 2 \\ 3 & 4 \end{bmatrix}\begin{bmatrix} -2 & 0 \\ 1 & 1 \end{bmatrix}$

   c. $\begin{bmatrix} 2 & 0 & 2 \\ 0 & -1 & -3 \\ 0 & 0 & 1 \end{bmatrix}\begin{bmatrix} 1 \\ 2 \\ 1 \end{bmatrix}$

3. Compute the transpose of the following matrices:

   a. $\begin{bmatrix} 1, & 2, & 3 \end{bmatrix}$

   b. $\begin{bmatrix} x & y \\ z & w \end{bmatrix}$

   c. $\begin{bmatrix} 1 & 2 \\ 3 & 4 \\ 5 & 6 \\ 7 & 8 \end{bmatrix}$

4. Let $A = \begin{bmatrix} 2 & 0 & 1 \\ 0 & -1 & -3 \\ 0 & 0 & 1 \end{bmatrix}$. Is $B = \begin{bmatrix} 1/2 & 0 & -1/2 \\ 0 & -1 & -3 \\ 0 & 0 & 1 \end{bmatrix}$ the inverse of A?

5. Let $A = \begin{bmatrix} 1 & 2 \\ 3 & 4 \end{bmatrix}$. Is $B = \begin{bmatrix} -2 & 1 \\ 3/2 & 1/2 \end{bmatrix}$ the inverse of A?

6. Write the following linear combinations as vector-matrix products:

    a. $v = 2(1,2,3) - 4(-5,0,-1) + 3(2,-2,3)$

    b. $v = 3(2,-4) + 2(1,4) - 1(-2,-3) + 5(1,1)$

7. Show that

$$AB = \begin{bmatrix} A_{11} & A_{12} & A_{13} \\ A_{21} & A_{22} & A_{23} \\ A_{31} & A_{32} & A_{33} \end{bmatrix} \begin{bmatrix} B_{11} & B_{12} & B_{13} \\ B_{21} & B_{22} & B_{23} \\ B_{31} & B_{32} & B_{33} \end{bmatrix} = \begin{bmatrix} \leftarrow & A_{1,*}B & \rightarrow \\ \leftarrow & A_{2,*}B & \rightarrow \\ \leftarrow & A_{3,*}B & \rightarrow \end{bmatrix}$$

8. Show that

$$Au = \begin{bmatrix} A_{11} & A_{12} & A_{13} \\ A_{21} & A_{22} & A_{23} \\ A_{31} & A_{32} & A_{33} \end{bmatrix} \begin{bmatrix} x \\ y \\ z \end{bmatrix} = xA_{*,1} + yA_{*,2} + zA_{*,3}$$

9. Show that $\left(A^{-1} \right)^T = \left(A^T \right)^{-1}$, assuming A is invertible.

10. Let $A = \begin{bmatrix} A_{11} & A_{12} \\ A_{21} & A_{22} \end{bmatrix}$, $B = \begin{bmatrix} B_{11} & B_{12} \\ B_{21} & B_{22} \end{bmatrix}$, and $C = \begin{bmatrix} C_{11} & C_{12} \\ C_{21} & C_{22} \end{bmatrix}$. Show that
    $A(BC) = (AB)C$. This shows that matrix multiplication is associative
    for 2×2 matrices. (In fact, matrix multiplication is associative for gen-
    eral sized matrices, whenever the multiplication is defined.)

Chapter 3

Transformations

We describe objects in our 3D worlds geometrically; that is, as a collection of triangles that approximate the exterior surfaces of the objects. It would be an uninteresting world if our objects remained motionless. Thus we are interested in methods for transforming geometry; examples of geometric transformations are translation, rotation, and scaling. In this chapter, we develop matrix equations, which can be used to transform points and vectors in 3D space.

Objectives:

- To learn the coordinate transformations for scaling, rotating, and translating geometry.
- To discover how several transformation matrices can be combined into one net transformation matrix through matrix-matrix multiplication.
- To find out how we can convert coordinates from one coordinate system to another, and how this change of coordinate transformation can be represented by a matrix.
- To become familiar with the subset of functions provided by the D3DX library used for constructing transformation matrices.

3.1 **Basic Transformations**

When programming using Direct3D, we use 4×4 matrices to represent transformations. The idea is this: We set the entries of a 4×4 matrix $\mathbf{M}$ to describe a specific transformation. Then we place the coordinates of a point or vector into the columns of a 1×4 row vector $\mathbf{v}$. The product $\mathbf{vM}$ results in a new row vector $\mathbf{v}'$ that represents the transformed point/vector.

We use 4×4 matrices because that particular size can represent all the transformations we need. A 3×3 sized matrix may at first seem more suitable to 3D; however, there are many types of transformations that we would like to use that cannot be described with a 3×3 matrix, such as translations, perspective projections, and reflections. Remember that we are working with a vector-matrix product, and so we are limited to the rules of matrix multiplication to perform transformations. Augmenting to a 4×4 matrix allows us to describe more transformations with a vector-matrix product.

We said that we place the coordinates of a point or vector in the columns of a 1×4 row vector. But our points and vectors have three coordinates, not four. So what do we place for the fourth coordinate? First, realize that when using a 4×4 matrix we must use a 1×4 row vector so that the multiplication is defined; the product of a 1×3 row vector and a 4×4 matrix is not defined. The 4-tuples used to write the coordinates of a 3D vector or point are called *homogeneous coordinates*, and what we place in the fourth w-coordinate depends on whether we are describing a point or a vector. Specifically, we write:

- $(x, y, z, 0)$ for vectors
- $(x, y, z, 1)$ for points

We will see later that setting $w = 1$ for points allows translations of points to work correctly, and setting $w = 0$ for vectors prevents the coordinates of vectors from being modified by translations. (We do not want to translate the coordinates of a vector, as that would change its direction and magnitude — translations should not alter the properties of vectors.) We now have enough background to look at some particular kinds of transformations we will be working with.

Note: The notation of homogeneous coordinates is consistent with the ideas shown in Figure 1.13. That is, the difference between two points $\mathbf{q} - \mathbf{p} = (q_x, q_y, q_z, 1) - (p_x, p_y, p_z, 1) = (q_x - p_x, q_y - p_y, q_z - p_z, 0)$ results in a vector, and a point plus a vector $\mathbf{p} + \mathbf{v} = (p_x, p_y, p_z, 1) + (v_x, v_y, v_z, 0) = (p_x + v_x, p_y + v_y, p_z + v_z, 1)$ results in a point.

3.1.1 **Scaling**

Scaling refers to changing the size of an object as shown in Figure 3.1.

Figure 3.1: The left pawn is the original object. The middle pawn is the original pawn scaled 2 units on the y-axis. The right pawn is the original pawn scaled 2 units on the x-axis.

The scaling matrix:

$$S = \begin{bmatrix} s_x & 0 & 0 & 0 \\ 0 & s_y & 0 & 0 \\ 0 & 0 & s_z & 0 \\ 0 & 0 & 0 & 1 \end{bmatrix}$$

scales geometry s_x units on the x-axis, s_y units on the y-axis, and s_z units on the z-axis.

The inverse of the scaling matrix is given by:

$$S^{-1} = \begin{bmatrix} 1/s_x & 0 & 0 & 0 \\ 0 & 1/s_y & 0 & 0 \\ 0 & 0 & 1/s_z & 0 \\ 0 & 0 & 0 & 1 \end{bmatrix}$$

Example 3.1

Suppose we have a square defined by a minimum point (–4, –4, 0) and a maximum point (4, 4, 0). Suppose now that we wish to scale the square 0.5 units on the x-axis, 2.0 units on the y-axis, and leave the z-axis unchanged. The corresponding scaling matrix is:

$$S = \begin{bmatrix} 0.5 & 0 & 0 & 0 \\ 0 & 2 & 0 & 0 \\ 0 & 0 & 1 & 0 \\ 0 & 0 & 0 & 1 \end{bmatrix}$$

Now to actually scale (transform) the square, we multiply both the minimum point and maximum point by this matrix:

$$[-4,-4,0,1] \begin{bmatrix} 0.5 & 0 & 0 & 0 \\ 0 & 2 & 0 & 0 \\ 0 & 0 & 1 & 0 \\ 0 & 0 & 0 & 1 \end{bmatrix} = [-2,-8,0,1]$$

$$[4,4,0,1] \begin{bmatrix} 0.5 & 0 & 0 & 0 \\ 0 & 2 & 0 & 0 \\ 0 & 0 & 1 & 0 \\ 0 & 0 & 0 & 1 \end{bmatrix} = [2,8,0,1]$$

The result is shown in Figure 3.2.

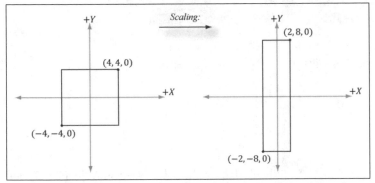

Figure 3.2: Scaling by one-half units on the *x*-axis and two units on the *y*-axis. Note that when looking down the negative *z*-axis, the geometry is basically 2D since *z* = 0.

3.1.2 **Rotation**

Often we will want to rotate geometry about some axis passing through the origin of the working coordinate system (see Figure 3.3).

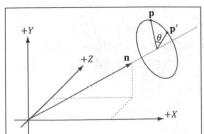

Figure 3.3: Clockwise rotation about an arbitrary axis **n**. The point **p** gets rotated by an angle θ to the point **p**′.

The following matrix rotates points/vectors about an arbitrary axis $\mathbf{n} = (x, y, z)$ by an angle θ:

$$\mathbf{R}_n = \begin{bmatrix} c+(1-c)x^2 & (1-c)xy+sz & (1-c)xz-sy & 0 \\ (1-c)xy-sz & c+(1-c)y^2 & (1-c)yz+sx & 0 \\ (1-c)xz+sy & (1-c)yz-sx & c+(1-c)z^2 & 0 \\ 0 & 0 & 0 & 1 \end{bmatrix}$$

where $c = \cos\theta$ and $s = \sin\theta$.

Note: In a left-handed coordinate system, positive angles go clockwise when looking down the positive axis of rotation.

Rotation matrices have an interesting property. The readers can verify that each row vector is unit length and the row vectors are mutually orthogonal. Thus the row vectors are *orthonormal* (i.e., mutually orthogonal and unit length). A matrix whose rows are orthonormal is said to be an *orthogonal matrix*. An orthogonal matrix has the attractive property that its inverse is actually equal to its transpose. Thus, the inverse of $\mathbf{R}_n$ is:

$$\mathbf{R}_n^{-1} = \mathbf{R}_n^T \begin{bmatrix} c+(1-c)x^2 & (1-c)xy-sz & (1-c)xz+sy & 0 \\ (1-c)xy+sz & c+(1-c)y^2 & (1-c)yz-sx & 0 \\ (1-c)xz-sy & (1-c)yz+sx & c+(1-c)z^2 & 0 \\ 0 & 0 & 0 & 1 \end{bmatrix}$$

In general, orthogonal matrices are desirable to work with since their inverses are easy and efficient to compute.

In particular, if we choose the x-, y-, and z-axes for rotation (i.e., $\mathbf{n} = (1, 0, 0)$, $\mathbf{n} = (0, 1, 0)$, and $\mathbf{n} = (0, 0, 1)$, respectively), then we get the x, y, and z rotation matrices:

$$\mathbf{R}_x = \begin{bmatrix} 1 & 0 & 0 & 0 \\ 0 & \cos\theta & \sin\theta & 0 \\ 0 & -\sin\theta & \cos\theta & 0 \\ 0 & 0 & 0 & 1 \end{bmatrix}, \mathbf{R}_y = \begin{bmatrix} \cos\theta & 0 & -\sin\theta & 0 \\ 0 & 1 & 0 & 0 \\ \sin\theta & 0 & \cos\theta & 0 \\ 0 & 0 & 0 & 1 \end{bmatrix}, \mathbf{R}_z = \begin{bmatrix} \cos\theta & \sin\theta & 0 & 0 \\ -\sin\theta & \cos\theta & 0 & 0 \\ 0 & 0 & 1 & 0 \\ 0 & 0 & 0 & 1 \end{bmatrix}$$

Example 3.2

Suppose we have a square defined by a minimum point (–1, 0, –1) and a maximum point (1, 0, 1). Suppose now that we wish to rotate the square –30° clockwise about the y-axis (i.e., 30° counterclockwise). Then the y-axis rotation matrix is:

$$
\mathbf{R}_y =
\begin{bmatrix}
\cos\theta & 0 & -\sin\theta & 0 \\
0 & 1 & 0 & 0 \\
\sin\theta & 0 & \cos\theta & 0 \\
0 & 0 & 0 & 1
\end{bmatrix}
=
\begin{bmatrix}
\cos(-30°) & 0 & -\sin(-30°) & 0 \\
0 & 1 & 0 & 0 \\
\sin(-30°) & 0 & \cos(-30°) & 0 \\
0 & 0 & 0 & 1
\end{bmatrix}
=
\begin{bmatrix}
\frac{\sqrt{3}}{2} & 0 & \frac{1}{2} & 0 \\
0 & 1 & 0 & 0 \\
-\frac{1}{2} & 0 & \frac{\sqrt{3}}{2} & 0 \\
0 & 0 & 0 & 1
\end{bmatrix}
$$

Now to actually rotate (transform) the square, we multiply both the minimum point and maximum point by this matrix:

$$
[-1, 0, -1, 1]
\begin{bmatrix}
\frac{\sqrt{3}}{2} & 0 & \frac{1}{2} & 0 \\
0 & 1 & 0 & 0 \\
-\frac{1}{2} & 0 & \frac{\sqrt{3}}{2} & 0 \\
0 & 0 & 0 & 1
\end{bmatrix}
\approx [-0.36, 0, -1.36, 1]
$$

$$
[1, 0, 1, 1]
\begin{bmatrix}
\frac{\sqrt{3}}{2} & 0 & \frac{1}{2} & 0 \\
0 & 1 & 0 & 0 \\
-\frac{1}{2} & 0 & \frac{\sqrt{3}}{2} & 0 \\
0 & 0 & 0 & 1
\end{bmatrix}
\approx [0.36, 0, 1.36, 1]
$$

The result is shown in Figure 3.4.

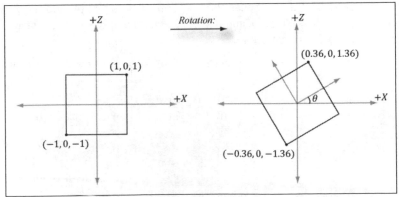

Figure 3.4: Rotating –30° clockwise around the y-axis. Note that when looking down the positive y-axis, the geometry is basically 2D since $y = 0$.

3.1.3 **Translation**

To translate a point **u**, we simply add a displacement vector **b** to it, to get the new point **u** + **b** (see Figure 3.5). Note that to translate an entire object, we translate every point on the object by the same vector **b**.

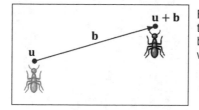

Figure 3.5: Displacing the position of the ant by some displacement vector **b**.

The translation matrix is given as follows:

$$\mathbf{T} = \begin{bmatrix} 1 & 0 & 0 & 0 \\ 0 & 1 & 0 & 0 \\ 0 & 0 & 1 & 0 \\ b_x & b_y & b_z & 1 \end{bmatrix}$$

If you multiply a point $\mathbf{u} = (u_x, u_y, u_z, 1)$ by this matrix, you get:

$$\mathbf{uT} = (u_x + b_x, u_y + b_y, u_z + b_z, 1) = \mathbf{u} + \mathbf{b}$$

The inverse of the translation matrix is given by:

$$\mathbf{T}^{-1} = \begin{bmatrix} 1 & 0 & 0 & 0 \\ 0 & 1 & 0 & 0 \\ 0 & 0 & 1 & 0 \\ -b_x & -b_y & -b_z & 1 \end{bmatrix}$$

Example 3.3

Suppose we have a square defined by a minimum point (–8, 2, 0) and a maximum point (–2, 8, 0). Suppose now that we wish to translate the square 12 units on the x-axis, –10 units on the y-axis, and leave the z-axis unchanged. The corresponding translation matrix is:

$$\mathbf{T} = \begin{bmatrix} 1 & 0 & 0 & 0 \\ 0 & 1 & 0 & 0 \\ 0 & 0 & 1 & 0 \\ 12 & -10 & 0 & 1 \end{bmatrix}$$

Now to actually translate (transform) the square, we multiply both the minimum point and maximum point by this matrix:

$$[-8,2,0,1]\begin{bmatrix} 1 & 0 & 0 & 0 \\ 0 & 1 & 0 & 0 \\ 0 & 0 & 1 & 0 \\ 12 & -10 & 0 & 1 \end{bmatrix} = [4,-8,0,1]$$

$$[-2,8,0,1]\begin{bmatrix} 1 & 0 & 0 & 0 \\ 0 & 1 & 0 & 0 \\ 0 & 0 & 1 & 0 \\ 12 & -10 & 0 & 1 \end{bmatrix} = [10,-2,0,1]$$

The result is shown in Figure 3.6.

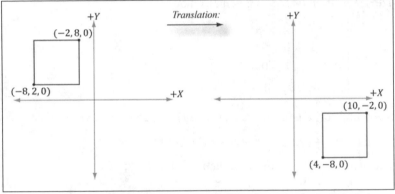

Figure 3.6: Translating 12 units on the *x*-axis and −10 units on the *y*-axis. Note that when looking down the negative *z*-axis, the geometry is basically 2D since *z* = 0.

3.2 **D3DX Transformation Functions**

In this section we summarize the D3DX-related functions for building the various transformation matrices.

```
// Constructs a scaling matrix:
D3DXMATRIX *WINAPI D3DXMatrixScaling(
    D3DXMATRIX *pOut,              // Returns S
    FLOAT sx, FLOAT sy, FLOAT sz);  // Scaling factors

// Constructs an x-axis rotation matrix:
D3DXMATRIX *WINAPI D3DXMatrixRotationX(
    D3DXMATRIX *pOut,      // Returns Rn, where n = (1, 0, 0)
    FLOAT Angle);          // Angle θ to rotate

// Constructs a y-axis rotation matrix:
D3DXMATRIX *WINAPI D3DXMatrixRotationY(
    D3DXMATRIX *pOut,      // Returns Rn, where n = (0, 1, 0)
    FLOAT Angle);          // Angle θ to rotate
```

```
// Constructs a z-axis rotation matrix:
D3DXMATRIX *WINAPI D3DXMatrixRotationZ(
    D3DXMATRIX *pOut,       // Returns Rn, where n = (0, 0, 1)
    FLOAT Angle);           // Angle θ to rotate

// Constructs an arbitrary axis rotation matrix:
D3DXMATRIX *WINAPI D3DXMatrixRotationAxis(
    D3DXMATRIX *pOut,       // Returns Rn
    CONST D3DXVECTOR3 *pV,  // Axis n to rotate about
    FLOAT Angle);           // Angle θ to rotate

// Constructs a translation matrix:
D3DXMATRIX *WINAPI D3DXMatrixTranslation(
    D3DXMATRIX *pOut,           // Returns T
    FLOAT x, FLOAT y, FLOAT z); // Translation factors
```

Note: For the rotation matrices, the angles are given in radians.
    Observe that the above D3DX functions return pointers to
D3DXMATRIX* objects; these pointers point to the same object as pOut,
thereby allowing us to pass the functions as parameters to other
functions (other D3DX functions do this also, which you may have
noticed in Chapters 1 and 2). For example,

```
D3DXMATRIX M, T;
D3DXMatrixTranspose(&T, D3DXMatrixRotationX(&M));
```

3.3 Composition of Transformations

Suppose $\mathbf{S}$ is a scaling matrix, $\mathbf{R}$ is a rotation matrix, and $\mathbf{T}$ is a translation
matrix. Assume we have a cube made up of eight vertices, $\mathbf{v}_i$, for
$i = 0, 1, ..., 7$, and we wish to apply these three transformations to each
vertex successively. The obvious way to do this is step-by-step:

$$\big((\mathbf{v}_i \mathbf{S})\mathbf{R}\big)\mathbf{T} = (\mathbf{v}_i' \mathbf{R})\mathbf{T} = \mathbf{v}_i'' \mathbf{T} = \mathbf{v}_i''' \text{ for } i = 0, 1, ..., 7$$

However, because matrix multiplication is associative, we can instead write
this equivalently as:

$$\mathbf{v}_i(\mathbf{SRT}) = \mathbf{v}_i''' \text{ for } i = 0, 1, ..., 7$$

We can think of the matrix $\mathbf{C} = \mathbf{SRT}$ as a matrix that encapsulates all three
transformations into one net affine transformation matrix. In other words,
matrix-matrix multiplication allows us to concatenate transforms.

    This has performance implications. To see this, assume that a 3D
object is composed of 20,000 points and that we want to apply these three
successive geometric transformations to the object. Using the step-by-step
approach, we would require $20,000 \times 3$ vector-matrix multiplications. On the
other hand, using the combined matrix approach requires 20,000 vector-
matrix multiplications and two matrix-matrix multiplications. Clearly, two

extra matrix-matrix multiplications is a cheap price to pay for the large savings in vector-matrix multiplications.

Note: Again, we point out that matrix multiplication is not commutative. This is even seen geometrically. For example, a rotation followed by a translation, which we can describe by the matrix product **RT**, does not result in the same transformation as the same translation followed by the same rotation, that is, **TR**. Figure 3.7 demonstrates this.

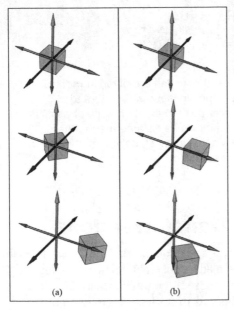

Figure 3.7: (a) Rotating first and then translating. (b) Translating first and then rotating.

(a)   (b)

3.4 Change of Coordinate Transformations

The scalar 100° C represents the temperature of boiling water relative to the Celsius scale. How do we describe the *same* temperature of boiling water relative to the Fahrenheit scale? In other words, what is the scalar, relative to the Fahrenheit scale, that represents the temperature of boiling water? To make this conversion (or change of frame), we need to know how the Celsius and Fahrenheit scales relate. They are related as follows: $T_F = \frac{9}{5}T_C + 32°$. Therefore, $T_F = \frac{9}{5}T_C + 32° = 212°$ F; that is, the temperature of boiling water is 212° Fahrenheit.

This example illustrates that we can convert a scalar k that describes some quantity relative to a frame A into a new scalar k' that describes the *same* quantity relative to a different frame B, provided that we know how frame A and B are related. In the following subsections, we look at a similar problem, but instead of scalars, we are interested in converting the coordinates of a point/vector relative to one frame into coordinates relative to a different frame (see Figure 3.8). We call the transformation that converts coordinates from one frame into coordinates of another frame a *change of coordinate transformation*.

It is worth emphasizing that in a change of coordinate transformation, we do not think of the geometry as changing; rather, we are changing the frame of reference, which thus changes the coordinate representation of the geometry. This is in contrast to how we usually think about rotations, translations, and scaling, where we think of actually physically moving or deforming the geometry.

In 3D computer graphics, since we employ multiple coordinate systems, we need to know how to convert from one to another. Because location is a property of points, but not of vectors, the change of coordinate transformation is different for points and vectors.

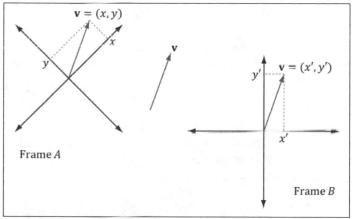

Figure 3.8: The *same* vector **v** has different coordinates when described relative to different frames.

3.4.1 **Vectors**

Consider Figure 3.9 in which we have two frames, A and B, and a vector **p**. Suppose we are given the coordinates $\mathbf{p}_A = (x, y)$ of **p** relative to frame A, and we wish to find the coordinates $\mathbf{p}_B = (x', y')$ of **p** relative to frame B. In other words, given the coordinates identifying a vector relative to one frame, how do we find the coordinates that identify the same vector relative to a different frame?

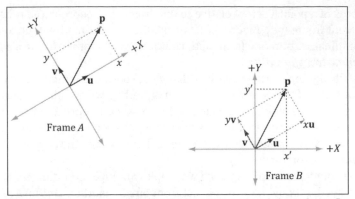

Figure 3.9: The geometry of finding the coordinates of **p** relative to frame *B*.

From Figure 3.9, it is clear that

$$\mathbf{p} = x\mathbf{u} + y\mathbf{v}$$

where **u** and **v** are unit vectors that aim, respectively, along the *x*- and *y*-axes of frame *A*. Expressing each vector in the above equation in frame *B* coordinates we get:

$$\mathbf{p}_B = x\mathbf{u}_B + y\mathbf{v}_B$$

Thus, if we are given $\mathbf{p}_A = (x, y)$ and we know the coordinates of the vectors **u** and **v** relative to frame *B*, that is if we know $\mathbf{u}_B = (u_x, u_y)$ and $\mathbf{v}_B = (v_x, v_y)$, then we can always find $\mathbf{p}_B = (x', y')$.

Generalizing to 3D, if $\mathbf{p}_A = (x, y, z)$, then

$$\mathbf{p}_B = x\mathbf{u}_B + y\mathbf{v}_B + z\mathbf{w}_B$$

where **u**, **v**, and **w** are unit vectors that aim, respectively, along the *x*-, *y*- and *z*-axes of frame *A*.

3.4.2 **Points**

The change of coordinate transformation for points is slightly different from the one for vectors; this is because location is important for points, so we cannot translate points as we translated the vectors in Figure 3.9.

Figure 3.10 shows the situation, and we see that the point **p** can be expressed by the equation:

$$\mathbf{p} = x\mathbf{u} + y\mathbf{v} + \mathbf{Q}$$

where **u** and **v** are unit vectors that aim, respectively, along the x- and y-axes of frame A, and **Q** is the origin of frame A. Expressing each vector/point in the above equation in frame B coordinates we get:

$$\mathbf{p}_B = x\mathbf{u}_B + y\mathbf{v}_B + \mathbf{Q}_B$$

Thus, if we are given $\mathbf{p}_A = (x, y)$ and we know the coordinates of the vectors **u** and **v**, and origin **Q** relative to frame B, that is if we know $\mathbf{u}_B = (u_x, u_y)$, $\mathbf{v}_B = (v_x, v_y)$, and $\mathbf{Q}_B = (Q_x, Q_y)$, then we can always find $\mathbf{p}_B = (x', y')$.

Generalizing to 3D, if $\mathbf{p}_A = (x, y, z)$, then

$$\mathbf{p}_B = x\mathbf{u}_B + y\mathbf{v}_B + z\mathbf{w}_B + \mathbf{Q}_B$$

where **u**, **v**, and **w** are unit vectors that aim, respectively, along the x-, y- and z-axes of frame A, and **Q** is the origin of frame A.

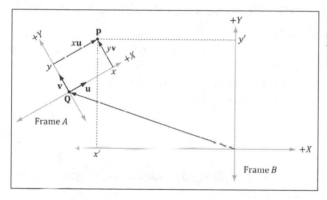

Figure 3.10: The geometry of finding the coordinates of **p** relative to frame B.

3.4.3 Matrix Representation

To review so far, the vector and point change of coordinate transformations are:

$$\left(x', y', z'\right) = x\mathbf{u}_B + y\mathbf{v}_B + z\mathbf{w}_B \qquad \text{for vectors}$$

$$\left(x', y', z'\right) = x\mathbf{u}_B + y\mathbf{v}_B + z\mathbf{w}_B + \mathbf{Q}_B \quad \text{for points}$$

If we use homogeneous coordinates, then we can handle vectors and points by one equation:

$$\left(x', y', z', w\right) = x\mathbf{u}_B + y\mathbf{v}_B + z\mathbf{w}_B + w\mathbf{Q}_B \qquad (3.1)$$

If $w = 0$, then this equation reduces to the change of coordinate transformation for vectors; if $w = 1$, then this equation reduces to the change of coordinate transformation for points. The advantage of Equation 3.1 is that it works for both vectors and points, provided we set the w-coordinates correctly; we no longer need two equations (one for vectors and one for points). Equation 2.3 says that we can write Equation 3.1 in the language of matrices:

$$[x', y', z', w] = [x, y, z, w] \begin{bmatrix} u_x & u_y & u_z & 0 \\ v_x & v_y & v_z & 0 \\ w_x & w_y & w_z & 0 \\ Q_x & Q_y & Q_z & 1 \end{bmatrix} = x\mathbf{u}_B + y\mathbf{v}_B + z\mathbf{w}_B + w\mathbf{Q}_B \quad (3.2)$$

where $\mathbf{Q}_B = (Q_x, Q_y, Q_z, 1)$, $\mathbf{u}_B = (u_x, u_y, u_z, 0)$, $\mathbf{v}_B = (v_x, v_y, v_z, 0)$, and $\mathbf{w}_B = (w_x, w_y, w_z, 0)$ describe the origin and axes of frame A with homogeneous coordinates relative to frame B. We call the 4×4 matrix in Equation 3.2 a *change of coordinate matrix* or *change of frame matrix*, and we say it converts (or maps) frame A coordinates into frame B coordinates.

3.4.4 Associativity and Change of Coordinate Matrices

Suppose now that we have three frames, F, G, and H. Moreover, let $\mathbf{A}$ be the change of frame matrix from F to G, and let $\mathbf{B}$ be the change of frame matrix from G to H. Suppose we have the coordinates $\mathbf{p}_F$ of a vector relative to frame F and we want the coordinates of the same vector relative to frame H, that is, we want $\mathbf{p}_H$. One way to do this is step-by-step:

$$(\mathbf{p}_F \mathbf{A})\mathbf{B} = \mathbf{p}_H$$

$$(\mathbf{p}_G)\mathbf{B} = \mathbf{p}_H$$

However, because matrix multiplication is associative, we can instead rewrite $(\mathbf{p}_F \mathbf{A})\mathbf{B} = \mathbf{p}_H$ as:

$$\mathbf{p}_F (\mathbf{A}\mathbf{B}) = \mathbf{p}_H$$

In this sense, the matrix product $\mathbf{C} = \mathbf{A}\mathbf{B}$ can be thought of as the change of frame matrix from F directly to H; it combines the effects of $\mathbf{A}$ and $\mathbf{B}$ into a net matrix. (The idea is like composition of functions.)

This has performance implications. To see this, assume that a 3D object is composed of 20,000 points and that we want to apply two successive change of frame transformations to the object. Using the step-by-step approach, we would require $20,000 \times 2$ vector-matrix multiplications. On the other hand, using the combined matrix approach requires 20,000 vector-matrix multiplications and one matrix-matrix multiplication to combine the two change of frame matrices. The one extra matrix-matrix multiplications is a cheap price to pay for the large savings in vector-matrix multiplications.

Note: Again, matrix multiplication is not commutative, so we expect that **AB** and **BA** do *not* represent the same composite transformation. More specifically, the order in which you multiply the matrices is the order in which the transformations are applied, and in general, it is not a commutative process.

3.4.5 **Inverses and Change of Coordinate Matrices**

Suppose that we are given $\mathbf{p}_B$ (the coordinates of a vector $\mathbf{p}$ relative to frame B), and we are given the change of coordinate matrix $\mathbf{M}$ from frame A to frame B; that is, $\mathbf{p}_B = \mathbf{p}_A\mathbf{M}$. We want to solve for $\mathbf{p}_A$. In other words, instead of mapping from frame A into frame B, we want the change of coordinate matrix that maps us from B into A. To find this matrix, suppose that $\mathbf{M}$ is invertible (i.e., $\mathbf{M}^{-1}$ exists). We can solve for $\mathbf{p}_A$ like so:

$\mathbf{p}_B = \mathbf{p}_A\mathbf{M}$

$\mathbf{p}_B\mathbf{M}^{-1} = \mathbf{p}_A\mathbf{M}\mathbf{M}^{-1}$ Multiply both sides of the equation by $\mathbf{M}^{-1}$.

$\mathbf{p}_B\mathbf{M}^{-1} = \mathbf{p}_A\mathbf{I}$ $\mathbf{MM}^{-1} = \mathbf{I}$, by definition of inverse.

$\mathbf{p}_B\mathbf{M}^{-1} = \mathbf{p}_A$ $\mathbf{p}_A\mathbf{I} = \mathbf{p}_A$, by definition of the identity matrix.

Thus the matrix $\mathbf{M}^{-1}$ is the change of coordinate matrix from B into A.

Figure 3.11 illustrates the relationship between a change of coordinate matrix and its inverse. Also note that all of the change of frame mappings that we do in this book will be invertible, so we won't have to worry about whether the inverse exists.

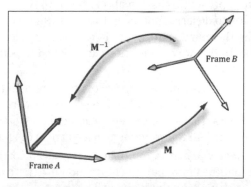

Figure 3.11: **M** maps from A into B and **M**⁻¹ maps from B into A.

Figure 3.12 shows how the matrix inverse property $(\mathbf{AB})^{-1} = \mathbf{B}^{-1}\mathbf{A}^{-1}$ can be interpreted in terms of change of coordinate matrices.

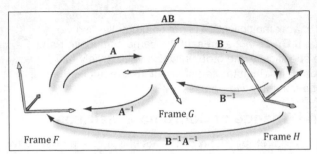

Figure 3.12: **A** maps from *F* into *G*, **B** maps from *G* into *H*, and **AB** maps from *F* directly into *H*. **B⁻¹** maps from *H* into *G*, **A⁻¹** maps from *G* into *F*, and **B⁻¹A⁻¹** maps from *H* directly into *F*.

3.5 **Summary**

- The fundamental transformation matrices — scaling, rotation, and translation — are given by:

$$
S = \begin{bmatrix} s_x & 0 & 0 & 0 \\ 0 & s_y & 0 & 0 \\ 0 & 0 & s_z & 0 \\ 0 & 0 & 0 & 1 \end{bmatrix} \quad
T = \begin{bmatrix} 1 & 0 & 0 & 0 \\ 0 & 1 & 0 & 0 \\ 0 & 0 & 1 & 0 \\ b_x & b_y & b_z & 1 \end{bmatrix}
$$

$$
R_n = \begin{bmatrix} c+(1-c)x^2 & (1-c)xy+sz & (1-c)xz-sy & 0 \\ (1-c)xy-sz & c+(1-c)y^2 & (1-c)yz+sx & 0 \\ (1-c)xz+sy & (1-c)yz-sx & c+(1-c)z^2 & 0 \\ 0 & 0 & 0 & 1 \end{bmatrix}
$$

- We use 4×4 matrices to represent transformations and 1×4 homogeneous coordinates to describe points and vectors, where we denote a point by setting the fourth component to $w = 1$ and we denote a vector by setting $w = 0$. In this way, translations are applied to points but not to vectors.

- A matrix is orthogonal if all of its row vectors are unit length and mutually orthogonal. An orthogonal matrix has the special property that its inverse is equal to its transpose, thereby making the inverse easy and efficient to compute. All the rotation matrices are orthogonal.

- From the associative property of matrix multiplication, we can combine several transformation matrices into one transformation matrix that represents the net effect of applying the individual matrices sequentially.

- Let $\mathbf{Q}_B$, $\mathbf{u}_B$, $\mathbf{v}_B$, and $\mathbf{w}_B$ describe the origin and x-, y-, and z-axes of frame A with coordinates relative to frame B, respectively. If a vector/point $\mathbf{p}$ has coordinates $\mathbf{p}_A = (x, y, x)$ relative to frame A, then the same vector/point relative to frame B has coordinates:

$$\mathbf{p}_B = (x', y', z') = x\mathbf{u}_B + y\mathbf{v}_B + z\mathbf{w}_B \qquad \text{For vectors (direction and magnitude)}$$

$$\mathbf{p}_B = (x', y', z') = \mathbf{Q}_B + x\mathbf{u}_B + y\mathbf{v}_B + z\mathbf{w}_B \ \text{For position vectors (points)}$$

These change of coordinate transformations can be written in terms of matrices using homogeneous coordinates.

■ Suppose we have three frames, F, G, and H, and let $\mathbf{A}$ be the change of frame matrix from F to G, and let $\mathbf{B}$ be the change of frame matrix from G to H. Using matrix-matrix multiplication, the matrix $\mathbf{C} = \mathbf{AB}$ can be thought of as the change of frame matrix F directly into H; that is, matrix-matrix multiplication combines the effects of $\mathbf{A}$ and $\mathbf{B}$ into one net matrix, and so we can write: $\mathbf{p}_F(\mathbf{AB}) = \mathbf{p}_H$.

■ If the matrix $\mathbf{M}$ maps frame A coordinates into frame B coordinates, then the matrix $\mathbf{M}^{-1}$ maps frame B coordinates into frame A coordinates.

3.6 **Exercises**

1. Prove that the rows of $\mathbf{R}_y$ are orthonormal.

2. Prove that $\mathbf{R}_y^{-1} = \mathbf{R}_y^T$.

3. Compute:

$$[x, y, z, 1]\begin{bmatrix} 1 & 0 & 0 & 0 \\ 0 & 1 & 0 & 0 \\ 0 & 0 & 1 & 0 \\ b_x & b_y & b_z & 1 \end{bmatrix} \text{ and } [x, y, z, 0]\begin{bmatrix} 1 & 0 & 0 & 0 \\ 0 & 1 & 0 & 0 \\ 0 & 0 & 1 & 0 \\ b_x & b_y & b_z & 1 \end{bmatrix}$$

Does the translation translate points? Does the translation translate vectors? Why does it not make sense to translate the coordinates of a vector in standard position?

4. Verify that the given scaling matrix inverse is indeed the inverse of the scaling matrix; that is, show, by directly doing the matrix multiplication, $\mathbf{SS}^{-1} = \mathbf{S}^{-1}\mathbf{S} = \mathbf{I}$. Similarly, verify that the given translation matrix inverse is indeed the inverse of the translation matrix; that is, show that $\mathbf{TT}^{-1} = \mathbf{T}^{-1}\mathbf{T} = \mathbf{I}$.

5. Suppose that we have frames A and B. Let $\mathbf{p}_A = (1, -2, 0)$ and $\mathbf{q}_A = (1, 2, 0)$ represent a point and force, respectively, relative to frame A. Moreover, let $\mathbf{Q}_B = (-6, 2, 0)$, $\mathbf{u}_B = \left(\frac{1}{\sqrt{2}}, \frac{1}{\sqrt{2}}, 0\right)$, $\mathbf{v}_B = \left(-\frac{1}{\sqrt{2}}, \frac{1}{\sqrt{2}}, 0\right)$, and $\mathbf{w}_B = (0, 0, 1)$ describe frame A with coordinates relative to frame B. Build the change of coordinate matrix that maps frame A coordinates

into frame B coordinates, and find $\mathbf{p}_B = (x, y, z)$ and $\mathbf{q}_B = (x, y, z)$. Draw a picture on graph paper to verify that your answer is reasonable.

6. Redo Example 3.1, but this time scale the square 1.5 units on the x-axis, 0.75 units on the y-axis, and leave the z-axis unchanged. Graph the geometry before and after the transformation to confirm your work.

7. Redo Example 3.2, but this time rotate the square –45° clockwise about the y-axis (i.e., 45° counterclockwise). Graph the geometry before and after the transformation to confirm your work.

8. Redo Example 3.3, but this time translate the square –5 units on the x-axis, –3 units on the y-axis, and 4 units on the z-axis. Graph the geometry before and after the transformation to confirm your work.

Part II

Direct3D Foundations

In this part, we study fundamental Direct3D concepts and techniques that are used throughout the rest of this book. With these fundamentals mastered, we can move on to writing more interesting applications. A brief description of the chapters in this part follows.

Chapter 4, "Direct3D Initialization"

In this chapter, we learn what Direct3D is about and how to initialize it in preparation for 3D drawing. Basic Direct3D topics are also introduced, such as surfaces, pixel formats, page flipping, depth buffering, and multisampling. We also learn how to measure time with the performance counter, which we use to compute the frames rendered per second. In addition, we show how to output 2D text and give some tips on debugging Direct3D applications. We develop and use our own application framework — not the SDK's framework.

Chapter 5, "The Rendering Pipeline"

In this long chapter, we provide a thorough introduction to the rendering pipeline, which is the sequence of steps necessary to generate a 2D image of the world based on what the virtual camera sees. We learn how to define 3D worlds, control the virtual camera, and draw 3D scenes.

Chapter 6, "Lighting"

This chapter shows how to create light sources and define the interaction between light and surfaces via materials. In particular, we show how to implement directional lights, point lights, and spotlights with vertex and pixel shaders.

Chapter 7, "Texturing"

This chapter describes texture mapping, which is a technique used to increase the realism of the scene by mapping 2D image data onto a 3D primitive. For example, using texture mapping, we can model a brick wall by applying a 2D brick wall image onto a 3D rectangle. Other key texturing topics covered include texture tiling and animated texture transformations.

Chapter 8, "Blending"

In this chapter, we look at a technique called blending, which allows us to implement a number of special effects like transparency. In addition, we discuss the intrinsic clip function, which enables us to mask out certain parts of an image; this can be used to implement fences and gates, for example. We also show how to implement a fog effect.

Chapter 9, "Stenciling"

This chapter describes the stencil buffer, which, like a stencil, allows us to block pixels from being drawn. To illustrate the ideas of this chapter, we include a thorough discussion on implementing planar reflections using the stencil buffer. An exercise describes an algorithm for using the stencil buffer to render the depth complexity of a scene and asks you to implement the algorithm.

Chapter 10, "The Geometry Shader"

This chapter shows how to program geometry shaders, which are special because they can create or destroy entire geometric primitives. Some applications include billboards, subdivisions, and particle systems. In addition, this chapter explains primitive IDs and texture arrays.

Chapter 4

Direct3D
Initialization

The initialization process of Direct3D requires us to be familiar with some basic Direct3D types and basic graphics concepts; the first section of this chapter addresses these requirements. We then detail the necessary steps to initialize Direct3D. After that, a small detour is taken to introduce accurate timing and the time measurements needed for real-time graphics applications. Finally, we explore the sample framework code, which is used to provide a consistent interface that all demo applications in this book follow.

Objectives:

- To obtain a basic understanding of Direct3D's role in programming 3D hardware.

- To understand the role COM plays with Direct3D.

- To learn fundamental graphics concepts, such as how 2D images are stored, page flipping, depth buffering, and multisampling.

- To learn how to use the performance counter functions for obtaining high-resolution timer readings.

- To find out how to initialize Direct3D.

- To become familiar with the general structure of the application framework that all the demos in this book employ.

4.1 **Preliminaries**

The Direct3D initialization process requires us to be familiar with some basic graphics concepts and Direct3D types. We introduce these ideas and types in this section, so that we do not have to digress in the next section.

4.1.1 **Direct3D Overview**

Direct3D is a low-level graphics API (application programming interface) that enables us to render 3D worlds using 3D hardware acceleration. Essentially, Direct3D provides the software interfaces through which we control the graphics hardware. For example, to instruct the graphics device to clear the render target (e.g., the screen), we would call the Direct3D method `ID3D10Device::ClearRenderTargetView`. Having the Direct3D layer between the application and the graphics hardware means we do not have to worry about the specifics of the 3D hardware, so long as it is a Direct3D 10-capable device.

A Direct3D 10-capable graphics device must support the entire Direct3D 10 capability set, with few exceptions (some things like the multisampling count still need to be queried). This is in contrast to Direct3D 9, where a device only had to support a subset of Direct3D 9 capabilities; consequently, if a Direct3D 9 application wanted to use a certain feature, it was necessary to first check if the available hardware supported that feature, as calling a Direct3D function not implemented by the hardware resulted in failure. In Direct3D 10, device capability checking is no longer necessary since it is now a strict requirement that a Direct3D 10 device implement the entire Direct3D 10 capability set.

4.1.2 **COM**

Component Object Model (COM) is the technology that allows DirectX to be programming language independent and have backward compatibility. We usually refer to a COM object as an interface, which for our purposes can be thought of and used as a C++ class. Most of the details of COM are hidden to us when programming DirectX with C++. The only thing that we must know is that we obtain pointers to COM interfaces through special functions or by the methods of another COM interface — we do not create a COM interface with the C++ `new` keyword. In addition, when we are done with an interface we call its `Release` method (all COM interfaces inherit functionality from the `IUnknown` COM interface, which provides the `Release` method) rather than `delete` it — COM objects perform their own memory management.

There is, of course, much more to COM, but more detail is not necessary for using DirectX effectively.

Note: COM interfaces are prefixed with a capital I. For example, the COM interface that represents a 2D texture is called `ID3D10Texture2D`.

4.1.3 Textures and Data Resource Formats

A 2D texture is a matrix of data elements. One use for 2D textures is to store 2D image data, where each element in the texture stores the color of a pixel. However, this is not the only usage; for example, in an advanced technique called normal mapping, each element in the texture stores a 3D vector instead of a color. Therefore, although it is common to think of textures as storing image data, they are really more general purpose than that. A 1D texture is like a 1D array of data elements, and a 3D texture is like a 3D array of data elements. As will be discussed in later chapters, textures are more than just arrays of data; they can have mipmap levels, and the GPU can do special operations on them, such as applying filters and multisampling. In addition, a texture cannot store arbitrary kinds of data; it can only store certain kinds of data formats, which are described by the `DXGI_FORMAT` enumerated type. Some example formats are:

- `DXGI_FORMAT_R32G32B32_FLOAT`: Each element has three 32-bit floating-point components.

- `DXGI_FORMAT_R16G16B16A16_UNORM`: Each element has four 16-bit components mapped to the [0, 1] range.

- `DXGI_FORMAT_R32G32_UINT`: Each element has two 32-bit unsigned integer components.

- `DXGI_FORMAT_R8G8B8A8_UNORM`: Each element has four 8-bit unsigned components mapped to the [0, 1] range.

- `DXGI_FORMAT_R8G8B8A8_SNORM`: Each element has four 8-bit signed components mapped to the [–1, 1] range.

- `DXGI_FORMAT_R8G8B8A8_SINT`: Each element has four 8-bit signed integer components mapped to the [–128, 127] range.

- `DXGI_FORMAT_R8G8B8A8_UINT`: Each element has four 8-bit unsigned integer components mapped to the [0, 255] range.

Note that the R, G, B, A letters are used to stand for red, green, blue, and alpha, respectively. Colors are formed as combinations of the basis colors red, green, and blue (e.g., equal values of red and green make yellow). The alpha channel or alpha component is generally used to control transparency. However, as we said earlier, textures need not store color information; for example, the format

```
DXGI_FORMAT_R32G32B32_FLOAT
```

has three floating-point components and can therefore store a 3D vector with floating-point coordinates. There are also *typeless* formats, where we just reserve memory and then specify how to reinterpret the data at a later time (sort of like a cast) when the texture is bound to the pipeline; for example, the following typeless format reserves elements with four 8-bit components, but does not specify the data type (e.g., integer, floating-point, unsigned integer):

```
DXGI_FORMAT_R8G8B8A8_TYPELESS
```

4.1.4 **The Swap Chain and Page Flipping**

To avoid flickering in animation, it is best to draw a frame of animation into an off-screen texture called the back buffer. Once the entire scene has been drawn to the back buffer for the given frame of animation, it is presented to the screen as one complete frame; in this way, the viewer does not watch as the frame gets drawn — the viewer only sees complete frames. The ideal time to present the frame to the screen is during the vertical blanking interval. To implement this, two texture buffers are maintained by the hardware, one called the *front buffer* and a second called the *back buffer*. The front buffer stores the image data currently being displayed on the monitor, while the next frame of animation is being drawn to the back buffer. After the frame has been drawn to the back buffer, the roles of the back buffer and front buffer are reversed: The back buffer becomes the front buffer and the front buffer becomes the back buffer for the next frame of animation. Swapping the roles of the back and front buffers is called *presenting*. Presenting is an efficient operation, as the pointer to the current front buffer and the pointer to the current back buffer just need to be swapped. Figure 4.1 illustrates the process.

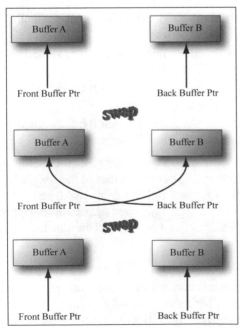

Figure 4.1: We first render to Buffer B, which is serving as the current back buffer. Once the frame is completed, the pointers are swapped and Buffer B becomes the front buffer and Buffer A becomes the new back buffer. We then render the next frame to Buffer A. Once the frame is completed, the pointers are swapped and Buffer A becomes the front buffer and Buffer B becomes the back buffer again.

The front and back buffer form a *swap chain*. In Direct3D, a swap chain is represented by the IDXGISwapChain interface. This interface stores the front and back buffer textures, as well as provides methods for resizing the buffers (IDXGISwapChain::ResizeBuffers) and presenting (IDXGISwapChain::Present). We will discuss these methods in detail in §4.5.

Using two buffers (front and back) is called *double buffering*. More than two buffers can be employed; using three buffers is called *triple buffering*. Two buffers are usually sufficient, however.

Note: Even though the back buffer is a texture (so an element should be called a *texel*), we often call an element a *pixel* since, in the case of the back buffer, it stores color information. Sometimes people will call an element of a texture a *pixel*, even if it doesn't store color information (e.g., "the pixels of a normal map").

4.1.5 Depth Buffering

The *depth buffer* is an example of a texture that does not contain image data, but rather depth information about a particular pixel. The possible depth values range from 0.0 to 1.0, where 0.0 denotes the closest an object can be to the viewer and 1.0 denotes the farthest an object can be from the viewer. There is a one-to-one correspondence between each element in the depth buffer and each pixel in the back buffer (i.e., the *ij*th element in the back buffer corresponds to the *ij*th element in the depth buffer). So if the back buffer had a resolution of 1280×1024, there would be 1280×1024 depth entries.

Figure 4.2: A group of objects that partially obscure each other.

Figure 4.2 shows a simple scene where some objects partially obscure the objects behind them. In order for Direct3D to determine which pixels of an object are in front of another, it uses a technique called *depth buffering* or *z-buffering*. Let us emphasize that with depth buffering, the order in which we draw the objects does not matter.

Remark: To handle the depth problem, one might suggest drawing the objects in the scene in the order of farthest to nearest. In this way, near objects will be painted over far objects, and the correct results should be rendered. This is how a painter would draw a scene. However, this method has its own problems — sorting a large data set and intersecting geometry. Besides, the graphics hardware gives us depth buffering for free.

To illustrate how depth buffering works, let's look at an example. Consider Figure 4.3, which shows the volume the viewer sees (left) and a 2D side view of that volume (right). From the figure, we observe that three different pixels compete to be rendered onto the pixel P on the view window. (Of course, we know the closest pixel should be rendered to P since it obscures the ones behind it, but the computer does not.) First, before any rendering takes place, the back buffer is cleared to a default color (like black or white), and the depth buffer is cleared to a default value — usually 1.0 (the farthest depth value a pixel can have). Now, suppose that the objects are rendered in the order of cylinder, sphere, and cone. The following table summarizes how the pixel P and its corresponding depth value are updated as the objects are drawn; a similar process happens for the other pixels.

Table 4.1

Operation	P	d	Description
Clear operation	Black	1.0	Pixel and corresponding depth entry initialized.
Draw cylinder	P_3	d_3	Since $d_3 \leq d = 1.0$, the depth test passes and we update the buffers by setting $P = P_3$ and $d = d_3$.
Draw sphere	P_1	d_1	Since $d_1 \leq d = d_3$, the depth test passes and we update the buffers by setting $P = P_1$ and $d = d_1$.
Draw cone	P_1	d_1	Since $d_2 > d = d_1$, the depth test fails and we do not update the buffers.

As you can see, we only update the pixel and its corresponding depth value in the depth buffer when we find a pixel with a smaller depth value. In this way, after all is said and done, the pixel that is closest to the viewer will be the one rendered. (You can try switching the drawing order around and working through this example again if you are still not convinced.)

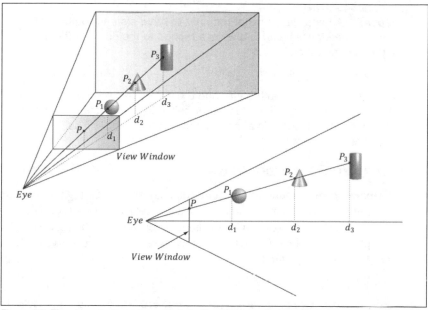

Figure 4.3: The view window corresponds to the 2D image (back buffer) we generate of the 3D scene. We see that three different pixels can be projected to the pixel P. Intuition tells us that P_1 should be written to P since it is closer to the viewer and blocks the other two pixels. The depth buffer algorithm provides a mechanical procedure for determining this on a computer. Note that we show the depth values relative to the 3D scene being viewed, but they are actually normalized to the range [0.0, 1.0] when stored in the depth buffer.

To summarize, depth buffering works by computing a depth value for each pixel and performing a depth test. The *depth test* compares the depths of pixels competing to be written to a particular pixel location on the back buffer. The pixel with the depth value closest to the viewer wins, and that is the pixel that gets written to the back buffer. This makes sense because the pixel closest to the viewer obscures the pixels behind it.

The depth buffer is a texture, so it must be created with certain data formats. The formats used for depth buffering are as follows:

- DXGI_FORMAT_D32_FLOAT_S8X24_UINT: Specifies a 32-bit floating-point depth buffer, with 8 bits (unsigned integer) reserved for the stencil buffer mapped to the [0, 255] range and 24 bits used for padding.

- DXGI_FORMAT_D32_FLOAT: Specifies a 32-bit floating-point depth buffer.

- DXGI_FORMAT_D24_UNORM_S8_UINT: Specifies an unsigned 24-bit depth buffer mapped to the [0, 1] range with 8 bits (unsigned integer) reserved for the stencil buffer mapped to the [0, 255] range.

- DXGI_FORMAT_D16_UNORM: Specifies an unsigned 16-bit depth buffer mapped to the [0, 1] range.

> **Note:**   An application is not required to have a stencil buffer, but if it does, the stencil buffer is always attached to the depth buffer. For example, the 32-bit format
>
> ```
> DXGI_FORMAT_D24_UNORM_S8_UINT
> ```
>
> uses 24 bits for the depth buffer and 8 bits for the stencil buffer. For this reason, the depth buffer is better called the depth/stencil buffer. Using the stencil buffer is a more advanced topic and will be explained in Chapter 9.

4.1.6 Texture Resource Views

A texture can be bound to different stages of the rendering pipeline; for example, it is common to use a texture as a render target (i.e., Direct3D draws into the texture) and as a shader resource (i.e., the texture will be sampled in a shader). A texture resource created for these two purposes would be given the bind flags:

```
D3D10_BIND_RENDER_TARGET | D3D10_BIND_SHADER_RESOURCE
```

indicating the two pipeline stages the texture will be bound to. Actually, resources are not directly bound to a pipeline stage; instead, their associated resource views are bound to different pipeline stages. For each way we wish to use a texture, Direct3D requires that we create a *resource view* of that texture at initialization time. This is mostly for efficiency, as the SDK documentation points out: "This allows validation and mapping in the runtime and driver to occur at view creation, minimizing type checking at bind time." So for the example of using a texture as a render target and shader resource, we would need to create two views: a render target view (ID3D10RenderTargetView) and a shader resource view (ID3D10ShaderResourceView). Resource views essentially do two things: They tell Direct3D how the resource will be used (i.e., what stage of the pipeline you will bind it to), and if the resource format was specified as typeless at creation time, then we must now state the type when creating a view. Thus, with typeless formats, it is possible for the elements of a texture to be viewed as floating-point values in one pipeline stage and as integers in another.

In order to create a specific view to a resource, the resource must be created with that specific bind flag. For instance, if the resource was not created with the D3D10_BIND_DEPTH_STENCIL bind flag (which indicates the texture will be bound to the pipeline as a depth/stencil buffer), then we cannot create an ID3D10DepthStencilView to that resource. If you try, you should get a Direct3D debug error like the following:

```
ERROR: ID3D10Device::CreateDepthStencilView: A DepthStencilView
cannot be created of a Resource that did not specify
D3D10_BIND_DEPTH_STENCIL.
```

We will have a chance to see code for creating a render target view and a depth/stencil view in §4.2 of this chapter. Creating a shader resource view will be seen in Chapter 7. Using a texture as a render target and shader resource will come much later in this book.

Note: The August 2007 SDK documentation says: "Creating a fully-typed resource restricts the resource to the format it was created with. This enables the runtime to optimize access ...." Therefore, you should only create a typeless resource if you really need it; otherwise, create a fully typed resource.

4.1.7 Multisampling

Because the pixels on a monitor are not infinitely small, an arbitrary line cannot be represented perfectly on the computer monitor. The upper line in Figure 4.4 illustrates a "stairstep" (*aliasing*) effect, which can occur when approximating a line by a matrix of pixels.

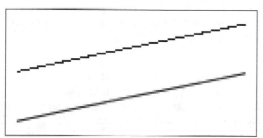

Figure 4.4: On the top we observe aliasing (the stairstep effect when trying to represent a line by a matrix of pixels). On the bottom, we see an antialiased line, which generates the final color of a pixel by sampling and using its neighboring pixels; this results in a smoother image and dilutes the stairstep effect.

Shrinking the pixel sizes by increasing the monitor resolution can alleviate the problem significantly to where the stairstep effect goes largely unnoticed.

When increasing the monitor resolution is not possible or not enough, we can apply antialiasing techniques. Direct3D supports an antialiasing technique called *multisampling*, which works by taking the neighboring pixels into consideration when computing the final color of a pixel. Thus, the technique is called multisampling because it uses multiple pixel samples to compute the final color of a pixel.

In the next section, we will be required to fill out a DXGI_SAMPLE_DESC structure. This structure has two members and is defined as follows:

```
typedef struct DXGI_SAMPLE_DESC {
    UINT Count;
    UINT Quality;
} DXGI_SAMPLE_DESC, *LPDXGI_SAMPLE_DESC;
```

The Count member specifies the number of samples to take per pixel, and the Quality member is used to specify the desired quality level. A higher quality is more expensive, so a trade-off between quality and speed must be made. The range of quality levels depends on the texture format and the number of samples to take per pixel. Use the following method to query the number of quality levels for a given texture format and sample count:

```
HRESULT ID3D10Device::CheckMultisampleQualityLevels(
    DXGI_FORMAT Format, UINT SampleCount, UINT *pNumQualityLevels);
```

This method returns 0 (zero) if the format and sample count combination is not supported by the device. Otherwise, the number of quality levels for the given combination will be returned through the pNumQualityLevels parameter. Valid quality levels for a texture format and sample count combination range from 0 to pNumQualityLevels −1.

In the demos of this book, we do not use multisampling. To indicate this, we set the sample count to 1 and the quality level to 0.

Note: A DXGI_SAMPLE_DESC structure needs to be filled out for both the swap chain buffer and the depth buffer. Both the back buffer and depth buffer must be created with the *same* multisampling settings; sample code illustrating this is given in the next section.

4.2 **Initializing Direct3D**

The following subsections show how to initialize Direct3D. Our process of initializing Direct3D can be broken down into the following steps:

1. Describe the characteristics of the swap chain we are going to create by filling out an instance of the DXGI_SWAP_CHAIN_DESC structure.

2. Create the ID3D10Device and IDXGISwapChain interfaces using the D3D10CreateDeviceAndSwapChain function.

3. Create a render target view to the swap chain's back buffer.

4. Create the depth/stencil buffer and its associated depth/stencil view.

5. Bind the render target view and depth/stencil view to the output merger stage of the rendering pipeline so that they can be used by Direct3D.

6. Set the viewport.

4.2.1 **Describe the Swap Chain**

Initializing Direct3D begins by filling out an instance of the
DXGI_SWAP_CHAIN_DESC structure, which describes the characteristics of the
swap chain we are going to create. This structure is defined as follows:

```
typedef struct DXGI_SWAP_CHAIN_DESC {
    DXGI_MODE_DESC BufferDesc;
    DXGI_SAMPLE_DESC SampleDesc;
    DXGI_USAGE BufferUsage;
    UINT BufferCount;
    HWND OutputWindow;
    BOOL Windowed;
    DXGI_SWAP_EFFECT SwapEffect;
    UINT Flags;
} DXGI_SWAP_CHAIN_DESC;
```

The DXGI_MODE_DESC type is another structure, defined as:

```
typedef struct DXGI_MODE_DESC
{
    UINT Width;                          // desired back buffer width
    UINT Height;                         // desired back buffer height
    DXGI_RATIONAL RefreshRate;           // display mode refresh rate
    DXGI_FORMAT Format;                  // back buffer pixel format
    DXGI_MODE_SCANLINE_ORDER ScanlineOrdering; // display scanline mode
    DXGI_MODE_SCALING Scaling;           // display scaling mode
} DXGI_MODE_DESC;
```

Note: In the following data member descriptions, we only cover
the common flags and options that are most important to a beginner
at this point. For a description of other flags and options, refer to the
SDK documentation.

- BufferDesc: This structure describes the properties of the back buffer
  we want to create. The main properties we are concerned with are the
  width and height and the pixel format; see the SDK documentation for
  details on the other properties.

- SampleDesc: The number of multisamples and quality level (see §4.1.7).
  In the demos of this book, we do not use multisampling. To indicate
  this, we set the sample count to 1 and the quality level to 0.

- BufferUsage: Specify DXGI_USAGE_RENDER_TARGET_OUTPUT since we are going
  to be rendering to the back buffer (i.e., use it as a render target).

- BufferCount: The number of back buffers to use in the swap chain; we
  usually only use one back buffer for double buffering, although you
  could use two for triple buffering.

- OutputWindow: A handle to the window we are rendering into.

- Windowed: Specify true to run in windowed mode or false for full-screen
  mode.

■ `SwapEffect`: Specify `DXGI_SWAP_EFFECT_DISCARD` in order to let the display driver select the most efficient presentation method.

■ `Flags`: Optional flags. If you specify `DXGI_SWAP_CHAIN_FLAG_ALLOW_MODE_SWITCH`, when the application is switching to full-screen mode it will choose a display mode that best matches the current back buffer settings. If this flag is not specified, when the application is switching to full-screen mode it will use the current desktop display mode. In our sample framework, we do not specify this flag, as using the current desktop display mode in full-screen mode works fine for our demos.

The following code shows how we fill out the `DXGI_SWAP_CHAIN_DESC` structure in our sample framework:

```
DXGI_SWAP_CHAIN_DESC sd;
sd.BufferDesc.Width  = mClientWidth;  // use window's client area dims
sd.BufferDesc.Height = mClientHeight;
sd.BufferDesc.RefreshRate.Numerator = 60;
sd.BufferDesc.RefreshRate.Denominator = 1;
sd.BufferDesc.Format = DXGI_FORMAT_R8G8B8A8_UNORM;
sd.BufferDesc.ScanlineOrdering = DXGI_MODE_SCANLINE_ORDER_UNSPECIFIED;
sd.BufferDesc.Scaling = DXGI_MODE_SCALING_UNSPECIFIED;

// No multisampling.
sd.SampleDesc.Count   = 1;
sd.SampleDesc.Quality = 0;

sd.BufferUsage  = DXGI_USAGE_RENDER_TARGET_OUTPUT;
sd.BufferCount  = 1;
sd.OutputWindow = mhMainWnd;
sd.Windowed     = true;
sd.SwapEffect   = DXGI_SWAP_EFFECT_DISCARD;
sd.Flags        = 0;
```

4.2.2 Create the Device and Swap Chain

After we describe the swap chain we want to create by filling out a `DXGI_SWAP_CHAIN_DESC` structure, we are ready to create the Direct3D 10 device (`ID3D10Device`) and swap chain (`IDXGISwapChain`). The `ID3D10Device` interface is the chief Direct3D interface and can be thought of as our software controller of the physical graphics device hardware; that is, through this interface we can interact with the hardware and instruct it to do things (such as clear the back buffer, bind resources to the various pipeline stages, and draw geometry). The device and swap chain can be created with the following function:

```
HRESULT WINAPI D3D10CreateDeviceAndSwapChain(
    IDXGIAdapter *pAdapter,
    D3D10_DRIVER_TYPE DriverType,
    HMODULE Software,
    UINT Flags,
```

```
    UINT SDKVersion,
    DXGI_SWAP_CHAIN_DESC *pSwapChainDesc,
    IDXGISwapChain **ppSwapChain,
    ID3D10Device **ppDevice);
```

- pAdapter: Specifies the display adapter we want the created device to represent. Specifying null for this parameter uses the primary display adapter. We always use the primary adapter in the sample programs of this book.

- DriverType: In general, you will always specify D3D10_DRIVER_TYPE_ HARDWARE for this parameter to use 3D hardware acceleration for rendering. Specifying D3D10_DRIVER_TYPE_REFERENCE creates a so-called reference device. The *reference device* is a software implementation of Direct3D with the goal of correctness (it is extremely slow since it is a software implementation). There are two reasons to use the reference device:

  - To test code your hardware does not support; for example, to test Direct3D 10.1 code when you do not have a Direct3D 10.1-capable graphics card.

  - To test for driver bugs. If you have code that works correctly with the reference device, but not with the hardware, then there is probably a bug in the hardware drivers.

- Software: This is used for supplying a software rasterizer. We always specify null since we are using hardware for rendering. Moreover, one must have a software rasterizer available in order to use one.

- Flags: Optional device creation flags. For release mode builds, this will generally be 0 (no extra flags); for debug mode builds, this should be D3D10_CREATE_DEVICE_DEBUG to enable the debug layer. When the debug flag is specified, Direct3D will send debug messages to the VC++ output window; Figure 4.5 shows an example of some of the error messages that can be output.

- SDKVersion: Always specify D3D10_SDK_VERSION.

- pSwapChainDesc: A pointer to the filled out DXGI_SWAP_CHAIN_DESC structure describing the swap chain we want to create.

- ppSwapChain: Returns the created swap chain.

- ppDevice: Returns the created device.

Here is an example call of this function:

```
DXGI_SWAP_CHAIN_DESC sd;

/* Initialize sd */

UINT createDeviceFlags = 0;
#if defined(DEBUG) || defined(_DEBUG)
    createDeviceFlags |= D3D10_CREATE_DEVICE_DEBUG;
```

```
#endif
ID3D10Device*    md3dDevice;
IDXGISwapChain*  mSwapChain;
D3D10CreateDeviceAndSwapChain(0, D3D10_DRIVER_TYPE_HARDWARE,
    0, createDeviceFlags, D3D10_SDK_VERSION,
    &sd, &mSwapChain, &md3dDevice);
```

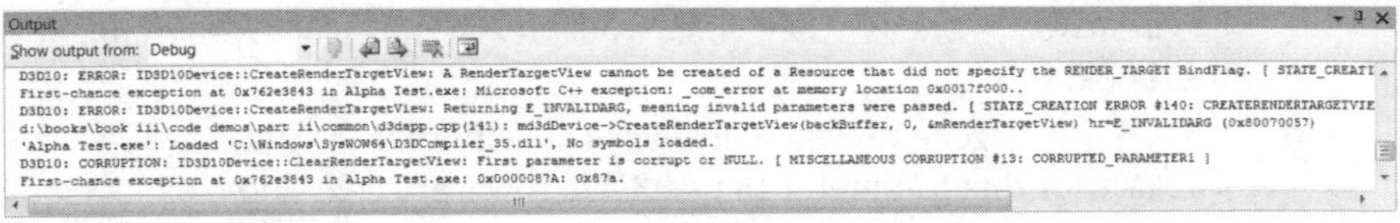

Figure 4.5: An example of Direct3D 10 debug output.

4.2.3 Create the Render Target View

As noted in §4.1.6, we do not bind a resource to a pipeline stage directly; instead, we must create a resource view to the resource and bind the view to the pipeline stage. In particular, in order to bind the back buffer to the output merger stage of the pipeline (so Direct3D can render onto it), we need to create a render target view to the back buffer. The following example code shows how this is done:

```
ID3D10RenderTargetView* mRenderTargetView;
ID3D10Texture2D* backBuffer;
mSwapChain->GetBuffer(0, __uuidof(ID3D10Texture2D),
    reinterpret_cast<void**>(&backBuffer));
md3dDevice->CreateRenderTargetView(backBuffer, 0, &mRenderTargetView);
ReleaseCOM(backBuffer);
```

- A pointer to the swap chain's back buffer is obtained using the `IDXGISwapChain::GetBuffer` method. The first parameter of this method is an index identifying the particular back buffer we want to get (in case there is more than one). In our demos, we only use one back buffer, and it has index 0. The second parameter is the interface type of the buffer, which is usually always a 2D texture (`ID3D10Texture2D`). The third parameter returns a pointer to the back buffer.

- To create the render target view, we use the `ID3D10Device::CreateRenderTargetView` method. The first parameter specifies the resource that will be used as the render target, which, in the example above, is the back buffer. The second parameter is a pointer to a `D3D10_RENDER_TARGET_VIEW_DESC`. Among other things, this structure describes the data type of the elements in the resource. If the resource was created with a typed format (i.e., not typeless), then this parameter can be null, which indicates to use the format the resource was created with. The third parameter returns a pointer to the create render target view object.

■ The call to IDXGISwapChain::GetBuffer increases the COM reference count to the back buffer, which is why we release it (ReleaseCOM) at the end of the code fragment.

4.2.4 **Create the Depth/Stencil Buffer and View**

We now need to create the depth/stencil buffer. As described in §4.1.5, the depth buffer is just a 2D texture that stores the depth information (and stencil information if using stenciling). To create a texture, we need to fill out a D3D10_TEXTURE2D_DESC structure describing the texture to create, and then call the ID3D10Device::CreateTexture2D method. The D3D10_TEXTURE2D_DESC structure is defined as follows:

```
typedef struct D3D10_TEXTURE2D_DESC {
    UINT Width;
    UINT Height;
    UINT MipLevels;
    UINT ArraySize;
    DXGI_FORMAT Format;
    DXGI_SAMPLE_DESC SampleDesc;
    D3D10_USAGE Usage;
    UINT BindFlags;
    UINT CPUAccessFlags;
    UINT MiscFlags;
} D3D10_TEXTURE2D_DESC;
```

■ Width: The width of the texture in texels.

■ Height: The height of the texture in texels.

■ MipLevels: The number of mipmap levels. Mipmaps are covered in Chapter 7, "Texturing." For creating the depth/stencil buffer, our texture only needs one mipmap level.

■ ArraySize: The number of textures in a texture array. For the depth/stencil buffer, we only need one texture.

■ Format: A member of the DXGI_FORMAT enumerated type specifying the format of the texels. For a depth/stencil buffer, this needs to be one of the formats shown in §4.1.5.

■ SampleDesc: The number of multisamples and quality level; see §4.1.7. In the demos of this book, we do not use multisampling. To indicate this, we set the sample count to 1 and the quality level to 0.

■ Usage: A member of the D3D10_USAGE enumerated type specifying how the texture will be used. The four usage values are:

　■ D3D10_USAGE_DEFAULT: Specify this usage if the GPU (graphics processing unit) will be reading and writing to the resource. The CPU cannot read or write to a resource with this usage. For the depth/stencil buffer, we specify D3D10_USAGE_DEFAULT since the GPU will be doing all the reading and writing to the depth/stencil buffer.

- **D3D10_USAGE_IMMUTABLE**: Specify this usage if the content of a resource never changes after creation. This allows for some potential optimizations, as the resource will be read-only by the GPU. The CPU cannot write to an immutable resource, except at creation time to initialize the resource. The CPU cannot read from an immutable resource.

- **D3D10_USAGE_DYNAMIC**: Specify this usage if the application (CPU) needs to update the data contents of the resource frequently (e.g., on a per-frame basis). A resource with this usage can be read by the GPU and written to by the CPU.

- **D3D10_USAGE_STAGING**: Specify this usage if the application (CPU) needs to be able to read a copy of the resource (i.e., the resource supports copying data from video memory to system memory).

- **BindFlags**: One or more flags ORed together, specifying where the resource will be bound to the pipeline. For a depth/stencil buffer, this needs to be D3D10_BIND_DEPTH_STENCIL. Some other bind flags for textures are:

  - **D3D10_BIND_RENDER_TARGET**: The texture will be bound as a render target to the pipeline.

  - **D3D10_BIND_SHADER_RESOURCE**: The texture will be bound as a shader resource to the pipeline.

- **CPUAccessFlags**: Specifies how the CPU will access the resource. If the CPU needs to write to the resource, specify D3D10_CPU_ACCESS_WRITE. A resource with write access must have usage D3D10_USAGE_DYNAMIC or D3D10_USAGE_STAGING. If the CPU needs to read from the buffer, specify D3D10_CPU_ACCESS_READ. A buffer with read access must have usage D3D10_USAGE_STAGING. For the depth/stencil buffer, only the GPU writes and reads to the depth/buffer; therefore, we can specify 0 for this value, as the CPU will not be reading or writing to the depth/stencil buffer.

- **MiscFlags**: Optional flags, which do not apply to the depth/stencil buffer, so set to 0.

Note: Throughout this book, we will see different examples of creating resources with different options; for example, different usage flags, bind flags, and CPU access flags. For now, just concentrate on the values we need to specify to create the depth/stencil buffer, and do not worry about every single option.

In addition, before using the depth/stencil buffer, we must create a depth/stencil view to be bound to the pipeline. This is done similarly to creating the render target view. The following code example shows how we create the depth/stencil texture and its corresponding depth/stencil view:

```
D3D10_TEXTURE2D_DESC depthStencilDesc;
depthStencilDesc.Width            = mClientWidth;
```

```
depthStencilDesc.Height              = mClientHeight;
depthStencilDesc.MipLevels           = 1;
depthStencilDesc.ArraySize           = 1;
depthStencilDesc.Format              = DXGI_FORMAT_D24_UNORM_S8_UINT;
depthStencilDesc.SampleDesc.Count    = 1; // multisampling must match
depthStencilDesc.SampleDesc.Quality  = 0; // swap chain values.
depthStencilDesc.Usage               = D3D10_USAGE_DEFAULT;
depthStencilDesc.BindFlags           = D3D10_BIND_DEPTH_STENCIL;
depthStencilDesc.CPUAccessFlags      = 0;
depthStencilDesc.MiscFlags           = 0;

ID3D10Texture2D* mDepthStencilBuffer;
ID3D10DepthStencilView* mDepthStencilView;

HR(md3dDevice->CreateTexture2D(
&depthStencilDesc, 0, &mDepthStencilBuffer));
HR(md3dDevice->CreateDepthStencilView(
mDepthStencilBuffer, 0, &mDepthStencilView));
```

Note: The second parameter of `CreateTexture2D` is a pointer to initial data to fill the texture with. However, since this texture is to be used as the depth/stencil buffer, we do not need to fill it ourselves with any data. Direct3D will write to the depth/stencil buffer directly when performing depth buffering and stencil operations. Thus, we specify null for the second parameter.

4.2.5 Bind the Views to the Output Merger Stage

Now that we have created views to the back buffer and depth buffer, we can bind these views to the output merger stage of the pipeline to make the resources the render target and depth/stencil buffer of the pipeline:

```
md3dDevice->OMSetRenderTargets(1, &mRenderTargetView, mDepthStencilView);
```

The first parameter is the number of render targets we are binding; we bind only one here, but more can be bound to render simultaneously to several render targets (an advanced technique). The second parameter is a pointer to the first element in an array of render target view pointers to bind to the pipeline. The third parameter is a pointer to the depth/stencil view to bind to the pipeline.

Note: We can set an array of render target views, but only one depth/stencil view.

4.2.6 Set the Viewport

Usually we like to draw the 3D scene to the entire back buffer. However, sometimes we only want to draw the 3D scene into a subrectangle of the back buffer, as shown in Figure 4.6.

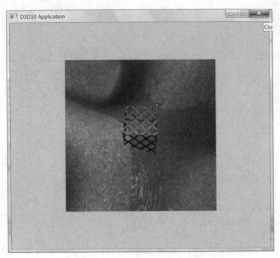

Figure 4.6: By modifying the viewport, we can draw the 3D scene into a subrectangle of the back buffer. The back buffer then gets presented to the client area of the window.

The subrectangle of the back buffer we draw into is called the *viewport* and it is described by the following structure:

```
typedef struct D3D10_VIEWPORT {
    INT TopLeftX;
    INT TopLeftY;
    UINT Width;
    UINT Height;
    FLOAT MinDepth;
    FLOAT MaxDepth;
} D3D10_VIEWPORT;
```

The first four data members define the viewport rectangle relative to the client area rectangle of the window we are drawing into. The MinDepth member specifies the minimum depth buffer value and MaxDepth specifies the maximum depth buffer value. Direct3D uses a depth buffer range of 0 to 1, so MinDepth and MaxDepth should be set to those values, respectively, unless a special effect is desired.

Once we have filled out the D3D10_VIEWPORT structure, we set the viewport with Direct3D with the ID3D10Device::RSSetViewports method. The following example creates and sets a viewport that draws onto the entire back buffer:

```
D3D10_VIEWPORT vp;
    vp.TopLeftX = 0;
    vp.TopLeftY = 0;
    vp.Width    = mClientWidth;
    vp.Height   = mClientHeight;
    vp.MinDepth = 0.0f;
    vp.MaxDepth = 1.0f;

    md3dDevice->RSSetViewports(1, &vp);
```

You could use the viewport to implement split screens for two-player game modes, for example. You would create two viewports, one for the left half of the screen and one for the right half of the screen. Then you would draw the 3D scene from the perspective of player one into the left viewport and draw the 3D scene from the perspective of player two into the right viewport.

4.3 **Timing and Animation**

To do animation correctly, we need to keep track of the time. In particular, we need to measure the amount of time that elapses between frames of animation. If the frame rate is high, these time intervals between frames will be very short; therefore, we need a timer with a high level of accuracy.

4.3.1 **The Performance Timer**

For accurate time measurements, we use the performance timer (or performance counter). To use the Win32 functions for querying the performance timer, we must #include <windows.h>.

The performance timer measures time in units called *counts*. We obtain the current time value, measured in counts, of the performance timer with the QueryPerformanceCounter function like so:

```
__int64 currTime;
    QueryPerformanceCounter((LARGE_INTEGER*)&currTime);
```

Observe that this function returns the current time value through its parameter, which is a 64-bit integer value.

To get the frequency (counts per second) of the performance timer, we use the QueryPerformanceFrequency function:

```
__int64 countsPerSec;
    QueryPerformanceFrequency((LARGE_INTEGER*)&countsPerSec);
```

Then the number of seconds (or fractions of a second) per count is just the reciprocal of the counts per second:

```
mSecondsPerCount = 1.0 / (double)countsPerSec;
```

Thus, to convert a time reading valueInCounts to seconds, we just multiply it by the conversion factor mSecondsPerCount

```
valueInSecs = valueInCounts * mSecondsPerCount;
```

The values returned by the QueryPerformanceCounter function are not particularly interesting in and of themselves. What we do is get the current time value using QueryPerformanceCounter, and then get the current time value a little later using QueryPerformanceCounter again. Then the time that elapsed between those two time calls is just the difference. That is, we always look at the relative difference between two time stamps to measure time, not the actual values returned by the performance counter. The following better illustrates the idea:

```
__int64 A = 0;
QueryPerformanceCounter((LARGE_INTEGER*)&A);

/* Do work */

__int64 B = 0;
QueryPerformanceCounter((LARGE_INTEGER*)&B);
```

So it took (B−A) counts to do the work, or (B−A)*mSecondsPerCount seconds to do the work.

Note: MSDN has the following remark about QueryPerform-anceCounter: "On a multiprocessor computer, it should not matter which processor is called. However, you can get different results on different processors due to bugs in the basic input/output system (BIOS) or the hardware abstraction layer (HAL)." You can use the SetThreadAffinityMask function so that the main application thread does not get switched to another processor.

4.3.2 Game Timer Class

In the next two sections, we will discuss the implementation of the following GameTimer class.

```
class GameTimer
{
public:
    GameTimer();

    float getGameTime()const;  // in seconds
    float getDeltaTime()const; // in seconds

    void reset(); // Call before message loop.
    void start(); // Call when unpaused.
    void stop();  // Call when paused.
    void tick();  // Call every frame.

private:
    double mSecondsPerCount;
    double mDeltaTime;

    __int64 mBaseTime;
    __int64 mPausedTime;
    __int64 mStopTime;
    __int64 mPrevTime;
    __int64 mCurrTime;

    bool mStopped;
};
```

The constructor, in particular, queries the frequency of the performance counter. The other member functions are discussed in the next two sections.

```
GameTimer::GameTimer()
: mSecondsPerCount(0.0), mDeltaTime(-1.0), mBaseTime(0),
  mPausedTime(0), mPrevTime(0), mCurrTime(0), mStopped(false)
{

    __int64 countsPerSec;
    QueryPerformanceFrequency((LARGE_INTEGER*)&countsPerSec);
    mSecondsPerCount = 1.0 / (double)countsPerSec;
}
```

Note: The `GameTimer` class and implementations are in the _GameTimer.h_ and _GameTimer.cpp_ files, which can be found in the _Common_ directory of the sample code.

4.3.3 **Time Elapsed between Frames**

When we render our frames of animation, we need to know how much time has elapsed between frames so that we can update our game objects based on how much time has passed. Computing the time elapsed between frames proceeds as follows: Let t_i be the time returned by the performance counter during the ith frame and let t_{i-1} be the time returned by the performance counter during the previous frame. Then the time elapsed between the t_{i-1} reading and the t_i reading is $\Delta t = t_i - t_{i-1}$. For real-time rendering, we typically require at least 30 frames per second for smooth animation (and we usually have much higher rates); thus, $\Delta t = t_i - t_{i-1}$ tends to be a relatively small number.

The following code shows how Δt is computed:

```
void GameTimer::tick()
{
    if( mStopped )
    {
        mDeltaTime = 0.0;
        return;
    }

    // Get the time this frame.
    __int64 currTime;
    QueryPerformanceCounter((LARGE_INTEGER*)&currTime);
    mCurrTime = currTime;

    // Time difference between this frame and the previous.
    mDeltaTime = (mCurrTime - mPrevTime)*mSecondsPerCount;

    // Prepare for next frame.
    mPrevTime = mCurrTime;
```

```
    // Force nonnegative. The DXSDK's CDXUTTimer mentions that if the
    // processor goes into a power save mode or we get shuffled to
    // another processor, then mDeltaTime can be negative.
    if(mDeltaTime < 0.0)
    {
        mDeltaTime = 0.0;
    }
}

float GameTimer::getDeltaTime()const
{
    return (float)mDeltaTime;
}
```

The function `tick` is called in the application message loop as follows:

```
int D3DApp::run()
{
    MSG msg = {0};

    mTimer.reset();

    while(msg.message != WM_QUIT)
    {
        // If there are Window messages then process them.
        if(PeekMessage( &msg, 0, 0, 0, PM_REMOVE ))
        {
            TranslateMessage( &msg );
            DispatchMessage( &msg );
        }
        // Otherwise, do animation/game stuff.
        else
        {
            mTimer.tick();

            if( !mAppPaused )
                updateScene(mTimer.getDeltaTime());
            else
                Sleep(50);

            drawScene();
        }
    }
    return (int)msg.wParam;
}
```

In this way, Δt is computed every frame and fed into the updateScene method so that the scene can be updated based on how much time has passed since the previous frame of animation. The implementation of the reset method is:

```
void GameTimer::reset()
{
    __int64 currTime;
```

```
QueryPerformanceCounter((LARGE_INTEGER*)&currTime);

mBaseTime = currTime;
mPrevTime = currTime;
mStopTime = 0;
mStopped  = false;
}
```

Some of the variables shown have not been discussed yet (see the next section). However, we see that this initializes mPrevTime to the current time when reset is called. It is important to do this because for the first frame of animation, there is no previous frame, and therefore, no previous time stamp t_{i-1}. Thus this value needs to be initialized in the reset method before the message loop starts.

4.3.4 **Game Time**

Another time measurement that can be useful is the amount of time that has elapsed since the application start, not counting paused time; we will call this *game time*. The following situation shows how this could be useful. Suppose the player has 300 seconds to complete a level. When the level starts, we can get the time t_{start}, which is the time elapsed since the application started. Then after the level has started, we can check the time t since the application started every so often. If $t - t_{start} > 300s$ (see Figure 4.7) then the player has been in the level for over 300 seconds and loses. Obviously in this situation we do not want to count any time the game was paused against the player.

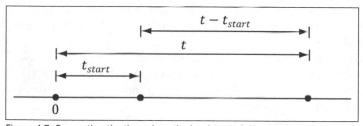

Figure 4.7: Computing the time since the level started. Note that we choose the application start time as the origin (zero), and measure time values relative to that frame of reference.

Another application of game time is when we want to animate a quantity as a function of time. For instance, suppose we wish to have a light orbit the scene as a function of time. Its position can be described by the parametric equations:

$$\begin{cases} x = 10\cos t \\ y = 20 \\ z = 10\sin t \end{cases}$$

Here t represents time, and as t (time) increases, the coordinates of the light are updated so that it moves in a circle with radius 10 in the $y = 20$ plane. Chapter 5 shows a sample program that animates the camera by describing its position as a function of time. For this kind of animation, we also do not want to count paused time; see Figure 4.8.

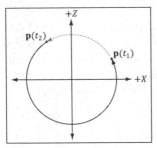

Figure 4.8: If we paused at t_1 and unpaused at t_2, and counted paused time, then when we unpause, the position will jump abruptly from $\mathbf{p}(t_1)$ to $\mathbf{p}(t_2)$.

To implement game time, we use the following variables:

```
__int64 mBaseTime;
__int64 mPausedTime;
__int64 mStopTime;
```

As we saw in §4.3.3, mBaseTime is initialized to the current time when reset was called. We can think of this as the time when the application started. In most cases, you will only call reset once before the message loop, so mBaseTime stays constant throughout the application's lifetime. The variable mPausedTime accumulates all the time that passes while we are paused. We need to accumulate this time, so we can subtract it from the total running time in order to not count paused time. The mStopTime variable gives us the time when the timer is stopped (paused); this is used to help us keep track of paused time.

Two important methods of the GameTimer class are stop and start. They should be called when the application is paused and unpaused, respectively, so that the GameTimer can keep track of paused time. The code comments explain the details of these two methods.

```
void GameTimer::stop()
{
    // If we are already stopped, then don't do anything.
    if( !mStopped )
    {
        __int64 currTime;
        QueryPerformanceCounter((LARGE_INTEGER*)&currTime);

        // Otherwise, save the time we stopped at, and set
        // the Boolean flag indicating the timer is stopped.
        mStopTime = currTime;
        mStopped  = true;
    }
}
```

```
void GameTimer::start()
{
    __int64 startTime;
    QueryPerformanceCounter((LARGE_INTEGER*)&startTime);

    // Accumulate the time elapsed between stop and start pairs.
    //
    //                      |<-------d------->|
    // ---------------*-----------------*------------> time
    //            mStopTime          startTime

    // If we are resuming the timer from a stopped state...
    if( mStopped )
    {
        // then accumulate the paused time.
        mPausedTime += (startTime - mStopTime);

        // Since we are starting the timer back up, the current
        // previous time is not valid, as it occurred while paused.
        // So reset it to the current time.
        mPrevTime = startTime;

        // no longer stopped...
        mStopTime = 0;
        mStopped  = false;
    }
}
```

Finally, the getGameTime member function, which returns the time elapsed since reset was called not counting paused time, is implemented as follows:

```
float GameTimer::getGameTime()const
{
    // If we are stopped, do not count the time that has passed since
    // we stopped.
    //
    // ----*---------------*----------------------------*------> time
    //  mBaseTime       mStopTime                     mCurrTime

    if( mStopped )
    {
        return (float)((mStopTime - mBaseTime)*mSecondsPerCount);
    }

    // The distance mCurrTime - mBaseTime includes paused time,
    // which we do not want to count. To correct this, we can subtract
    // the paused time from mCurrTime:
    //
    // (mCurrTime - mPausedTime) - mBaseTime
    //
    //                      |<-------d------->|
    // ====*---------------*-----------------*------------*------> time
    //  mBaseTime       mStopTime         startTime    mCurrTime
```

```
    else
    {
        return (float)
            (((mCurrTime-mPausedTime)-mBaseTime)*mSecondsPerCount);
    }
}
```

4.4 Text Output

It is important to be able to display textual information to the user. For example, you may want your game to display subtitles or game statistics (e.g., the number of units killed). In our demos, we will want to display the average number of frames per second and the average time elapsed between frames. To display text, the D3DX library provides the ID3DX10Font interface.

To obtain a pointer to an ID3DX10Font object, we first must fill out an instance of the D3DX10_FONT_DESC structure to describe the characteristics of the font we want to create. Once that is done, a pointer to an ID3DX10Font object can be obtained with the D3DX10CreateFontIndirect function. The following code illustrates:

```
D3DX10_FONT_DESC fontDesc;
fontDesc.Height          = 24;
fontDesc.Width           = 0;
fontDesc.Weight          = 0;
fontDesc.MipLevels       = 1;
fontDesc.Italic          = false;
fontDesc.CharSet         = DEFAULT_CHARSET;
fontDesc.OutputPrecision = OUT_DEFAULT_PRECIS;
fontDesc.Quality         = DEFAULT_QUALITY;
fontDesc.PitchAndFamily  = DEFAULT_PITCH | FF_DONTCARE;
wcscpy(fontDesc.FaceName, L"Times New Roman");

ID3DX10Font* mFont;
D3DX10CreateFontIndirect(md3dDevice, &fontDesc, &mFont);
```

The first parameter of the D3DX10CreateFontIndirect function takes a pointer to a valid ID3D10Device object. The second parameter is a pointer to a D3DX10_FONT_DESC instance describing the font to create; a pointer to the created font object is returned through the third parameter.

The main method of ID3DX10Font we will be using is the ID3DX10Font::DrawText method; this method has the following prototype:

```
INT ID3DX10Font::DrawText(
    LPD3DX10SPRITE pSprite,
    LPCTSTR pString,
    INT Count,
    LPRECT pRect,
    UINT Format,
    D3DXCOLOR Color
);
```

- pSprite: Pointer to an ID3DX10Sprite interface. This can be null, but if you are doing a lot of text drawing per frame, it is more efficient to supply your own sprite interface; see the SDK documentation for details. Because we only call ID3DX10Font::DrawText once per frame to output the frame statistics, we specify null in our sample code.

- pString: Pointer to the string to draw.

- Count: The number of characters in the string. We can specify –1 if the string is null terminating.

- pRect: Pointer to a RECT structure, relative to the window's client area, that defines the area to which the text is to be drawn and formatted.

- Format: Optional flags that specify how the text should be formatted in the RECT specified by pRect. In the sample call below, we specify DT_NOCLIP, which means the text will not be clipped if it goes outside the boundaries of pRect. Other common flags are DT_CENTER and DT_VCENTER; these flags center the text horizontally and vertically, respectively, inside the rectangle specified by pRect.

- Color: The text color. As we will learn in the next chapter, a color is represented by the D3DXCOLOR class. An instance of this class has four floating-point data members, describing the red, green, blue, and alpha components of the color.

Here is an example call:

```
// We specify DT NOCLIP, so we do not care about width/height of the rect.
const D3DXCOLOR BLACK(0.0f, 0.0f, 0.0f, 1.0f);
RECT R = {5, 5, 0, 0};
mFont->DrawText(0, L"Hello, Direct3D!", -1, &R, DT_NOCLIP, BLACK);
```

4.5 The Demo Application Framework

The demos in this book use code from the _d3dUtil.h_, _d3dApp.h_, and _d3dApp.cpp_ files, which can be downloaded from the book's website. These common files, which are used in every demo application, reside in a _Common_ directory for Parts II and III of the book, so that the files are not duplicated in each project. The _d3dUtil.h_ file contains useful utility code, and the _d3dApp.h_ and _d3dApp.cpp_ files contain the core Direct3D application class code that is used to encapsulate a Direct3D application. The reader is encouraged to study these files after reading this chapter, as we do not cover every line of code in these files (e.g., we do not show how to create a window, as basic Win32 programming is a prerequisite of this book). The goal of this framework was to hide the window creation code and Direct3D initialization code; by hiding this code, we feel it makes the demos less distracting, as you can focus only on the specific details the sample code is trying to illustrate.

4.5.1 **D3DApp**

The D3DApp class is the base Direct3D application class, which provides functions for creating the main application window, running the application message loop, handling window messages, and initializing Direct3D. Moreover, the class defines the framework functions for the demo applications. Clients are to derive from D3DApp, override the virtual framework functions, and instantiate only a single instance of the derived D3DApp class. The D3DApp class is defined as follows:

```
class D3DApp
{
public:
    D3DApp(HINSTANCE hInstance);
    virtual ~D3DApp();

    HINSTANCE getAppInst();
    HWND      getMainWnd();

    int run();

    // Framework methods.  Derived client class overrides these methods
    // to implement specific application requirements.

    virtual void initApp();
    virtual void onResize(); // reset projection/etc.
    virtual void updateScene(float dt);
    virtual void drawScene();
    virtual LRESULT msgProc(UINT msg, WPARAM wParam, LPARAM lParam);

protected:
    void initMainWindow();
    void initDirect3D();

protected:
    HINSTANCE mhAppInst; // application instance handle
    HWND      mhMainWnd; // main window handle
    bool      mAppPaused; // is the application paused?
    bool      mMinimized; // is the application minimized?
    bool      mMaximized; // is the application maximized?
    bool      mResizing;  // are the resize bars being dragged?

    // Used to keep track of the "delta-time" and game time (§4.3).
    GameTimer mTimer;

    // A string to store the frame statistics for output. We display
    // the average frames per second and the average time it takes
    // to render one frame.
    std::wstring mFrameStats;

    // The D3D10 device (§4.2.2), the swap chain for page flipping
    // (§4.1.4), the 2D texture for the depth/stencil buffer (§4.1.5),
```

```
// and the render target and depth/stencil views (§4.1.6). We
// also store a font pointer (§4.4) so that we can render the
// frame statistics to the screen.
ID3D10Device*      md3dDevice;
IDXGISwapChain*    mSwapChain;
ID3D10Texture2D*   mDepthStencilBuffer;
ID3D10RenderTargetView*  mRenderTargetView;
ID3D10DepthStencilView*  mDepthStencilView;
ID3DX10Font* mFont;

// The following variables are initialized in the D3DApp constructor
// to default values. However, you can override the values in the
// derived class to pick different defaults.

// Hardware device or reference device? D3DApp defaults to
// D3D10_DRIVER_TYPE_HARDWARE.
D3D10_DRIVER_TYPE md3dDriverType;

// Window title/caption. D3DApp defaults to "D3D10 Application".
std::wstring mMainWndCaption;

// Color to clear the background. D3DApp defaults to blue.
D3DXCOLOR mClearColor;

// Initial size of the window's client area. D3DApp defaults to
// 800x600.  Note, however, that these values change at run time
// to reflect the current client area size as the window is resized.
int mClientWidth;
int mClientHeight;
};
```

We have used comments in the above code to describe some of the data members; the methods are discussed in the subsequent sections.

4.5.2 Non-Framework Methods

- D3DApp: The constructor simply initializes the data members to default values.

- ~D3DApp: The destructor releases the COM interfaces the D3DApp acquires.

- getAppInst: Trivial access function returns a copy of the application instance handle.

- getMainWnd: Trivial access function returns a copy of the main window handle.

- run: This method wraps the application message loop. It uses the Win32 PeekMessage function so that it can process our game logic when no messages are present. The implementation of this function is shown in Appendix A.

- initMainWindow: Initializes the main application window; we assume the reader is familiar with basic Win32 window initialization.

■   `initDirect3D`: Initializes Direct3D by implementing the steps discussed
    in §4.2.

4.5.3 **Framework Methods**

For each sample application in this book, we consistently override five virtual functions of `D3DApp`. These five functions are used to implement the
code specific to the particular sample. The benefit of this setup is that all
the initialization code, message handling, etc., is implemented in the `D3DApp`
class, so that the derived class only needs to focus on the specific code of
the demo application. Here is a description of the framework methods:

■   `initApp`: Use this method for initialization code for the application, such
    as allocating resources, initializing objects, and setting up lights. The
    `D3DApp` implementation of this method calls `initMainWindow` and
    `initDirect3D`; therefore, you should call the `D3DApp` version of this
    method in your derived implementation first, like this:

```
void AlphaTestApp::initApp()
{
    D3DApp::initApp();

    /* Rest of initialization code goes here */
}
```

so that the `ID3D10Device` is available for the rest of your initialization
code. (Direct3D resource acquisition generally requires a valid
`ID3D10Device`.) In addition, the `D3DApp` implementation also creates an
`ID3DX10Font` object, which should be used to output the frame statistics;
the font creation code was shown in §4.4.

■   `onResize`: This method is called by `D3DApp::msgProc` when a `WM_SIZE`
    message is received. When the window is resized, some Direct3D
    properties need to be changed, as they depend on the client area
    dimensions. In particular, the back buffer and depth/stencil buffers need
    to be recreated to match the new client area of the window. The back
    buffer can be resized by calling the `IDXGISwapChain::ResizeBuffers`
    method. The depth/stencil buffer needs to be destroyed and then
    remade based on the new dimension. In addition, the render target and
    depth/stencil views need to be recreated. The `D3DApp` implementation of
    `onResize` handles the code necessary to resize the back and
    depth/stencil buffers; see the source code for the straightforward
    details. In addition to the buffers, other properties depend on the size
    of the client area (e.g., the projection matrix), so this method is part of
    the framework because the client code may need to execute some of its
    own code when the window is resized.

■   `updateScene`: This method is called every frame and should be used to
    update the 3D application over time (e.g., perform animation and
    collision detection, check for user input, calculate the frames per

second, etc.). The D3DApp implementation of this method computes the average frames per second and time elapsed per frame, and stores the result in the mFrameStats string. In this way, by calling the D3DApp implementation of this method, you get the frame statistics ready for output. See §4.5.4 for details on how the frame statistics are computed.

- drawScene: This method is invoked every frame and is used to draw the current frame of our 3D scene. The D3DApp implementation of this method simple clears the back buffer and depth/stencil buffer to prepare for drawing (it is common to always reset these buffers before drawing a new frame so that the values from the previous frame are not "left over"):

```
void D3DApp::drawScene()
{
    // Clear the render target to the color specified by mClearColor.
    md3dDevice->ClearRenderTargetView(mRenderTargetView, mClearColor);

    // Clear the depth buffer to 1.0, and clear the stencil buffer
    // to 0.
    md3dDevice->ClearDepthStencilView(mDepthStencilView,
        D3D10_CLEAR_DEPTH|D3D10_CLEAR_STENCIL, 1.0f, 0);
}
```

- msgProc: This method implements the window procedure function for the main application window. Generally, you only need to override this method if there is a message you need to handle that D3DApp::msgProc does not handle (or does not handle to your liking). The D3DApp implementation of this method is explored in §4.5.5.

Note: When you override these methods, you typically always want to call the base implementation from the derived implementation. For example, if you override msgProc, but do not call D3DApp::msgProc from the derived implementation, then you won't get the message handling that D3DApp::msgProc provides. Likewise, if you override updateScene, but do not call D3DApp::updateScene from the derived implementation, then you won't get the frame statistics calculated for you.

4.5.4 **Frame Statistics**

It is common for games and graphics applications to measure the number of frames being rendered per second (FPS). To do this, we simply count the number of frames processed (and store it in a variable n) over some specified time period t. Then, the average FPS over the time period t is $fps_{avg} = n/t$. If we set $t = 1$, then $fps_{avg} = n/1 = n$. In our code, we use $t = 1$ since it avoids a division, and moreover, one second gives a pretty good average — it is not too long and not too short. The code to compute the FPS is provided by the D3DApp implementation of updateScene:

```
void D3DApp::updateScene(float dt)
{
    // Code computes the average frames per second, and also the
    // average time it takes to render one frame.

    static int frameCnt = 0;
    static float t_base = 0.0f;

    frameCnt++;

    // Compute averages over one second period.
    if( (mTimer.getGameTime() - t_base) >= 1.0f )
    {
        float fps = (float)frameCnt; // fps = frameCnt / 1
        float mspf = 1000.0f / fps;

        std::wostringstream outs;
        outs.precision(6);
        outs << L"FPS: " << fps << L"\n"
             << "Milliseconds: Per Frame: " << mspf;

        // Save the stats in a string for output.
        mFrameStats = outs.str();

        // Reset for next average.
        frameCnt = 0;
        t_base  += 1.0f;
    }
}
```

This method would be called every frame in order to count the frames.

In addition to computing the FPS, the above code also computes the number of milliseconds it takes, on average, to process a frame:

```
float mspf = 1000.0f / fps;
```

Note: The seconds per frame is just the reciprocal of the FPS, but we multiply by 1000 ms / 1 s to convert from seconds to milliseconds (recall there are 1000 ms per second).

The idea behind this line is to compute the time, in milliseconds, it takes to render a frame; this is a different quantity than FPS (but observe this value can be derived from the FPS). In actuality, the time it takes to render a frame is more useful than the FPS, as we may directly see the increase/decrease in time it takes to render a frame as we modify our scene. On the other hand, the FPS does not immediately tell us the increase/decrease in time as we modify our scene. Moreover, as [Dunlop03] points out in his article *FPS versus Frame Time*, due to the non-linearity of the FPS curve, using the FPS can give misleading results. For example, consider situation (1): Suppose our application is running at 1000 FPS, taking 1 ms (millisecond) to render a frame. If the frame rate drops to 250 FPS, then it takes 4 ms to render a frame. Now consider situation (2): Suppose that our application is running at 100 FPS, taking 10 ms to render a frame. If the frame rate drops to about 76.9 FPS, then it takes about 13 ms to render a frame. In both situations, the rendering per frame increased by 3 ms, and thus both represent the same increase in time it takes to render a frame. Reading the FPS is not as straightforward. The drop from 1000 FPS to 250 FPS seems much more drastic than the drop from 100 FPS to 76.9 FPS; however, as we have just shown, they actually represent the same increase in time it takes to render a frame.

4.5.5 **The Message Handler**

The window procedure we implement for our application framework does the bare minimum. In general, we won't be working very much with Win32 messages anyway. In fact, the core of our application code gets executed during idle processing (i.e., when no window message is present). Still, there are some important messages we do need to process. Because of the length of the window procedure, we do not embed all the code here; rather, we just explain the motivation behind each message we handle. We encourage the reader to download the source code files and spend some time becoming familiar with the application framework code, as it is the foundation of every sample for this book.

The first message we handle is the WM_ACTIVATE message. This message is sent when an application becomes activated or deactivated. We implement it like so:

```
case WM_ACTIVATE:
    if( LOWORD(wParam) == WA_INACTIVE )
    {
        mAppPaused = true;
        mTimer.stop();
    }
    else
    {
        mAppPaused = false;
        mTimer.start();
    }
    return 0;
```

As you can see, when our application becomes deactivated, we set the data member mAppPaused to true, and when our application becomes active, we set the data member mAppPaused to false. In addition, when the application is paused, we stop the timer, and then resume the timer once the application becomes active again. If we look back at the implementation to D3DApp::run (§4.3.3), we find that if our application is paused, then we do not update our application code, but instead free some CPU cycles back to the OS; in this way, our application does not hog CPU cycles when it is inactive.

The next message we handle is the WM_SIZE message. Recall that this message is called when the window is resized. The main reason for handling this message is that we want the back and depth/stencil buffer dimensions to match the dimensions of the client area rectangle (so no stretching occurs). Thus, every time the window is resized, we want to resize the buffer dimensions. The code to resize the buffers is implemented in D3DApp::onResize. As already stated, the back buffer can be resized by calling the IDXGISwapChain::ResizeBuffers method. The depth/stencil buffer needs to be destroyed and then remade based on the new dimensions. In addition, the render target and depth/stencil views need to be recreated. If the user is dragging the resize bars, we must be careful because dragging the resize bars sends continuous WM_SIZE messages, and we do not want to continuously resize the buffers. Therefore, if we determine that the user is resizing by dragging, we actually do nothing (except pause the application) until the user is done dragging the resize bars. We can do this by handling the WM_EXITSIZEMOVE message. This message is sent when the user releases the resize bars.

```
// WM_ENTERSIZEMOVE is sent when the user grabs the resize bars.
case WM_ENTERSIZEMOVE:
    mAppPaused = true;
    mResizing  = true;
    mTimer.stop();
    return 0;

// WM_EXITSIZEMOVE is sent when the user releases the resize bars.
// Here we reset everything based on the new window dimensions.
case WM_EXITSIZEMOVE:
    mAppPaused = false;
    mResizing  = false;
    mTimer.start();
    onResize();
    return 0;
```

Finally, the last three messages we handle are trivially implemented and so we just show the code:

```
// WM_DESTROY is sent when the window is being destroyed.
case WM_DESTROY:
    PostQuitMessage(0);
    return 0;

// The WM_MENUCHAR message is sent when a menu is active and the user
// presses a key that does not correspond to any mnemonic or accelerator
// key.
case WM_MENUCHAR:
    // Don't beep when we alt-enter.
    return MAKELRESULT(0, MNC_CLOSE);

// Catch this message to prevent the window from becoming too small.
case WM_GETMINMAXINFO:
```

```
((MINMAXINFO*)lParam)->ptMinTrackSize.x = 200;
((MINMAXINFO*)lParam)->ptMinTrackSize.y = 200;
return 0;
```

4.5.6 Going Full Screen

The IDXGISwapChain interface created with D3D10CreateDeviceAndSwapChain automatically catches the Alt+Enter key combination and will switch the application to full-screen mode. Pressing Alt+Enter while in full-screen mode will switch back to windowed mode. During the mode switch, the application window will be resized, which sends a WM_SIZE message to the application; this gives the application a chance to resize the back and depth/stencil buffers to match the new screen dimensions. Also, if switching to full-screen mode, the window style will change to one that works for the full screen if necessary. You can use the Visual Studio Spy++ tool to sec the Windows messages that are generated by pressing Alt+Enter for the demo applications that use the sample framework.

One of the exercises at the end of this chapter explores how you can disable the default Alt+Enter functionality should you need to.

Note: The reader may wish to review the DXGI_SWAP_CHAIN_ DESC::Flags description in §4.1.4.

4.5.7 The Init Direct3D Demo

Now that we have discussed the application framework, let's make a small application using it. The program requires almost no real work on our part since the parent class D3DApp does most of the work required for this demo. The main thing to note is how we derive a class from D3DApp and implement the framework functions, where we will write our sample-specific code. All of the programs in this book will follow the same template.

```
#include "d3dApp.h"

class InitDirect3DApp : public D3DApp
{
public:
    InitDirect3DApp(HINSTANCE hInstance);
    ~InitDirect3DApp();

    void initApp();
    void onResize();
    void updateScene(float dt);
    void drawScene();
};

int WINAPI WinMain(HINSTANCE hInstance, HINSTANCE prevInstance,
                   PSTR cmdLine, int showCmd)
{
```

```
    // Enable run-time memory check for debug builds.
#if defined(DEBUG) | defined(_DEBUG)
    _CrtSetDbgFlag( _CRTDBG_ALLOC_MEM_DF | _CRTDBG_LEAK_CHECK_DF );
#endif


    InitDirect3DApp theApp(hInstance);

    theApp.initApp();

    return theApp.run();
}

InitDirect3DApp::InitDirect3DApp(HINSTANCE hInstance)
: D3DApp(hInstance)
{
}

InitDirect3DApp::~InitDirect3DApp()
{
if( md3dDevice )
        md3dDevice->ClearState();
}

void InitDirect3DApp::initApp()
{
    D3DApp::initApp();
}

void InitDirect3DApp::onResize()
{
    D3DApp::onResize();
}

void InitDirect3DApp::updateScene(float dt)
{
    D3DApp::updateScene(dt);
}

void InitDirect3DApp::drawScene()
{
    D3DApp::drawScene();

    // We specify DT_NOCLIP, so we do not care about width/height
    // of the rect.
    RECT R = {5, 5, 0, 0};
    mFont->DrawText(0, mFrameStats.c_str(), -1, &R, DT_NOCLIP, BLACK);

    mSwapChain->Present(0, 0);
}
```

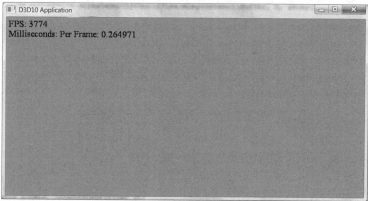

Figure 4.9: A screenshot of the sample program for Chapter 4.

4.6 **Debugging Direct3D Applications**

In order to shorten the code and minimize distractions, we omit most error handling in this book. However, we do implement a macro to check the HRESULT return codes returned by many Direct3D functions. Our macro is defined as follows in *d3dUtil.h*:

```
#if defined(DEBUG) | defined(_DEBUG)
    #ifndef HR
    #define HR(x)                                                  \
    {                                                              \
        HRESULT hr = (x);                                          \
        if(FAILED(hr))                                             \
        {                                                          \
            DXTrace(__FILE__, (DWORD)__LINE__, hr, L#x, true);    \
        }                                                          \
    }                                                              \
    #endif
#else
    #ifndef HR
    #define HR(x) (x)
    #endif
#endif
```

If the returned function's return code indicates failure, then we pass the return code into the DXTrace function (#include <dxerr.h>) and link *dxerr.lib*:

```
HRESULT WINAPI DXTraceW(const char* strFile, DWORD dwLine,
    HRESULT hr, const WCHAR* strMsg, BOOL bPopMsgBox);
```

This function displays a nice message box indicating the file and line number where the error occurred, as well as a textual description of the error and the name of the function that generated the error; Figure 4.10 shows an example. Note that if you specify false for the last parameter of DXTrace, then instead of a message box, the debug info will be output to the Visual C++ output window. Observe that the macro HR does nothing if we are not in debug mode. Also, HR must be a macro and not a function; otherwise __FILE__ and __LINE__ would refer to the file and line of the function implementation instead of the file and line where the function HR was called.

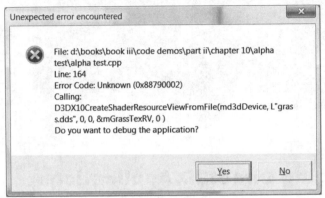

Figure 4.10: The message box displayed by the DXTrace function if a Direct3D function returns an error.

Now we just use this macro to surround a Direct3D function that returns an HRESULT as this example shows:

```
HR(D3DX10CreateShaderResourceViewFromFile(md3dDevice,
     L"grass.dds", 0, 0, &mGrassTexRV, 0 ));
```

This works well for debugging our demos, but a real application should handle errors more robustly.

Note: The L#x turns the HR macro's argument token into a Unicode string. In this way, we can output to the message box the function call that caused the error.

4.7 **Summary**

■   Direct3D can be thought of as a mediator between the programmer and the graphics hardware. For example, the programmer calls Direct3D functions to bind resource views to the hardware rendering pipeline, to configure the output of the rendering pipeline, and to draw 3D geometry.

■   In Direct3D 10, a Direct3D 10-capable graphics device must support the entire Direct3D 10 capability set, with few exceptions. Therefore, there is no need to do device capability checking, as there was with Direct3D 9.

- Component Object Model (COM) is the technology that allows DirectX to be language independent and have backward compatibility. Direct3D programmers don't need to know the details of COM and how it works; they need only to know how to acquire COM interfaces and how to release them.

- A 1D texture is like a 1D array of data elements, a 2D texture is like a 2D array of data elements, and a 3D texture is like a 3D array of data elements. The elements of a texture must have a format described by a member of the DXGI_FORMAT enumerated type. Textures typically contain image data, but they can contain other data, too, such as depth information (e.g., the depth buffer). The GPU can do special operations on textures, such as filter and multisample them.

- In Direct3D, resources are not bound to the pipeline directly. Instead, a resource view is bound to the pipeline. Different views of a single resource may be created. In this way, a single resource may be bound to different stages of the rendering pipeline. If a resource was created with a typeless format, then the type must be specified at view creation.

- The ID3D10Device interface is the chief Direct3D interface and can be thought of as our software controller of the physical graphics device hardware; that is, through this interface we can interact with the hardware and instruct it to do things (such as clear the back buffer, bind resources to the various pipeline stages, and draw geometry).

- The performance counter is a high-resolution timer that provides accurate timing measurements needed for measuring small time differentials, such as the time elapsed between frames. The performance timer works in time units called _counts_. The QueryPerformanceFrequency function outputs the counts per second of the performance timer, which can then be used to convert from units of counts to seconds. The current time value of the performance timer (measured in counts) is obtained with the QueryPerformanceCounter function.

- To compute the frames per second (FPS), we count the number of frames processed over some time interval Δt. Let n be the number of frames counted over time Δt; the average frames per second over that time interval is $fps_{avg} = \frac{n}{\Delta t}$. The frame rate can give misleading conclusions about performance; the time it takes to process a frame is more informative. The amount of time, in seconds, spent processing a frame is the reciprocal of the frame rate, i.e., $1/fps_{avg}$.

- To facilitate text output, the D3DX library provides the ID3DX10Font interface. A pointer to an object of this type can be obtained with the D3DX10CreateFontIndirect function. Once a pointer has been obtained, use the ID3DX10Font::DrawText method to draw a string to the screen.

- The sample framework is used to provide a consistent interface that all demo applications in this book follow. The code provided in the *d3dUtil.h*, *d3dApp.h*, and *d3dApp.cpp* files wrap standard initialization code that every application must implement. By wrapping this code up, we hide it, which allows the samples to be more focused on demonstrating the current topic.

- For debug mode builds, create the Direct3D device with the D3D10_CREATE_DEVICE_DEBUG flag to enable the debug layer. When the debug flag is specified, Direct3D will send debug messages to the VC++ output window. Also use the debug version of the D3DX library (i.e., *d3dx10d.lib*) for debug builds.

4.8 **Exercises**

1. Instead of using D3D10CreateDeviceAndSwapChain to create the device and swap chain at once, you can use D3D10CreateDevice and IDXGIFactory::CreateSwapChain to create the device and swap chain separately. In particular, this allows you to create several swap chains, which can be useful for applications that render into multiple windows (one swap chain is used for each window). To create an IDXGIFactory instance, use the CreateDXGIFactory function. To use the DXGI functions, you will need to link *dxgi.lib* to your project.

2. Modify the previous exercise solution by disabling the Alt+Enter functionality to switch between full-screen and windowed mode; use the IDXGIFactory::MakeWindowAssociation method and specify the DXGI_MWA_NO_WINDOW_CHANGES flag so that DXGI does not monitor the message queue. Note that the IDXGIFactory::MakeWindowAssociation method needs to be called after IDXGIFactory::CreateSwapChain is called.

3. Some systems have more than one adapter (video card), and the application may wish to let the user choose which one to use, instead of always using the default adapter. Use the IDXGIFactory::EnumAdapters method to determine how many adapters are on your system.

4. For each adapter the system possesses, IDXGIFactory::EnumAdapters outputs a pointer to a filled out IDXGIAdapter interface. This interface can be used to query information about the adapter. Use the IDXGIAdapter::CheckInterfaceSupport method to see if the adapters on your system support Direct3D 10.

5. An adapter has outputs associated with it (e.g., a monitor). You can use the IDXGIAdapter::EnumOutputs method to enumerate the outputs for a particular adapter. Use this method to determine the number of outputs for the default adapter.

6. Each output has a list of supported display modes (DXGI_MODE_DESC) for a given pixel format. For each output (IDXGIOutput), show the width,

height, and refresh rate of each display mode the output supports for the DXGI_FORMAT_R8G8B8A8_UNORM format using the IDXGIOutput::GetDisplayModeList method.

The listing below shows example output for Exercises 3, 4, 5, and 6. It is useful to use the OutputDebugString function for quick output to the VC++ output window.

```
*** NUM ADAPTERS = 1
*** D3D10 SUPPORTED FOR ADAPTER 0
*** NUM OUTPUTS FOR DEFAULT ADAPTER = 1
***WIDTH = 640 HEIGHT = 480 REFRESH = 60000/1000
***WIDTH = 640 HEIGHT = 480 REFRESH = 72000/1000
***WIDTH = 640 HEIGHT = 480 REFRESH = 75000/1000
***WIDTH = 720 HEIGHT = 480 REFRESH = 56250/1000
***WIDTH = 720 HEIGHT = 480 REFRESH = 56250/1000
***WIDTH = 720 HEIGHT = 480 REFRESH = 60000/1000
***WIDTH = 720 HEIGHT = 480 REFRESH = 60000/1000
***WIDTH = 720 HEIGHT = 480 REFRESH = 72188/1000
***WIDTH = 720 HEIGHT = 480 REFRESH = 72188/1000
***WIDTH = 720 HEIGHT = 480 REFRESH = 75000/1000
***WIDTH = 720 HEIGHT = 480 REFRESH = 75000/1000
***WIDTH = 720 HEIGHT = 576 REFRESH = 56250/1000
***WIDTH = 720 HEIGHT = 576 REFRESH = 56250/1000
***WIDTH = 720 HEIGHT = 576 REFRESH = 60000/1000
***WIDTH = 720 HEIGHT = 576 REFRESH = 60000/1000
***WIDTH = 720 HEIGHT = 576 REFRESH = 72188/1000
***WIDTH = 720 HEIGHT = 576 REFRESH = 72188/1000
***WIDTH = 720 HEIGHT = 576 REFRESH = 75000/1000
***WIDTH = 720 HEIGHT = 576 REFRESH = 75000/1000
***WIDTH = 800 HEIGHT = 600 REFRESH = 56250/1000
***WIDTH = 800 HEIGHT = 600 REFRESH = 60000/1000
***WIDTH = 800 HEIGHT = 600 REFRESH = 60000/1000
***WIDTH = 800 HEIGHT = 600 REFRESH = 72188/1000
***WIDTH = 800 HEIGHT = 600 REFRESH = 75000/1000
***WIDTH = 848 HEIGHT = 480 REFRESH = 60000/1000
***WIDTH = 848 HEIGHT = 480 REFRESH = 60000/1000
***WIDTH = 848 HEIGHT = 480 REFRESH = 70069/1000
***WIDTH = 848 HEIGHT = 480 REFRESH = 70069/1000
***WIDTH = 848 HEIGHT = 480 REFRESH = 75029/1000
***WIDTH = 848 HEIGHT = 480 REFRESH = 75029/1000
***WIDTH = 960 HEIGHT = 600 REFRESH = 60000/1000
***WIDTH = 960 HEIGHT = 600 REFRESH = 60000/1000
***WIDTH = 960 HEIGHT = 600 REFRESH = 70069/1000
***WIDTH = 960 HEIGHT = 600 REFRESH = 70069/1000
***WIDTH = 960 HEIGHT = 600 REFRESH = 75029/1000
***WIDTH = 960 HEIGHT = 600 REFRESH = 75029/1000
***WIDTH = 1024 HEIGHT = 768 REFRESH = 60000/1000
***WIDTH = 1024 HEIGHT = 768 REFRESH = 60000/1000
***WIDTH = 1024 HEIGHT = 768 REFRESH = 70069/1000
***WIDTH = 1024 HEIGHT = 768 REFRESH = 75029/1000
***WIDTH = 1152 HEIGHT = 864 REFRESH = 60000/1000
***WIDTH = 1152 HEIGHT = 864 REFRESH = 60000/1000
```

```
***WIDTH = 1152 HEIGHT =  864 REFRESH = 75000/1000
***WIDTH = 1280 HEIGHT =  720 REFRESH = 60000/1000
***WIDTH = 1280 HEIGHT =  720 REFRESH = 60000/1000
***WIDTH = 1280 HEIGHT =  720 REFRESH = 60000/1001
***WIDTH = 1280 HEIGHT =  768 REFRESH = 60000/1000
***WIDTH = 1280 HEIGHT =  768 REFRESH = 60000/1000
***WIDTH = 1280 HEIGHT =  800 REFRESH = 60000/1000
***WIDTH = 1280 HEIGHT =  800 REFRESH = 60000/1000
***WIDTH = 1280 HEIGHT =  960 REFRESH = 60000/1000
***WIDTH = 1280 HEIGHT =  960 REFRESH = 60000/1000
***WIDTH = 1280 HEIGHT = 1024 REFRESH = 60000/1000
***WIDTH = 1280 HEIGHT = 1024 REFRESH = 60000/1000
***WIDTH = 1280 HEIGHT = 1024 REFRESH = 75025/1000
***WIDTH = 1360 HEIGHT =  768 REFRESH = 60000/1000
***WIDTH = 1360 HEIGHT =  768 REFRESH = 60000/1000
***WIDTH = 1600 HEIGHT = 1200 REFRESH = 60000/1000
```

7. Experiment with modifying the viewport settings to draw the scene into a subrectangle of the back buffer. For example, try:

```
D3D10_VIEWPORT vp;
    vp.TopLeftX = 100;
    vp.TopLeftY = 100;
    vp.Width    = 400;
    vp.Height   = 300;
    vp.MinDepth = 0.0f;
    vp.MaxDepth = 1.0f;
```

Chapter 5

The Rendering Pipeline

The primary theme of this chapter is the rendering pipeline. Given a geometric description of a 3D scene with a positioned and oriented virtual camera, the *rendering pipeline* refers to the entire sequence of steps necessary to generate a 2D image based on what the virtual camera sees (Figure 5.1). Before we begin coverage of the rendering pipeline, we have two short stops: First, we discuss some elements of the 3D illusion (i.e., the illusion that we are looking into a 3D world through a flat 2D monitor screen); and second, we explain how colors will be represented and worked with mathematically and in Direct3D code.

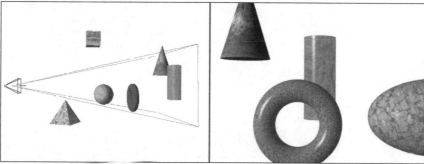

Figure 5.1: The image on the left shows some objects set up in the 3D world with a camera positioned and aimed. The "pyramid" volume specifies the volume of space that the viewer can see; objects (and parts of objects) outside this volume are not seen. The image on the right shows the 2D image created based on what the camera "sees."

Objectives:

- ■ To discover several key signals used to convey a realistic sense of volume and spatial depth in a 2D image.
- ■ To find out how we represent 3D objects in Direct3D.
- ■ To learn how we model the virtual camera.
- ■ To understand the rendering pipeline — the process of taking a geometric description of a 3D scene and generating a 2D image from it.

5.1 **The 3D Illusion**

Before we embark on our journey of 3D computer graphics, a simple question remains outstanding: How do we display a 3D world with depth and volume on a flat 2D monitor screen? Fortunately for us, this problem has been well studied, as artists have been painting 3D scenes on 2D canvases for centuries. In this section, we outline several key techniques that make an image look 3D, even though it is actually drawn on a 2D plane.

Suppose that you have encountered a railroad track that doesn't curve, but goes along a straight line for a long distance. The railroad rails always remain parallel to each other, but if you stand on the track and look down its path, you will observe that the two railroad rails seem to get closer and closer together as their distance from you increases, and eventually they appear to converge at an infinite distance. This is one observation that characterizes our human viewing system: Parallel lines of vision converge to a *vanishing point*, as shown in Figure 5.2.

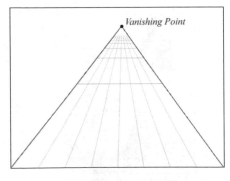

Figure 5.2: Parallel lines converge to a vanishing point. Artists sometimes call this *linear perspective*.

Another simple observation of how humans see things is that the size of an object appears to diminish with depth; that is, objects near us look bigger than objects far away. For example, a house far away on a hill will look very small, while a tree near us will look very large in comparison. Figure 5.3 shows a simple scene where parallel rows of columns are placed behind each other, one after another. The columns are actually all the same size, but as their depths increase from the viewer, they appear smaller and smaller. Also notice how the columns are converging to the vanishing point at the horizon.

Figure 5.3: Here, all the columns are of the same size, but a viewer observes a diminishing in size with respect to depth phenomenon.

Object overlap is another reality we experience. Object overlap refers to the fact that opaque objects obscure parts (or all) of the objects behind them. This is important, as it tells us the depth ordering relationship of the objects in the scene. We already discussed (in Chapter 4) how Direct3D uses a depth buffer to figure out which pixels are being obscured and thus should not be drawn. However, for completeness, we reshow the situation again in Figure 5.4.

Figure 5.4: A group of objects that partially obscure each other because they overlap.

Consider Figure 5.5. On the left we have an unlit sphere, and on the right we have a lit sphere. As you can see, the sphere on the left looks rather flat — maybe it is not even a sphere at all, but just a 2D circle! Thus, lighting and shading play a very important role in depicting the solid form and volume of 3D objects.

Figure 5.5: (a) An unlit sphere that looks 2D. (b) A lit sphere that looks 3D.

Finally, Figure 5.6 shows a spaceship and its shadow. The shadow serves two key purposes. First, it tells us the origin of the light source in the scene. And secondly, it provides us with a rough idea of how high off the ground the spaceship is.

Figure 5.6: A spaceship and its shadow. The shadow implies the location of the light source in the scene and also gives an idea of the spaceship's height off the ground.

The observations just discussed, no doubt, are intuitively obvious from our day-to-day experiences. Nonetheless, it is helpful to explicitly write down what we know and keep these observations in mind as we study and work on 3D computer graphics.

5.2 **Model Representation**

A solid 3D *object* is represented by a *triangle mesh* approximation, and consequently, triangles form the basic building blocks of the objects we model. As Figure 5.7 implies, we can approximate any real-world 3D object by a triangle mesh. Generally speaking, the greater the triangle density of the mesh, the better the approximation. Of course, the more triangles we use, the more processing power is required, so a balance must be made based on the hardware power of the application's target audience. In addition to triangles, it is sometimes useful to draw lines or points. For example, a curve could be graphically drawn by a sequence of short line segments one pixel thick.

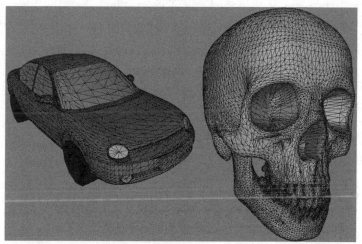

Figure 5.7: (Left) A car approximated by a relatively low-density triangle mesh. (Right) A skull approximated by a higher density triangle mesh.

The large number of triangles used in Figure 5.7 makes one thing clear: It would be extremely cumbersome to manually list the triangles of a 3D model. For all but the simplest models, special 3D applications called *3D modelers* are used to generate and manipulate 3D objects. These modelers allow the user to build complex and realistic meshes in a visual and interactive environment with a rich tool set, thereby making the entire modeling process much easier. Examples of popular modelers used for game development are 3ds Max (http://www.autodesk.com/3dsmax), LightWave 3D (http://www.newtek.com/lightwave/), Maya (http://www.autodesk.com/ maya), and Softimage|XSI (www.softimage.com). Nevertheless, for Part II of this book, we will generate our 3D models manually by hand or via a mathematical formula (the triangle list for cylinders and spheres, for example, can easily be generated with parametric formulas). In Part III of this book, we show how to load and display 3D models exported from 3D modeling programs.

5.3 **Basic Computer Color**

Computer monitors emit a mixture of red, green, and blue light through each pixel. When the light mixture enters the eye and strikes an area of the retina, cone receptor cells are stimulated and neural impulses are sent down the optic nerve toward the brain. The brain interprets the signal and generates a color. As the light mixture varies, the cells are stimulated differently, which in turn generates a different color in the mind. Figure 5.8 shows how mixing red, green, and blue produces different colors; it also shows different intensities of red. By using different intensities for each color component and mixing them together, we can describe all the colors we need to display realistic images.

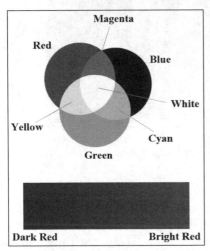

Figure 5.8: (Top) The mixing of pure red, green, and blue colors to get new colors. (Bottom) Different shades of red found by controlling the intensity of red light. A full-color version of this image is available in the download for this book, and is named Figure 5_8.bmp.

The best way to get comfortable with describing colors by RGB (red, green, blue) values is to use a paint program like Adobe Photoshop, or even the Win32 Color dialog box (Figure 5.9), and experiment with different RGB combinations to see the colors they produce.

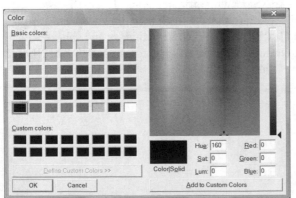

Figure 5.9: The Color dialog box.

A monitor has a maximum intensity of red, green, and blue light it can emit. To describe the intensities of light, it is useful to use a normalized range from 0 to 1. 0 denotes no intensity and 1 denotes the full intensity. Intermediate values denote intermediate intensities. For example, the values (0.25, 0.67, 1.0) mean the light mixture consists of 25% intensity of red light, 67% intensity of green light, and 100% intensity of blue light. As this example implies, we can represent a color by a 3D color vector (r, g, b), where $0 \leq r, g, b \leq 1$, and each color component describes the intensity of red, green, and blue light, respectively, in the mixture.

5.3.1 Color Operations

Some vector operations also apply to color vectors. For example, we can add color vectors to get new colors:

$$(0.0, 0.5, 0.0) + (0.0, 0.0, 0.25) = (0.0, 0.5, 0.25)$$

By combining a medium-intensity green color with a low-intensity blue color, we get a dark-green color.

Colors can also be subtracted to get new colors:

$$(1, 1, 1) - (1, 1, 0) = (0, 0, 1)$$

That is, we start with white and subtract out the red and green parts, and we end up with blue.

Scalar multiplication also makes sense. Consider the following:

$$0.5(1, 1, 1) = (0.5, 0.5, 0.5)$$

That is, we start with white and multiply by 0.5, and we end up with a medium shade of gray. On the other hand, the operation $2(0.25, 0.0, 0.0) = (0.5, 0.0, 0.0)$ doubles the intensity of the red component.

Obviously expressions like the dot product and cross product do not make sense for color vectors. However, color vectors do get their own special color operation called *modulation* or *componentwise* multiplication. It is defined as:

$$(c_r, c_g, c_b) \otimes (k_r, k_g, k_b) = (c_r k_r, c_g k_g, c_b k_b)$$

This operation is mainly used in lighting equations. For example, suppose we have an incoming ray of light with color (r, g, b) and it strikes a surface that reflects 50% red light, 75% green light, and 25% blue light, and absorbs the rest. Then the color of the reflected light ray is given by:

$$(r, g, b) \otimes (0.5, 0.75, 0.25) = (0.5r, 0.75g, 0.25b)$$

So we can see that the light ray lost some intensity when it struck the surface, since the surface absorbed some of the light.

When doing color operations, it is possible that your color components extend outside the [0, 1] interval; consider the equation, (1, 0.1, 0.6) + (0.0, 0.3, 0.5) = (1, 0.4, 1.1), for example. Since 1.0 represents the maximum intensity of a color component, you cannot increase it. Thus 1.1 is just as intense as 1.0. So what we do is clamp $1.1 \to 1.0$. Likewise, a monitor cannot emit negative light, so any negative color component (which could result from a subtraction operation) should be clamped to 0.0.

5.3.2 **128-Bit Color**

It is common to incorporate an additional color component called the *alpha component*. The alpha component is often used to denote the opacity of a color, which is useful in blending (see Chapter 8). (Since we are not using blending yet, just set the alpha component to 1 for now.)

Including the alpha component means we can represent a color by a 4D color vector (r, g, b, a) where $0 \le r, g, b, a \le 1$. To represent a color with 128 bits, we use a floating-point value for each component. The D3DX library provides the following structure, complete with helpful overloaded operators:

```
typedef struct D3DXCOLOR
{
#ifdef __cplusplus
public:
    D3DXCOLOR() {};
    D3DXCOLOR(UINT argb);
    D3DXCOLOR(CONST FLOAT *);
    D3DXCOLOR(CONST D3DXFLOAT16 *);
    D3DXCOLOR(FLOAT r, FLOAT g, FLOAT b, FLOAT a);

    // casting
    operator UINT () const;

    operator FLOAT* ();
    operator CONST FLOAT* () const;

    // assignment operators
    D3DXCOLOR& operator += (CONST D3DXCOLOR&);
    D3DXCOLOR& operator -= (CONST D3DXCOLOR&);
    D3DXCOLOR& operator *= (FLOAT);
    D3DXCOLOR& operator /= (FLOAT);

    // unary operators
    D3DXCOLOR operator + () const;
    D3DXCOLOR operator - () const;

    // binary operators
    D3DXCOLOR operator + (CONST D3DXCOLOR&) const;
    D3DXCOLOR operator - (CONST D3DXCOLOR&) const;
    D3DXCOLOR operator * (FLOAT) const;
```

```
    D3DXCOLOR operator / (FLOAT) const;

    friend D3DXCOLOR operator * (FLOAT, CONST D3DXCOLOR&);

    BOOL operator == (CONST D3DXCOLOR&) const;
    BOOL operator != (CONST D3DXCOLOR&) const;

#endif //__cplusplus
    FLOAT r, g, b, a;
} D3DXCOLOR, *LPD3DXCOLOR;
```

For componentwise multiplication, the D3DX library provides the following function:

```
D3DXCOLOR* D3DXColorModulate(
    D3DXCOLOR* pOut,     // Returns (cᵣ, c_g, c_b, c_a) ⊗ (kᵣ, k_g, k_b, k_a)
    CONST D3DXCOLOR* pC1, // (cᵣ, c_g, c_b, c_a)
    CONST D3DXCOLOR* pC2  // (kᵣ, k_g, k_b, k_a)
);
```

5.3.3 32-Bit Color

To represent a color with 32 bits, a byte is given to each component. Since each color is given an 8-bit byte, we can represent 256 different shades for each color component — 0 being no intensity, 255 being full intensity, and intermediate values being intermediate intensities. A byte per color component may seem small, but when we look at all the combinations ($256 \times 256 \times 256 = 16,777,216$), we see that millions of distinct colors can be represented.

A 32-bit color can be converted to a 128-bit color by mapping the integer range [0, 255] onto the real-valued interval [0, 1]. This is done by dividing by 255. That is, if $0 \le n \le 255$ is an integer, then $0 \le \frac{n}{255} \le 1$ gives the intensity in the normalized range from 0 to 1. For example, the 32-bit color (80, 140, 200, 255) becomes:

$$\left(80, 140, 200, 255\right) \rightarrow \left(\frac{80}{255}, \frac{140}{255}, \frac{200}{255}, \frac{255}{255}\right) \approx \left(0.31, 0.55, 0.78, 1.0\right)$$

On the other hand, a 128-bit color can be converted to a 32-bit color by multiplying each component by 255 and rounding to the nearest integer. For example:

$$\left(0.3, 0.6, 0.9, 1.0\right) \rightarrow \left(0.3 \cdot 255, 0.6 \cdot 255, 0.9 \cdot 255, 1.0 \cdot 255\right) = \left(77, 153, 230, 255\right)$$

Additional bit operations must usually be done when converting a 32-bit color to a 128-bit color and conversely because the 8-bit color components are usually packed into a 32-bit integer value (e.g., an unsigned int). The D3DXCOLOR class has a constructor that takes an unsigned integer (UINT) and constructs a D3DXCOLOR object from it. Figure 5.10 shows how the 8-bit color components are packed into a UINT. Note that this is just one way to pack the color components. Another format might be ABGR or RGBA, instead of ARGB; however, the D3DXCOLOR class assumes the ARGB layout. The D3DXCOLOR class also overloads operator UINT, so that a D3DXCOLOR object can be cast to a 32-bit color value packed into a UINT with format ARGB.

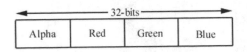

Figure 5.10: A 32-bit color, where a byte is allocated for each color component alpha, red, green, and blue.

Typically, 128-bit color values are used where many color operations will take place (e.g., in a pixel shader); in this way, we have many bits of accuracy for the calculations so arithmetic errors do not accumulate too much. The final pixel color, however, is usually stored in a 32-bit color value in the back buffer; current physical display devices cannot take advantage of the higher resolution color [Verth04].

5.4 Overview of the Rendering Pipeline

Given a geometric description of a 3D scene with a positioned and oriented virtual camera, the *rendering pipeline* refers to the entire sequence of steps necessary to generate a 2D image based on what the virtual camera sees. Figure 5.11 shows a diagram of the stages that make up the rendering pipeline, as well as memory resources off to the side. An arrow going from the memory pool to a stage means the stage can access the memory as input; for example, the pixel shader stage may need to read data from a texture resource stored in memory. An arrow going from a stage to memory means the stage writes to memory; for example, the output merger stage writes data to textures such as the back buffer and depth/stencil buffer. Observe that the arrow for the output merger stage is bidirectional. The subsequent sections give an overview of each stage of the rendering pipeline.

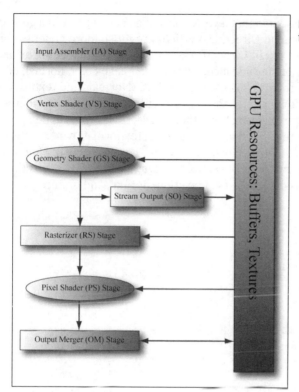

Figure 5.11: The stages of the rendering pipeline.

5.5 **The Input Assembler Stage**

The *input assembler* (IA) stage reads geometric data (vertices and indices) from memory and uses it to assemble geometric primitives (e.g., triangles, lines). (Indices are covered in a later subsection, but briefly, they define how the vertices should be put together to form the primitives.)

5.5.1 **Vertex Layouts**

Mathematically, the vertices of a triangle are where two edges meet; the vertices of a line are the endpoints. For a single point, the point itself is the vertex. Figure 5.12 illustrates vertices pictorially.

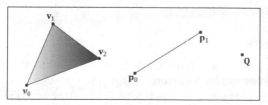

Figure 5.12: A triangle defined by the three vertices v_0, v_1, v_2; a line defined by the two vertices p_0, p_1; a point defined by the vertex u.

From Figure 5.12, it seems that a vertex is just a special point in a geometric primitive. However, in Direct3D, vertices are much more general than that. Essentially, a vertex in Direct3D can consist of additional properties besides spatial location; for instance, a vertex can have color, normal, or texture coordinate properties associated with it. (Normals and texture coordinates are discussed in later chapters.) Direct3D gives us the flexibility to construct our own vertex format; in other words, it allows us to define the components of a vertex. To create a custom vertex format, we first create a structure that holds the vertex data we choose. For instance, the following illustrates two different kinds of vertex formats; one consists of position and color, and the second consists of position, normal, and texture coordinates.

```
struct Vertex1
{
    D3DXVECTOR3 pos;
    D3DXCOLOR color;
};

struct Vertex2
{
    D3DXVECTOR3 pos;
    D3DXVECTOR3 normal;
    D3DXVECTOR2 texC;
};
```

Once we have defined a vertex structure, we need to provide Direct3D with a description of our vertex structure so that it knows what to do with each component. This description is provided to Direct3D in the form of an *input layout* (ID3D10InputLayout). An input layout is specified by an array of D3D10_INPUT_ELEMENT_DESC elements. Each element in the D3D10_INPUT_ELEMENT_DESC array describes one component in the vertex structure. So if the vertex structure has two components, then the corresponding D3D10_INPUT_ELEMENT_DESC array will have two elements. The D3D10_INPUT_ELEMENT_DESC structure is defined as:

```
typedef struct D3D10_INPUT_ELEMENT_DESC {
    LPCSTR SemanticName;
    UINT SemanticIndex;
    DXGI_FORMAT Format;
    UINT InputSlot;
    UINT AlignedByteOffset
    D3D10_INPUT_CLASSIFICATION InputSlotClass;
    UINT InstanceDataStepRate;
} D3D10_INPUT_ELEMENT_DESC;
```

■   SemanticName: A string to associate with the element. This can be any valid variable name. Semantics are used to map elements in the vertex structure to elements in the vertex shader input signature (see Figure 5.13).

- SemanticIndex: An index to attach to a semantic. The motivation for this is also illustrated in Figure 5.13; that is, a vertex structure may have more than one set of texture coordinates, for example, so rather than introducing a new semantic name, we can just attach an index to the end. A semantic with no index specified in the shader code defaults to index 0; for instance, POSITION is equivalent to POSITION0 in Figure 5.13.

- Format: A member of the DXGI_FORMAT enumerated type specifying the format of the element; here are some common examples of formats used:

```
DXGI_FORMAT_R32_FLOAT          // 1D 32-bit float scalar
DXGI_FORMAT_R32G32_FLOAT       // 2D 32-bit float vector
DXGI_FORMAT_R32G32B32_FLOAT    // 3D 32-bit float vector
DXGI_FORMAT_R32G32B32A32_FLOAT // 4D 32-bit float vector

DXGI_FORMAT_R8_UINT            // 1D 8-bit unsigned integer scalar
DXGI_FORMAT_R16G16_SINT        // 2D 16-bit signed integer vector
DXGI_FORMAT_R32G32B32_UINT     // 3D 32-bit unsigned integer vector
DXGI_FORMAT_R8G8B8A8_SINT      // 4D 8-bit signed integer vector
```

- InputSlot: Specifies the input slot index this element will come from. Direct3D supports 16 input slots (indexed as 0-15) through which you can feed vertex data. For instance, if a vertex consisted of position and color elements, you could either feed both elements through a single input slot, or you could split the elements up and feed the position elements through the first input slot and feed the color elements through the second input slot. Direct3D will then use the elements from the different input slots to assemble the vertices. In this book, we only use one input slot, but Exercise 2 at the end of this chapter asks you to experiment with two.

- AlignedByteOffset: For a single input slot, this is the offset, in bytes, from the start of the vertex structure to the start of the vertex component. For example, in the following vertex structure, the element pos has a 0-byte offset since its start coincides with the start of the vertex structure; the element normal has a 12-byte offset because we have to skip over the bytes of pos to get to the start of normal; the element texC has a 24-byte offset because we need to skip over the bytes of pos and normal to get to the start of texC.

```
struct Vertex2
{
        D3DXVECTOR3 pos;    // 0-byte offset
        D3DXVECTOR3 normal; // 12-byte offset
        D3DXVECTOR2 texC;   // 24-byte offset
};
```

■ `InputSlotClass`: Specify `D3D10_INPUT_PER_VERTEX_DATA` for now; the other option is used for the advanced technique of instancing.

■ `InstanceDataStepRate`: Specify 0 for now; other values are only used for the advanced technique of instancing.

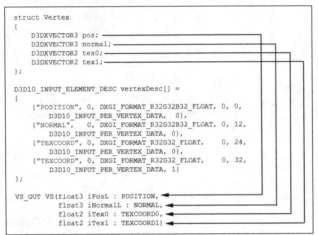

```
struct Vertex
{
    D3DXVECTOR3 pos;
    D3DXVECTOR3 normal;
    D3DXVECTOR2 tex0;
    D3DXVECTOR2 tex1;
};

D3D10_INPUT_ELEMENT_DESC vertexDesc[] =
{
    {"POSITION", 0, DXGI_FORMAT_R32G32B32_FLOAT, 0, 0,
        D3D10_INPUT_PER_VERTEX_DATA, 0},
    {"NORMAL",   0, DXGI_FORMAT_R32G32B32_FLOAT, 0, 12,
        D3D10_INPUT_PER_VERTEX_DATA, 0},
    {"TEXCOORD", 0, DXGI_FORMAT_R32G32_FLOAT,    0, 24,
        D3D10_INPUT_PER_VERTEX_DATA, 0},
    {"TEXCOORD", 0, DXGI_FORMAT_R32G32_FLOAT,    0, 32,
        D3D10_INPUT_PER_VERTEX_DATA, 1}
};

VS_OUT VS(float3 iPosL : POSITION,
          float3 iNormalL : NORMAL,
          float2 iTex0 : TEXCOORD0,
          float2 iTex1 : TEXCOORD1)
```

Figure 5.13: Each element in the vertex structure is described by a corresponding element in the `D3D10_INPUT_ELEMENT_DESC` array. The semantic name and index provide a way to map vertex elements to the corresponding parameters of the vertex shader.

For the previous two example vertex structures, `Vertex1` and `Vertex2`, the corresponding `D3D10_INPUT_ELEMENT_DESC` arrays would be:

```
D3D10_INPUT_ELEMENT_DESC desc1[] =
{
    {"POSITION", 0, DXGI_FORMAT_R32G32B32_FLOAT, 0, 0,
        D3D10_INPUT_PER_VERTEX_DATA, 0},
    {"COLOR", 0, DXGI_FORMAT_R32G32B32A32_FLOAT, 0, 12,
        D3D10_INPUT_PER_VERTEX_DATA, 0}
};

D3D10_INPUT_ELEMENT_DESC desc2[] =
{
    {"POSITION", 0, DXGI_FORMAT_R32G32B32_FLOAT, 0, 0,
        D3D10_INPUT_PER_VERTEX_DATA, 0},
    {"NORMAL", 0, DXGI_FORMAT_R32G32B32_FLOAT, 0, 12,
        D3D10_INPUT_PER_VERTEX_DATA, 0},
    {"TEXCOORD", 0, DXGI_FORMAT_R32G32_FLOAT, 0, 24,
        D3D10_INPUT_PER_VERTEX_DATA, 0}
};
```

Once an input layout has been specified by an array of `D3D10_INPUT_ELEMENT_DESC` elements, we can obtain a pointer to an `ID3D10InputLayout` interface, which represents an input layout, using the `ID3D10Device::CreateInputLayout` method:

```
HRESULT ID3D10Device::CreateInputLayout(
    const D3D10_INPUT_ELEMENT_DESC *pInputElementDescs,
    UINT NumElements,
    const void *pShaderBytecodeWithInputSignature,
    SIZE_T BytecodeLength,
    ID3D10InputLayout **ppInputLayout);
```

- pInputElementDescs: An array of D3D10_INPUT_ELEMENT_DESC elements describing the vertex structure.

- NumElements: The number of elements in the D3D10_INPUT_ELEMENT_DESC elements array.

- pShaderBytecodeWithInputSignature: A pointer to the shader byte-code of the input signature of the vertex shader.

- BytecodeLength: The byte size of the vertex shader signature data passed into the previous parameter.

- ppInputLayout: Returns a pointer to the created input layout.

The third parameter needs some elaboration. Essentially, a vertex shader expects a certain vertex format for each vertex it processes. The elements in the vertex structure need to be mapped to their corresponding inputs in the vertex shader; Figure 5.13 alludes to this. By passing in the vertex shader signature when the input layout is created, Direct3D can create the mapping from the vertex structure to the shader inputs at creation time (as opposed to "draw time," which was the case in Direct3D 9). An input layout can be reused across different shaders, provided the input signatures are exactly the same.

The following code provides an example to illustrate how the ID3D10Device::CreateInputLayout method is invoked. Note that the code involves some topics we have not discussed yet (such as ID3D10Effect). Essentially, an effect encapsulates one or more passes, and a vertex shader is associated with each pass. So from the effect, we can get a pass description (D3D10_PASS_DESC), from which we can get to the input signature of the vertex shader.

```
ID3D10Effect* mFX;
ID3D10EffectTechnique* mTech;
ID3D10InputLayout* mVertexLayout;

/* ...create the effect... */

mTech = mFX->GetTechniqueByName("ColorTech");
D3D10_PASS_DESC PassDesc;
mTech->GetPassByIndex(0)->GetDesc(&PassDesc);
HR(md3dDevice->CreateInputLayout(vertexDesc, 3,
    PassDesc.pIAInputSignature, PassDesc.IAInputSignatureSize,
    &mVertexLayout));
```

After an input layout has been created, it is still not bound to the device yet. The last step is to bind the input layout you want to use to the device, as the following code shows:

```
ID3D10InputLayout* mVertexLayout;

/* ...create the input layout... */

md3dDevice->IASetInputLayout(mVertexLayout);
```

If some objects you are drawing use one input layout, and other objects you are drawing require a different layout, then you need to structure your code like this:

```
md3dDevice->IASetInputLayout(mVertexLayout1);
/* ...draw objects using input layout 1... */

md3dDevice->IASetInputLayout(mVertexLayout2);
/* ...draw objects using input layout 2... */
```

In other words, when an input layout is bound to the device, it does not change until you overwrite it.

5.5.2 Vertex Buffers

In order for the GPU to access an array of vertices, they need to be placed in a special resource structure called a *buffer*, which is represented by the ID3D10Buffer interface. A buffer that stores vertices is called a *vertex buffer*. To create a vertex buffer, we need to perform the following steps:

1. Fill out a D3D10_BUFFER_DESC structure describing the buffer we are going to create.

2. Fill out a D3D10_SUBRESOURCE_DATA structure that specifies the data we want to initialize the buffer contents with.

3. Call ID3D10Device::CreateBuffer to create the buffer.

The D3D10_BUFFER_DESC structure is defined as follows:

```
typedef struct D3D10_BUFFER_DESC {
    UINT ByteWidth;
    D3D10_USAGE Usage;
    UINT BindFlags;
    UINT CPUAccessFlags;
    UINT MiscFlags;
} D3D10_BUFFER_DESC;
```

■   ByteWidth: The size, in bytes, of the vertex buffer we are going to create.

■   Usage: A member of the D3D10_USAGE enumerated type specifying how the buffer will be used. The four usage values are:

■ D3D10_USAGE_DEFAULT: Specify this usage if the GPU will be reading and writing to the resource. The CPU cannot read or write to a resource with this usage.

■ D3D10_USAGE_IMMUTABLE: Specify this usage if the contents of a resource never change after creation. This allows for some potential optimizations, as the resource will be read-only by the GPU. The CPU cannot write to an immutable resource, except at creation time to initialize the resource. The CPU cannot read from an immutable resource.

■ D3D10_USAGE_DYNAMIC: Specify this usage if the application (CPU) needs to update the data contents of the resource frequently (e.g., on a per-frame basis). A resource with this usage can be read by the GPU and written to by the CPU.

■ D3D10_USAGE_STAGING: Specify this usage if the application (CPU) needs to be able to read a copy of the resource (i.e., the resource supports copying data from video memory to system memory).

■ BindFlags: For a vertex buffer, specify D3D10_BIND_VERTEX_BUFFER.

■ CPUAccessFlags: Specifies how the CPU will access the buffer. If the CPU needs to update the buffer by writing to it, specify D3D10_CPU_ACCESS_WRITE. A buffer with write access must have usage D3D10_USAGE_DYNAMIC or D3D10_USAGE_STAGING. If the CPU needs to read from the buffer, specify D3D10_CPU_ACCESS_READ. A buffer with read access must have usage D3D10_USAGE_STAGING.

Only specify these flags if you need them. In general, the CPU reading from a Direct3D resource is slow. The CPU writing to a resource is faster, but there is still the overhead of having to transfer the updated data back to video memory. It is best to not specify any of these flags (if possible), and let the resource sit in video memory where only the GPU writes and reads to it.

■ MiscFlags: We do not need any of the miscellaneous flags for vertex buffers; specify 0 and see the D3D10_RESOURCE_MISC_FLAG enumerated type in the SDK documentation for further info.

The D3D10_SUBRESOURCE_DATA structure is defined as follows:

```
typedef struct D3D10_SUBRESOURCE_DATA {
    const void *pSysMem;
    UINT SysMemPitch;
    UINT SysMemSlicePitch;
} D3D10_SUBRESOURCE_DATA;
```

■ pSysMem: A pointer to a system memory array that contains the data to initialize the vertex buffer with. If the buffer can store n vertices, then the system array must contain at least n vertices so that the entire buffer can be initialized.

■ SysMemPitch: Not used for vertex buffers.

■ `SysMemSlicePitch`: Not used for vertex buffers.

The following code creates an immutable vertex buffer that is initialized with the eight vertices of a cube centered at the origin. The buffer is immutable because the cube geometry never needs to change once it is created — it always remains a cube. Moreover, we associate with each vertex a different color; these vertex colors will be used to color the cube, as we will see later in this chapter.

```
Vertex vertices[] =
{
    {D3DXVECTOR3(-1.0f, -1.0f, -1.0f), WHITE},
    {D3DXVECTOR3(-1.0f, +1.0f, -1.0f), BLACK},
    {D3DXVECTOR3(+1.0f, +1.0f, -1.0f), RED},
    {D3DXVECTOR3(+1.0f, -1.0f, -1.0f), GREEN},
    {D3DXVECTOR3(-1.0f, -1.0f, +1.0f), BLUE},
    {D3DXVECTOR3(-1.0f, +1.0f, +1.0f), YELLOW},
    {D3DXVECTOR3(+1.0f, +1.0f, +1.0f), CYAN},
    {D3DXVECTOR3(+1.0f, -1.0f, +1.0f), MAGENTA},
};

D3D10_BUFFER_DESC vbd;
vbd.Usage = D3D10_USAGE_IMMUTABLE;
vbd.ByteWidth = sizeof(Vertex) * 8;
vbd.BindFlags = D3D10_BIND_VERTEX_BUFFER;
vbd.CPUAccessFlags = 0;
vbd.MiscFlags = 0;

D3D10_SUBRESOURCE_DATA vinitData;
vinitData.pSysMem = vertices;

ID3D10Buffer* mVB;
HR(md3dDevice->CreateBuffer(
    &vbd,        // description of buffer to create
    &vinitData,  // data to initialize buffer with
    &mVB));      // return the created buffer
```

where the `Vertex` type and colors are defined as follows:

```
struct Vertex
{
    D3DXVECTOR3 pos;
    D3DXCOLOR   color;
};

const D3DXCOLOR WHITE(1.0f, 1.0f, 1.0f, 1.0f);
const D3DXCOLOR BLACK(0.0f, 0.0f, 0.0f, 1.0f);
const D3DXCOLOR RED(1.0f, 0.0f, 0.0f, 1.0f);
const D3DXCOLOR GREEN(0.0f, 1.0f, 0.0f, 1.0f);
const D3DXCOLOR BLUE(0.0f, 0.0f, 1.0f, 1.0f);
const D3DXCOLOR YELLOW(1.0f, 1.0f, 0.0f, 1.0f);
const D3DXCOLOR CYAN(0.0f, 1.0f, 1.0f, 1.0f);
const D3DXCOLOR MAGENTA(1.0f, 0.0f, 1.0f, 1.0f);
```

After a vertex buffer has been created, it needs to be bound to an input slot of the device in order to feed the vertices to the pipeline as input. This is done with the following method:

```
void ID3D10Device::IASetVertexBuffers(
    UINT StartSlot,
    UINT NumBuffers,
    ID3D10Buffer *const *ppVertexBuffers,
    const UINT *pStrides,
    const UINT *pOffsets);
```

- ■　StartSlot: The input slot to start binding vertex buffers to. There are 16 input slots indexed as 0-15.

- ■　NumBuffers: The number of vertex buffers we are binding to the input slots, starting at StartSlot.

- ■　ppVertexBuffers: Pointer to the first element of an array of vertex buffers.

- ■　pStrides: Pointer to the first element of an array of strides (one for each vertex buffer and the *i*th stride corresponds to the *i*th vertex buffer). A *stride* is the size, in bytes, of an element in the corresponding vertex buffer.

- ■　pOffsets: Pointer to the first element of an array of offsets (one for each vertex buffer and the *i*th offset corresponds to the *i*th vertex buffer). This is an offset, in bytes, from the start of the vertex buffer to the position in the vertex buffer from which the input assembly should start reading the data. You would use this if you wanted to skip over some data at the front of the vertex buffer.

A vertex buffer will stay bound to an input slot until you change it. So you may structure your code like the following if you are using more than one vertex buffer:

```
ID3D10Buffer* mVB1; // stores vertices of type Vertex1
ID3D10Buffer* mVB2; // stores vertices of type Vertex2

/*...Create the vertex buffers...*/

UINT stride = sizeof(Vertex1);
UINT offset = 0;
md3dDevice->IASetVertexBuffers(0, 1, &mVB1, &stride, &offset);
/* ...draw objects using vertex buffer 1... */

stride = sizeof(Vertex2);
offset = 0;
md3dDevice->IASetVertexBuffers(0, 1, &mVB2, &stride, &offset);
/* ...draw objects using vertex buffer 2... */
```

Setting a vertex buffer to an input slot does not draw the vertices; it only makes them ready to be fed into the pipeline. The final step to actually draw the vertices is done with the ID3D10Device::Draw method:

```
void ID3D10Device::Draw(UINT VertexCount, UINT StartVertexLocation);
```

The two parameters define a contiguous subset of vertices in the vertex buffer to draw, as shown in Figure 5.14.

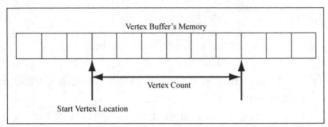

Figure 5.14: StartVertexLocation specifies the index (zero-based) of the first vertex in the vertex buffer to begin drawing. VertexCount specifies the number of vertices to draw.

5.5.3 **Primitive Topology**

A vertex buffer just stores a list of vertices in contiguous memory. However, it does not say how these vertices should be put together to form geometric primitives. For example, should every two vertices in the vertex buffer be interpreted as a line or should every three vertices in the vertex buffer be interpreted as a triangle? We tell Direct3D how to form geometric primitives from the vertex data by specifying the *primitive topology*:

```
void ID3D10Device::IASetPrimitiveTopology(
    D3D10_PRIMITIVE_TOPOLOGY Topology);

typedef enum D3D10_PRIMITIVE_TOPOLOGY
{
    D3D10_PRIMITIVE_TOPOLOGY_UNDEFINED = 0,
    D3D10_PRIMITIVE_TOPOLOGY_POINTLIST = 1,
    D3D10_PRIMITIVE_TOPOLOGY_LINELIST = 2,
    D3D10_PRIMITIVE_TOPOLOGY_LINESTRIP = 3,
    D3D10_PRIMITIVE_TOPOLOGY_TRIANGLELIST = 4,
    D3D10_PRIMITIVE_TOPOLOGY_TRIANGLESTRIP = 5,
    D3D10_PRIMITIVE_TOPOLOGY_LINELIST_ADJ = 10,
    D3D10_PRIMITIVE_TOPOLOGY_LINESTRIP_ADJ = 11,
    D3D10_PRIMITIVE_TOPOLOGY_TRIANGLELIST_ADJ = 12,
    D3D10_PRIMITIVE_TOPOLOGY_TRIANGLESTRIP_ADJ = 13,
} D3D10_PRIMITIVE_TOPOLOGY;
```

All subsequent drawing calls will use the currently set primitive topology until the topology is changed. The following code illustrates:

```
md3dDevice->IASetPrimitiveTopology(D3D10_PRIMITIVE_TOPOLOGY_LINELIST);
/* ...draw objects using line list... */

md3dDevice->IASetPrimitiveTopology(D3D10_PRIMITIVE_TOPOLOGY_TRIANGLELIST);
/* ...draw objects using triangle list... */

md3dDevice->IASetPrimitiveTopology(
    D3D10_PRIMITIVE_TOPOLOGY_TRIANGLESTRIP);
/* ...draw objects using triangle strip... */
```

The following subsections elaborate on the different primitive topologies. In this book, we use triangle lists with few exceptions; Exercise 3 at the end of this chapter asks you to experiment with the other primitive topologies.

5.5.3.1 *Point List*

A point list is specified by D3D10_PRIMITIVE_TOPOLOGY_POINTLIST. With a point list, every vertex in the draw call is drawn as an individual point, as shown in Figure 5.15a.

5.5.3.2 *Line Strip*

A line strip is specified by D3D10_PRIMITIVE_TOPOLOGY_LINESTRIP. With a line strip, the vertices in the draw call are connected to form lines (see Figure 5.15b); so $n + 1$ vertices induces n lines.

5.5.3.3 *Line List*

A line list is specified by D3D10_PRIMITIVE_TOPOLOGY_LINELIST. With a line list, every two vertices in the draw call form an individual line (see Figure 5.15c); so $2n$ vertices induces n lines. The difference between a line list and strip is that the lines in the line list may be disconnected, whereas a line strip automatically assumes they are connected; by assuming connectivity, fewer vertices can be used since each interior vertex is shared by two lines.

5.5.3.4 *Triangle Strip*

A triangle strip is specified by D3D10_PRIMITIVE_TOPOLOGY_TRIANGLESTRIP. With a triangle strip, it is assumed the triangles are connected as shown in Figure 5.15d to form a strip. By assuming connectivity, we see that vertices are shared between adjacent triangles, and n vertices induce $n - 2$ triangles.

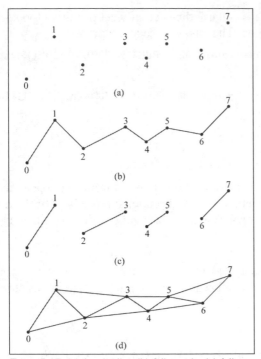

Figure 5.15: (a) A point list. (b) A line strip. (c) A line list. (d) A triangle strip.

Note: Observe that the winding order for even triangles in a triangle strip differs from the odd triangles, thereby causing culling issues (see §5.9.2). To fix this problem, the GPU internally swaps the order of the first two vertices of even triangles so that they are consistently ordered like the odd triangles.

5.5.3.5 *Triangle List*

A triangle list is specified by D3D10_PRIMITIVE_TOPOLOGY_TRIANGLELIST. With a triangle list, every three vertices in the draw call form an individual triangle (see Figure 5.16a); so $3n$ vertices induces n triangles. The difference between a triangle list and strip is that the triangles in the triangle list may be disconnected, whereas a triangle strip assumes they are connected.

5.5.3.6 *Primitives with Adjacency*

A triangle list with adjacency is where, for each triangle, you also include its three neighboring triangles called *adjacent triangles*; see Figure 5.16b to observe how these triangles are defined. This is used for the geometry shader, where certain geometry shading algorithms need access to the adjacent triangles. In order for the geometry shader to get those adjacent triangles, the adjacent triangles need to be submitted to the pipeline in the vertex/index buffers along with the triangle itself, and the D3D10_PRIMITIVE_ TOPOLOGY_TRIANGLELIST_ADJ topology must be specified so that the pipeline knows how to construct the triangle and its adjacent triangles from the vertex buffer. Note that the vertices of adjacent primitives are only used as input into the geometry shader — they are not drawn. If there is no geometry shader, the adjacent primitives are still not drawn (see Exercise 3f).

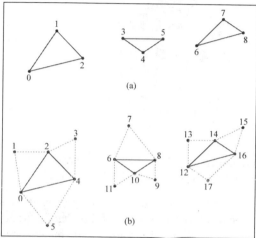

Figure 5.16: (a) A triangle list. (b) A triangle list with adjacency — observe that each triangle requires six vertices to describe it and its adjacent triangles. Thus 6*n* vertices induces *n* triangles with adjacency info.

It is also possible to have a line list with adjacency, line strip with adjacency, and triangle strip with adjacency primitives; see the SDK documentation for details.

5.5.4 Indices and Index Buffers

As already mentioned, triangles are the basic building blocks for solid 3D objects. The following code shows the vertex arrays used to construct a quad and octagon using triangle lists (i.e., every three vertices form a triangle).

```
Vertex quad[6] = {
    v0, v1, v2, // Triangle 0
    v0, v2, v3, // Triangle 1
};

Vertex octagon[24] = {
    v0, v1, v2, // Triangle 0
    v0, v2, v3, // Triangle 1
    v0, v3, v4, // Triangle 2
    v0, v4, v5, // Triangle 3
    v0, v5, v6, // Triangle 4
```

```
    v0, v6, v7, // Triangle 5
    v0, v7, v8, // Triangle 6
    v0, v8, v1  // Triangle 7
};
```

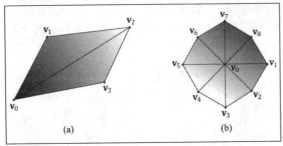

Figure 5.17: (a) A quad built from two triangles. (b) An octagon built from eight triangles.

Note: The order in which you specify the vertices of a triangle is important and is called the *winding order*; see §5.9.2 for details.

As Figure 5.17 illustrates, the triangles that form a 3D object share many of the same vertices. More specifically, each triangle of the quad in Figure 5.17a shares the vertices v_0 and v_2. While duplicating two vertices is not too bad, the duplication is worse in the octagon example (Figure 5.17b), as every triangle duplicates the center vertex v_0, and each vertex on the perimeter of the octagon is shared by two triangles. In general, the number of duplicate vertices increases as the detail and complexity of the model increases.

There are two reasons why we do not want to duplicate vertices:

■ Increased memory requirements. (Why store the same vertex data more than once?)

■ Increased processing by the graphics hardware. (Why process the same vertex data more than once?)

Triangle strips can help the duplicate vertex problem in some situations, provided the geometry can be organized in a strip-like fashion. However, triangle lists are more flexible (the triangles need not be connected), and so it is worth devising a method to remove duplicate vertices for triangle lists. The solution is to use *indices*. It works like this: We create a vertex list and an index list. The vertex list consists of all the *unique* vertices, and the index list contains values that index into the vertex list to define how the vertices are to be put together to form triangles. Returning to the shapes in Figure 5.17, the vertex list of the quad would be constructed as follows:

```
Vertex v[4] = {v0, v1, v2, v3};
```

Then the index list needs to define how the vertices in the vertex list are to be put together to form the two triangles.

```
DWORD indexList[6] = {0, 1, 2, // Triangle 0
                      0, 2, 3}; // Triangle 1
```

In the index list, every three elements define a triangle. So the above index list says, "form triangle 0 by using the vertices v[0], v[1], and v[2], and form triangle 1 by using the vertices v[0], v[2], and v[3]."

Similarly, the vertex list for the octagon would be constructed as follows:

```
Vertex v[9] = {v0, v1, v2, v3, v4, v5, v6, v7, v8};
```

and the index list would be:

```
DWORD indexList[24] = {
    0, 1, 2, // Triangle 0
    0, 2, 3, // Triangle 1
    0, 3, 4, // Triangle 2
    0, 4, 5, // Triangle 3
    0, 5, 6, // Triangle 4
    0, 6, 7, // Triangle 5
    0, 7, 8, // Triangle 6
    0, 8, 1  // Triangle 7
};
```

After the unique vertices in the vertex list are processed, the graphics card can use the index list to put the vertices together to form the triangles. Observe that we have moved the "duplication" over to the index list, but this is not bad since:

- Indices are simply integers and do not take up as much memory as a full vertex structure (and vertex structures can get big as we add more components to them).

- With good vertex cache ordering, the graphics hardware won't have to process duplicate vertices (too often).

Because indices need to be accessed by the GPU, they need to be placed in a special resource structure: an *index buffer*. Creating an index buffer is very similar to creating a vertex buffer, except that the index buffer stores indices instead of vertices. Therefore, rather than repeating a discussion similar to the one carried out for vertex buffers, we just show an example of creating an index buffer:

```
DWORD indices[24] = {
    0, 1, 2, // Triangle 0
    0, 2, 3, // Triangle 1
    0, 3, 4, // Triangle 2
    0, 4, 5, // Triangle 3
    0, 5, 6, // Triangle 4
    0, 6, 7, // Triangle 5
    0, 7, 8, // Triangle 6
    0, 8, 1  // Triangle 7
};
```

```
// Describe the index buffer we are going to create. Observe the
// D3D10_BIND_INDEX_BUFFER bind flag
D3D10_BUFFER_DESC ibd;
ibd.Usage = D3D10_USAGE_IMMUTABLE;
ibd.ByteWidth = sizeof(DWORD) * 24;
ibd.BindFlags = D3D10_BIND_INDEX_BUFFER;
ibd.CPUAccessFlags = 0;
ibd.MiscFlags = 0;

// Specify the data to initialize the index buffer.
D3D10_SUBRESOURCE_DATA iinitData;
iinitData.pSysMem = indices;

// Create the index buffer.
ID3D10Buffer* mIB;
HR(md3dDevice->CreateBuffer(&ibd, &iinitData, &mIB));
```

As with vertex buffers, and other Direct3D resources for that matter, before we can use it, we need to bind it to the pipeline. An index buffer is bound to the input assembler stage with the `ID3D10Device::IASetIndexBuffer` method. Below is an example call:

```
md3dDevice->IASetIndexBuffer(mIB, DXGI_FORMAT_R32_UINT, 0);
```

The second parameter specifies the format of the indices. In our example, we are using 32-bit unsigned integers (`DWORD`); therefore, we specified `DXGI_FORMAT_R32_UINT`. You could alternatively use 16-bit unsigned integers if you wanted to save memory and did not need the extra range. Just remember that in addition to specifying the format in the `IASetIndexBuffer` method, the `D3D10_BUFFER_DESC::ByteWidth` data member depends on the format as well, so make sure they are consistent to avoid problems. Note that `DXGI_FORMAT_R16_UINT` and `DXGI_FORMAT_R32_UINT` are the only formats supported for index buffers. The third parameter is an offset, measured in bytes, from the start of the index buffer to the position in the index buffer from which the input assembly should start reading the data. You would use this if you wanted to skip over some data at the front of the index buffer.

Finally, when using indices, we must use the `DrawIndexed` method instead of `Draw`:

```
void ID3D10Device::DrawIndexed(
    UINT IndexCount,
    UINT StartIndexLocation,
    INT BaseVertexLocation);
```

■ `IndexCount`: The number of indices that will be used in this draw call. This need not be every index in the index buffer; that is, you can draw a contiguous subset of indices.

■ `StartIndexLocation`: Index to an element in the index buffer that marks the starting point from which to begin reading indices.

■ `BaseVertexLocation`: An integer to be added to the indices used in this draw call.

To illustrate these parameters, consider the following situation. Suppose we have three objects: a sphere, box, and cylinder. Each object has its own vertex buffer and its own index buffer. The indices in each local index buffer are relative to the corresponding local vertex buffer. Now suppose that we combine the vertices and indices of the sphere, box, and cylinder into one global vertex and index buffer, as shown in Figure 5.18. After this merger, the indices are no longer correct (the indices index into the corresponding local vertex buffers, not the global one); thus the indices need to be recomputed to index correctly into the global vertex buffer. The original box indices were computed with the assumption that the box's vertices ran through the indices 0, 1, ..., `numBoxVertices-1`. But after the merger, they run from `firstBoxVertexPos`, `firstBoxVertexPos+1`, ..., `firstBoxVertexPos+ numBoxVertices-1`. Therefore, to update the indices, we need to add `firstBoxVertexPos` to every box index. Likewise, we need to add `firstCylVertexPos` to every cylinder index. Note that the sphere's indices do not need to be changed (since the first sphere vertex position is 0). In general, the new indices of an object are computed by adding the position of the object's first vertex, relative to the global vertex buffer, to each index. Thus, given the first vertex position of the object relative to the global vertex buffer (i.e., the `BaseVertexLocation`), Direct3D can recompute the indices for us internally in the draw call. We can then draw the sphere, box, and cylinder one-by-one with the following three calls:

```
md3dDevice->DrawIndexed(numSphereIndices, 0, 0);
md3dDevice->DrawIndexed(numBoxIndices, firstBoxIndex, firstBoxVertexPos);
md3dDevice->DrawIndexed(numCylIndices, firstCylIndex, firstCylVertexPos);
```

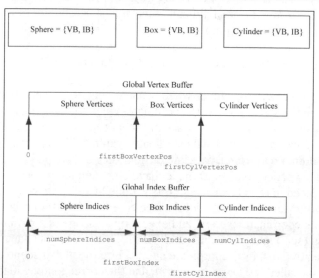

Figure 5.18: Merging several vertex buffers into one large vertex buffer, and merging several index buffers into one large index buffer.

5.6 **The Vertex Shader Stage**

After the primitives have been assembled, the vertices are fed into the vertex shader stage. The vertex shader can be thought of as a function that inputs a vertex and outputs a vertex. Every vertex drawn will be pumped through the vertex shader; in fact, we can conceptually think of the following happening on the hardware:

```
for(UINT i = 0; i < numVertices; ++i)
    outputVertex[i] = VertexShader(inputVertex[i]);
```

The vertex shader function is something we implement, but it is executed by the GPU for each vertex, so it is very fast.

Many special effects such as transformations, lighting, and displacement mapping can be done in the vertex shader. Remember that not only do we have access to the input vertex data, but we can also access textures and other data stored in memory, such as transformation matrices and scene lights.

We will see many examples of different vertex shaders throughout this book; so by the end, you should have a good idea of what can be done with them. For our first code example, however, we will just use the vertex shader to transform vertices. The following subsections explain the kind of transformations that generally need to be done.

5.6.1 **Local Space and World Space**

Suppose for a moment that you are working on a film and your team has to construct a miniature version of a train scene for some special effect shots. In particular, suppose that you are tasked with making a small bridge. Now, you would not construct the bridge in the middle of the scene, where you would likely have to work from a difficult angle and be careful not to mess up the other miniatures that compose the scene. Instead, you would work on the bridge at your workbench away from the scene. Then when it is all done, you would place the bridge at its correct position and angle in the scene.

3D artists do something similar when constructing 3D objects. Instead of building an object's geometry with coordinates relative to a global scene coordinate system (*world space*), they specify them relative to a local coordinate system (*local space*); the local coordinate system will usually be some convenient coordinate system located near the object and aligned with the object. Once the vertices of the 3D model have been defined in local space, the model is placed in the global scene; this is done by us specifying where we want the origin and axes of the local space coordinate system relative to the global scene coordinate system, and executing a change of coordinate transformation (see Figure 5.19 and recall §3.4). The process of changing coordinates relative to a local coordinate system into the global scene coordinate system is called the *world transform*, and the corresponding matrix is called the *world matrix*. After each object has been transformed from its local space to the world space, all the objects are relative to the same coordinate system (the world space). If you want to define an object directly in the world space, then you can supply an identity world matrix.

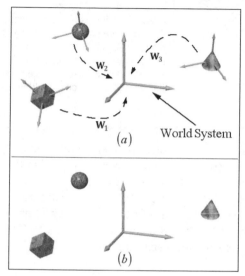

Figure 5.19: (a) The vertices of each object are defined with coordinates relative to their own local coordinate system. In addition, we define the position and orientation of each local coordinate system relative to the world space coordinate system based on where we want the object in the scene. Then we execute a change of coordinate transformation to make all coordinates relative to the world space system. (b) After the world transform, all the objects' vertices have coordinates relative to the same world system.

Defining each model relative to its own local coordinate system has several advantages:

- It is easier. For instance, usually in local space the object will be centered at the origin and symmetrical with respect to one of the major axes. As another example, the vertices of a cube are much easier to specify if we choose a local coordinate system with the origin centered at the cube and with axes orthogonal to the cube faces (see Figure 5.20).

- The object may be reused across multiple scenes, in which case it makes no sense to hardcode the object's coordinates relative to a particular scene. Instead, it is better to store its coordinates relative to a local coordinate system and then define, via a change of coordinate matrix, how the local coordinate system and world coordinate system are related for each scene.

- Finally, sometimes we draw the same object more than once, but in different positions, orientations, and scales (e.g., a tree object may be reused several times to build a forest). It would be wasteful to duplicate the object's data for each instance. Instead, we store a single copy of the geometry relative to its local space. Then we draw the object several times, but each time with a different world matrix to specify the position, orientation, and scale of the instance in the world space.

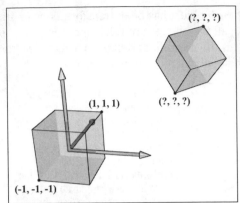

Figure 5.20: The vertices of a cube are easily specified when the cube is centered at the origin and axis-aligned with the coordinate system. It is not so easy to specify the coordinates when the cube is at an arbitrary position and orientation with respect to the coordinate system. Therefore, when we construct the geometry of an object, we usually always choose a convenient coordinate system near the object and aligned with the object, from which to build the object around.

As §3.4.3 shows, the world matrix for an object is given by describing its local space with coordinates relative to the world space, and placing these coordinates in the rows of a matrix. If $\mathbf{Q}_W = (Q_x, Q_y, Q_z, 1)$, $\mathbf{u}_W = (u_x, u_y, u_z, 0)$, $\mathbf{v}_W = (v_x, v_y, v_z, 0)$, and $\mathbf{w}_W = (w_x, w_y, w_z, 0)$ describe, respectively, the origin and x-, y-, and z-axes of a local space with homogeneous coordinates relative to world space, then we know from §3.4.3 that the change of coordinate matrix from local space to world space is:

$$\mathbf{W} = \begin{bmatrix} u_x & u_y & u_z & 0 \\ v_x & v_y & v_z & 0 \\ w_x & w_y & w_z & 0 \\ Q_x & Q_y & Q_z & 1 \end{bmatrix}$$

5.6.2 View Space

In order to form a 2D image of the scene, we must place a virtual camera in the scene. The camera specifies what volume of the world the viewer can see and thus what volume of the world we need to generate a 2D image of. Let us attach a local coordinate system (called *view space*, *eye space*, or *camera space*) to the camera as shown in Figure 5.21; that is, the camera sits at the origin looking down the positive z-axis, the x-axis aims to the right of the camera, and the y-axis aims above the camera. Instead of describing our scene vertices relative to the world space, it is convenient for later stages of the rendering pipeline to describe them relative to the camera coordinate system. The change of coordinate transformation from world space to view space is called the *view transform*, and the corresponding matrix is called the *view matrix*.

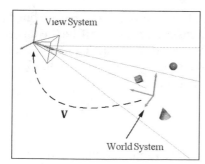

Figure 5.21: Convert the coordinates of vertices relative to the world space to make them relative to the camera space.

If $\mathbf{Q}_W = (Q_x, Q_y, Q_z, 1)$, $\mathbf{u}_W = (u_x, u_y, u_z, 0)$, $\mathbf{v}_W = (v_x, v_y, v_z, 0)$, and $\mathbf{w}_W = (w_x, w_y, w_z, 0)$ describe, respectively, the origin and x-, y-, and z-axes of view space with homogeneous coordinates relative to world space, then we know from §3.4.3 that the change of coordinate matrix from view space to world space is:

$$\mathbf{W} = \begin{bmatrix} u_x & u_y & u_z & 0 \\ v_x & v_y & v_z & 0 \\ w_x & w_y & w_z & 0 \\ Q_x & Q_y & Q_z & 1 \end{bmatrix}$$

However, this is not the transformation we want. We want the reverse transformation from world space to view space. But recall from §3.4.5 that reverse transformation is just given by the inverse. Thus $\mathbf{W}^{-1}$ transforms from world space to view space.

The world coordinate system and view coordinate system generally differ by position and orientation, so it makes intuitive sense that $\mathbf{W} = \mathbf{RT}$ (i.e., the world matrix can be decomposed into a rotation followed by a translation). This form makes the inverse easier to compute:

$$\mathbf{V} = \mathbf{W}^{-1} = (\mathbf{RT})^{-1} = \mathbf{T}^{-1}\mathbf{R}^{-1} = \mathbf{T}^{-1}\mathbf{R}^{T}$$

$$= \begin{bmatrix} 1 & 0 & 0 & 0 \\ 0 & 1 & 0 & 0 \\ 0 & 0 & 1 & 0 \\ -Q_x & -Q_y & -Q_z & 1 \end{bmatrix} \begin{bmatrix} u_x & v_x & w_x & 0 \\ u_y & v_y & w_y & 0 \\ u_z & v_z & w_z & 0 \\ 0 & 0 & 0 & 1 \end{bmatrix} = \begin{bmatrix} u_x & v_x & w_x & 0 \\ u_y & v_y & w_y & 0 \\ u_z & v_z & w_z & 0 \\ -\mathbf{Q}\cdot\mathbf{u} & -\mathbf{Q}\cdot\mathbf{v} & -\mathbf{Q}\cdot\mathbf{w} & 1 \end{bmatrix}$$

So the view matrix has the form:

$$\mathbf{V} = \begin{bmatrix} u_x & v_x & w_x & 0 \\ u_y & v_y & w_y & 0 \\ u_z & v_z & w_z & 0 \\ -\mathbf{Q}\cdot\mathbf{u} & -\mathbf{Q}\cdot\mathbf{v} & -\mathbf{Q}\cdot\mathbf{w} & 1 \end{bmatrix}$$

We now show an intuitive way to construct the vectors needed to build the view matrix. Let **Q** be the position of the camera and let **T** be the target point at which the camera is aimed. Furthermore, let μ be the unit vector that describes the "up" direction of the world space. Referring to Figure 5.22, the direction the camera is looking is given by:

$$\mathbf{w} = \frac{\mathbf{T} - \mathbf{Q}}{\|\mathbf{T} - \mathbf{Q}\|}$$

This vector describes the local z-axis of the camera. A unit vector that aims to the "right" of **w** is given by:

$$\mathbf{u} = \frac{\mu \times \mathbf{w}}{\|\mu \times \mathbf{w}\|}$$

This vector describes the local x-axis of the camera. Finally, a vector that describes the local y-axis of the camera is given by:

$$\mathbf{v} = \mathbf{w} \times \mathbf{u}$$

Since **w** and **u** are orthogonal unit vectors, **w** × **u** is necessarily a unit vector, and so it does not need to be normalized.

Thus, given the position of the camera, the target point, and the world "up" direction, we were able to derive the local coordinate system of the camera, which can be used to form the view matrix.

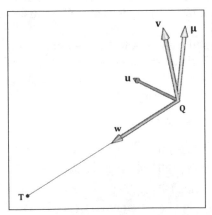

Figure 5.22: Constructing the camera coordinate system given the camera position, a target point, and a world "up" vector.

The D3DX library provides the following function for computing the view matrix based on the just described process:

```
D3DXMATRIX * D3DXMatrixLookAtLH(
    D3DXMATRIX *pOut,           // Outputs resulting view matrix V
    CONST D3DXVECTOR3 *pEye,    // Input camera position Q
    CONST D3DXVECTOR3 *pAt,     // Input target point T
    CONST D3DXVECTOR3 *pUp);    // Input world up vector μ
```

Usually the world's *y*-axis corresponds to the "up" direction, so the "up" vector is usually μ = (0, 1, 0). As an example, suppose we want to position the camera at the point (5, 3, –10) relative to the world space, and have the camera look at the origin of the world (0, 0, 0). We can build the view matrix by writing:

```
D3DXVECTOR3 position(5.0f, 3.0f, -10.0f);
D3DXVECTOR3 target(0.0f, 0.0f, 0.0f);
D3DXVECTOR3 worldUp(0.0f, 1.0f, 0.0f);

D3DXMATRIX V;
D3DXMatrixLookAtLH(&V, &position, &target, &worldUp);
```

5.6.3 Projection and Homogeneous Clip Space

So far we have described the position and orientation of the camera in the world, but there is another component to a camera, which is the volume of space the camera sees. This volume is described by a *frustum* (Figure 5.23), which is a pyramid with its tip cut off at the near plane.

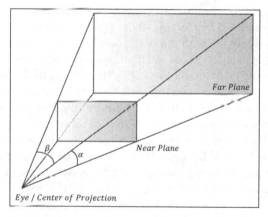

Figure 5.23: A frustum defines the volume of space that the camera "sees."

Our next task is to project the 3D geometry inside the frustum onto a 2D projection window. The projection must be done in such a way that parallel lines converge to a vanishing point, and as the 3D depth of an object increases, the size of its projection diminishes; a perspective projection does this, and is illustrated in Figure 5.24. We call the line from a vertex to the eye point the *vertex's line of projection*. Then we define the *perspective projection transformation* as the transformation that transforms a 3D vertex **v** to the point **v**′ where its line of projection intersects the 2D projection plane; we say that **v**′ is the projection of **v**. The projection of a 3D object refers to the projection of all the vertices that make up the object.

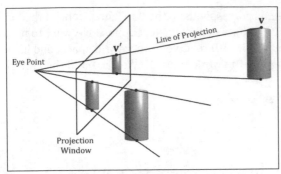

Figure 5.24: Both cylinders in 3D space are the same size but are placed at different depths. The projection of the cylinder closer to the eye is bigger than the projection of the farther cylinder. Geometry inside the frustum is projected onto a projection window; geometry outside the frustum gets projected onto the projection plane, but will lie outside the projection window.

5.6.3.1 *Defining a Frustum*

We can define a frustum in view space, with the center of projection at the origin and looking down the positive z-axis, by the following four quantities: a near plane n, far plane f, vertical field of view angle α, and aspect ratio r. Note that in view space, the near plane and far plane are parallel to the xy-plane; thus we simply specify their distance from the origin along the z-axis. The aspect ratio is defined by $r = w/h$ where w is the width of the projection window and h is the height of the projection window (units in view space). The projection window is essentially the 2D image of the scene in view space. The image here will eventually be mapped to the back buffer; therefore, we like the ratio of the projection window dimensions to be the same as the ratio of the back buffer dimensions. So the ratio of the back buffer dimensions is usually specified as the aspect ratio (it is a ratio so it has no units). For example, if the back buffer dimensions are 800×600, then we specify $r = \frac{800}{600} \approx 1.333$. If the aspect ratio of the projection window and the back buffer were not the same, then a nonuniform scaling would be necessary to map the projection window to the back buffer, which would cause distortion (e.g., a circle on the projection window might get stretched into an ellipse when mapped to the back buffer).

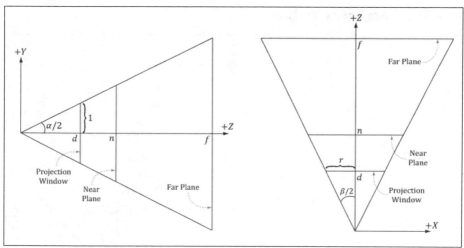

Figure 5.25: Deriving the horizontal field of view angle β given the vertical field of view angle α and the aspect ratio r.

To see how r helps us find β, consider Figure 5.25. Note that the actual dimensions of the projection window are not important, just the aspect ratio. Therefore, we will choose the convenient height of 2, and thus the width must be:

$$r = \frac{w}{h} = \frac{w}{2} \Rightarrow w - 2r$$

In order to have the specified vertical field of view α, the projection window must be placed a distance d from the origin:

$$\tan\left(\frac{\alpha}{2}\right) = \frac{1}{d} \Rightarrow d = \cot\left(\frac{\alpha}{2}\right)$$

Looking at the xz-plane in Figure 5.25, we now see that:

$$\tan\left(\frac{\beta}{2}\right) = \frac{r}{d} = \frac{r}{\cot\left(\dfrac{\alpha}{2}\right)}$$

$$= r \cdot \tan\left(\frac{\alpha}{2}\right)$$

So given the vertical field of view angle α and the aspect ratio r, we can always get the horizontal field of view angle β.

5.6.3.2 *Projecting Vertices*

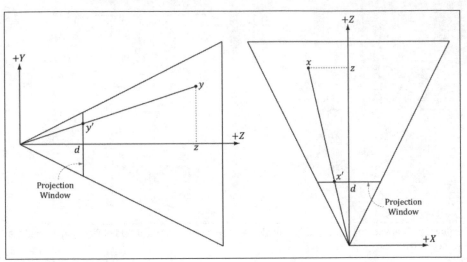

Figure 5.26: Similar triangles.

Refer to Figure 5.26. Given a point (x, y, z), we wish to find its projection (x', y', d) on the projection plane $z = d$. By considering the x- and y-coordinates separately and using similar triangles, we find:

$$\frac{x'}{d} = \frac{x}{z} \Rightarrow x' = \frac{xd}{z} = \frac{x\cot(\alpha/2)}{z} = \frac{x}{z\tan(\alpha/2)}$$

and

$$\frac{y'}{d} = \frac{y}{z} \Rightarrow y' = \frac{yd}{z} = \frac{y\cot(\alpha/2)}{z} = \frac{y}{z\tan(\alpha/2)}$$

Observe that a point (x, y, z) is inside the frustum if and only if

$$-r \le x' \le r$$
$$-1 \le y' \le 1$$
$$n \le z \le f$$

5.6.3.3 *Normalized Device Coordinates (NDC)*

The coordinates of the projected points in the preceding section are computed in view space. In view space, the projection window has a height of 2 and a width of $2r$, where r is the aspect ratio. The problem with this is that the dimensions depend on the aspect ratio. This means we would need to tell the hardware the aspect ratio, since the hardware will later need to do some operations that involve the dimensions of the projection window (such as map it to the back buffer). It would be more convenient if we could remove this dependency on the aspect ratio. The solution is to scale the projected x-coordinate from the interval $[-r, r]$ to $[-1, 1]$ like so:

$$-r \leq x' \leq r$$
$$-1 \leq x'/r \leq 1$$

After this mapping, the x- and y-coordinates are said to be *normalized device coordinates* (NDC) (the z-coordinate has not yet been normalized), and a point (x, y, z) is inside the frustum if and only if

$$-1 \leq x'/r \leq 1$$
$$-1 \leq y' \leq 1$$
$$n \leq z \leq f$$

The transformation from view space to NDC space can be viewed as a unit conversion. We have the relationship that one NDC unit equals r units in view space (i.e., 1 ndc $= r$ vs) on the x-axis. So given x view space units, we can use this relationship to convert units:

$$x\,\text{vs} \cdot \frac{1\,\text{ndc}}{r\,\text{vs}} = \frac{x}{r}\,\text{ndc}$$

We can modify our projection formulas to give us the projected x- and y-coordinates directly in NDC coordinates:

$$x' = \frac{x}{rz\tan(\alpha/2)}$$
$$y' = \frac{y}{z\tan(\alpha/2)}$$

(5.1)

Note that in NDC coordinates, the projection window has a height of 2 and a width of 2. So now the dimensions are fixed, and the hardware need not know the aspect ratio, but it is our responsibility to always supply the projected coordinates in NDC space (the graphics hardware assumes we will).

5.6.3.4 *Writing the Projection Equations with a Matrix*

For uniformity, we would like to express the projection transformation by a matrix. However, Equation 5.1 is nonlinear, so it does not have a matrix representation. The "trick" is to separate it into two parts: a linear part and a nonlinear part. The nonlinear part is the divide by z. As will be discussed in the next section, we are going to normalize the z-coordinate; this means we will not have the original z-coordinate around for the divide. Therefore, we must save the input z-coordinate before it is transformed; to do this, we take advantage of homogeneous coordinates, and copy the input z-coordinate to the output w-coordinate. In terms of matrix multiplication, this is done by setting entry [2][3] = 1 and entry [3][3] = 0 (zero-based indices). Our projection matrix looks like this:

$$\mathbf{P} = \begin{bmatrix} \dfrac{1}{r\tan(\alpha/2)} & 0 & 0 & 0 \\ 0 & \dfrac{1}{\tan(\alpha/2)} & 0 & 0 \\ 0 & 0 & A & 1 \\ 0 & 0 & B & 0 \end{bmatrix}$$

Note that we have placed constants (to be determined in the next section) A and B into the matrix; these constants will be used to transform the input z-coordinate into the normalized range. Multiplying an arbitrary point $(x, y, z, 1)$ by this matrix gives:

$$[x, y, z, 1] \begin{bmatrix} \dfrac{1}{r\tan(\alpha/2)} & 0 & 0 & 0 \\ 0 & \dfrac{1}{\tan(\alpha/2)} & 0 & 0 \\ 0 & 0 & A & 1 \\ 0 & 0 & B & 0 \end{bmatrix} = \left[\dfrac{x}{r\tan(\alpha/2)}, \dfrac{y}{\tan(\alpha/2)}, Az + B, z \right] \quad (5.2)$$

After multiplying by the projection matrix (the linear part), we complete the transformation by dividing each coordinate by $w = z$ (the nonlinear part):

$$\left[\dfrac{x}{r\tan(\alpha/2)}, \dfrac{y}{\tan(\alpha/2)}, Az + B, z \right] \xrightarrow{\textit{divide by } w} \left[\dfrac{x}{rz\tan(\alpha/2)}, \dfrac{y}{z\tan(\alpha/2)}, A + \dfrac{B}{z}, 1 \right] \quad (5.3)$$

Incidentally, you may wonder about a possible divide by zero; however, the near plane should be greater than zero, so such a point would be clipped (§5.8). The divide by w is sometimes called the *perspective divide* or *homogeneous divide*. We see that the projected x- and y-coordinates agree with Equation 5.1.

5.6.3.5 *Normalized Depth Value*

It may seem that after projection we can discard the original 3D z-coordinate, as all the projected points now lay on the 2D projection window, which forms the 2D image seen by the eye. However, we still need 3D depth information around for the depth buffering algorithm. Just like Direct3D wants the projected x- and y-coordinates in a normalized range, Direct3D wants the depth coordinates in the normalized range [0, 1]. Therefore, we must construct an order preserving function $g(z)$ that maps the interval $[n, f]$ onto [0, 1]. Because the function is order preserving, if $z_1, z_2 \in [n, f]$ and $z_1 < z_2$, then $g(z_1) < g(z_2)$. Therefore, even though the depth values have been transformed the relative depth relationships remain intact, so we can still correctly compare depths in the normalized interval, which is all we need for the depth buffering algorithm.

Mapping $[n, f]$ onto [0, 1] can be done with scaling and translation. However, this approach will not integrate into our current projection strategy. We see from Equation 5.3 that the z-coordinate undergoes the transformation:

$$g(z) = A + \frac{B}{z}$$

We now need to choose A and B subject to the constraints:

Condition 1: $g(n) = A + B/n = 0$ (the near plane gets mapped to 0)

Condition 2: $g(f) = A + B/f = 1$ (the far plane gets mapped to 1)

Solving condition 1 for B yields: $B = -An$. Substituting this into condition 2 and solving for A gives:

$$A + \frac{-An}{f} = 1$$

$$\frac{Af - An}{f} = 1$$

$$Af - An = f$$

$$A = \frac{f}{f - n}$$

Therefore,

$$g(z) = \frac{f}{f - n} - \frac{nf}{(f - n)z}$$

A graph of g (Figure 5.27) shows it is strictly increasing (order preserving) and nonlinear. It also shows that most of the range is "used up" by depth values close to the near plane. Consequently, the majority of the depth values get mapped to a small subset of the range. This can lead to depth buffer precision problems (the computer can no longer distinguish between slightly different transformed depth values due to finite numerical representation). The general advice is to make the near and far planes as close as possible to minimize depth precision problems.

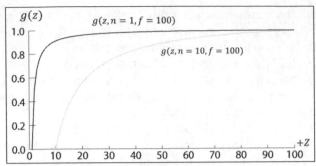

Figure 5.27: Graph of $g(z)$ for different near planes.

Now that we have solved for A and B, we can state the full *perspective projection matrix*:

$$\mathbf{P} = \begin{bmatrix} \dfrac{1}{r\tan(\alpha/2)} & 0 & 0 & 0 \\ 0 & \dfrac{1}{\tan(\alpha/2)} & 0 & 0 \\ 0 & 0 & \dfrac{f}{f-n} & 1 \\ 0 & 0 & \dfrac{-nf}{f-n} & 0 \end{bmatrix}$$

After multiplying by the projection matrix, but before the perspective divide, geometry is said to be in *homogeneous clip space* or *projection space*. After the perspective divide, the geometry is said to be in normalized device coordinates (NDC).

5.6.3.6 *D3DXMatrixPerspectiveFovLH*

A perspective projection matrix can be built with the following D3DX function:

```
D3DXMATRIX *D3DXMatrixPerspectiveFovLH(
    D3DXMATRIX* pOut,  // returns projection matrix
    FLOAT fovY,        // vertical field of view angle in radians
    FLOAT Aspect,      // aspect ratio = width / height
    FLOAT zn,          // distance to near plane
    FLOAT zf           // distance to far plane
);
```

The following code snippet illustrates how to use `D3DXMatrixPerspectiveFovLH`. Here, we specify a 45° vertical field of view, a near plane at $z = 1$, and a far plane at $z = 1000$ (these lengths are in view space).

```
D3DXMATRIX proj;
D3DXMatrixPerspectiveFovLH(
    &proj, D3DX_PI * 0.25f,
    (float)width / (float)height, 1.0, 1000.0f);
```

5.6.4 Example Vertex Shader

Below is an implementation of the simple vertex shader we use for this chapter's demos:

```
cbuffer cbPerObject
{
    float4x4 gWVP;
};

void VS(float3 iPosL  : POSITION,
        float4 iColor : COLOR,
        out float4 oPosH  : SV_POSITION,
        out float4 oColor : COLOR)
{
    // Transform to homogeneous clip space.
    oPosH = mul(float4(iPosL, 1.0f), gWVP);

    // Just pass vertex color into the pixel shader.
    oColor = iColor;
}
```

Shaders are written in a language called the High-Level Shading Language (HLSL), which has similar syntax to C++, so it is easy to learn. Appendix B provides a concise reference to the HLSL. Our approach to teaching the HLSL and programming shaders will be example based. That is, as we progress through the book, we will introduce any new HLSL concepts we need in order to implement the demo at hand. Shaders are usually written in text-based files called *effect files* (.fx). We will discuss effect files later in this chapter, but for now, we will just concentrate on the vertex shader.

Here, the vertex shader is the function called VS. Note that you can give the vertex shader any valid function name. This vertex shader has four parameters; the first two are input parameters, and the last two are output parameters (indicated by the out keyword). The HLSL does not have references or pointers, so to return multiple values from a function, you need to use either structures or out parameters.

The first two input parameters correspond to data members in our custom vertex structure. The parameter semantics ": POSITION" and ": COLOR" are used for mapping the elements in the vertex structure to the vertex shader input parameters, as Figure 5.28 shows.

```
struct Vertex
{
    D3DXVECTOR3 pos;
    D3DXCOLOR    color;
};

D3D10_INPUT_ELEMENT_DESC vertexDesc[] =
{
    {"POSITION", 0, DXGI_FORMAT_R32G32B32_FLOAT, 0, 0,
        D3D10_INPUT_PER_VERTEX_DATA, 0},
    {"COLOR",    0, DXGI_FORMAT_R32G32B32A32_FLOAT, 0, 12,
        D3D10_INPUT_PER_VERTEX_DATA, 0}
};

void VS(float3 iPosL  : POSITION,
        float4 iColor : COLOR,
        out float4 oPosH  : SV_POSITION,
        out float4 oColor : COLOR)
{
    // Transform to homogeneous clip space.
    oPosH = mul(float4(iPosL, 1.0f), gWVP);

    // Just pass vertex color into the pixel shader.
    oColor = iColor;
}
```

Figure 5.28: Each vertex element has an associated semantic specified by the D3D10_INPUT_ELEMENT_DESC array. Each parameter of the vertex shader also has an attached semantic. The semantics are used to match vertex elements with vertex shader parameters.

The output parameters also have attached semantics (": SV_POSITION" and ": COLOR"). These are used to map vertex shader outputs to the corresponding inputs of the next stage (either the geometry shader or pixel shader). Note that the SV_POSITION semantic is special (SV stands for system value). It is used to denote the vertex shader output element that holds the vertex position. The vertex position needs to be handled differently than other vertex attributes because it is involved in operations the other attributes are not involved in, such as clipping.

The actual body implementation of the vertex shader is quite straight-forward. The first line transforms the vertex position from local space to homogeneous clip space by multiplying by a 4×4 matrix gWVP, which represents the combined world, view, and projection matrix:

```
oPosH = mul(float4(iPosL, 1.0f), gWVP);
```

The constructor syntax float4(iPosL, 1.0f) constructs a 4D vector and is equivalent to float4(iPosL.x, iPosL.y, iPosL.z, 1.0f); because we know the positions of vertices are points and not vectors, we place a 1 in the fourth component ($w = 1$). The float2 and float3 types represent 2D and 3D vectors, respectively. The matrix variable gWVP lives in a constant buffer, which will be discussed in the next section. The built-in function mul is used for the vector-matrix multiplication. Incidentally, the mul function is overloaded for matrix multiplications of different sizes; for example, you can use it to multiply two 4×4 matrices, two 3×3 matrices, or a 1×3 vector and a 3×3 matrix. The last line in the shader body just copies the input color to the output parameter so that the color will be fed into the next stage of the pipeline:

```
    oColor = iColor;
```

We can equivalently rewrite the above vertex shader using structures:

```
cbuffer cbPerObject
{
    float4x4 gWVP;
};

struct VS_IN
{
    float3 posL  : POSITION;
    float4 color : COLOR;
};

struct VS_OUT
{
    float4 posH : SV_POSITION;
    float4 color : COLOR;
};

VS_OUT VS(VS_IN input)
{
    VS_OUT output;

    output.posH = mul(float4(input.posL, 1.0f), gWVP);
    output.color = input.color;

    return output;
}
```

Note: If there is no geometry shader, then the vertex shader must at least do the projection transformation because this is the space the hardware expects the vertices to be in when leaving the vertex shader (if there is no geometry shader). If there is a geometry shader, the job of projection can be deferred to the geometry shader.

Note: A vertex shader (or geometry shader) does not do the perspective divide; it just does the projection matrix part. The perspective divide will be done later by the hardware.

5.6.5 Constant Buffers

Above the example vertex shader in the previous section was the code:

```
cbuffer cbPerObject
{
    float4x4 gWVP;
};
```

This code defines a `cbuffer` object (constant buffer) called `cbPerObject`. *Constant buffers* are just blocks of data that can store different variables that may be accessed by a shader. In this example, the constant buffer stores a single 4×4 matrix called `gWVP`, representing the combined world, view, and projection matrices used to transform a point from local space to homogeneous clip space. In HLSL, a 4×4 matrix is declared by the built-in `float4x4` type; to declare a 3×4 matrix and a 2×2 matrix, for example, you would use the `float3x4` and `float2x2` types, respectively. Data in constant buffers does not vary per vertex, but through the effects framework (§5.13), the C++ application code can update the contents of a constant buffer at run time. This provides a means for the C++ application code and the effect code to communicate. For instance, because the world matrix varies per object, the combined world, view, and projection matrix varies per object; therefore, when using the above vertex shader to draw multiple objects, we would need to update the `gWVP` variable appropriately before drawing each object.

The general advice is to create constant buffers based on the frequency in which you need to update their contents. For instance, you may create the following constant buffers:

```
cbuffer cbPerObject
{
    float4x4 gWVP;
};

cbuffer cbPerFrame
{
    float3 gLightDirection;
    float3 gLightPosition;
    float4 gLightColor;
};

cbuffer cbRarely
{
    float4 gFogColor;
    float gFogStart;
    float gFogEnd;
};
```

In this example, we use three constant buffers. The first constant buffer stores the combined world, view, and projection matrix. This variable depends on the object, so it must be updated on a per-object basis. That is, if we are rendering 100 objects per frame, then we will be updating this variable 100 times per frame. The second constant buffer stores scene light variables. Here, we are assuming that the lights are animated and so need to be updated once every frame of animation. The last constant buffer stores variables used to control fog. Here, we are assuming that the scene fog rarely changes (e.g., maybe it only changes at certain times of day in the game).

The motivation for dividing up the constant buffers is efficiency. When a constant buffer is updated, all its variables must be updated; therefore, it is efficient to group them based on their update frequency to minimize redundant updates.

5.7 The Geometry Shader Stage

The geometry shader stage is optional, and we do not use it until Chapter 10, so we will be brief here. The geometry shader inputs entire primitives. For example, if we were drawing triangle lists, then the input to the geometry shader would be the three vertices defining the triangle. (Note that the three vertices will have already passed through the vertex shader.) The main advantage of the geometry shader is that it can create or destroy geometry. For example, the input primitive can be expanded into one or more other primitives, or the geometry shader can choose not to output a primitive based on some condition. This is in contrast to a vertex shader, which cannot create vertices: it inputs one vertex and outputs one vertex. A common example of the geometry shader is to expand a point into a quad or to expand a line into a quad.

We also notice the "stream output" arrow from Figure 5.11. That is, the geometry shader can stream out vertex data into a buffer in memory, which can later be drawn. This is an advanced technique, and will be discussed in a later chapter.

Note: Vertex positions leaving the geometry shader must be transformed to homogeneous clip space.

5.8 The Clipping Stage

Geometry completely outside the viewing frustum needs to be discarded, and geometry that intersects the boundary of the frustum must be clipped, so that only the interior part remains; see Figure 5.29 for the idea illustrated in 2D.

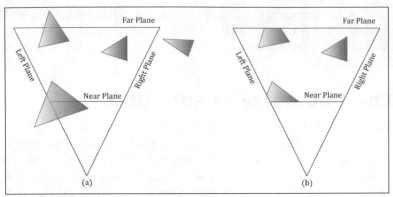

Figure 5.29: (a) Before clipping. (b) After clipping.

We can think of the *frustum* as being the region bounded by six planes: the top, bottom, left, right, near, and far planes. To clip a polygon against the frustum, we clip it against each frustum plane one-by-one. When clipping a polygon against a plane (see Figure 5.30), the part in the positive half-space of the plane is kept, and the part in the negative half-space is discarded. Clipping a convex polygon against a plane will always result in a convex polygon. Because the hardware does clipping for us, we will not cover the details here; instead, we refer the reader to the popular Sutherland-Hodgeman clipping algorithm [Sutherland74]. It basically amounts to finding the intersection points between the plane and polygon edges, and then ordering the vertices to form the new clipped polygon.

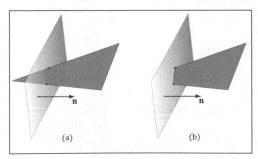

Figure 5.30: (a) Clipping a triangle against a plane. (b) The clipped triangle. Note that the clipped triangle is not a triangle, but a quad. Thus the hardware will need to triangulate the resulting quad, which is a straight-forward process for convex polygons.

[Blinn78] describes how clipping can be done in 4D homogeneous space. After the perspective divide, points $\left(\frac{x}{w}, \frac{y}{w}, \frac{z}{w}, 1\right)$ inside the view frustum are in normalized device coordinates and bounded as follows:

$$-1 \le x/w \le 1$$
$$-1 \le y/w \le 1$$
$$0 \le z/w \le 1$$

So in homogeneous clip space, before the divide, 4D points (x, y, z, w) inside the frustum are bounded as follows:

$$-w \leq x \leq w$$
$$-w \leq y \leq w$$
$$0 \leq z \leq w$$

That is, the points are bounded by the simple 4D planes:

Left: $w = -x$

Right: $w = x$

Bottom: $w = -y$

Top: $w = y$

Near: $z = 0$

Far: $z = w$

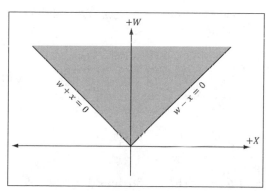

Figure 5.31: The frustum boundaries in the *xw*-plane in homogeneous clip space.

Once we know the frustum plane equations in homogeneous space, we can apply a clipping algorithm (such as Sutherland-Hodgeman). Note that the mathematics of the segment/plane intersection test generalizes to $\mathbb{R}^4$, so we can do the test with 4D points and the 4D planes in homogeneous clip space.

5.9 **The Rasterization Stage**

The main job of the rasterization stage is to compute pixel colors from the projected 3D triangles.

5.9.1 **Viewport Transform**

After clipping, the hardware can do the perspective divide to transform from homogeneous clip space to normalized device coordinates (NDC). Once vertices are in NDC space, the 2D x- and y-coordinates forming the 2D image are transformed to a rectangle on the back buffer called the viewport (recall §4.2.6). After this transform, the x- and y-coordinates are in units of pixels. Usually the viewport transformation does not modify the z-coordinate, as it is used for depth buffering, but it can by modifying the MinDepth and MaxDepth values of the D3D10_VIEWPORT structure. The MinDepth and MaxDepth values must be between 0 and 1.

5.9.2 Backface Culling

A triangle has two sides. To distinguish between the two sides we use the following convention. If the triangle vertices are ordered $\mathbf{v}_0$, $\mathbf{v}_1$, $\mathbf{v}_2$, then we compute the triangle normal $\mathbf{n}$ like so:

$$\mathbf{e}_0 = \mathbf{v}_1 - \mathbf{v}_0$$

$$\mathbf{e}_1 = \mathbf{v}_2 - \mathbf{v}_0$$

$$\mathbf{n} = \frac{\mathbf{e}_0 \times \mathbf{e}_1}{\|\mathbf{e}_0 \times \mathbf{e}_1\|}$$

The side the normal vector emanates from is the *front side* and the other side is the *back side*. Figure 5.32 illustrates this.

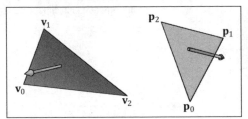

Figure 5.32: The triangle on the left is front-facing from our viewpoint, and the triangle on the right is back-facing from our viewpoint.

We say that a triangle is *front-facing* if the viewer sees the front side of a triangle, and we say a triangle is *back-facing* if the viewer sees the back side of a triangle. From our perspective of Figure 5.32, the left triangle is front-facing while the right triangle is back-facing. Moreover, from our perspective, the left triangle is ordered clockwise while the right triangle is ordered counterclockwise. This is no coincidence: With the convention we have chosen (i.e., the way we compute the triangle normal), a triangle ordered clockwise (with respect to the viewer) is front-facing, and a triangle ordered counterclockwise (with respect to the viewer) is back-facing.

Now, most objects in 3D worlds are enclosed solid objects. Suppose we agree to construct the triangles for each object in such a way that the normals are always aimed outward. Then, the camera does not see the back-facing triangles of a solid object because the front-facing triangles occlude the back-facing triangles; Figure 5.33 illustrates this in 2D and 5.34 in 3D. Because the front-facing triangles occlude the back-facing triangles, it makes no sense to draw them. *Backface culling* refers to the process of discarding back-facing triangles from the pipeline. This can potentially reduce the number of triangles that need to be processed by half.

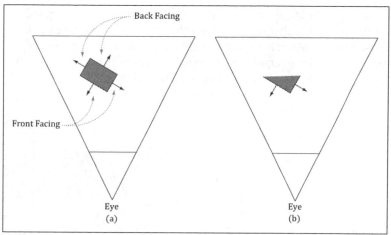

Figure 5.33: (a) A solid object with front-facing and back-facing triangles. (b) The scene after culling the back-facing triangles. Note that backface culling does not affect the final image since the back-facing triangles are occluded by the front-facing ones.

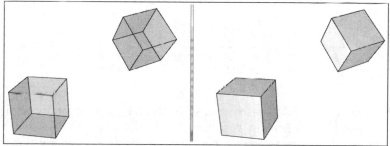

Figure 5.34: (Left) We draw the cubes with transparency so that you can see all six sides. (Right) We draw the cubes as solid blocks. Note that we do not see the three back-facing sides since the three front-facing sides occlude them — thus the back-facing triangles can actually be discarded from further processing and no one will notice.

By default, Direct3D treats triangles with a clockwise winding order (with respect to the viewer) as front-facing, and triangles with a counterclockwise winding order (with respect to the viewer) as back-facing. However, this convention can be reversed with a Direct3D render state setting.

5.9.3 Vertex Attribute Interpolation

Recall that we define a triangle by specifying its vertices. In addition to position, we can attach attributes to vertices such as colors, normal vectors, and texture coordinates. After the viewport transform, these attributes need to be interpolated for each pixel covering the triangle. Vertex depth values also need to get interpolated so that each pixel has a depth value for the depth buffering algorithm. The vertex attributes are interpolated in screen space in such a way that the attributes are interpolated linearly across the triangle in 3D space (see Figure 5.35); this requires the so-called *perspective correct interpolation*. Essentially, interpolation allows us to use the vertex values to compute values for the interior pixels.

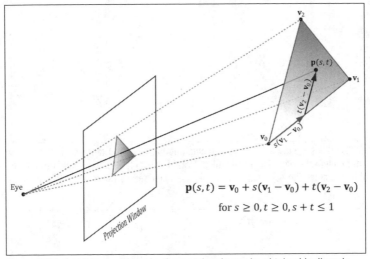

$$\mathbf{p}(s, t) = \mathbf{v}_0 + s(\mathbf{v}_1 - \mathbf{v}_0) + t(\mathbf{v}_2 - \mathbf{v}_0)$$

$$\text{for } s \geq 0, t \geq 0, s + t \leq 1$$

Figure 5.35: An attribute value $\mathbf{p}(s, t)$ on a triangle can be obtained by linearly interpolating between the attribute values at the vertices of the triangle.

The mathematical details of perspective correct attribute interpolation is not something we need to worry about since the hardware does it for us; however, the interested reader may find the mathematical derivation in [Eberly01].

5.10 The Pixel Shader Stage

As discussed thus far, vertex attributes output from the vertex shader (or geometry shader) are interpolated across the triangle. The interpolated values are then fed into the pixel shader as input. Assuming there is no geometry shader, Figure 5.36 illustrates the path vertex data takes up to now.

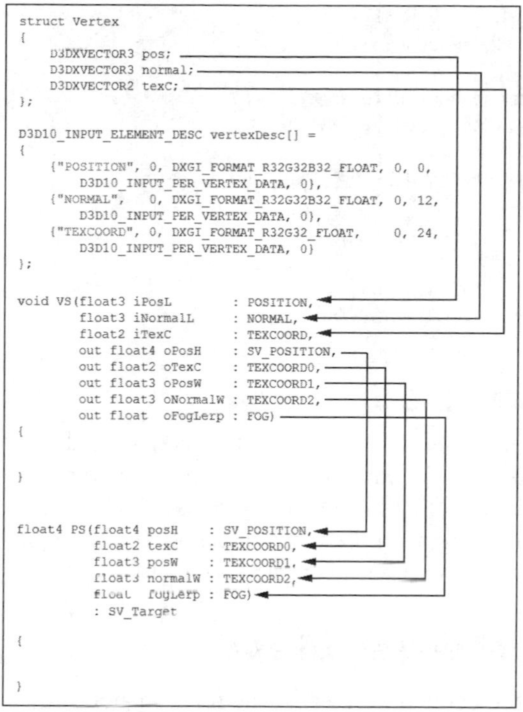

```
struct Vertex
{
    D3DXVECTOR3 pos;
    D3DXVECTOR3 normal;
    D3DXVECTOR2 texC;
};

D3D10_INPUT_ELEMENT_DESC vertexDesc[] =
{
    {"POSITION", 0, DXGI_FORMAT_R32G32B32_FLOAT, 0, 0,
        D3D10_INPUT_PER_VERTEX_DATA, 0},
    {"NORMAL",   0, DXGI_FORMAT_R32G32B32_FLOAT, 0, 12,
        D3D10_INPUT_PER_VERTEX_DATA, 0},
    {"TEXCOORD", 0, DXGI_FORMAT_R32G32_FLOAT,    0, 24,
        D3D10_INPUT_PER_VERTEX_DATA, 0}
};

void VS(float3 iPosL      : POSITION,
        float3 iNormalL   : NORMAL,
        float2 iTexC      : TEXCOORD,
        out float4 oPosH  : SV_POSITION,
        out float2 oTexC  : TEXCOORD0,
        out float3 oPosW  : TEXCOORD1,
        out float3 oNormalW : TEXCOORD2,
        out float  oFogLerp : FOG)
{


}

float4 PS(float4 posH    : SV_POSITION,
          float2 texC    : TEXCOORD0,
          float3 posW    : TEXCOORD1,
          float3 normalW : TEXCOORD2,
          float  fogLerp : FOG)
          : SV_Target
{


}
```

Figure 5.36: Each vertex element has an associated semantic specified by the D3D10_INPUT_ELEMENT_DESC array. Each parameter of the vertex shader also has an attached semantic. The semantics are used to match vertex elements with vertex shader parameters. Likewise, each output from the vertex shader has an attached semantic, and each pixel shader input parameter has an attached semantic. These semantics are used to map vertex shader outputs into the pixel shader input parameters.

A pixel shader is like a vertex shader in that it is a function executed for each pixel fragment. Given the pixel shader input, the job of the pixel shader is to calculate a color value for the pixel fragment. We note that the pixel fragment may not survive and make it onto the back buffer; for example, it might be clipped in the pixel shader (the HLSL includes a `clip` function that can discard a pixel fragment from further processing), occluded by another pixel fragment with a smaller depth value, or discarded by a later pipeline test like the stencil buffer test. Therefore, a pixel on the back buffer may have several pixel fragment candidates; this is the distinction between what is meant by "pixel fragment" and "pixel," although sometimes the terms are used interchangeably, but context usually makes it clear what is meant.

Below is a simple pixel shader that corresponds to the vertex shader given in §5.6.4. For completeness, the vertex shader is shown again.

```
cbuffer cbPerObject
{
    float4x4 gWVP;
};

void VS(float3 iPosL : POSITION,
        float4 iColor : COLOR,
```

```
            out float4 oPosH  : SV_POSITION,
            out float4 oColor : COLOR)
{
    // Transform to homogeneous clip space.
    oPosH = mul(float4(iPosL, 1.0f), gWVP);

    // Just pass vertex color into the pixel shader.
    oColor = iColor;
}

float4 PS(float4 posH  : SV_POSITION,
          float4 color : COLOR) : SV_TARGET
{
    return color;
}
```

In this example, the pixel shader simply returns the interpolated color value. Notice that the pixel shader input exactly matches the vertex shader output; this is a requirement. The pixel shader returns a 4D color value, and the SV_TARGET semantic following the function parameter listing indicates the return value should be the render target format.

5.11 The Output Merger Stage

After pixel fragments have been generated by the pixel shader, they move to the output merger (OM) stage of the rendering pipeline. In this stage, some pixel fragments may be rejected (e.g., from the depth or stencil buffer tests). Pixel fragments that are not rejected are written to the back buffer. Blending is also done in this stage, where a pixel may be blended with the pixel currently on the back buffer instead of overriding it completely. Some special effects like transparency are implemented with blending; Chapter 8 is devoted to blending.

5.12 Render States

Direct3D is basically a state machine. Things stay in their current state until we change them. For example, we saw in §5.5 that the vertex and index buffers bound to the input assembler stage of the pipeline stay there until we bind different ones; likewise, the currently set primitive topology stays in effect until it is changed. In addition, Direct3D has state groups that encapsulate settings that can be used to configure Direct3D:

■ ID3D10RasterizerState: This interface represents a state group used to configure the rasterization stage of the pipeline.

■ ID3D10BlendState: This interface represents a state group used to configure blending operations. We will discuss these states in the chapter on blending (Chapter 8); by default, blending is disabled, so we do not need to worry about it for now.

■ `ID3D10DepthStencilState`: This interface represents a state group used to configure the depth and stencil tests. We will discuss these states in Chapter 9; by default, stenciling is disabled, so we do not need to worry about it for now. The default depth test settings are set to do the standard depth test as described in §4.1.5.

Right now, the only state block interface that concerns us is the `ID3D10RasterizerState` interface. We can create an interface of this type by filling out a `D3D10_RASTERIZER_DESC` structure and then calling the method:

```
HRESULT ID3D10Device::CreateRasterizerState(
    const D3D10_RASTERIZER_DESC *pRasterizerDesc,
    ID3D10RasterizerState **ppRasterizerState);
```

The first parameter is just the filled out `D3D10_RASTERIZER_DESC` structure describing the rasterizer state block to create; the second parameter is used to return a pointer to the created `ID3D10RasterizerState` interface.

The `D3D10_RASTERIZER_DESC` structure is defined as follows:

```
typedef struct D3D10_RASTERIZER_DESC {
    D3D10_FILL_MODE FillMode;
    D3D10_CULL_MODE CullMode;
    BOOL FrontCounterClockwise;
    INT DepthBias;
    FLOAT DepthBiasClamp;
    FLOAT SlopeScaledDepthBias;
    BOOL DepthClipEnable;
    BOOL ScissorEnable;
    BOOL MultisampleEnable;
    BOOL AntialiasedLineEnable;
} D3D10_RASTERIZER_DESC;
```

Most of these members are advanced or not used very often; therefore, we refer you to the SDK documentation for the descriptions of each member. However, the first three are worth discussing here.

■ `FillMode`: Specify `D3D10_FILL_WIREFRAME` for wireframe rendering or `D3D10_FILL_SOLID` for solid rendering.

■ `CullMode`: Specify `D3D10_CULL_NONE` to disable culling, `D3D10_CULL_BACK` to cull back-facing triangles, or `D3D10_CULL_FRONT` to cull front-facing triangles.

■ `FrontCounterClockwise`: Specify `false` if you want triangles ordered clockwise (with respect to the camera) to be treated as front-facing and triangles ordered counterclockwise (with respect to the camera) to be treated as back-facing. Specify `true` if you want triangles ordered counterclockwise (with respect to the camera) to be treated as front-facing and triangles ordered clockwise (with respect to the camera) to be treated as back-facing.

Once an ID3D10RasterizerState object has been created, we can update the device with the new state block:

```
void ID3D10Device::RSSetState(ID3D10RasterizerState *pRasterizerState);
```

The following code shows how to create a rasterize state that disables backface culling:

```
D3D10_RASTERIZER_DESC rsDesc;
ZeroMemory(&rsDesc, sizeof(D3D10_RASTERIZER_DESC));
rsDesc.FillMode = D3D10_FILL_SOLID;
rsDesc.CullMode = D3D10_CULL_NONE;
rsDesc.FrontCounterClockwise = false;

HR(md3dDevice->CreateRasterizerState(&rsDesc, &mNoCullRS));
```

Note that for an application, you may need several different ID3D10RasterizerState objects. So what you would do is create them all at initialization time, and then switch between them as needed in the application update/draw code. For example, let's suppose you have two objects, and you wanted to draw the first one in wireframe mode and the second in solid mode. Then you would have two ID3D10RasterizerState objects and you would switch between them when drawing your objects:

```
// Create render state objects at initialization time.
ID3D10RasterizerState* mWireframeRS;
ID3D10RasterizerState* mSolidRS;
...


// Switch between the render state objects in the draw function.
md3dDevice->RSSetState(mSolidRS);
DrawObject();

md3dDevice->RSSetState(mWireframeRS);
DrawObject();
```

It should be noted that Direct3D never restores states to the previous setting. Therefore, you should always set the states you need when drawing an object. Making incorrect assumptions about the current state of the device will lead to incorrect output.

Each state block has a default state. We can revert to the default state by calling the RSSetState method with null:

```
md3dDevice->RSSetState( 0 );
```

5.13 **Effects**

5.13.1 **Effect Files**

We have discussed vertex shaders, pixel shaders, and to a lesser extent, geometry shaders. We have also discussed constant buffers, which can be used to store "global" variables accessible to the shaders. Such code is commonly written in an effect file (.fx), which is just a text file (just like C++ code is written in .h/.cpp files). In addition to housing shaders and constant buffers, an effect also contains at least one _technique_. In turn, a technique contains at least one _pass_.

■ technique10: A technique consists of one or more passes that are used to create a specific rendering technique. For each pass, the geometry is rendered in a different way, and the results of each pass are combined in some way to achieve the desired result. For example, a terrain rendering technique may use a multi-pass texturing technique. Note that multi-pass techniques are usually expensive because the geometry is redrawn for each pass; however, multi-pass techniques are required to implement some rendering techniques.

■ pass: A pass consists of a vertex shader, optional geometry shader, a pixel shader, and render states. These components indicate how to render the geometry for this pass.

Below is the effect file for the demos in this chapter:

```
cbuffer cbPerObject
{
    float4x4 gWVP;
};

void VS(float3 iPosL  : POSITION,
        float4 iColor : COLOR,
        out float4 oPosH  : SV_POSITION,
        out float4 oColor : COLOR)
{
    // Transform to homogeneous clip space.
    oPosH = mul(float4(iPosL, 1.0f), gWVP);

    // Just pass vertex color into the pixel shader.
    oColor = iColor;
}

float4 PS(float4 posH  : SV_POSITION,
          float4 color : COLOR) : SV_Target
{
    return color;
}
```

```
technique10 ColorTech
{
    pass P0
    {
        SetVertexShader( CompileShader( vs_4_0, VS() ) );
        SetGeometryShader( NULL );
        SetPixelShader( CompileShader( ps_4_0, PS() ) );
    }
}
```

Note: Points and vectors can live in many different spaces (e.g., local space, world space, view space, homogeneous clip space). When reading code, it might not be obvious which coordinate system the coordinates of the point/vector are relative to. Therefore, we often use the following suffixes to denote the space: L (for local space), W (for world space), V (for view space), and H (for homogeneous clip space). Here are some examples:

```
float3 iPosL;      // local space
float3 gEyePosW;   // world space
float3 normalV;    // view space
float4 posH;       // homogeneous clip space
```

We mentioned that passes consist of render states. That is, state blocks can be created and set directly in an effect file. This is convenient when the effect requires specific render states to work; in contrast, some effects may work with variable render state settings, in which case we prefer to set the states at the application level in order to facilitate easy state switching. The following code shows how to create and set a rasterizer state block in an effect file.

```
RasterizerState Wireframe
{
    FillMode = Wireframe;
    CullMode = Back;
    FrontCounterClockwise = false;
};

technique10 ColorTech
{
    pass P0
    {
        SetVertexShader( CompileShader( vs_4_0, VS() ) );
        SetGeometryShader( NULL );
        SetPixelShader( CompileShader( ps_4_0, PS() ) );

        SetRasterizerState(Wireframe);
    }
}
```

Observe that the right-hand values in the rasterizer state object definition are basically the same as in the C++ case, except the prefixes are omitted (e.g., D3D10_FILL_ and D3D10_CULL_ are omitted).

Note: Because an effect is typically written in an external .fx file, it can be modified without having to recompile the source code.

5.13.2 **Creating an Effect**

An effect is represented by the ID3D10Effect interface, which we create with the following D3DX function:

```
HRESULT D3DX10CreateEffectFromFile(
    LPCTSTR pFileName,
    CONST D3D10_SHADER_MACRO *pDefines,
    ID3D10Include *pInclude,
    LPCSTR pProfile,
    UINT HLSLFlags,
    UINT FXFlags,
    ID3D10Device *pDevice,
    ID3D10EffectPool *pEffectPool,
    ID3DX10ThreadPump *pPump,
    ID3D10Effect **ppEffect,
    ID3D10Blob **ppErrors);
    HRESULT *pttResult
```

- pFileName: The name of the .fx file that contains the effect source code we want to compile.
- pDefines: Advanced option we do not use; see the SDK documentation.
- pInclude: Advanced option we do not use; see the SDK documentation.
- pProfile: A string specifying the shader version we are using. For Direct3D 10, we use shader version 4.0.
- HLSLFlags: Flags to specify how the shader code should be compiled. There are quite a few of these flags listed in the SDK documentation, but the only three we use in this book are:
  - D3D10_SHADER_ENABLE_STRICTNESS: Forces IEEE strictness.
  - D3D10_SHADER_DEBUG: Compiles the shaders in debug mode.
  - D3D10_SHADER_SKIP_OPTIMIZATION: Instructs the compiler to skip optimizations (useful for debugging).
- FXFlags: Advanced options we do not use; see the SDK documentation.
- pDevice: A pointer to the Direct3D device.
- pEffectPool: Advanced option we do not use; see the SDK documentation.
- pPump: Advanced option we do not use; see the SDK documentation.
- ppEffect: Returns a pointer to the created effect.
- ppErrors: Returns a pointer to a string containing the compilation errors, if any. Note that the type ID3D10Blob is just a generic chunk of

memory, so it must be cast to the appropriate type before use (see the example below).

■ pttResult: Use only for pPump; we specify null in this book.

Here is an example call of this function:

```
DWORD shaderFlags = D3D10_SHADER_ENABLE_STRICTNESS;
#if defined( DEBUG ) || defined( _DEBUG )
    shaderFlags |= D3D10_SHADER_DEBUG;
    shaderFlags |= D3D10_SHADER_SKIP_OPTIMIZATION;
#endif

ID3D10Blob* compilationErrors = 0;
HRESULT hr = 0;
hr = D3DX10CreateEffectFromFile(L"color.fx", 0, 0, "fx_4_0",
    shaderFlags, 0, md3dDevice, 0, 0, &mFX, &compilationErrors, 0);
if(FAILED(hr))
{
    if( compilationErrors )
    {
        MessageBoxA(0, (char*)compilationErrors->GetBufferPointer(),
                    0, 0);
        ReleaseCOM(compilationErrors);
    }
    DXTrace(__FILE__, (DWORD)__LINE__, hr, L"D3DX10CreateEffectFromFile",
            true);
}
```

5.13.3 Interfacing with Effects from the C++ Application

The C++ application code typically needs to communicate with the effect; in particular, the C++ application usually needs to update variables in the constant buffers. For example, suppose that we had the following constant buffer defined in an effect file:

```
cbuffer cbPerObject
{
    float4x4 gWVP;
    float4 gColor;
    float gSize;
    int gIndex;
    bool gOptionOn;
};
```

Through the ID3D10Effect interface, we can obtain pointers to the variables in the constant buffer:

```
ID3D10EffectMatrixVariable* fxWVPVar;
ID3D10EffectVectorVariable* fxColorVar;
ID3D10EffectScalarVariable* fxSizeVar;
ID3D10EffectScalarVariable* fxIndexVar;
ID3D10EffectScalarVariable* fxOptionOnVar;
```

```
fxWVPVar      = mFX->GetVariableByName("gWVP")->AsMatrix();
fxColorVar    = mFX->GetVariableByName("gColor")->AsVector();
fxSizeVar     = mFX->GetVariableByName("gSize")->AsScalar();
fxIndexVar    = mFX->GetVariableByName("gIndex")->AsScalar();
fxOptionOnVar = mFX->GetVariableByName("gOptionOn")->AsScalar();
```

The `ID3D10Effect::GetVariableByName` method returns a pointer of type `ID3D10EffectVariable`. This is a generic effect variable type; to obtain a pointer to the specialized type (e.g., matrix, vector, scalar), you must use the appropriate `As*****` method (e.g., `AsMatrix`, `AsVector`, `AsScalar`).

Once we have pointers to the variables, we can update them through the C++ interface. Here are some examples:

```
fxWVPVar->SetMatrix( (float*)&M ); // assume M is of type D3DXMATRIX
fxColorVar->SetFloatVector( (float*)&v ); // assume v is of type
                                          // D3DXVECTOR4
fxSizeVar->>SetFloat( 5.0f );
fxIndexVar->SetInt( 77 );
fxOptionOnVar->SetBool( true );
```

Note that these calls update an internal cache in the effect object, and are not transferred over to GPU memory until we apply the rendering pass (see §5.13.4). This ensures one update to GPU memory instead of many small updates, which would be inefficient.

Note: An effect variable need not be specialized. For example, you can write:

```
ID3D10EffectVariable* mfxEyePosVar;
mfxEyePosVar = mFX->GetVariableByName("gEyePosW");
...
mfxEyePosVar->SetRawValue(&mEyePos, 0, sizeof(D3DXVECTOR3));
```

This is useful for setting variables of arbitrary size (e.g., general structures). Note that the `ID3D10EffectVectorVariable` interface assumes 4D vectors, so you will need to use `ID3D10EffectVariable`, as above, if you want to use 3D vectors.

In addition to constant buffer variables, it is necessary to obtain a pointer to the technique objects stored in the effect. This is done like so:

```
ID3D10EffectTechnique* mTech;
mTech = mFX->GetTechniqueByName("ColorTech");
```

The single parameter this method takes is the string name of the technique you wish to obtain a pointer to.

5.13.4 **Using Effects to Draw**

To use a technique to draw geometry, we simply need to make sure the variables in the constant buffers are up to date. Then we just loop over each pass in the technique, apply the pass, and draw the geometry:

```
mWVP = mWorld*mView*mProj;
mfxWVPVar->SetMatrix((float*)&mWVP);

D3D10_TECHNIQUE_DESC techDesc;
mTech->GetDesc( &techDesc );
for(UINT p = 0; p < techDesc.Passes; ++p)
{
    mTech->GetPassByIndex( p )->Apply(0);

    mBox.draw();
}
```

When the geometry is drawn in a pass, it will be drawn with the shaders and render states set by that pass. This example assumed we have a Box class (of which mBox is an instance of) that knows how to draw itself. The ID3D10EffectTechnique::GetPassByIndex method returns a pointer to an ID3D10EffectPass interface, which represents the pass with the specified index. In the current version of Direct3D 10, the ID3D10EffectPass::Apply method's single parameter is unused, and 0 should be specified. The Apply method updates the constant buffers stored in GPU memory, binds the shader programs to the pipeline, and applies any render states the pass sets.

If you need to change the values of variables in a constant buffer between draw calls, then you will have to call Apply to update the changes before drawing the geometry:

```
for(UINT i = 0; i < techDesc.Passes; ++i)
{
    ID3D10EffectPass* pass = mTech->GetPassByIndex(i);

    // Set combined world-view-projection matrix for land geometry.
    mWVP = mLandWorld*mView*mProj;
    mfxWVPVar->SetMatrix((float*)&mWVP);
    pass->Apply(0);
    mLand.draw();

    // Set combined world-view-projection matrix for wave geometry.
    mWVP = mWavesWorld*mView*mProj;
    mfxWVPVar->SetMatrix((float*)&mWVP);
    pass->Apply(0);
    mWaves.draw();
}
```

5.14 **Colored Cube Demo**

At last we have covered enough material to present a simple demo that renders a colored cube. This example essentially puts everything we have discussed in this chapter up to now into a single program. The reader should study the code and refer to the previous sections of the chapter until every line is understood. Note that the program uses the "color.fx" effect, as written in §5.13.1. We also mention that the code utilizes a user-defined Box class, the code of which follows the ColoredCubeApp implementation code below.

```
//========================================================================
// Color Cube App.cpp by Frank Luna (C) 2008 All Rights Reserved.
//
// Demonstrates coloring.
//
// Controls:
//        'A'/'D'/'W'/'S' - Rotate
//
//========================================================================

#include "d3dApp.h"
#include "Box.h"

class ColoredCubeApp : public D3DApp
{
public:
    ColoredCubeApp(HINSTANCE hInstance);
    ~ColoredCubeApp();

    void initApp();
    void onResize();
    void updateScene(float dt);
    void drawScene();

private:
    void buildFX();
    void buildVertexLayouts();

private:

    Box mBox;

    ID3D10Effect* mFX;
    ID3D10EffectTechnique* mTech;
    ID3D10InputLayout* mVertexLayout;
    ID3D10EffectMatrixVariable* mfxWVPVar;

    D3DXMATRIX mView;
    D3DXMATRIX mProj;
    D3DXMATRIX mWVP;

    float mTheta;
    float mPhi;
};

int WINAPI WinMain(HINSTANCE hInstance, HINSTANCE prevInstance,
                    PSTR cmdLine, int showCmd)
{
    // Enable run-time memory check for debug builds.
```

```cpp
#if defined(DEBUG) | defined(_DEBUG)
    _CrtSetDbgFlag( _CRTDBG_ALLOC_MEM_DF | _CRTDBG_LEAK_CHECK_DF );
#endif

    ColoredCubeApp theApp(hInstance);

    theApp.initApp();

    return theApp.run();
}

ColoredCubeApp::ColoredCubeApp(HINSTANCE hInstance)
: D3DApp(hInstance), mFX(0), mTech(0), mVertexLayout(0),
  mfxWVPVar(0), mTheta(0.0f), mPhi(PI*0.25f)
{
    D3DXMatrixIdentity(&mView);
    D3DXMatrixIdentity(&mProj);
    D3DXMatrixIdentity(&mWVP);
}

ColoredCubeApp::~ColoredCubeApp()
{
    if( md3dDevice )
        md3dDevice->ClearState();

    ReleaseCOM(mFX);
    ReleaseCOM(mVertexLayout);
}

void ColoredCubeApp::initApp()
{
    D3DApp::initApp();

    mBox.init(md3dDevice, 1.0f);

    buildFX();
    buildVertexLayouts();
}

void ColoredCubeApp::onResize()
{
    D3DApp::onResize();

    float aspect = (float)mClientWidth/mClientHeight;
    D3DXMatrixPerspectiveFovLH(&mProj, 0.25f*PI, aspect, 1.0f, 1000.0f);
}

void ColoredCubeApp::updateScene(float dt)
{
    D3DApp::updateScene(dt);

    // Update angles based on input to orbit camera around box.
```

```
    if(GetAsyncKeyState('A') & 0x8000) mTheta -= 2.0f*dt;
    if(GetAsyncKeyState('D') & 0x8000) mTheta += 2.0f*dt;
    if(GetAsyncKeyState('W') & 0x8000) mPhi -= 2.0f*dt;
    if(GetAsyncKeyState('S') & 0x8000) mPhi += 2.0f*dt;

    // Restrict the angle mPhi.
    if( mPhi < 0.1f ) mPhi = 0.1f;
    if( mPhi > PI-0.1f ) mPhi = PI-0.1f;

    // Convert Spherical to Cartesian coordinates: mPhi measured from +y
    // and mTheta measured counterclockwise from -z.
    float x =  5.0f*sinf(mPhi)*sinf(mTheta);
    float z = -5.0f*sinf(mPhi)*cosf(mTheta);
    float y =  5.0f*cosf(mPhi);

    // Build the view matrix.
    D3DXVECTOR3 pos(x, y, z);
    D3DXVECTOR3 target(0.0f, 0.0f, 0.0f);
    D3DXVECTOR3 up(0.0f, 1.0f, 0.0f);
    D3DXMatrixLookAtLH(&mView, &pos, &target, &up);
}

void ColoredCubeApp::drawScene()
{
    D3DApp::drawScene();

    // Restore default states, input layout, and primitive topology
    // because mFont->DrawText changes them.  Note that we can
    // restore the default states by passing null.
    md3dDevice->OMSetDepthStencilState(0, 0);
    float blendFactors[] = {0.0f, 0.0f, 0.0f, 0.0f};
    md3dDevice->OMSetBlendState(0, blendFactors, 0xffffffff);
    md3dDevice->IASetInputLayout(mVertexLayout);
    md3dDevice->IASetPrimitiveTopology(D3D10_PRIMITIVE_TOPOLOGY_
                                        TRIANGLELIST);


    // set constants
    mWVP = mView*mProj;
    mfxWVPVar->SetMatrix((float*)&mWVP);

    D3D10_TECHNIQUE_DESC techDesc;
    mTech->GetDesc( &techDesc );
    for(UINT p = 0; p < techDesc.Passes; ++p)
    {
        mTech->GetPassByIndex( p )->Apply(0);

        mBox.draw();
    }

    // We specify DT_NOCLIP, so we do not care about width/height
    // of the rect.
    RECT R = {5, 5, 0, 0};
```

```
    mFont->DrawText(0, mFrameStats.c_str(), -1, &R, DT_NOCLIP, BLACK);

    mSwapChain->Present(0, 0);
}

void ColoredCubeApp::buildFX()
{
    DWORD shaderFlags = D3D10_SHADER_ENABLE_STRICTNESS;
#if defined( DEBUG ) || defined( _DEBUG )
    shaderFlags |= D3D10_SHADER_DEBUG;
    shaderFlags |= D3D10_SHADER_SKIP_OPTIMIZATION;
#endif
    ID3D10Blob* compilationErrors = 0;
    HRESULT hr = 0;
    hr = D3DX10CreateEffectFromFile(L"color.fx", 0, 0,
        "fx_4_0", shaderFlags, 0, md3dDevice, 0, 0, &mFX,
        compilationErrors, 0);
    if(FAILED(hr))
    {
        if( compilationErrors )
        {
            MessageBoxA(0,
                (char*)compilationErrors->GetBufferPointer(), 0, 0);
            ReleaseCOM(compilationErrors);
        }
        DXTrace(__FILE__, (DWORD)__LINE__, hr,
            L"D3DX10CreateEffectFromFile", true);
    }

    mTech = mFX->GetTechniqueByName("ColorTech");

    mfxWVPVar = mFX->GetVariableByName("gWVP")->AsMatrix();
}

void ColoredCubeApp::buildVertexLayouts()
{
    // Create the vertex input layout.
    D3D10_INPUT_ELEMENT_DESC vertexDesc[] =
    {
        {"POSITION", 0, DXGI_FORMAT_R32G32B32_FLOAT, 0, 0,
         D3D10_INPUT_PER_VERTEX_DATA, 0},
        {"COLOR", 0, DXGI_FORMAT_R32G32B32A32_FLOAT, 0, 12,
         D3D10_INPUT_PER_VERTEX_DATA, 0}
    };

    // Create the input layout
    D3D10_PASS_DESC PassDesc;
    mTech->GetPassByIndex(0)->GetDesc(&PassDesc);
    HR(md3dDevice->CreateInputLayout(vertexDesc, 2,
        PassDesc.pIAInputSignature,
        PassDesc.IAInputSignatureSize, &mVertexLayout));
}
```

```
//=======================================================================
// Box.h by Frank Luna (C) 2008 All Rights Reserved.
//=======================================================================

#ifndef BOX_H
#define BOX_H

#include "d3dUtil.h"

class Box
{
public:

    Box();
    ~Box();

    void init(ID3D10Device* device, float scale);
    void draw();

private:
    DWORD mNumVertices;
    DWORD mNumFaces;

    ID3D10Device* md3dDevice;
    ID3D10Buffer* mVB;
    ID3D10Buffer* mIB;
};


#endif // BOX_H
```

```
//=======================================================================
// Box.cpp by Frank Luna (C) 2008 All Rights Reserved.
//=======================================================================

#include "Box.h"
#include "Vertex.h"

Box::Box()
: mNumVertices(0), mNumFaces(0), md3dDevice(0), mVB(0), mIB(0)
{
}

Box::~Box()
{
    ReleaseCOM(mVB);
    ReleaseCOM(mIB);
}

void Box::init(ID3D10Device* device, float scale)
{
    md3dDevice = device;
```

```
mNumVertices = 8;
mNumFaces    = 12; // 2 per quad

// Create vertex buffer
Vertex vertices[] =
{
    {D3DXVECTOR3(-1.0f, -1.0f, -1.0f), WHITE},
    {D3DXVECTOR3(-1.0f, +1.0f, -1.0f), BLACK},
    {D3DXVECTOR3(+1.0f, +1.0f, -1.0f), RED},
    {D3DXVECTOR3(+1.0f, -1.0f, -1.0f), GREEN},
    {D3DXVECTOR3(-1.0f, -1.0f, +1.0f), BLUE},
    {D3DXVECTOR3(-1.0f, +1.0f, +1.0f), YELLOW},
    {D3DXVECTOR3(+1.0f, +1.0f, +1.0f), CYAN},
    {D3DXVECTOR3(+1.0f, -1.0f, +1.0f), MAGENTA},
};

// Scale the box.
for(DWORD i = 0; i < mNumVertices; ++i)
    vertices[i].pos *= scale;


D3D10_BUFFER_DESC vbd;
vbd.Usage = D3D10_USAGE_IMMUTABLE;
vbd.ByteWidth = sizeof(Vertex) * mNumVertices;
vbd.BindFlags = D3D10_BIND_VERTEX_BUFFER;
vbd.CPUAccessFlags = 0;
vbd.MiscFlags = 0;
D3D10_SUBRESOURCE_DATA vinitData;
vinitData.pSysMem = vertices;
HR(md3dDevice->CreateBuffer(&vbd, &vinitData, &mVB));


// Create the index buffer

DWORD indices[] = {
    // front face
    0, 1, 2,
    0, 2, 3,

    // back face
    4, 6, 5,
    4, 7, 6,

    // left face
    4, 5, 1,
    4, 1, 0,

    // right face
    3, 2, 6,
    3, 6, 7,

    // top face
```

```
        1, 5, 6,
        1, 6, 2,

        // bottom face
        4, 0, 3,
        4, 3, 7
    };

    D3D10_BUFFER_DESC ibd;
    ibd.Usage = D3D10_USAGE_IMMUTABLE;
    ibd.ByteWidth = sizeof(DWORD) * mNumFaces*3;
    ibd.BindFlags = D3D10_BIND_INDEX_BUFFER;
    ibd.CPUAccessFlags = 0;
    ibd.MiscFlags = 0;
    D3D10_SUBRESOURCE_DATA iinitData;
    iinitData.pSysMem = indices;
    HR(md3dDevice->CreateBuffer(&ibd, &iinitData, &mIB));
}

void Box::draw()
{
    UINT stride = sizeof(Vertex);
    UINT offset = 0;
    md3dDevice->IASetVertexBuffers(0, 1, &mVB, &stride, &offset);
    md3dDevice->IASetIndexBuffer(mIB, DXGI_FORMAT_R32_UINT, 0);
    md3dDevice->DrawIndexed(mNumFaces*3, 0, 0);
}
```

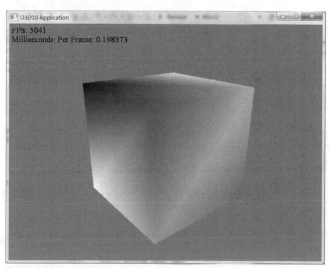

Figure 5.37: Screenshot of the cube demo.

5.15 **Peaks and Valleys Demo**

This chapter also includes a "Peaks and Valleys" demo. It uses the same Direct3D methods as the Colored Cube demo, except that it draws more complicated geometry. In particular, it shows how to construct a triangle grid mesh procedurally; such geometry turns out to be particularly useful for terrain and water rendering, among other things.

The graph of a "nice" real-valued function $y = f(x, z)$ is a surface. We can approximate the surface by constructing a grid in the xz-plane, where every quad is built from two triangles, and then applying the function to each grid point; see Figure 5.38.

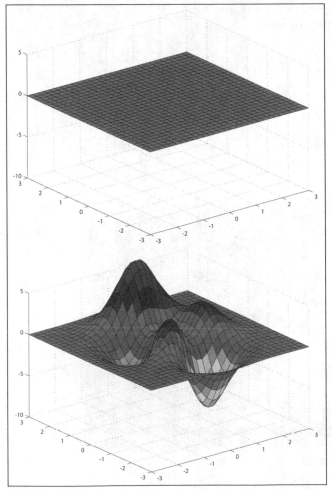

Figure 5.38: (Top) Lay down a grid in the xz-plane. (Bottom) For each grid point, apply the function $f(x, z)$ to obtain the y-coordinate. The plot of the points $(x, f(x, z), z)$ gives the graph of a surface.

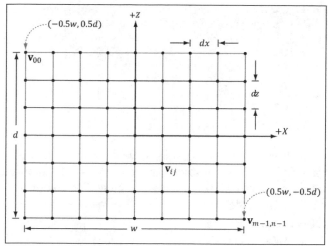

Figure 5.39: Grid construction.

So the main task is how to build the grid in the xz-plane. A grid of $m \times n$ vertices induces $(m - 1) \times (n - 1)$ quads (or cells), as shown in Figure 5.39. If the cell spacing along the x-axis is dx, and the cell spacing along the z-axis is dz, then the grid has a width $w = (n - 1) \cdot dx$ and depth $d = (m - 1) \cdot dz$. To generate the vertices, we start at the upper-left corner and incrementally compute the vertex coordinates row-by-row. The coordinates of the ijth grid vertex in the xz-plane are given by:

$$\mathbf{v}_{ij} = \left(-0.5w + j \cdot dx, 0.5d - i \cdot dz\right)$$

After we have obtained the xz-coordinates of the grid point, we get the height (y-coordinate) by applying the function $f(x, z)$. The following code does this, and sets $dx = dz$ so that the cells are square.

```
float halfWidth = (n-1)*dx*0.5f;
float halfDepth = (m-1)*dx*0.5f;
for(DWORD i = 0; i < m; ++i)
{
    float z = halfDepth - i*dx;
    for(DWORD j = 0; j < n; ++j)
    {
        float x = -halfWidth + j*dx;

        // Graph of this function looks like a mountain range.
        float y = getHeight(x,z);

        vertices[i*n+j].pos = D3DXVECTOR3(x, y, z);

        // Color the vertex based on its height.
        if( y < -10.0f )
            vertices[i*n+j].color = BEACH_SAND;
```

```
          else if( y < 5.0f )
              vertices[i*n+j].color = LIGHT_YELLOW_GREEN;
          else if( y < 12.0f )
              vertices[i*n+j].color = DARK_YELLOW_GREEN;
          else if( y < 20.0f )
              vertices[i*n+j].color = DARKBROWN;
          else
              vertices[i*n+j].color = WHITE;
      }
  }
```

In addition to computing the vertex positions, we color the vertices based on the altitude; for example, low altitudes are colored a sandy color, and the peaks of the hills are colored white to represent snow. The colors are defined in the *d3dUtil.h* header file:

```
const D3DXCOLOR WHITE(1.0f, 1.0f, 1.0f, 1.0f);
const D3DXCOLOR BEACH_SAND(1.0f, 0.96f, 0.62f, 1.0f);
const D3DXCOLOR LIGHT_YELLOW_GREEN(0.48f, 0.77f, 0.46f, 1.0f);
const D3DXCOLOR DARK_YELLOW_GREEN(0.1f, 0.48f, 0.19f, 1.0f);
const D3DXCOLOR DARKBROWN(0.45f, 0.39f, 0.34f, 1.0f);
```

The function $f(x, z)$ we have used in this demo is given by:

```
float PeaksAndValleys::getHeight(float x, float z)const
{
    return 0.3f*( z*sinf(0.1f*x) + x*cosf(0.1f*z) );
}
```

Its graph looks like a terrain with hills and valleys.

After we have computed the vertices, we need to define the grid triangles by specifying the indices. To do this, we iterate over each quad, again row-by-row starting at the top-left corner, and compute the indices to define the two triangles of the quad. As shown in Figure 5.40, for an $m \times n$ vertex grid, the linear array indices of the two triangles are computed as follows:

$$\Delta ABC = \left(i \cdot n + j, \quad i \cdot n + j + 1, \quad (i+1) \cdot n + j\right)$$

$$\Delta CBD = \left((i+1) \cdot n + j, \quad i \cdot n + j + 1, \quad (i+1) \cdot n + j + 1\right)$$

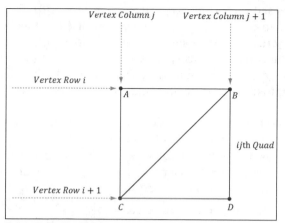

Figure 5.40: The indices of the *ij*th quad's vertices.

Here is the corresponding code:

```
// Iterate over each quad and compute indices.
int k = 0;
for(DWORD i = 0; i < m-1; ++i)
{
    for(DWORD j = 0; j < n-1; ++j)
    {
        indices[k]   = i*n+j;
        indices[k+1] = i*n+j+1;
        indices[k+2] = (i+1)*n+j;

        indices[k+3] = (i+1)*n+j;
        indices[k+4] = i*n+j+1;
        indices[k+5] = (i+1)*n+j+1;

        k += 6; // next quad
    }
}
```

The vertices and indices are, of course, placed in vertex and index buffers. The rest of the code is similar to the Cube demo.

5.16 **Dynamic Vertex Buffers**

Thus far we have worked with static buffers, which are fixed at initialization time. In contrast, the contents of a dynamic buffer change, usually per frame. Dynamic buffers are usually used when we need to animate something. For example, suppose we are doing a wave simulation, and we solve the wave equation for the solution function $f(x, z, t)$. This function represents the wave height at each point in the xz-plane at time t. If we were to use this function to draw the waves, we would use a triangle grid mesh like we did with the peaks and valleys, and apply $f(x, z, t)$ to each grid point in order to obtain the wave heights at the grid points. Because this function also depends on time t (i.e., the wave surface changes with time), we would need to reapply this function to the grid points a short time later (say every 1/30th of a second) to get a smooth animation. Thus, we need a dynamic vertex buffer in order to update the heights of the triangle grid mesh vertices as time passes.

Recall that in order to make a buffer dynamic, we must specify the usage D3D10_USAGE_DYNAMIC; in addition, since we will be writing to the buffer, we need the CPU access flag D3D10_CPU_ACCESS_WRITE. Then we can use the ID3D10Buffer::Map function to obtain a pointer to the start of the buffer memory block and write to it, as the following code shows:

```
// Update the vertex buffer with the new solution.
Vertex* v = 0;
HR(mVB->Map(D3D10_MAP_WRITE_DISCARD, 0, (void**)&v ));

for(DWORD i = 0; i < mNumVertices; ++i)
{
    v[i].pos = mCurrSolution[i];
    v[i].color = D3DXCOLOR(0.0f, 0.0f, 0.0f, 1.0f);
}

mVB->Unmap();
```

The ID3D10Buffer::Unmap function must be called when you are done updating the buffer. The argument D3D10_MAP_WRITE_DISCARD passed into the first parameter of the Map function instructs the hardware to discard the buffer and return a pointer to a newly allocated buffer; this prevents the hardware from stalling by allowing the hardware to continue rendering from the discarded buffer while we write to the newly allocated buffer. Another option is the D3D10_MAP_WRITE_NO_OVERWRITE value. This flag tells the hardware we are only going to write to uninitialized parts of the buffer; this also prevents the hardware from stalling by allowing the hardware to continue rendering previously written geometry at the same time we write to the uninitialized parts of the buffer. The D3D10_MAP_READ flag is used for staging buffers, where you need to read a copy of the GPU buffer.

There is some overhead when using dynamic buffers, as the new data must be transferred from CPU memory back up to GPU memory. Therefore, static buffers should be preferred to dynamic buffers, provided static buffers will work. The latest versions of Direct3D have introduced new features to lessen the need for dynamic buffers. For instance:

■ Simple animations may be done in a vertex shader.

■ Through render to texture and vertex texture fetch functionality, it is possible to implement a wave simulation like the one described above that runs completely on the GPU.

■ The geometry shader provides the ability for the GPU to create or destroy primitives, a task that would normally need to be done on the CPU without a geometry shader.

Index buffers can be dynamic, too. However, in the Waves demo, the triangle topology remains constant and only the vertex heights change; therefore, only the vertex buffer needs to be dynamic.

The Waves demo for this chapter uses a dynamic vertex buffer to implement a simple wave simulation like the one described at the beginning of this section. For this book, we are not concerned with the actual algorithm details for the wave simulation (see [Lengyel02] for that), but more with the process so as to illustrate dynamic buffers: Update the simulation on CPU and then update the vertex buffer accordingly using Map/Unmap.

Note: In the Waves demo, we render the waves in wireframe mode; this is because without lighting it is difficult to see the wave motion in solid fill mode.

Note: We mention again that this demo could be implemented on the GPU using more advanced methods such as render to texture functionality and vertex texture fetch. Because we have not covered these topics yet, we do the wave simulation on the CPU and update the new vertices using dynamic vertex buffers.

5.17 **Summary**

■ We can simulate 3D scenes on 2D images by employing several techniques based on the way we see things in real life. We observe parallel lines converge to vanishing points, the size of objects diminish with depth, objects obscure the objects behind them, lighting and shading depict the solid form and volume of 3D objects, and shadows imply the location of light sources and indicate the position of objects relative to other objects in the scene.

■ We approximate objects with triangle meshes. We can define each triangle by specifying its three vertices. In many meshes, vertices are shared among triangles; indexed lists can be used to avoid vertex duplication.

■ Colors are described by specifying an intensity of red, green, and blue. The additive mixing of these three colors at different intensities allows us to describe millions of colors. To describe the intensities of red, green, and blue, it is useful to use a normalized range from 0 to 1. 0 denotes no intensity, 1 denotes the full intensity, and intermediate values denote intermediate intensities. It is common to incorporate an additional color component, called the _alpha component_. The alpha component is often used to denote the opacity of a color, which is useful in blending. Including the alpha component means we can represent a color by a 4D color vector (r, g, b, a) where $0 \le r, g, b, a \le 1$. In Direct3D, colors are represented by the D3DXCOLOR class. Color vectors are added, subtracted, and scaled just like regular vectors, except that we must clamp their components to the $[0, 1]$ interval. The other vector operations such as the dot product and cross product do not make sense for color vectors. The symbol $\otimes$ denotes componentwise multiplication and it is defined as: $(c_1, c_2, c_3, c_4) \otimes (k_1, k_2, k_3, k_4) = (c_1 k_1, c_2 k_2, c_3 k_3, c_4 k_4)$.

- Given a geometric description of a 3D scene and a positioned and aimed virtual camera in that scene, the *rendering pipeline* refers to the entire sequence of steps necessary to generate a 2D image that can be displayed on a monitor screen based on what the virtual camera sees.

- The rendering pipeline can be broken down into the following major stages: the input assembly (IA) stage, the vertex shader (VS) stage, the geometry shader (GS) stage, the clipping stage, the rasterization stage (RS), the pixel shader (PS) stage, and the output merger (OM) stage.

- Render states are states the device maintains that affect how geometry is rendered. Render states remain in effect until changed, and the current values are applied to the geometry of any subsequent drawing operations. All render states have initial default states. Direct3D divides render states into three state blocks: the rasterizer state (ID3D10RasterizerState), the blend state (ID3D10BlendState), and the depth/stencil state (ID3D10DepthStencilState). Render states can be created and set at the C++ application level or in effect files.

- A Direct3D effect (ID3D10Effect) encapsulates at least one rendering technique. A rendering technique contains the code that specifies how to render 3D geometry in a particular way. A rendering technique consists of at least one rendering pass. For each rendering pass, the geometry is rendered. A multi-pass technique requires rendering the geometry several times to achieve the desired result. Each pass consists of the vertex shader, optional geometry shader, pixel shader, and the render states used to draw the geometry for that pass. The vertex, geometry and pixel shaders may access variables in the constant buffers defined in the effect file, as well as texture resources.

- Dynamic buffers are used when the contents of the buffer need to be updated frequently at run time (e.g., every frame or every 1/30th of a second). A dynamic buffer must be created with the D3D10_USAGE_DYNAMIC usage and the D3D10_CPU_ACCESS_WRITE CPU access flag. Use the ID3D10Buffer::Map and ID3D10Buffer::Unmap methods to update the buffer.

5.18 **Exercises**

1. Write the D3D10_INPUT_ELEMENT_DESC array for the following vertex structure:

    ```
    struct Vertex
    {
        D3DXVECTOR3 pos;
        D3DXVECTOR3 tangent;
        D3DXVECTOR3 binormal;
        D3DXVECTOR3 normal;
        D3DXVECTOR2 tex0;
        D3DXCOLOR color;
    };
    ```

2. Redo the Colored Cube demo, but this time use two vertex buffers (and two input slots) to feed the pipeline with vertices — one that stores the position element and the other that stores the color element. Your D3D10_INPUT_ELEMENT_DESC array will look like this:

    ```
    D3D10_INPUT_ELEMENT_DESC vertexDesc[] =
    {
        {"POSITION", 0, DXGI_FORMAT_R32G32B32_FLOAT, 0, 0,
            D3D10_INPUT_PER_VERTEX_DATA, 0},
        {"COLOR", 0, DXGI_FORMAT_R32G32B32A32_FLOAT, 1, 0,
            D3D10_INPUT_PER_VERTEX_DATA, 0}
    };
    ```

    The position element is hooked up to input slot 0, and the color element is hooked up to input slot 1. Moreover note that the D3D10_INPUT_ELEMENT_DESC::AlignedByteOffset is 0 for both elements; this is because the position and color elements are no longer interleaved in a single input slot.

3. Draw

    a. A point list like the one shown in Figure 5.15a.

    b. A line strip like the one shown in Figure 5.15b.

    c. A line list like the one shown in Figure 5.15c.

    d. A triangle strip like the one shown in Figure 5.15d.

    e. A triangle list like the one shown in Figure 5.16a.

    f. A triangle adjacency list like the one shown in Figure 5.16b.

4. Construct the vertex and index list of a pyramid, as shown in Figure 5.41, and draw it. Color the base vertices green and the tip vertex red.

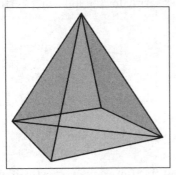

Figure 5.41: The triangles of a pyramid.

5. Modify the Colored Cube demo by applying the following transformation to each vertex in the vertex shader prior to transforming to world space:

```
iPosL.xy += 0.5f*sin(iPosL.x)*sin(3*gTime);
iPosL.z  *= 0.6f + 0.4f*sin(2*gTime);
```

The `gTime` constant buffer variable corresponds to the current `GameTimer::getGameTime()` value. This will animate the vertices as a function of time by distorting them periodically with the sine function.

6. Merge the vertices of a box and pyramid into one large vertex buffer. Also merge the indices of the box and pyramid into one large index buffer (but do not update the index values). Then draw the box and pyramid one-by-one using the parameters of `ID3D10Device::DrawIndexed`. Use the world transformation matrix so that the box and pyramid are disjointed in world space.

7. Modify the Colored Cube demo by rendering the cube in wireframe mode. Do this in two different ways:

   a. By setting the rasterization render state from the C++ code by calling `ID3D10Device::RSSetState`.

   b. By setting the rasterization render state from the effect file by calling `SetRasterizerState()` in the effect pass.

8. Modify the Colored Cube demo by disabling backface culling (`CullMode = None`); also try culling front faces instead of back faces (`CullMode = Front`). Do this in two different ways:

   a. By setting the rasterization render state from the C++ code by calling `ID3D10Device::RSSetState`.

   b. By setting the rasterization render state from the effect file by calling `SetRasterizerState()` in the effect pass. Output your results in wireframe mode so that you can see the difference.

9. Relative to the world coordinate system, suppose that the camera is positioned at $(-20, 35, -50)$ and looking at the point $(10, 0, 30)$. Compute the view matrix, assuming $(0, 1, 0)$ describes the "up" direction in the world.

10. Consider the following perspective projection matrix:

$$\begin{bmatrix} 1.86603 & 0 & 0 & 0 \\ 0 & 3.73205 & 0 & 0 \\ 0 & 0 & 1.02564 & 1 \\ 0 & 0 & -5.12821 & 0 \end{bmatrix}$$

Find the vertical field of view angle α the aspect ratio r, and the near and far plane values that were used to build this matrix.

11. If vertex data is taking up a significant amount of memory, then reducing from 128-bit color values to 32-bit color values may be worthwhile. Modify the Colored Cube demo by using a 32-bit color value instead of a 128-bit color value in the vertex structure. Your vertex structure and corresponding vertex input description will look like this:

```
struct Vertex
{
    D3DXVECTOR3 pos;
    UINT    color;
};

D3D10_INPUT_ELEMENT_DESC vertexDesc[] =
{
    {"POSITION", 0, DXGI_FORMAT_R32G32B32_FLOAT, 0, 0,
        D3D10_INPUT_PER_VERTEX_DATA, 0},
    {"COLOR",    0, DXGI_FORMAT_R8G8B8A8_UNORM, 0, 12,
        D3D10_INPUT_PER_VERTEX_DATA, 0}
};
```

Hint: The 8-bit color components need to be packed into a UINT in the format ABGR, *not* RGBA; this is because the byte order is reversed in *little-endian* format. The conversion from ARGB (which D3DXCOLOR returns) to ABGR can be done with a function like the following:

```
D3DX10INLINE UINT ARGB2ABGR(UINT argb)
{
    BYTE A = (argb >> 24) & 0xff;
    BYTE R = (argb >> 16) & 0xff;
    BYTE G = (argb >>  8) & 0xff;
    BYTE B = (argb >>  0) & 0xff;

    return (A << 24) | (B << 16) | (G << 8) | (R << 0);
}
```

12. Modify the Colored Cube demo by changing the viewport to only render to a subrectangle of the output window.

Chapter 6

Lighting

Figure 6.1 shows how important lighting and shading are in conveying the solid form and volume of an object. The unlit sphere on the left looks like a flat 2D circle, whereas the lit sphere on the right does look 3D. In fact, our visual perception of the world depends on light and its interaction with materials, and consequently, much of the problem of generating photo-realistic scenes has to do with physically accurate lighting models.

Figure 6.1: (a) An unlit sphere looks 2D. (b) A lit sphere looks 3D.

Of course, in general, the more accurate the model, the more computationally expensive it is; thus a balance must be reached between realism and speed. For example, 3D special FX scenes for films can be much more complex and utilize more realistic lighting models than games because the frames for a film are pre-rendered, so they can afford to take hours or days to process a frame. Games, on the other hand, are real-time applications, and therefore, the frames need to be drawn at a rate of at least 30 frames per second.

Note that the lighting model explained and implemented in this book is largely based on the one described in [Möller02].

Objectives:

■ To gain a basic understanding of the interaction between lights and materials.

■ To understand the differences between local illumination and global illumination.

■ To find out how we can mathematically describe the direction a point on a surface is "facing" so that we can determine the angle at which incoming light strikes the surface.

■ To learn how to correctly transform normal vectors.

■ To be able to distinguish between ambient, diffuse, and specular light.

■ To learn how to implement directional lights, point lights, and spotlights.

■ To understand how to vary light intensity as a function of depth by controlling attenuation parameters.

6.1 Light and Material Interaction

When using lighting, we no longer specify vertex colors directly; rather, we specify materials and lights, and then apply a lighting equation, which computes the vertex colors for us based on light/material interaction. This leads to a much more realistic coloring of the object (compare the spheres in Figure 6.1 again).

Materials can be thought of as the properties that determine how light interacts with the surface of an object. For example, the colors of light a surface reflects and absorbs, and also the reflectivity, transparency, and shininess are all parameters that make up the material of the surface. In this chapter, however, we only concern ourselves with the colors of light a surface reflects and absorbs, and shininess.

In our model, a light source can emit various intensities of red, green, and blue light; in this way, we can simulate many light colors. When light travels outward from a source and collides with an object, some of that light may be absorbed and some may be reflected (for transparent objects, such as glass, some of the light passes through the medium, but we do not consider transparency here). The reflected light now travels along its new path and may strike other objects where some light is again absorbed and reflected. A light ray may strike many objects before it is fully absorbed. Presumably, some light rays eventually travel into the eye (see Figure 6.2) and strike the light receptor cells (called cones and rods) on the retina.

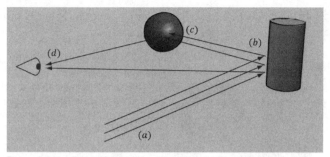

Figure 6.2: (a) Flux of incoming white light. (b) The light strikes the cylinder and some rays are absorbed and other rays are scattered toward the eye and the sphere. (c) The light reflecting off the cylinder toward the sphere is absorbed or reflected again and travels into the eye. (d) The eye receives incoming light that determines what the person sees.

According to the *trichromatic* theory (see [Santrock03]), the retina contains three kinds of colored light receptors, each sensitive to red, green, or blue light (with some overlap). The incoming RGB light stimulates its corresponding light receptors to varying intensities based on the strength of the light. As the light receptors are stimulated (or not), neural impulses are sent down the optic nerve toward the brain, where the brain generates an image in your head based on the stimulus of the light receptors. (Of course, if you close/cover your eyes, the receptor cells receive no stimulus and the brain registers this as black.)

For example, consider Figure 6.2 again. Suppose that the material of the cylinder reflects 75% red light and 75% green light and absorbs the rest, and the sphere reflects 25% red light and absorbs the rest. Also suppose that pure white light is being emitted from the light source. As the light rays strike the cylinder, all the blue light is absorbed and only 75% red and green light is reflected (i.e., a medium-high intensity yellow). This light is then scattered — some of it travels into the eye and some of it travels toward the sphere. The part that travels into the eye primarily stimulates the red and green cone cells to a semi-high degree; hence, the viewer sees the cylinder as a semi-bright shade of yellow. Now, the other light rays travel toward the sphere and strike it. The sphere reflects 25% red light and absorbs the rest; thus, the diluted incoming red light (medium-high intensity red) is diluted further and reflected, and all of the incoming green light is absorbed. This remaining red light then travels into the eye and primarily stimulates the red cone cells to a low degree. Thus the viewer sees the sphere as a dark shade of red.

The lighting models we (and most real-time applications) adopt in this book are called *local illumination models*. With a local model, each object is lit independently of another object, and only the light directly emitted from light sources is taken into account in the lighting process (i.e., light that has bounced off other scene objects to strike the object currently being lit is ignored). Figure 6.3 shows a consequence of this model.

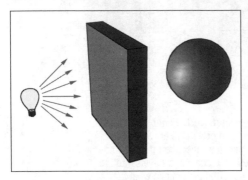

Figure 6.3: Physically, the wall blocks the light rays emitted by the light bulb and the sphere is in the shadow of the wall. However, in a local illumination model, the sphere is lit as if the wall were not there.

On the other hand, global illumination models light objects by taking into consideration not only the light directly emitted from light sources, but also the indirect light that has bounced off other objects in the scene. These are called global illumination models because they take everything in the global scene into consideration when lighting an object. Global illumination models are generally prohibitively expensive for real-time games (but come very close to generating photorealistic scenes); however, there is research being done in real-time global illumination methods.

6.2 **Normal Vectors**

A *face normal* is a unit vector that describes the direction a polygon is facing (i.e., it is orthogonal to all points on the polygon), as shown in Figure 6.4a. A *surface normal* is a unit vector that is orthogonal to the tangent plane of a point on a surface, as shown in Figure 6.4b. Observe that surface normals determine the direction a point on a surface is "facing."

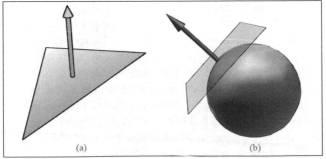

(a) (b)

Figure 6.4: (a) The face normal is orthogonal to all points on the face. (b) The surface normal is the vector that is orthogonal to the tangent plane of a point on a surface.

For lighting calculations, we need to find the surface normal at each point on the surface of a triangle mesh so that we can determine the angle at which light strikes the point on the mesh surface. To obtain surface normals, we specify the surface normals only at the vertex points (so-called _vertex normals_). Then, in order to obtain a surface normal approximation at each point on the surface of a triangle mesh, these vertex normals will need to be interpolated across the triangle during rasterization (recall §5.9.3 and see Figure 6.5).

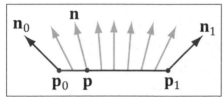

Figure 6.5: The vertex normals n_0 and n_1 are defined at the segment vertex points p_0 and p_1. A normal vector n for a point p in the interior of the line segment is found by linearly interpolating (weighted average) between the vertex normals; that is, $n = n_0 + t(n_1 - n_0)$, where t is such that $p = p_0 + t(p_1 - p_0)$. Although we illustrated normal interpolation over a line segment for simplicity, the idea straight-forwardly generalizes to interpolating over a 3D triangle.

6.2.1 **Computing Normal Vectors**

To find the face normal of a triangle $\Delta p_0 p_1 p_2$, we first compute two vectors that lie on the triangle's edges:

$$u = p_1 - p_0$$

$$v = p_2 - p_0$$

Then the face normal is:

$$n = \frac{u \times v}{\|u \times v\|}$$

Below is a function that computes the face normal of the front side (§5.9.2) of a triangle from the three vertex points of the triangle.

```
void ComputeNormal(const D3DXVECTOR3& p0,
                   const D3DXVECTOR3& p1,
                   const D3DXVECTOR3& p2,
                   D3DXVECTOR3& out)
{
    D3DXVECTOR3 u = p1 - p0;
    D3DXVECTOR3 v = p2 - p0;

    D3DXVec3Cross(&out, &u, &v);
    D3DXVec3Normalize(&out, &out);
}
```

For a differentiable surface, we can use calculus to find the normals of points on the surface. Unfortunately, a triangle mesh is not differentiable. The technique that is generally applied to triangle meshes is called *vertex normal averaging*. The vertex normal $\mathbf{n}$ for an arbitrary vertex $\mathbf{v}$ in a mesh is found by averaging the face normals of every polygon in the mesh that shares the vertex $\mathbf{v}$. For example, in Figure 6.6, four polygons in the mesh share the vertex $\mathbf{v}$; thus, the vertex normal for $\mathbf{v}$ is given by:

$$\mathbf{n}_{avg} = \frac{\mathbf{n}_0 + \mathbf{n}_1 + \mathbf{n}_2 + \mathbf{n}_3}{\left\| \mathbf{n}_0 + \mathbf{n}_1 + \mathbf{n}_2 + \mathbf{n}_3 \right\|}$$

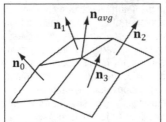

Figure 6.6: The middle vertex is shared by the neighboring four polygons, so we approximate the middle vertex normal by averaging the four polygon face normals.

In the above example, we do not need to divide by 4, as we would in a typical average, since we normalize the result. Note also that more sophisticated averaging schemes can be constructed; for example, a weighted average might be used where the weights are determined by the areas of the polygons (e.g., polygons with larger areas have more weight than polygons with smaller areas).

The following pseudocode shows how this averaging can be implemented given the vertex and index list of a triangle mesh:

```
// Input:
// 1. An array of vertices (mVertices). Each vertex has a
//    position component (pos) and a normal component (normal).
// 2. An array of indices (mIndices).

// For each triangle in the mesh:
for(DWORD i = 0; i < mNumTriangles; ++i)
{
    // indices of the ith triangle
    DWORD i0 = mIndices[i*3+0];
    DWORD i1 = mIndices[i*3+1];
    DWORD i2 = mIndices[i*3+2];

    // vertices of ith triangle
    Vertex v0 = mVertices[i0];
    Vertex v1 = mVertices[i1];
    Vertex v2 = mVertices[i2];

    // compute face normal
    D3DXVECTOR3 e0 = v1.pos - v0.pos;
```

```
        D3DXVECTOR3 e1 = v2.pos - v0.pos;
        D3DXVECTOR3 faceNormal;
        D3DXVec3Cross(&faceNormal, &e0, &e1);

        // This triangle shares the following three vertices,
        // so add this face normal into the average of these
        // vertex normals.
        mVertices[i0].normal += faceNormal;
        mVertices[i1].normal += faceNormal;
        mVertices[i2].normal += faceNormal;
    }

    // For each vertex v, we have summed the face normals of all
    // the triangles that share v, so now we just need to normalize.
    for(DWORD i = 0; i < mNumVertices; ++i)
        D3DXVec3Normalize(&mVertices[i].normal, &mVertices[i].normal);
```

6.2.2 Transforming Normal Vectors

Consider Figure 6.7a, where we have a tangent vector $\mathbf{u} = \mathbf{v}_1 - \mathbf{v}_0$ orthogonal to a normal vector $\mathbf{n}$. If we apply a nonuniform scaling transformation $\mathbf{A}$, we see from Figure 6.7b that the transformed tangent vector $\mathbf{u}\mathbf{A} = \mathbf{v}_1\mathbf{A} - \mathbf{v}_0\mathbf{A}$ does not remain orthogonal to the transformed normal vector $\mathbf{n}\mathbf{A}$.

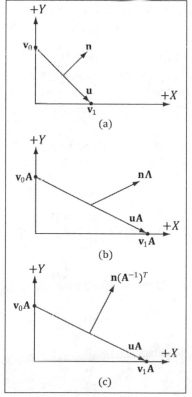

Figure 6.7: (a) The surface normal before transformation. (b) After scaling by 2 units on the x-axis the normal is no longer orthogonal to the surface. (c) The surface normal correctly transformed by the inverse-transpose of the scaling transformation.

So our problem is this: Given a transformation matrix $\mathbf{A}$ that transforms points and vectors (non-normal), we want to find a transformation matrix $\mathbf{B}$ that transforms normal vectors such that the transformed tangent vector is orthogonal to the transformed normal vector (i.e., $\mathbf{uA} \cdot \mathbf{nB} = 0$). To do this, let's first start with something we know: We know that the normal vector $\mathbf{n}$ is orthogonal to the tangent vector $\mathbf{u}$.

$\mathbf{u} \cdot \mathbf{n} = 0$	Tangent vector orthogonal to normal vector
$\mathbf{u}\mathbf{n}^T = 0$	Rewriting the dot product as a matrix multiplication
$\mathbf{u}(AA^{-1})\mathbf{n}^T = 0$	Inserting the identity matrix $\mathbf{I} = \mathbf{AA}^{-1}$
$(\mathbf{uA})(\mathbf{A}^{-1}\mathbf{n}^T) = 0$	Associative property of matrix multiplication
$(\mathbf{uA})\left((\mathbf{A}^{-1}\mathbf{n}^T)^T\right)^T = 0$	Transpose property $(\mathbf{A}^T)^T = \mathbf{A}$
$(\mathbf{uA})\left(\mathbf{n}(\mathbf{A}^{-1})^T\right)^T = 0$	Transpose property $(\mathbf{AB})^T = \mathbf{B}^T\mathbf{A}^T$
$\mathbf{uA} \cdot \mathbf{n}(\mathbf{A}^{-1})^T = 0$	Rewriting the matrix multiplication as a dot product
$\mathbf{uA} \cdot \mathbf{nB} = 0$	Transformed tangent vector orthogonal to transformed normal vector

Thus $\mathbf{B} = (\mathbf{A}^{-1})^T$ (the inverse-transpose of $\mathbf{A}$) does the job in transforming normal vectors so that they are perpendicular to the associated transformed tangent vector $\mathbf{uA}$.

Note that if the matrix is orthogonal ($\mathbf{A}^T = \mathbf{A}^{-1}$), then $\mathbf{B} = (\mathbf{A}^{-1})^T = (\mathbf{A}^T)^T = \mathbf{A}$; that is, we do not need to compute the inverse-transpose, since $\mathbf{A}$ does the job in this case. In summary, when transforming a normal vector by a nonuniform or shear transformation, use the inverse-transpose.

Note: In this book, we only use uniform scaling and rigid body transformations to transform normals, so using the inverse-transpose is not necessary.

Note: Even with the inverse-transpose transformation, normal vectors may lose their unit length; thus, they may need to be renormalized after the transformation.

6.3 **Lambert's Cosine Law**

Light that strikes a surface point head-on is more intense than light that
just glances a surface point (see Figure 6.8).

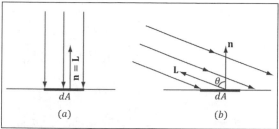

Figure 6.8: Consider a small area element _dA_. (a) The area _dA_
receives the most light when the normal vector **n** and light
vector **L** are aligned. (b) The area _dA_ receives less light as the
angle θ between **n** and **L** increases (as depicted by the light
rays that miss the surface _dA_).

So the idea is to come up with a function that returns different intensities
based on the alignment of the vertex normal and the _light vector_. (Observe
that the light vector is the vector from the surface to the light source; that
is, it is aimed in the opposite direction the light rays travel.) The function
should return maximum intensity when the vertex normal and light vector
are perfectly aligned (i.e., the angle θ between them is 0°), and it should
smoothly diminish in intensity as the angle between the vertex normal and
light vector increases. If $\theta > 90°$, then the light strikes the back of a surface
and so we set the intensity to 0. _Lambert's cosine law_ gives the function we
seek, which is given by

$$f(\theta) = \max(\cos\theta, 0) = \max(\mathbf{L} \cdot \mathbf{n}, 0)$$

where **L** and **n** are unit vectors. Figure 6.9 shows a plot of $f(\theta)$ to see how
the intensity, ranging from 0.0 to 1.0 (i.e., 0% to 100%), varies with θ.

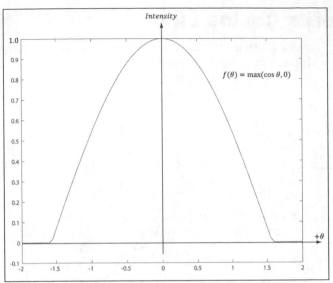

Figure 6.9: Plot of the function $f(\theta) = \max(\cos\theta, 0) = \max(\mathbf{L} \cdot \mathbf{n}, 0)$ for $-2 \le \theta \le 2$. Note that $\pi/2 \approx 1.57$.

6.4 Diffuse Lighting

Consider a rough surface, as in Figure 6.10. When light strikes a point on such a surface, the light rays scatter in various random directions; this is called a *diffuse reflection*. In our approximation for modeling this kind of light/surface interaction, we stipulate that the light scatters equally in all directions above the surface; consequently, the reflected light will reach the eye no matter the viewpoint (eye position). Therefore, we do not need to take the viewpoint into consideration (i.e., the diffuse lighting calculation is viewpoint independent), and the color of a point on the surface will always look the same no matter the viewpoint.

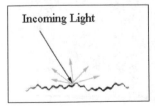

Figure 6.10: Incoming light scatters in random directions when striking a diffuse surface. The idea is that the surface is rough at a microscopic level.

We break the calculation of diffuse lighting into two parts. For the first part, we specify a diffuse light color and a diffuse material color. The diffuse material specifies the amount of incoming diffuse light that the surface reflects and absorbs; this is handled with a componentwise color multiplication. For example, suppose some point on a surface reflects 50% incoming red light, 100% green light, and 75% blue light, and the incoming light color is 80% intensity white light. Hence the incoming diffuse light color is given by $\mathbf{c}_D = (0.8, 0.8, 0.8)$ and the diffuse material color is given by $\mathbf{m}_D = (0.5, 1.0, 0.75)$; then the amount of light reflected off the point is given by:

$$\mathbf{c}_D \otimes \mathbf{m}_D = (0.8, 0.8, 0.8) \otimes (0.5, 1.0, 0.75) = (0.4, 0.8, 0.6)$$

Note: The diffuse material may vary over the surface; that is, different points on the surface may have different diffuse material values. For example, consider a terrain mix of sand, grass, dirt, and snow; each of these terrain components reflects and absorbs light differently, and so the material values would need to vary over the surface of the terrain. In our Direct3D lighting implementation, we handle this by specifying a diffuse material value per vertex. These per-vertex attributes are then interpolated across the triangle during rasterization. In this way, we obtain a diffuse material value for each point on the surface of the triangle mesh.

To finish the diffuse lighting calculation, we simply include Lambert's cosine law (which controls how much of the original light the surface receives based on the angle between the surface normal and light vector). Let $\mathbf{c}_D$ be the diffuse light color, $\mathbf{m}_D$ be the diffuse material color, and $k_D = \max(\mathbf{L} \cdot \mathbf{n}, 0)$, where $\mathbf{L}$ is the light vector and $\mathbf{n}$ is the surface normal. Then the amount of diffuse light reflected off a point is given by:

$$LitColor = k_D \cdot \mathbf{c}_D \otimes \mathbf{m}_D \tag{6.1}$$

6.5 **Ambient Lighting**

As stated earlier, our lighting model does not take into consideration indirect light that has bounced off other objects in the scenes. However, much of the light we see in the real world is indirect. For example, a hallway connected to a room might not be in the direct line of sight with a light source in the room, but the light bounces off the walls in the room and some of it may make it into the hallway, thereby lightening it up a bit. As a second example, suppose we are sitting in a room with a teapot on a desk and there is one light source in the room. Only one side of the teapot is in the direct line of sight of the light source; nevertheless, the back side of the teapot would not be pitch black. This is because some light scatters off the walls or other objects in the room and eventually strikes the back side of the teapot.

To sort of hack this indirect light, we introduce an ambient term to the lighting equation:

$$\mathbf{c}_A \otimes \mathbf{m}_A$$

The color c_A specifies the total amount of indirect (ambient) light a surface receives from a light source. The ambient material color m_A specifies the amount of incoming ambient light that the surface reflects and absorbs. All ambient light does is uniformly brighten up the object a bit — there is no real physics calculation at all. The idea is that the indirect light has scattered and bounced around the scene so many times that it strikes the object equally in every direction.

Note: In our implementation, we require that $m_A = m_D$; for example, if the surface reflects red diffuse light, then it also reflects red ambient light. Some other implementations allow m_A to be different from m_D for greater flexibility.

Combining the ambient term with the diffuse term, our new lighting equation looks like this:

$$LitColor = c_A \otimes m_A + k_D \cdot c_D \otimes m_D \qquad (6.2)$$

6.6 Specular Lighting

Consider a smooth surface, as shown in Figure 6.11. When light strikes such a surface, the light rays reflect sharply in a general direction through a *cone of reflectance*; this is called a *specular reflection*. In contrast to diffuse light, specular light might not travel into the eye because it reflects in a specific direction; the specular lighting calculation is viewpoint dependent. This means that as the position of the eye changes within the scene, the amount of specular light it receives will change.

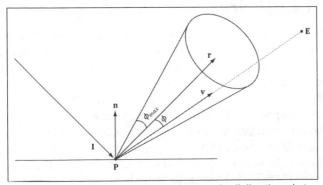

Figure 6.11: Specular reflections do not scatter in all directions, but instead reflect in a general cone of reflection whose size we can control with a parameter. If **v** is in the cone, the eye receives specular light; otherwise, it does not. The closer **v** is aligned with **r**, the more specular light the eye receives.

The cone the specular light reflects through is defined by an angle ϕ_{max} with respect to the reflection vector **r**. Intuitively, it makes sense to vary the specular light intensity based on the angle ϕ between the reflected vector **r** and the *view vector* $\mathbf{v} = \frac{\mathbf{E} - \mathbf{P}}{\|\mathbf{E} - \mathbf{P}\|}$ (i.e., the unit vector from the surface point **P** to the eye position **E**) in the following way: We stipulate that the specular light intensity is maximized when $\phi = 0$ and smoothly decreases to 0 as ϕ approaches ϕ_{max}. To model this mathematically, we modify the function used in Lambert's cosine law. Figure 6.12 shows the graph of the cosine function for different powers of $p \geq 1$ (i.e., $p = 1$, $p = 8$, and $p = 128$). Essentially, by choosing different values for p, we indirectly control the cone angle ϕ_{max} where the light intensity drops to 0. The parameter p can be used to control the shininess of a surface; that is, highly polished surfaces will have a smaller cone of reflectance (the light reflects more sharply) than less shiny surfaces. So you would use a larger p for shiny surfaces than you would for matte surfaces.

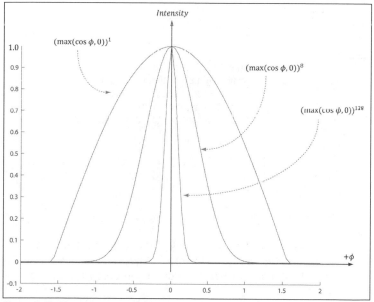

Figure 6.12: Plots of the cosine functions with different powers of $p \geq 1$.

We now define the specular term of our lighting model:

$$k_S \cdot \mathbf{c}_S \otimes \mathbf{m}_S$$

$$k_S = \begin{cases} (\max(\cos\phi, 0))^p, & \mathbf{L} \cdot \mathbf{n} > 0 \\ 0, & \mathbf{L} \cdot \mathbf{n} \leq 0 \end{cases} = \begin{cases} (\max(\mathbf{v} \cdot \mathbf{r}, 0))^p, & \mathbf{L} \cdot \mathbf{n} > 0 \\ 0, & \mathbf{L} \cdot \mathbf{n} \leq 0 \end{cases}$$

The color $\mathbf{c}_S$ specifies the amount of specular light the light source emits. The specular material color $\mathbf{m}_S$ specifies the amount of incoming specular light that the surface reflects and absorbs. The factor k_S scales the intensity of the specular light based on the angle between $\mathbf{r}$ and $\mathbf{v}$. Figure 6.14 shows it is possible for a surface to receive no diffuse light ($\mathbf{L} \cdot \mathbf{n} < 0$), but to receive specular light. However, if the surface receives no diffuse light, then it makes no sense for the surface to receive specular light, so we set $k_S = 0$ in this case.

Note: The specular power p should always be ≥ 1.

Our new lighting model is:

$$LitColor = \mathbf{c}_A \otimes \mathbf{m}_A + k_D \cdot \mathbf{c}_D \otimes \mathbf{m}_D + k_S \cdot \mathbf{c}_S \otimes \mathbf{m}_S \tag{6.3}$$

$$k_D = \max(\mathbf{L} \cdot \mathbf{n}, 0)$$

$$k_S = \begin{cases} (\max(\mathbf{v} \cdot \mathbf{r}, 0))^p, & \mathbf{L} \cdot \mathbf{n} > 0 \\ 0, & \mathbf{L} \cdot \mathbf{n} \leq 0 \end{cases}$$

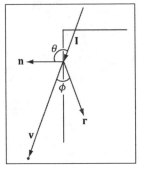

Figure 6.13: The eye can receive specular light even though the light strikes the back of a surface. This is incorrect, so we must detect this situation and set $k_S = 0$ in this case.

Note: The reflection vector is given by $\mathbf{r} = \mathbf{I} - 2(\mathbf{n} \cdot \mathbf{I})\mathbf{n}$ (see Figure 6.14). (It is assumed that $\mathbf{n}$ is a unit vector.) However, we can actually use the HLSL intrinsic `reflect` function to compute $\mathbf{r}$ for us in a shader program.

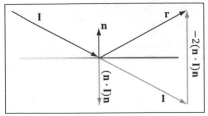

Figure 6.14: Geometry of reflection.

Observe that $\mathbf{I}$, the incident vector, is the direction of the incoming light (i.e., opposite direction of the light vector $\mathbf{L}$).

6.7 **Brief Recap**

In our model, a light source emits three different kinds of light:

- Ambient light: to model indirect lighting.
- Diffuse light: to model the direct lighting of relatively rough surfaces.
- Specular light: to model the direct lighting of relatively smooth surfaces.

Correspondingly, a surface point has the following material properties associated with it:

- Ambient material: the amount of ambient light the surface reflects and absorbs.
- Diffuse material: the amount of diffuse light the surface reflects and absorbs.
- Specular material: the amount of specular light the surface reflects and absorbs.
- Specular exponent: an exponent used in the specular lighting calculation, which controls the cone of reflectance and thus how shiny the surface is. The smaller the cone, the smoother/shinier the surface.

The reason for breaking lighting up into three components like this is for the flexibility; an artist has several degrees of freedom to tweak to obtain the desired output. Figure 6.15 shows how these three components work together.

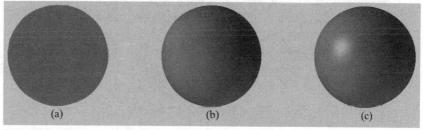

Figure 6.15: (a) Sphere colored with ambient light only, which uniformly brightens it. (b) Ambient and diffuse lighting combined. There is now a smooth transition from bright to dark due to Lambert's cosine law. (c) Ambient, diffuse, and specular lighting. The specular lighting yields a specular highlight.

As mentioned in the Note in §6.4, we define material values at the vertex level. These values are then linearly interpolated across the 3D triangle to obtain material values at each surface point of the triangle mesh. Our vertex structure looks like this:

```
struct Vertex
{
    D3DXVECTOR3 pos;
```

```
        D3DXVECTOR3 normal;
        D3DXCOLOR   diffuse;
        D3DXCOLOR   spec; // (r, g, b, specPower);
};

D3D10_INPUT_ELEMENT_DESC vertexDesc[] =
{
    {"POSITION", 0, DXGI_FORMAT_R32G32B32_FLOAT, 0,
        0, D3D10_INPUT_PER_VERTEX_DATA, 0},
    {"NORMAL", 0, DXGI_FORMAT_R32G32B32_FLOAT, 0,
        12, D3D10_INPUT_PER_VERTEX_DATA, 0},
    {"DIFFUSE", 0, DXGI_FORMAT_R32G32B32A32_FLOAT, 0,
        24, D3D10_INPUT_PER_VERTEX_DATA, 0},
    {"SPECULAR", 0, DXGI_FORMAT_R32G32B32A32_FLOAT, 0,
        40, D3D10_INPUT_PER_VERTEX_DATA, 0}
};
```

Recall that we have no ambient component because in our implementation we set $\mathbf{m}_A = \mathbf{m}_D$. Also, notice that we embed the specular power exponent p into the fourth component of the specular material color. This is because the alpha component is not needed for lighting, so we might as well use the empty slot to store something useful. The alpha component of the diffuse material will be used too — for alpha blending, as will be shown in a later chapter.

Note: In some cases, large groups of vertices will share the same material values (see Figure 6.16), so it is wasteful to duplicate them. It may be more memory efficient to remove the material values from the vertex structure, sort the scene geometry into batches by material, set the material values in a constant buffer, and render like this pseudocode:

```
Set material for batch 1 to constant buffer
Draw geometry in batch 1

Set material for batch 2 to constant buffer
Draw geometry in batch 2

...

Set material for batch n to constant buffer
Draw geometry in batch n
```

With this approach, the material information is fed into the shader programs through a constant buffer, rather than from the vertex data. However, this approach becomes inefficient if the batches are too small (there is some overhead in updating the constant buffer, as well as in Direct3D draw calls). A hybrid approach may be best: Use per-vertex materials when needed, and use constant buffer materials when they suffice. As always, you should customize the code based

on your specific application requirements and the required trade-off
between detail and speed.

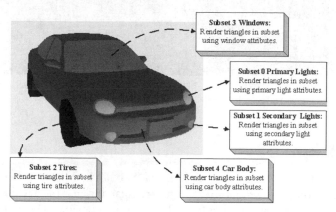

Figure 6.16: A car mesh divided into five material attribute groups.

Finally, we remind the reader that we need normal vectors at each point on
the surface of a triangle mesh so that we can determine the angle at which
light strikes a point on the mesh surface (for Lambert's cosine law). In
order to obtain a normal vector approximation at each point on the surface
of the triangle mesh, we specify normals at the vertex level. These vertex
normals will be interpolated across the triangle during rasterization.

Thus far we have discussed the components of light, but we have not
discussed specific kinds of light sources. The next three sections describe
how to implement parallel lights, point lights, and spotlights.

6.8 **Parallel Lights**

A parallel light (or directional light) approximates a light source that is very
far away. Consequently, we can approximate all incoming light rays from
this light as parallel to each other (see Figure 6.17). A parallel light source
is defined by a vector, which specifies the direction the light rays travel.
Because the light rays are parallel, they all use the same direction vector.
The light vector aims in the opposite direction the light rays travel. A common example of a real directional light source is the Sun (see Figure 6.18).

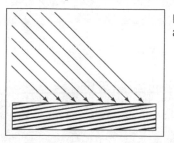

Figure 6.17: Parallel light rays striking
a surface.

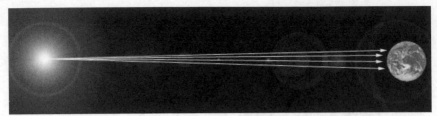

Figure 6.18: The figure is not drawn to scale, but if you select a small surface area on the Earth, the light rays from the Sun striking that area are approximately parallel.

6.9 **Point Lights**

A good physical example of a point light is a light bulb; it radiates spherically in all directions (see Figure 6.19). In particular, for an arbitrary point **P**, there exists a light ray originating from the point light position **Q** traveling toward the point. As usual, we define the light vector to go in the opposite direction; that is, the direction from point **P** to the point light source **Q**:

$$\mathbf{L} = \frac{\mathbf{Q} - \mathbf{P}}{\|\mathbf{Q} - \mathbf{P}\|}$$

Essentially, the only difference between point lights and parallel lights is how the light vector is computed — it varies from point to point for point lights, but remains constant for parallel lights.

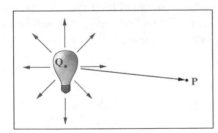

Figure 6.19: Point lights radiate in every direction; in particular, for an arbitrary point **P** there exists a light ray originating from the point source **Q** toward **P**.

6.9.1 **Attenuation**

Physically, light intensity weakens as a function of distance based on the inverse squared law. That is to say, the light intensity at a point a distance d away from the light source is given by:

$$I(d) = \frac{I_0}{d^2}$$

where I_0 is the light intensity at a distance $d = 1$ from the light source. However, this formula does not always give aesthetically pleasing results. Thus, instead of worrying about physical accuracy, we use a more general function that gives the artist/programmer some parameters to control (i.e., the artist/programmer experiments with different parameter values until he is satisfied with the result). The typical formula used to scale light intensity is:

$$I(d) = \frac{I_0}{a_0 + a_1 d + a_2 d^2}$$

We call a_0, a_1, and a_2 *attenuation parameters*, and they are to be supplied by the artist or programmer. For example, if you actually want the light intensity to weaken with the inverse distance, then set $a_0 = 0$, $a_1 = 1$, and $a_2 = 0$. If you want the actual inverse square law, then set $a_0 = 0$, $a_1 = 0$, and $a_2 = 1$.

Incorporating attenuation into the lighting equation, we get:

$$LitColor = \frac{\mathbf{c}_A \otimes \mathbf{m}_A + k_D \cdot \mathbf{c}_D \otimes \mathbf{m}_D + k_S \cdot \mathbf{c}_S \otimes \mathbf{m}_S}{a_0 + a_1 d + a_2 d^2} \qquad (6.4)$$

$$k_D = \max(\mathbf{L} \cdot \mathbf{n}, 0)$$

$$k_S = \begin{cases} (\max(\mathbf{v} \cdot \mathbf{r}, 0))^p, & \mathbf{L} \cdot \mathbf{n} > 0 \\ 0, & \mathbf{L} \cdot \mathbf{n} \leq 0 \end{cases}$$

6.9.2 Range

For point lights, we include an additional *range* parameter (see §6.11.1 and §6.11.3). A point whose distance from the light source is greater than the range does not receive any light from that light source. This parameter is useful for localizing a light to a particular area. Even though the attenuation parameters weaken the light intensity with distance, it is still useful to be able to explicitly define the max range of the light source. The range parameter is also useful for shader optimization. As we will soon see in our shader code, if the point is out of range, then we can return early and skip the lighting calculations with dynamic branching. The range parameter does not affect parallel lights, which model light sources very far away.

6.10 Spotlights

A good physical example of a spotlight is a flashlight. Essentially, a spotlight has a position $\mathbf{Q}$, is aimed in a direction $\mathbf{d}$, and radiates light through a cone (see Figure 6.20).

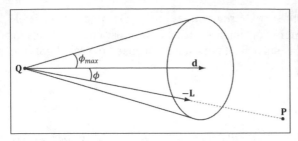

Figure 6.20: A spotlight has a position **Q**, is aimed in a direction **d**, and radiates light through a cone with angle ϕ_{max}.

To implement a spotlight, we begin as we do with a point light. The light vector is given by:

$$\mathbf{L} = \frac{\mathbf{Q} - \mathbf{P}}{\|\mathbf{Q} - \mathbf{P}\|}$$

where **P** is the position of the point being lit and **Q** is the position of the spotlight. Observe from Figure 6.20 that **P** is inside the spotlight's cone (and therefore receives light) if and only if the angle ϕ between $-\mathbf{L}$ and **d** is smaller than the cone angle ϕ_{max}. Moreover, all the light in the spotlight's cone should not be of equal intensity; the light at the center of the cone should be the most intense and the light intensity should fade to 0 (zero) as ϕ increases from 0 to ϕ_{max}.

So how do we control the intensity falloff as a function of ϕ, and how do we control the size of the spotlight's cone? Well, we can play the same game we did with the specular cone of reflectance. That is, we use the function:

$$k_{spot}(\phi) = \left(\max(\cos\phi, 0)\right)^{S} = \left(\max(-\mathbf{L} \cdot \mathbf{d}, 0)\right)^{S}$$

Refer back to Figure 6.12 for the graph of this function. As you can see, the intensity smoothly fades as ϕ increases, which is one of the characteristics we want; additionally, by altering the exponent s, we can indirectly control ϕ_{max} (the angle the intensity drops to 0); that is to say, we can shrink or expand the spotlight cone by varying s. For example, if we set $s = 8$, the cone has approximately a 45° half angle.

So the spotlight equation is just like the point light equation, except that we multiply by the spotlight factor to scale the light intensity based on where the point is with respect to the spotlight cone:

$$LitColor = k_{spot} \cdot \frac{\mathbf{c}_A \otimes \mathbf{m}_A + k_D \cdot \mathbf{c}_D \otimes \mathbf{m}_D + k_S \cdot \mathbf{c}_S \otimes \mathbf{m}_S}{a_0 + a_1 d + a_2 d^2} \qquad (6.5)$$

$$k_D = \max(\mathbf{L} \cdot \mathbf{n}, 0)$$

$$k_S = \begin{cases} \left(\max(\mathbf{v} \cdot \mathbf{r}, 0)\right)^{p}, & \mathbf{L} \cdot \mathbf{n} > 0 \\ 0, & \mathbf{L} \cdot \mathbf{n} \leq 0 \end{cases}$$

$$k_{spot} = \left(\max(-\mathbf{L} \cdot \mathbf{d}, 0)\right)^S$$

6.11 **Implementation**

6.11.1 **Lighting Structures**

In an effect file, we define the following `Light` structure to represent either a parallel light, a point light, or a spotlight. Not all the members are used for each light.

```
struct Light
{
    float3 pos;
    float3 dir;
    float4 ambient;
    float4 diffuse;
    float4 spec;
    float3 att; // attenuation parameters (a0, a1, a2)
    float  spotPower;
    float  range;
};
```

- `pos`: The position of the light (ignored for directional lights).
- `dir`: The direction of the light (ignored for point lights).
- `ambient`: The amount of ambient light emitted by the light source.
- `diffuse`: The amount of diffuse light emitted by the light source.
- `spec`: The amount of specular light emitted by the light source.
- `att`: Stores the three attenuation constants in the format (a_0, a_1, a_2). Attenuation constants are only applied to point lights and spotlights.
- `spotPower`: The exponent used in the spotlight calculation to control the spotlight cone; this value only applies to spotlights.
- `range`: The range of the light (ignored for directional lights).

This next structure (also defined in an effect file) stores the information at a surface point needed to light that point; that is, it stores the surface point itself, its normal, and the diffuse and specular material values at that point. At the moment, it matches our vertex structure (§6.7); however, our vertex structure is subject to change, but `SurfaceInfo` will not.

```
struct SurfaceInfo
{
    float3 pos;
    float3 normal;
    float4 diffuse;
    float4 spec;
};
```

6.11.2 **Implementing Parallel Lights**

The following HLSL function outputs the lit surface color of Equation 6.3 given a parallel light source, the position of the eye, and the surface point information.

```
float3 ParallelLight(SurfaceInfo v, Light L, float3 eyePos)
{
    float3 litColor = float3(0.0f, 0.0f, 0.0f);

    // The light vector aims opposite the direction the light rays travel.
    float3 lightVec = -L.dir;

    // Add the ambient term.
    litColor += v.diffuse * L.ambient;

    // Add diffuse and specular term, provided the surface is in
    // the line of sight of the light.

    float diffuseFactor = dot(lightVec, v.normal);
    [branch]
    if( diffuseFactor > 0.0f )
    {
        float specPower  = max(v.spec.a, 1.0f);
        float3 toEye     = normalize(eyePos - v.pos);
        float3 R         = reflect(-lightVec, v.normal);
        float specFactor = pow(max(dot(R, toEye), 0.0f), specPower);

        // diffuse and specular terms
        litColor += diffuseFactor * v.diffuse * L.diffuse;
        litColor += specFactor * v.spec * L.spec;
    }

    return litColor;
}
```

This code breaks Equation 6.3 down over several lines. The following intrinsic HLSL functions were used: dot, normalize, reflect, pow, and max, which are, respectively, the vector dot product function, vector normalization function, vector reflection function, power function, and maximum function. Descriptions of most of the HLSL intrinsic functions can be found in Appendix B, along with a quick primer on other HLSL syntax. One thing to note, however, is that when two vectors are multiplied with operator*, the multiplication is done componentwise.

6.11.3 **Implementing Point Lights**

The following HLSL function outputs the lit color of Equation 6.4 given a point light source, the position of the eye, and the surface point information.

```
float3 PointLight(SurfaceInfo v, Light L, float3 eyePos)
{
    float3 litColor = float3(0.0f, 0.0f, 0.0f);

    // The vector from the surface to the light.
    float3 lightVec = L.pos - v.pos;

    // The distance from surface to light.
    float d = length(lightVec);

    if( d > L.range )
        return float3(0.0f, 0.0f, 0.0f);

    // Normalize the light vector.
    lightVec /= d;

    // Add the ambient light term.
    litColor += v.diffuse * L.ambient;

    // Add diffuse and specular term, provided the surface is in
    // the line of sight of the light.

    float diffuseFactor = dot(lightVec, v.normal);
    [branch]
    if( diffuseFactor > 0.0f )
    {
        float specPower  = max(v.spec.a, 1.0f);
        float3 toEye     = normalize(eyePos - v.pos);
        float3 R         = reflect(-lightVec, v.normal);
        float specFactor = pow(max(dot(R, toEye), 0.0f), specPower);

        // diffuse and specular terms
        litColor += diffuseFactor * v.diffuse * L.diffuse;
        litColor += specFactor * v.spec * L.spec;
    }

    // attenuate
    return litColor / dot(L.att, float3(1.0f, d, d*d));
}
```

6.11.4 Implementing Spotlights

The following HLSL function outputs the lit color of Equation 6.5 given a spotlight source, the position of the eye, and the surface point information.

```
float3 Spotlight(SurfaceInfo v, Light L, float3 eyePos)
{
    float3 litColor = PointLight(v, L, eyePos);

    // The vector from the surface to the light.
    float3 lightVec = normalize(L.pos - v.pos);

    float s = pow(max(dot(-lightVec, L.dir), 0.0f), L.spotPower);
```

```
    // Scale color by spotlight factor.
    return litColor*s;
}
```

Observe that a spotlight works just like a point light except that it is scaled based on where the surface point is with respect to the spotlight cone.

6.12 Lighting Demo

In our Lighting demo, we will have one light source active at a time. However, the user can change the active light by pressing one of the following keys: 1 (for parallel light), 2 (for point light), or 3 (for spotlight). The directional light remains fixed, but the point light and spotlight animate. The Lighting demo builds off the Waves demo from the previous chapter and uses the PeaksAndValleys class to draw a land mass, and the Waves class to draw a water mass. The effect file is given in §6.12.1, which makes use of the structures and functions defined in §6.11.

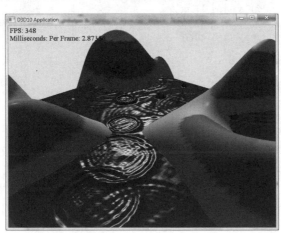

Figure 6.21: Screenshot of the Lighting demo.

6.12.1 Effect File

```
//===========================================================================
// lighting.fx by Frank Luna (C) 2008 All Rights Reserved.
//
// Transforms and lights geometry.
//===========================================================================

#include "lighthelper.fx"

cbuffer cbPerFrame
{
    Light gLight;
    int gLightType;
```

```
        float3 gEyePosW;
};

cbuffer cbPerObject
{
    float4x4 gWorld;
    float4x4 gWVP;
};

struct VS_IN
{
    float3 posL    : POSITION;
    float3 normalL : NORMAL;
    float4 diffuse : DIFFUSE;
    float4 spec    : SPECULAR;
};

struct VS_OUT
{
    float4 posH    : SV_POSITION;
    float3 posW    : POSITION;
    float3 normalW : NORMAL;
    float4 diffuse : DIFFUSE;
    float4 spec    : SPECULAR;
};

VS_OUT VS(VS_IN vIn)
{
    VS_OUT vOut;

    // Transform to world space.
    vOut.posW    = mul(float4(vIn.posL, 1.0f), gWorld);
    vOut.normalW = mul(float4(vIn.normalL, 0.0f), gWorld);

    // Transform to homogeneous clip space.
    vOut.posH = mul(float4(vIn.posL, 1.0f), gWVP);

    // Output vertex attributes for interpolation across triangle.
    vOut.diffuse = vIn.diffuse;
    vOut.spec    = vIn.spec;

    return vOut;
}

float4 PS(VS_OUT pIn) : SV_Target
{
    // Interpolating normal can make it not be of unit length so
    // normalize it.
    pIn.normalW = normalize(pIn.normalW);

    SurfaceInfo v = {pIn.posW, pIn.normalW, pIn.diffuse, pIn.spec};

    float3 litColor;
```

```
    if( gLightType == 0 ) // Parallel
    {
        litColor = ParallelLight(v, gLight, gEyePosW);
    }
    else if( gLightType == 1 ) // Point
    {
        litColor = PointLight(v, gLight, gEyePosW);
    }
    else // Spot
    {
        litColor = Spotlight(v, gLight, gEyePosW);
    }

    return float4(litColor, pIn.diffuse.a);
}

technique10 LightTech
{
    pass P0
    {
        SetVertexShader( CompileShader( vs_4_0, VS() ) );
        SetGeometryShader( NULL );
        SetPixelShader( CompileShader( ps_4_0, PS() ) );
    }
}
```

6.12.2 Structure Packing

The preceding effect file has a constant buffer with a Light instance. We would like to be able to set this value with one function call. Therefore, in the C++ code we define a structure very similar to the HLSL Light structure:

```
struct Light
{
    Light()
    {
        ZeroMemory(this, sizeof(Light));
    }

    D3DXVECTOR3 pos;
    float pad1;        // not used
    D3DXVECTOR3 dir;
    float pad2;        // not used
    D3DXCOLOR ambient;
    D3DXCOLOR diffuse;
    D3DXCOLOR specular;
    D3DXVECTOR3 att;
    float spotPow;
    float range;
};
```

The issue with the "pad" variables is to make the C++ structure match the HLSL structure. In the HLSL, structure padding occurs so that elements are packed into 4D vectors, with the restriction that a single element cannot be split across two 4D vectors. Consider the following example:

```
struct S
{
    float3 pos;
    float3 dir;
};
```

If we have to pack the data into 4D vectors, you might think it is done like this:

```
vector 1: (pos.x, pos.y, pos.z, dir.x)
vector 2: (dir.y, dir.z, empty, empty)
```

However, this splits the element dir across two 4D vectors, which is not allowed — an element is not allowed to straddle a 4D vector boundary. Therefore, it has to be packed like this:

```
vector 1: (pos.x, pos.y, pos.z, empty)
vector 2: (dir.x, dir.y, dir.z, empty)
```

Thus, the "pad" variables in our C++ structure are able to correspond to those empty slots in the padded HLSL structure (since C++ does not follow the same packing rules as HLSL).

If we have a structure like this:

```
struct S
{
    float3 v;
    float  s;
    float2 p;
    float3 q;
};
```

The structure would be padded and the data will be packed into three 4D vectors like so:

```
vector 1: (v.x, v.y, v.z, s)
vector 2: (p.x, p.y, empty, empty)
vector 3: (q.x, q.y, q.z, empty)
```

And a final example, the structure:

```
struct S
{
    float2 u;
    float2 v;
    float a0;
    float a1;
    float a2;
};
```

would be padded and packed like so:

```
vector 1: (u.x, u.y, v.x, v.y)
vector 2: (a0, a1, a2, empty)
```

6.12.3 C++ Application Code

In the application class, we have an array of three Lights, and also an integer that identifies the currently selected light by indexing into the light array:

```
Light mLights[3];
int mLightType; // 0 (parallel), 1 (point), 2 (spot)
```

They are initialized in the initApp method:

```
void LightingApp::initApp()
{
    D3DApp::initApp();

    mClearColor = D3DXCOLOR(0.9f, 0.9f, 0.9f, 1.0f);

    mLand.init(md3dDevice, 129, 129, 1.0f);
    mWaves.init(md3dDevice, 201, 201, 0.5f, 0.03f, 4.0f, 0.4f);


    buildFX();
    buildVertexLayouts();

    mLightType = 0;

    // Parallel light.
    mLights[0].dir      = D3DXVECTOR3(0.57735f, -0.57735f, 0.57735f);
    mLights[0].ambient  = D3DXCOLOR(0.2f, 0.2f, 0.2f, 1.0f);
    mLights[0].diffuse  = D3DXCOLOR(1.0f, 1.0f, 1.0f, 1.0f);
    mLights[0].specular = D3DXCOLOR(1.0f, 1.0f, 1.0f, 1.0f);

    // Point light--position is changed every frame to animate.
    mLights[1].ambient  = D3DXCOLOR(0.4f, 0.4f, 0.4f, 1.0f);
    mLights[1].diffuse  = D3DXCOLOR(1.0f, 1.0f, 1.0f, 1.0f);
    mLights[1].specular = D3DXCOLOR(1.0f, 1.0f, 1.0f, 1.0f);
    mLights[1].att.x    = 0.0f;
    mLights[1].att.y    = 0.1f;
    mLights[1].att.z    = 0.0f;
    mLights[1].range    = 50.0f;

    // Spotlight--position and direction changed every frame to animate.
    mLights[2].ambient  = D3DXCOLOR(0.4f, 0.4f, 0.4f, 1.0f);
    mLights[2].diffuse  = D3DXCOLOR(1.0f, 1.0f, 1.0f, 1.0f);
    mLights[2].specular = D3DXCOLOR(1.0f, 1.0f, 1.0f, 1.0f);
    mLights[2].att.x    = 1.0f;
    mLights[2].att.y    = 0.0f;
    mLights[2].att.z    = 0.0f;
```

```
    mLights[2].spotPow   = 64.0f;
    mLights[2].range     = 10000.0f;
}
```

As mentioned, the point light and spotlight are animated; this is done in the updateScene method:

```
void LightingApp::updateScene(float dt)
{
    /* ...Irrelevant code omitted... */

    // Set the light type based on user input.
    if(GetAsyncKeyState('1') & 0x8000)   mLightType = 0;
    if(GetAsyncKeyState('2') & 0x8000)   mLightType = 1;
    if(GetAsyncKeyState('3') & 0x8000)   mLightType = 2;

    // The point light circles the scene as a function of time,
    // staying 7 units above the land's or water's surface.
    mLights[1].pos.x = 50.0f*cosf( mTimer.getGameTime() );
    mLights[1].pos.z = 50.0f*sinf( mTimer.getGameTime() );
    mLights[1].pos.y = Max(mLand.getHeight(
        mLights[1].pos.x, mLights[1].pos.z), 0.0f) + 7.0f;


    // The spotlight takes on the camera position and is aimed in the
    // same direction the camera is looking. In this way, it looks
    // like we are holding a flashlight.
    mLights[2].pos - mEyePos;
    D3DXVec3Normalize(&mLights[2].dir, &(target-mEyePos));
}
```

The point light basically follows a circular trajectory in the *xz*-plane, but always travels above the land or water. The spotlight is positioned at the eye and is aimed in the same direction the eye looks; this makes it look like the viewer is holding the light like a flashlight.

Finally, the selected light is set to the effect before rendering:

```
void LightingApp::drawScene()
{
    /* ...Irrelevant code omitted... */

    // Set per frame constants.
    // ID3D10EffectVariable* mfxEyePosVar;
    // ID3D10EffectVariable* mfxLightVar;
    // ID3D10EffectScalarVariable* mfxLightType;
    mfxEyePosVar->SetRawValue(&mEyePos, 0, sizeof(D3DXVECTOR3));
    mfxLightVar->SetRawValue(&mLights[mLightType], 0, sizeof(Light));
    mfxLightType->SetInt(mLightType);

    /* ...Render the scene code omitted... */
}
```

6.12.4 **Normal Computation**

Because our terrain surface is given by a function $y = f(x, z)$, we can compute the normal vectors directly using calculus, rather than the normal averaging technique described in §6.2.1. To do this, for each point on the surface, we form two tangent vectors in the $+x$ and $+z$ directions by taking the partial derivatives:

$$\mathbf{T}_x = \left(1, \frac{\partial f}{\partial x}, 0\right)$$

$$\mathbf{T}_z = \left(0, \frac{\partial f}{\partial z}, 1\right)$$

These two vectors lie in the tangent plane of the surface point. Taking the cross product then gives the normal vector:

$$\mathbf{n} = \mathbf{T}_z \times \mathbf{T}_x = \left(-\frac{\partial f}{\partial x}, 1, -\frac{\partial f}{\partial z}\right)$$

The function we use to generate the land mesh is:

$$f(x, z) = 0.3z \cdot \sin(0.1x) + 0.3x \cdot \cos(0.1z)$$

The partial derivatives are:

$$\frac{\partial f}{\partial x} = 0.03z \cdot \cos(0.1x) + 0.3\cos(0.1z)$$

$$\frac{\partial f}{\partial z} = 0.3\sin(0.1x) - 0.03x \cdot \sin(0.1z)$$

The surface normal at a surface point $(x, f(x, z), z)$ is thus given by:

$$\mathbf{n}(x, z) = \begin{bmatrix} -0.03z \cdot \cos(0.1x) - 0.3\cos(0.1z) \\ 1 \\ -0.3\sin(0.1x) + 0.03x \cdot \sin(0.1z) \end{bmatrix}$$

We note that this surface normal is not of unit length, so it needs to be normalized before performing the lighting calculations.

In particular, we do the above normal calculation at each vertex point to get the vertex normals:

```
D3DXVECTOR3 normal;
normal.x = -0.03f*z*cosf(0.1f*x) - 0.3f*cosf(0.1f*z);
normal.y = 1.0f;
normal.z = -0.3f*sinf(0.1f*x) + 0.03f*x*sinf(0.1f*z);
D3DXVec3Normalize(&vertices[i*n+j].normal, &normal);
```

The normal vectors for the water surface are done in a similar way, except that we do not have a formula for the water. However, tangent vectors at each vertex point can be approximated using a finite difference scheme (see [Lengyel02] or any numerical analysis book).

Note: If your calculus is rusty, don't worry; it will not play a major role in this book. Right now it is useful because we are using mathematical surfaces to generate our geometry so that we have some interesting objects to draw. Eventually, we will load 3D meshes from files that were exported from 3D modeling programs.

6.13 **Summary**

- With lighting, we no longer specify per-vertex colors but instead define scene lights and per-vertex materials. Materials can be thought of as the properties that determine how light interacts with a surface of an object. The per-vertex materials are interpolated across the face of the triangle to obtain material values at each surface point of the triangle mesh. The lighting equations then compute a surface color the eye sees based on the interaction between the light and surface materials; other parameters are also involved, such as the surface normal and eye position.

- A _surface normal_ is a unit vector that is orthogonal to the tangent plane of a point on a surface. Surface normals determine the direction a point on a surface is "facing." For lighting calculations, we need the surface normal at each point on the surface of a triangle mesh so that we can determine the angle at which light strikes the point on the mesh surface. To obtain surface normals, we specify the surface normals only at the vertex points (so-called _vertex normals_). Then, in order to obtain a surface normal approximation at each point on the surface of a triangle mesh, these vertex normals will be interpolated across the triangle during rasterization. For arbitrary triangle meshes, vertex normals are typically approximated via a technique called normal averaging. If the matrix $\mathbf{A}$ is used to transform points and vectors (non-normal vectors), then $(\mathbf{A}^{-1})^T$ should be used to transform surface normals.

- A parallel (directional) light approximates a light source that is very far away. Consequently, we can approximate all incoming light rays as parallel to each other. A physical example of a directional light is the Sun relative to the Earth. A point light emits light in _every_ direction. A physical example of a point light is a light bulb. A spotlight emits light through a cone. A physical example of a spotlight is a flashlight.

■ Ambient light models indirect light that has scattered and bounced around the scene so many times that it strikes the object equally in every direction, thereby uniformly brightening it up. Diffuse light travels in a particular direction, and when it strikes a surface, it reflects equally in all directions. Diffuse light should be used to model rough and or matte surfaces. Specular light travels in a particular direction, and when it strikes a surface, it reflects sharply in one general direction, thereby causing a bright shine that can only be seen at some angles. Specular light should be used to model smooth and polished surfaces.

6.14 **Exercises**

1. Modify the Lighting demo of this chapter so that the directional light only emits red light, the point light only emits green light, and the spot-light only emits blue light. Colored lights can be useful for different game moods; for example, a red light might be used to signify emergency situations.

2. Modify the Lighting demo of this chapter by changing the specular power material component, which controls the "shininess" of the surface. Try $p = 8, p = 32, p = 64, p = 128, p = 256,$ and $p = 512$.

3. One characteristic of "toon" lighting (cartoon styled lighting) is the abrupt transition from one color shade to the next (in contrast with a smooth transition) as shown in Figure 6.22. This can be implemented by computing k_d and k_s in the usual way (Equation 6.5), but then transforming them by discrete functions like the following before using them in the pixel shader:

$$k_d' = f(k_d) = \begin{cases} 0.4 & \text{if} -\infty < k_d \leq 0.0 \\ 0.6 & \text{if } 0.0 < k_d \leq 0.5 \\ 1.0 & \text{if } 0.5 < k_d \leq 1.0 \end{cases}$$

$$k_s' = g(k_s) = \begin{cases} 0.0 & \text{if } 0.0 \leq k_s \leq 0.1 \\ 0.5 & \text{if } 0.1 < k_s \leq 0.8 \\ 0.8 & \text{if } 0.8 < k_s \leq 1.0 \end{cases}$$

Modify the Lighting demo of this chapter to use this sort of toon shading. (Note: The functions f and g above are just sample functions to start with, and can be tweaked until you get the results you want.)

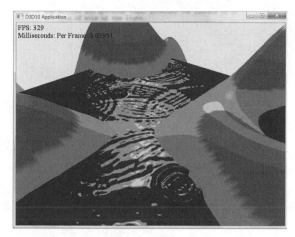

Figure 6.22: Screenshot of the toon shader.

4. Modify the Lighting demo of this chapter to use one point light and one spotlight. Note that light is just summed together; that is, if c_1 is the lit color of a surface point from one light source and c_2 is the lit color of a surface point from another light source, the total lit color of the surface point is $c_1 + c_2$.

5. Modify the Lighting demo of this chapter so that the angle of the spotlight's cone can be increased or decreased based on the user's keyboard input.

Chapter 7

Texturing

Our demos are getting a little more interesting, but real-world objects typically have more details than per-vertex colors can capture. *Texture mapping* is a technique that allows us to map image data onto a triangle, thereby enabling us to increase the details and realism of our scene significantly. For instance, we can build a cube and turn it into a crate by mapping a crate texture on each side (see Figure 7.1).

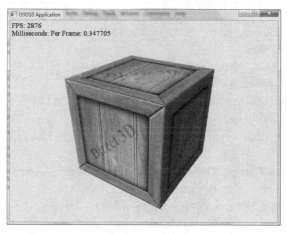

Figure 7.1: The Crate demo creates a cube with a crate texture.

Objectives:

- To learn how to specify the part of a texture that gets mapped to a triangle.
- To find out how to create and enable textures.
- To learn how textures can be filtered to create a smoother image.
- To discover how to tile a texture several times with address modes.
- To find out how multiple textures can be combined to create new textures and special effects.
- To learn how to create some basic effects via texture animation.

7.1 **Texture and Resource Recap**

Recall that we learned about and have been using textures since Chapter 4; in particular, that the depth buffer and back buffer are 2D texture objects represented by the ID3D10Texture2D interface. For easy reference, in this first section we review much of the material on textures we have already covered in Chapter 4.

A 2D texture is a matrix of data elements. One use for 2D textures is to store 2D image data, where each element in the texture stores the color of a pixel. However, this is not the only usage; for example, in an advanced technique called *normal mapping*, each element in the texture stores a 3D vector instead of a color. Therefore, although it is common to think of textures as storing image data, they are really more general-purpose than that. A 1D texture (ID3D10Texture1D) is like a 1D array of data elements, and a 3D texture (ID3D10Texture3D) is like a 3D array of data elements. The 1D, 2D, and 3D texture interfaces all inherit from ID3D10Resource.

As will be discussed later in this chapter, textures are more than just arrays of data; they can have mipmap levels, and the GPU can do special operations on them, such as applying filters and multisampling. However, textures are not arbitrary chunks of data; they can only store certain kinds of data formats, which are described by the DXGI_FORMAT enumerated type. Some example formats are:

- DXGI_FORMAT_R32G32B32_FLOAT: Each element has three 32-bit floating-point components.
- DXGI_FORMAT_R16G16B16A16_UNORM: Each element has four 16-bit components mapped to the [0, 1] range.
- DXGI_FORMAT_R32G32_UINT: Each element has two 32-bit unsigned integer components.
- DXGI_FORMAT_R8G8B8A8_UNORM: Each element has four 8-bit unsigned components mapped to the [0, 1] range.
- DXGI_FORMAT_R8G8B8A8_SNORM: Each element has four 8-bit signed components mapped to the [–1, 1] range.
- DXGI_FORMAT_R8G8B8A8_SINT: Each element has four 8-bit signed integer components mapped to the [–128, 127] range.
- DXGI_FORMAT_R8G8B8A8_UINT: Each element has four 8-bit unsigned integer components mapped to the [0, 255] range.

Note that the R, G, B, A letters stand for red, green, blue, and alpha, respectively. However, as we said earlier, textures need not store color information; for example, the format

```
DXGI_FORMAT_R32G32B32_FLOAT
```

has three floating-point components and can therefore store a 3D vector with floating-point coordinates (not necessarily a color vector). There are also *typeless* formats, where we just reserve memory and then specify how to reinterpret the data at a later time (sort of like a cast) when the texture is bound to the rendering pipeline. For example, the following typeless format reserves elements with four 8-bit components, but does not specify the data type (e.g., integer, floating-point, unsigned integer):

```
DXGI_FORMAT_R8G8B8A8_TYPELESS
```

A texture can be bound to different stages of the rendering pipeline; a common example is to use a texture as a render target (i.e., Direct3D draws into the texture) and as a shader resource (i.e., the texture will be sampled in a shader). A texture resource created for these two purposes would be given the bind flags:

```
D3D10_BIND_RENDER_TARGET | D3D10_BIND_SHADER_RESOURCE
```

indicating the two pipeline stages the texture will be bound to. Actually, resources are not directly bound to a pipeline stage; instead their associated resource views are bound to different pipeline stages. For each way we are going to use a texture, Direct3D requires that we create a *resource view* of that texture at initialization time. This is mostly for efficiency, as the SDK documentation points out: "This allows validation and mapping in the runtime and driver to occur at view creation, minimizing type checking at bind time." So for the example of using a texture as a render target and shader resource, we would need to create two views: a render target view (ID3D10RenderTargetView) and a shader resource view (ID3D10ShaderResource-View). Resource views essentially do two things: They tell Direct3D how the resource will be used (i.e., what stage of the pipeline you will bind it to), and if the resource format was specified as typeless at creation time, then we must now state the type when creating a view. Thus, with typeless for mats, it is possible for the elements of a texture to be viewed as floating-point values in one pipeline stage and as integers in another.

Note: The August 2008 SDK documentation says: "Creating a fully-typed resource restricts the resource to the format it was created with. This enables the runtime to optimize access [...]." Therefore, you should only create a typeless resource if you really need it; otherwise, create a fully typed resource.

In order to create a specific view to a resource, the resource must be created with that specific bind flag. For instance, if the resource was not created with the D3D10_BIND_SHADER_RESOURCE bind flag (which indicates the texture will be bound to the pipeline as a depth/stencil buffer), then we cannot create an ID3D10ShaderResourceView to that resource. If you try, you'll likely get a Direct3D debug error like the following:

```
D3D10: ERROR: ID3D10Device::CreateShaderResourceView: A ShaderResourceView
cannot be created of a Resource that did not specify the D3D10_BIND_
SHADER_RESOURCE BindFlag.
```

In this chapter, we will only be interested in binding textures as shader resources so that our pixel shaders can sample the textures and use them to color pixels.

7.2 **Texture Coordinates**

Direct3D uses a texture coordinate system that consists of a u-axis that runs horizontally to the image and a v-axis that runs vertically to the image. The coordinates, (u, v) such that $0 \le u, v \le 1$, identify an element on the texture called a *texel*. Notice that the v-axis is positive in the "down" direction (see Figure 7.2). Also, notice the normalized coordinate interval, [0, 1], which is used because it gives Direct3D a dimension-independent range to work with; for example, (0.5, 0.5) always specifies the middle texel no matter if the actual texture dimension is 256×256, 512×1024, or 2048×2048 in pixels. Likewise, (0.25, 0.75) identifies the texel a quarter of the total width in the horizontal direction, and three-quarters of the total height in the vertical direction. For now, texture coordinates are always in the range [0, 1], but later we explain what can happen when you go outside this range.

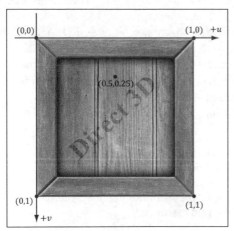

Figure 7.2: The texture coordinate system, sometimes called texture space.

For each 3D triangle, we want to define a corresponding triangle on the texture that is to be mapped onto the 3D triangle (see Figure 7.3).

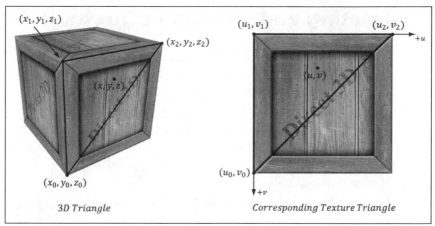

Figure 7.3: On the left is a triangle in 3D space, and on the right we define a 2D triangle on the texture that is going to be mapped onto the 3D triangle. For an arbitrary point (x, y, z) on the 3D triangle, its texture coordinates (u, v) are found by linearly interpolating the vertex texture coordinates across the 3D triangle. In this way, every point on the triangle has a corresponding texture coordinate.

To do this, we modify our vertex structure once again and add a pair of texture coordinates that identify a point on the texture. So now every 3D point has a corresponding 2D texture point. Thus, every 3D triangle defined by three vertices also defines a 2D triangle in texture space (i.e., we have associated a 2D texture triangle for every 3D triangle).

```
struct Vertex
{
    D3DXVECTOR3 pos;
    D3DXVECTOR3 normal;
    D3DXVECTOR2 texC;
};

D3D10_INPUT_ELEMENT_DESC vertexDesc[] =
{
    {"POSITION", 0, DXGI_FORMAT_R32G32B32_FLOAT, 0, 0,
        D3D10_INPUT_PER_VERTEX_DATA, 0},
    {"NORMAL", 0, DXGI_FORMAT_R32G32B32_FLOAT, 0, 12,
        D3D10_INPUT_PER_VERTEX_DATA, 0},
    {"TEXCOORD", 0, DXGI_FORMAT_R32G32_FLOAT, 0, 24,
        D3D10_INPUT_PER_VERTEX_DATA, 0},
};
```

7.3 **Creating and Enabling a Texture**

Texture data is usually read from an image file stored on disk and loaded into an ID3D10Texture2D object (see D3DX10CreateTextureFromFile). However, texture resources are not bound directly to the rendering pipeline; instead, you create a shader resource view (ID3D10ShaderResourceView) to the texture, and then bind the view to the pipeline. So two steps need to be taken:

1. Call D3DX10CreateTextureFromFile to create the ID3D10Texture2D object from an image file stored on disk.

2. Call ID3D10Device::CreateShaderResourceView to create the corresponding shader resource view to the texture.

Both of these steps can be done at once with the following D3DX function:

```
HRESULT D3DX10CreateShaderResourceViewFromFile(
    ID3D10Device *pDevice,
    LPCTSTR pSrcFile,
    D3DX10_IMAGE_LOAD_INFO *pLoadInfo,
    ID3DX10ThreadPump *pPump,
    ID3D10ShaderResourceView **ppShaderResourceView,
    HRESULT *pHResult
);
```

■   pDevice: Pointer to the D3D device to create the texture with.

■   pSrcFile: Filename of the image to load.

■   pLoadInfo: Optional image info; specify null to use the information from the source image. For example, if we specify null here, then the source image dimensions will be used as the texture dimensions; also a full mipmap chain will be generated (§7.4.2). This is usually what we always want and a good default choice.

■   pPump: Used to spawn a new thread for loading the resource. To load the resource in the working thread, specify null. In this book, we will always specify null.

■   ppShaderResourceView: Returns a pointer to the created shader resource view of the texture loaded from file.

■   pHResult: Specify null if null was specified for pPump.

This function can load any of the following image formats: BMP, JPG, PNG, DDS, TIFF, GIF, and WMP (see D3DX10_IMAGE_FILE_FORMAT).

Note: Sometimes we will refer to a texture and its corresponding shader resource view interchangeably. For example, we might say we are binding the texture to the pipeline, even though we are really binding its view.

For example, to create a texture from an image called *WoodCrate01.dds*, we would write the following:

```
ID3D10ShaderResourceView* mDiffuseMapRV;
HR(D3DX10CreateShaderResourceViewFromFile(md3dDevice,
    L"WoodCrate01.dds", 0, 0, &mDiffuseMapRV, 0 ));
```

Once a texture is loaded, we need to set it to an effect variable so that it can be used in a pixel shader. A 2D texture object in an .fx file is represented by the Texture2D type; for example, we declare a texture variable in an effect file like so:

```
// Nonnumeric values cannot be added to a cbuffer.
Texture2D gDiffuseMap;
```

As the comment notes, texture objects are placed outside of constant buffers. We can obtain a pointer to an effect's Texture2D object (which is a shader resource variable) from our C++ application code as follows:

```
ID3D10EffectShaderResourceVariable* mfxDiffuseMapVar;
mfxDiffuseMapVar = mFX->GetVariableByName(
    "gDiffuseMap")->AsShaderResource();
```

Once we have obtained a pointer to an effect's Texture2D object, we can update it through the C++ interface like so:

```
// Set the C++ texture resource view to the effect texture variable.
mfxDiffuseMapVar->SetResource(mDiffuseMapRV);
```

As with other effect variables, if we need to change them between draw calls, we must call Apply:

```
// set grass texture
mfxDiffuseMapVar->SetResource(mGrassMapRV);
pass->Apply(0);
mLand.draw();

// set water texture
mfxDiffuseMapVar->SetResource(mWaterMapRV);
pass->Apply(0);
mWaves.draw();
```

Note: A texture resource can actually be used by any shader (vertex, geometry, or pixel). For now, we will just be using them in pixel shaders. As we mentioned, textures are essentially special arrays, so it is not hard to imagine that array data could be useful in vertex and geometry shader programs too.

7.4 **Filters**

7.4.1 **Magnification**

The elements of a texture map should be thought of as discrete color samples from a continuous image; they should not be thought of as rectangles with areas. So the question is: What happens if we have texture coordinates (u, v) that do not coincide with one of the texel points? This can happen in the following situation: Suppose the player zooms in on a wall in the scene so that the wall covers the entire screen. For the sake of example, suppose the monitor resolution is 1024×1024 and the wall's texture resolution is 256×256. This illustrates texture *magnification* — we are trying to cover many pixels with a few texels. In our example, between every texel point lies four pixels. Each pixel will be given a pair of unique texture coordinates when the vertex texture coordinates are interpolated across the triangle. Thus there will be pixels with texture coordinates that do not coincide with one of the texel points. Given the colors at the texels we can approximate the colors between texels using interpolation. There are two methods of interpolation graphics hardware supports: constant interpolation and linear interpolation. In practice, linear interpolation is almost always used.

Figure 7.4 illustrates these methods in 1D: Suppose we have a 1D texture with 256 samples and an interpolated texture coordinate $u = 0.126484375$. This normalized texture coordinate refers to the $0.126484375 \times 256 = 32.38$ texel. Of course, this value lies between two of our texel samples, so we must use interpolation to approximate it.

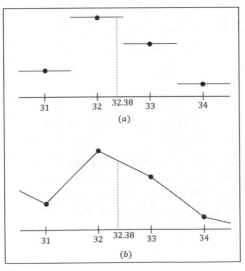

(a)

(b)

Figure 7.4: (a) Given the texel points, we construct a piecewise constant function to approximate values between the texel points; this is sometimes called *nearest neighbor point sampling*, as the value of the nearest texel point is used. (b) Given the texel points, we construct a piecewise linear function to approximate values between texel points.

2D linear interpolation is called *bilinear interpolation* and is illustrated in Figure 7.5. Given a pair of texture coordinates between four texels, we do two 1D linear interpolations in the u-direction, followed by one 1D interpolation in the v-direction.

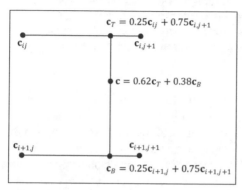

$$c_T = 0.25c_{ij} + 0.75c_{i,j+1}$$

c_{ij} $c_{i,j+1}$

$$c = 0.62c_T + 0.38c_B$$

$c_{i+1,j}$ $c_{i+1,j+1}$

$$c_B = 0.25c_{i+1,j} + 0.75c_{i+1,j+1}$$

Figure 7.5: Here we have four texel points c_{ij}, $c_{i,j+1}$, $c_{i+1,j}$, and $c_{i+1,j+1}$. We want to approximate the color of c, which lies between these four texel points, using interpolation. In this example, c lies 0.75 units to the right of c_{ij} and 0.38 units below c_{ij}. We first do a 1D linear interpolation between the top two colors to get c_T. Likewise, we do a 1D linear interpolation between the bottom two colors to get c_B. Finally, we do a 1D linear interpolation between c_T and c_B to get c.

Figure 7.6 shows the difference between constant and linear interpolation. As you can see, constant interpolation has the characteristic of creating a blocky looking image. Linear interpolation is smoother, but still will not look as good as if we had real data (e.g., a higher resolution texture) instead of derived data via interpolation.

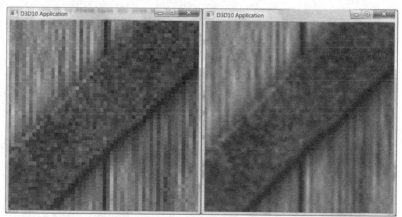

Figure 7.6: We zoom in on a cube with a crate texture so that magnification occurs. On the left we use constant interpolation, which results in a blocky appearance; this makes sense because the interpolating function has discontinuities (Figure 7.4a), which makes the changes abrupt rather than smooth. On the right we use linear filtering, which results in a smoother image due to the continuity of the interpolating function.

One thing to note about this discussion is that there is no real way to get around magnification in an interactive 3D program where the virtual eye is free to move around and explore. From some distances, the textures will look great, but will start to break down as the eye gets too close to them. Using higher resolution textures can help.

Note: In the context of texturing, using constant interpolation to find texture values for texture coordinates between texels is also called *point filtering*. And using linear interpolation to find texture values for texture coordinates between texels is also called *linear filtering*. Point and linear filtering is the terminology Direct3D uses.

7.4.2 Minification

Minification is the opposite of magnification. In minification, too many texels are being mapped to too few pixels. For instance, consider the following situation where we have a wall with a 256×256 texture mapped over it. The eye, looking at the wall, keeps moving back so that the wall gets smaller and smaller until it only covers 64×64 pixels on screen. So now we have 256×256 texels getting mapped to 64×64 screen pixels. In this situation, texture coordinates for pixels will still generally not coincide with any of the texels of the texture map, so constant and linear interpolation filters still apply to the minification case. However, there is more that can be done with minification. Intuitively, a sort of average downsampling of the 256×256 texels should be taken to reduce it to 64×64. The technique of mipmapping offers an efficient approximation for this at the expense of some extra memory. At initialization time (or asset creation time), smaller versions of the texture are made by downsampling the image to create a mipmap chain (see Figure 7.7). Thus the averaging work is precomputed for the mipmap sizes. At run time, the graphics hardware will do two different things based on the mipmap settings specified by the programmer:

- Pick and use the mipmap level that best matches the screen geometry resolution for texturing, applying constant or linear interpolation as needed. This is called *point filtering* for mipmaps because it is like constant interpolation — you just choose the nearest mipmap level and use that for texturing.

- Pick the two nearest mipmap levels that best match the screen geometry resolution for texturing (one will be bigger and one will be smaller than the screen geometry resolution). Next, apply constant or linear filtering to both of these mipmap levels to produce a texture color for each one. Finally, interpolate between these two texture color results. This is called *linear filtering* for mipmaps because it is like linear interpolation — you linearly interpolate between the two nearest mipmap levels.

By choosing the best texture levels of detail from the mipmap chain, the amount of minification is greatly reduced.

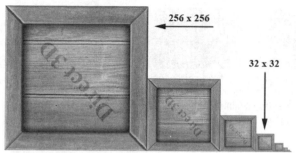

Figure 7.7: A chain of mipmaps; each successive mipmap is half the size, in each dimension, of the previous mipmap level of detail down to 1 × 1.

7.4.2.1 *Creating Mipmaps*

Mipmap levels can be created by artists directly, or they can be created by filtering algorithms.

Some image file formats like DDS (DirectDraw Surface format) can stores mipmap levels directly in the data file; in this case, the data simply needs to be read — no run-time work is needed to compute the mipmap levels algorithmically. The DirectX Texture Tool can generate a mipmap chain for a texture and export it to a DDS file. If an image file does not contain a complete mipmap chain, the functions D3DX10CreateShaderResourceView-FromFile or D3DX10CreateTextureFromFile will create a mipmap chain for you using some specified filtering algorithm (see D3DX10_IMAGE_LOAD_INFO and in particular the MipFilter data member in the SDK documentation). Thus we see that mipmapping is essentially automatic. The D3DX10 functions will automatically generate a mipmap chain for us if the source file doesn't already contain one. And as long as mipmapping is enabled, the hardware will choose the right mipmap level to use at run time.

7.4.3 **Anisotropic Filtering**

Another type of filter that can be used is called an *anisotropic filter*. This filter helps alleviate the distortion that occurs when the angle between a polygon's normal vector and a camera's look vector is wide (e.g., when a polygon is orthogonal to the view window). This filter is the most expensive, but can be worth the cost for correcting the distortion artifacts. Figure 7.8 shows a screenshot comparing anisotropic filtering with linear filtering.

Figure 7.8: The top face of the crate is nearly orthogonal to the view window. (Left) Using linear filtering, the top of the crate is badly blurred. (Right) Anisotropic filtering does a better job of rendering the top face of the crate from this angle.

7.5 Sampling Textures

We saw that a Texture2D object represents a texture in an effect file. However, there is another object associated with a texture, called a SamplerState object (or sampler). A sampler object is where we define the filters to use with a texture. Here are some examples:

```
// Use linear filtering for minification, magnification, and mipmapping.
SamplerState mySampler0
{
    Filter = MIN_MAG_MIP_LINEAR;
};

// Use linear filtering for minification, point filtering for
// magnification, and point filtering for mipmapping.
SamplerState mySampler1
{
    Filter = MIN_LINEAR_MAG_MIP_POINT;
};

// Use point filtering for minification, linear filtering for
// magnification, and point filtering for mipmapping.
SamplerState mySampler2
{
    Filter = MIN_POINT_MAG_LINEAR_MIP_POINT;
};

// Use anisotropic interpolation for minification, magnification,
// and mipmapping.
SamplerState mySampler3
{
    Filter = ANISOTROPIC;
};
```

You can figure out the other possible permutations from these examples, or you can look up the D3D10_FILTER enumerated type in the SDK documentation. We will see shortly that other properties are associated with a sampler, but for now this is all we need for our first demo.

Now, given a pair of texture coordinates for a pixel in the pixel shader, we actually sample a texture using the following syntax:

```
struct VS_OUT
{
    float4 posH    : SV_POSITION;
    float3 posW    : POSITION;
    float3 normalW : NORMAL;
    float2 texC    : TEXCOORD;
};

Texture2D gDiffuseMap;

SamplerState gTriLinearSam
{
    Filter = MIN_MAG_MIP_LINEAR;
};

float4 PS(VS_OUT pIn) : SV_Target
{
    // Get color from texture.
    float4 diffuse = gDiffuseMap.Sample( gTriLinearSam, pIn.texC );
    ...
```

As you can see, to sample a texture, we use the `Texture2D::Sample` method. We pass a `SamplerState` object for the first parameter, and we pass in the pixel's (u, v) texture coordinates for the second parameter. This method returns the interpolated color from the texture map at the specified (u, v) point using the filtering methods specified by the `SamplerState` object.

7.6 Textures as Materials

In Chapter 6, "Lighting," we specified diffuse and specular materials per vertex, with the understanding that the diffuse material would also double as the ambient material. Now with texturing, we do away with per-vertex materials and think of the colors in the texture map as describing the materials of the surface. This leads to per-pixel materials, which offer finer resolution than per-vertex materials since many texels generally cover a triangle. That is, every pixel will get interpolated texture coordinates (u, v); these texture coordinates are then used to sample the texture to get a color that describes the surface materials of that pixel.

With this setup, we need two texture maps: a diffuse map and a specular map. The diffuse map specifies how much diffuse light a surface reflects and absorbs on a per-pixel basis. Likewise, the specular map specifies how much specular light a surface reflects and absorbs on a per-pixel basis. As we did in the previous chapter, we set the ambient material to be equal to the diffuse material; thus no additional ambient map is required. Figure 7.9 shows the advantage of having a specular map — we can get very fine per-pixel control over which parts of a triangle are shiny and reflective and which parts are matte.

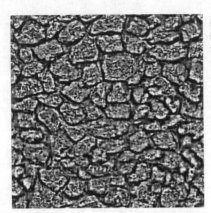

Figure 7.9: A specular map used to control the specular material at a pixel level.

For surfaces that are not shiny or for surfaces where the shininess is already baked into the diffuse map (i.e., the artist embedded specular highlights directly into the diffuse map), we just use a black texture for the specular map. Our calculations could be made more efficient by introducing a constant buffer flag and some code like this:

```
bool gSpecularEnabled;

...

if(gSpecularEnabled)
    // sample specular texture map

...

if(gSpecularEnabled)
    // do specular part of lighting equation
```

Thus we could skip specular lighting calculations if the application indicated it was unnecessary to perform them. However, for the purposes of our demos, we will just leave things as is, and do the calculations with a default black texture if the surface reflects zero specular light.

Note: Even though our shader code works with specular maps, in this book we will not take full advantage of the per-pixel control this offers. The main reason for this is that specular maps take time to author, and should really be done by a texture artist.

7.7 **Crate Demo**

We now review the key points of adding a crate texture to a cube (as shown in Figure 7.1). This demo builds off of the Colored Cube demo of Chapter 5 by replacing coloring with lighting and texturing.

7.7.1 **Specifying Texture Coordinates**

The Box::init method is responsible for creating and filling out the vertex and index buffers for the box geometry. The index buffer code is unchanged from the Colored Cube demo, and the only change to the vertex buffer code is that we need to add normals and texture coordinates (which are shown in bold). For brevity, we only show the vertex definitions for the front and back faces.

```
struct Vertex
{
    Vertex(){}
    Vertex(float x,  float y,  float z,
           float nx, float ny, float nz,
           float u,  float v)
           : pos(x,y,z), normal(nx,ny,nz), texC(u,v){}

    D3DXVECTOR3 pos;
    D3DXVECTOR3 normal;
    D3DXVECTOR2 texC;
};

void Box::init(ID3D10Device* device, float scale)
{
    md3dDevice = device;

    mNumVertices = 24;
    mNumFaces    = 12; // 2 per quad

    // Create vertex buffer
    Vertex v[24];

    // Fill in the front face vertex data.
    v[0] = Vertex(-1.0f, -1.0f, -1.0f, 0.0f, 0.0f, -1.0f, 0.0f, 1.0f);
    v[1] = Vertex(-1.0f,  1.0f, -1.0f, 0.0f, 0.0f, -1.0f, 0.0f, 0.0f);
    v[2] = Vertex( 1.0f,  1.0f, -1.0f, 0.0f, 0.0f, -1.0f, 1.0f, 0.0f);
    v[3] = Vertex( 1.0f, -1.0f, -1.0f, 0.0f, 0.0f, -1.0f, 1.0f, 1.0f);

    // Fill in the back face vertex data.
    v[4] = Vertex(-1.0f, -1.0f, 1.0f, 0.0f, 0.0f, 1.0f, 1.0f, 1.0f);
    v[5] = Vertex( 1.0f, -1.0f, 1.0f, 0.0f, 0.0f, 1.0f, 0.0f, 1.0f);
    v[6] = Vertex( 1.0f,  1.0f, 1.0f, 0.0f, 0.0f, 1.0f, 0.0f, 0.0f);
    v[7] = Vertex(-1.0f,  1.0f, 1.0f, 0.0f, 0.0f, 1.0f, 1.0f, 0.0f);
```

Refer back to Figure 7.3 if you need help seeing why the texture coordinates are specified this way.

7.7.2 **Creating the Texture**

We create the diffuse and specular map textures from files (technically the shader resource views to the textures) at initialization time as follows:

```
// CrateApp data members
ID3D10ShaderResourceView* mDiffuseMapRV;
ID3D10ShaderResourceView* mSpecMapRV;

void CrateApp::initApp()
{
    D3DApp::initApp();

    mClearColor = D3DXCOLOR(0.9f, 0.9f, 0.9f, 1.0f);

    buildFX();
    buildVertexLayouts();

    mCrateMesh.init(md3dDevice, 1.0f);

    HR(D3DX10CreateShaderResourceViewFromFile(md3dDevice,
        L"WoodCrate01.dds", 0, 0, &mDiffuseMapRV, 0));

    HR(D3DX10CreateShaderResourceViewFromFile(md3dDevice,
        L"defaultspec.dds", 0, 0, &mSpecMapRV, 0));

    mParallelLight.dir      = D3DXVECTOR3(0.57735f, -0.57735f, 0.57735f);
    mParallelLight.ambient  = D3DXCOLOR(0.4f, 0.4f, 0.4f, 1.0f);
    mParallelLight.diffuse  = D3DXCOLOR(1.0f, 1.0f, 1.0f, 1.0f);
    mParallelLight.specular = D3DXCOLOR(1.0f, 1.0f, 1.0f, 1.0f);
}
```

7.7.3 **Setting the Texture**

Texture data is typically accessed in a pixel shader. In order for the pixel shader to access it, we need to set the texture view (`ID3D10ShaderResource-View`) to a `Texture2D` object in the .fx file. This is done as follows:

```
mfxDiffuseMapVar->SetResource(mDiffuseMapRV);
mfxSpecMapVar->SetResource(mSpecMapRV);
```

where `mfxDiffuseMapVar` and `mfxSpecMapVar` are of type `ID3D10EffectShader-ResourceVariable`; that is, they are pointers to the `Texture2D` objects in the effect file:

```
// [C++ code]
// Get pointers to effect file variables.
mfxDiffuseMapVar = mFX->GetVariableByName("gDiffuseMap")->
    AsShaderResource();
mfxSpecMapVar    = mFX->GetVariableByName("gSpecMap")->AsShaderResource();

// [.FX code]
```

```
// Effect file texture variables.
Texture2D gDiffuseMap;
Texture2D gSpecMap;
```

7.7.4 Texture Effect

Below is the texture effect file, which ties together what we have discussed thus far.

```
//===========================================================================
// tex.fx by Frank Luna (C) 2008 All Rights Reserved.
//
// Transforms, lights, and textures geometry.
//===========================================================================

#include "lighthelper.fx"

cbuffer cbPerFrame
{
    Light gLight;
    float3 gEyePosW;
};

cbuffer cbPerObject
{
    float4x4 gWorld;
    float4x4 gWVP;
    float4x4 gTexMtx;
};

// Nonnumeric values cannot be added to a cbuffer.
Texture2D gDiffuseMap;
Texture2D gSpecMap;

SamplerState gTriLinearSam
{
    Filter = MIN_MAG_MIP_LINEAR;
};

struct VS_IN
{
    float3 posL    : POSITION;
    float3 normalL : NORMAL;
    float2 texC    : TEXCOORD;
};

struct VS_OUT
{
    float4 posH    : SV_POSITION;
    float3 posW    : POSITION;
    float3 normalW : NORMAL;
    float2 texC    : TEXCOORD;
};
```

```
VS_OUT VS(VS_IN vIn)
{
    VS_OUT vOut;

    // Transform to world space.
    vOut.posW    = mul(float4(vIn.posL, 1.0f), gWorld);
    vOut.normalW = mul(float4(vIn.normalL, 0.0f), gWorld);

    // Transform to homogeneous clip space.
    vOut.posH = mul(float4(vIn.posL, 1.0f), gWVP);

    // Output vertex attributes for interpolation across triangle.
    vOut.texC    = mul(float4(vIn.texC, 0.0f, 1.0f), gTexMtx);

    return vOut;
}

float4 PS(VS_OUT pIn) : SV_Target
{
    // Get materials from texture maps.
    float4 diffuse = gDiffuseMap.Sample(gTriLinearSam, pIn.texC);
    float4 spec    = gSpecMap.Sample(gTriLinearSam, pIn.texC);

    // Map [0,1] --> [0,256]
    spec.a *= 256.0f;

    // Interpolating normal can make it not be of unit length so
    // normalize it.
    float3 normalW = normalize(pIn.normalW);

    // Compute the lit color for this pixel.
    SurfaceInfo v = {pIn.posW, normalW, diffuse, spec};
    float3 litColor = ParallelLight(v, gLight, gEyePosW);

    return float4(litColor, diffuse.a);
}

technique10 TexTech
{
    pass P0
    {
        SetVertexShader( CompileShader( vs_4_0, VS() ) );
        SetGeometryShader( NULL );
        SetPixelShader( CompileShader( ps_4_0, PS() ) );
    }
}
```

One constant buffer variable we have not discussed is gTexMtx. This variable is used in the vertex shader to transform the input texture coordinates:

```
vOut.texC = mul(float4(vIn.texC, 0.0f, 1.0f), gTexMtx);
```

Texture coordinates are 2D points in the texture plane. Thus, we can translate, rotate, and scale them like any other point. In this demo, we use an identity matrix transformation so that the input texture coordinates are left unmodified. However, as we will see in §7.9 some special effects can be obtained by transforming texture coordinates. Note that to transform the 2D texture coordinates by a 4×4 matrix, we augment it to a 4D vector:

```
vIn.texC ---> float4(vIn.texC, 0.0f, 1.0f)
```

After the multiplication is done, the resulting 4D vector is implicitly cast back to a 2D vector by throwing away the z and w components. That is,

```
vOut.texC = mul(float4(vIn.texC, 0.0f, 1.0f), gTexMtx);
```

is equivalent to:

```
vOut.texC = mul(float4(vIn.texC, 0.0f, 1.0f), gTexMtx).xy;
```

One other line of code we must discuss is:

```
// Map [0,1] --> [0,256]
spec.a *= 256.0f;
```

Recall that the alpha channel of the specular map stores the specular power exponent. However, when a texture is sampled, its components are returned in the normalized [0, 1] range. Thus we must rescale this interval to a value that is reasonable for a specular power exponent. We decided on the scaling range [0, 256]. This means we can have a maximum specular power exponent of 256, which is high enough in practice.

7.8 **Address Modes**

A texture, combined with constant or linear interpolation, defines a vector-valued function $(r, g, b, a) = T(u, v)$. That is, given the texture coordinates $(u, v) \in [0, 1]^2$, the texture function T returns a color (r, g, b, a). Direct3D allows us to extend the domain of this function in four different ways (called _address modes_): _wrap, border color, clamp,_ and _mirror._

■ Wrap: Extends the texture function by repeating the image at every integer junction (see Figure 7.10).

■ Border color: Extends the texture function by mapping each (u, v) not in $[0, 1]^2$ to some color specified by the programmer (see Figure 7.11).

■ Clamp: Extends the texture function by mapping each (u, v) not in $[0, 1]^2$ to the color $T(u_0, v_0)$, where (u_0, v_0) is the nearest point to (u, v) contained in $[0, 1]^2$ (see Figure 7.12).

■ Mirror: Extends the texture function by mirroring the image at every integer junction (see Figure 7.13).

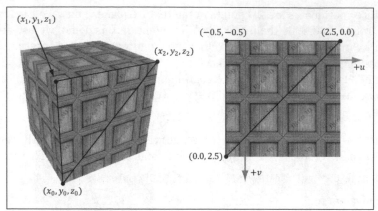

Figure 7.10: Wrap address mode.

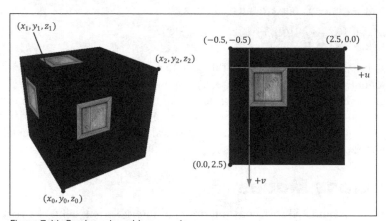

Figure 7.11: Border color address mode.

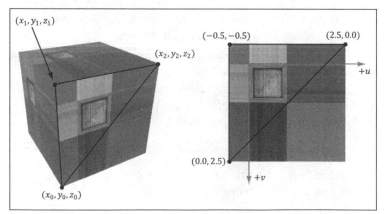

Figure 7.12: Clamp address mode.

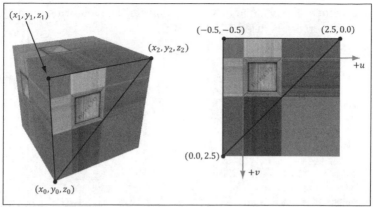

Figure 7.13: Mirror address mode.

Since an address mode is always specified (wrap mode is the default), texture coordinates outside the [0, 1] range are always defined.

The wrap address mode is probably the most often employed; it allows us to tile a texture repeatedly over some surface. This effectively enables us to increase the texture resolution without supplying additional data (although the extra resolution is repetitive). With tiling, it is often desirable for the texture to be seamless. For example, the crate texture is not seamless, as you can see the repetition clearly. Figure 7.14 shows a seamless brick texture repeated 2×3 times.

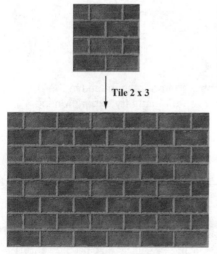

Tile 2 x 3

Figure 7.14: A brick texture tiled 2 × 3 times. Because the texture is seamless, the repetition pattern is harder to notice.

Address modes are specified in sampler objects. The following examples were used to create Figures 7.10 to 7.13:

```
SamplerState gTriLinearSam
{
    Filter = MIN_MAG_MIP_LINEAR;
    AddressU = WRAP;
    AddressV = WRAP;
};

SamplerState gTriLinearSam
{
    Filter = MIN_MAG_MIP_LINEAR;
    AddressU = BORDER;
    AddressV = BORDER;

    // Blue border color
    BorderColor = float4(0.0f, 0.0f, 1.0f, 1.0f);
};

SamplerState gTriLinearSam
{
    Filter = MIN_MAG_MIP_LINEAR;
    AddressU = CLAMP;
    AddressV = CLAMP;
};

SamplerState gTriLinearSam
{
    Filter = MIN_MAG_MIP_LINEAR;
    AddressU = MIRROR;
    AddressV = MIRROR;
};
```

Note: Observe that you can control the address modes in the *u* and *v* directions independently. The reader might try experimenting with this.

7.9 Transforming Textures

As stated earlier, texture coordinates represent 2D points in the texture plane. Thus, we can translate, rotate, and scale them like we could any other point. Here are some example uses for transforming textures:

■ A brick texture is stretched along a wall. The wall vertices currently have texture coordinates in the range [0, 1]. We scale the texture coordinates by 4 to scale them to the range [0, 4], so that the texture will be repeated 4×4 times across the wall.

- We have cloud textures stretched over a clear blue sky. By translating the texture coordinates as a function of time, the clouds are animated over the sky.

- Texture rotation is sometimes useful for particle-like effects; for example, to rotate a fireball texture over time.

Texture coordinate transformations are done just like regular transformations. We specify a transformation matrix, and multiply the texture coordinate vector by the matrix. For example:

```
// Constant buffer variable
float4x4 gTexMtx;

// In shader program
vOut.texC = mul(float4(vIn.texC, 0.0f, 1.0f), gTexMtx);
```

Note that since we are working with 2D texture coordinates, we only care about transformations done to the first two coordinates. For instance, if the texture matrix translated the z-coordinate, it would have no effect on the resulting texture coordinates.

7.10 **Land Tex Demo**

In this demo, we add textures to our land and water scene. The first key issue is that we tile a grass texture over the land. Because the land mesh is a large surface, if we simply stretched a texture over it, then too few texels would cover each triangle. In other words, there is not enough texture resolution for the surface; we would thus get magnification artifacts. Therefore, we repeat the grass texture over the land mesh to get more resolution. The second key issue is that we scroll the water texture over the water geometry as a function of time. This added motion makes the water a bit more convincing. Figure 7.15 shows a screenshot of the demo.

Figure 7.15:
Screenshot of the
Land Tex demo.

7.10.1 **Grid Texture Coordinate Generation**

Figure 7.16 shows an $m \times n$ grid in the xz-plane and a corresponding grid in the normalized texture space domain $[0, 1]^2$. From the figure, it is clear that the texture coordinates of the ijth grid vertex in the xz-plane are the coordinates of the ijth grid vertex in the texture space. The texture space coordinates of the ijth vertex are:

$$u_{ij} = j \cdot \Delta u$$

$$v_{ij} = i \cdot \Delta v$$

where $\Delta u = \frac{1}{n-1}$ and $\Delta v = \frac{1}{m-1}$.

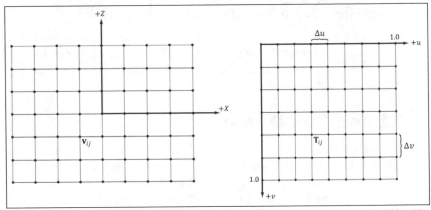

Figure 7.16: The texture coordinates of the grid vertex $\mathbf{v}_{ij}$ in xz-space are given by the ijth grid vertex $\mathbf{T}_{ij}$ in uv-space.

Thus, we use the following code to generate texture coordinates for the land mesh:

```
float du = 1.0f / (n-1);
float dv = 1.0f / (m-1);
for(DWORD i = 0; i < m; ++i)
{
    float z = halfDepth - i*dx;
    for(DWORD j = 0; j < n; ++j)
    {
        float x = -halfWidth + j*dx;

        // Graph of this function looks like a mountain range.
        float y = getHeight(x, z);

        vertices[i*n+j].pos = D3DXVECTOR3(x, y, z);

        // Stretch texture over grid.
        vertices[i*n+j].texC.x = j*du;
        vertices[i*n+j].texC.y = i*dv;
```

7.10.2 **Texture Tiling**

We said we wanted to tile a grass texture over the land mesh. But so far the texture coordinates we have computed lie in the unit domain $[0, 1]^2$, so no tiling will occur. To tile the texture, we specify the wrap address mode and scale the texture coordinates by 5 using a texture transformation matrix. Thus the texture coordinates are mapped to the domain $[0, 5]^2$ so that the texture is tiled 5×5 times across the land mesh surface:

```
D3DXMATRIX S;
D3DXMatrixScaling(&S, 5.0f, 5.0f, 1.0f);
D3DXMATRIX landTexMtx = S;
...
mfxTexMtxVar->SetMatrix((float*)&landTexMtx);
...
pass->Apply(0);
mLand.draw();
```

7.10.3 **Texture Animation**

To scroll a water texture over the water geometry, we translate the texture coordinates in the texture plane as a function of time. Provided the displacement is small for each frame, this gives the illusion of a smooth animation. We use the wrap address mode along with a seamless texture so that we can seamlessly translate the texture coordinates around the texture space plane. The following code shows how we calculate the offset vector for the water texture, and how we build and set the water's texture matrix:

```
// Animate water texture as a function of time in the update function.
mWaterTexOffset.y += 0.1f*dt;
mWaterTexOffset.x = 0.25f*sinf(4.0f*mWaterTexOffset.y);


...


// Scale texture coordinates by 5 units to map [0,1]-->[0,5]
// so that the texture repeats five times in each direction.
D3DXMATRIX S;
D3DXMatrixScaling(&S, 5.0f, 5.0f, 1.0f);

// Translate the texture.
D3DXMATRIX T;
D3DXMatrixTranslation(&T, mWaterTexOffset.x, mWaterTexOffset.y, 0.0f);

// Scale and translate the texture.
D3DXMATRIX waterTexMtx = S*T;
...
mfxTexMtxVar->SetMatrix((float*)&waterTexMtx);
...
pass->Apply(0);
mWaves.draw();
```

7.11 **Compressed Texture Formats**

The GPU memory requirements for textures add up quickly as your virtual worlds grow with hundreds of textures (remember we need to keep all these textures in GPU memory to apply them quickly). To help alleviate memory overload, Direct3D supports compressed texture formats: BC1, BC2, BC3, BC4, and BC5.

- BC1 (DXGI_FORMAT_BC1_UNORM): Use this format if you need to compress a format that supports three color channels, and only a 1-bit (on/off) alpha component.

- BC2 (DXGI_FORMAT_BC2_UNORM): Use this format if you need to compress a format that supports three color channels, and only a 4-bit alpha component.

- BC3 (DXGI_FORMAT_BC3_UNORM): Use this format if you need to compress a format that supports three color channels, and an 8-bit alpha component.

- BC4 (DXGI_FORMAT_BC4_UNORM): Use this format if you need to compress a format that contains one color channel (e.g., a grayscale image).

- BC5 (DXGI_FORMAT_BC5_UNORM): Use this format if you need to compress a format that supports two color channels.

For more information on these formats, look up "Block Compression" in the index of the SDK documentation.

Note: A compressed texture can only be used as an input to the shader stage of the rendering pipeline.

Note: Because the block compression algorithms work with 4×4 pixel blocks, the dimensions of the texture must be multiples of 4.

The advantage of these formats is that they can be stored compressed in GPU memory, and then decompressed on the fly by the GPU when needed.

If you have a file that contains uncompressed image data, you can have Direct3D convert it to a compressed format at load time by using the pLoadInfo parameter of the D3DX10CreateShaderResourceViewFromFile function. For example, consider the following code, which loads a BMP file:

```
D3DX10_IMAGE_LOAD_INFO loadInfo;
loadInfo.Format = DXGI_FORMAT_BC3_UNORM;

HR(D3DX10CreateShaderResourceViewFromFile(md3dDevice,
    L"darkbrick.bmp", &loadInfo, 0, &mTexMapRV, 0 ));

// Get the actual 2D texture from the resource view.
ID3D10Texture2D* tex;
mTexMapRV->GetResource((ID3D10Resource**)&tex);
```

```
// Get the description of the 2D texture.
D3D10_TEXTURE2D_DESC texDesc;
tex->GetDesc(&texDesc);
```

Figure 7.17a shows what texDesc looks like in the debugger; we see that it has the desired compressed texture format. If instead we specified null for the pLoadInfo parameter, then the format from the source image is used (Figure 7.17b), which is the uncompressed DXGI_FORMAT_R8G8B8A8_UNORM format.

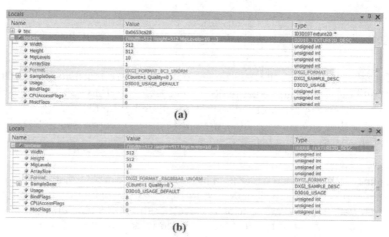

Figure 7.17: (a) The texture is created with the DXGI_FORMAT_BC3_UNORM compressed format. (b) The texture is created with the DXGI_FORMAT_R8G8B8A8_UNORM uncompressed format.

Alternatively, you can use the DDS (DirectDraw Surface) format, which can store compressed textures directly. To do this, load your image file into the DirectX Texture Tool (*DXTex.exe*) located in the SDK directory: *D:\Microsoft DirectX SDK (November 2007)\Utilities\Bin\x86*. Then go to Menu>Format>Change Surface Format and choose DXT1, DXT2, DXT3, DXT4, or DXT5. Then save the file as a DDS file. These formats are actually Direct3D 9 compressed texture formats, but DXT1 is the same as BC1, DXT2 and DXT3 are the same as BC2, and DXT4 and DXT5 are the same as BC3. As an example, if we save a file as DXT1 and load it using D3DX10CreateShaderResourceViewFromFile, the texture will have format DXGI_FORMAT_BC1_UNORM:

```
// water2.dds is DXT1 format
HR(D3DX10CreateShaderResourceViewFromFile(md3dDevice,
    L"water2.dds", 0, 0, &mWaterMapRV, 0 ));

// Get the actual 2D texture from the resource view.
ID3D10Texture2D* tex,
mWaterMapRV->GetResource((ID3D10Resource **)&tex);
```

```
// Get the description of the 2D texture.
D3D10_TEXTURE2D_DESC texDesc;
tex->GetDesc(&texDesc);
```

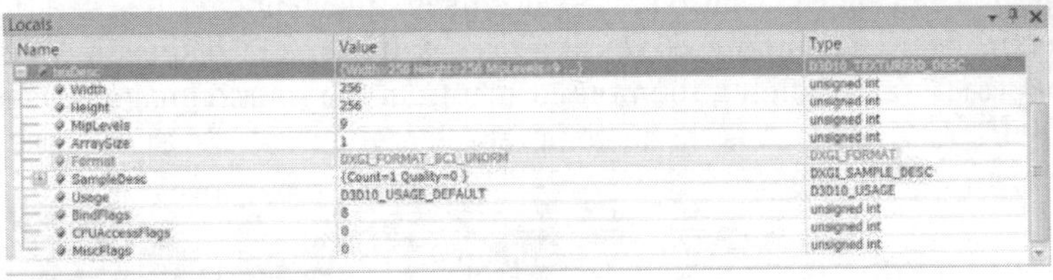

Figure 7.18: The texture is created with the `DXGI_FORMAT_BC1_UNORM` format.

Note that if the DDS file uses one of the compressed formats, we can specify null for the `pLoadInfo` parameter, and `D3DX10CreateShaderResourceViewFromFile` will use the compressed format specified by the file.

Another advantage of storing your textures compressed in DDS files is that they also take up less disk space.

Note: You can also generate mipmap levels (Menu>Format>Generate Mip Maps) in the DirectX Texture Tool, and save them in a DDS file as well. In this way, the mipmap levels are precomputed and stored with the file so that they do not need to be computed at load time (they just need to be loaded).

Note: Direct3D 10 has extended the DDS format from previous versions to include support for texture arrays. Texture arrays will be discussed and used later in this book.

7.12 **Summary**

- Texture coordinates are used to define a triangle on the texture that gets mapped to the 3D triangle.
- We can create textures from image files stored on disk using the `D3DX10CreateShaderResourceViewFromFile` function.
- We can filter textures by using the minification, magnification, and mipmap filter sampler states.
- Address modes define what Direct3D is supposed to do with texture coordinates outside the [0, 1] range. For example, should the texture be tiled, mirrored, clamped, etc.?
- Texture coordinates can be scaled, rotated, and translated just like other points. By incrementally transforming the texture coordinates by a small amount each frame, we animate the texture.
- By using the compressed Direct3D texture formats BC1, BC2, BC3, BC4, or BC5, we can save a considerable amount of GPU memory.

7.13 **Exercises**

1. Experiment with the Crate demo by changing the texture coordinates and using different address mode combinations.

2. Using the DirectX Texture Tool, we can manually specify each mipmap level (File>Open Onto This Surface). Create a DDS file with a mipmap chain like the one in Figure 7.19, with a different textual description or color on each level so that you can easily distinguish between each mipmap level. Modify the Crate demo by using this texture and have the camera zoom in and out so that you can explicitly see the mipmap levels changing. Try both point and linear mipmap filtering.

Figure 7.19: A mipmap chain manually constructed so that each level is easily distinguishable.

3. Given two textures of the same size, we can combine them via different operations to obtain a new image. More generally, this is called *multi-texturing*, where multiple textures are used to achieve a result. For example, we can add, subtract, or (componentwise) multiply the corresponding texels of two textures. Figure 7.20 shows the result of componentwise multiplying two textures to get a fireball-like result. For this exercise, modify the Crate demo by combining the two source textures in Figure 7.20 in a pixel shader to produce the fireball texture over each cube face. (The image files for this exercise may be downloaded from the book's website at www.d3dcoder.net and the publisher's website at www.wordware.com/files/0535dx10.)

Figure 7.20: Componentwise multiply corresponding texels of two textures (flare.dds and flarealpha.dds) to produce a new texture.

4. Modify the solution to Exercise 3 by rotating the fireball texture as a function of time over each cube face.

5. This chapter's downloadable directory contains a folder with 120 frames of a fire animation designed to be played over 4 seconds (30 frames per second). Figure 7.21 shows the first 30 frames. Modify the Crate demo by playing this animation over each face of the cube. (*Hint*: Load the images into an array of 120 texture objects. Start by using the first frame texture, and every 1/30th of a second, increment to the next frame texture. After the 120th frame texture, roll back to the first texture and repeat the process.) This is sometimes called *page flipping*, because it is reminiscent of flipping the pages in a flip book.

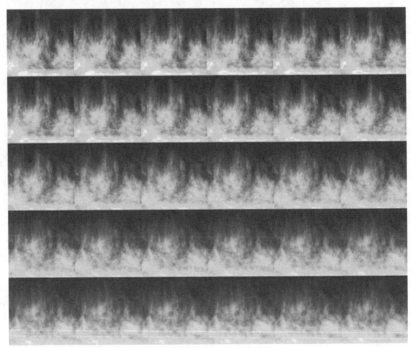

Figure 7.21: Frames of a precomputed fire animation.

Chapter 8

Blending

Consider Figure 8.1. We start rendering the frame by first drawing the terrain followed by the wooden crate, so that the terrain and crate pixels are on the back buffer. We then draw the water surface to the back buffer using *blending*, so that the water pixels are combined with the terrain and crate pixels on the back buffer in such a way that the terrain and crate show through the water. In this chapter, we examine blending techniques that allow us to blend (combine) the pixels that we are currently rasterizing (so-called *source* pixels) with the pixels that were previously rasterized to the back buffer (so-called *destination* pixels). This technique enables us, among other things, to render semi-transparent objects such as water and glass.

Figure 8.1: A semi-transparent water surface.

Objectives:

- To understand how blending works and how to use it with Direct3D.
- To learn about the different blend modes that Direct3D supports.

- To find out how the alpha component can be used to control the transparency of a primitive.
- To learn how we can prevent a pixel from being drawn to the back buffer altogether by employing the HLSL `clip` function.

8.1 **The Blending Equation**

Let $\mathbf{C}_{src}$ be the color of the ijth pixel we are currently rasterizing (the source pixel), and let $\mathbf{C}_{dst}$ be the color of the ijth pixel currently on the back buffer (the destination pixel). Without blending, $\mathbf{C}_{src}$ would overwrite $\mathbf{C}_{dst}$ (assuming it passes the depth/stencil test) and become the new color of the ijth back buffer pixel. But with blending, $\mathbf{C}_{src}$ and $\mathbf{C}_{dst}$ are combined to get the new color $\mathbf{C}$ that will overwrite $\mathbf{C}_{dst}$ (i.e., the blended color $\mathbf{C}$ will be written to the ijth pixel of the back buffer). Direct3D uses the following blending equation to blend the source and destination pixel colors:

$$\mathbf{C} = \mathbf{C}_{src} \otimes \mathbf{F}_{src} \boxplus \mathbf{C}_{dst} \otimes \mathbf{F}_{dst}$$

The colors $\mathbf{F}_{src}$ (source blend factor) and $\mathbf{F}_{dst}$ (destination blend factor) may be any of the values described in §8.3, and they allow us to modify the original source and destination pixels in a variety of ways, allowing for different effects to be achieved. The $\boxplus$ operator may be any of the binary operators defined in §8.2.

The above blending equation holds only for the RGB components of the colors. The alpha component is actually handled by a separate, similar equation:

$$A = A_{src} F_{src} \boxplus A_{dst} F_{dst}$$

The equation is essentially the same, but it is possible for the blend factors and binary operation to be different. The motivation for separating RGB from alpha is simply so that we can process them independently, and hence, differently.

Note: Blending the alpha components is needed much less frequently than blending the RGB components. In particular, in this book, we will never need to blend source and destination alpha values, although alpha values will be involved in our RGB blending. This is mainly because we do not care about the back buffer alpha values. Back buffer alpha values are only important if you have some algorithm that requires destination alpha values.

8.2 **Blend Operations**

The binary ⊞ operator used in the blending equation may be one of the following:

```
typedef enum D3D10_BLEND_OP
{
    D3D10_BLEND_OP_ADD = 1,            C = Csrc ⊗ Fsrc + Cdst ⊗ Fdst
    D3D10_BLEND_OP_SUBTRACT = 2,       C = Csrc ⊗ Fsrc - Cdst ⊗ Fdst
    D3D10_BLEND_OP_REV_SUBTRACT = 3,   C = Cdst ⊗ Fdst - Csrc ⊗ Fsrc
    D3D10_BLEND_OP_MIN = 4,            C = min(Csrc ⊗ Fsrc, Cdst ⊗ Fdst)
    D3D10_BLEND_OP_MAX = 5,            C = max(Csrc ⊗ Fsrc, Cdst ⊗ Fdst)
} D3D10_BLEND_OP;
```

These same operators also work for the alpha blending equation. Also, you can specify a different operator for RGB and alpha. For example, it is possible to add the two RGB terms, but subtract the two alpha terms:

$$C = C_{src} \otimes F_{src} + C_{dst} \otimes F_{dst}$$

$$A = A_{src} F_{src} - A_{dst} F_{dst}$$

8.3 **Blend Factors**

By setting different combinations for the source and destination blend factors, dozens of different blending effects may be achieved. We will illustrate some combinations in §8.5, but you will need to experiment with others to get a feel for what they do. The following list describes the basic blend factors, which apply to both F_{src} and F_{dst}. See the D3D10_BLEND enumerated type in the SDK documentation for some additional advanced blend factors. Letting $C_{src} = (r_s, g_s, b_s)$, $A_{src} = a_s$, $C_{dst} = (r_d, g_d, b_d)$, $A_{dst} = a_d$, F being either F_{src} or F_{dst}, and F being either F_{src} or F_{dst}, we have:

- D3D10_BLEND_ZERO: $F = (0, 0, 0)$ and $F = 0$
- D3D10_BLEND_ONE: $F = (1, 1, 1)$ and $F = 1$
- D3D10_BLEND_SRC_COLOR: $F = (r_s, g_s, b_s)$
- D3D10_BLEND_INV_SRC_COLOR: $F = (1 - r_s, 1 - g_s, 1 - b_s)$
- D3D10_BLEND_SRC_ALPHA: $F = (a_s, a_s, a_s)$ and $F = a_s$
- D3D10_BLEND_INV_SRC_ALPHA: $F = (1 - a_s, 1 - a_s, 1 - a_s)$ and $F = 1 - a_s$
- D3D10_BLEND_DEST_ALPHA: $F = (a_d, a_d, a_d)$ and $F = a_d$
- D3D10_BLEND_INV_DEST_ALPHA: $F = (1 - a_d, 1 - a_d, 1 - a_d)$ and $F = 1 - a_d$
- D3D10_BLEND_DEST_COLOR: $F = (r_d, g_d, b_d)$
- D3D10_BLEND_INV_DEST_COLOR: $F = (1 - r_d, 1 - g_d, 1 - b_d)$
- D3D10_BLEND_SRC_ALPHA_SAT: $F = (a'_s, a'_s, a'_s)$ and $F = a'_s$
  where $a'_s = \text{clamp}(a_s, 0, 1)$

- D3D10_BLEND_BLEND_FACTOR: $\mathbf{F} = (r, g, b)$ and $F = a$, where the color (r, g, b, a) is supplied to the second parameter of the ID3D10Device::OMSet-BlendState method (§8.4). This allows you to specify the blend factor color to use directly; however, it is constant until you change the blend state.

- D3D10_BLEND_INV_BLEND_FACTOR: $\mathbf{F} = (1 - r, 1 - g, 1 - b)$ and $F = 1 - a$, where the color (r, g, b, a) is supplied by the second parameter of the ID3D10Device::OMSetBlendState method (§8.4). This allows you to specify the blend factor color to use directly; however, it is constant until you change the blend state.

Note: The clamp function is defined as:

$$\text{clamp}(x,a,b) = \begin{cases} x, & a \le x \le b \\ a, & x < a \\ b, & x > b \end{cases}$$

All of these blend factors apply to the RGB blending equation. For the alpha blending equation, blend factors ending with _COLOR are *not allowed*.

8.4 Blend State

We have talked about the blending operators and blend factors, but where do we set these values with Direct3D? These blend settings are controlled by the ID3D10BlendState interface. Such an interface is found by filling out a D3D10_BLEND_DESC structure and then calling ID3D10Device::CreateBlendState:

```
HRESULT ID3D10Device::CreateBlendState(
    const D3D10_BLEND_DESC *pBlendStateDesc,
    ID3D10BlendState **ppBlendState);
```

- pBlendStateDesc: Pointer to the filled out D3D10_BLEND_DESC structure describing the blend state to create.

- ppBlendState: Returns a pointer to the created blend state interface.

The D3D10_BLEND_DESC structure is defined like so:

```
typedef struct D3D10_BLEND_DESC {
    BOOL AlphaToCoverageEnable;
    BOOL BlendEnable[8];
    D3D10_BLEND SrcBlend;
    D3D10_BLEND DestBlend;
    D3D10_BLEND_OP BlendOp;
    D3D10_BLEND SrcBlendAlpha;
    D3D10_BLEND DestBlendAlpha;
    D3D10_BLEND_OP BlendOpAlpha;
    UINT8 RenderTargetWriteMask[8];
} D3D10_BLEND_DESC;
```

■ `AlphaToCoverageEnable`: Specify `true` to enable alpha-to-coverage, which is a multisampling technique useful when rendering foliage or wire fence textures. Specify `false` to disable alpha-to-coverage.

■ `BlendEnable`: Specify `true` to enable blending and `false` to disable it. This is an array of eight since it is possible to have eight render targets simultaneously bound to the output merger stage, and we can enable/disable blending individually for each render target separately. In this book, we will always use index 0 (corresponding to the first render target) since we only use one render target.

■ `SrcBlend`: A member of the `D3D10_BLEND` enumerated type that specifies the source blend factor F_{src} for RGB blending.

■ `DestBlend`: A member of the `D3D10_BLEND` enumerated type that specifies the destination blend factor F_{dst} for RGB blending.

■ `BlendOp`: A member of the `D3D10_BLEND_OP` enumerated type that specifies the RGB blending operator.

■ `SrcBlendAlpha`: A member of the `D3D10_BLEND` enumerated type that specifies the source blend factor F_{src} for alpha blending.

■ `DestBlendAlpha`: A member of the `D3D10_BLEND` enumerated type that specifies the destination blend factor F_{dst} for alpha blending.

■ `BlendOpAlpha`: A member of the `D3D10_BLEND_OP` enumerated type that specifies the alpha blending operator.

■ `RenderTargetWriteMask`: A combination of one or more of the following flags:

```
typedef enum D3D10_COLOR_WRITE_ENABLE
{
    D3D10_COLOR_WRITE_ENABLE_RED = 1,
    D3D10_COLOR_WRITE_ENABLE_GREEN = 2,
    D3D10_COLOR_WRITE_ENABLE_BLUE = 4,
    D3D10_COLOR_WRITE_ENABLE_ALPHA = 8,
    D3D10_COLOR_WRITE_ENABLE_ALL =
        (D3D10_COLOR_WRITE_ENABLE_RED | D3D10_COLOR_WRITE_ENABLE_GREEN |
        D3D10_COLOR_WRITE_ENABLE_BLUE | D3D10_COLOR_WRITE_ENABLE_ALPHA),
} D3D10_COLOR_WRITE_ENABLE;
```

These flags control which color channels in the back buffer are written to after blending. For example, you could disable writes to the RGB channels and only write to the alpha channel, by specifying `D3D10_COLOR_WRITE_ENABLE_ALPHA`. This flexibility can be useful for advanced techniques. When blending is disabled, the color returned from the pixel shader is used with no write mask applied. Again, there are eight of these fields, one corresponding to each of the eight potential render targets.

To bind a blend state object to the output merger stage of the pipeline, we call:

```
void ID3D10Device::OMSetBlendState(
    ID3D10BlendState *pBlendState,
    const FLOAT BlendFactor[4],
    UINT SampleMask);
```

- ■ pBlendState: A pointer to the blend state object to enable with the device.

- ■ BlendFactor: An array of four floats defining an RGBA color vector. This color vector is used as a blend factor when D3D10_BLEND_BLEND_FACTOR or D3D10_BLEND_INV_BLEND_FACTOR is specified.

- ■ SampleMask: Multisampling can take up to 32 samples. This 32-bit integer value is used to enable/disable the samples. For example, if you turn off the fifth bit, then the fifth sample will not be taken. Of course, disabling the fifth sample only has any consequence if you are actually using multisampling with at least five samples. If an application is using single sampling, then only the first bit of this parameter matters (see Exercise 1). Generally the default of 0xffffffff is used, which does not disable any samples.

As with the other state blocks, there is a default blend state (blending disabled); if you call OMSetBlendState with null, then it restores the default blend state. We note that blending does require additional per-pixel work, so only enable it if you need it, and turn it off when you are done.

The following code shows an example of creating and setting a blend state:

```
D3D10_BLEND_DESC blendDesc = {0};
blendDesc.AlphaToCoverageEnable = false;
blendDesc.BlendEnable[0] = true;
blendDesc.SrcBlend = D3D10_BLEND_SRC_ALPHA;
blendDesc.DestBlend = D3D10_BLEND_INV_SRC_ALPHA;
blendDesc.BlendOp = D3D10_BLEND_OP_ADD;
blendDesc.SrcBlendAlpha = D3D10_BLEND_ONE;
blendDesc.DestBlendAlpha = D3D10_BLEND_ZERO;
blendDesc.BlendOpAlpha = D3D10_BLEND_OP_ADD;
blendDesc.RenderTargetWriteMask[0] = D3D10_COLOR_WRITE_ENABLE_ALL;

ID3D10BlendState* mTransparentBS;
HR(md3dDevice->CreateBlendState(&blendDesc, &mTransparentBS));

...

float blendFactors[] = {0.0f, 0.0f, 0.0f, 0.0f};
md3dDevice->OMSetBlendState(mTransparentBS, blendFactors, 0xffffffff);
```

As with other state block interfaces, you should create them all at application initialization time, and then just switch between the state interfaces as needed.

A blend state object can also be set and defined in an effect file:

```
BlendState blend
{
    BlendEnable[0] = TRUE;
    SrcBlend = SRC_COLOR;
    DestBlend = INV_SRC_ALPHA;
    BlendOp = ADD;
    SrcBlendAlpha = ZERO;
    DestBlendAlpha = ZERO;
    BlendOpAlpha = ADD;
    RenderTargetWriteMask[0] = 0x0F;
};

technique10 Tech
{
    pass P0
    {
        ...

        // Use "blend" for this pass.
        SetBlendState(blend, float4(0.0f, 0.0f, 0.0f, 0.0f), 0xffffffff);
    }
}
```

The values you assign to the blend state object are like those you assign to the C++ structure, except without the prefix. For example, instead of specifying D3D10_BLEND_SRC_COLOR we just specify SRC_COLOR in the effect code.

8.5 **Examples**

In the following subsections, we look at some blend factor combinations used to get specific effects. In these examples, we only look at RGB blending, because, as we mentioned earlier, we do not need back buffer alpha values for any algorithm in this book. Thus it doesn't matter what alpha value we write to the back buffer.

8.5.1 **No Color Write**

Suppose that we want to keep the original destination pixel exactly as it is and not overwrite it or blend it with the source pixel currently being rasterized. This can be useful, for example, if you just want to write to the depth/stencil buffer, and not the back buffer. To do this, set the source pixel blend factor to D3D10_BLEND_ZERO, the destination blend factor to D3D10_BLEND_ONE, and the blend operator to D3D10_BLEND_OP_ADD. With this setup, the blending equation reduces to:

$$\mathbf{C} = \mathbf{C}_{src} \otimes \mathbf{F}_{src} \boxplus \mathbf{C}_{dst} \otimes \mathbf{F}_{dst}$$
$$\mathbf{C} = \mathbf{C}_{src} \otimes (0,0,0) + \mathbf{C}_{dst} \otimes (1,1,1)$$
$$\mathbf{C} = \mathbf{C}_{dst}$$

8.5.2 **Adding/Subtracting**

Suppose that we want to add the source pixels and the destination pixels (see Figure 8.2). To do this, set the source blend factor to D3D10_BLEND_ONE, the destination blend factor to D3D10_BLEND_ONE, and the blend operator to D3D10_BLEND_OP_ADD. With this setup, the blending equation reduces to:

$$\mathbf{C} = \mathbf{C}_{src} \otimes \mathbf{F}_{src} \boxplus \mathbf{C}_{dst} \otimes \mathbf{F}_{dst}$$

$$\mathbf{C} = \mathbf{C}_{src} \otimes (1,1,1) + \mathbf{C}_{dst} \otimes (1,1,1)$$

$$\mathbf{C} = \mathbf{C}_{src} + \mathbf{C}_{dst}$$

Source pixels can be subtracted from the destination pixels by replacing D3D10_BLEND_OP_ADD with D3D10_BLEND_OP_SUBTRACT or D3D10_BLEND_OP_REV_SUBTRACT (see Figure 8.3).

Figure 8.2: Adding source and destination color. Adding creates a brighter image since color is being added.

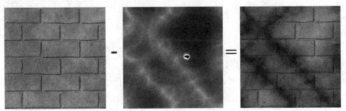

Figure 8.3: Subtracting source color from destination color. Subtraction creates a darker image since color is being removed.

8.5.3 **Multiplying**

Suppose that we want to multiply a source pixel with its corresponding destination pixel (see Figure 8.4). To do this, we set the source blend factor to D3D10_BLEND_ZERO, the destination blend factor to D3D10_BLEND_SRC_COLOR, and the blend operator to D3D10_BLEND_OP_ADD. With this setup, the blending equation reduces to:

$$\mathbf{C} = \mathbf{C}_{src} \otimes \mathbf{F}_{src} \boxplus \mathbf{C}_{dst} \otimes \mathbf{F}_{dst}$$
$$\mathbf{C} = \mathbf{C}_{src} \otimes (0,0,0) + \mathbf{C}_{dst} \otimes \mathbf{C}_{src}$$
$$\mathbf{C} = \mathbf{C}_{dst} \otimes \mathbf{C}_{src}$$

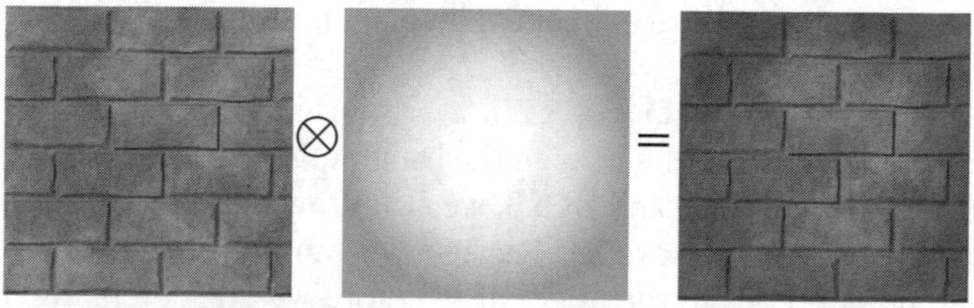

Figure 8.4: Multiplying source color and destination color.

8.5.4 **Transparency**

Let the source alpha component a_s be thought of as a percentage that controls the opacity of the source pixel (e.g., 0.0 alpha means 0% opaque, 0.4 means 40% opaque, and 1.0 means 100% opaque). The relationship between opacity and transparency is simply $T = 1 - A$, where A is opacity and T is transparency. For instance, if something is 0.4 opaque, then it is $1 - 0.4 = 0.6$ transparent. Now suppose that we want to blend the source and destination pixels based on the opacity of the source pixel. To do this, set the source blend factor to D3D10_BLEND_SRC_ALPHA, the destination blend factor to D3D10_BLEND_INV_SRC_ALPHA, and the blend operator to D3D10_BLEND_OP_ADD. With this setup, the blending equation reduces to:

$$\mathbf{C} = \mathbf{C}_{src} \otimes \mathbf{F}_{src} \boxplus \mathbf{C}_{dst} \otimes \mathbf{F}_{dst}$$
$$\mathbf{C} = \mathbf{C}_{src} \otimes (a_s, a_s, a_s) + \mathbf{C}_{dst} \otimes (1 - a_s, 1 - a_s, 1 - a_s)$$
$$\mathbf{C} = a_s \mathbf{C}_{dst} \otimes (1 - a_s) \mathbf{C}_{src}$$

For example, suppose $a_s = 0.25$, which is to say the source pixel is only 25% opaque. Then when the source and destination pixels are blended together, we expect the final color will be a combination of 25% of the source pixel and 75% of the destination pixel (the pixel "behind" the source pixel), since the source pixel is 75% transparent. The equation above gives us precisely this:

$$\mathbf{C} = a_s \mathbf{C}_{dst} \otimes (1 - a_s) \mathbf{C}_{src}$$
$$\mathbf{C} = 0.25 \mathbf{C}_{dst} \otimes 0.75 \mathbf{C}_{src}$$

Using this blending method, we can draw a transparent object like the one in Figure 8.1. It should be noted that with this blending method, the order in which you draw the objects matters. We use the following rule:

> _Draw objects that do not use blending first. Next, sort the objects that use blending by their distance from the camera. Finally, draw the objects that use blending in a back-to-front order._

The reason for the back-to-front draw order is so that objects are blended with the objects behind them. If an object is transparent, we can see through it to see the scene behind it. Therefore, it is necessary that all the pixels behind the transparent object be written to the back buffer first, so that we can blend the transparent source pixels with the destination pixels of the scene behind it.

For the blending method in §8.5.1, draw order does not matter since it simply prevents source pixel writes to the back buffer. For the blending methods discussed in §8.5.2 and §8.5.3, we still draw non-blended objects first and blended objects last; this is because we want to first lay all the non-blended geometry onto the back buffer before we start blending. However, we do not need to sort the objects that use blending. This is because the operations are commutative. That is, if you start with a back buffer pixel color $\mathbf{B}$, and then do n additive/subtractive/multiplicative blends to that pixel, the order does not matter:

$$\mathbf{B}' = \mathbf{B} + \mathbf{C}_0 + \mathbf{C}_1 + \cdots + \mathbf{C}_{n-1}$$
$$\mathbf{B}' = \mathbf{B} - \mathbf{C}_0 - \mathbf{C}_1 - \cdots - \mathbf{C}_{n-1}$$
$$\mathbf{B}' = \mathbf{B} \otimes \mathbf{C}_0 \otimes \mathbf{C}_1 \otimes \cdots \otimes \mathbf{C}_{n-1}$$

8.5.5 Blending and the Depth Buffer

When blending with additive/subtractive/multiplicative blending, an issue arises with the depth test. For the sake of example, we will explain only with additive blending, but the same idea holds for subtractive/multiplicative blending. If we are rendering a set S of objects with additive blending, the idea is that the objects in S do not obscure each other; instead, their colors are meant to simply accumulate (see Figure 8.5). Therefore, we do not want to perform the depth test between objects in S. In this situation, without a back-to-front draw ordering, one of the objects in S would obscure another object in S, thus causing the pixel fragments to be rejected due to the depth test, which means that object's pixel colors would not be accumulated into the blend sum. We can disable the depth test between objects in S by disabling writes to the depth buffer while rendering objects in S. Because depth writes are disabled, the depths of an object in S drawn with additive blending will not be written to the depth buffer; hence, this object will not obscure any later drawn object in S behind it due to the depth test. Note that we only disable depth writes while drawing the objects in S (the set of objects drawn with additive blending). Depth reads and the depth test are still enabled. This is so that non-blended geometry (which is drawn before blended geometry) will still obscure blended geometry behind it. For example, if you have a set of additively blended objects behind a wall, you will not see the blended objects because the solid wall obscures them. How to disable depth writes and, more generally, configure the depth test settings will be covered in the next chapter.

Figure 8.5: With additive blending, the intensity is greater near the source point where more particles are overlapping and being added together. As the particles spread out, the intensity weakens because there are fewer particles overlapping and being added together.

8.6 **Alpha Channels**

The example from §8.5.4 showed that source alpha components can be used in RGB blending to control transparency. The source color used in the blending equation comes from the pixel shader. As we saw in the last chapter, we return the diffuse material's alpha value as the alpha output of the pixel shader. Thus the alpha channel of the diffuse map is used to control transparency.

```
float4 PS(VS_OUT pIn) : SV_Target
{
    // Get materials from texture maps.
    float4 diffuse = gDiffuseMap.Sample( gTriLinearSam, pIn.texC );
    float4 spec    = gSpecMap.Sample( gTriLinearSam, pIn.texC );

    ...

    return float4(litColor, diffuse.a);
}
```

You can generally add an alpha channel in any popular image editing software, such as Adobe Photoshop, and then save the image to a format that supports an alpha channel (e.g., 32-bit BMP format or DDS format). However, here we show an alternative way to insert an alpha channel using the DXTex utility program that was discussed in the previous chapter.

We start by assuming we have two images — a color RGB image and a grayscale image — that will be inserted into the alpha channel (see Figure 8.6).

Figure 8.6: An RGB image (left) and a grayscale image (right). The grayscale image will be inserted into the alpha channel of the texture.

RGB Channels   **Alpha Channel**

Now, open the DXTex tool and open the **fire_rgb.bmp** file located in this chapter's demo folder. The fire texture is automatically loaded in as a 24-bit RGB texture (i.e., D3DFMT_R8G8B8), with 8 bits of red, 8 bits of green, and 8 bits of blue per pixel. We need to change the texture to a format that supports an alpha channel, such as a 32-bit ARGB texture format D3DFMT_A8R8G8B8 or a compressed format that supports alpha like D3DFMT_DXT5. Select **Format** from the menu bar and choose **Change Surface Format**. A dialog box pops up, as shown in Figure 8.7. Select the **DXT5** format and click **OK**.

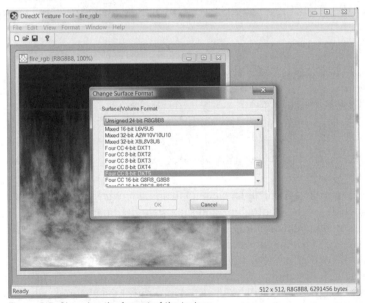

Figure 8.7: Changing the format of the texture.

This creates a compressed texture with an alpha channel. Our next task is to load data into the alpha channel. We will load the 8-bit grayscale map shown in Figure 8.6 into the alpha channel. Select **File** from the menu bar, and then choose **Open Onto Alpha Channel Of This Texture**, followed by **Format>Generate Mip Maps.** A dialog box will pop up, asking you to locate the image file that contains the data you want to load into the alpha channel. Select the **fire_a.bmp** file that is located in this chapter's demo folder. Figure 8.8 shows the program after the alpha channel data has been inserted — the texture is transparently blended with a background color. The background color can be changed by choosing **View** from the menu bar, then **Change Background Color....** You can also choose **View>Alpha Channel Only** to only view the alpha channel.

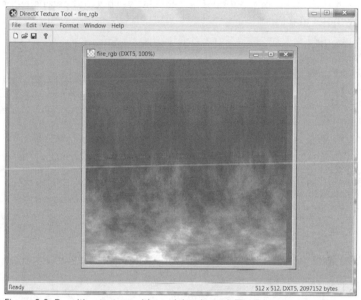

Figure 8.8: Resulting texture with an alpha channel. The fire texture is transparently blended against a blue background color.

Now save the texture with the name of your choice (e.g., fire.dds).

8.7 **Transparent Water Demo**

For this demo (see Figure 8.1), we modify the Land Tex demo from the previous chapter by making the water transparent. Figure 8.9 shows the alpha map we use. This alpha map was designed based on the land mesh so that the water is most transparent near the shore, and then gradually becomes less transparent as the water depth increases.

Figure 8.9: The water texture's alpha channel. The idea was to make deep areas more opaque and shallow regions more transparent.

For the most part, this demo is exactly like the one from the previous chapter except that we have to enable blending before we draw the water with the transparency blend factors. However, there is another minor issue. Recall that we are tiling the water texture over the water surface. Clearly, we do not want to tile the alpha channel over the water surface as it was designed globally based on the water depth with respect to the land mesh — if we tiled it, the alpha channel would no longer correspond to the water depth. Therefore, we will need to sample the texture twice — once using the transformed texture coordinate to get the tiled RGB color, and again using the unmodified texture coordinates in the range [0, 1] to get the alpha component. The relevant vertex and pixel shader code now looks like this:

```
struct VS_IN
{
    float3 posL    : POSITION;
    float3 normalL : NORMAL;
    float2 texC    : TEXCOORD;
};

struct VS_OUT
{
    float4 posH    : SV_POSITION;
    float3 posW    : POSITION;
    float3 normalW : NORMAL;
    float2 texC0   : TEXCOORD0;
    float2 texC1   : TEXCOORD1;
};

VS_OUT VS(VS_IN vIn)
{
    VS_OUT vOut;

    ...

    // Output vertex attributes for interpolation across triangle.
    vOut.texC0 = vIn.texC;
    vOut.texC1 = mul(float4(vIn.texC, 0.0f, 1.0f), gTexMtx);

    return vOut;
}

float4 PS(VS_OUT pIn) : SV_Target
{
    // Get materials from texture maps.
    float  alpha   = gDiffuseMap.Sample( gTriLinearSam, pIn.texC0 ).a;
    float4 diffuse = gDiffuseMap.Sample( gTriLinearSam, pIn.texC1 );
    float4 spec    = gSpecMap.Sample( gTriLinearSam, pIn.texC1 );

    ...

    return float4(litColor, alpha);
}
```

8.8 **Clipping Pixels**

Sometimes we want to completely reject a source pixel from being further processed. This can be done with the intrinsic HLSL `clip(x)` function. This function can only be called in a pixel shader, and it discards the current pixel from further processing if x < 0. This function is useful for rendering wire fence textures, for example, like the one shown in Figure 8.10. That is, it is useful for rendering pixels where a pixel is either completely opaque or completely transparent.

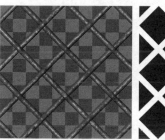 

RGB Channels   **Alpha Channel**

Figure 8.10: A wire fence texture with its alpha channel. The pixels with black alpha values will be rejected by the `clip` function and not drawn; hence, only the wire fence remains. Essentially, the alpha channel is used to mask out the non-fence pixels from the texture.

In the pixel shader, we grab the diffuse alpha component. If it is a small value close to 0, which indicates that the pixel is completely transparent, then we clip the pixel from further processing.

```
float4 PS(VS_OUT pIn) : SV_Target
{
    // Get materials from texture maps.
    float alpha = gDiffuseMap.Sample( gTriLinearSam, pIn.texC0 ).a;

    // Discard pixel if texture alpha < 0.25f. Note that we do this
    // test as soon as possible so that we can potentially exit the shader
    // early, thereby skipping the rest of the shader code.
    clip(alpha - 0.25f);

    ...
```

Note that the same result can be obtained using blending, but this is more efficient. For one thing, no blending calculation needs to be done. Also, the draw order does not matter. And furthermore, by discarding a pixel early from the pixel shader, the remaining pixel shader instructions can be skipped (no point in doing the calculations for a discarded pixel).

Note: Due to filtering, the alpha channel can get blurred a bit, so you should leave some buffer room when clipping pixels. For example, clip pixels with alpha values close to 0, but not necessarily exactly zero.

Figure 8.11 shows a screenshot of the Clip Pixel demo. Most of the code is like the Transparent Water demo, except that we use the new wire fence texture, and add the `clip` test to the pixel shader code. One other change worth mentioning is that, because we can now see through the box with the fence texture, we want to disable backface culling:

```
D3D10_RASTERIZER_DESC rsDesc;
ZeroMemory(&rsDesc, sizeof(D3D10_RASTERIZER_DESC));
rsDesc.FillMode = D3D10_FILL_SOLID;
rsDesc.CullMode = D3D10_CULL_NONE;

HR(md3dDevice->CreateRasterizerState(&rsDesc, &mNoCullRS));

...

// Since the gate texture has transparent regions, we can
// see through it, and thus see the backsides of the triangles.
// Therefore, we don't want to backface cull in this case.
md3dDevice->RSSetState(mNoCullRS);
pass->Apply(0);
mBox.draw();
md3dDevice->RSSetState(0); // restore default
```

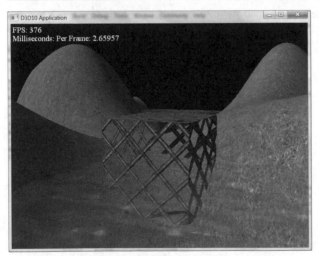

Figure 8.11: Screenshot of the Clip Pixel demo.

8.9 Fog

To simulate certain types of weather conditions in our games, we need to be able to implement a fog effect (see Figure 8.12). In addition to the obvious purposes of fog, fog provides some fringe benefits. For example, it can mask distant rendering artifacts and prevent popping. *Popping* refers to an object that was previously behind the far plane all of a sudden coming in front of the frustum, due to camera movement, and thus becoming visible;

it seems to "pop" into the scene abruptly. By having a layer of fog in the distance, the popping is hidden. Note that if your scene takes place on a clear day, you may still wish to include a subtle amount of fog at far distances, because, even on clear days, distant objects such as mountains appear hazy and lose contrast as a function of depth. We can use fog to simulate this *atmospheric perspective* phenomenon.

Figure 8.12: Screenshot of the Fog demo.

Our strategy for implementing fog works as follows: We specify a fog color, a fog start distance from the camera, and a fog range (i.e., the range from the fog start distance until the fog completely hides any objects). Then the color of a point on a triangle is a weighted average of its usual color and the fog color:

$$foggedColor = litColor + s(fogColor - litColor)$$
$$= (1-s) \cdot litColor + s \cdot fogColor$$

The parameter s ranges from 0 to 1 and is a function of the distance between the camera position and the surface point. As the distance between a surface point and the eye increases, the point becomes more and more obscured by the fog. The parameter s is defined as follows:

$$s = \text{saturate}\left(\frac{dist(\mathbf{p},\mathbf{E}) - fogStart}{fogRange}\right)$$

where dist(**p**, **E**) is the distance between the surface point **p** and the camera position **E**. The saturate function clamps the argument to the range [0, 1]:

$$saturate(x) = \begin{cases} x, & 0 \le x \le 1 \\ 0, & x < 0 \\ 1, & x > 1 \end{cases}$$

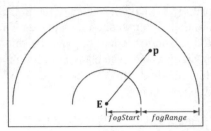

Figure 8.13: The distance of a point from the eye and the *fogStart* and *fogRange* parameters.

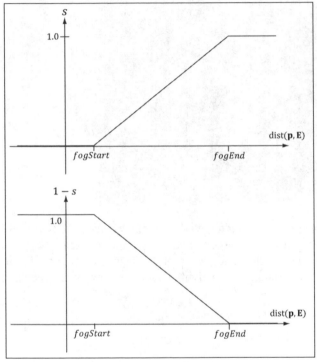

Figure 8.14: (Top) A plot of *s* (the fog color weight) as a function of distance. (Bottom) A plot of 1 − *s* (the lit color weight) as a function of distance. As *s* increases, (1 − *s*) decreases the same amount.

Figure 8.14 shows a plot of *s* as a function of distance. We see that when dist($\mathbf{p}$, $\mathbf{E}$) ≤ *fogStart*, *s* = 0 and the fogged color is given by:

$$foggedColor = litColor$$

In other words, the fog does not modify the color of vertices whose distance from the camera is less than *fogStart*. This makes sense based on the name *fogStart*; the fog does not start affecting the color until the distance from the camera is at least that of *fogStart*.

Let *fogEnd* = *fogStart* + *fogRange*. When dist($\mathbf{p}$, $\mathbf{E}$) ≥ *fogEnd*, *s* = 1 and the fogged color is given by:

$$foggedColor = fogColor$$

In other words, the fog completely hides the surface point at distances greater than or equal to _fogEnd_, so all you see is the fog color.

When _fogStart_ < dist($\mathbf{p}$, $\mathbf{E}$) < _fogEnd_, we see that s linearly ramps up from 0 to 1 as dist($\mathbf{p}$, $\mathbf{E}$) increases from _fogStart_ to _fogEnd_. This means that as the distance increases, the fog color gets more and more weight while the original color gets less and less weight. This makes sense, of course, because as the distance increases, the fog obscures more and more of the surface point.

The following shader code shows how fog is implemented. We compute the distance and interpolation parameter at the vertex level, and then interpolate that over the triangle pixels. The interpolation is done at the pixel level, after we have computed the lit color.

```
cbuffer cbFixed
{
    // For this demo, we hardcode the fog values. However, in a real
    // application, the program may want to change the fog settings
    // at run time; for example, to fade the fog in and out based on
    // the time of day or the location of the game player.

    float  gFogStart = 5.0f;
    float  gFogRange = 140.0f;
    float3 gFogColor = {0.7f, 0.7f, 0.7f};
};

struct VS_IN
{
    float3 posL    : POSITION;
    float3 normalL : NORMAL;
    float2 texC    : TEXCOORD;
};

struct VS_OUT
{
    float4 posH    : SV_POSITION;
    float3 posW    : POSITION;
    float3 normalW : NORMAL;
    float2 texC0   : TEXCOORD0;
    float2 texC1   : TEXCOORD1;
    float  fogLerp : FOG;
};

VS_OUT VS(VS_IN vIn)
{
    VS_OUT vOut;

    ...

    float d       = distance(vOut.posW, gEyePosW);
    vOut.fogLerp = saturate( (d - gFogStart) / gFogRange );
```

```
      return vOut;
}

float4 PS(VS_OUT pIn) : SV_Target
{
    ...

    // Compute the lit color for this pixel.
    SurfaceInfo v = {pIn.posW, normalW, diffuse, spec};
    float3 litColor = ParallelLight(v, gLight, gEyePosW);

    // Blend the fog color and the lit color.
    float3 foggedColor = lerp(litColor, gFogColor, pIn.fogLerp);

    return float4(foggedColor, alpha);
}
```

8.10 **Summary**

- Blending is a technique that allows us to blend (combine) the pixels that we are currently rasterizing (so-called *source* pixels) with the pixels that were previously rasterized to the back buffer (so-called *destination* pixels). This technique enables us, among other things, to render semi-transparent objects such as water and glass.

- The blending equation is:

$$C = C_{src} \otimes F_{src} \boxplus C_{dst} \otimes F_{dst}$$
$$A = A_{src} F_{src} \boxplus A_{dst} F_{dst}$$

Note that RGB components are blended independently of alpha components. The $\boxplus$ binary operator can be one of the operators defined by the D3D10_BLEND_OP enumerated type.

- F_{src}, F_{dst}, F_{src}, and F_{dst} are called blend factors, and they provide a means for customizing the blending equation. They can be a member of the D3D10_BLEND enumerated type. For the alpha blending equation, blend factors ending with _COLOR are *not allowed*.

- Source alpha information comes from the diffuse material. In our framework, the diffuse material is defined by a texture map, and the texture's alpha channel stores the alpha information.

- Source pixels can be completely rejected from further processing using the intrinsic HLSL clip(x) function. This function can only be called in a pixel shader, and it discards the current pixel from further processing if x < 0. Among other things, this function is useful for efficiently rendering pixels where a pixel is either completely opaque or completely transparent (it is used to reject completely transparent pixels — pixels with an alpha value near zero).

■ Use fog to model various weather effects and atmospheric perspective, to hide distant rendering artifacts, and to hide popping. In our linear fog model, we specify a fog color, a fog start distance from the camera, and a fog range. The color of a point on a triangle is a weighted average of its usual color and the fog color:

$$foggedColor = litColor + s(fogColor - litColor)$$
$$= (1 - s) \cdot litColor + s \cdot fogColor$$

The parameter s ranges from 0 to 1 and is a function of the distance between the camera position and the surface point. As the distance between a surface point and the eye increases, the point becomes more and more obscured by the fog.

8.11 **Exercises**

1. Modify the Transparent Water demo by using the following line before drawing the water:

```
md3dDevice->OMSetBlendState(mTransparentBS, blendFactors, 0xfffffffe);
```

This turns off the first bit, which disables the first sample. Since we are not using multisampling (which is like using multisampling with one sample), this will prevent the water pixels from being drawn.

2. Experiment with different blend operation and blend factor combinations.

3. Modify the Transparent Water demo by drawing the water first. Explain the results.

4. Suppose _fogStart_ = 10 and _fogRange_ = 200. Compute _foggedColor_ for when

a. dist($\mathbf{p}$, $\mathbf{E}$) = 160

b. dist($\mathbf{p}$, $\mathbf{E}$) = 110

c. dist($\mathbf{p}$, $\mathbf{E}$) = 60

d. dist($\mathbf{p}$, $\mathbf{E}$) = 30

Chapter 9

Stenciling

The stencil buffer is an off-screen buffer we can use to achieve special effects. The stencil buffer has the same resolution as the back buffer and depth buffer, such that the ijth pixel in the stencil buffer corresponds with the ijth pixel in the back buffer and depth buffer. Recall from the note in §4.1.5 that when a stencil buffer is specified, the stencil buffer always shares the depth buffer. As the name suggests, the stencil buffer works as a stencil and allows us to block the rendering of certain pixel fragments to the back buffer.

For instance, when implementing a mirror we need to reflect an object across the plane of the mirror; however, we only want to draw the reflection into the mirror. We can use the stencil buffer to block the rendering of the reflection unless it is being drawn into the mirror (see Figure 9.1).

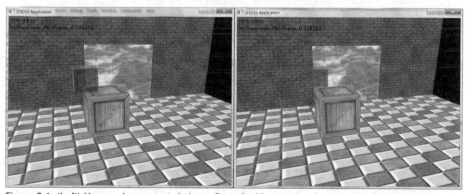

Figure 9.1: (Left) Here we have a crate being reflected without using the stencil buffer. We see that the reflected crate is always reflected regardless of whether the reflection is in the mirror. (Right) By using the stencil buffer, we can block the reflected crate from being rendered unless it is being drawn in the mirror.

The stencil buffer (and also the depth buffer) is controlled via the ID3D10DepthStencilState interface. Like blending, the interface offers a flexible and powerful set of capabilities. Learning to use the stencil buffer effectively comes best by studying existing example applications. Once you understand a few applications of the stencil buffer, you will have a better idea of how it can be used for your own specific needs.

Objectives:

■ To find out how to control the depth and stencil buffer settings with the ID3D10DepthStencilState interface.

■ To learn how to implement mirrors by using the stencil buffer to prevent reflections from being drawn to non-mirror surfaces.

■ To learn how to measure depth complexity using the stencil buffer.

9.1 **Depth/Stencil Formats and Clearing**

Recalling that the depth/stencil buffer is a texture, it must be created with certain data formats. The formats used for depth/stencil buffering are as follows:

■ DXGI_FORMAT_D32_FLOAT_S8X24_UINT: Specifies a 32-bit floating-point depth buffer, with 8 bits (unsigned integer) reserved for the stencil buffer mapped to the [0, 255] range and 24 bits used for padding.

■ DXGI_FORMAT_D24_UNORM_S8_UINT: Specifies an unsigned 24-bit depth buffer mapped to the [0, 1] range with 8 bits (unsigned integer) reserved for the stencil buffer mapped to the [0, 255] range.

In our D3DApp framework, when we create the depth buffer we specify:

```
depthStencilDesc.Format = DXGI_FORMAT_D24_UNORM_S8_UINT;
```

Also, the stencil buffer should be reset to some value at the beginning of each frame. This is done with the following method (which also clears the depth buffer):

```
void ID3D10Device::ClearDepthStencilView(
    ID3D10DepthStencilView *pDepthStencilView,
    UINT ClearFlags, FLOAT Depth, UINT8 Stencil);
```

■ pDepthStencilView: Pointer to the view of the depth/stencil buffer we want to clear.

■ ClearFlags: Specify D3D10_CLEAR_DEPTH to clear the depth buffer only, D3D10_CLEAR_STENCIL to clear the stencil buffer only, or D3D10_CLEAR_DEPTH | D3D10_CLEAR_STENCIL to clear both.

■ Depth: The float value to set each pixel in the depth buffer to; it must be a floating-point number x such that $0 \leq x \leq 1$.

■ Stencil: The integer value to set each pixel of the stencil buffer to; it must be an integer n such that $0 \leq n \leq 255$.

In our D3DApp framework, we call this function in the D3DApp::drawScene method:

```
void D3DApp::drawScene()
{
    md3dDevice->ClearRenderTargetView(mRenderTargetView, mClearColor);
    md3dDevice->ClearDepthStencilView(mDepthStencilView,
        D3D10_CLEAR_DEPTH|D3D10_CLEAR_STENCIL, 1.0f, 0);
}
```

9.2 The Stencil Test

As previously stated, we can use the stencil buffer to block rendering to certain areas of the back buffer. The decision to block a particular pixel from being written is decided by the *stencil test*, which is given by the following:

```
if( StencilRef & StencilReadMask ◁ Value & StencilReadMask )
        accept pixel
    else
        reject pixel
```

The stencil test is performed as pixels get rasterized, assuming stenciling is enabled, and takes two operands:

- A left-hand-side (LHS) operand that is determined by ANDing an application-defined *stencil reference value* (StencilRef) with an application-defined *masking value* (StencilReadMask).

- A right-hand-side (RHS) operand that is determined by ANDing the entry already in the stencil buffer of the particular pixel we are testing (Value) with an application-defined masking value (StencilReadMask).

The stencil test then compares the LHS with the RHS as specified by an application-chosen *comparison function* ◁, which returns a true or false value. We write the pixel to the back buffer if the test evaluates to true (assuming the depth test also passes). If the test evaluates to false, then we block the pixel from being written to the back buffer. And of course, if a pixel is rejected due to failing the stencil test, it is not written to the depth buffer either.

The ◁ operator is any one of the functions defined in the D3D10_ COMPARISON_FUNC enumerated type:

```
typedef enum D3D10_COMPARISON_FUNC
{
    D3D10_COMPARISON_NEVER = 1,
    D3D10_COMPARISON_LESS = 2,
    D3D10_COMPARISON_EQUAL = 3,
    D3D10_COMPARISON_LESS_EQUAL = 4,
    D3D10_COMPARISON_GREATER = 5,
    D3D10_COMPARISON_NOT_EQUAL = 6,
    D3D10_COMPARISON_GREATER_EQUAL = 7,
```

```
    D3D10_COMPARISON_ALWAYS = 8,
} D3D10_COMPARISON_FUNC;
```

- ■ D3D10_COMPARISON_NEVER: The function always returns false.
- ■ D3D10_COMPARISON_LESS: Replace ⊴ with the < operator.
- ■ D3D10_COMPARISON_EQUAL: Replace ⊴ with the == operator.
- ■ D3D10_COMPARISON_LESS_EQUAL: Replace ⊴ with the ≤ operator.
- ■ D3D10_COMPARISON_GREATER: Replace ⊴ with the > operator.
- ■ D3D10_COMPARISON_NOT_EQUAL: Replace ⊴ with the ! = operator.
- ■ D3D10_COMPARISON_GREATER_EQUAL: Replace ⊴ with the ≥ operator.
- ■ D3D10_COMPARISON_ALWAYS: The function always returns true.

9.3 The Depth/Stencil State Block

The first step to creating an ID3D10DepthStencilState interface is to fill out a D3D10_DEPTH_STENCIL_DESC instance:

```
typedef struct D3D10_DEPTH_STENCIL_DESC {
    BOOL DepthEnable;
    D3D10_DEPTH_WRITE_MASK DepthWriteMask;
    D3D10_COMPARISON_FUNC DepthFunc;
    BOOL StencilEnable;
    UINT8 StencilReadMask;
    UINT8 StencilWriteMask;
    D3D10_DEPTH_STENCILOP_DESC FrontFace;
    D3D10_DEPTH_STENCILOP_DESC BackFace;
} D3D10_DEPTH_STENCIL_DESC;
```

9.3.1 Depth Settings

- ■ DepthEnable: Specify true to enable the depth test; specify false to disable it. When depth testing is disabled, the draw order matters, and a pixel fragment will be drawn even if it is behind an occluding object (review §4.1.5). If the depth test is disabled, elements in the depth buffer are *not* updated either, regardless of the DepthWriteMask setting.

- ■ DepthWriteMask: This can be either D3D10_DEPTH_WRITE_MASK_ZERO or D3D10_DEPTH_WRITE_MASK_ALL, but not both. Assuming DepthEnable is set to true, D3D10_DEPTH_WRITE_MASK_ZERO disables writes to the depth buffer, but depth testing will still occur. D3D10_DEPTH_WRITE_MASK_ALL enables writes to the depth buffer; new depths will be written provided the depth and stencil test both pass.

- ■ DepthFunc: Specify one of the members of the D3D10_COMPARISON_FUNC enumerated type to define the depth test comparison function. Usually this is always D3D10_COMPARISON_LESS so that the usual depth test is performed, as described in §4.1.5. That is, a pixel fragment is accepted provided its depth value is less than the depth of the previous pixel written to the back buffer. But as you can see, Direct3D allows you to customize the depth test if necessary.

9.3.2 Stencil Settings

- `StencilEnable`: Specify true to enable the stencil test; specify false to disable it.

- `StencilReadMask`: The `StencilReadMask` used in the stencil test:

```
if(StencilRef & StencilReadMask ⊴ Value & StencilReadMask)
    accept pixel
else
    reject pixel
```

The default does not mask any bits:

```
#define D3D10_DEFAULT_STENCIL_READ_MASK (0xff)
```

- `StencilWriteMask`: When the stencil buffer is being updated, we can mask off certain bits from being written to with the write mask. For example, if you wanted to prevent the top four bits from being written to, you could use the write mask of 0x0f. The default value does not mask any bits:

```
#define D3D10_DEFAULT_STENCIL_WRITE_MASK (0xff)
```

- `FrontFace`: A filled-out `D3D10_DEPTH_STENCILOP_DESC` structure indicating how the stencil buffer works for front-facing triangles.

- `BackFace`: A filled-out `D3D10_DEPTH_STENCILOP_DESC` structure indicating how the stencil buffer works for back-facing triangles.

```
typedef struct D3D10_DEPTH_STENCILOP_DESC {
    D3D10_STENCIL_OP StencilFailOp;
    D3D10_STENCIL_OP StencilDepthFailOp;
    D3D10_STENCIL_OP StencilPassOp;
    D3D10_COMPARISON_FUNC StencilFunc;
} D3D10_DEPTH_STENCILOP_DESC;
```

- `StencilFailOp`: A member of the `D3D10_STENCIL_OP` enumerated type describing how the stencil buffer should be updated when the stencil test fails for a pixel fragment.

- `StencilDepthFailOp`: A member of the `D3D10_STENCIL_OP` enumerated type describing how the stencil buffer should be updated when the stencil test passes but the depth test fails for a pixel fragment.

- `StencilPassOp`: A member of the `D3D10_STENCIL_OP` enumerated type describing how the stencil buffer should be updated when the stencil test and depth test both pass for a pixel fragment.

- `StencilFunc`: A member of the `D3D10_COMPARISON_FUNC` enumerated type to define the stencil test comparison function.

```
typedef enum D3D10_STENCIL_OP
{
    D3D10_STENCIL_OP_KEEP = 1,
    D3D10_STENCIL_OP_ZERO = 2,
    D3D10_STENCIL_OP_REPLACE = 3,
    D3D10_STENCIL_OP_INCR_SAT = 4,
    D3D10_STENCIL_OP_DECR_SAT = 5,
    D3D10_STENCIL_OP_INVERT = 6,
    D3D10_STENCIL_OP_INCR = 7,
    D3D10_STENCIL_OP_DECR = 8,
} D3D10_STENCIL_OP;
```

- D3D10_STENCIL_OP_KEEP: Specifies to not change the stencil buffer; that is, keep the value currently there.

- D3D10_STENCIL_OP_ZERO: Specifies to set the stencil buffer entry to 0.

- D3D10_STENCIL_OP_REPLACE: Specifies to replace the stencil buffer entry with the stencil-reference value (StencilRef) used in the stencil test. Note that the StencilRef value is set when we bind the depth/stencil state block to the rendering pipeline (§9.3.3).

- D3D10_STENCIL_OP_INCR_SAT: Specifies to increment the stencil buffer entry. If the incremented value exceeds the maximum value (e.g., 255 for an 8-bit stencil buffer), then we clamp the entry to that maximum.

- D3D10_STENCIL_OP_DECR_SAT: Specifies to decrement the stencil buffer entry. If the decremented value is less than 0, then we clamp the entry to 0.

- D3D10_STENCIL_OP_INVERT: Specifies to invert the bits of the stencil buffer entry.

- D3D10_STENCIL_OP_INCR: Specifies to increment the stencil buffer entry. If the incremented value exceeds the maximum value (e.g., 255 for an 8-bit stencil buffer), then we wrap to 0.

- D3D10_STENCIL_OP_DECR: Specifies to decrement the stencil buffer entry. If the decremented value is less than 0, then we wrap to the maximum allowed value.

Note: The BackFace settings are irrelevant in this case, since we do not render back-facing polygons due to backface culling. However, sometimes we do need to render back-facing polygons for certain graphics algorithms, or for transparent geometry (like the wire fence box, where we could see through the box to see the back sides). In these cases, the BackFace settings are relevant.

9.3.3 Creating and Binding a Depth/Stencil State

After we have filled out a D3D10_DEPTH_STENCIL_DESC structure, we can obtain a pointer to an ID3D10DepthStencilState interface with the following method:

```
HRESULT ID3D10Device::CreateDepthStencilState(
    const D3D10_DEPTH_STENCIL_DESC *pDepthStencilDesc,
    ID3D10DepthStencilState **ppDepthStencilState);
```

■ pDepthStencilDesc: Pointer to a filled-out D3D10_DEPTH_STENCIL_DESC structure describing the depth/stencil state block we want to create.

■ ppDepthStencilState: Returns a pointer to the created ID3D10DepthStencilState interface.

Once an ID3D10DepthStencilState interface is created, we bind it to the output merger stage of the pipeline with the following method:

```
void ID3D10Device::OMSetDepthStencilState(
    ID3D10DepthStencilState *pDepthStencilState,
    UINT StencilRef);
```

■ pDepthStencilState: Pointer to the depth/stencil state block to set.

■ StencilRef: The 32-bit stencil reference value to use in the stencil test.

As with the other state groups, a default depth/stencil state exists (basically the usual depth test with stenciling disabled). The default depth/stencil state can be restored by passing null for the first parameter of OMSetDepthStencilState:

```
// restore default
md3dDevice->OMSetDepthStencilState(0, 0);
```

9.3.4 Depth/Stencil States in Effect Files

A depth/stencil state can also be directly defined and set in an effect file:

```
DepthStencilState NoDepthWritesDSS
{
    DepthEnable    = false;
    DepthWriteMask = Zero;

    StencilEnable    = true;
    StencilReadMask  = 0xff;
    StencilWriteMask = 0xff;

    FrontFaceStencilFunc = Always;
    FrontFaceStencilPass = Incr;
    FrontFaceStencilFail = Keep;

    BackFaceStencilFunc = Always;
    BackFaceStencilPass = Incr;
    BackFaceStencilFail = Keep;
};
```

```
...

technique10 LayDepthTech
{
    pass P0
    {
        SetVertexShader( CompileShader( vs_4_0, LayDepthVS() ) );
        SetGeometryShader( NULL );
        SetPixelShader( CompileShader( ps_4_0, LayDepthPS() ) );

        SetDepthStencilState(NoDepthWritesDSS, 0);
    }
}
```

The values you assign to the depth/stencil state object are like those you assign to the C++ structure, except without the prefix. For example, instead of specifying D3D10_STENCIL_OP_INCR we just specify INCR in the effect code. Incidentally, the state values we specify are not case sensitive; for example, INCR is equivalent to Incr.

9.4 Mirror Demo

Many surfaces in nature serve as mirrors and allow us to see the reflections of objects. This section describes how we can simulate mirrors for our 3D applications. Note that for simplicity, we reduce the task of implementing mirrors to planar surfaces only. For instance, a shiny car can display a reflection; however, a car's body is smooth, round, and not planar. Instead, we render reflections such as those displayed in a shiny marble floor or in a mirror hanging on a wall — in other words, mirrors that lie on a plane.

Implementing mirrors programmatically requires us to solve two problems. First, we must learn how to reflect an object about an arbitrary plane so that we can draw the reflection correctly. Second, we must only display the reflection in a mirror; that is, we must somehow "mark" a surface as a mirror and then, as we are rendering, only draw the reflected object if it is in a mirror. Refer back to Figure 9.1, which first introduced this concept.

The first problem is easily solved with some analytic geometry, which is discussed in Appendix C. The second problem can be solved using the stencil buffer.

9.4.1 **Overview**

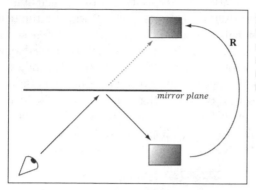

Figure 9.2: The eye sees the box reflection through the mirror. To simulate this, we reflect the box across the mirror plane and render the reflected box as usual.

Figure 9.2 shows that to draw a reflection of an object, we just need to reflect it over the mirror plane. However, this introduces problems, as seen in Figure 9.1. Namely, the reflection of the object (the crate in this case) is rendered on surfaces that are not mirrors (like the walls, for example). The reflection should only be seen through the mirror. We can solve this problem using the stencil buffer because the stencil buffer allows us to block rendering to certain areas on the back buffer. Thus we can use the stencil buffer to block the rendering of the reflected crate if it is not being rendered into the mirror. The following steps outline how this can be accomplished:

1. Render the floor, walls, mirror, and crate to the back buffer as normal. Note that this step does not modify the stencil buffer.

2. Clear the stencil buffer to 0. Figure 9.3 shows the back buffer and stencil buffer at this point.

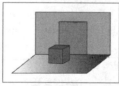 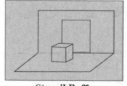

Back Buffer   **Stencil Buffer**

Figure 9.3: The scene rendered to the back buffer and the stencil buffer cleared to 0 (denoted by light gray color). The black outlines drawn on the stencil buffer illustrate the relationship between the back buffer pixels and the stencil buffer pixels — they do not indicate any data drawn on the stencil buffer.

3. Render the mirror to the stencil buffer. Set the stencil test to always succeed (`D3D10_COMPARISON_ALWAYS`) and specify that the stencil buffer entry should be replaced (`D3D10_STENCIL_OP_REPLACE`) with 1 if the test passes. If the depth test fails, we specify `D3D10_STENCIL_OP_KEEP` so that the stencil buffer is not changed if the depth test fails (this can happen if the crate obscures part of the mirror). Since we are only rendering the mirror to the stencil buffer, it follows that all the pixels in the stencil buffer will be 0 except for the pixels that correspond to the visible part of the mirror — they will have a 1. Figure 9.4 shows the updated stencil buffer. Essentially, we are marking the visible pixels of the mirror in the stencil buffer.

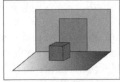 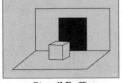

Back Buffer **Stencil Buffer**

Figure 9.4: Rendering the mirror to the stencil buffer, we are essentially marking the pixels in the stencil buffer that correspond to the visible parts of the mirror. The solid black area on the stencil buffer denotes stencil entries set to 1. Note that the area on the stencil buffer occluded by the crate does not get set to 1 since it fails the depth test (the crate is in front of that part of the mirror).

4. Now we render the reflected crate to the back buffer and stencil buffer. But recall that we only will render to the back buffer if the stencil test passes. This time, we set the stencil test to only succeed if the value in the stencil buffer is 1. In this way, the reflected crate will only be rendered to areas that have a 1 in their corresponding stencil buffer entry. Since the areas in the stencil buffer that correspond to the visible parts of the mirror are the only entries that have a 1, it follows that the reflected crate will only be rendered into the visible parts of the mirror.

9.4.2 Defining the Depth/Stencil States

To implement the previously described algorithm, we need two depth/stencil states. The first is used when drawing the mirror to mark the mirror pixels on the stencil buffer. The second is used to draw the reflected crate so that it is only drawn into the visible mirror.

```
D3D10_DEPTH_STENCIL_DESC dsDesc;
dsDesc.DepthEnable      = true;
dsDesc.DepthWriteMask   = D3D10_DEPTH_WRITE_MASK_ALL;
dsDesc.DepthFunc        = D3D10_COMPARISON_LESS;
dsDesc.StencilEnable    = true;
```

```
dsDesc.StencilReadMask  = 0xff;
dsDesc.StencilWriteMask = 0xff;

// Always pass the stencil test, and replace the
// current stencil value with the stencil reference value 1.
dsDesc.FrontFace.StencilFailOp      = D3D10_STENCIL_OP_KEEP;
dsDesc.FrontFace.StencilDepthFailOp = D3D10_STENCIL_OP_KEEP;
dsDesc.FrontFace.StencilPassOp      = D3D10_STENCIL_OP_REPLACE;
dsDesc.FrontFace.StencilFunc        = D3D10_COMPARISON_ALWAYS;

// We are not rendering backfacing polygons, so these
// settings do not matter.
dsDesc.BackFace.StencilFailOp       = D3D10_STENCIL_OP_KEEP;
dsDesc.BackFace.StencilDepthFailOp  = D3D10_STENCIL_OP_KEEP;
dsDesc.BackFace.StencilPassOp       = D3D10_STENCIL_OP_REPLACE;
dsDesc.BackFace.StencilFunc         = D3D10_COMPARISON_ALWAYS;

// Create the depth/stencil state used to draw the mirror
// to the stencil buffer.
HR(md3dDevice->CreateDepthStencilState(&dsDesc, &mDrawMirrorDSS));

// Only pass the stencil test if the value in the stencil
// buffer equals the stencil reference value.
dsDesc.DepthEnable       = true;
dsDesc.DepthWriteMask    = D3D10_DEPTH_WRITE_MASK_ZERO;
dsDesc.DepthFunc         = D3D10_COMPARISON_ALWAYS;
dsDesc.FrontFace.StencilPassOp = D3D10_STENCIL_OP_KEEP;
dsDesc.FrontFace.StencilFunc   = D3D10_COMPARISON_EQUAL;

// Create the depth/stencil state used to draw the reflected
// crate to the back buffer.
HR(md3dDevice->CreateDepthStencilState(&dsDesc, &mDrawReflectionDSS));
```

Note that when drawing the reflected crate, we set the depth test to always pass. This is because the reflected crate is behind the wall, so the wall actually occludes it. In other words, if we used the normal depth test comparison function, the reflected crate would not be drawn since the depth test would fail. Moreover, we disable depth writes, as we should not update the depth buffer with the depths of the reflected crate that lies behind the wall/mirror.

9.4.3 Blending the Reflection

Our mirror, as shown in Figure 9.1, is not a perfect mirror and it has a texture of its own. Therefore, we blend the reflected crate with the mirror so that the final color is a weighted average of the reflected crate color and the mirror color. In other words, the crate is not reflected perfectly off the mirror — only a percentage of it is; the remaining percentage of color comes from the interaction between the light and mirror material.

Note that the crate texture does not have a source alpha — the WoodCrate01.dds image has no alpha channel. So how does this blending work? Well, we use `D3D10_BLEND_BLEND_FACTOR` as the source blend factor and `D3D10_BLEND_INV_BLEND_FACTOR` as the destination blend factor; this allows us to specify the blend factor color in the `OMSetBlendState` method:

```
// Set blend state.
float blendf[] = {0.65f, 0.65f, 0.65f, 1.0f};
md3dDevice->OMSetBlendState(mDrawReflectionBS, blendf, 0xffffffff);

mCrateMesh.draw();

// Restore default blend state.
md3dDevice->OMSetBlendState(0, blendf, 0xffffffff);
```

These settings give the following blending equation:

$$\mathbf{C} = 0.65 \cdot \mathbf{C}_{src} + 0.45 \cdot \mathbf{C}_{dst}$$

So we see 65% of the color comes from the crate and 45% of the color comes from the mirror. For reference, the following code shows how we create the blend state interface:

```
D3D10_BLEND_DESC blendDesc = {0};
blendDesc.AlphaToCoverageEnable = false;
blendDesc.BlendEnable[0] = true;
blendDesc.SrcBlend       = D3D10_BLEND_BLEND_FACTOR;
blendDesc.DestBlend      = D3D10_BLEND_INV_BLEND_FACTOR;
blendDesc.BlendOp        = D3D10_BLEND_OP_ADD;
blendDesc.SrcBlendAlpha  = D3D10_BLEND_ONE;
blendDesc.DestBlendAlpha = D3D10_BLEND_ZERO;
blendDesc.BlendOpAlpha   = D3D10_BLEND_OP_ADD;
blendDesc.RenderTargetWriteMask[0] = D3D10_COLOR_WRITE_ENABLE_ALL;

HR(md3dDevice->CreateBlendState(&blendDesc, &mDrawReflectionBS));
```

9.4.4 Drawing the Scene

The following code illustrates our draw method. We have omitted irrelevant details, such as setting constant buffer values, for brevity and clarity (see the Mirror demo example code for the full details).

```
ID3D10EffectPass* pass = mTech->GetPassByIndex( p );

//
// Draw the floor and walls
//
...
drawRoom(pass);
//
// Draw the crate
//
...
mCrateMesh.draw();
//
```

```
// Draw the mirror to the back buffer and stencil buffer last
//
...
md3dDevice->OMSetDepthStencilState(mDrawMirrorDSS, 1);
drawMirror(pass);
md3dDevice->OMSetDepthStencilState(0, 0);


//
// Draw reflected crate in mirror.
//

// Build reflection matrix to reflect the crate.
D3DXPLANE mirrorPlane(0.0f, 0.0f, 1.0f, 0.0f); // xy plane
D3DXMATRIX R;
D3DXMatrixReflect(&R, &mirrorPlane);
D3DXMATRIX W = mCrateWorld*R;
...
// Reflect the light source as well.
D3DXVECTOR3 oldDir = mParallelLight.dir;
D3DXVec3TransformNormal(&mParallelLight.dir, &mParallelLight.dir, &R);
mfxLightVar->SetRawValue(&mParallelLight, 0, sizeof(Light));
pass->Apply(0);

md3dDevice->>RSSetState(mCullCWRS);
float blendf[] = {0.65f, 0.65f, 0.65f, 1.0f};
md3dDevice->OMSetBlendState(mDrawReflectionBS, blendf, 0xffffffff);

md3dDevice->OMSetDepthStencilState(mDrawReflectionDSS, 1);
mCrateMesh.draw();
md3dDevice->OMSetDepthStencilState(0, 0);

md3dDevice->OMSetBlendState(0, blendf, 0xffffffff);
md3dDevice->RSSetState(0);
mParallelLight.dir = oldDir; // restore
```

Note: When a triangle is reflected across a plane, its winding order does not reverse, and thus, its face normal does not reverse. Hence, outward-facing normals become inward-facing normals (see Figure 9.5) after reflection. To correct this, we tell Direct3D to interpret triangles with a counterclockwise winding order as front-facing and triangles with a clockwise winding order as back-facing (this is the opposite of our usual convention — §5.9.2). This effectively reflects the normal directions so that they are outward facing after reflection. We reverse the winding order convention by setting the following rasterizer state:

```
D3D10_RASTERIZER_DESC rsDesc;
ZeroMemory(&rsDesc, sizeof(D3D10_RASTERIZER_DESC));
rsDesc.FillMode = D3D10_FILL_SOLID;
rsDesc.CullMode = D3D10_CULL_BACK;
rsDesc.FrontCounterClockwise = true;
```

```
HR(md3dDevice->CreateRasterizerState(&rsDesc, &mCullCWRS));
```

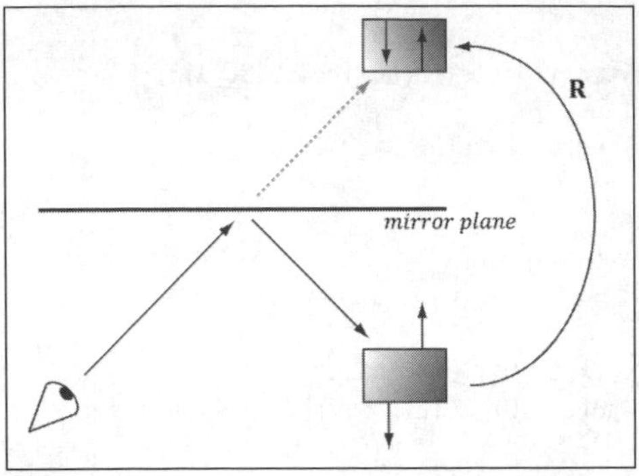

Figure 9.5: The polygon normals do not get reversed with reflection, which makes them inward facing after reflection.

Note: When we draw the reflected crate, we also need to reflect the light source across the mirror plane. Otherwise, the lighting in the reflection would not be accurate.

9.5 **Summary**

- The stencil buffer is an off-screen buffer we can use to block the rendering of certain pixel fragments to the back buffer. The stencil buffer is shared with the depth buffer and thus has the same resolution as the depth buffer. Valid depth/stencil buffer formats are DXGI_FORMAT_D32_FLOAT_S8X24_UINT and DXGI_FORMAT_D24_UNORM_S8_UINT.

- The decision to block a particular pixel from being written is decided by the *stencil test*, which is given by the following:

```
if( StencilRef & StencilReadMask ⊴ Value & StencilReadMask )
        accept pixel
    else
        reject pixel
```

where the ⊴ operator is any one of the functions defined in the D3D10_COMPARISON_FUNC enumerated type. The StencilRef, StencilReadMask, StencilReadMask, and comparison operator ⊴ are all application-defined quantities set with the Direct3D depth/stencil API. The Value quantity is the current value in the stencil buffer.

- The first step to creating an ID3D10DepthStencilState interface is to fill out a D3D10_DEPTH_STENCIL_DESC instance, which describes the depth/stencil state we want to create. After we have filled out a D3D10_DEPTH_STENCIL_DESC structure, we can obtain a pointer to an ID3D10DepthStencilState interface with the ID3D10Device::CreateDepthStencilState method. Finally, we bind a depth/stencil state block to the output merger stage of the pipeline with the ID3D10Device::OMSetDepthStencilState method.

9.6 **Exercises**

1. Modify the Mirror demo in the following way. First draw a wall with the following depth settings:

```
depthStencilDesc.DepthEnable    = false;
depthStencilDesc.DepthWriteMask = D3D10_DEPTH_WRITE_MASK_ALL;
depthStencilDesc.DepthFunc      = D3D10_COMPARISON_LESS;
```

Next, draw a box behind the wall with these depth settings:

```
depthStencilDesc.DepthEnable    = true;
depthStencilDesc.DepthWriteMask = D3D10_DEPTH_WRITE_MASK_ALL;
depthStencilDesc.DepthFunc      = D3D10_COMPARISON_LESS;
```

Does the wall occlude the box? Explain. What happens if you use the following to draw the wall instead?

```
depthStencilDesc.DepthEnable    = true;
depthStencilDesc.DepthWriteMask = D3D10_DEPTH_WRITE_MASK_ALL;
depthStencilDesc.DepthFunc      = D3D10_COMPARISON_LESS;
```

Note that this exercise does not use the stencil buffer, so that should be disabled.

2. Modify the Mirror demo by not reversing the triangle winding order convention. Does the reflected crate render correctly?

3. Modify the Mirror demo by disabling the stencil test when rendering the reflected crate. Does the reflected crate render only into the mirror?

4. Modify the Transparent Water demo from Chapter 8 to draw a cylinder (with no caps) at the center of the scene. Texture the cylinder with the 60-frame animated electric bolt animation found in this chapter's directory using additive blending. Figure 9.6 shows an example of the output. (*Hint*: Refer back to §8.5.5 for the depth states to use when rendering additive blending geometry.)

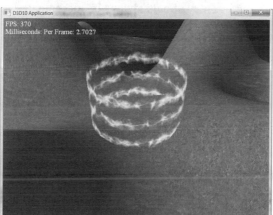

Figure 9.6: Sample screenshot of the solution to Exercise 4.

5. *Depth complexity* refers to the number of pixel fragments that compete, via the depth test, to be written to a particular entry in the back buffer. For example, a pixel we have drawn may be overwritten by a pixel that is closer to the camera (and this can happen several times before the closest pixel is actually figured out once the entire scene has been drawn). The pixel *P* in Figure 9.7 has a depth complexity of three since three pixel fragments compete for the pixel.

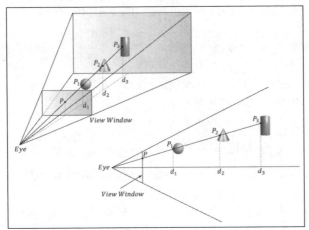

Figure 9.7: Multiple pixel fragments competing to be rendered to a single pixel on the projection window. In this scene, the pixel *P* has a depth complexity of three.

Potentially, the graphics card could fill a pixel several times each frame. This *overdraw* has performance implications, as the graphics card is wasting time processing pixels that eventually get overridden and are never seen. Consequently, it is useful to measure the depth complexity in a scene for performance analysis.

We can measure the depth complexity as follows: Render the scene and use the stencil buffer as a counter; that is, each pixel in the stencil buffer is originally cleared to zero, and every time a pixel fragment is processed, increment its count with D3D10_STENCIL_OP_INCR. The corresponding stencil buffer entry should always be incremented for every pixel fragment no matter what, so use the stencil comparison function D3D10_COMPARISON_ALWAYS. Then, for example, after the frame has been drawn, if the *ij*th pixel has a corresponding entry of five in the stencil buffer, then we know that five pixel fragments were processed for that pixel during that frame (i.e., the pixel has a depth complexity of five). Note that when counting the depth complexity, technically you only need to render the scene to the stencil buffer.

To visualize the depth complexity (stored in the stencil buffer), proceed as follows:

a. Associate a color c_k for each level of depth complexity k. For example, blue for a depth complexity of one, green for a depth complexity of two, red for a depth complexity of three, and so on.

(In very complex scenes where the depth complexity for a pixel could get very large, you probably do not want to associate a color for each level. Instead, you could associate a color for a range of disjoint levels. For example, pixels with depth complexity 1 to 5 are colored blue, pixels with depth complexity 6 to 10 are colored green, and so on.)

b. Set the stencil buffer operation to D3D10_STENCIL_OP_KEEP so that we do not modify it anymore. (We modify the stencil buffer with D3DSTENCILOP_INCR when we are counting the depth complexity as the scene is rendered, but when writing the code to visualize the stencil buffer, we only need to *read* from the stencil buffer and we should not *write* to it.)

c. For each level of depth complexity k:

1) Set the stencil comparison function to D3D10_COMPARISON_EQUAL and set the stencil reference value to k.

2) Draw a quad of color c_k that covers the entire projection window. Note that this will only color the pixels that have a depth complexity of k because of the preceding set stencil comparison function and reference value.

With this setup, we have colored each pixel based on its depth complexity uniquely, and so we can easily study the depth complexity of the scene. For this exercise, render the depth complexity of the scene used in the Clip Pixel demo from Chapter 8. Figure 9.8 shows a sample screenshot.

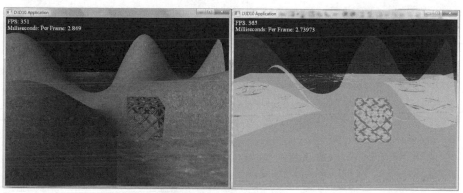

Figure 9.8: Sample screenshot of the solution to exercise 5.

Note: The depth test occurs in the output merger stage of the pipeline, which occurs after the pixel shader stage. This means that a pixel fragment is processed through the pixel shader, even if it may ultimately be rejected by the depth test. However, modern hardware does an "early z-test" where the depth test is performed before the pixel shader. This way, a rejected pixel fragment will be discarded before being processed by a potentially expensive pixel shader. To take advantage of this optimization, you should try to render your non-blended game objects in front-to-back order with respect to the camera; in this way, the nearest objects will be drawn first, and objects behind them will fail the early z-test and not be processed further. This can be a significant performance benefit if your scene suffers from lots of overdraw due to a high depth complexity. We are not able to control the early z-test through the Direct3D API; the graphics driver is the one that decides if it is possible to perform the early z-test. For example, if a pixel shader modifies the pixel fragment's depth value, then the early z-test is not possible, as the pixel shader must be executed before the depth test since the pixel shader modifies depth values. The opposite of this strategy is to render in back-to-front order, which would mean every pixel fragment would be processed only to be overwritten by a pixel in front of it.

Note: We mentioned the ability to modify the depth of a pixel in the pixel shader. How does that work? A pixel shader can actually output a structure, not just a single color vector as we have been doing thus far:

```
struct PS_OUT
{
    float4 color : SV_Target;
    float depth  : SV_Depth;
};

PS_OUT PS(VS_OUT pIn)
{
    PS_OUT pOut;

    // ... usual pixel work

    pOut.color = float4(litColor, alpha);

    // set pixel depth in normalized [0, 1] range
    pOut.depth = pIn.posH.z - 0.05f;

    return pOut;
}
```

The z-coordinate of the SV_Position element (pIn.posH.z) gives the unmodified pixel depth value. Using the special system value semantic SV_Depth, the pixel shader can output a modified depth value.

Chapter 10

The Geometry Shader

The geometry shader stage is an optional stage that sits between the vertex and pixel shader stages. While the vertex shader inputs vertices, the geometry shader inputs entire primitives. For example, if we were drawing triangle lists, then the geometry shader program would be executed for each triangle T in the list:

```
for(UINT i = 0; i < numTriangles; ++i)
    OutputPrimitiveList = GeometryShader( T[i].vertexList );
```

Notice the three vertices of each triangle are input into the geometry shader. The main advantage of the geometry shader is that it can create or destroy geometry. For example, the input primitive can be expanded into one or more other primitives, or the geometry shader can choose not to output a primitive based on some condition. Note that the output primitives need not be the same type as the input primitive; for instance, a common application of the geometry shader is to expand a point into a quad (two triangles).

The primitives output from the geometry shader are defined by a vertex list. Vertex positions leaving the geometry shader must be transformed to homogeneous clip space. After the geometry shader stage, we have a list of vertices defining primitives in homogeneous clip space. These vertices are projected (homogeneous divide), and then rasterization occurs as usual.

Objectives:

- To learn how to program geometry shaders.
- To understand how the billboard algorithm can be implemented efficiently using the geometry shader.
- To discover auto-generated primitive IDs and some of their applications.

- To learn how to create and use texture arrays, and understand why they are useful.

10.1 **Programming Geometry Shaders**

Programming geometry shaders is a lot like programming vertex or pixel shaders, but there are some differences. The following code shows the general form:

```
[maxvertexcount(N)]
void ShaderName (
    PrimitiveType InputVertexType InputName [NumElements],
    inout StreamOutputObject<OutputVertexType> OutputName)
{
    // Geometry shader body...
}
```

We must first specify the maximum number of vertices the geometry shader will output for a single invocation. This is done by setting the max vertex count before the shader definition:

```
[maxvertexcount(N)]
```

where N is the maximum number of vertices the geometry shader will output for a single invocation. The number of vertices a geometry shader can output per invocation is variable, but it cannot exceed the defined maximum.

The geometry shader takes two parameters: an input parameter and an output parameter. (Actually, it can take more, but that is a special topic; see §10.2.4.) The input parameter is always an array of vertices — one vertex for a point, two for a line, three for a triangle, four for a line with adjacency, and six for a triangle with adjacency. The vertex type of the input vertices is the vertex type returned by the vertex shader (e.g., VS_OUT). The input parameter must be prefixed by a primitive type, describing the type of primitives being input into the geometry shader. This can be any one of the following:

- point: The input primitives are points.
- line: The input primitives are lines (lists or strips).
- triangle: The input primitives are triangles (lists or strips).
- lineadj: The input primitives are lines with adjacency (lists or strips).
- triangleadj: The input primitives are triangles with adjacency (lists or strips).

Note: The input primitive into a geometry shader is always a complete primitive (e.g., two vertices for a line, three vertices for a triangle). Thus the geometry shader does not need to distinguish between lists and strips. For example, if you are drawing triangle strips, the geometry shader is still executed for every triangle in the strip, and the three vertices of each triangle are passed into the geometry shader as input.

The output parameter always has the `inout` modifier. Additionally, the output parameter is always a stream type. A stream type stores a list of vertices that define the geometry the geometry shader is outputting. A geometry shader adds a vertex to the outgoing stream list using the intrinsic `Append` method:

```
void StreamOutputObject<OutputVertexType>::Append(OutputVertexType v);
```

A stream type is a template type, where the template argument is used to specify the vertex type of the outgoing vertices (e.g., `GS_OUT`). There are three possible stream types:

- `PointStream<OutputVertexType>`: A list of vertices defining a point list.
- `LineStream<OutputVertexType>`: A list of vertices defining a line strip.
- `TriangleStream<OutputVertexType>`: A list of vertices defining a triangle strip.

The vertices output by a geometry shader form primitives; the type of output primitive is indicated by the stream type (`PointStream`, `LineStream`, `TriangleStream`). For lines and triangles, the output primitive is always a strip. Line and triangle lists, however, can be simulated by using the intrinsic `RestartStrip` method:

```
void StreamOutputObject<OutputVertexType>::RestartStrip();
```

For example, if you wanted to output triangle lists, then you would call `RestartStrip` each time three vertices were appended to the output stream.

Below are some specific examples of geometry shader signatures:

```
// EXAMPLE 1: GS outputs at most 4 vertices. The input primitive is
// a line. The output is a triangle strip.
//
[maxvertexcount(4)]
void GS(line VS_OUT gIn[2],
    inout TriangleStream<GS_OUT> triStream)
{
    // Geometry shader body...
}
//
// EXAMPLE 2: GS outputs at most 32 vertices. The input primitive is
// a triangle. The output is a triangle strip.
//
[maxvertexcount(32)]
```

```
void GS(triangle VS_OUT gIn[3],
    inout TriangleStream<GS_OUT> triStream)
{
    // Geometry shader body...
}
//
// EXAMPLE 3: GS outputs at most 4 vertices. The input primitive
// is a point. The output is a triangle strip.
//
[maxvertexcount(4)]
void GS(point VS_OUT gIn[1],
    inout TriangleStream<GS_OUT> triStream)
{
    // Geometry shader body...
}
```

The following geometry shader illustrates the Append and RestartStrip methods; it inputs a triangle, subdivides it (see Figure 10.1), and outputs the four subdivided triangles:

```
struct VS_OUT
{
    float3 posL    : POSITION;
    float3 normalL : NORMAL;
    float4 diffuse : DIFFUSE;
    float4 spec    : SPECULAR;
};

struct GS_OUT
{
    float4 posH    : SV_POSITION;
    float3 posW    : POSITION;
    float3 normalW : NORMAL;
    float4 diffuse : DIFFUSE;
    float4 spec    : SPECULAR;
};

[maxvertexcount(8)]
void GS(triangle VS_OUT gIn[3],
    inout TriangleStream<GS_OUT> triStream)
{
    GS_OUT gOut;

    // Same materials for all vertices.
    gOut.diffuse = gIn[0].diffuse;
    gOut.spec    = gIn[0].spec;

    // Use face normal for vertex normals.
    float3 e0 = gIn[1].posL - gIn[0].posL;
    float3 e1 = gIn[2].posL - gIn[0].posL;
    float3 n  = normalize( cross(e0, e1) );

    gOut.normalW = mul(float4(n, 0.0f), gWorld);
```

```
// Compute edge midpoints.
float3 m0 = 0.5f*(gIn[0].posL+gIn[1].posL);
float3 m1 = 0.5f*(gIn[1].posL+gIn[2].posL);
float3 m2 = 0.5f*(gIn[2].posL+gIn[0].posL);

//        1
//        *
//       / \
//      /   \
//   m0*-----*m1
//    / \   / \
//   /   \ /   \
//  *-----*-----*
//  0    m2     2

float3 v[6];
v[0] = gIn[0].posL;
v[1] = m0;
v[2] = m2;
v[3] = m1;
v[4] = gIn[2].posL;
v[5] = gIn[1].posL;

// We can draw the subdivision in two strips:
//     Strip 1: bottom three triangles
//     Strip 2: top triangle

for(int i = 0; i < 5; ++i)
{
    gOut.posW    = mul(float4(v[i], 1.0f), gWorld);
    gOut.posH    = mul(float4(v[i], 1.0f), gWVP);
    triStream.Append(gOut);
}
triStream.RestartStrip();

gOut.posW    = mul(float4(v[1], 1.0f), gWorld);
gOut.posH    = mul(float4(v[1], 1.0f), gWVP);
triStream.Append(gOut);

gOut.posW    = mul(float4(v[5], 1.0f), gWorld);
gOut.posH    = mul(float4(v[5], 1.0f), gWVP);
triStream.Append(gOut);

gOut.posW    = mul(float4(v[3], 1.0f), gWorld);
gOut.posH    = mul(float4(v[3], 1.0f), gWVP);
triStream.Append(gOut);
}
```

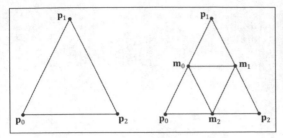

Figure 10.1: Subdividing a triangle into four equally sized triangles. Observe that the three new vertices are the midpoints along the edges of the original triangle.

Once a geometry shader has been implemented, we must bind it to an effect pass if it is to be used when rendering:

```
technique10 TreeBillboardTech
{
    pass P0
    {
        SetVertexShader(CompileShader(vs_4_0, VS()));
        SetGeometryShader(CompileShader(gs_4_0, GS()));
        SetPixelShader(CompileShader(ps_4_0, PS()));
    }
}
```

Note: Given an input primitive, the geometry shader can choose not to output it. In this way, geometry is "destroyed" by the geometry shader, which can be useful for some algorithms.

Note: If you do not output enough vertices to complete a primitive in a geometry shader, then the partial primitive is discarded.

10.2 **Tree Billboards Demo**

10.2.1 Overview

When trees are far away, a *billboarding* technique is used for efficiency. That is, instead of rendering the geometry for a fully 3D tree, a picture of a 3D tree is painted on the quad (see Figure 10.2). From a distance, you cannot tell that a billboard is being used. However, the trick is to make sure that the billboard always faces the camera (otherwise the illusion would break).

Assuming the y-axis is up and the xz-plane is the ground plane, the tree billboards will generally be aligned with the y-axis and just face the camera in the xz-plane. Figure 10.3 shows the local coordinate systems of several billboards from a bird's-eye view — notice that the billboards are "looking" at the camera.

Figure 10.2: A tree billboard texture with alpha channel.

RGB Channel   Alpha Channel

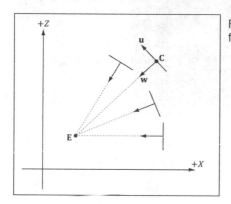

Figure 10.3: Billboards facing the camera.

So given the center position $\mathbf{C} = (C_x, C_y, C_z)$ of a billboard in world space and the position of the camera $\mathbf{E} = (E_x, E_y, E_z)$ in world space, we have enough information to describe the local coordinate system of the billboard relative to the world space:

$$\mathbf{w} = \frac{(E_x - C_x, 0, E_z - C_z)}{\|(E_x - C_x, 0, E_z - C_z)\|}$$

$$\mathbf{v} = (0, 1, 0)$$

$$\mathbf{u} = \mathbf{v} \times \mathbf{w}$$

And recall that the world matrix takes the form:

$$\mathbf{W} = \begin{bmatrix} u_x & u_y & u_z & 0 \\ v_x & v_y & v_z & 0 \\ w_x & w_y & w_z & 0 \\ C_x & C_y & C_z & 1 \end{bmatrix}$$

Note that the billboard matrix differs for each billboard, so it must be computed for each billboard.

For this demo, we will construct a list of point primitives (D3D10_PRIMITIVE_TOPOLOGY_POINTLIST) that lie slightly above a land mass. These points represent the centers of the billboards we want to draw. In the geometry shader, we will expand these points into billboard quads. In addition, we will compute the world matrix of the billboard in the geometry shader. Figure 10.4 shows a screenshot of the demo.

Figure 10.4: Screenshot of the Tree Billboards demo.

As Figure 10.4 shows, this sample builds off the Clip Pixel demo from Chapter 8. Most of the billboard-specific code occurs in the *TreeSprites.h*, *TreeSprites.cpp*, and *tree.fx* files.

Note: An inefficient implementation of billboards would draw the billboards one-by-one: For each billboard, the CPU would compute the world matrix, set the world matrix to the effect file, and then draw the billboard. With our approach, all the billboards can be drawn with a single draw call, and the GPU computes the world matrix instead of the CPU, thereby freeing the CPU to do other work.

10.2.2 **Vertex Structure**

We use the following vertex structure for our billboard points:

```
struct TreeVertex
{
    D3DXVECTOR3 centerW;
    D3DXVECTOR2 sizeW;
};

D3D10_INPUT_ELEMENT_DESC vertexDesc[] =
{
    {"POSITION", 0, DXGI_FORMAT_R32G32B32_FLOAT, 0, 0,
            D3D10_INPUT_PER_VERTEX_DATA, 0},
    {"SIZE", 0, DXGI_FORMAT_R32G32_FLOAT, 0, 12,
            D3D10_INPUT_PER_VERTEX_DATA, 0},
};
```

The vertex stores a point that represents the center position of the billboard in world space. It also includes a size member, which stores the width/height of the billboard (scaled to world space units); this is so the geometry shader knows how large the billboard should be after expansion (see Figure 10.5). By having the size vary per vertex, we can easily allow for billboards of different sizes.

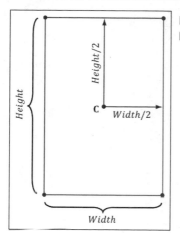

Figure 10.5: Expanding a point into a quad.

Excepting texture arrays (see §10.3), the other C++ code in the _TreeSprites.h/.cpp_ files should be routine Direct3D code by now (creating vertex buffers, effects, invoking draw methods, etc.). Thus we will now turn our attention to the _tree.fx_ file.

10.2.3 Effect File

Since this is our first demo with a geometry shader, we will show the entire effect file here so that you can see how it fits together with the vertex and pixel shaders and the other effect objects. This effect also introduces some new objects that we have not discussed yet (SV_PrimitiveID and Texture2DArray); these items will be discussed next. For now, mainly focus on the geometry shader program GS, which expands a point into a quad and aligns the quad to face the camera, as described in §10.2.1.

```
//===========================================================
// tree.fx by Frank Luna (C) 2008 All Rights Reserved.
//
// Uses the geometry shader to expand points into y-axis
// aligned billboards.
//===========================================================

#include "lighthelper.fx"

cbuffer cbPerFrame
{
```

```
    Light gLight;
    float3 gEyePosW;
    float4x4 gViewProj;
};

// Nonnumeric values cannot be added to a cbuffer.
Texture2DArray gDiffuseMapArray;

SamplerState gTriLinearSam
{
    Filter = MIN_MAG_MIP_LINEAR;
    AddressU = Wrap;
    AddressV = Wrap;
};

struct VS_IN
{
    float3 centerW : POSITION;
    float2 sizeW   : SIZE;
};

struct VS_OUT
{
    float3 centerW : POSITION;
    float2 sizeW   : SIZE;
};

struct GS_OUT
{
    float4 posH    : SV_POSITION;
    float3 posW    : POSITION;
    float3 normalW : NORMAL;
    float2 texC    : TEXCOORD;
    uint primID    : SV_PrimitiveID;
};

VS_OUT VS(VS_IN vIn)
{
    VS_OUT vOut;

    // Just pass data into geometry shader stage.
    vOut.centerW = vIn.centerW;
    vOut.sizeW   = vIn.sizeW;

    return vOut;
}

[maxvertexcount(4)]
void GS(point VS_OUT gIn[1],
    uint primID : SV_PrimitiveID,
    inout TriangleStream<GS_OUT> triStream)
{
    //
```

```
// Compute 4 triangle strip vertices (quad) in local space.
// The quad faces down the +z axis in local space.
//
float halfWidth  = 0.5f*gIn[0].sizeW.x;
float halfHeight = 0.5f*gIn[0].sizeW.y;

float4 v[4];
v[0] = float4(-halfWidth, -halfHeight, 0.0f, 1.0f);
v[1] = float4(+halfWidth, -halfHeight, 0.0f, 1.0f);
v[2] = float4(-halfWidth, +halfHeight, 0.0f, 1.0f);
v[3] = float4(+halfWidth, +halfHeight, 0.0f, 1.0f);
//
// Compute texture coordinates to stretch texture over quad.
//
float2 texC[4];
texC[0] = float2(0.0f, 1.0f);
texC[1] = float2(1.0f, 1.0f);
texC[2] = float2(0.0f, 0.0f);
texC[3] = float2(1.0f, 0.0f);
//
// Compute world matrix so that billboard is aligned with
// the y-axis and faces the camera.
//
float3 up = float3(0.0f, 1.0f, 0.0f);
float3 look = gEyePosW - gIn[0].centerW;
look.y = 0.0f; // y-axis aligned, so project to xz-plane
look = normalize(look);
float3 right = cross(up, look);

float4x4 W;
W[0] = float4(right,            0.0f);
W[1] = float4(up,               0.0f);
W[2] = float4(look,             0.0f);
W[3] - float4(gIn[0].centerW, 1.0f);

float4x4 WVP = mul(W,gViewProj);

//
// Transform quad vertices to world space and output
// them as a triangle strip.
//
GS_OUT gOut;
[unroll]
for(int i = 0; i < 4; ++i)
{
    gOut.posH    = mul(v[i], WVP);
    gOut.posW    = mul(v[i], W);
    gOut.normalW = look;
    gOut.texC    = texC[i];
    gOut.primID  = primID;

    triStream.Append(gOut);
}
```

```
}

float4 PS(GS_OUT pIn) : SV_Target
{
    // Get materials from texture maps.
    float3 uvw = float3(pIn.texC, pIn.primID%4);
    float4 diffuse = gDiffuseMapArray.Sample( gTriLinearSam, uvw );

    // Discard pixel if texture alpha < 0.25.  Note that we do this
    // test as soon as possible so that we can potentially exit the shader
    // early, thereby skipping the rest of the shader code.
    clip(diffuse.a - 0.25f);

    // Don't light tree billboards, just use texture color.

    return diffuse;
}

technique10 TreeBillboardTech
{
    pass P0
    {
        SetVertexShader( CompileShader(   vs_4_0, VS() ) );
        SetGeometryShader( CompileShader( gs_4_0, GS() ) );
        SetPixelShader( CompileShader(    ps_4_0, PS() ) );
    }
}
```

10.2.4 **SV_PrimitiveID**

The geometry shader in this example takes a special unsigned integer parameter with the semantic SV_PrimitiveID.

```
[maxvertexcount(4)]
void GS(point VS_OUT gIn[1],
    uint primID : SV_PrimitiveID,
    inout TriangleStream<GS_OUT> triStream);
```

When this semantic is specified, it tells the input assembler stage to automatically generate a primitive ID for each primitive. When a draw call is executed to draw n primitives, the first primitive is labeled 0, the second primitive is labeled 1, and so on, until the last primitive in the draw call is labeled $n-1$. In our billboard example, the geometry shader does not use this ID (although a geometry shader could); instead, the geometry shader writes the primitive ID to the outgoing vertices, thereby passing it on to the pixel shader stage. The pixel shader uses the primitive ID to index into a texture array, which leads us to the next section.

Note: If a geometry shader is not present, the primitive ID parameter can be added to the parameter list of the pixel shader:

```
float4 PS(VS_OUT pIn, uint primID : SV_PrimitiveID) : SV_Target
{
// Pixel shader body...
}
```

However, if a geometry shader is present, then the primitive ID parameter must occur in the geometry shader signature. Then the geometry shader can use the primitive ID or pass it on to the pixel shader stage (or both).

Note: It is also possible to have the input assembler generate a vertex ID. To do this, add an additional parameter of type `uint` to the vertex shader signature with the semantic `SV_VertexID`. The following vertex shader signature shows how this is done:

```
VS_OUT VS(VS_IN vIn, uint vertID : SV_VertexID)
{
// vertex shader body...
}
```

For a `Draw` call, the vertices in the draw call will be labeled with IDs 0, 1, ..., $n-1$, where n is the number of vertices in the draw call. For a `DrawIndexed` call, the vertex IDs correspond to the vertex index values.

10.3 **Texture Arrays**

10.3.1 **Overview**

A texture array stores an array of textures. In C++ code, a texture array is represented by the `ID3D10Texture2D` interface (the same one used for single textures). When creating an `ID3D10Texture2D` object, there is actually a property called `ArraySize` that can be set to specify the number of texture elements the texture stores. However, since we have been relying on D3DX for creating textures, we haven't explicitly set this data member. In an effect file, a texture array is represented by the `Texture2DArray` type:

```
Texture2DArray gDiffuseMapArray;
```

Now, you have to be wondering why we need texture arrays. Why not just do this:

```
Texture2D TexArray[4];

...

float4 PS(GS_OUT pIn) : SV_Target
{
    float4 c = TexArray[pIn.texIndex].Sample(gTriLinearSam, pIn.texC);
```

This will give an error saying that "sampler array index must be a literal expression." In other words, it does not like how the array index varies per pixel. This code would work if we specified a literal array index:

```
float4 c = TexArray[2].Sample(gTriLinearSam, pIn.texC);
```

But this is less powerful than the first scenario.

10.3.2 Sampling a Texture Array

In the Tree Billboards demo, we sample a texture array with the following code:

```
float3 uvw = float3(pIn.texC, pIn.primID%4);
float4 diffuse = gDiffuseMapArray.Sample( gTriLinearSam, uvw );
```

When using a texture array, three texture coordinates are required. The first two texture coordinates are the usual 2D texture coordinates; the third texture coordinate is an index into the texture array. For example, 0.0 is the index to the first texture in the array, 1.0 is the index to the second texture in the array, 2.0 is the index to the third texture in the array, and so on.

In the Tree Billboards demo, we use a texture array with four texture elements, each with a different tree texture (see Figure 10.6). However, because we are drawing more than four primitives, the primitive IDs will become greater than three. Thus, we take the primitive ID modulo 4 (pIn.primID % 4) to map the primitive ID to 0, 1, 2, or 3, which are valid array indices for an array with four elements.

Figure 10.6: Tree billboard images.

One of the advantages of using texture arrays is that we are able to draw a collection of primitives, with different textures, in one draw call. Normally, we would have to do something like this (pseudocode):

```
SetTextureA();
DrawPrimitivesWithTextureA();

SetTextureB();
DrawPrimitivesWithTextureB();

...

SetTextureZ();
DrawPrimitivesWithTextureZ();
```

Each set and draw call has some overhead associated with it. With texture arrays, we could reduce this to one set and one draw call:

```
SetTextureArray();
DrawPrimitivesWithTextureArray();
```

10.3.3 Loading Texture Arrays

At the time of this writing, there is no D3DX function to load a set of images from file into a texture array. Thus, we have to do this task our selves. The process is summarized as follows:

1. Create each texture from file individually one-by-one.
2. Create the texture array.
3. Copy each individual texture into the elements of the texture array.
4. Create a shader resource view to the texture array.

The following code shows the details.

```
void TreeSprites::buildShaderResourceView()
{
    //
    // Load the texture elements individually from file. These textures
    // won't be used by the GPU (0 bind flags), they are just used to
    // load the image data from file. We use the STAGING usage so the
    // CPU can read the resource.
    //

    std::wstring filenames[4] =
    {
        L"tree0.dds",
        L"tree1.dds",
        L"tree2.dds",
        L"tree3.dds"
    };

    ID3D10Texture2D* srcTex[4];
    for(UINT i = 0; i < 4; ++i)
    {
        D3DX10_IMAGE_LOAD_INFO loadInfo;

        loadInfo.Width  = D3DX10_FROM_FILE;
```

```
        loadInfo.Height = D3DX10_FROM_FILE;
        loadInfo.Depth  = D3DX10_FROM_FILE;
        loadInfo.FirstMipLevel = 0;
        loadInfo.MipLevels = D3DX10_FROM_FILE;
        loadInfo.Usage = D3D10_USAGE_STAGING;
        loadInfo.BindFlags = 0;
        loadInfo.CpuAccessFlags = D3D10_CPU_ACCESS_WRITE |
                D3D10_CPU_ACCESS_READ;
        loadInfo.MiscFlags = 0;
        loadInfo.Format = DXGI_FORMAT_R8G8B8A8_UNORM;
        loadInfo.Filter = D3DX10_FILTER_NONE;
        loadInfo.MipFilter = D3DX10_FILTER_NONE;
        loadInfo.pSrcInfo  = 0;

        HR(D3DX10CreateTextureFromFile(md3dDevice,
                filenames[i].c_str(),
                &loadInfo, 0,
                (ID3D10Resource**)&srcTex[i], 0));
    }

    //
    // Create the texture array.  Each element in the texture
    // array has the same format/dimensions.
    //

    D3D10_TEXTURE2D_DESC texElementDesc;
    srcTex[0]->GetDesc(&texElementDesc);

    D3D10_TEXTURE2D_DESC texArrayDesc;
    texArrayDesc.Width              = texElementDesc.Width;
    texArrayDesc.Height             = texElementDesc.Height;
    texArrayDesc.MipLevels          = texElementDesc.MipLevels;
    texArrayDesc.ArraySize          = 4;
    texArrayDesc.Format             = DXGI_FORMAT_R8G8B8A8_UNORM;
    texArrayDesc.SampleDesc.Count   = 1;
    texArrayDesc.SampleDesc.Quality = 0;
    texArrayDesc.Usage              = D3D10_USAGE_DEFAULT;
    texArrayDesc.BindFlags          = D3D10_BIND_SHADER_RESOURCE;
    texArrayDesc.CPUAccessFlags     = 0;
    texArrayDesc.MiscFlags          = 0;

    ID3D10Texture2D* texArray = 0;
    HR(md3dDevice->CreateTexture2D(&texArrayDesc, 0, &texArray));

    //
    // Copy individual texture elements into texture array.
    //

    // for each texture element...
    for(UINT i = 0; i < 4; ++i)
    {
        // for each mipmap level...
        for(UINT j = 0; j < texElementDesc.MipLevels; ++j)
```

```
        {
            D3D10_MAPPED_TEXTURE2D mappedTex2D;
            srcTex[i]->Map(j, D3D10_MAP_READ, 0, &mappedTex2D);

            md3dDevice->UpdateSubresource(texArray,
            D3D10CalcSubresource(j, i, texElementDesc.MipLevels),
            0, mappedTex2D.pData, mappedTex2D.RowPitch, 0);

            srcTex[i]->Unmap(j);
        }
    }
    //
    // Create a resource view to the texture array.
    //

    D3D10_SHADER_RESOURCE_VIEW_DESC viewDesc;
    viewDesc.Format = texArrayDesc.Format;
    viewDesc.ViewDimension = D3D10_SRV_DIMENSION_TEXTURE2DARRAY;
    viewDesc.Texture2DArray.MostDetailedMip = 0;
    viewDesc.Texture2DArray.MipLevels = texArrayDesc.MipLevels;
    viewDesc.Texture2DArray.FirstArraySlice = 0;
    viewDesc.Texture2DArray.ArraySize = 4;

    HR(md3dDevice->CreateShaderResourceView(
            texArray, &viewDesc, &mTreeMapArrayRV));

    //
    // Cleanup--we only need the resource view.
    //

    ReleaseCOM(texArray);

    for(UINT i = 0; i < 4; ++i)
        ReleaseCOM(srcTex[i]);
```

The ID3D10Device::UpdateSubresource method uses the CPU to copy memory from one subresource to another (see the SDK documentation for a description of the parameters).

10.3.4 Texture Subresources

Now that we have discussed texture arrays, we can talk about subresources. Figure 10.7 shows an example of a texture array with several textures. In turn, each texture has its own mipmap chain. The Direct3D API uses the term *array slice* to refer to an element in a texture along with its complete mipmap chain. The Direct3D API uses the term *mip slice* to refer to all the mipmaps at a particular level in the texture array. A *subresource* refers to a single mipmap level in a texture array element.

Given the texture array index and a mipmap level, we can access a subresource in a texture array. However, the subresources can also be labeled by a linear index; Direct3D uses a linear index ordered as shown in Figure 10.8.

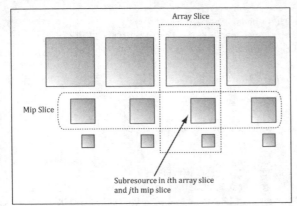

Figure 10.7: A texture array with four textures. Each texture has three mipmap levels.

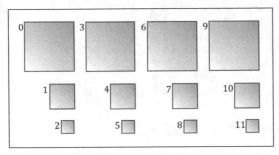

Figure 10.8: Subresources in a texture array labeled with a linear index.

The following utility function is used to compute the linear subresource index given the mip level, array index, and the number of mipmap levels:

```
inline UINT D3D10CalcSubresource(
    UINT MipSlice, UINT ArraySlice, UINT MipLevels);
```

10.4 **Summary**

- The geometry shader stage is an optional stage that sits between the vertex and pixel shader stages. The geometry shader is invoked for each primitive sent through the input assembler. The geometry shader can output zero, one, or more primitives. The output primitive type may be different from the input primitive type. The vertices of the output primitives should be transformed to homogeneous clip space before leaving the geometry shader. The primitives output from the geometry shader next enter the rasterization stage of the rendering pipeline. Geometry shaders are programmed side-by-side with vertex and pixel shaders in effect files.

- The billboard technique is where a quad textured with an image of an object is used instead of a true 3D model of the object. For objects far away, the viewer cannot tell a billboard is being used. The advantage of billboards is that the GPU does not have to waste processing time rendering a full 3D object when a textured quad will suffice. This technique can be useful for rendering forests of trees, where true 3D geometry is used for trees near the camera, and billboards are used for trees in the distance. In order for the billboard trick to work, the billboard must always face the camera.

■ A special parameter of type `uint` and semantic `SV_PrimitiveID` can be added to the parameter list of a geometry shader as the following example shows:

```
[maxvertexcount(4)]
void GS(point VS_OUT gIn[1],
        uint primID : SV_PrimitiveID,
        inout TriangleStream<GS_OUT> triStream);
```

When this semantic is specified, it tells the input assembler stage to automatically generate a primitive ID for each primitive. When a draw call is executed to draw n primitives, the first primitive is labeled 0, the second primitive is labeled 1, and so on, until the last primitive in the draw call is labeled $n-1$. If a geometry shader is not present, the primitive ID parameter can be added to the parameter list of the pixel shader:

```
float4 PS(VS_OUT pIn, uint primID : SV_PrimitiveID) : SV_Target
{
    // Pixel shader body...
}
```

However, if a geometry shader is present, then the primitive ID parameter must occur in the geometry shader signature. Then the geometry shader can use the primitive ID or pass it on to the pixel shader stage (or both).

■ A texture array stores an array of textures. In C++ code, a texture array is represented by the `ID3D10Texture2D` interface (the same one used for single textures). In an effect file, a texture array is represented by the `Texture2DArray` type. When using a texture array, three texture coordinates are required. The first two texture coordinates are the usual 2D texture coordinates; the third texture coordinate is an index into the texture array. For example, 0.0 is the index to the first texture in the array, 1.0 is the index to the second texture in the array, 2.0 is the index to the third texture in the array, and so on. One of the advantages of using texture arrays is that we are able to draw a collection of primitives, with different textures, in one draw call. Each primitive will have an index into the texture array, which indicates which texture to apply to the primitive.

10.5 **Exercises**

1. Consider a circle, drawn with a line strip, in the xz-plane. Expand the line strip into a cylinder with no caps using the geometry shader.

2. An icosahedron is a rough approximation of a sphere. By subdividing each triangle (see Figure 10.1), and projecting the new vertices onto the sphere, a better approximation is obtained. (Projecting a vertex onto a unit sphere simply amounts to normalizing the position vector, as the heads of all unit vectors coincide with the surface of the unit sphere.) For this exercise, build and render an icosahedron. Use a geometry shader to subdivide the icosahedron based on its distance from the camera. For example, if $d < 15$, then subdivide the original icosahedron twice; if $15 \leq d < 30$, then subdivide the original icosahedron once; if $d \geq 30$, then just render the original icosahedron. The idea here is to only use a high number of polygons if the object is close to the camera; if the object is far away, then a coarser mesh will suffice, and we need not waste GPU power processing more polygons than needed. Figure 10.9 shows the three LOD levels side-by-side in wireframe and solid (lit) mode.

Note: The lighting in Figure 10.9 looks wrong because of the phong shading model used, which assumes the underlying surface is smooth. It does not work for faceted geometry like the icosahedron (it is trying to smooth out the facets); however, it works better to model a sphere once more triangles are added.

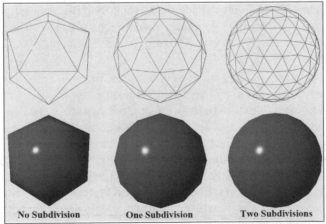

Figure 10.9: Subdivision of an icosahedron with vertices projected onto the unit sphere.

The vertex and index list for an icosahedron are given below. The vertices are constructed to already lie on the unit sphere.

```
const float X = 0.525731f;
const float Z = 0.850651f;

// 12 unique vertices
D3DXVECTOR3 pos[12] =
{
    D3DXVECTOR3(-X, 0.0f, Z),  D3DXVECTOR3(X, 0.0f, Z),
    D3DXVECTOR3(-X, 0.0f, -Z), D3DXVECTOR3(X, 0.0f, -Z),
    D3DXVECTOR3(0.0f, Z, X),   D3DXVECTOR3(0.0f, Z, -X),
    D3DXVECTOR3(0.0f, -Z, X),  D3DXVECTOR3(0.0f, -Z, -X),
    D3DXVECTOR3(Z, X, 0.0f),   D3DXVECTOR3(-Z, X, 0.0f),
    D3DXVECTOR3(Z, -X, 0.0f),  D3DXVECTOR3(-Z, -X, 0.0f)
};

// 20 triangles
DWORD k[60] =
{
    1,4,0,   4,9,0,   4,5,9,   8,5,4,   1,8,4,
    1,10,8,  10,3,8,  8,3,5,   3,2,5,   3,7,2,
    3,10,7,  10,6,7,  6,11,7,  6,0,11,  6,1,0,
    10,1,6,  11,0,9,  2,11,9,  5,2,9,   11,2,7
};
```

3. A simple explosion effect can be simulated by translating triangles in the direction of their face normals as a function of time. This simulation can be implemented in a geometry shader. For each triangle input into the geometry shader, the geometry shader computes the face normal **n**, and then translates the three triangle vertices, $\mathbf{p}_0$, $\mathbf{p}_1$, and $\mathbf{p}_2$, in the direction **n** based on the time t since the explosion started:

    $$\mathbf{p}'_i = \mathbf{p}_i + t\mathbf{n} \quad \text{for} \quad i = 0, 1, 2$$

    The face normal **n** need not be unit length, and can be scaled accordingly to control the speed of the explosion. One could even make the scale depend on the primitive ID, so that each primitive travels at a different speed. Use an icosahedron (not subdivided) as a sample mesh for implementing this effect.

4. This exercise shows that for a Draw call, the vertices in the draw call will be labeled with IDs 0, 1, ..., $n - 1$, where n is the number of vertices in the draw call. It also shows that for a DrawIndexed call, the vertex IDs correspond to the vertex index values.

    Modify the Tree Billboards demo in the following way. First, change the vertex shader to the following:

```
VS_OUT VS(VS_IN vIn, uint vertID : SV_VertexID)
{
    VS_OUT vOut;

    // Just pass data into geometry shader stage.
```

```
        vOut.centerW  = vIn.centerW;
        vOut.sizeW    = float2(2+vertID, 2+vertID);

        return vOut;
}
```

In other words, we size the tree billboard based on the vertex ID of its center. Now run the program; when drawing 16 billboards, the sizes should range from 2 to 17. Now modify the `TreeSprites::draw` method as follows. Instead of using a single draw call to draw all 16 points at once, use four like so:

```
md3dDevice->Draw(4, 0);

md3dDevice->Draw(4, 4);

md3dDevice->Draw(4, 8);

md3dDevice->Draw(4, 12);
```

Now run the program. This time, the sizes should range from 2 to 5. Because each draw call draws four vertices, the vertex IDs range from 0 to 3 for each draw call. Now use an index buffer and four `DrawIndexed` calls. After running the program, the sizes should return to the range of 2 to 17. This is because when using `DrawIndexed`, the vertex IDs correspond to the vertex index values.

5. Modify the Tree Billboards demo in the following way. First, remove the "modulo 4" from the pixel shader:

```
float3 uvw = float3(pIn.texC, pIn.primID);
```

Now run the program. Since we are drawing 16 primitives, with primitive IDs ranging from 0 to 15, these IDs go outside the array bounds. However, this does not cause an error, as the out-of-bounds index will be clamped to the highest valid index (three in this case). Now instead of using a single draw call to draw all 16 points at once, use four like so:

```
md3dDevice->Draw(4, 0);

md3dDevice->Draw(4, 4);

md3dDevice->Draw(4, 8);

md3dDevice->Draw(4, 12);
```

Run the program again. This time there is no clamping. Because each draw call draws four primitives, the primitive IDs range from 0 to 3 for each draw call. Thus the primitive IDs can be used as indices without going out of bounds. This shows that the primitive ID "count" resets to 0 with each draw call.

Part III

Direct3D Topics

In this part, we focus on applying Direct3D to implement several 3D applications, demonstrating techniques such as terrain rendering, sky rendering, working with meshes, particle systems, picking, environment mapping, normal mapping, and shadow mapping. A brief description of the chapters in this part follows.

Chapter 11, "Cube Mapping"

In this chapter, we show how to reflect environments onto arbitrary meshes with environment mapping; in addition, we use an environment map to texture a sky sphere.

Chapter 12, "Normal Mapping"

This chapter shows how to get detailed real-time lighting results using normal maps.

Chapter 13, "Shadow Mapping"

In this chapter we discuss shadow mapping, which is a real-time shadowing technique that shadows arbitrary geometry (it is not limited to planar shadows). In addition, we learn how to render to a texture and how projective texturing works.

Chapter 14, "Meshes"

This chapter shows how to load complex models from files and work with the ID3DX10Mesh interface.

Chapter 15, "Picking"

This chapter shows how to determine the particular 3D object (or 3D primitive) that the user has selected with the mouse. Picking is often a necessity in 3D games and applications where the user interacts with the 3D world with the mouse. We also show how to compute the bounding box and sphere of a mesh.

Chapter 16, "Terrain Rendering"

This chapter shows how to create, texture, light, and render 3D terrains using heightmaps and a multi-texturing technique. Furthermore, we show how to smoothly "walk" the camera over the terrain.

Chapter 17, "Particle Systems and Stream Output"

In this chapter, we learn how to model systems that consist of many small particles that all behave in a similar manner. For example, particle systems can be used to model falling snow and rain, fire and smoke, rocket trails, and sprinkler droplets from fountains.

Chapter 11

Cube Mapping

In this chapter, we study cube maps, which are basically arrays of six textures interpreted in a special way. With cube mapping, we can easily texture a sky or model reflections.

The Cube Map demo file for this chapter is located in the download files.

Objectives:

■ To learn what cube maps are and how to sample them in HLSL code.

■ To discover how to create cube maps with the DirectX Texture Tool.

■ To find out how we can use cube maps to model reflections.

■ To learn how we can texture a sky dome with cube maps.

11.1 **Cube Mapping**

The idea of cube mapping is to store six textures and to visualize them as the faces of a cube — hence the name cube map — centered and axis-aligned about some coordinate system. Since the cube texture is axis-aligned, each face corresponds with a direction along the three major axes; therefore, it is natural to reference a particular face on a cube map based on the axis direction ($\pm X$, $\pm Y$, $\pm Z$) that intersects the face. For the purposes of identifying a cube map face, Direct3D provides the D3D10_TEXTURECUBE_FACE enumerated type:

```
typedef enum D3D10_TEXTURECUBE_FACE
{
    D3D10_TEXTURECUBE_FACE_POSITIVE_X = 0,
    D3D10_TEXTURECUBE_FACE_NEGATIVE_X = 1,
    D3D10_TEXTURECUBE_FACE_POSITIVE_Y = 2,
    D3D10_TEXTURECUBE_FACE_NEGATIVE_Y = 3,
    D3D10_TEXTURECUBE_FACE_POSITIVE_Z = 4,
    D3D10_TEXTURECUBE_FACE_NEGATIVE_Z = 5,
} D3D10_TEXTURECUBE_FACE;
```

A cube map is stored in a texture array with six elements:

- Index 0 refers to the +X face.
- Index 1 refers to the –X face.
- Index 2 refers to the +Y face.
- Index 3 refers to the –Y face.
- Index 4 refers to the +Z face.
- Index 5 refers to the –Z face.

In contrast to 2D texturing, we can no longer identify a texel with 2D texture coordinates. To identify a texel in a cube map, we use 3D texture coordinates, which define a 3D *lookup* vector **v** originating at the origin. The texel of the cube map that **v** intersects (see Figure 11.1) is the texel corresponding to the 3D coordinates of **v**. The concepts of texture filtering discussed in Chapter 7 apply in the case **v** intersects a point between texel samples.

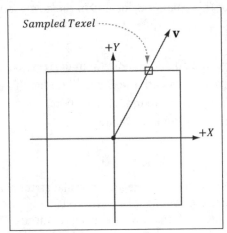

Figure 11.1: We illustrate in 2D for simplicity; in 3D the square becomes a cube. The square denotes a cube map centered and axis-aligned with some coordinate system. We shoot a vector **v** from the origin. The texel **v** intersects is the sampled texel. In this illustration, **v** intersects the cube face corresponding to the +Y-axis.

Note: The magnitude of the lookup vector is unimportant; only the direction matters. Two vectors with the same direction but different magnitudes will sample the same point in the cube map.

In the HLSL, a cube texture is represented by the `TextureCube` type. The following code fragment illustrates how we sample a cube map:

```
TextureCube gCubeMap;

SamplerState gTriLinearSam
{
    Filter = MIN_MAG_MIP_LINEAR;
    AddressU = Wrap;
    AddressV = Wrap;
};
```

```
...

// in pixel shader
float3 v = float3(x,y,z); // some lookup vector
float4 color = gCubeMap.Sample(gTriLinearSam, v);
```

Note: The lookup vector should be in the same space the cube map is relative to. For example, if the cube map is relative to the world space (i.e., the cube faces are axis-aligned with the world space axes), then the lookup vector should have world space coordinates.

11.2 **Environment Maps**

The primary application of cube maps is *environment mapping*. The idea is to position a camera at the center of some object O in the scene with a 90° field of view angle (both vertically and horizontally). Then have the camera look down the positive x-axis, negative x-axis, positive y-axis, negative y-axis, positive z-axis, and negative z-axis, and take a picture of the scene (excluding the object O) from each of these six viewpoints. Because the field of view angle is 90°, these six images will have captured the entire surrounding environment (see Figure 11.2) from the perspective of the object O. We then store these six images of the surrounding environment in a cube map, which leads to the name environment map. In other words, an *environment map* is a cube map where the cube faces store the surrounding images of an environment.

Figure 11.2: An example of an environment map after "unfolding" the cube map. Imagine refolding these six faces into a 3D box, and then imagine being at the center of the box. From every direction you look, you see the surrounding environment.

The above description suggests that we need to create an environment map for each object that is to use environment mapping. Often, however, an environment map is used to only capture distant "background" information, which means many nearby objects can share the same environment map. For example, in Figure 11.3, all the spheres share the environment map shown in Figure 11.2. Note that this environment map does not capture the local columns or floor of the scene; it only captures the distant mountains and sky (i.e., the scene background). Although the background environment map is, in some sense, incomplete, it works well in practice.

Figure 11.3: Screenshot of the Cube Map demo.

If the axis directions the camera looks down to build the environment map images are the world space axes, then the environment map is said to be generated relative to the world space. You could, of course, capture the environment from a different orientation (say the local space of an object). However, the lookup vector coordinates must be in the space the cube map is relative to.

Note that the six images for the environment map are generally not taken in a Direct3D program, although they could be (see Exercise 2). Because cube maps just store texture data, their contents are often pre-generated by an artist (just like the 2D textures we've been using). Consequently, we do not need to use real-time rendering to compute the images of a cube map. That is, we can create a scene in a 3D world editor, and then pre-render the six cube map face images in the editor. For outdoor environment maps, the program Terragen (http://www.planetside.co.uk/terragen/) is commonly used (free for personal use), and can create photorealistic outdoor scenes. The environment maps we create for this book, such as the one shown in Figure 11.2, were made with Terragen.

Note: If you choose to try out Terragen, you need to go to the Camera Settings dialog box and set the zoom factor to 1.0 to achieve a 90° field of view. Also, be sure to set your output image dimensions to be equal so that both the vertical and horizontal field of view angles are the same, namely 90°.

Once we have created the six cube map images using some program, we need to create a cube map texture, which stores all six. The DDS texture image format we have been using readily supports cube maps, and we can use the DirectX Texture Tool to create a cube map from our six textures. Open the DirectX Texture Tool (ships with the DirectX SDK: *C:\Microsoft DirectX SDK (November 2007)\Utilities\Bin\x86*) and first go to the **File** menu and select **New Texture**. From the dialog box that pops up (Figure 11.4), select **Cubemap Texture** as the texture type, enter the dimensions that match the dimensions of the six images, and choose a surface format. (Use a compressed format like DXT1; high-resolution cube maps can eat up a lot of memory since there are six textures being stored.)

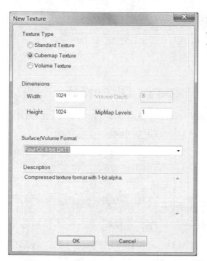

Figure 11.4: Creating a new cube texture with the DirectX Texture Tool.

Now we have an empty cube map. Go to the **View** menu, select **Cube Map Face**, and pick the face along the axis you want to view in the window (Figure 11.5). (All of these faces are initially empty.) Select any face to start with, and then go to the **File** menu and select **Open Onto This Cubemap Face**, which will launch a dialog box that asks you for the file you want to load onto the currently selected cube map face. Choose the image corresponding to this cube map face. Repeat this process for the remaining five cube map faces so that each cube map face has the desired image inserted onto it. When you are done, save the DDS to the file that now stores your cube map.

Figure 11.5: Selecting a face of the cube map to view in the DirectX Texture Tool.

11.2.1 Loading and Using Cube Maps in Direct3D

Conveniently, the `D3DX10CreateTextureFromFile` function can load a DDS file that stores a cube map into an `ID3D10Texture2D` object:

```
D3DX10_IMAGE_LOAD_INFO loadInfo;
loadInfo.MiscFlags = D3D10_RESOURCE_MISC_TEXTURECUBE;

ID3D10Texture2D* tex = 0;
HR(D3DX10CreateTextureFromFile(md3dDevice, filename.c_str(),
        &loadInfo, 0, (ID3D10Resource**)&tex, 0) );
```

The only requirement is that we specify the `D3D10_RESOURCE_MISC_TEXTURECUBE` flag so that it knows we are loading a cube texture. An `ID3D10Texture2D` object stores the six textures of a cube map as a texture array.

Once the texture data is loaded, we create a shader resource view to it in the following way:

```
D3D10_TEXTURE2D_DESC texDesc;
tex->GetDesc(&texDesc);

D3D10_SHADER_RESOURCE_VIEW_DESC viewDesc;
viewDesc.Format = texDesc.Format;
viewDesc.ViewDimension = D3D10_SRV_DIMENSION_TEXTURECUBE;
viewDesc.TextureCube.MipLevels = texDesc.MipLevels;
viewDesc.TextureCube.MostDetailedMip = 0;

ID3D10ShaderResourceView* rv = 0;
HR(md3dDevice->CreateShaderResourceView(tex, &viewDesc, &rv));

ReleaseCOM(tex);
```

Everything here is pretty standard, except that we must specify the
D3D10_SRV_DIMENSION_TEXTURECUBE flag to indicate this is a view to a cube
texture.

   After we have obtained an ID3D10ShaderResourceView* to the cube texture, we can set it to a TextureCube variable in an effect file with the
ID3D10EffectShaderResourceVariable::SetResource method:

```
// .fx variable
TextureCube gCubeMap;

// .cpp code
ID3D10EffectShaderResourceVariable* mfxCubeMapVar;


mfxCubeMapVar = fx::CubeMapFX->GetVariableByName("gCubeMap")
                   ->AsShaderResource();

...

mfxCubeMapVar->SetResource( rv );
```

11.3 **Texturing a Sky**

In this section we use an environment map to texture a sky. We create an
ellipsoid that surrounds the entire scene (we use an ellipsoid to create a
flatter sky surface). To create the illusion of distant mountains far in the
horizon and a sky, we texture the ellipsoid using an environment map by the
method shown in Figure 11.6. In this way, the environment map is projected
onto the ellipsoid's surface.

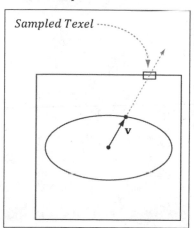

Figure 11.6: We illustrate in 2D for
simplicity; in 3D the square becomes a
cube and the ellipse becomes an ellipsoid.
We assume that the sky and environment
map are centered about the same origin.
Then to texture a point on the surface of
the ellipsoid, we use the vector from the
origin to the surface point as the lookup
vector into the cube map. This projects the
cube map onto the ellipsoid.

We assume that the sky ellipsoid is infinitely far away (i.e., it is centered
about the world space but has infinite radius), so no matter how the camera
moves in the world, we never appear to get closer or farther from the surface of the sky ellipsoid. To implement this infinitely faraway sky, we simply

center the sky ellipsoid about the camera in world space so that it is always centered about the camera. Consequently, as the camera moves, we are getting no closer to the surface of the ellipsoid. If we did not do this, and we let the camera move closer to the sky surface, the whole illusion would break down, as the trick we use to simulate the sky would be obvious.

The effect file for the sky is given below:

```
cbuffer cbPerFrame
{
    float4x4 gWVP;
};

TextureCube gCubeMap;

SamplerState gTriLinearSam
{
    Filter = MIN_MAG_MIP_LINEAR;
    AddressU = Wrap;
    AddressV = Wrap;
};

struct VS_IN
{
    float3 posL : POSITION;
};

struct VS_OUT
{
    float4 posH : SV_POSITION;
    float3 texC : TEXCOORD;
};

VS_OUT VS(VS_IN vIn)
{
    VS_OUT vOut;

    // set z = w so that z/w = 1 (i.e., skydome always on far plane).
    vOut.posH = mul(float4(vIn.posL, 1.0f), gWVP).xyww;

    // use local vertex position as cube map lookup vector.
    vOut.texC = vIn.posL;

    return vOut;
}

float4 PS(VS_OUT pIn) : SV_Target
{
    return gCubeMap.Sample(gTriLinearSam, pIn.texC);
}

RasterizerState NoCull
{
```

```
        CullMode = None;
};

DepthStencilState LessEqualDSS
{
    // Make sure the depth function is LESS_EQUAL and not just LESS.
    // Otherwise, the normalized depth values at z = 1 (NDC) will
    // fail the depth test if the depth buffer was cleared to 1.
    DepthFunc = LESS_EQUAL;
};

technique10 SkyTech
{
    pass P0
    {
        SetVertexShader( CompileShader( vs_4_0, VS() ) );
        SetGeometryShader( NULL );
        SetPixelShader( CompileShader( ps_4_0, PS() ) );

        SetRasterizerState(NoCull);
        SetDepthStencilState(LessEqualDSS, 0);
    }
}
```

Note: In the past, applications would draw the sky first and use it as a replacement to clearing the render target and depth/stencil buffer. However, the "ATI Radeon HD 2000 Programming Guide" (http://ati.amd.com/developer/SDK/AMD_SDK_Samples_May2007/Documentations/ATI_Radeon_HD_2000_programming_guide.pdf) now advises against this for the following reasons. First, the depth/stencil buffer needs to be explicitly cleared for internal hardware depth optimizations to perform well. The situation is similar with render targets. Second, typically most of the sky is occluded by other geometry such as buildings and terrain. Therefore, if we draw the sky first, then we are wasting resources by drawing pixels that will only get overridden later by geometry closer to the camera. Therefore, it is now recommended to always clear, and to draw the sky last.

11.4 Modeling Reflections

As described in the previous section, an environment map works well for the purposes of texturing a sky. However, the other main application of environment maps is to model reflections for arbitrary objects (only the images in the environment map are reflected with this technique). Figure 11.7 illustrates how reflections are done with environment maps. The surface acts like a mirror: The eye looks at **p** and sees the environment reflected off **p**.

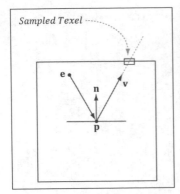

Figure 11.7: Here **e** is the eye point, and **n** is the surface normal at the point **p**. The texel that gets mapped to a point **p** on the surface is given by the reflection vector **v** (i.e., we use **v** as the lookup vector), which is the reflection of the vector from **e** to **p** about the surface. In this way, the eye sees the reflected environment.

We compute the reflection vector per pixel and then use it to sample the environment map:

```
if( gCubeMapEnabled )
{
    float3 incident = pIn.posW - gEyePosW;
    float3 refW = reflect(incident, normalW);
    float4 reflectedColor = gCubeMap.Sample(gTriLinearSam, refW);
    litColor += (gReflectMtrl*reflectedColor).rgb;
}
```

In general, a pixel's color is not completely determined by the reflected color (only mirrors are 100% reflective). Therefore, we modify our lighting equation to include a reflection term $c_R \otimes m_R$. Here c_R is the color sampled from the environment map and m_R is an application-controlled material value indicating how much of c_R the surface reflects into the eye. For example, if the surface only reflects red light, then you could set $m_R = (1,0,0)$ so that only red light from the environment map makes it into the eye.

Thus far we have been specifying materials with texture maps (e.g., we have diffuse and specular textures). It would be natural then to add a reflection map so that we could have finer control of the reflectivity c_R of a surface at the pixel level. (For example, some parts of a shield may be reflective and other parts not as reflective.) However, this flexibility is overkill for the purposes of our demo applications. So what we will do is store c_R as an element in a constant buffer. We can update this value as needed to change the reflectivity, but the general idea is that we will keep it the same for a group of related geometry (i.e., a collection of related triangles will share the same reflectivity value so that we do not have to update c_R often). In the above code fragment, the variable

```
float4 gReflectMtrl;
```

corresponds to c_R.

One issue with including the additional reflection term to the lighting equation is oversaturation. With the addition of the reflection term, we are now adding more color to the pixel, which may brighten it up too much. Basically, if we are adding additional color from the reflection term, then we must take away color from one of the other terms to achieve a balance. This is usually done by scaling down the ambient and diffuse material factors so that less ambient and diffuse light are reflected off the surface. Another approach is to average the color sampled from the environment map with the usual lit pixel color **s**:

$$\mathbf{f} = t\mathbf{c}_R + (1-t)\mathbf{s} \quad \text{for} \quad 0 \le t \le 1$$

In this way, as we add in the color sampled from the environment map with weight t, we equally take away color from the usual lit pixel color to keep a balance. So here the parameter t controls the reflectivity of the surface.

Figure 11.8 shows that reflections via environment mapping do not work well for flat surfaces.

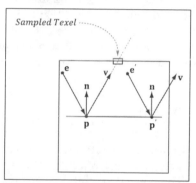

Figure 11.8: The reflection vector corresponding to two different points, **p** and **p'**, when the eye is at positions **e** and **e'**, respectively.

This is because the reflection vector does not tell the whole story, as it does not incorporate position; we really need a reflection ray and to intersect the ray with the environment map. A ray has position and direction, whereas a vector just has direction. From the figure, we see that the two reflection rays, $\mathbf{r}(t) = \mathbf{p} + t\mathbf{v}$ and $\mathbf{r}'(t) = \mathbf{p}' + t\mathbf{v}$, intersect different texels of the cube map, and thus should be colored differently. However, because both rays have the same direction vector **v**, and the direction vector **v** is solely used for the cube map lookup, the same texel gets mapped to **p** and **p'** when the eye is at **e** and **e'**, respectively. For flat objects this defect of environment mapping is very noticeable. For curvy surfaces, this shortcoming of environment mapping goes largely unnoticed since the curvature of the surface causes the reflection vector to vary. See [Brennan02] for an approximate solution to this problem.

11.5 **New Application Code**

This section gives a brief overview of some of the new classes and namespaces we will be using in Part III of this book. As always, the actual source code should be examined for further clarification.

11.5.1 **Texture Manager**

Later on we will be loading mesh data from files that store the filenames of the textures that need to be applied to the mesh. Because some meshes will share the same textures, these textures could be loaded more than once if care is not taken to prevent duplication. From now on we will use the TextureMgr class to create textures. This class will prevent textures from being loaded and created twice. In addition, this class provides methods for creating texture arrays, cube textures, and random textures. We use random textures for the particle system in Chapter 17. Note that the TextureMgr class also handles destroying the texture resources, so the main application code does not need to do this. The TextureMgr class is a singleton and a reference to the one and only instance that can be obtained with the GetResourceMgr() function.

11.5.2 **Global Effects and Input Layouts**

As we progress through this part of the book, we will eventually start using several effects (ID3D10Effect) and input layouts (ID3D10InputLayout) per project. We only need one instance of each effect in our project. Likewise, we only need one instance of each input layout used in our project. It is convenient to create and destroy all these unique instances in one location. Moreover, we provide global access to them through a namespace so that they can easily be shared across different types of objects that may need them. For example, many different classes we create may share the same input layout or effect. This organization works well for the scope of our demo applications. Readers wishing to avoid global variables can develop their own management system.

We define all the effects of our project in the *Effects.h* header file like so:

```
namespace fx
{
    extern ID3D10Effect* SkyFX;
    extern ID3D10Effect* CubeMapFX;

    void InitAll(ID3D10Device* device);
    void DestroyAll();
};
```

The fx::InitAll function is implemented in the *Effects.cpp* file and creates all the effects. It must be called before using any of the effects. For example, we call it early in the derived D3DApp::initApp method. Likewise, fx::DestroyAll destroys all the effects; it should be called in the destructor of the derived application class.

We define all of our input layouts in the *InputLayouts.h* header file like so:

```
namespace InputLayout
{
    extern ID3D10InputLayout* Pos;
    extern ID3D10InputLayout* PosNormalTex;

    void InitAll(ID3D10Device* device);
    void DestroyAll();
};
```

The InputLayout::InitAll and InputLayout::DestroyAll functions work analogously to the fx versions, and they are implemented in *InputLayouts.cpp*.

These files (*Effects.h/.cpp* and *InputLayouts.h/.cpp*) will be updated on a per-project basis to reflect the effects and input layouts the project requires.

11.5.3 New 3D Object Classes

The demos of this chapter and the next two make use of the Quad, Box, Cylinder, and Sphere classes that we have implemented. These just provide some simple test meshes for our demos. The Quad and Box geometry is quite straightforward to create in code. Generating the Cylinder and Sphere geometry requires a little more bookkeeping. The reader can study the code if desired; however, although it is a good exercise to be able to construct such geometry in code, it is not terribly important since most mesh data is generated by artists in 3D modeling applications. Therefore, you can treat these classes as block boxes if desired.

The public interfaces of these classes are as follows:

```
class Quad
{
public:
    Quad();
    ~Quad();

    void init(ID3D10Device* device, DWORD m, DWORD n, float dx);
    void draw();
};
```

The Quad::init method constructs an **m** × **n** triangle grid in the *xz*-plane of its local space with cell spacing dx.

```
class Box
{
public:

    Box();
```

```
    ~Box();

    void init(ID3D10Device* device, float scale);
    void draw();
};
```

The Box::init method constructs a cube centered at the origin of its local space with width scale.

```
class Cylinder
{
public:
    Cylinder();
    ~Cylinder();

    void init(ID3D10Device* device, float topRadius, float bottomRadius,
            float height, UINT numSlices, UINT numStacks);

    void draw();
};
```

The Cylinder::init method constructs a cylinder in its local space as shown in Figure 11.9.

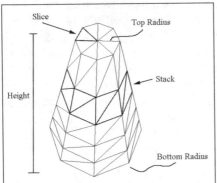

Figure 11.9: In this illustration, the cylinder has eight slices and five stacks. The slices and stacks control the level of tessellation. Note that the top and bottom radii can differ so that we can create cone-shaped objects, not just pure cylinders.

```
class Sphere
{
public:
    Sphere();
    ~Sphere();

    void init(ID3D10Device* device, float radius,
    UINT numSlices, UINT numStacks);
    void draw();
};
```

The Sphere::init method constructs a sphere centered at the origin of its local space with radius radius. The number of slices and stacks work to tessellate the sphere in a way analogous to the cylinder (see Figure 11.10).

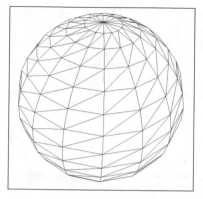

Figure 11.10: The idea of slices and stacks also apply to a sphere to control the level of tessellation.

Note: These classes compute vertex positions, normal vectors, and texture coordinates. In the next chapter, these classes will be updated to also include tangent vectors, which are needed for normal mapping.

11.6 Summary

- A cube map consists of six textures that we visualize as the faces of a cube. In Direct3D 10, a cube map can be represented by the `ID3D10Texture2D` interface as a texture array (§10.3). In the HLSL, a cube map is represented by the `TextureCube` type. To identify a texel in a cube map, we use 3D texture coordinates, which define a 3D *lookup* vector **v** originating at the center of the cube map. The texel of the cube map that **v** intersects is the texel corresponding to the 3D coordinates of **v**.

- An environment map captures the surrounding environment about a point with six images. These images can then be stored in a cube map. With environment maps we can easily texture a sky or approximate reflections.

- Cube maps can be made from six individual images using the DirectX Texture Tool. Cube maps can then be saved to file with the DDS image format. Because cube maps store six 2D textures, which can consume a lot of memory, a compressed DDS format should be used. The `D3DX10CreateTextureFromFile` function can load a DDS file that stores a cube map into an `ID3D10Texture2D` object as a texture array.

11.7 Exercises

1. Experiment with different `gReflectMtrl` values in the Cube Map demo. Also try to make the cylinders and box reflective.

2. In §11.2, we described how to create the textures of a cube map in a separate 3D rendering program like Terragen. However, suppose that

you want animated clouds or birds that fly in the sky. With a pre-generated cube map, you cannot capture these changing objects. One solution is to build the cube map at run time. That is, every frame you position the camera in the scene that is to be the origin of the cube map, and then render the scene six times into each cube map face along each coordinate axis direction. Since the cube map is rebuilt every frame, it will capture changing objects in the environment.

For this exercise, study the "CubeMapGS" DirectX SDK sample to see how they implement dynamic cube maps in a single pass with the geometry shader. You can find an explanatory overview of the sample by looking up "CubeMapGS" in the index of the SDK documentation.

Chapter 12

Normal Mapping

In Chapter 7, we introduced texture mapping, which enabled us to map fine details from an image onto our triangles. However, our normal vectors are still defined at the coarser vertex level and interpolated over the triangle. In this chapter, we study a popular method for specifying surface normals at a higher resolution.

The Normal Map demo for this chapter is available in the download files.

Objectives:

- To understand why we need normal mapping.
- To discover how normal maps are stored.
- To learn how normal maps can be created.
- To determine the coordinate system the normal vectors in normal maps are stored relative to, and how it relates to the object space coordinate system of a 3D triangle.
- To learn how to implement normal mapping in a vertex and pixel shader.

12.1 Motivation

Consider Figure 12.1 from the Cube Map demo of the preceding chapter (see the download files). The specular highlights on the cone-shaped columns do not look right — they look unnaturally smooth compared to the bumpiness of the brick texture. This is because the underlying mesh geometry is smooth, and we have merely applied the image of bumpy bricks over the smooth cylindrical surface. However, the lighting calculations are performed based on the mesh geometry (in particular, the interpolated vertex normals), and not the texture image. Thus the lighting is not completely consistent with the texture.

Figure 12.1: Smooth
specular highlights.

Ideally, we would tessellate the mesh geometry so much that the actual bumps and crevices of the bricks could be modeled by the underlying geometry. Then the lighting and texture could be made consistent. However, tessellating a mesh to such a resolution is not practical due to the huge increase in vertex and triangle count.

Another possible solution would be to bake the lighting details directly into the textures. However, this will not work if the lights are allowed to move, as the texel colors will remain fixed as the lights move.

Thus our goal is to find a way to implement dynamic lighting such that the fine details that show up in the texture map also show up in the lighting. Since textures provide us with the fine details to begin with, it is natural to look for a texture mapping solution to this problem. Figure 12.2 shows the same scene with normal mapping; we can see now that the dynamic lighting is much more consistent with the brick texture.

Figure 12.2: Bumpy
specular highlights.

12.2 **Normal Maps**

A *normal map* is a texture, but instead of storing RGB data at each texel, we store a compressed x-coordinate, y-coordinate, and z-coordinate in the red component, green component, and blue component, respectively. These coordinates define a normal vector; thus a normal map stores a normal vector at each pixel. Figure 12.3 shows an example of how to visualize a normal map.

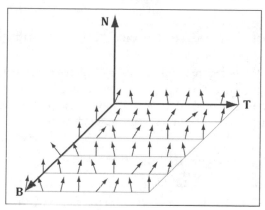

Figure 12.3: Normals stored in a normal map relative to a texture space coordinate system defined by the vectors **T** (x-axis), **B** (y-axis), and **N** (z-axis). The **T** vector runs right horizontally to the texture image, the **B** vector runs down vertically to the texture image, and **N** is orthogonal to the texture plane.

For illustration, we will assume a 24-bit image format, which reserves a byte for each color component, and therefore, each color component can range from 0 to 255. (A 32-bit format could be employed where the alpha component goes unused or stores some other scalar value. Also, a floating-point format could be used in which no compression is necessary, but this requires more memory, of course.)

Note: As Figure 12.3 shows, the vectors are generally mostly aligned with the z-axis. That is, the z-coordinate has the largest magnitude. Consequently, normal maps usually appear mostly blue when viewed as a color image. This is because the z-coordinate is stored in the blue channel and since it has the largest magnitude, this color dominates.

So how do we compress a unit vector into this format? First note that for a unit vector, each coordinate always lies in the range [–1, 1]. If we shift and scale this range to [0, 1] and multiply by 255 and truncate the decimal, the result will be an integer in the range 0 to 255. That is, if x is a coordinate in the range [–1, 1], then the integer part of $f(x)$ is an integer in the range 0 to 255, where f is defined by

$$f(x) = (0.5x + 0.5) \cdot 255$$

So to store a unit vector in a 24-bit image, we just apply f to each coordinate and write the coordinate to the corresponding color channel in the texture map.

The next question is how to reverse the compression process; that is, given a compressed texture coordinate in the range 0 to 255, how can we recover its true value in the interval [–1, 1]? The answer is to simply invert the function f, which after a little thought, can be seen to be:

$$f^{-1}(x) = \frac{2x}{255} - 1$$

That is, if x is an integer in the range 0 to 255, then $f^{-1}(x)$ is a floating-point number in the range [–1, 1].

We will not have to do the compression process ourselves, as we will use a Photoshop plug-in to convert images to normal maps. However, when we sample a normal map in a pixel shader, we will have to do part of the inverse process to uncompress it. When we sample a normal map in a shader like this:

```
float3 normalT = gNormalMap.Sample( gTriLinearSam, pIn.texC );
```

the color vector normalT will have normalized components (r, g, b) such that $0 \le r, g, b \le 1$. Thus, the method has already done part of the uncompressing work for us (namely the divide by 255, which transforms an integer in the range 0 to 255 to the floating-point interval [0, 1]). We complete the transformation by shifting and scaling each component in [0, 1] to [–1, 1] with the function $g: [0, 1] \rightarrow [-1, 1]$ defined by:

$$g(x) = 2x - 1$$

In code, we apply this function to each color component like this:

```
// Uncompress each component from [0,1] to [-1,1].
normalT = 2.0f*normalT - 1.0f;
```

This works because the scalar 1.0 is augmented to the vector (1, 1, 1) so that the expression makes sense and is done componentwise.

Note: The Photoshop plug-in is available at http://developer. nvidia.com/object/nv_texture_tools.html. There are other tools available for generating normal maps such as http://www.crazybump. com/. Also, there are tools that can generate normal maps from high-resolution meshes (see http://developer.nvidia .com/object/ melody_home.html).

12.3 **Texture/Tangent Space**

Consider a 3D texture mapped triangle. For the sake of discussion, suppose that there is no distortion in the texture mapping; in other words, mapping the texture triangle onto the 3D triangle requires only a rigid body transformation (translation and rotation). Now, suppose that the texture is like a decal. So we pick up the decal, translate it, and rotate it onto the 3D triangle. Figure 12.4 shows how the texture space axes relate to the 3D triangle: They are tangent to the triangle and lie in the plane of the triangle. The texture coordinates of the triangle are, of course, relative to the texture space coordinate system. Incorporating the triangle face normal **N**, we obtain a 3D _TBN-basis_ in the plane of the triangle that we call _texture space_ or _tangent space_. Note that the tangent space generally varies from triangle to triangle (see Figure 12.5).

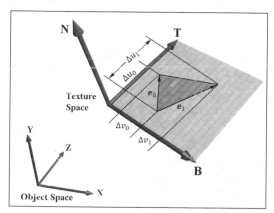

Figure 12.4: The relationship between the texture space of a triangle and the object space.

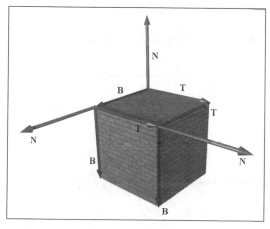

Figure 12.5: The texture space is different for each face of the box.

Now, as Figure 12.3 shows, the normal vectors in a normal map are defined relative to the texture space. But our lights are defined in world space. In order to do lighting, the normal vectors and lights need to be in the same space. So our first step is to relate the tangent space coordinate system with the object space coordinate system the triangle vertices are relative to. Once we are in object space, we can use the world matrix to get from object space to world space (the details of this are covered in the next section). Let $\mathbf{v}_0$, $\mathbf{v}_1$, and $\mathbf{v}_2$ define the three vertices of a 3D triangle with corresponding texture coordinates (u_0, v_0), (u_1, v_1), and (u_2, v_2) that define a triangle in the texture plane relative to the texture space axes (i.e., $\mathbf{T}$ and $\mathbf{B}$). Let $\mathbf{e}_0 = \mathbf{v}_1 - \mathbf{v}_0$ and $\mathbf{e}_1 = \mathbf{v}_2 - \mathbf{v}_0$ be two edge vectors of the 3D triangle with corresponding texture triangle edge vectors $(\Delta u_0, \Delta v_0) = (u_1 - u_0, v_1 - v_0)$ and $(\Delta u_1, \Delta v_1) = (u_2 - u_0, v_2 - v_0)$. From Figure 12.4, it is clear that

$$\mathbf{e}_0 = \Delta u_0 \mathbf{T} + \Delta v_0 \mathbf{B}$$
$$\mathbf{e}_1 = \Delta u_1 \mathbf{T} + \Delta v_1 \mathbf{B}$$

Representing the vectors with coordinates relative to object space, we get the matrix equation:

$$\begin{bmatrix} e_{0,x} & e_{0,y} & e_{0,z} \\ e_{1,x} & e_{1,y} & e_{1,z} \end{bmatrix} = \begin{bmatrix} \Delta u_0 & \Delta v_0 \\ \Delta u_1 & \Delta v_1 \end{bmatrix} \begin{bmatrix} T_x & T_y & T_z \\ B_x & B_y & B_z \end{bmatrix}$$

Note that we know the object space coordinates of the triangle vertices; hence we know the object space coordinates of the edge vectors, so the matrix

$$\begin{bmatrix} e_{0,x} & e_{0,y} & e_{0,z} \\ e_{1,x} & e_{1,y} & e_{1,z} \end{bmatrix}$$

is known. Likewise, we know the texture coordinates, so the matrix

$$\begin{bmatrix} \Delta u_0 & \Delta v_0 \\ \Delta u_1 & \Delta v_1 \end{bmatrix}$$

is known. Solving for the $\mathbf{T}$ and $\mathbf{B}$ object space coordinates we get:

$$\begin{bmatrix} T_x & T_y & T_z \\ B_x & B_y & B_z \end{bmatrix} = \begin{bmatrix} \Delta u_0 & \Delta v_0 \\ \Delta u_1 & \Delta v_1 \end{bmatrix}^{-1} \begin{bmatrix} e_{0,x} & e_{0,y} & e_{0,z} \\ e_{1,x} & e_{1,y} & e_{1,z} \end{bmatrix}$$

$$= \frac{1}{\Delta u_0 \Delta v_1 - \Delta v_0 \Delta u_1} \begin{bmatrix} \Delta v_1 & -\Delta v_0 \\ -\Delta u_1 & \Delta u_0 \end{bmatrix} \begin{bmatrix} e_{0,x} & e_{0,y} & e_{0,z} \\ e_{1,x} & e_{1,y} & e_{1,z} \end{bmatrix}$$

In the above, we used the fact that the inverse of a matrix $\mathbf{A} = \begin{bmatrix} a & b \\ c & d \end{bmatrix}$ is given by:

$$\mathbf{A}^{-1} = \frac{1}{ad - bc}\begin{bmatrix} d & -b \\ -c & a \end{bmatrix}$$

Note that the vectors $\mathbf{T}$ and $\mathbf{B}$ are generally not unit length in object space, and if there is texture distortion, they will not be orthonormal either.

The $\mathbf{T}$, $\mathbf{B}$, and $\mathbf{N}$ vectors are commonly referred to as the _tangent_, _binormal_ (or _bitangent_), and _normal_ vectors, respectively.

12.4 **Vertex Tangent Space**

In the previous section, we derived a tangent space per triangle. However, if we use this texture space for normal mapping, we will get a triangulated appearance since the tangent space is constant over the face of the triangle. Therefore, we specify tangent vectors per vertex, and we do the same averaging trick that we did with vertex normals to approximate a smooth surface:

1. The tangent vector $\mathbf{T}$ for an arbitrary vertex $\mathbf{v}$ in a mesh is found by averaging the tangent vectors of every triangle in the mesh that shares the vertex $\mathbf{v}$.

2. The bitangent vector $\mathbf{B}$ for an arbitrary vertex $\mathbf{v}$ in a mesh is found by averaging the bitangent vectors of every triangle in the mesh that shares the vertex $\mathbf{v}$.

After averaging, the TBN-bases will generally need to be orthonormalized, so that the vectors are mutually orthogonal and of unit length. This is usually done using the Gram-Schmidt procedure. Code is available on the web for building a per-vertex tangent space for an arbitrary triangle mesh: http://www.terathon.com/code/tangent.php.

In our system, we will not store the bitangent vector $\mathbf{B}$ directly in memory. Instead, we will compute $\mathbf{B} = \mathbf{N} \times \mathbf{T}$ when we need $\mathbf{B}$, where $\mathbf{N}$ is the usual averaged vertex normal. Hence, our vertex structure looks like this:

```
struct Vertex
{
    D3DXVECTOR3 pos;
    D3DXVECTOR3 tangent;
    D3DXVECTOR3 normal;
    D3DXVECTOR2 texC;
};
```

For our Normal Map demo, we will continue to use the Quad, Box, Cylinder, and Sphere classes. We have updated these classes to include a tangent vector per vertex. The object space coordinates of the tangent vector $\mathbf{T}$ is easily specified at each vertex for the Quad and Box (see Figure 12.5). For the Cylinder and Sphere, the tangent vector $\mathbf{T}$ at each vertex can be found by forming the vector-valued function of two variables $\mathbf{P}(u, v)$ of the cylinder/sphere and computing $\partial \mathbf{P} / \partial u$, where the parameter u is also used as the u-texture coordinate.

12.5 **Transforming between Tangent Space and Object Space**

At this point, we have an orthonormal TBN-basis at each vertex in a mesh. Moreover, we have the coordinates of the TBN vectors relative to the object space of the mesh. So now that we have the coordinates of the TBN-basis relative to the object space coordinate system, we can transform coordinates from tangent space to object space with the matrix:

$$\mathbf{M}_{object} = \begin{bmatrix} T_x & T_y & T_z \\ B_x & B_y & B_z \\ N_x & N_y & N_z \end{bmatrix}$$

Since this matrix is orthogonal, its inverse is its transpose. Thus, the change of coordinate matrix from object space to tangent space is:

$$\mathbf{M}_{tangent} = \mathbf{M}_{object}^{-1} = \mathbf{M}_{object}^{T} = \begin{bmatrix} T_x & B_x & N_x \\ T_y & B_y & N_y \\ T_z & B_z & N_z \end{bmatrix}$$

In our shader program, we will actually want to transform the normal vector from tangent space to world space for lighting. One way would be to transform the normal from tangent space to object space first, and then use the world matrix to transform from object space to world space:

$$\mathbf{n}_{world} = (\mathbf{n}_{tangent} \mathbf{M}_{object}) \mathbf{M}_{world}$$

However, since matrix multiplication is associative, we can do it like this:

$$\mathbf{n}_{world} = \mathbf{n}_{tangent} (\mathbf{M}_{object} \mathbf{M}_{world})$$

And note that

$$\mathbf{M}_{object} \mathbf{M}_{world} = \begin{bmatrix} \leftarrow \mathbf{T} \rightarrow \\ \leftarrow \mathbf{B} \rightarrow \\ \leftarrow \mathbf{N} \rightarrow \end{bmatrix} \mathbf{M}_{world} = \begin{bmatrix} \leftarrow \mathbf{T}' \rightarrow \\ \leftarrow \mathbf{B}' \rightarrow \\ \leftarrow \mathbf{N}' \rightarrow \end{bmatrix} = \begin{bmatrix} T'_x & T'_y & T'_z \\ B'_x & B'_y & B'_z \\ N'_x & N'_y & N'_z \end{bmatrix}$$

where $\mathbf{T}' = \mathbf{T} \cdot \mathbf{M}_{world}$, $\mathbf{B}' = \mathbf{B} \cdot \mathbf{M}_{world}$, and $\mathbf{N}' = \mathbf{N} \cdot \mathbf{M}_{world}$. So to go from tangent space directly to world space, we just have to describe the tangent basis in world coordinates, which can be done by transforming the TBN-basis from object space coordinates to world space coordinates.

Note: We will only be interested in transforming vectors (not points). Thus, we only need a 3×3 matrix. Recall that the fourth row of an affine matrix is for translation, but we do not translate vectors.

12.6 **Shader Code**

We summarize the general process for normal mapping:

1.   Create the desired normal maps from some art or utility program and store them in an image file. Create 2D textures from these files when the program is initialized.

2.   For each triangle, compute the tangent vector **T**. Obtain a per-vertex tangent vector for each vertex **v** in a mesh by averaging the tangent vectors of every triangle in the mesh that shares the vertex **v**. (In our demo, we use simple geometry and are able to specify the tangent vectors directly, but this averaging process would need to be done if using arbitrary triangle meshes made in a 3D modeling program.)

3.   In the vertex shader, transform the vertex normal and tangent vector to world space and output the results to the pixel shader.

4.   Using the interpolated tangent vector and normal vector, we build the TBN-basis at each pixel point on the surface of the triangle. We use this basis to transform the sampled normal vector from the normal map from tangent space to world space. We then have a world space normal vector from the normal map to use for our usual lighting calculations.

The entire normal mapping effect is shown below for completeness, with the parts relevant to normal mapping in bold.

```
#include "lighthelper.fx"

cbuffer cbPerFrame
{
    Light gLight;
    float3 gEyePosW;
};

cbuffer cbPerObject
{
    float4x4 gWorld;
    float4x4 gWVP;
    float4x4 gTexMtx;
    float4 gReflectMtrl;
    bool gCubeMapEnabled;
};
```

```
// Nonnumeric values cannot be added to a cbuffer.
Texture2D gDiffuseMap;
Texture2D gSpecMap;
Texture2D gNormalMap;
TextureCube gCubeMap;

SamplerState gTriLinearSam
{
    Filter = MIN_MAG_MIP_LINEAR;
    AddressU = Wrap;
    AddressV = Wrap;
};

struct VS_IN
{
    float3 posL     : POSITION;
    float3 tangentL : TANGENT;
    float3 normalL  : NORMAL;
    float2 texC     : TEXCOORD;
};

struct VS_OUT
{
    float4 posH     : SV_POSITION;
    float3 posW     : POSITION;
    float3 tangentW : TANGENT;
    float3 normalW  : NORMAL;
    float2 texC     : TEXCOORD;
};

VS_OUT VS(VS_IN vIn)
{
    VS_OUT vOut;

    // Transform to world space space.
    vOut.posW     = mul(float4(vIn.posL, 1.0f), gWorld);
    vOut.tangentW = mul(float4(vIn.tangentL, 0.0f), gWorld);
    vOut.normalW  = mul(float4(vIn.normalL, 0.0f), gWorld);

    // Transform to homogeneous clip space.
    vOut.posH = mul(float4(vIn.posL, 1.0f), gWVP);

    // Output vertex attributes for interpolation across triangle.
    vOut.texC = mul(float4(vIn.texC, 0.0f, 1.0f), gTexMtx);

    return vOut;
}

float4 PS(VS_OUT pIn) : SV_Target
{
    float4 diffuse = gDiffuseMap.Sample( gTriLinearSam, pIn.texC );

    // Kill transparent pixels.
```

```
    clip(diffuse.a - 0.15f);

    float4 spec    = gSpecMap.Sample( gTriLinearSam, pIn.texC );
    float3 normalT = gNormalMap.Sample( gTriLinearSam, pIn.texC );

    // Map [0,1] --> [0,256]
    spec.a *= 256.0f;

    // Uncompress each component from [0,1] to [-1,1].
    normalT = 2.0f*normalT - 1.0f;

    // build orthonormal basis
    float3 N = normalize(pIn.normalW);
    float3 T = normalize(pIn.tangentW - dot(pIn.tangentW, N)*N);
    float3 B = cross(N,T);

    float3x3 TBN = float3x3(T, B, N);

    // Transform from tangent space to world space.
    float3 bumpedNormalW = normalize(mul(normalT, TBN));

    // Compute the lit color for this pixel using normal from normal map.
    SurfaceInfo v = {pIn.posW, bumpedNormalW, diffuse, spec};
    float3 litColor = ParallelLight(v, gLight, gEyePosW);

    [branch]
    if( gCubeMapEnabled )
    {
        float3 incident = pIn.posW - gEyePosW;
        float3 refW = reflect(incident, bumpedNormalW);
        float4 reflectedColor = gCubeMap.Sample(gTriLinearSam, refW);
        litColor += (gReflectMtrl*reflectedColor).rgb;
    }

    return float4(litColor, diffuse.a);
}

technique10 NormalMapTech
{
    pass P0
    {
        SetVertexShader( CompileShader( vs_4_0, VS() ) );
        SetGeometryShader( NULL );
        SetPixelShader( CompileShader( ps_4_0, PS() ) );
    }
}
```

Two lines that might not be clear are these:

```
float3 N = normalize(pIn.normalW);
float3 T = normalize(pIn.tangentW - dot(pIn.tangentW, N)*N);
```

After the interpolation, the tangent vector and normal vector may not be orthonormal. This code makes sure **T** is orthonormal to **N** by subtracting off any component of **T** along the direction **N** (see Figure 12.6).

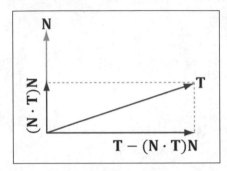

Figure 12.6: Since $\|\mathbf{N}\| = 1$, $\text{proj}_{\mathbf{N}}(\mathbf{T}) = (\mathbf{T} \cdot \mathbf{N})\mathbf{N}$. The vector $\mathbf{T} - \text{proj}_{\mathbf{N}}(\mathbf{T})$ is the portion of **T** orthogonal to **N**.

12.7 **Summary**

- The strategy of normal mapping is to texture our polygons with normal maps. We then have per-pixel normals, which capture the fine details of a surface like bumps, scratches, and crevices. We then use these per-pixel normals from the normal map in our lighting calculations, instead of the interpolated vertex normals.

- A normal map is a texture, but instead of storing RGB data at each texel, we store a compressed x-coordinate, y-coordinate, and z-coordinate in the red component, green component, and blue component, respectively. We use various tools to generate normal maps, such as the ones located at http://developer.nvidia.com/object/nv_texture_tools.html, http://www.crazybump.com/, and http://developer.nvidia.com/object/melody_home.html.

- The coordinates of the normals in a normal map are relative to the texture space coordinate system. Consequently, to do lighting calculations, we need to transform the normal from the texture space to the world space so that the lights and normals are in the same coordinate system. The TBN-bases built at each vertex facilitate the transformation from texture space to world space.

12.8 **Exercises**

1. Download the NVIDIA normal map plug-in (http://developer.nvidia.com/object/nv_texture_tools.html) and experiment with making different normal maps with it. Try your normal maps out in this chapter's demo application.

2. Investigate `D3DX10ComputeNormalMap` and use it to create a normal map from a heightmap. Essentially, a heightmap is a grayscale image that defines the heights of a surface (see §16.1). Use `D3DX10SaveTextureToFile` to export your normal map to file as a Windows bitmap image (`D3DX10_IFF_BMP`).

Chapter 13 . . . .

Shadow Mapping

Shadows indicate to the observer where light originates and helps convey the relative locations of objects in a scene. This chapter provides an introduction to the basic shadow mapping algorithm, which is a popular method for modeling dynamic shadows in games and 3D applications. For an introductory book, we focus only on the basic shadow mapping algorithm; more sophisticated shadowing techniques, such as cascading shadow maps [Engel06] which give better quality results, are built by extending the basic shadow mapping algorithm. Before we can discuss the shadow mapping algorithm, we must introduce two techniques the shadow mapping algorithm utilizes: render to texture and projective texturing.

Objectives:

- To understand the basic shadow mapping algorithm.
- To discover how to render to a texture.
- To learn how projective texturing works.
- To find out about orthographic projections.

13.1 Render to Texture

Thus far, we have been rendering to the swap chain's back buffer surface; that is to say, the back buffer has been the render target. However, the back buffer need not always be the render target; we can render to a different texture. For example, Figure 13.1 shows an application of rendering to texture to implement a radar map. In this section, we show how to update a texture at run time by rendering into it every frame; after we render to this texture, we can bind the texture as a shader input and map it onto geometry.

Figure 13.1: The scene is rendered to a texture from a bird's-eye view. Then, when we render the scene as normal from the player's eye, we map the texture onto a quad in the bottom-right corner of the screen to display the radar map (i.e., the scene from the bird's-eye view).

To facilitate render to texture, we implement a class called DrawableTex2D. This class encapsulates the resource views to two textures: a color map, which we bind as the render target, and a depth map, which we bind as the depth/stencil buffer. We incorporate a depth buffer since, just as we want to do depth buffering when we render the scene to the back buffer, we will want to do depth buffering when we render a scene to a texture. The class definition is given below:

```
class DrawableTex2D
{
public:
    DrawableTex2D();
    ~DrawableTex2D();

    void init(ID3D10Device* device, UINT width, UINT height,
        bool hasColorMap, DXGI_FORMAT colorFormat);

    ID3D10ShaderResourceView* colorMap();
    ID3D10ShaderResourceView* depthMap();

    void begin();
    void end();

private:
    DrawableTex2D(const DrawableTex2D& rhs);
    DrawableTex2D& operator=(const DrawableTex2D& rhs);

    void buildDepthMap();
    void buildColorMap();
private:
    UINT mWidth;
    UINT mHeight;
    DXGI_FORMAT mColorMapFormat;
```

```
ID3D10Device* md3dDevice;

ID3D10ShaderResourceView* mColorMapSRV;
ID3D10RenderTargetView* mColorMapRTV;

ID3D10ShaderResourceView* mDepthMapSRV;
ID3D10DepthStencilView* mDepthMapDSV;

D3D10_VIEWPORT mViewport;
};
```

13.1.1 Constructor/Destructor/Accessors

The following implementations are trivial, but we include them for
completeness:

```
DrawableTex2D::DrawableTex2D()
: mWidth(0), mHeight(0), mColorMapFormat(DXGI_FORMAT_UNKNOWN),
  md3dDevice(0), mColorMapSRV(0), mColorMapRTV(0), mDepthMapSRV(0),
  mDepthMapDSV(0)
{
    ZeroMemory(&mViewport, sizeof(D3D10_VIEWPORT));
}

DrawableTex2D::~DrawableTex2D()
{
    ReleaseCOM(mColorMapSRV);
    ReleaseCOM(mColorMapRTV);

    ReleaseCOM(mDepthMapSRV);
    ReleaseCOM(mDepthMapDSV);
}

ID3D10ShaderResourceView* DrawableTex2D::colorMap()
{
    return mColorMapSRV;
}

ID3D10ShaderResourceView* DrawableTex2D::depthMap()
{
    return mDepthMapSRV;
}
```

The `DrawableTex2D::colorMap` and `DrawableTex2D::depthMap` methods return
shader resource views, so that we can bind the respective texture to a
shader stage in order to sample the texture in a shader.

13.1.2 DrawableTex2D::init

The `DrawableTex2D::init` method is implemented like so:

```
void DrawableTex2D::init(ID3D10Device* device, UINT width, UINT height,
                         bool hasColorMap, DXGI_FORMAT colorFormat)
{
```

```
        mWidth  = width;
        mHeight = height;

        mColorMapFormat = colorFormat;

        md3dDevice = device;

        buildDepthMap();

        // shadow maps don't need color maps, for example
        if( hasColorMap )
            buildColorMap();

        mViewport.TopLeftX = 0;
        mViewport.TopLeftY = 0;
        mViewport.Width    = width;
        mViewport.Height   = height;
        mViewport.MinDepth = 0.0f;
        mViewport.MaxDepth = 1.0f;
    }
```

The width and height parameters specify the dimensions of the color and depth/stencil buffers. The colorFormat parameter specifies the pixel format of the color buffer. The hasColorMap parameter indicates whether a DrawableTex2D instance has a color map. For example, to implement shadow mapping, we do not need a color map — we only need a depth buffer. The viewport indicates the subrectangle of the render target (and depth/stencil buffer) to draw to. In our implementation, we draw to the entire render target (and depth/stencil buffer) by having the viewport dimensions match the buffer dimensions.

13.1.3 **DrawableTex2D::buildDepthMap**

The following code builds the depth map. We specify the bind flags

```
    texDesc.BindFlags = D3D10_BIND_DEPTH_STENCIL |
                        D3D10_BIND_SHADER_RESOURCE;
```

so that we can bind the texture as a depth/stencil buffer and as a shader input. Note that the texture format is typeless (DXGI_FORMAT_R32_TYPELESS) when we create the texture. The format needs to be typeless because the format depends on the view. The shader resource view uses the format DXGI_FORMAT_R32_FLOAT and the depth/stencil view uses the format DXGI_FORMAT_D32_FLOAT.

```
    void DrawableTex2D::buildDepthMap()
    {
        ID3D10Texture2D* depthMap = 0;

        D3D10_TEXTURE2D_DESC texDesc;

        texDesc.Width     = mWidth;
```

```
texDesc.Height      = mHeight;
texDesc.MipLevels = 1;
texDesc.ArraySize = 1;
texDesc.Format      = DXGI_FORMAT_R32_TYPELESS;
texDesc.SampleDesc.Count   = 1;
texDesc.SampleDesc.Quality = 0;
texDesc.Usage             = D3D10_USAGE_DEFAULT;
texDesc.BindFlags         = D3D10_BIND_DEPTH_STENCIL |
                            D3D10_BIND_SHADER_RESOURCE;
texDesc.CPUAccessFlags = 0;
texDesc.MiscFlags       = 0;

HR(md3dDevice->CreateTexture2D(&texDesc, 0, &depthMap));

D3D10_DEPTH_STENCIL_VIEW_DESC dsvDesc;
dsvDesc.Format = DXGI_FORMAT_D32_FLOAT;
dsvDesc.ViewDimension = D3D10_DSV_DIMENSION_TEXTURE2D;
dsvDesc.Texture2D.MipSlice = 0;
HR(md3dDevice->CreateDepthStencilView(depthMap,
        &dsvDesc, &mDepthMapDSV));

D3D10_SHADER_RESOURCE_VIEW_DESC srvDesc;
srvDesc.Format = DXGI_FORMAT_R32_FLOAT;
srvDesc.ViewDimension = D3D10_SRV_DIMENSION_TEXTURE2D;
srvDesc.Texture2D.MipLevels - texDesc.MipLevels;
srvDesc.Texture2D.MostDetailedMip = 0;
HR(md3dDevice->CreateShaderResourceView(depthMap,
        &srvDesc, &mDepthMapSRV));

// View saves a reference to the texture so we can
// release our reference.
ReleaseCOM(depthMap);
}
```

You might wonder why the depth buffer should be allowed to be bound to a shader input. It seems the depth buffer would just be needed for the depth buffer algorithm to accurately generate the color buffer, and that we would only want to bind the color buffer as a shader input. In actuality, the depth buffer is precisely the texture we want to project onto geometry to implement the shadow mapping algorithm. Thus, it is useful to also allow the depth buffer to be bound as a shader input.

13.1.4 **DrawableTex2D::buildColorMap**

The following code builds the color map. It is analogous to the `DrawableTex2D::buildDepthMap` method. However, one difference is that we specify the flag:

```
texDesc.MiscFlags = D3D10_RESOURCE_MISC_GENERATE_MIPS;
```

When this flag is specified, it allows the hardware to generate the lower mipmap levels (see §13.1.6).

```
void DrawableTex2D::buildColorMap()
{
    ID3D10Texture2D* colorMap = 0;

    D3D10_TEXTURE2D_DESC texDesc;

    texDesc.Width        = mWidth;
    texDesc.Height       = mHeight;
    texDesc.MipLevels = 0;
    texDesc.ArraySize = 1;
    texDesc.Format       = mColorMapFormat;
    texDesc.SampleDesc.Count    = 1;
    texDesc.SampleDesc.Quality = 0;
    texDesc.Usage           = D3D10_USAGE_DEFAULT;
    texDesc.BindFlags       = D3D10_BIND_RENDER_TARGET |
                              D3D10_BIND_SHADER_RESOURCE;
    texDesc.CPUAccessFlags = 0;
    texDesc.MiscFlags       = D3D10_RESOURCE_MISC_GENERATE_MIPS;

    HR(md3dDevice->CreateTexture2D(&texDesc, 0, &colorMap));

    // Null description means to create a view to all mipmap levels
    // using the format the texture was created with.
    HR(md3dDevice->CreateRenderTargetView(colorMap, 0, &mColorMapRTV));
    HR(md3dDevice->CreateShaderResourceView(colorMap, 0, &mColorMapSRV));

    // View saves a reference to the texture so we can
    // release our reference.
    ReleaseCOM(colorMap);
}
```

13.1.5 DrawableTex2D::begin

The structure for drawing to a texture is as follows:

```
DrawableTex2D::begin();

// Draw geometry here to texture

DrawableTex2D::end();
```

That is, the DrawableTex2D::begin method needs to be called before we can draw to the texture, and the DrawableTex2D::end method should be called when we are done drawing to the texture.

The DrawableTex2D::begin method changes the render target of the output merger stage from the back buffer to the texture. It also sets the new viewport that corresponds to the texture. Finally, it clears the color map (if it exists) and the depth map to default values.

```
void DrawableTex2D::begin()
{
    ID3D10RenderTargetView* renderTargets[1] = {mColorMapRTV};
    md3dDevice->OMSetRenderTargets(1, renderTargets, mDepthMapDSV);
```

```
    md3dDevice->RSSetViewports(1, &mViewport);

    // only clear if we actually created a color map.
    if( mColorMapRTV )
    md3dDevice->ClearRenderTargetView(mColorMapRTV, BLACK);

    md3dDevice->ClearDepthStencilView(mDepthMapDSV,
            D3D10_CLEAR_DEPTH, 1.0f, 0);
}
```

If a color map does not exist, then mColorMapRTV will be null, and we are
binding a null render target. This is fine, and it disables any pixels from
being written since there is no render target for them to be written to.
Depth values are still written to the depth buffer, however. It might sound
odd to draw to the depth buffer but not the color buffer, but as we will soon
see, for shadow mapping we only need to draw to the depth buffer.

Note: When binding a null render target, you do not pass in null
for the render target array parameter. Instead you must pass in a
valid array of ID3D10RenderTargetView pointers, where the elements
are null. That is, note the distinction between:

```
    // Incorrect
    md3dDevice->OMSetRenderTargets(1, 0, mDepthMapDSV);

    // Correct
    ID3D10RenderTargetView* renderTargets[1] = {0};
    md3dDevice->OMSetRenderTargets(1, renderTargets, mDepthMapDSV);
```

13.1.6 **DrawableTex2D::end**

As mentioned, when we render to texture to generate a color map, we
usually want to map the generated texture onto some geometry, as was
illustrated in Figure 13.1. However, since we had Direct3D generate the
texture at run time, we do not have the lower mipmap levels. We can
have Direct3D generate the lower mipmap levels using the
ID3D10Device::GenerateMips method. In order to call this method on a shader
resource view, the original texture must have been created with the
D3D10_RESOURCE_MISC_GENERATE_MIPS flag.

```
void DrawableTex2D::end()
{
    // After we have drawn to the color map, have the hardware generate
    // the lower mipmap levels.

    if( mColorMapSRV )
            md3dDevice->GenerateMips(mColorMapSRV);
}
```

As mentioned, `DrawableTex2D::end` should be called when we are done rendering to the texture. This is because we do not want to generate the mipmap levels until after we are done drawing to the texture for the current frame.

13.2 **Orthographic Projections**

Thus far in this book we have been using a perspective projection. The key property of perspective projection is that objects more distant from the camera are perceived as smaller. This agrees with how we perceive things in real life. Another type of projection is an *orthographic projection*. Such projections are primarily used in 3D science or engineering applications, where it is desirable to have parallel lines remain parallel after projection. However, orthographic projections will enable us to model shadows that parallel lights generate. With an orthographic projection, the viewing volume is a box axis-aligned with the view space with width w, height h, near plane n, and far plane f that looks down the positive z-axis of view space (see Figure 13.2). These numbers, defined relative to the view space coordinate system, define the box view volume.

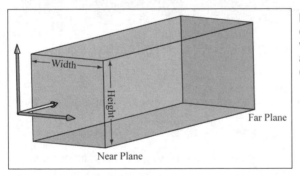

Figure 13.2: The orthographic viewing volume is a box that is axis-aligned with the view coordinate system.

With an orthographic projection, the lines of projection are parallel to the view space z-axis (Figure 13.3). And we see that the 2D projection of a vertex (x, y, z) is just (x, y).

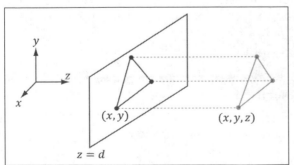

Figure 13.3: The orthographic projection of points onto the projection plane. The lines of projection are parallel to the view space z-axis with an orthographic projection.

As with perspective projection, we want to maintain relative depth information, and we want normalized device coordinates (NDC). To transform the view volume from view space to NDC space, we need to rescale and shift to map the view space view volume $\left[-\frac{w}{2}, \frac{w}{2}\right] \times \left[-\frac{h}{2}, \frac{h}{2}\right] \times [n, f]$ to the NDC space view volume $[-1, 1] \times [-1, 1] \times [0, 1]$. We can determine this mapping by working coordinate-by-coordinate. For the first two coordinates, it is easy to see that the intervals differ only by a scaling factor:

$$\frac{2}{w} \cdot \left[-\frac{w}{2}, \frac{w}{2}\right] = [-1, 1]$$

$$\frac{2}{h} \cdot \left[-\frac{h}{2}, \frac{h}{2}\right] = [-1, 1]$$

For the third coordinate, we need to map $[n, f] \to [0, 1]$. We assume the mapping takes the form $g(z) = az + b$ (i.e., a scaling and translation). We have the conditions $g(n) = 0$ and $g(f) = 1$, which allow us to solve for a and b:

$$an + b = 0$$
$$af + b - 1$$

The first equation implies $b = -an$. Plugging this into the second equation we get:

$$af - an = 1$$

$$a - \frac{1}{f - n}$$

And so:

$$-\frac{n}{f - n} = b$$

Thus,

$$g(z) = \frac{z}{f - n} - \frac{n}{f - n}$$

The reader may wish to graph $g(z)$ over the domain $[n, f]$ for various n and f such that $f > n$.

Finally, the orthographic transformation from view space coordinates (x, y, z) to NDC space coordinates (x', y', z') is:

$$x' = \frac{2}{w} x$$

$$y' = \frac{2}{h} y$$

$$z' = \frac{z}{f - n} - \frac{n}{f - n}$$

Or in terms of matrices:

$$[x', y', z', 1] = [x, y, z, 1] \begin{bmatrix} \frac{2}{w} & 0 & 0 & 0 \\ 0 & \frac{2}{h} & 0 & 0 \\ 0 & 0 & \frac{1}{f-n} & 0 \\ 0 & 0 & \frac{n}{n-f} & 1 \end{bmatrix}$$

The 4 × 4 matrix in the above equation is the *orthographic projection matrix*.

Recall that with the perspective projection transform, we had to split it into two parts: a linear part described by the projection matrix, and a non-linear part described by the divide by w. In contrast, the orthographic projection transformation is completely linear — there is no divide by w. Multiplying by the orthographic projection matrix takes us directly into NDC coordinates.

13.3 **Projective Texture Coordinates**

Projective texturing is so-called because it allows us to project a texture onto arbitrary geometry, much like a slide projector. Figure 13.4 shows an example of projective texturing.

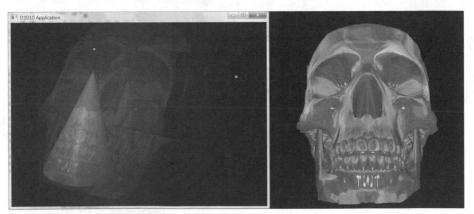

Figure 13.4: The skull texture (right) is projected onto the scene geometry (left).

Projective texturing can be useful on its own for modeling slide projectors, but as we will see in §13.4, it is also used as an intermediate step for shadow mapping.

The key to projective texturing is to generate texture coordinates for each pixel in such a way that the applied texture looks like it has been projected onto the geometry. We will call such generated texture coordinates *projective texture coordinates*.

From Figure 13.5, we see that the texture coordinates (u, v) identify the texel that should be projected onto the 3D point **p**. But the coordinates

(u, v) precisely identify the projection of **p** on the projection window, relative to a texture space coordinate system on the projection window. So the strategy of generating projective texture coordinates is as follows:

1. Project the point **p** onto the light's projection window and transform the coordinates to NDC space.

2. Transform the projected coordinates from NDC space to texture space, thereby effectively turning them into texture coordinates.

Step 1 can be implemented by thinking of the light projector as a camera. We define a view matrix **V** and projection matrix **P** for the light projector. Together, these matrices essentially define the position, orientation, and frustum of the light projector in the world. The matrix **V** transforms coordinates from world space to the coordinate system of the light projector. Once the coordinates are relative to the light coordinate system, the projection matrix, along with the homogeneous divide, are used to project the vertices onto the projection plane of the light. Recall from §5.6.3 that after the homogeneous divide, the coordinates are in NDC space.

Step 2 is accomplished by transforming from NDC space to texture space via the following change of coordinate transformation:

$$u = 0.5x + 0.5$$
$$v = -0.5y + 0.5$$

Here, $u, v \in [0, 1]$ provided $x, y \in [-1, 1]$. We scale the y-coordinate by a negative to invert the axis because the positive y-axis in NDC coordinates goes in the direction opposite to the positive v-axis in texture coordinates.

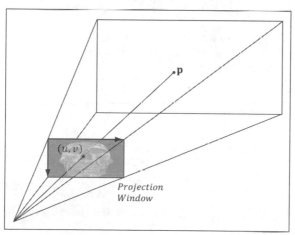

Figure 13.5: The texel identified by the coordinates (u, v) relative to the texture space on the projection window is projected onto the point **p** by following the line of sight from the light origin to the point **p**.

13.3.1 **Code Implementation**

The code for generating projective texture coordinates is shown below:

```
struct VS_OUT
{
    float4 posH      : SV_POSITION;
    float3 posW      : POSITION;
    float3 tangentW  : TANGENT;
    float3 normalW   : NORMAL;
    float2 texC      : TEXCOORD0;
    float4 projTexC  : TEXCOORD1;
};

VS_OUT VS(VS_IN vIn)
{
    VS_OUT vOut;

    [...]

    // Transform to light's projective space.
    vOut.projTexC = mul(float4(vIn.posL, 1.0f), gLightWVP);

    [...]

    return vOut;
}

float4 PS(VS_OUT pIn) : SV_Target
{
    // Complete projection by doing division by w.
    projTexC.xyz /= projTexC.w;

    // Transform from NDC space to texture space.
    projTexC.x = +0.5f*projTexC.x + 0.5f;
    projTexC.y = -0.5f*projTexC.y + 0.5f;

    // Depth in NDC space.
    float depth = projTexC.z;

    // Sample the texture using the projective tex-coords.
    float4 c = gTextureMap.Sample(gSampler, projTexC.xy);

    [...]
}
```

13.3.2 **Points Outside the Frustum**

In the rendering pipeline, geometry outside the frustum is clipped. However, when we generate projective texture coordinates by projecting the geometry from the point of view of the light projector, no clipping is done — we simply project vertices. Consequently, geometry outside the projector's frustum receives projective texture coordinates outside the [0, 1] range.

Projective texture coordinates outside the [0, 1] range function just like normal texture coordinates outside the [0, 1] range based on the enabled address mode (see §7.8) used when sampling the texture.

We do not want to projectively texture any geometry outside the projector's frustum because it does not make sense (such geometry receives no light from the projector). To handle this, we can use conditional statements to check if a projected point is outside the projector's frustum in NDC coordinates:

```
if( projTexC.x < -1.0f || projTexC.x > 1.0f ||
    projTexC.y < -1.0f || projTexC.y > 1.0f ||
    projTexC.z < 0.0f )

    // then not in light volume
```

Another strategy is to associate a spotlight (see §6.10) with the projector so that anything outside the spotlight's field of view cone is not lit (i.e., the surface receives no projected light). The advantage of using a spotlight is that the light intensity from the projector is strongest at the center of the spotlight cone, and can smoothly fade out as the angle ϕ between $-\mathbf{L}$ and $\mathbf{d}$ increases (where $\mathbf{L}$ is the light vector to the surface point and $\mathbf{d}$ is the direction of the spotlight).

13.3.3 Orthographic Projections

So far we have illustrated projective texturing using perspective projections (frustum shaped volumes). However, instead of using a perspective projection for the projection process, we could have used an orthographic projection. In this case, the texture is projected in the direction of the z-axis of the light through a box.

Everything we have talked about with projective texture coordinates also applies when using an orthographic projection, except for a couple of things. First, with an orthographic projection, the spotlight strategy used to handle points outside the projector's volume does not work. This is because a spotlight cone approximates the volume of a frustum to some degree, but it does not approximate a box. However, we can still use conditional statements to check if a projected point is outside the projector's volume. This is because an orthographic projection still generates NDC coordinates and a point (x, y, z) is inside the volume if and only if:

$$-1 \le x \le 1$$
$$-1 \le y \le 1$$
$$0 \le z \le 1$$

Second, with an orthographic projection, we do not need to do the divide by w; that is, we do not need the line:

```
// Complete projection by doing division by w.
    projTexC.xyz /= projTexC.w;
```

This is because after an orthographic projection, the coordinates are already in NDC space. This is faster, because it avoids the per-pixel division required for perspective projection. On the other hand, leaving in the division does not hurt because it divides by 1 (an orthographic projection does not change the w-coordinate, so w will be 1). If we leave the division by w in the shader code, then the shader code works for both perspective and orthographic projections uniformly. The trade-off for this uniformity is that you do a superfluous division with an orthographic projection.

13.4 **Shadow Mapping**

13.4.1 **Algorithm Description**

The idea of the shadow mapping algorithm is to render to texture the scene depth from the viewpoint of the light into a depth buffer called a *shadow map*. After this is done, the shadow map will contain the depth values of all the visible pixels from the perspective of the light. (Pixels occluded by other pixels will not be in the shadow map because they will fail the depth test and either be overwritten or never written.)

To render the scene from the viewpoint of the light, we need to define a light view matrix that transforms coordinates from world space to the space of the light and a light projection matrix, which describes the volume light emits through in the world. This can be either a frustum volume (perspective projection) or box volume (orthographic projection). A frustum light volume can be used to model spotlights by embedding the spotlight cone inside the frustum. A box light volume can be used to model parallel lights. However, the parallel light is now bounded and only passes through the box volume; therefore, it may only strike a subset of the scene (see Figure 13.6).

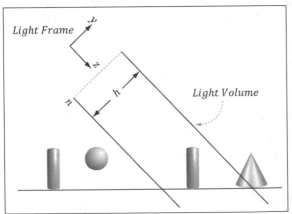

Figure 13.6: Parallel light rays travel through the light volume, so only a subset of the scene inside the volume receives light.

Once we have built the shadow map, we render the scene as normal from the perspective of the camera. For each pixel p rendered, we also compute its depth from the light source, which we denote by $d(p)$. In addition, using projective texturing, we sample the shadow map along the line of sight from the light source to the pixel p to get the depth value $s(p)$; this value is the depth of the pixel closest to the light along the line of sight from the position of the light to p. Then, from Figure 13.7, we see that a pixel p is not in shadow if and only if $d(p) = s(p)$. Due to floating-point inaccuracy, it is problematic to compare two floating-point numbers for equality; therefore, we usually say that a pixel is not in shadow if and only if $d(p) \leq s(p) + \varepsilon$, where $\varepsilon > 0$ is some small number determined by experimenting.

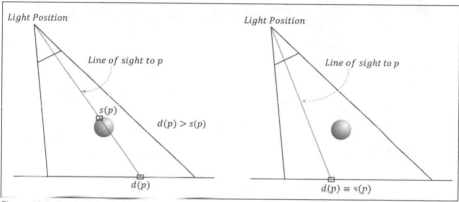

Figure 13.7: On the left, the depth of the pixel p from the light is $d(p)$. However, the depth of the pixel nearest to the light along the same line of sight has depth $s(p)$, and $s(p) < d(p)$. We conclude, therefore, that p is in shadow. On the right, the depth of the pixel p from the light is $d(p)$ and it also happens to be the pixel nearest to the light along the line of sight (that is, $s(p) = d(p)$), so we conclude p is not in shadow.

Note: The depth values compared are in NDC coordinates. This is because the shadow map, which is a depth buffer, stores the depth values in NDC coordinates. How this is done exactly will be clear when we look at the code.

13.4.2 Building the Shadow Map

The first step in shadow mapping is building the shadow map. To do this, we create a DrawableTex2D instance. For shadow mapping, we only need the depth values, so we create the texture with no color map:

```
mShadowMap.init(md3dDevice, 1024, 1024, false, DXGI_FORMAT_UNKNOWN);
```

We then define a light view matrix and projection matrix, and render the scene into the shadow map:

```
mShadowMap.begin();

drawSceneToShadowMap();

mShadowMap.end();
```

The effect file we use for rendering the scene from the perspective of the light is quite simple. For one thing, we only need a position element and texture coordinates element:

```
cbuffer cbPerFrame
{
    float4x4 gLightWVP;
};

// Nonnumeric values cannot be added to a cbuffer.
Texture2D gDiffuseMap;

SamplerState gTriLinearSam
{
    Filter = MIN_MAG_MIP_LINEAR;
    AddressU = Wrap;
    AddressV = Wrap;
};

struct VS_IN
{
    float3 posL     : POSITION;
    float3 tangentL : TANGENT;
    float3 normalL  : NORMAL;
    float2 texC     : TEXCOORD;
};

struct VS_OUT
{
    float4 posH : SV_POSITION;
    float2 texC : TEXCOORD;
};

VS_OUT VS(VS_IN vIn)
{
    VS_OUT vOut;

    vOut.posH = mul(float4(vIn.posL, 1.0f), gLightWVP);

    vOut.texC = vIn.texC;

    return vOut;
}
```

```
void PS(VS_OUT pIn)
{
    float4 diffuse = gDiffuseMap.Sample( gTriLinearSam, pIn.texC );

    // Don't write transparent pixels to the shadow map.
    clip(diffuse.a - 0.15f);
}


technique10 BuildShadowMapTech
{
    pass P0
    {
        SetVertexShader( CompileShader( vs_4_0, VS() ) );
        SetGeometryShader( NULL );
        SetPixelShader( CompileShader( ps_4_0, PS() ) );
    }
}
```

Notice that the pixel shader does not return a value because we only need to output depth values. The pixel shader is solely used to clip pixel fragments with zero or low alpha values, which we assume indicate complete transparency. For example, consider the tree leaf texture in Figure 13.8; here, we only want to draw the pixels with white alpha values to the shadow map.

Figure 13.8: Leaf texture.

13.4.3 Restore Rendering to the Back Buffer

When we render to a texture, we change the render target, depth/stencil buffer, and viewport. Therefore, after rendering to a texture, we need to restore the old values. This is done with the D3DApp::resetOMTargets-AndViewport method. The way it is used and its implementation are given below:

```
mShadowMap.begin();

drawSceneToShadowMap();

mShadowMap.end();

// restore rendering to back buffer
resetOMTargetsAndViewport();

// Render scene to back buffer

...

void D3DApp::resetOMTargetsAndViewport()
{
    md3dDevice->OMSetRenderTargets(1, &mRenderTargetView,
        mDepthStencilView);

    D3D10_VIEWPORT vp;
    vp.TopLeftX = 0;
    vp.TopLeftY = 0;
    vp.Width    = mClientWidth;
    vp.Height   = mClientHeight;
    vp.MinDepth = 0.0f;
    vp.MaxDepth = 1.0f;

    md3dDevice->RSSetViewports(1, &vp);
}
```

13.4.4 **The Shadow Factor**

The shadow factor is a new factor we add to the lighting equation. The shadow factor is a scalar in the range 0 to 1. A value of 0 indicates a point is in shadow, and a value of 1 indicates a point is not in shadow. With filtering (§13.4.6), we will see that a point can also be partially in shadow, in which case the shadow factor will be between 0 and 1. In our model, the shadow factor will be multiplied against the diffuse and specular lighting terms:

```
litColor += shadowFactor * diffuseFactor * v.diffuse * L.diffuse;
litColor += shadowFactor * specFactor * v.spec * L.spec;
```

The shadow factor does not affect ambient light since that is indirect light, and it also does not affect reflective light coming from the environment map. Our lighting functions have been updated to take a shadow factor parameter. For example:

```
float3 ParallelLight(SurfaceInfo v, Light L, float3 eyePos,
                     float shadowFactor)
{
    ...
}
```

13.4.5 **The Shadow Map Test**

We now show the effect code used to draw the scene from the camera's viewpoint after the shadow map has been built. The key issue is computing $d(p)$ and $s(p)$ for each pixel p. The value $d(p)$ is found by transforming the point to the NDC space of the light; then the z-coordinate gives the normalized depth value of the point from the light source. The value $s(p)$ is found by projecting the shadow map onto the scene through the light's view volume using projective texturing. Note that with this setup, both $d(p)$ and $s(p)$ are measured in the NDC space of the light, so they can be compared. The relevant code is in bold.

```
#include "lighthelper.fx"

static const float SHADOW_EPSILON = 0.001f;
static const float SMAP_SIZE = 1024.0f;
static const float SMAP_DX = 1.0f / SMAP_SIZE;

cbuffer cbPerFrame
{
    Light gLight;
    float3 gEyePosW;
};

cbuffer cbPerObject
{
    float4x4 gLightWVP;
    float4x4 gWorld;
    float4x4 gWVP;
    float4x4 gTexMtx;
    float4 gReflectMtrl;
    bool gCubeMapEnabled;
};

// Nonnumeric values cannot be added to a cbuffer.
Texture2D gDiffuseMap;
Texture2D gSpecMap;
Texture2D gNormalMap;
Texture2D gShadowMap;
TextureCube gCubeMap;

SamplerState gShadowSam
{
    Filter = MIN_MAG_MIP_POINT;
    AddressU = Clamp;
    AddressV = Clamp;
};

SamplerState gTriLinearSam
{
    Filter = MIN_MAG_MIP_LINEAR;
    AddressU = Wrap;
```

```
     AddressV = Wrap;
};

struct VS_IN
{
    float3 posL     : POSITION;
    float3 tangentL : TANGENT;
    float3 normalL  : NORMAL;
    float2 texC     : TEXCOORD;
};

struct VS_OUT
{
    float4 posH     : SV_POSITION;
    float3 posW     : POSITION;
    float3 tangentW : TANGENT;
    float3 normalW  : NORMAL;
    float2 texC     : TEXCOORD0;
    float4 projTexC : TEXCOORD1;
};

VS_OUT VS(VS_IN vIn)
{
    VS_OUT vOut;

    // Transform to world space space.
    vOut.posW     = mul(float4(vIn.posL, 1.0f), gWorld);
    vOut.tangentW = mul(float4(vIn.tangentL, 0.0f), gWorld);
    vOut.normalW  = mul(float4(vIn.normalL, 0.0f), gWorld);

    // Transform to homogeneous clip space.
    vOut.posH = mul(float4(vIn.posL, 1.0f), gWVP);

    // Generate projective tex-coords to project shadow map onto scene.
    vOut.projTexC = mul(float4(vIn.posL, 1.0f), gLightWVP);

    // Output vertex attributes for interpolation across triangle.
    vOut.texC = mul(float4(vIn.texC, 0.0f, 1.0f), gTexMtx);

    return vOut;
}

float CalcShadowFactor(float4 projTexC)
{
    // Complete projection by doing division by w.
    projTexC.xyz /= projTexC.w;

    // Points outside the light volume are in shadow.
    if( projTexC.x < -1.0f || projTexC.x > 1.0f ||
        projTexC.y < -1.0f || projTexC.y > 1.0f ||
        projTexC.z < 0.0f )
        return 0.0f;
```

```
        // Transform from NDC space to texture space.
        projTexC.x = +0.5f*projTexC.x + 0.5f;
        projTexC.y = -0.5f*projTexC.y + 0.5f;

        // Depth in NDC space.
        float depth = projTexC.z;


        // Sample shadow map to get nearest depth to light.
        float s0 = gShadowMap.Sample(gShadowSam,
            projTexC.xy).r;
        float s1 = gShadowMap.Sample(gShadowSam,
            projTexC.xy + float2(SMAP_DX, 0)).r;
        float s2 = gShadowMap.Sample(gShadowSam,
            projTexC.xy + float2(0, SMAP_DX)).r;
        float s3 = gShadowMap.Sample(gShadowSam,
            projTexC.xy + float2(SMAP_DX, SMAP_DX)).r;

        // Is the pixel depth <= shadow map value?
        float result0 = depth <= s0 + SHADOW_EPSILON;
        float result1 = depth <= s1 + SHADOW_EPSILON;
        float result2 = depth <= s2 + SHADOW_EPSILON;
        float result3 = depth <= s3 + SHADOW_EPSILON;

        // Transform to texel space.
        float2 texelPos = SMAP_SIZE*projTexC.xy;

        // Determine the interpolation amounts.
        float2 t = frac( texelPos );

        // Interpolate results.
        return lerp(lerp(result0, result1, t.x),
                    lerp(result2, result3, t.x), t.y);
}

float4 PS(VS_OUT pIn) : SV_Target
{
    float4 diffuse = gDiffuseMap.Sample( gTriLinearSam, pIn.texC );

    // Kill transparent pixels.
    clip(diffuse.a - 0.15f);

    float4 spec    = gSpecMap.Sample( gTriLinearSam, pIn.texC );
    float3 normalT = gNormalMap.Sample( gTriLinearSam, pIn.texC );

    // Map [0,1] --> [0,256]
    spec.a *= 256.0f;

    // Uncompress each component from [0,1] to [-1,1].
    normalT = 2.0f*normalT - 1.0f;

    // build orthonormal basis
    float3 N = normalize(pIn.normalW);
```

```
    float3 T = normalize(pIn.tangentW - dot(pIn.tangentW, N)*N);
    float3 B = cross(N,T);

    float3x3 TBN = float3x3(T, B, N);

    // Transform from tangent space to world space.
    float3 bumpedNormalW = normalize(mul(normalT, TBN));

    float shadowFactor = CalcShadowFactor(pIn.projTexC);

    // Compute the lit color for this pixel.
    SurfaceInfo v = {pIn.posW, bumpedNormalW, diffuse, spec};
    float3 litColor = ParallelLight(v, gLight, gEyePosW, shadowFactor);

    [branch]
    if( gCubeMapEnabled )
    {
        float3 incident = pIn.posW - gEyePosW;
        float3 refW = reflect(incident, bumpedNormalW);
        float4 reflectedColor = gCubeMap.Sample(gTriLinearSam, refW);
        litColor += (gReflectMtrl*reflectedColor).rgb;
    }

    return float4(litColor, diffuse.a);
}

technique10 ShadowTech
{
    pass P0
    {
        SetVertexShader( CompileShader( vs_4_0, VS() ) );
        SetGeometryShader( NULL );
        SetPixelShader( CompileShader( ps_4_0, PS() ) );
    }
}
```

13.4.6 Filtering and the Shadow Map Test

The projective texture coordinates (u, v) used to sample the shadow map generally will not coincide with a texel in the shadow map. Usually, the coordinates will hit between four texels. With color texturing, this is solved with bilinear interpolation (§7.4). However, [Kilgard01] points out that we should not average depth values, as this can lead to incorrect results about a pixel being flagged in shadow. (For the same reason, we also cannot generate mipmaps for the shadow map.) Instead of interpolating the depth values, we interpolate the results. That is, we use point filtering (MIN_MAG_MIP_POINT) and sample the texture with coordinates (u,v), $(u+\Delta x,v)$, $(u,v+\Delta x)$, $(u+\Delta x,v+\Delta x)$, where $\Delta x = 1/\text{SHADOW\_MAP\_SIZE}$. Since we are using point sampling, these four points will hit the nearest four texels $\mathbf{s}_0$, $\mathbf{s}_1$, $\mathbf{s}_2$, and $\mathbf{s}_3$, respectively, surrounding (u, v), as shown in

Figure 13.9. We then do the shadow map test for each of these sampled depths and bilinearly interpolate the shadow map results:

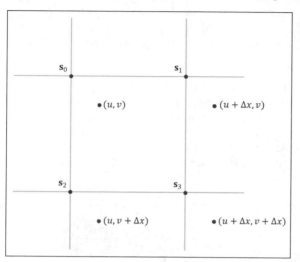

Figure 13.9: Taking four shadow map samples.

```
static const float SHADOW_EPSILON = 0.001f;
static const float SMAP_SIZE = 1024.0f;
static const float SMAP_DX = 1.0f / SMAP_SIZE;

...

// Sample shadow map to get nearest depth to light.
    float s0 = gShadowMap.Sample(gShadowSam,
        projTexC.xy).r;
    float s1 = gShadowMap.Sample(gShadowSam,
        projTexC.xy + float2(SMAP_DX, 0)).r;
    float s2 = gShadowMap.Sample(gShadowSam,
        projTexC.xy + float2(0, SMAP_DX)).r;
    float s3 = gShadowMap.Sample(gShadowSam,
        projTexC.xy + float2(SMAP_DX, SMAP_DX)).r;

    // Is the pixel depth <= shadow map value?
    float result0 = depth <= s0 + SHADOW_EPSILON;
    float result1 = depth <= s1 + SHADOW_EPSILON;
    float result2 = depth <= s2 + SHADOW_EPSILON;
    float result3 = depth <= s3 + SHADOW_EPSILON;

    // Transform to texel space.
    float2 texelPos = SMAP_SIZE*projTexC.xy;

    // Determine the interpolation amounts.
    float2 t = frac( texelPos );

    // Interpolate results.
    return lerp(lerp(result0, result1, t.x),
```

```
lerp(result2, result3, t.x), t.y);
```

In this way, it is not an all-or-nothing situation; a pixel can be partially in shadow. For example, if two of the samples are in shadow and two are not in shadow, then the pixel is 50% in shadow. This creates a smoother transition from shadowed pixels to non-shadowed pixels (see Figure 13.10).

Note: The HLSL `frac` function returns the fractional part of a floating-point number (i.e., the mantissa). For example, if `SMAP_SIZE` = 1024 and `projTex.xy` = (0.23, 0.68), then `texelPos` = (235.52, 696.32) and `frac(texelPos)` = (0.52, 0.32). These fractions tell us how much to interpolate between the samples. The HLSL `lerp(x, y, s)` function is the linear interpolation function and returns $x + s(y - x) = (1 - s)x + sy$.

Figure 13.10: In the top image, observe the "stairstepping" artifacts on the shadow boundary. On the bottom image, these aliasing artifacts are smoothed out a bit with filtering.

Note: Even with our filtering, the shadows are still very hard and the aliasing artifacts can still be unsatisfactory close up. More aggressive methods can be used; see [Uralsky05], for example. We also note that using a higher-resolution shadow map helps, but can be cost prohibitive.

13.4.7 Rendering the Shadow Map

For the Shadow Map demo (available in the download files), we also render the shadow map onto a quad that occupies the lower-left corner of the screen. This allows us to see what the shadow map looks like for each frame. Recall that the shadow map is just a depth buffer texture with the

D3D10_BIND_SHADER_RESOURCE flag, so it can also be used to texture a surface. The shadow map is rendered as a grayscale image since it stores a one-dimensional value at each pixel (a depth value). Figure 13.11 shows a screenshot of the demo.

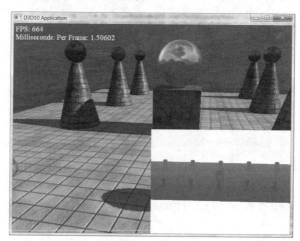

Figure 13.11: Screenshot of the Shadow Map demo.

13.5 **Summary**

- The back buffer need not always be the render target; we can render to a different texture. Rendering to texture provides an efficient way for the GPU to update the contents of a texture at run time. After we have rendered to a texture, we can bind the texture as a shader input and map it onto geometry. Many special effects require render to texture functionality, such as shadow maps, water simulations, and general-purpose GPU programming.

- With an orthographic projection, the viewing volume is a box (see Figure 13.2) with width w, height h, near plane n, and far plane f, and the lines of projection are parallel to the view space z-axis. Such projections are primarily used in 3D science or engineering applications, where it is desirable to have parallel lines remain parallel after projection. However, we can use orthographic projections to model shadows generated by parallel lights.

- Projective texturing is so-called because it allows us to project a texture onto arbitrary geometry, much like a slide projector. The key to projective texturing is to generate texture coordinates for each pixel in such a way that the applied texture looks like it has been projected onto the geometry. Such texture coordinates are called _projective texture coordinates_. We obtain the projective texture coordinates for a pixel by projecting it onto the projection plane of the projector, and then mapping it to the texture coordinate system.

■ Shadow mapping is a real-time shadowing technique that shadows arbitrary geometry (it is not limited to planar shadows). The idea of shadow mapping is to render the depth of the scene from the light's viewpoint into a shadow map, after which the shadow map stores the depth of all pixels visible from the light's perspective. We then render the scene again from the camera's perspective, and we project the shadow map onto the scene using projective texturing. Let $s(p)$ be the depth value projected onto a pixel p from the shadow map and let $d(p)$ be the depth of the pixel from the light source. Then p is in shadow if $s(p) < d(p)$; that is, if the projected pixel depth is less than the depth of the pixel, then there must exist a pixel closer to the light which occludes p, thereby casting p in shadow.

13.6 **Exercises**

1. Write a program that simulates a slide projector by projecting a texture onto the scene. Experiment with both perspective and orthographic projections.

2. Modify the solution to Exercise 1 by using conditional statements so that points outside the projector's frustum do not receive light.

3. Modify the solution to Exercise 1 by using a spotlight so that points outside the spotlight cone do not receive any light from the projector.

4. Modify this chapter's demo application by using a perspective projection. Note that the ε used for bias in the shadow map test that worked for an orthographic projection might not work well for a perspective projection. So you may need to tweak ε. When using a perspective projection, notice that the depth map is heavily biased to white (1.0). Does this make sense considering the graph in Figure 5.27?

5. Experiment with the following shadow map resolutions: 2048×2048, 1024×1024, 512×512, 256×256. Be sure to also update the effect constants that depend on the size:

```
static const float SMAP_SIZE = 1024.0f;
static const float SMAP_DX = 1.0f / SMAP_SIZE;
```

6. Derive the matrix that maps the box $[l, r] \times [b, t] \times [n, f] \rightarrow [-1, 1] \times [-1, 1] \times [0, 1]$. This is an "off-center" orthographic view volume (i.e., the box is not centered about the view space origin). See `D3DXMatrixOrthoOffCenterLH`.

Chapter 14

Meshes

Our main topic to study in this chapter is the `ID3DX10Mesh` interface. Besides grouping the vertex and index buffer of a mesh, this interface organizes geometry data (vertices and indices) into subsets, which allow for efficient rendering.

Objectives:

- To learn how to use the `ID3DX10Mesh` interface for storing and rendering mesh data.
- To find out how to create, optimize, and render an `ID3DXMesh` object.
- To find out how to load data from file into an `ID3DX10Mesh` instance.
- To become familiar with several D3DX mesh-related utility functions.

14.1 **ID3DX10MeshBuffer**

The `ID3DX10MeshBuffer` interface is a generic data structure that the `ID3DX10Mesh` interface uses to return a contiguous block of data. It has only three methods:

```
SIZE_T ID3DX10MeshBuffer::GetSize();
HRESULT ID3DX10MeshBuffer::Map(void **ppData, SIZE_T *pSize);
HRESULT ID3DX10MeshBuffer::Unmap();
```

- `GetSize`: Returns the size of the buffer, in bytes.
- `Map`: Returns a pointer to the start of the internal mesh data through its first parameter. You can use this pointer to read from or write to the data. The size of the buffer, in bytes, is returned through the second parameter.
- `Unmap`: Call this method when you are done reading from or writing to the data.

Note that the Map method returns a void*. This enables generic chunks of data to be returned. The concrete type the void* needs to be cast to depends on the context. For example, the ID3DX10Mesh::GetIndexBuffer method returns a pointer to an ID3DX10MeshBuffer instance containing the index data. If the mesh was created with 16-bit indices, then you would cast the void pointer to a WORD*; if the mesh was created with 32-bit indices, then you would cast the void pointer to a DWORD*.

14.2 **Geometry Info**

The following ID3DX10Mesh methods have to do with the vertices and indices of the mesh:

■ HRESULT ID3DX10Mesh::GetIndexBuffer(ID3DX10MeshBuffer
        **ppIndexBuffer);

This method returns a pointer to an ID3DX10MeshBuffer instance containing the index data through the ppIndexBuffer parameter.

■ UINT ID3DX10Mesh::GetVertexBufferCount();

Returns the number of vertex buffers in the mesh. A mesh can utilize multiple vertex buffers, each bound to a different input slot (recall Exercise 2 of Chapter 5). For example, one vertex buffer stores the position element and another stores the color element. The D3D10_INPUT_ELEMENT_DESC array describing the format of the vertices of the mesh will indicate if multiple slots are to be used. That is, if the elements of the D3D10_INPUT_ELEMENT_DESC array are bound to different input slots, then multiple vertex buffers will be used.

■ HRESULT ID3DX10Mesh::GetVertexBuffer(UINT iBuffer,
        ID3DX10MeshBuffer **ppVertexBuffer);

The first parameter specifies the index of the vertex buffer to get. If the mesh has n vertex buffers, then the vertex buffers are labeled with indices from 0 to $n-1$. A pointer to an ID3DX10MeshBuffer instance containing the vertex buffer data is returned through the second parameter.

■ UINT ID3DX10Mesh::GetVertexCount();

This method returns the number of vertices in the mesh.

■ UINT ID3DX10Mesh::GetFaceCount();

This method returns the number of faces (triangles) in the mesh.

■ UINT ID3DX10Mesh::GetFlags();

This method returns the flags the mesh was created with. This can be zero, one, or both of the following flags (the flags are combined with bitwise OR):

  ■ D3DX10_MESH_32_BIT: The mesh uses 32-bit indices. If this flag is not specified, then the mesh uses 16-bit indices.

- D3DX10_MESH_GS_ADJACENCY: The mesh has adjacency info, in which case it should be rendered with the D3D10_PRIMITIVE_TOPOLOGY_TRIANGLELIST_ADJ primitive topology. If this flag is not specified, then the mesh is rendered with D3D10_PRIMITIVE_TOPOLOGY_TRIANGLELIST primitive topology.

- HRESULT ID3DX10Mesh::GetVertexDescription(
      CONST D3D10_INPUT_ELEMENT_DESC **ppDesc,
      UINT *pDeclCount);

  This method returns a constant pointer to an array of elements of type D3D10_INPUT_ELEMENT_DESC, which describes the format of the vertices in the mesh. Note that you should not delete the returned pointer, as it points to internal memory maintained by the mesh. The second parameter returns the number of elements in the array. Here is an example code fragment:

```
const D3D10_INPUT_ELEMENT_DESC* vDesc;
UINT cnt = 0;
mMeshData->GetVertexDescription(&vDesc, &cnt);

for(UINT i = 0; i < cnt; ++i)
{
OutputDebugStringA(vDesc[i].SemanticName);
OutputDebugStringA("\n");
}
```

For a mesh created with the vertex format described by:

```
D3D10_INPUT_ELEMENT_DESC vertexDesc[] =
{
    {"POSITION", 0, DXGI_FORMAT_R32G32B32_FLOAT, 0, 0,
        D3D10_INPUT_PER_VERTEX_DATA, 0},
    {"TANGENT", 0, DXGI_FORMAT_R32G32B32_FLOAT, 0, 12,
        D3D10_INPUT_PER_VERTEX_DATA, 0},
    {"NORMAL", 0, DXGI_FORMAT_R32G32B32_FLOAT, 0, 24,
        D3D10_INPUT_PER_VERTEX_DATA, 0},
    {"TEXCOORD", 0, DXGI_FORMAT_R32G32_FLOAT, 0, 36,
        D3D10_INPUT_PER_VERTEX_DATA, 0}
};
```

this outputs:

```
POSITION
TANGENT
NORMAL
TEXCOORD
```

- HRESULT ID3DX10Mesh::SetIndexData(CONST void *pData, UINT cIndices);

  This method lets you set the index data of the mesh. The first parameter is a pointer to the array of indices to set. The second parameter is the number of indices being set. Note that the first parameter needs to be a `void*` since we could be setting 16-bit or 32-bit indices. Here is an example code fragment:

```
DWORD* indices = new DWORD[numTriangles*3];

// Read the index data from a file.
for(UINT i = 0; i < numTriangles; ++i)
{
    fin >> indices[i*3+0];
    fin >> indices[i*3+1];
    fin >> indices[i*3+2];
}
HR(mMeshData->SetIndexData(indices, numTriangles*3));
delete[] indices;
```

■ `HRESULT ID3DX10Mesh::SetVertexData(UINT iBuffer, CONST void *pData);`

This method lets you set the vertex data of the mesh. The first parameter specifies the index of the vertex buffer we are going to set. If the mesh has *n* vertex buffers, then the vertex buffers are labeled with indices from 0 to *n*–1. The second parameter is a pointer to the array of vertices to set. Note that the second parameter needs to be a `void*` since the vertex format of a mesh may be variable across meshes. Here is an example code fragment:

```
struct MeshVertex
{
    D3DXVECTOR3 pos;
    D3DXVECTOR3 tangent;
    D3DXVECTOR3 normal;
    D3DXVECTOR2 texC;
};

wistream& operator>>(wistream& is, D3DXVECTOR3& v)
{
    is >> v.x >> v.y >> v.z;
    return is;
}

wistream& operator>>(wistream& is, D3DXVECTOR2& v)
{
    is >> v.x >> v.y;
    return is;
}

MeshVertex* verts = new MeshVertex[numVertices];

// Read the vertex data from a file.
for(UINT i = 0; i < numVertices; ++i)
{
    fin >> ignore; // Position:
    fin >> verts[i].pos;
```

```
        fin >> ignore; // Tangent:
        fin >> verts[i].tangent;

        fin >> ignore; // Normal:
        fin >> verts[i].normal;

        fin >> ignore; // Tex-Coords:
        fin >> verts[i].texC;
    }
    HR(mMeshData->SetVertexData(0, verts));

    delete[] verts;
```

14.3 **Subsets and the Attribute Buffer**

A *subset* is a group of geometry that should be rendered with the same effect, textures, render states, etc.

A mesh consists of one or more subsets. These subsets are groups of triangles in the mesh that can all be rendered using the same attribute. By same *attribute* we mean the same effect, textures, and render states. Figure 14.1 illustrates how a mesh representing a car may be divided into several subsets.

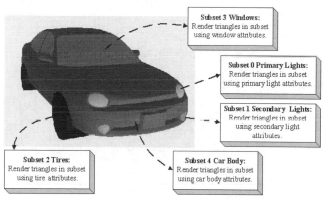

Figure 14.1: A car broken up by subset. Here only the materials per subset differ, but we could also imagine textures being added and differing as well. In addition, the render states may differ; for example, the glass windows may be rendered with alpha blending for transparency.

We label each subset by specifying a unique positive integer value for that subset. This value can be any number that can be stored in a UINT. For instance, in Figure 14.1 we labeled the subsets 0, 1, 2, 3, and 4.

Each triangle in a mesh is given an *attribute ID* that specifies the subset the triangle lives in. For example, from Figure 14.1, the triangles that make up the tires of the car would have an attribute ID of 2 to indicate they live in subset 2. Similarly, the triangles that make up the body of the car have an attribute ID equal to 4 to indicate they live in subset 4.

The attribute IDs for the triangles are stored in a mesh's *attribute buffer*, which is a UINT array. Since each face has an entry in the attribute buffer, the number of elements in the attribute buffer is equal to the number of faces in the mesh. The ith entry in the attribute buffer corresponds with the ith triangle in the mesh. Recalling that every three entries in the index buffer defines a triangle (assuming triangle lists), triangle 0 is defined by the first three entries in the index buffer, triangle 1 by the next three entries in the index buffer, and so on. In general, the ith triangle is defined by the three index buffer entries:

```
// Vertex buffer indices of ith triangle
DWORD A = IndexBuffer[i*3+0];
DWORD B = IndexBuffer[i*3+1];
DWORD C = IndexBuffer[i*3+2];
```

and the vertices of the ith triangle are derived by:

```
// Vertices of ith triangle
Vertex v0 = VertexBuffer[A];
Vertex v1 = VertexBuffer[B];
Vertex v2 = VertexBuffer[C];
```

Figure 14.2 shows this correspondence:

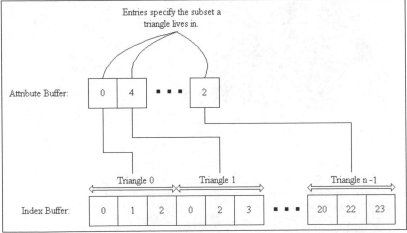

Figure 14.2: The correspondence between the triangles defined in the index buffer and the entries in the attribute buffer. We see that triangle 0 exists in subset 0, triangle 1 exists in subset 4, and triangle n–1 exists in subset 2.

We can access the attribute buffer with the following method:

```
HRESULT ID3DX10Mesh::GetAttributeBuffer(
    ID3DX10MeshBuffer **ppAttributeBuffer);
```

This method returns a pointer to an ID3DX10MeshBuffer instance containing the attribute buffer data through its parameter ppAttributeBuffer. Since each element in the attribute buffer is a UINT, the data pointer returned by ID3DX10MeshBuffer::Map should be cast to a UINT*. And to reiterate, the number of elements in the attribute buffer array is the same as the number of triangles in the mesh.

If we only need to set the attribute buffer, then we can use the following method:

```
HRESULT ID3DX10Mesh::SetAttributeData(CONST UINT *pData);
```

The following code fragment illustrates how this is used:

```
UINT* attributeBuffer = new UINT[numTriangles];

// read the attribute data from file
for(UINT i = 0; i < numTriangles; ++i)
{
    fin >> attributeBuffer[i];
}

// set the attribute data to the mesh
HR(mMeshData->SetAttributeData(attributeBuffer));

delete[] attributeBuffer;
```

14.4 **Drawing**

The ID3DX10Mesh interface provides the ID3DX10Mesh::DrawSubset(UINT AttribId) method to draw all the triangles of the mesh that live in the subset specified by the AttribId argument. For instance, to draw all the triangles that live in subset 2, we would write:

```
Mesh->DrawSubset(2);
```

Therefore, to draw an entire mesh, we must draw all the subsets of the mesh. It is convenient to label subsets in the order 0, 1, 2, ..., $n-1$, where n is the number of subsets, and to have a corresponding material array, such that index i refers to the material associated with subset i. This allows us to render the entire mesh using a simple loop:

```
D3D10_TECHNIQUE_DESC techDesc;
mTech->GetDesc( &techDesc );

for(UINT p = 0; p < techDesc.Passes; ++p)
{
    ID3D10EffectPass* pass = mTech->GetPassByIndex(p);

    for(UINT subsetID = 0; subsetID < mDiffuseTextures.size(); ++subsetID)
    {
        // Bind shader resource variables needed to render
        // the ith subset.
```

```
            mfxDiffuseMapVar->SetResource(mDiffuseTextures[subsetID]);
            mfxSpecMapVar->SetResource(mSpecTextures[subsetID]);
            mfxNormalMapVar->SetResource(mNormalTextures[subsetID]);

            pass->Apply(0);
            mMeshData->DrawSubset(subsetID);
        }
    }
```

14.5 **Adjacency Information**

For certain mesh operations, such as optimizing, it is necessary to know the triangles that are adjacent to a given triangle. A mesh's *adjacency buffer* stores this information. The adjacency buffer is a UINT array, where each entry contains an index identifying a triangle in the mesh (e.g., an adjacency buffer entry containing the index refers to the *i*th triangle of the mesh). Since each triangle has three edges, it can have up to three adjacent triangles (see Figure 14.3). Therefore, the adjacency buffer must have GetFaceCount()*3 many elements — three possible adjacent triangles for every triangle in the mesh. If an edge of a triangle does not have an adjacent triangle, then the adjacency buffer entry for that edge stores a –1.

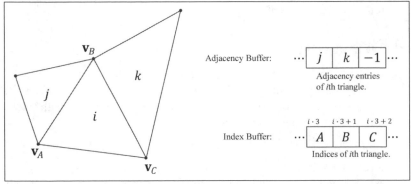

Figure 14.3: Suppose the *i*th triangle in the mesh is defined by the vertices $\mathbf{v}_A$, $\mathbf{v}_B$, and $\mathbf{v}_C$. The first adjacency entry identifies the triangle adjacent to the first edge, $\mathbf{v}_A$ to $\mathbf{v}_B$; the second adjacency entry identifies the triangle adjacent to the second edge, $\mathbf{v}_B$ to $\mathbf{v}_C$; and the third adjacency entry identifies the triangle adjacent to the third edge, $\mathbf{v}_C$ to $\mathbf{v}_A$.

The following method is used to compute the adjacency buffer of a mesh:

```
HRESULT ID3DX10Mesh::GenerateAdjacencyAndPointReps(
          FLOAT Epsilon);
```

Let **p** and **q** be two distinct vertices in the mesh. This method treats **p** and **q** as coincident (i.e., overlapping/at the same position) if and only if $\|\mathbf{p} - \mathbf{q}\| < \varepsilon$. In other words, ε (Epsilon) specifies how far two vertices can differ in position and still be considered equal. This information is needed because we need to know when face edges coincide to build the adjacency buffer (and knowing when vertices coincide enables us to figure out when edges coincide). The actual adjacency buffer this method generates is stored internally with the mesh. Here is an example of how this function could be called:

```
HR(mMeshData->GenerateAdjacencyAndPointReps(0.001f));
```

If we are using units of meters, this means that if two points are within a millimeter distance, then they will be treated as the same.

To access the adjacency buffer data, we use the following method:

```
HRESULT ID3DX10Mesh::GetAdjacencyBuffer(
        ID3DX10MeshBuffer **ppAdjacency);
```

Each element in the adjacency buffer is a UINT and there are GetFaceCount()*3 elements in the adjacency buffer.

14.6 **Optimizing**

The vertices and indices of a mesh can be reorganized to render the mesh more efficiently. When we do this, we say that we are *optimizing* a mesh, and we use the following method to do this:

```
HRESULT ID3DX10Mesh::Optimize(
    UINT Flags,
    UINT *pFaceRemap,
    LPD3D10BLOB *ppVertexRemap);
```

- Flags: A combination of one or more bit flags from the D3DX10_MESHOPT enumerated type (combined with bitwise OR) that tells the method what kind of optimizations to perform. The two flags commonly used together are:

    - D3DX10_MESHOPT_ATTR_SORT: Sorts the geometry by attribute and generates an attribute table. This allows DrawSubset to be more efficient (see §14.7). Observe that a triangle can belong to only one subset, but a vertex could belong to more than one due to the use of indices (i.e., a vertex could be referenced by triangles in different subsets). In order to sort the vertices by subset then, D3DX10_MESHOPT_ATTR_SORT duplicates vertices that are shared among different subsets so that each vertex belongs to only one subset. If you do not want this duplication of vertices, then specify the D3DX10_MESHOPT_DO_NOT_SPLIT flag.

    - D3DX10_MESHOPT_VERTEX_CACHE: A *vertex cache* is a hardware buffer that saves processed vertices. If a vertex is referenced again by other indices and it is in the cache, then it does not need to be processed again. This optimization reorganized the geometry of the mesh to take better advantage of the vertex cache.

- pFaceRemap: Pointer to a UINT array to be filled with the face remap information. The array should be of size GetFaceCount() (i.e., one element for each face). When a mesh is optimized, its faces may be moved around in the index buffer. The face remap info tells where an unoptimized face has moved. That is, `j = pFaceRemap[i]` means the *i*th face in the unoptimized mesh has been moved to the *j*th face in the optimized mesh. If you do not need this info, pass 0.

■ `ppVertexRemap`: Address of a pointer to an `ID3D10Blob` that will be filled with the vertex remap info. The number of elements in this buffer should be `GetVertexCount()` of the optimized mesh. When a mesh is optimized, its vertices may be moved around the vertex buffer. The vertex remap info tells where the original vertices have moved. That is,

```
ID3D10Blob* vertexRemap;
/* Call Optimize()... */
DWORD j = ((DWORD*)vertexRemap->GetBufferPointer())[i];
```

means the *i*th vertex in the unoptimized mesh has been moved to the *j*th vertex in the optimized mesh. If you do not need this info, pass 0.

You must call `ID3DX10Mesh::GenerateAdjacencyAndPointReps` to generate the adjacency buffer before calling `ID3DX10Mesh::Optimize`. Here is an example call:

```
HR(mMeshData->GenerateAdjacencyAndPointReps(0.001f));
HR(mMeshData->Optimize(D3DX10_MESHOPT_ATTR_SORT|
                       D3DX10_MESHOPT_VERTEX_CACHE,0,0));
```

14.7 **The Attribute Table**

When a mesh is optimized with the `D3DX10_MESHOPT_ATTR_SORT` flag (and assuming `D3DX10_MESHOPT_DO_NOT_SPLIT` was not specified), the geometry of the mesh is sorted by its attributes so that the geometry of a particular subset exists as a contiguous block in the vertex/index buffers (see Figure 14.4).

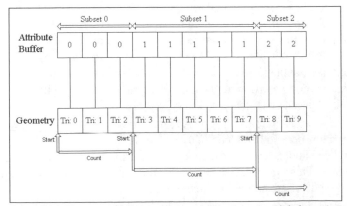

Figure 14.4: The geometry in a mesh is sorted by the subset it belongs to.

In addition to sorting the geometry, the D3DX10_MESHOPT_ATTR_SORT optimization builds an attribute table. The attribute table is an array of D3DX10_ATTRIBUTE_RANGE structures. Each entry in the attribute table corresponds to a subset of the mesh and specifies the block of memory in the vertex/index buffers where the geometry for the subset resides. The D3DX10_ATTRIBUTE_RANGE structure is defined as:

```
typedef struct D3DX10_ATTRIBUTE_RANGE {
    UINT AttribId;
    UINT FaceStart;
    UINT FaceCount;
    UINT VertexStart;
    UINT VertexCount;
} D3DX10_ATTRIBUTE_RANGE, *LPD3DX10_ATTRIBUTE_RANGE;
```

- AttribId: The subset ID.
- FaceStart: An offset into the index buffer (FaceStart * 3) identifying the start of the triangles that are associated with this subset.
- FaceCount: The number of faces (triangles) in this subset.
- VertexStart: An offset into the vertex buffer identifying the start of the vertices that are associated with this subset.
- VertexCount: The number of vertices in this subset.

We can easily see the members of the D3DX10_ATTRIBUTE_RANGE structure at work graphically in Figure 14.4. The attribute table for the mesh corresponding to Figure 14.3 would have three entries — one to correspond with each subset. With the attribute table built, rendering a subset can be done very efficiently, for only a quick lookup in the attribute table is required to find the geometry block of a particular subset. Note that without an attribute table, rendering a subset would require a linear search of the entire attribute buffer to find the geometry that exists in the particular subset we are drawing.

Note: If D3DX10_MESHOPT_DO_NOT_SPLIT was specified, then it is possible that the vertex ranges for each subset would overlap (i.e., not be disjoint). In this case, the vertex range, [VertexStart, VertexStart + VertexCount], includes all the vertices for a subset, but it could additionally include vertices that are not part of the subset. This follows from the fact that the vertices cannot be sorted by subset if a vertex can belong to more than one subset, which it can when D3DX10_MESHOPT_DO_NOT_SPLIT is specified.

To access the attribute table of a mesh we use the following method:

```
HRESULT ID3DX10Mesh::GetAttributeTable(
    D3DX10_ATTRIBUTE_RANGE *pAttribTable,
    UINT *pAttribTableSize
);
```

This method can do two things: It can return the number of attributes in the attribute table, or it can fill an array of D3DX10_ATTRIBUTE_RANGE structures with the attribute data.

To get the number of elements in the attribute table, we pass in 0 as the first argument:

```
UINT numSubsets = 0;
mesh->GetAttributeTable(0, &numSubsets);
```

Once we know the number of elements in the attribute table, we can fill a D3DX10_ATTRIBUTE_RANGE array with the actual attribute table by writing:

```
D3DX10_ATTRIBUTE_RANGE* attTable = new D3DX10_ATTRIBUTE_RANGE[numSubsets];
mesh->GetAttributeTable(attTable, &numSubsets);
```

14.8 **Cloning**

Sometimes we will need to copy the data from one mesh to another. This is accomplished with the ID3DX10Mesh::CloneMesh method.

```
HRESULT ID3DX10Mesh::CloneMesh(
    UINT Flags,
    LPCSTR pPosSemantic,
    CONST D3D10_INPUT_ELEMENT_DESC *pDeclaration,
    UINT DeclCount,
    ID3DX10Mesh **ppCloneMesh
);
```

■ Flags: Mesh creation flags. This can be zero, one, or both of the following flags (the flags are combined with bitwise OR):

  ■ D3DX10_MESH_32_BIT: The mesh uses 32-bit indices. If this flag is not specified, then the mesh uses 16-bit indices.

  ■ D3DX10_MESH_GS_ADJACENCY: The mesh has adjacency info, in which case it should be rendered with the D3D10_PRIMITIVE_TOPOLOGY_TRIANGLELIST_ADJ primitive topology. If this flag is not specified, then the mesh is rendered with D3D10_PRIMITIVE_TOPOLOGY_TRIANGLELIST primitive topology.

■ pPosSemantic: The semantic name of the vertex element that stores the vertex position.

■ pDeclaration: A pointer to the first element in a D3D10_INPUT_ELEMENT_DESC array that describes the vertex format we want for the new cloned mesh.

■ DeclCount: The number of elements in the preceding D3D10_INPUT_ELEMENT_DESC array.

■ ppCloneMesh: Returns a pointer to the new cloned mesh.

Notice that this method allows the flags and vertex format of the destination mesh to be different from the source mesh. Thus, in addition to just copying data, this function is useful if the flags or vertex format of the destination mesh need to be different from the source mesh. However, suppose that the source mesh and destination mesh have the following two vertex formats:

```
// Source
struct SourceVertex
{
    D3DXVECTOR3 pos;
    D3DXVECTOR3 normal;
};

// Destination
struct DestinationVertex
{
    D3DXVECTOR3 pos;
    D3DXVECTOR3 normal;
    D3DXVECTOR2 texC;
};
```

When the source mesh is copied to the destination mesh, the texture coordinates of the destination mesh vertices will be uninitialized. This is because the source mesh does not have texture coordinates, so there are no texture coordinates to copy over. The application will manually have to initialize the texture coordinates in the destination mesh.

Note: The destination mesh vertex format must contain the vertex elements of the source mesh. For example, if you have:

```
struct SourceVertex
{
    D3DXVECTOR3 pos;
    D3DXVECTOR3 tangent;
    D3DXVECTOR3 normal;
    D3DXVECTOR2 texC;
};

struct DestinationVertex
{
    D3DXVECTOR3 pos;
    D3DXVECTOR3 normal;
};
```

Then the clone method will throw an exception.

Note: If you need to render a mesh with adjacency info, be sure to call `ID3DX10Mesh::GenerateGSAdjacency` first. This method uses the mesh's adjacency info to recreate the index buffer so that the indices define triangle lists with adjacency primitives.

14.9 **Commit to Device**

The ID3DX10Mesh interface stores vertices and indices in vertex and index buffers with the staging usage D3D10_USAGE_STAGING. Basically, this is a system memory copy of the geometry data. The CPU can efficiently read from and write to these buffers. For example, when ID3DX10Mesh::GetVertexBuffer is called, you are getting access to the system memory vertex buffer. When we call ID3DX10Mesh::SetIndexData, the system memory index buffer is being set. Therefore, before we can render the mesh, the system memory vertex/index data needs to be copied into hardware vertex/index buffers. This amounts to copying the vertex/index data into vertex/index buffers with usage like D3D10_USAGE_DEFAULT with no CPU access flags, which will place the vertex/index buffer in GPU memory for efficient rendering. The following method does this for us:

```
HR(mMeshData->CommitToDevice());
```

Any CPU reads from the mesh will read from the system memory copy. Any modifications to the mesh will be made to the system memory copy. After you modify the mesh data and want the changes to take effect in the rendered output, you need to again call the ID3DX10Mesh::CommitToDevice method. Otherwise, your modifications will have no effect on the rendered output.

Note: If you need access to the hardware vertex/index buffers after calling ID3DX10Mesh::CommitToDevice, then use the following methods:

```
HRESULT GetDeviceVertexBuffer(
  UINT iBuffer,
  ID3D10Buffer **ppVertexBuffer
);

HRESULT GetDeviceIndexBuffer(
  ID3D10Buffer **ppIndexBuffer
);
```

14.10 **Creating a Mesh**

Thus far we have discussed many of the methods of the ID3DX10Mesh interface, but we have not shown how to create an instance of this type. This is done with the following function:

```
HRESULT D3DX10CreateMesh(
    ID3D10Device *pDevice,
    CONST D3D10_INPUT_ELEMENT_DESC *pDeclaration,
    UINT DeclCount,
    LPCSTR pPositionSemantic,
    UINT VertexCount,
```

```
        UINT FaceCount,
        UINT Options,
        ID3DX10Mesh **ppMesh
);
```

- pDevice: The device associated with the mesh.

- pDeclaration: A pointer to the first element in a
  D3D10_INPUT_ELEMENT_DESC array that describes the vertex format of the
  mesh we are creating.

- DeclCount: The number of elements in the preceding
  D3D10_INPUT_ELEMENT_DESC array.

- pPositionSemantic: The semantic name of the vertex element that
  stores the vertex position.

- VertexCount: The number of vertices the mesh will have.

- FaceCount: The number of faces the mesh will have.

- Options: Mesh creation flags. This can be zero, one, or both of the
  following flags (the flags are combined with bitwise OR):

  - D3DX10_MESH_32_BIT: The mesh uses 32-bit indices. If this flag is not
    specified, then the mesh uses 16-bit indices.

  - D3DX10_MESH_GS_ADJACENCY: The mesh has adjacency info, in which
    case it should be rendered with the D3D10_PRIMITIVE_TOPOLOGY_
    TRIANGLELIST_ADJ primitive topology. If this flag is not specified,
    then the mesh is rendered with D3D10_PRIMITIVE_TOPOLOGY_
    TRIANGLELIST primitive topology.

- ppMesh: Outputs the created mesh.

Here is an example call:

```
D3D10_INPUT_ELEMENT_DESC vertexDesc[] =
{
    {"POSITION", 0, DXGI_FORMAT_R32G32B32_FLOAT, 0, 0,
        D3D10_INPUT_PER_VERTEX_DATA, 0},
    {"TANGENT", 0, DXGI_FORMAT_R32G32B32_FLOAT, 0, 12,
        D3D10_INPUT_PER_VERTEX_DATA, 0},
    {"NORMAL", 0, DXGI_FORMAT_R32G32B32_FLOAT, 0, 24,
        D3D10_INPUT_PER_VERTEX_DATA, 0},
    {"TEXCOORD", 0, DXGI_FORMAT_R32G32_FLOAT, 0, 36,
        D3D10_INPUT_PER_VERTEX_DATA, 0}
};

ID3DX10Mesh* mMeshData;
HR(D3DX10CreateMesh(device, vertexDesc, 4,
        "POSITION", numVertices,
        numTriangles, D3DX10_MESH_32_BIT, &mMeshData));
```

14.11 **Mesh Viewer Demo**

The demo for this chapter loads several meshes from file and sets them into ID3DX10Mesh instances. See Figure 14.5 for a screenshot. The file format is very simple and consists of four parts. The first part is the header, and indicates the number of materials, triangles, and vertices in the mesh. The second part includes three texture filenames for each material in the mesh; these filenames reference the diffuse, specular, and normal texture maps for the material. The third part lists all the mesh vertices. The fourth part lists three indices per triangle, followed by the subset ID the triangle lives in. The file (.m3d for model 3D) is a text file, so you can open it up and have a look at it in Notepad, for example. Here is an abridged look at one of the files:

```
***************m3d-File-Header***************
#Materials 1
#Vertices 192
#Triangles 204


***************Materials********************
pillar01_diffuse.dds
pillar01_spec.dds
pillar01_normal.dds


***************Vertices*********************
Position: -4.749955 3.420444 -4.744714
Tangent: 0.001683 1.784455E-11 -0.9999986
Normal: -0.9999986 -4.999998E-05 -0.001682999
Tex-Coords: 0.473722 0.095042

Position: -4.749567 -4.235451 -4.749567
Tangent: 0.0004 2.091744E-10 -0.9999999
Normal: -0.9999999 -0.000372 -0.0003999999
Tex-Coords: 0.47395 0.454225

...

***************Triangles********************
0 1 2 0
2 1 3 0
3 1 4 0

...
```

The code that loads the mesh data from file and sets it into an ID3DX10Mesh instance is located in the *Mesh.h/.cpp* files. These files define a Mesh class that encapsulates an ID3DX10Mesh instance, as well as the textures and effect handles needed to render it.

Figure 14.5: Screenshot of the Mesh Viewer demo.

14.12 **Summary**

- An ID3DX10Mesh contains a vertex, index, and attribute buffer. The vertex and index buffer hold the geometry of the mesh (vertices and triangles). The attribute buffer contains a corresponding entry for each triangle and specifies the subset a triangle belongs to. The ID3DX10Mesh class internally uses indexed triangle lists or indexed triangle lists with adjacency (if the D3DX10_MESH_GS_ADJACENCY flag was specified).

- A mesh can be optimized with the ID3DX10Mesh::Optimize method. Optimization reorganizes the geometry of the mesh to make rendering more efficient. Optimizing a mesh with D3DX10_MESHOPT_ATTR_SORT generates an attribute table; an attribute table allows the mesh to render an entire subset using a simple lookup into the table.

- The adjacency info of a mesh is a UINT array that contains three entries for every triangle in the mesh. The three entries corresponding to a particular triangle specify the triangles that are adjacent to that triangle. Adjacency info can be generated with the ID3DX10Mesh::GenerateAdjacencyAndPointReps method. This method must be called before optimizing the mesh.

- A mesh can be copied with the ID3DX10Mesh::Clone method. In addition to simply copying the mesh, the ID3DX10Mesh::Clone method allows us to change the mesh options and vertex format of the output mesh.

- We can create a mesh using the D3DX10CreateMesh function. We can then manually write data to the mesh using the appropriate methods: ID3DX10Mesh::SetVertexData, ID3DX10Mesh::SetIndexData, and ID3DX10Mesh::SetAttributeData.

- Before drawing a mesh, remember to call the ID3DX10Mesh::CommitToDevice method. A subset of a mesh is drawn with the ID3DX10Mesh::DrawSubset method.

14.13 **Exercises**

1. Manually create a mesh and fill it with cube data. Put the geometry of each face in its own subset so that there are six subsets. Optimize the mesh to build an attribute table. Finally, draw the cube mesh using a different texture for each cube face.

Chapter 15

Picking

In this chapter, we discuss the problem of determining the 3D object (or primitive) the user picked with the mouse cursor (see Figure 15.1). In other words, given the 2D screen coordinates of the mouse cursor, can we determine the 3D object that was projected onto that point? To solve this problem, in some sense, we must work backward; that is to say, we typically transform from 3D space to screen space, but here we transform from screen space back to 3D space. Of course, we already have a slight problem: A 2D screen point does not correspond to a unique 3D point (i.e., more than one 3D point could be projected onto the same 2D projection window point — see Figure 15.2). Thus, there is some ambiguity in determining which object is really picked. However, this is not such a big problem, as the closest object to the camera is usually the one we want.

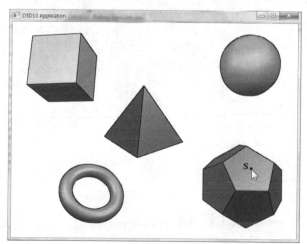

Figure 15.1: The user picking the dodecahedron.

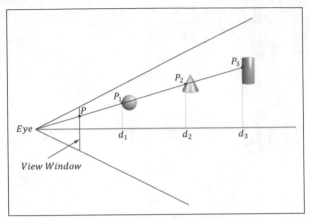

Figure 15.2: A side view of the frustum. Observe that several points in 3D space can get projected onto a point on the projection window.

Consider Figure 15.3, which shows the viewing frustum. Here **p** is the point on the projection window that corresponds to the clicked screen point **s**. Now, we see that if we shoot a *picking ray*, originating at the eye position, through **p**, we will intersect the object whose projection surrounds **p**, namely the cylinder in this example. Therefore, our strategy is as follows: Once we compute the picking ray, we can iterate through each object in the scene and test if the ray intersects it. The object that the ray intersects is the object that was picked by the user. As mentioned, the ray may intersect several scene objects (or none at all if nothing was picked) if the objects are along the ray's path but with different depth values. In this case, we can just take the intersected object nearest to the camera as the picked object.

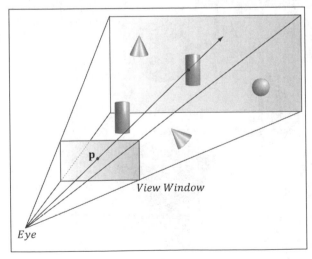

Figure 15.3: A ray shooting through **p** will intersect the object whose projection surrounds **p**. Note that the projected point **p** on the projection window corresponds to the clicked screen point **s**.

Objectives:

■ To learn how to implement the picking algorithm and to understand how it works. We break picking down into the following four steps:

1. Given the clicked screen point **s**, find its corresponding point on the projection window and call it **p**.

2. Compute the picking ray in view space. That is the ray originating at the origin, in view space, which shoots through **p**.

3. Transform the picking ray and the models to be tested with the ray into the same space.

4. Determine the object the picking ray intersects. The nearest (from the camera) intersected object corresponds to the picked screen object.

■ To learn about bounding volumes, why they are useful, and how to create them using D3DX functions.

15.1 Screen to Projection Window Transform

The first task is to transform the clicked screen point to normalized device coordinates (see §5.6.3.3). Recall that the viewport matrix transforms vertices from normalized device coordinates to screen space:

$$
\mathbf{M} = \begin{bmatrix} \dfrac{Width}{2} & 0 & 0 & 0 \\ 0 & -\dfrac{Height}{2} & 0 & 0 \\ 0 & 0 & MaxDepth - MinDepth & 0 \\ TopLeftX + \dfrac{Width}{2} & TopLeftY + \dfrac{Height}{2} & MinDepth & 1 \end{bmatrix}
$$

The variables of the viewport matrix refer to those of the D3D10_VIEWPORT structure:

```
typedef struct D3D10_VIEWPORT {
    INT TopLeftX;
    INT TopLeftY;
    UINT Width;
    UINT Height;
    FLOAT MinDepth;
    FLOAT MaxDepth;
} D3D10_VIEWPORT;
```

Generally, for a game, the viewport is the entire back buffer and the depth buffer range is 0 to 1. Thus, *TopLeftX* = 0, *TopLeftY* = 0, *MinDepth* = 0, *MaxDepth* = 1, *Width* = w, and *Height* = h, where w and h are the width and height of the back buffer, respectively. Assuming this is indeed the case, the viewport matrix simplifies to:

$$
\mathbf{M} = \begin{bmatrix} w/2 & 0 & 0 & 0 \\ 0 & -h/2 & 0 & 0 \\ 0 & 0 & 1 & 0 \\ w/2 & h/2 & 0 & 1 \end{bmatrix}
$$

Now let $\mathbf{p}_{ndc} = (x_{ndc}, y_{ndc}, z_{ndc}, 1)$ be a point in normalized device space (i.e., $-1 \le x_{ndc} \le 1, -1 \le y_{ndc} \le 1$, and $0 \le z_{ndc} \le 1$). Transforming $\mathbf{p}_{ndc}$ to screen space yields:

$$
\begin{bmatrix} x_{ndc}, y_{ndc}, z_{ndc}, 1 \end{bmatrix} \begin{bmatrix} w/2 & 0 & 0 & 0 \\ 0 & -h/2 & 0 & 0 \\ 0 & 0 & 1 & 0 \\ w/2 & h/2 & 0 & 1 \end{bmatrix} = \begin{bmatrix} \dfrac{x_{ndc}w + w}{2}, & \dfrac{-y_{ndc}h + h}{2}, & z_{ndc}, & 1 \end{bmatrix}
$$

The coordinate z_{ndc} is just used by the depth buffer and we are not concerned with any depth coordinates for picking. The 2D screen point $\mathbf{p}_s = (x_s, y_s)$ corresponding to $\mathbf{p}_{ndc}$ is just the transformed x- and y-coordinates:

$$
x_s = \frac{x_{ndc}w + w}{2}
$$

$$
y_s = \frac{-y_{ndc}h + h}{2}
$$

The above equation gives us the screen point $\mathbf{p}_s$ in terms of the normalized device point $\mathbf{p}_{ndc}$ and the viewport dimensions. However, in our picking situation, we are initially given the screen point $\mathbf{p}_s$ and the viewport dimensions, and we want to find $\mathbf{p}_{ndc}$. Solving the above equations for $\mathbf{p}_{ndc}$ yields:

$$
x_{ndc} = \frac{2x_s}{w} - 1
$$

$$
y_{ndc} = -\frac{2y_s}{h} + 1
$$

We now have the clicked point in NDC space. But to shoot the picking ray, we really want the screen point in view space. Recall from §5.6.3.3 that we mapped the projected point from view space to NDC space by dividing the x-coordinate by the aspect ratio r:

$$
-r \le x' \le r
$$

$$
-1 \le x'/r \le 1
$$

Thus, to get back to view space, we just need to multiply the x-coordinate in NDC space by the aspect ratio. The clicked point in view space is thus:

$$x_v = r\left(\frac{2s_x}{w} - 1\right)$$

$$y_v = -\frac{2s_y}{h} + 1$$

Note: The projected y-coordinate in view space is the same in NDC space. This is because we chose the height of the projection window in view space to cover the interval [−1, 1].

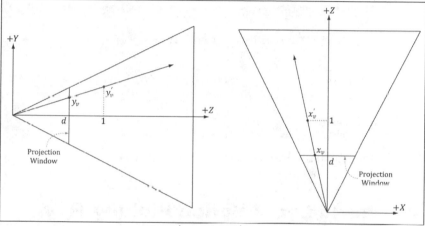

Figure 15.4: By similar triangles, $\dfrac{y_v}{d} = \dfrac{y'_v}{1}$ and $\dfrac{x_v}{d} = \dfrac{x'_v}{1}$.

Now recall from §5.6.3.1 that the projection window lies at a distance $d = \cot\left(\frac{\alpha}{2}\right)$ from the origin, where a is the vertical field of view angle. So we could shoot the picking ray through the point (x_v, y_v, d) on the projection window. However, this requires that we compute $d = \cot\left(\frac{\alpha}{2}\right)$. A simpler way is to observe from Figure 15.4 that:

$$x'_v = \frac{x_v}{d} = \frac{x_v}{\cot\left(\frac{\alpha}{2}\right)} = x_v \cdot \tan\left(\frac{\alpha}{2}\right) = \left(\frac{2s_x}{w} - 1\right)r\tan\left(\frac{\alpha}{2}\right)$$

$$y'_v = \frac{y_v}{d} = \frac{y_v}{\cot\left(\frac{\alpha}{2}\right)} = y_v \cdot \tan\left(\frac{\alpha}{2}\right) = \left(-\frac{2s_y}{h} + 1\right)\tan\left(\frac{\alpha}{2}\right)$$

Recalling that $\mathbf{P}_{00} = \frac{1}{r\tan(\frac{\alpha}{2})}$ and $\mathbf{P}_{11} = \frac{1}{\tan(\frac{\alpha}{2})}$ in the projection matrix, we can rewrite this as:

$$x'_v = \left(\frac{2s_x}{w} - 1\right)/\mathbf{P}_{00}$$

$$y'_v = \left(-\frac{2s_y}{h} + 1\right)/\mathbf{P}_{11}$$

Thus, we can shoot our picking ray through the point $\left(x'_v, y'_v, 1\right)$ instead. Note that this yields the same picking ray as the one shot through the point $\left(x_v, y_v, d\right)$. The code that computes the picking ray in view space is given below:

```
void PickingApp::pick(int sx, int sy)
{
    D3DXMATRIX P = GetCamera().proj();

    // Compute picking ray in view space.
    float vx = (+2.0f*sx/mClientWidth  - 1.0f)/P(0,0);
    float vy = (-2.0f*sy/mClientHeight + 1.0f)/P(1,1);

    D3DXVECTOR3 rayOrigin(0.0f, 0.0f, 0.0f);
    D3DXVECTOR3 rayDir(vx, vy, 1.0f);
```

Note that the ray originates from the origin in view space since the eye sits at the origin in view space.

15.2 World/Local Space Picking Ray

So far we have the picking ray in view space, but this is only useful if our objects are in view space as well. Because the view matrix transforms geometry from world space to view space, the inverse of the view matrix transforms geometry from view space to world space. If $\mathbf{r}_v(t) = \mathbf{q} + t\mathbf{u}$ is the view space picking ray and $\mathbf{V}$ is the view matrix, then the world space picking ray is given by:

$$\mathbf{r}_w(t) = \mathbf{q}\mathbf{V}^{-1} + t\mathbf{u}\mathbf{V}^{-1}$$
$$= \mathbf{q}_w + t\mathbf{u}_w$$

Note that the ray origin $\mathbf{q}$ is transformed as a point (i.e., $q_w = 1$) and the ray direction $\mathbf{u}$ is transformed as a vector (i.e., $u_w = 0$).

A world space picking ray can be useful in some situations where you have some objects defined in world space. However, most of the time, the geometry of an object is defined relative to the object's own local space. Therefore, to perform the ray/object intersection test, we must transform the ray into the local space of the object. If $\mathbf{W}$ is the world matrix of an object, the matrix $\mathbf{W}^{-1}$ transforms geometry from world space to the local space of the object. Thus the local space picking ray is:

$$\mathbf{r}_L(t) = \mathbf{q}_w \mathbf{W}^{-1} + t\mathbf{u}_w \mathbf{W}^{-1}$$

Generally, each object in the scene has its own local space. Therefore, the ray must be transformed to the local space of each scene object to do the intersection test.

One might suggest transforming the meshes to world space and doing the intersection test there. However, this is too expensive. A mesh may contain thousands of vertices, and all those vertices would need to be transformed to world space. It is much more efficient to just transform the ray to the local spaces of the objects.

The following code shows how the picking ray is transformed from view space to the local space of an object:

```
// Tranform to world space.
D3DXMATRIX V = GetCamera().view();

D3DXMATRIX inverseV;
D3DXMatrixInverse(&inverseV, 0, &V);

D3DXVec3TransformCoord(&rayOrigin, &rayOrigin, &inverseV);
D3DXVec3TransformNormal(&rayDir, &rayDir, &inverseV);

// Transform to the mesh's local space.
D3DXMATRIX inverseW;
D3DXMatrixInverse(&inverseW, 0, &mMeshWorld);

D3DXVec3TransformCoord(&rayOrigin, &rayOrigin, &inverseW);
D3DXVec3TransformNormal(&rayDir, &rayDir, &inverseW);
```

The D3DXVec3TransformCoord and D3DXVec3TransformNormal functions take 3D vectors as parameters, but note that with the D3DXVec3TransformCoord function there is an understood $w = 1$ for the fourth component. On the other hand, with the D3DXVec3TransformNormal function there is an understood $w = 0$ for the fourth component. Thus we can use D3DXVec3TransformCoord to transform points and we can use D3DXVec3TransformNormal to transform vectors.

15.3 **Ray/Mesh Intersection**

Once we have the picking ray and a mesh in the same space, we can perform the intersection test to see if the picking ray intersects the mesh. The following method iterates through each triangle in the mesh and does a ray/triangle intersection test. If the ray intersects one of the triangles, then it must have hit the mesh the triangle belongs to. Otherwise, the ray misses the mesh.

```
HRESULT ID3DX10Mesh::Intersect(
    D3DXVECTOR3 *pRayPos,
    D3DXVECTOR3 *pRayDir,
```

```
    UINT *pHitCount,
    UINT *pFaceIndex,
    float *pU,
    float *pV,
    float *pDist,
    ID3D10Blob **ppAllHits
);
```

- pRayPos: The ray position in the same space as the mesh geometry.
- pRayDir: The ray direction in the same space as the mesh geometry.
- pHitCount: Returns the number of times the ray intersected the mesh. For a complex mesh with overlapping parts, the ray may pierce several triangles of the mesh.
- pFaceIndex: The index of the nearest intersected triangle along the ray. If there are n triangles in a mesh, then the triangles are indexed from 0 to n–1. Assuming triangle lists, Triangle 0 is defined by the first three entries in the index buffer, Triangle 1 is defined by the next three entries in the index buffer, and so on, and Triangle n–1 is defined by the last three entries in the index buffer.
- pU: The u barycentric coordinate of the nearest intersection point.
- pV: The v barycentric coordinate of the nearest intersection point.
- pDist: The parameter t_0 such that $\mathbf{r}(t_0) = \mathbf{q} + t_0\mathbf{u}$ yields the nearest intersection point.
- ppAllHits: The address of an ID3D10Blob pointer. This returned interface contains an array of D3DX10_INTERSECT_INFO structures. The size of this array equals the value returned by the pHitCount parameter. This array describes the details of every intersection point.

```
typedef struct D3DX10_INTERSECT_INFO {
    UINT FaceIndex;
    FLOAT U;
    FLOAT V;
    FLOAT Dist;
} D3DX10_INTERSECT_INFO, *LPD3DX10_INTERSECT_INFO;
```

To understand the (u, v) barycentric coordinates, consider Figure 15.5. We fix an origin at one vertex, say $\mathbf{v}_0$, of the triangle, and form two vectors along the edges of the triangle. This forms a skewed coordinate system in the plane of the triangle. The coordinates (u, v) identify the point in the plane of the triangle given by $\mathbf{p}(u,v) = \mathbf{v}_0 + u(\mathbf{v}_1 - \mathbf{v}_0) + v(\mathbf{v}_2 - \mathbf{v}_0)$. A point is in the triangle if and only if $u \geq 0$, $v \geq 0$, and $u + v \leq 1$.

The following code shows how we use this method to test the intersection of a ray with a mesh:

```
    Mesh mSceneMesh;

...

ID3DX10Mesh* d3dxmesh = mSceneMesh.d3dxMesh();
```

```
UINT hitCount;
float u,v,t;
ID3D10Blob* allHits;
d3dxmesh->Intersect(&rayOrigin, &rayDir, &hitCount,
&mPickedTriangle, &u, &v, &t, &allHits);

ReleaseCOM(allHits);
```

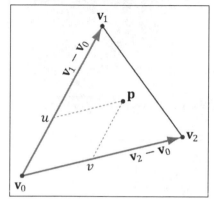

Figure 15.5: The point **p** in the plane of the triangle has coordinates (u, v) relative to the skewed coordinate system with origin $\mathbf{v}_0$ and axes $\mathbf{v}_1 - \mathbf{v}_0$ and $\mathbf{v}_2 - \mathbf{v}_0$.

15.4 **Bounding Volumes**

Performing a ray intersection test for every triangle in the scene adds up in computation time. Even for meshes not near the picking ray, we would still have to iterate over each triangle to conclude the ray misses the mesh; this is wasteful and inefficient. A popular strategy is to approximate the mesh with a simple bounding volume, like a sphere or box (see Figure 15.6 on the following page). Then, instead of testing the intersection of the ray with the mesh, we first test the intersection of the ray with the bounding volume. If the ray misses the bounding volume, then the ray necessarily misses the triangle mesh and so there is no need to do further calculations. If the ray intersects the bounding volume, then we do the more precise ray/mesh test. Assuming that the ray will miss most bounding volumes in the scene, this saves us many ray/triangle intersection tests.

Note that doing one ray/sphere or ray/box intersection test is much faster than doing a ray/triangle intersection test for every triangle in the mesh. For example, Figure 15.7 shows that a ray $\mathbf{r}(t) = \mathbf{q} + t\mathbf{u}$ misses a sphere with center $\mathbf{c}$ and radius r, if

$$\mathbf{v} \cdot \mathbf{u} < 0 \text{ and } \|\mathbf{v}\| < r$$

or

$$b^2 > r^2$$

where $b^2 = c^2 - a^2 = \|\mathbf{v}\|^2 - \|\text{proj}_\mathbf{u}(\mathbf{v})\|^2$ by the Pythagorean theorem.

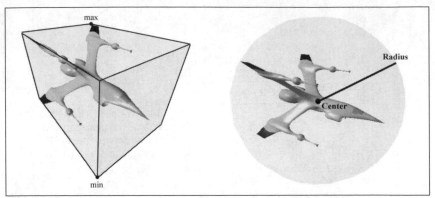

Figure 15.6: A mesh rendered with its AABB and bounding sphere.

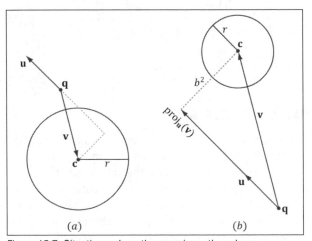

Figure 15.7: Situations where the ray misses the sphere.

15.4.1 **Computing an Axis-Aligned Bounding Box**

The *axis-aligned bounding box* (AABB) of a mesh is a box, with its faces parallel to the major axes, that tightly surrounds the mesh. An AABB can be described by a minimum point $\mathbf{v}_{min}$ and a maximum point $\mathbf{v}_{max}$ (see Figure 15.8). The minimum point $\mathbf{v}_{min}$ is found by searching through all the vertices of the mesh and finding the minimum x-, y-, and z-coordinates, and the maximum point $\mathbf{v}_{max}$ is found by searching through all the vertices of the mesh and finding the maximum x-, y-, and z-coordinates. The following code shows how this is done:

```
void Mesh::getAABB(D3DXVECTOR3& vMin, D3DXVECTOR3& vMax)
{
    ID3DX10MeshBuffer* vb = 0;
```

```
    HR(mMeshData->GetVertexBuffer(0, &vb));

    MeshVertex* vertices = 0;
    SIZE_T size;
    HR(vb->Map((void**)&vertices, &size));

    vMin = D3DXVECTOR3(+INFINITY, +INFINITY, +INFINITY);
    vMax = D3DXVECTOR3(-INFINITY, -INFINITY, -INFINITY);

    for(UINT i = 0; i < mMeshData->GetVertexCount(); ++i)
    {
        D3DXVec3Minimize(&vMin, &vMin, &vertices[i].pos);
        D3DXVec3Maximize(&vMax, &vMax, &vertices[i].pos);
    }

    HR(vb->Unmap());

    ReleaseCOM(vb);
}
```

The `D3DXVec3Minimize` and `D3DXVec3Maximize` functions return the vectors:

$$\mathbf{min}(\mathbf{u}, \mathbf{v}) = \Big(\min(u_x, v_x), \min(u_y, v_y), \min(u_z, v_z) \Big)$$

$$\mathbf{max}(\mathbf{u}, \mathbf{v}) = \Big(\max(u_x, v_x), \max(u_y, v_y), \max(u_z, v_z) \Big)$$

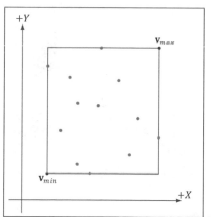

Figure 15.8: The axis-aligned bounding box (AABB) of a set of points.

15.4.2 Rotations and Axis-Aligned Bounding Boxes

Figure 15.9 shows that a box axis-aligned in one coordinate system may not be axis-aligned in a different coordinate system. In particular, if we compute the AABB of a mesh in local space, it gets transformed to an oriented bounding box (OBB) in world space. However, we can always transform the ray into the local space of the mesh and do the intersection there where the box is axis-aligned.

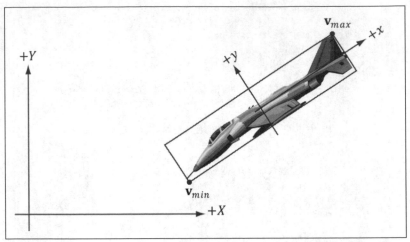

Figure 15.9: The bounding box is axis-aligned with the *xy*-frame, but not with the *XY*-frame.

Alternatively, we can recompute the AABB in the world space, but this can result in a "fatter" box that is a poorer approximation to the actual volume (see Figure 15.10).

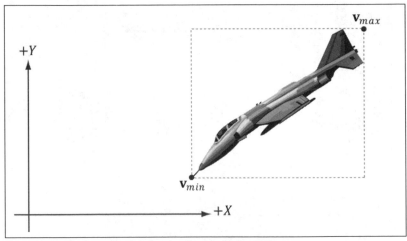

Figure 15.10: The bounding box is axis-aligned with the *XY*-frame.

15.4.3 **Computing a Bounding Sphere**

The *bounding sphere* of a mesh is a sphere that tightly surrounds the mesh. A bounding sphere can be described with a center point and radius. To compute the bounding sphere of a mesh, we first compute its AABB. We then take the center of the AABB as the center of the bounding sphere:

$$\mathbf{c} = 0.5(\mathbf{v}_{min} + \mathbf{v}_{max})$$

The radius is then taken to be the maximum distance between any vertex $\mathbf{p}$ in the mesh from the center $\mathbf{c}$:

$$r = \max\{\|\mathbf{c} - \mathbf{p}\|: \mathbf{p} \in mesh\}$$

15.4.4 **Scaling and Bounding Spheres**

Suppose we compute the bounding sphere of a mesh in local space. After the world transform, the bounding sphere may not tightly surround the mesh due to scaling. Thus the radius needs to be rescaled accordingly. To compensate for nonuniform scaling, we must scale the radius by the largest scaling component so that the sphere encapsulates the transformed mesh. Another possible strategy is to avoid scaling altogether by having all your meshes modeled to the same scale of the game world. This way, models will not need to be rescaled once they are loaded into the application.

15.5 **Demo Application**

The demo for this chapter, Picking, modifies the previous Mesh Viewer demo by allowing the user to pick a triangle of the tree mesh with the right mouse button. The index of the picked triangle is given by the `pFaceIndex` parameter from the `ID3DX10Mesh::Intersect` method. This index is then used to obtain the vertices of the picked triangle. We then redraw this triangle again using a green color with transparency blending; this gives the picked triangle a green highlighted look (see Figure 15.11).

Figure 15.11: The picked triangle is highlighted.

15.6 **Summary**

- Picking is the technique used to determine the 3D object that corresponds to the 2D projected object displayed on the screen that the user clicked with the mouse.

- The picking ray is found by shooting a ray, originating at the origin of the view space, through the point on the projection window that corresponds to the clicked screen point.

- We can transform a ray $r(t) = q + tu$ by transforming its origin q and direction u by a transformation matrix. Note that the origin is transformed as a point ($w = 1$) and the direction is treated as a vector ($w = 0$).

- To test if a ray has intersected an object, we can test if the ray intersected a triangle that composes the object with ID3DX10Mesh:: Intersect. Alternatively, we can test if the ray intersects a bounding volume of the object, such as a bounding sphere or axis-aligned bounding box (AABB). The functions D3DXBoxBoundProbe and D3DXSphereBoundProbe can be used for ray/AABB and ray/sphere intersection tests, respectively.

15.7 **Exercises**

1. Modify the demo of this chapter by allowing the user to pick any triangle of any mesh in the scene. (*Hint*: Put the meshes in an array and iterate over them in the picking code.)

2. Modify the demo of this chapter in the following way. Instead of using the ID3DX10Mesh::Intersect method, compute the AABB of the tree mesh and use the D3DXBoxBoundProbe function to determine if the picking ray intersects the AABB.

   ```
   BOOL D3DXBoxBoundProbe(
       CONST D3DXVECTOR3 *pMin,
       CONST D3DXVECTOR3 *pMax,
       CONST D3DXVECTOR3 *pRayPosition,
       CONST D3DXVECTOR3 *pRayDirection
   );
   ```

   This function returns true if the ray defined by pRayPosition and pRayDirection intersects the AABB defined by pMin and pMax. It returns false if the ray misses. Note that the ray and AABB must be in the same space if the function is to work correctly.

Also, render a box representing the AABB over your mesh with transparency blending so that you can visually test your ray/box picking code. To do this, compute the box geometry in the local space of the mesh to match the AABB. Then, for rendering, use the same world matrix for the box as used for the mesh it approximates. The rendered box will look like an oriented bounding box (OBB) since it is not axis-aligned in view space, but it is axis-aligned with the local space of the mesh.

Chapter 16

Terrain Rendering

The idea of terrain rendering is to start off with a flat grid (top of Figure 16.1). Then we adjust the heights (i.e., the y-coordinates) of the vertices in such a way that the mesh models smooth transitions from mountain to valley, thereby simulating a terrain (middle of Figure 16.1). And, of course, we apply a nice texture to render sandy beaches, grassy hills, rocky cliffs, and snowy mountains (bottom of Figure 16.1).

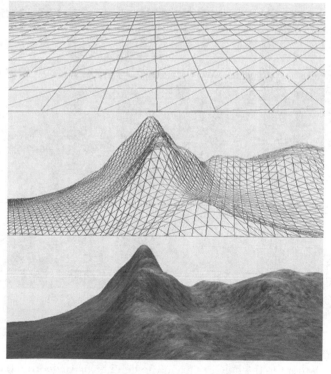

Figure 16.1: (Top) A triangle grid. (Middle) A triangle grid with smooth height transitions used to create hills and valleys. (Bottom) A lit and textured terrain.

Objectives:

- To learn how to generate height info for a terrain that results in smooth transitions between mountains and valleys.
- To find out how to light and texture the terrain.
- To discover a way to keep the camera or other objects planted on the terrain surface.

16.1 **Heightmaps**

We use a heightmap to describe the hills and valleys of our terrain. A *heightmap* is a matrix, where each element specifies the height of a particular vertex in the terrain grid. That is, there exists an entry in the heightmap for each grid vertex, and the *ij*th heightmap entry provides the height for the *ij*th vertex. Typically, a heightmap is graphically represented as a grayscale map in an image editor, where black denotes the lowest elevation, white denotes the highest elevation, and shades of gray represent in-between heights. Figure 16.2 shows a few examples of heightmaps and the corresponding terrains they construct.

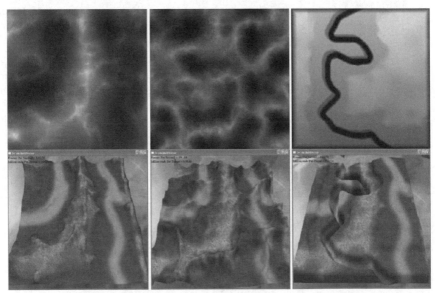

Figure 16.2: Examples of heightmaps. Observe how the heights, as described by the dark and light areas in the heightmaps, build different terrain surfaces.

When we store our heightmaps on disk, we usually allocate a byte of memory for each element in the heightmap, so the height can range from 0 to 255. The range 0 to 255 is enough to preserve the transition between heights of our terrain, but in our application we may need to extend the scale beyond the 0 to 255 range in order to match the scale of our 3D world. For example, if our unit of measure in the 3D world is feet, then 0 to 255 does not give us enough values to represent anything interesting. For this reason, when we load the data into our applications, we allocate a `float` for each height element. This allows us to then scale well beyond the 0 to 255 range to match any scale necessary; moreover, it also enables us to filter the heightmap and generate height values that are between integer numbers.

Note: In §5.15 we created a "terrain" using a mathematical function. That is an example of a procedurally generated terrain. However, it is difficult to come up with a function that precisely describes the terrain you want. Heightmaps give more flexibility because they can be edited by an artist.

16.1.1 Creating a Heightmap

Heightmaps can be generated procedurally or in an image editor such as Adobe Photoshop. Using paint filters to generate different chaotic heightmap patterns can prove to be a good start, and then the heightmap can be manually tweaked by taking advantage of your paint editor's tools. Note that applying the blur filter is useful to smooth out rough edges in the heightmap.

The program Terragen (http://www.planetside.co.uk/terragen/) can generate heightmaps procedurally, and it also provides tools for modifying the heightmap (or the heightmap can be exported, and then imported and modified in a separate paint program like Photoshop). The program Bryce (http://www.daz3d.com/i.x/software/bryce/) also has many procedural algorithms for generating heightmaps, as well as a built-in heightmap editor. Dark Tree (http://www.darksim.com/) is a powerful procedural texture authoring program, which, in particular, can be used for creating grayscale heightmaps.

Once you have finished drawing your heightmap, you need to save it as an 8-bit RAW file. RAW files simply contain the bytes of the image one after another. This makes it very easy to read the image into our programs. If your software asks you to save the RAW file with a header, specify no header. Figure 16.3 shows the export dialog for Terragen.

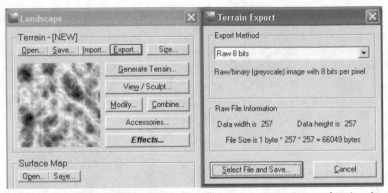

Figure 16.3: (Left) The landscape generator allows you to generate a random terrain procedurally and also to manually sculpt the terrain with brush tools. (Right) The export dialog for Terragen. Observe the export method selected is the 8-bit RAW format.

Note: You do not have to use the RAW format to store your heightmaps; you can use any format that suits your needs. The RAW format is just one example of a format that we can use. We decided to use the RAW format because many image editors can export to this format and it is very easy to load the data in a RAW file into our program demos. The demos in this book use 8-bit RAW files (i.e., each element in the heightmap is an 8-bit integer).

Note: If 256 height steps is too coarse for your needs, you may consider storing 16-bit heightmaps, where each height entry is described by a 16-bit integer. Terragen can also export 16-bit RAW heightmaps.

16.1.2 Loading a RAW File

Since a RAW file is nothing more than a contiguous block of bytes (where each byte is a heightmap entry), we can easily read in the block of memory with one std::ifstream::read call, as is done in this next method:

```
void Terrain::loadHeightmap()
{
    // A height for each vertex
    std::vector<unsigned char> in( mInfo.NumRows * mInfo.NumCols );

    // Open the file.
    std::ifstream inFile;
    inFile.open(mInfo.HeightmapFilename.c_str(), std::ios_base::binary);

    if(inFile)
    {
        // Read the RAW bytes.
```

```
        inFile.read((char*)&in[0], (std::streamsize)in.size());

        // Done with file.
        inFile.close();
    }


    // Copy the array data into a float array, and scale
    // and offset the heights.
    mHeightmap.resize(mInfo.NumRows * mInfo.NumCols, 0);
    for(UINT i = 0; i < mInfo.NumRows * mInfo.NumCols; ++i)
    {
        mHeightmap[i] = (float)in[i] * mInfo.HeightScale
                    + mInfo.HeightOffset;
    }
}
```

The mInfo variable is a member of the Terrain class and is an instance of the following structure, which describes various properties of the terrain:

```
struct InitInfo
{
    // Filename of RAW heightmap data.
    std::wstring HeightmapFilename;

    // Texture filenames used for texturing the terrain.
    std::wstring LayerMapFilename0;
    std::wstring LayerMapFilename1;
    std::wstring LayerMapFilename2;
    std::wstring LayerMapFilename3;
    std::wstring LayerMapFilename4;
    std::wstring BlendMapFilename;

    // Scale and translation to apply to heights after they have
    // been loaded from the heightmap.
    float HeightScale;
    float HeightOffset;

    // Dimensions of the heightmap, and dimensions of the vertex grid
    // (i.e., if there is an m x n vertex grid, then the heightmap
    // should also be m x n so that there is a corresponding height
    // for each vertex).
    UINT NumRows;
    UINT NumCols;

    // The cell spacing along the x- and z-axes (see Figure 16.4).
    float CellSpacing;
};
```

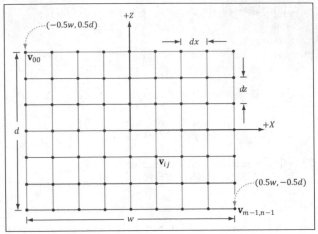

Figure 16.4: Grid properties.

Note: The reader may wish to review §5.15 for more information about grid construction.

16.1.3 Smoothing

One of the problems of using an 8-bit heightmap is that it means we can only represent 256 discrete height steps. Consequently, we cannot model the height values shown in Figure 16.5a; instead, we end up with Figure 16.5b. This truncation creates a "rougher" terrain than may have been intended. Of course, once we truncate we cannot recover the original height values, but by smoothing out Figure 16.5b, we can get something that is closer to 16.5a.

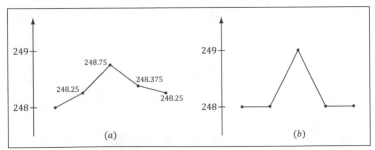

Figure 16.5: (a) Floating-point height values in the range [0, 255]. (b) Height values clamped to the nearest integer.

So what we do is load the heightmap into memory by reading the raw bytes. We then copy the byte array into a float array so that we have floating-point precision. Then we apply a filter to the floating-point heightmap, which smoothes the heightmap out, making the difference in heights between adjacent elements less drastic. The filtering algorithm we use is quite basic. A new filtered heightmap pixel is computed by averaging itself along with its eight neighbor pixels (see Figure 16.6):

$$\widetilde{h}_{i,j} = \frac{h_{i-1,j-1} + h_{i-1,j} + h_{i-1,j+1} + h_{i,j-1} + h_{i,j} + h_{i,j+1} + h_{i+1,j-1} + h_{i+1,j} + h_{i+1,j+1}}{9}$$

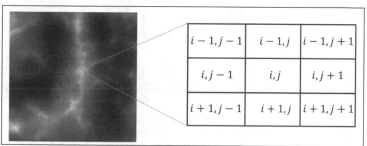

Figure 16.6: The height of the *ij*th vertex is found by averaging the *ij*th heightmap entry together with its eight neighbor heights.

In the case that we are on the edge of the heightmap, where a pixel does not have eight neighbor pixels, then we just take the average of the pixel itself with as many neighboring pixels as possible.

Here is the implementation of the function that averages the *ij*th pixel in the heightmap:

```
bool Terrain::inBounds(UINT i, UINT j)
{
    return
        i >= 0 && i < mInfo.NumRows &&
        j >= 0 && j < mInfo.NumCols;
}

float Terrain::average(UINT i, UINT j)
{
    // Function computes the average height of the ijth element.
    // It averages itself with its eight neighbor pixels. Note
    // that if a pixel is missing a neighbor, we just don't include it
    // in the average -- that is, edge pixels don't have a neighbor pixel.
    //
    // ----------
    // | 1| 2| 3|
    // ----------
    // |4 |ij| 6|
    // ----------
    // | 7| 8| 9|
    // ----------

    float avg = 0.0f;
```

```
        float num = 0.0f;

        for(UINT m = i-1; m <= i+1; ++m)
        {
            for(UINT n = j-1; n <= j+1; ++n)
            {
                if( inBounds(m,n) )
                {
                    avg += mHeightmap[m*mInfo.NumCols + n];
                    num += 1.0f;
                }
            }
        }

        return avg / num;
}
```

The function inBounds returns true if the entry is on the heightmap and false otherwise. So if we try to sample an element adjacent to an entry on an edge that is not part of the heightmap, then inBounds returns false, and we do not include it in our average — it does not exist.

To smooth the entire heightmap, we just apply average to each heightmap entry:

```
void Terrain::smooth()
{
    std::vector<float> dest( mHeightmap.size() );

    for(UINT i = 0; i < mInfo.NumRows; ++i)
    {
        for(UINT j = 0; j < mInfo.NumCols; ++j)
        {
            dest[i*mInfo.NumCols+j] = average(i,j);
        }
    }

    // Replace the old heightmap with the filtered one.
    mHeightmap = dest;
}
```

16.2 **Texturing**

Recall §7.10 where we tiled a grass texture over a land mass. We tiled the texture to increase the resolution (i.e., to increase the number of texel samples that covered a triangle on the land mass). We want to do the same thing here; however, we do not want to be limited to a single grass texture. We would like to create terrains depicting sand, grass, dirt, rock, and snow, all at the same time. You might suggest creating one large texture that contains the sand, grass, dirt, etc., and stretch it over the terrain. But this would lead us back to the resolution problem — the terrain geometry is so large, we would require an impractically large texture to have enough color samples to get a decent resolution. Instead, we take a multitexturing approach that works like transparency alpha blending.

The idea is to have a separate texture for each terrain layer (e.g., one each for grass, dirt, rock, etc.) These textures will be tiled over the terrain for high resolution. For the sake of example, suppose we have three terrain layers (grass, dirt, and rock); these layers are then combined as shown in Figure 16.7.

Terrain RGB   **Layer Maps**   **Blend Maps**

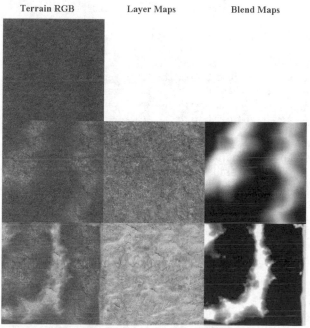

Figure 16.7: (Top) First lay down the zeroth layer (grass) as the current terrain color. (Middle) Now blend the current terrain color with the first layer (dirt) via the transparency alpha blending equation; the blend map supplies the source alpha component. (Bottom) Finally, blend the current terrain color with the second layer (rock) via the transparency alpha blending equation; the blend map supplies the source alpha component.

The above process should be reminiscent of transparency alpha blending. The blend map, which stores the source alpha of the layer we are writing, indicates the opacity of the source layer, thereby allowing us to control how much of the source layer overwrites the existing terrain color. This enables us to color some parts of the terrain with grass, some parts with dirt, and others with snow, or various blends of all three.

Figure 16.7 illustrates the process with three color maps. In our code, we use five. In order to combine the five color maps, we require four grayscale *blend maps*. We can pack these four grayscale blend maps into a single RGBA texture (the red channel stores the first blend map, the green channel the second blend map, the blue channel the third blend map, and the alpha channel the fourth blend map). Thus, a total of six textures are needed to implement this. The following terrain pixel shader code shows how our texture blending is implemented:

```
float4 c0 = gLayer0.Sample( gTriLinearSam, pIn.tiledUV );
float4 c1 = gLayer1.Sample( gTriLinearSam, pIn.tiledUV );
float4 c2 = gLayer2.Sample( gTriLinearSam, pIn.tiledUV );
float4 c3 = gLayer3.Sample( gTriLinearSam, pIn.tiledUV );
float4 c4 = gLayer4.Sample( gTriLinearSam, pIn.tiledUV );

float4 t = gBlendMap.Sample( gTriLinearSam, pIn.stretchedUV );

float4 C = c0;          // Lay down the 0th layer
C = lerp(C, c1, t.r); // Blend C with the 1st layer
C = lerp(C, c2, t.g); // Blend C with the 2nd layer
C = lerp(C, c3, t.b); // Blend C with the 3rd layer
C = lerp(C, c4, t.a); // Blend C with the 4th layer
```

Note: The blend maps generally depend on the heightmap of the terrain. Therefore, we do not embed the blend maps into the alpha channels of the color maps. If we did, then the color maps would only work for a particular heightmap. By keeping the color maps and blend maps separate, we can reuse the color maps for many different terrains. On the other hand, different blend maps will be constructed for each terrain.

Note: Unlike the layer textures, the blend maps are not tiled, as we stretch them over the entire terrain surface. This is necessary since we use the blend map to mark regions of the terrain where we want a particular texture to show through, so the blend map must be global and cover the whole terrain. You might wonder whether this is acceptable or if excessive magnification occurs. Indeed, magnification will occur and the blend maps will be distorted by the texture filtering when it is stretched over the entire terrain, but the blend maps are not where we get our details from (we get them from the tiled textures). The blend maps merely mark the general regions of the terrain where (and how much) a particular texture contributes. So if the blend maps get a bit distorted and blurred, it will not significantly affect the end result — perhaps a bit of dirt will blend in with a bit of grass, for example, and this actually provides a smoother transition between layers.

16.3 **Lighting**

For the terrain, we use a rather coarse lighting model. We drop the specular term on the assumption that the terrain layers will not be shiny. We also do the ambient and diffuse lighting at the vertex level using the vertex normal, and then interpolate the result. Although vertex lighting is coarser than per-pixel lighting, when combined with the texturing, the results are good. Moreover, this is much cheaper than per-pixel lighting. Essentially, the texturing gives the high-frequency details of the terrain, while the lighting broadly shades the terrain.

We compute the shade factor (which is a combination of the diffuse and ambient factors) in the vertex shader as follows:

```
vOut.shade = saturate(max(dot(normalW, gDirToSunW), 0.0f) + 0.1f);
```

We use a directional light (the Sun is the light source), and `gDirToSunW` is the unit light vector directed toward the Sun (it is set as an effect constant):

```
// C++ Code
void Terrain::setDirectionToSun(const D3DXVECTOR3& v)
{
    D3DXVECTOR4 temp(v.x, v.y, v.z, 0.0f);
    mfxDirToSunVar->SetFloatVector((float*)temp);
}

// FX Code
cbuffer cbPerFrame
{
    float4x4 gWorld;
    float4x4 gWVP;
    float4 gDirToSunW;
};
```

The normalized vertex normal in world space is `normalW`. The 0.1 is essentially our ambient material used to brighten up the shade. (The shade is a grayscale value, so it can be represented by a single scalar.) The `saturate` intrinsic HLSL function simply clamps the result to [0, 1] (the shade factor could go outside this range due to adding the ambient factor 0.1, so we need to clamp it). For simplicity, we hardcode the value 0.1, but the program could be modified to store the ambient material in a constant buffer, and let the C++ application set it.

Note: If necessary, review the mathematics behind the diffuse lighting calculation from Chapter 6.

You can think of this shade value as a grayscale color, which when multiplied with a color vector darkens the color. For example, if the shade factor is 0.25, then multiplying it with a color will reduce a color to one-fourth its intensity; if the shade factor is 1.0, then multiplying it with a color leaves the original color unmodified. So basically, the shade factor is a percentage based on the diffuse and ambient lighting calculation (i.e., how much incoming light the surface receives) that specifies how much of a pixel color to keep or discard.

The shading factor is output from the vertex shader, interpolated, and then fed into the pixel shader, where it is multiplied against the texture color to form the final pixel color:

```
// Multiply the final blended texture color by the shade.
C *= pIn.shade;
```

16.4 Terrain FX

Below is the entire terrain effect:

```
#include "lighthelper.fx"

cbuffer cbPerFrame
{
    float4x4 gWorld;
    float4x4 gWVP;
    float4 gDirToSunW;
};

cbuffer cbFixed
{
    float gTexScale = 20;
};

// Nonnumeric values cannot be added to a cbuffer.
Texture2D gLayer0;
Texture2D gLayer1;
Texture2D gLayer2;
Texture2D gLayer3;
Texture2D gLayer4;
Texture2D gBlendMap;

SamplerState gTriLinearSam
{
    Filter = MIN_MAG_MIP_LINEAR;
    AddressU = Wrap;
    AddressV = Wrap;
};

struct VS_IN
{
    float3 posL    : POSITION;
    float3 normalL : NORMAL;
    float2 texC    : TEXCOORD;
};

struct VS_OUT
```

```
{
    float4 posH       : SV_POSITION;
    float shade       : SHADE;
    float2 tiledUV    : TEXCOORD0;
    float2 stretchedUV : TEXCOORD1;
};

VS_OUT VS(VS_IN vIn)
{
    VS_OUT vOut;

    vOut.posH = mul(float4(vIn.posL, 1.0f), gWVP);

    float4 normalW = mul(float4(vIn.normalL, 0.0f), gWorld);

    vOut.shade = saturate(max(dot(normalW, gDirToSunW), 0.0f) + 0.1f);

    // Generate tiled texture coordinates for tiling the layers.
    vOut.tiledUV    = gTexScale*vIn.texC;

    // Stretched texture coordinates in [0, 1] range for blend maps.
    vOut.stretchedUV = vIn.texC;

    return vOut;
}

float4 PS(VS_OUT pIn) : SV_Target
{
    float4 c0 = gLayer0.Sample( gTriLinearSam, pIn.tiledUV );
    float4 c1 = gLayer1.Sample( gTriLinearSam, pIn.tiledUV );
    float4 c2 = gLayer2.Sample( gTriLinearSam, pIn.tiledUV );
    float4 c3 = gLayer3.Sample( gTriLinearSam, pIn.tiledUV );
    float4 c4 = gLayer4.Sample( gTriLinearSam, pIn.tiledUV );

    float4 t = gBlendMap.Sample( gTriLinearSam, pIn.stretchedUV );

    float4 C = c0;
    C = lerp(C, c1, t.r);
    C = lerp(C, c2, t.g);
    C = lerp(C, c3, t.b);
    C = lerp(C, c4, t.a);

    C *= pIn.shade;

    return C;
}

technique10 TerrainTech
{
    pass P0
    {
        SetVertexShader( CompileShader( vs_4_0, VS() ) );
        SetGeometryShader( NULL );
```

```
SetPixelShader( CompileShader( ps_4_0, PS() ) );
    }
}
```

Note: The input vertex texture coordinates are in the range [0, 1]. In other words, they stretch the texture over the terrain. The constant buffer element

```
float gTexScale = 20;
```

is used to scale the input texture coordinates outside the [0, 1] range for tiling. In the above code, we set `gTexScale = 20` so that the tiled texture coordinates are in the range [0, 20]; that is, the texture is tiled 20 times over the terrain. For simplicity, we hardcode the texture scaling value directly in the effect file, but you can get a handle to the variable and set it from the C++ code.

16.5 **Terrain Height**

A common task is to get the height of the terrain surface given the x- and z-coordinates. This is useful for placing objects on the surface of the terrain, or for placing the camera slightly above the terrain surface to simulate the player walking on the terrain.

The heightmap gives us the height of a terrain vertex at the grid points. However, we need the heights of the terrain between vertices. Therefore, we have to do interpolation to form a continuous surface $y = h(x, z)$ representing the terrain given the discrete heightmap sampling. Since the terrain is approximated by a triangle mesh, it makes sense to use linear interpolation so that our height function agrees with the underlying terrain mesh geometry.

To begin to solve this, our first goal is to figure out which cell the x- and z-coordinates lie in. (Note: We assume the coordinates x and z are relative to the local space of the terrain.) The following code does this; it tells us the row and column of the cell in which the x- and z-coordinates are located.

```
// Transform from terrain local space to "cell" space.
float c = (x + 0.5f*width()) / mInfo.CellSpacing;
float d = (z - 0.5f*depth()) / -mInfo.CellSpacing;

// Get the row and column we are in.
int row = (int)floorf(d);
int col = (int)floorf(c);
```

Figures 16.8a and b explain what this code does. Essentially, we are transforming to a new coordinate system where the origin is at the upper-leftmost terrain vertex, the positive z-axis goes down, and each unit is scaled so that it corresponds to one cell space. Now in this coordinate system, it is clear by Figure 16.8b that the row and column of the cell is just given by floor(z) and floor(x), respectively. In the figure example, the point is in row four and column one (using zero-based indices). (Recall that the C++ `floor(t)` function evaluates to the greatest integer less than or equal to t.) Observe also that `row` and `col` give the indices of the upper-left vertex of the cell.

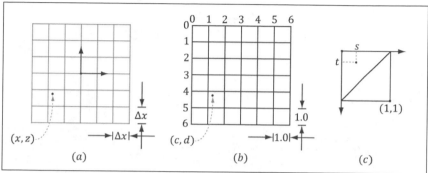

Figure 16.8: (a) The point in the xz-plane relative to the terrain coordinate system has coordinates (x, z). (b) We pick a new coordinate where the origin is the upper-leftmost grid vertex, the positive z-axis goes down, and each unit is scaled so that it corresponds to one cell space. The point has coordinates (c, d) relative to this coordinate system. This transformation involves a translation and scaling. Once in this new coordinate system, finding the row and column of the cell we are in is trivial. (c) We introduce a third coordinate system, which has its origin at the upper-left vertex of the cell in which the point is located. The point has coordinates (s, t) relative to this coordinate system. Transforming the coordinates into this system involves only a simple translation to offset the coordinates. Observe that if $s + t \leq 1$, we are in the "upper" triangle; otherwise, we are in the "lower" triangle.

Now that we know the cell we are in, we grab the heights of the four cell vertices from the heightmap:

```
// Grab the heights of the cell we are in.
// A*--*B
// | /|
// |/ |
// C*--*D
float A = mHeightmap[row*mInfo.NumCols + col];
float B = mHeightmap[row*mInfo.NumCols + col + 1];
float C = mHeightmap[(row+1)*mInfo.NumCols + col];
float D = mHeightmap[(row+1)*mInfo.NumCols + col + 1];
```

At this point we know the cell we are in and the heights of the four vertices of that cell. Now we need to find the height (y-coordinate) of the terrain surface at the particular x- and z-coordinates. This is a little tricky since the cell can be slanted in a couple of directions; see Figure 16.9.

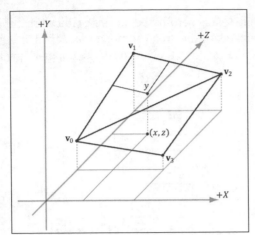

Figure 16.9: The height (*y*-coordinate) of the terrain surface at the particular *x*- and *z*-coordinates.

In order to find the height, we need to know which triangle of the cell we are in (recall our cells are rendered as two triangles). To find the triangle we are in, we are going to change our coordinates so that the coordinates (c, d) are described relative to the cell coordinate system (see Figure 16.8c). This simple change of coordinates involves only translations and is done as follows:

```
float s = c - (float)col;
float t = d - (float)row;
```

Then, if $s + t \leq 1$ we are in the "upper" triangle ΔABC; otherwise, we are in the "lower" triangle ΔDCB.

Now we explain how to find the height if we are in the "upper" triangle. The process is similar for the "lower" triangle, and, of course, the code for both follows shortly. To find the height if we are in the "upper" triangle, we first construct two vectors, $\mathbf{u} = (\Delta x, B - A, 0)$ and $\mathbf{v} = (0, C - A, \Delta z)$, on the sides of the triangle originating from the terminal point $\mathbf{Q}$ as Figure 16.10a shows. Then we linearly interpolate along $\mathbf{u}$ by s, and we linearly interpolate along $\mathbf{v}$ by t. Figure 16.10b illustrates these interpolations. The y-coordinate of the point $\mathbf{Q} + s\mathbf{u} + t\mathbf{v}$ gives the height based on the given x- and z-coordinates (recall the geometric interpretation of vector addition to see this).

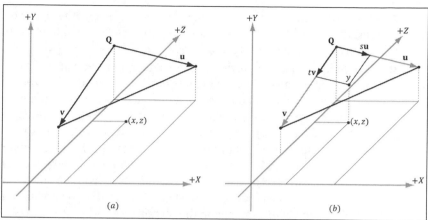

Figure 16.10: (a) Computing two vectors on the upper triangle edges. (b) The height is the _y_-coordinate of the vector.

Note that since we are only concerned about the interpolated height value we can just interpolate the _y_ components and ignore the other components. Thus the height is obtained by the sum $A + su_y + tv_y$.

Thus the conclusion of the `Terrain::getHeight` code is:

```
// If upper triangle ABC.
if( s + t <= 1.0f)
{
    float uy = B - A;
    float vy = C - A;
    return A + s*uy + t*vy;
}
else // lower triangle DCB.
{
    float uy = C - D;
    float vy = B - D;
    return D + (1.0f-s)*uy + (1.0f-t)*vy;
}
```

16.6 **Summary**

- We can model terrains using triangle grids where the height of each vertex is specified in such a way that hills and valleys are simulated.

- A heightmap is a matrix where each element specifies the height of a particular vertex in the terrain grid. There exists an entry in the heightmap for each grid vertex, and the _ij_th heightmap entry provides the height for the _ij_th vertex. A heightmap is commonly represented visually as a grayscale map, where black denotes the lowest elevation, white denotes the highest elevation, and shades of gray represent in-between heights.

■ We texture the terrain by blending layers over each other (e.g., grass, dirt, rock, snow). Blend maps are used to control the amount each layer contributes to the final terrain image.

■ The heightmap gives us the height of a terrain vertex at the grid points, but we also need the heights of the terrain between vertices. Therefore, we have to do interpolation to form a continuous surface $y = h(x, z)$ representing the terrain given the discrete heightmap sampling. Since the terrain is approximated by a triangle mesh, it makes sense to use linear interpolation so that our height function agrees with the underlying terrain mesh geometry. Having the height function of the terrain is useful for placing objects on the surface of the terrain, or for placing the camera slightly above the terrain surface to simulate the player walking on the terrain.

16.7 **Exercises**

1. Use the `Terrain::getHeight` function to fix the camera slightly above the terrain surface to simulate that the camera is walking on the terrain. Figure 16.11 shows that you should move the camera in the direction tangent to the terrain surface, not in the "Look" direction.

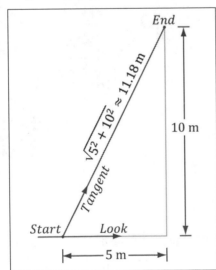

Figure 16.11: Suppose the camera is positioned at "Start" and moving in the "Look" direction. Also suppose that the camera has a speed of 5 m/s (meters per second). In one second, the camera will have traveled 5 m in the "Look" direction, but then the height will be adjusted to "End" so the camera stays on top of the terrain. In reality, then, the camera did not move 5 m in one second; it traveled a total distance of 11.18 m in one second, which is incorrect — the camera unnaturally sped up. To fix this, we always move the camera 5 m/s in a direction tangent to the surface.

Chapter 17

Particle Systems and Stream Output

In this chapter, we concern ourselves with the task of modeling a collection of particles (usually small) that all behave in a similar yet somewhat random manner; we call such a collection of particles a *particle system*. Particle systems can be used to simulate a wide range of phenomena such as fire, rain, smoke, explosions, sprinklers, magic spell effects, and projectiles.

Objectives:

■ To learn how to store and render particles efficiently using the geometry shader and stream output functionality.

■ To find out how we can make our particles move in a physically realistic way using basic physics concepts.

■ To design a flexible particle system framework that makes it easy to create new custom particle systems.

17.1 Particle Representation

A *particle* is a very small object that is usually modeled as a point mathematically. It follows then that a point primitive (D3D10_PRIMITIVE_TOPOLOGY_POINTLIST) would be a good candidate to display particles. However, a point primitive is rasterized as a single pixel. This does not give us much flexibility, as we would like to have particles of various sizes and even map entire textures onto these particles. Therefore, we will take a strategy like we used for the tree billboards from Chapter 10: We will store the particles using points, but then expand them into quads that face the camera in the geometry shader. In contrast to the tree billboards, which were aligned with the world's *y*-axis, the particle billboards will fully face the camera (see Figure 17.1).

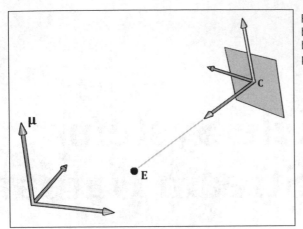

Figure 17.1: The world and billboard frames. The billboard faces the eye position **E**.

If we know the world coordinates of the world's up vector μ, the billboard's center position **C**, and the eye position **E**, then we can describe the billboard's local frame in world coordinates, which gives us the billboard's world matrix:

$$\mathbf{W} = \begin{bmatrix} u_x & u_y & u_z & 0 \\ v_x & v_y & v_z & 0 \\ w_x & w_y & w_z & 0 \\ C_x & C_y & C_z & 1 \end{bmatrix}$$

In addition to position and size, our particles will have other attributes. Our vertex structure for particles looks like this:

```
struct ParticleVertex
{
    D3DXVECTOR3 initialPos;
    D3DXVECTOR3 initialVel;
    D3DXVECTOR2 size;
    float age;
    unsigned int type;
};
```

Note: We need not expand a point into a quad, necessarily. For example, using line lists to render rain works pretty well. We can use a different geometry shader to expand points to lines. Basically, in our system, each particle system will have its own effect file. The effect file implements the details specific to the particular kind of particle system it is associated with.

17.2 **Particle Motion**

We would like our particles to move in a physically realistic way. For simplicity, in this book, we restrict ourselves to a constant net acceleration; for example, acceleration due to gravity. (We can also make loose approximations by making acceleration due to other forces constant as well, such as wind.) In addition, we do not do any collision detection with our particles.

Let $\mathbf{p}(t)$ describe the position of a particle (at time t) moving along a curve. The instantaneous velocity of the particle at time t is:

$$\mathbf{v}(t) = \mathbf{p}'(t)$$

The instantaneous acceleration of the particle at time t is:

$$\mathbf{a}(t) = \mathbf{v}'(t) = \mathbf{p}''(t)$$

Recall the following from calculus:

- An antiderivative of a function $\mathbf{f}(t)$ is any function $\mathbf{F}(t)$ such that the derivative of $\mathbf{F}(t)$ is $\mathbf{f}(t)$; that is, $\mathbf{F}'(t) = \mathbf{f}(t)$.

- If $\mathbf{F}(t)$ is any antiderivative of $\mathbf{f}(t)$ and $\mathbf{c}$ is any constant, then $\mathbf{F}(t) + \mathbf{c}$ is also an antiderivative of $\mathbf{f}(t)$. Moreover, every antiderivative of $\mathbf{f}(t)$ has the form $\mathbf{F}(t) + \mathbf{c}$.

- To denote an arbitrary antiderivative of $\mathbf{f}(t)$, we use the integral notation $\int \mathbf{f}(t)dt = \mathbf{F}(t) + \mathbf{c}$.

From the definitions of velocity and acceleration, it is evident that the velocity function is an antiderivative of the acceleration function, and the position function is an antiderivative of the velocity function. Thus we have:

$$\mathbf{p}(t) = \int \mathbf{v}(t)dt$$

$$\mathbf{v}(t) = \int \mathbf{a}(t)dt$$

Now, suppose that the acceleration is constant (i.e., it does not vary with time). Also suppose that we know the initial particle velocity $\mathbf{v}(0) = \mathbf{v}_0$ and the initial particle position $\mathbf{p}(0) = \mathbf{p}_0$ at time $t = 0$. Then the velocity function is found by integrating the constant acceleration:

$$\mathbf{v}(t) = \int \mathbf{a}(t)dt = t\mathbf{a} + \mathbf{c}$$

To find the constant $\mathbf{c}$, we use our initial velocity:

$$\mathbf{v}(0) = 0 \cdot \mathbf{a} + \mathbf{c} = \mathbf{c} = \mathbf{v}_0$$

So the velocity function is

$$\mathbf{v}(t) = t\mathbf{a} + \mathbf{v}_0$$

To find the position function, we integrate the just found velocity function:

$$\mathbf{p}(t) = \int \mathbf{v}(t)dt = \int (t\mathbf{a}+\mathbf{v}_0)dt = \frac{1}{2}t^2\mathbf{a}+t\mathbf{v}_0+\mathbf{k}$$

To find the constant $\mathbf{k}$, we use our initial position:

$$\mathbf{p}(0) = \frac{1}{2}\cdot 0\cdot\mathbf{a}+0\cdot\mathbf{v}_0+\mathbf{k} = \mathbf{k} = \mathbf{p}_0$$

So the position function is

$$\mathbf{p}(t) = \frac{1}{2}t^2\mathbf{a}+t\mathbf{v}_0+\mathbf{p}_0$$

In other words, the trajectory $\mathbf{p}(t)$ of a particle (i.e., its position at any time $t \geq 0$) is completely determined by its initial position, initial velocity, and the constant of acceleration. This is reasonable because if we know where we are starting, how fast and in which direction we are going initially, and we know how we are accelerating for all time, then we ought to be able to figure out the path we followed.

Let's look at an example. Suppose you have a mini-cannon sitting at the origin of a coordinate system and aimed at a 30° angle measured from the x-axis (see Figure 17.2). So in this coordinate system, $\mathbf{p}_0 = (0, 0, 0)$ (i.e., the initial position of a cannonball is at the origin), and the constant acceleration due to gravity is $\mathbf{a} = (0, -9.8, 0)\mathrm{m}/\mathrm{s}^2$ (i.e, acceleration due to gravity is 9.8 meters per second squared). In addition, suppose that from previous tests, we have determined that at the instant the cannon fires, the cannonball has an initial speed of 50 meters per second. Thus, the initial velocity is $\mathbf{v}_0 = 50(\cos 30°, \sin 30°, 0)\mathrm{m}/\mathrm{s} \approx (43.3, 25.0, 0)\mathrm{m}/\mathrm{s}$. (Remember, velocity is speed and direction so we multiply the speed by the unit direction vector $(\cos 30°, \sin 30°, 0)$.) Thus the trajectory of the cannonball is given by:

$$\mathbf{p}(t) = \frac{1}{2}t^2\mathbf{a}+t\mathbf{v}_0+\mathbf{p}_0$$

$$= \frac{1}{2}t^2(0, -9.8, 0)\mathrm{m}/\mathrm{s}^2 + t(43.3, 25.0, 0)\,\mathrm{m}/\mathrm{s}$$

If we plot this in the xy-plane (z-coordinate is always 0), we get Figure 17.2, which is the trajectory we would expect with gravity.

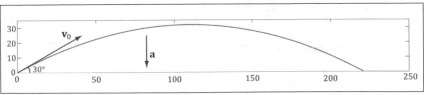

Figure 17.2: The path the particle follows in the xy-plane over time (the time dimension is not shown), given the initial position and velocity, and undergoing constant acceleration due to gravity.

Note: You can also choose not to use the function derived above. If you already know the trajectory function $\mathbf{p}(t)$ you want your particles to take, then you can just program it directly. For example, if you want your particles to follow an elliptical trajectory, then you can just use the parametric equations of an ellipse for $\mathbf{p}(t)$.

17.3 Randomness

In a particle system, we want the particles to behave similarly, but not exactly the same; in other words, we want to add some randomness to the system. For example, if we are modeling raindrops, we do not want all the raindrops to fall in exactly the same way; we want them to fall from different positions, at slightly different angles, and at slightly different speeds. To facilitate randomness functionality required for particle systems, we use the RandF and RandUnitVec3 functions implemented in *d3dUtil.h/.cpp*:

```
// Returns random float in [0, 1).
D3DX10INLINE float RandF()
{
    return (float)(rand()) / (float)RAND_MAX;
}


// Returns random float in [a, b).
D3DX10INLINE float RandF(float a, float b)
{
    return a + RandF()*(b-a);
}


// Returns random vector on the unit sphere.
D3DX10INLINE D3DXVECTOR3 RandUnitVec3()
{
    D3DXVECTOR3 v(RandF(-1.0f, 1.0f),
                  RandF(-1.0f, 1.0f),
                  RandF(-1.0f, 1.0f));
    D3DXVec3Normalize(&v, &v);
    return v;
}
```

The above functions work for C++ code, but we will also need random numbers in shader code. Generating random numbers in a shader is trickier since we do not have a shader random number generator. So what we do is create a 1D texture with four floating-point components (DXGI_FORMAT_R32G32B32A32_FLOAT). We fill the texture with random 4D vectors with coordinates in the interval [1, –1]. The texture will be sampled with the wrap address mode so that we can use unbounded texture coordinates outside the interval [0, 1]. The shader code will then sample this texture to get a random number. There are different ways to sample the random texture. If each particle has a different x-coordinate, we could use the x-coordinate as a texture coordinate to get a random number. However, this will not work very well if many of the particles have the same *x*-coordinate, as then they would all sample the same value in the texture, which would not be very random. Another approach is to use the current game time value as a texture coordinate. This way, particles generated at different times would get different random values. However, this means particles generated at the same time will have the same values. This can be a problem if the particle system needs to emit several particles at once. When generating many particles at the same time, we can add a different texture coordinate offset value to the game time so that we sample different points on the texture map, and hence get different random values. For example, if we were looping 20 times to create 20 particles, we could use the loop index (appropriately scaled) to offset the texture coordinate used to sample the random texture. This way, we would get 20 different random values.

The following code shows how to generate a random texture:

```
void TextureMgr::buildRandomTex()
{
    //
    // Create the random data.
    //
    D3DXVECTOR4 randomValues[1024];

    for(int i = 0; i < 1024; ++i)
    {
        randomValues[i].x = RandF(-1.0f, 1.0f);
        randomValues[i].y = RandF(-1.0f, 1.0f);
        randomValues[i].z = RandF(-1.0f, 1.0f);
        randomValues[i].w = RandF(-1.0f, 1.0f);
    }

    D3D10_SUBRESOURCE_DATA initData;
    initData.pSysMem = randomValues;
    initData.SysMemPitch = 1024*sizeof(D3DXVECTOR4);
    initData.SysMemSlicePitch = 1024*sizeof(D3DXVECTOR4);
    //
    // Create the texture.
    //
    D3D10_TEXTURE1D_DESC texDesc;
    texDesc.Width = 1024;
    texDesc.MipLevels = 1;
    texDesc.Format = DXGI_FORMAT_R32G32B32A32_FLOAT;
    texDesc.Usage = D3D10_USAGE_IMMUTABLE;
    texDesc.BindFlags = D3D10_BIND_SHADER_RESOURCE;
    texDesc.CPUAccessFlags = 0;
    texDesc.MiscFlags = 0;
    texDesc.ArraySize = 1;

    ID3D10Texture1D* randomTex = 0;
    HR(md3dDevice->CreateTexture1D(&texDesc, &initData, &randomTex));
    //
    // Create the resource view.
```

```
//
D3D10_SHADER_RESOURCE_VIEW_DESC viewDesc;
viewDesc.Format = texDesc.Format;
viewDesc.ViewDimension = D3D10_SRV_DIMENSION_TEXTURE1D;
viewDesc.Texture1D.MipLevels = texDesc.MipLevels;
viewDesc.Texture1D.MostDetailedMip = 0;

HR(md3dDevice->CreateShaderResourceView(randomTex,
                &viewDesc, &mRandomTexRV));

ReleaseCOM(randomTex);
}
```

Note that for a random texture, we only need one mipmap level. To sample a texture with only one mipmap, we use the `SampleLevel` intrinsic function. This function allows us to explicitly specify the mipmap level we want to sample. The first parameter to this function is the sampler, the second parameter is the texture coordinates (only one for a 1D texture), and the third parameter is the mipmap level (which should be 0 in the case of a texture with only one mipmap level).

The following shader function is used to get a random vector on the unit sphere:

```
float3 RandUnitVec3(float offset)
{
    // Use game time plus offset to sample random texture.
    float u = (gGameTime + offset);

    // coordinates in [-1,1]
    float3 v = gRandomTex.SampleLevel(gTriLinearSam, u, 0);

    // project onto unit sphere
    return normalize(v);
}
```

17.4 **Blending and Particle Systems**

Particle systems are usually drawn with some form of blending. For effects like fire and magic spells, we want the color intensity to brighten at the location of the particles. For this effect, additive blending works well. That is, we just add the source and destination colors together. However, particles are also typically transparent; therefore, we must scale the source particle color by its opacity; that is, we use the blend parameters:

```
SrcBlend = SRC_ALPHA;
DestBlend = ONE;
BlendOp = ADD;
```

This gives the blending equation:

$$\mathbf{C} = a_s \mathbf{C}_{src} + \mathbf{C}_{dst}$$

In other words, the amount of color the source particle contributes to the sum is determined by its opacity: The more opaque the particle is, the more color it contributes. An alternative approach is to premultiply the texture with its opacity (described by the alpha channel) so that the texture color is diluted based on its opacity. Then we use the diluted texture. In this case, we can use the blend parameters:

```
SrcBlend = ONE;
DestBlend = ONE;
BlendOp = ADD;
```

This is because we essentially precomputed $a_s\mathbf{C}_{src}$ and baked it directly into the texture data.

Additive blending also has the nice effect of brightening up areas proportional to the particle concentration there (due to additive accumulation of the colors); thus, areas where the concentration is high appear extra bright, which is usually what we want (see Figure 17.3).

Figure 17.3: With additive blending, the intensity is greater near the source point where more particles are overlapping and being added together. As the particles spread out, the intensity weakens because there are fewer particles overlapping and being added together.

For things like smoke, additive blending does not work because adding the colors of a bunch of overlapping smoke particles would eventually brighten up the smoke so that it is no longer dark. Blending with the subtraction operator (D3D10_BLEND_OP_REV_SUBTRACT) would work better for smoke, where the smoke particles would subtract color from the destination. In this way, higher concentrations of smoke particles would result in blacker color, giving the illusion of thick smoke, whereas lower concentrations of smoke particles would result in a mild tint, giving the illusion of thin smoke. However, while this works well for black smoke, it does not work well for light gray smoke, or steam. Another possibility for smoke is to use transparency blending, where we just think of smoke particles as semi-transparent objects, and use transparency blending to render them. The main problem with transparency blending is sorting the particles in a system in back-to-front order with respect to the eye. This can be expensive and impractical. Due to the random nature of particle systems, this rule can sometimes be broken without noticeable rendering errors. Note that if many particle systems are in a scene, the systems should still be sorted in back-to-front order; we just do not sort the particles of a system relative to each other. Also note that when using blending, the discussions in §8.5.4 and §8.5.5 apply.

17.5 **Stream Output**

We know that the GPU can write to textures. For example, the GPU handles writing to the depth/stencil buffer, and also the back buffer. A new feature in Direct3D 10 is the stream output (SO) stage. The SO stage allows the GPU to actually write geometry (in the form of a vertex list) to a vertex buffer V bound to the SO stage of the pipeline. Specifically, the vertices output from the geometry shader are written (or streamed out) to V. The geometry in V can then be drawn later. Figure 17.4 illustrates the idea. Stream output will play an important role in our particle system framework.

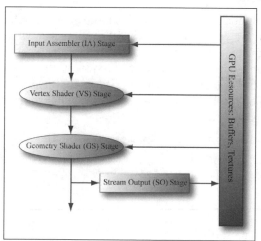

Figure 17.4: Primitives are pumped through the pipeline. The geometry shader outputs primitives that are streamed out to vertex buffers in GPU memory.

17.5.1 **Creating a Geometry Shader for Stream Output**

When using stream output, the geometry shader must be created specially. The following code shows how this is done in an effect file:

```
GeometryShader gsStreamOut = ConstructGSWithSO(
    CompileShader( gs_4_0, GS() ),
    "POSITION.xyz; VELOCITY.xyz; SIZE.xy; AGE.x; TYPE.x");

technique10 SOTech
{
```

```
        pass P0
        {
            SetVertexShader( CompileShader( vs_4_0, VS() ) );
            SetGeometryShader( gsStreamOut );
            SetPixelShader( CompileShader( ps_4_0, PS() ));
        }
    }
```

The first parameter of ConstructGSWithSO is just the compiled geometry shader. The second parameter is a string that describes the format of the vertices being streamed out (i.e., the format of the vertices the geometry shader outputs). In the above example, the vertex format is:

```
struct Vertex
{
    float3 initialPosW : POSITION;
    float3 initialVelW : VELOCITY;
    float2 sizeW       : SIZE;
    float  age         : AGE;
    uint   type        : TYPE;
};
```

17.5.2 **Stream Output Only**

When using stream output under normal conditions, the geometry shader output is streamed out to the vertex buffer *and* still continues down to the next stage of the rendering pipeline (rasterization). If you want a rendering technique that only streams out data, and does not render it, then the pixel shader and depth stencil buffer must be disabled. (Disabling the pixel shader and depth/stencil buffer disables rasterization.) The following technique shows how this is done:

```
DepthStencilState DisableDepth
{
    DepthEnable = FALSE;
    DepthWriteMask = ZERO;
};

GeometryShader gsStreamOut = ConstructGSWithSO(
    CompileShader( gs_4_0, StreamOutGS() ),
    "POSITION.xyz; VELOCITY.xyz; SIZE.xy; AGE.x; TYPE.x" );

technique10 StreamOutTech
{
    pass P0
    {
        SetVertexShader( CompileShader( vs_4_0, StreamOutVS() ) );
        SetGeometryShader( gsStreamOut );

        // disable pixel shader for stream output only
        SetPixelShader(NULL);
```

```
        // we must also disable the depth buffer for stream output only
        SetDepthStencilState( DisableDepth, 0 );
    }
}
```

In our particle system, we will use a stream output-only technique. This technique will be used solely to create and destroy particles (i.e., update the particle system). Every frame:

1. The current particle list will be drawn with stream output only. This does not render any particles to the screen since the rasterization unit is disabled.

2. The geometry shader of this pass will create/destroy particles based on various conditions that vary from particle system to particle system.

3. The updated particle list will be streamed out to a vertex buffer.

The application will then draw the updated particle list for that frame using a different rendering technique. The main reason for using two techniques is that the geometry shaders just do different things. For the stream output-only technique, the geometry shader inputs particles, updates them, and outputs particles. For the drawing technique, the geometry shader is tasked with expanding the point into a quad that faces the camera. As the geometry shaders do not even output the same type of primitives, we need two geometry shaders.

To summarize, we need two techniques for rendering our particle systems on the GPU:

■ A stream output-only technique used to update the particle system.

■ A rendering technique used to draw the particle system.

In previous Direct3D versions, the update step would have been performed on the CPU.

Note: Particle physics could also be incrementally updated in the stream output-only pass. However, in our setup, we have an explicit position function **p**(t). So we do not need to incrementally update the position/velocity of the particle in the stream output-only pass. The ParticlesGS SDK sample does use the stream output-only pass for updating physics, however, because it uses a different physics model.

17.5.3 **Creating a Vertex Buffer for Stream Output**

In order to bind a vertex buffer to the SO stage so that the GPU can write vertices to it, it must be created with the D3D10_BIND_STREAM_OUTPUT bind flag. Generally, a vertex buffer used as a stream output target will also be used as an input into the pipeline later (i.e., it will be bound to the IA stage so that the contents can be drawn). Therefore, we must also specify the

D3D10_BIND_VERTEX_BUFFER bind flag. The following code fragment shows an example of creating a vertex buffer for stream output usage:

```
D3D10_BUFFER_DESC vbd;
vbd.Usage = D3D10_USAGE_DEFAULT;
vbd.ByteWidth = sizeof(Vertex) * MAX_VERTICES;
vbd.BindFlags = D3D10_BIND_VERTEX_BUFFER | D3D10_BIND_STREAM_OUTPUT;
vbd.CPUAccessFlags = 0;
vbd.MiscFlags = 0;

HR(md3dDevice->CreateBuffer(&vbd, 0, &mStreamOutVB));
```

Note that the buffer memory is left uninitialized. This is because the GPU will be writing the vertex data to it. Also note that the buffer has a finite size, so care should be taken not to stream out so many vertices that the maximum is exceeded.

17.5.4 Binding to the SO Stage

A vertex buffer created with the D3D10_BIND_STREAM_OUTPUT bind flag can be bound to the SO stage of the pipeline for writing with the following method:

```
void ID3D10Device::SOSetTargets(
    UINT NumBuffers,
    ID3D10Buffer *const *ppSOTargets,
    const UINT *pOffsets);
```

- NumBuffers: The number of vertex buffers to bind to the SO stage as a target. The maximum is four.
- ppSOTargets: An array of vertex buffers to bind to the SO stage.
- pOffsets: An array of offsets, one for each vertex buffer, indicating the start position the SO stage should begin writing vertices to.

Note: There are four output slots for stream output. If less than four buffers are bound to the SO stage, the other slots are set to null. For example, if you only bind to slot 0 (the first slot), then slots 1, 2, and 3 are set to null.

17.5.5 Unbinding from the Stream Output Stage

After we have streamed out vertices to a vertex buffer, we may want to draw the primitives those vertices define. However, a vertex buffer cannot be bound to the SO stage and the IA stage at the same time. To unbind a vertex buffer from the SO stage, we just need to bind a different buffer to the SO stage in its place (which can be null). The following code unbinds a vertex buffer from slot 0 by binding a null buffer:

```
ID3D10Buffer* bufferArray[1] = {0};
md3dDevice->SOSetTargets(1, bufferArray, &offset);
```

17.5.6 **Auto Draw**

The geometry streamed out to a vertex buffer can be variable. So how many vertices do we draw? Fortunately, Direct3D keeps track of the count internally, and we can use the ID3D10Device::DrawAuto method to draw the geometry written to a vertex buffer with SO:

```
void ID3D10Device::DrawAuto();
```

Remarks:

- Before calling DrawAuto, we must first bind the vertex buffer (which was used as a stream output target) to input slot 0 of the IA stage. The DrawAuto method should only be used when a vertex buffer with the D3D10_BIND_STREAM_OUTPUT bind flag is bound to input slot 0 of the IA stage.

- We must still specify the vertex input layout of the vertices in the stream output vertex buffer when drawing with DrawAuto.

- DrawAuto does not use indices, since the geometry shader only outputs entire primitives defined by vertex lists.

17.5.7 **Ping-Ponging Vertex Buffers**

As already stated, a vertex buffer cannot be bound to the SO stage and the IA stage at the same time. Therefore, a ping-pong scheme is used. When drawing with stream output, we use two vertex buffers. One will serve as the input buffer, and the other will serve as the output buffer. On the next rendering frame, the roles of the two buffers are reversed. The buffer just streamed to becomes the new input buffer, and the old input buffer becomes the new stream output target. The following table shows three iterations using vertex buffers V_0 and V_1.

	Input Vertex Buffer Bound to IA Stage	Output Vertex Buffer Bound to SO Stage
Frame *i*	V_0	V_1
Frame *i* + 1	V_1	V_0
Frame *i* + 2	V_0	V_1

17.6 **GPU-Based Particle System**

Particle systems generally emit and destroy particles over time. The seemingly natural way to do this would be to use a dynamic vertex buffer and keep track of spawning and killing particles on the CPU. Then the vertex buffer would be filled with the currently living particles and drawn. However, we now know from the previous section that a separate stream output-only pass can handle this spawn/kill update cycle completely on the

GPU. The motivation for this is efficiency — there is some overhead whenever the CPU needs to upload data to the GPU; furthermore, it moves work from the CPU over to the GPU, which frees the CPU for other tasks like AI or physics. In this section, we explain the general details of our particle system framework.

17.6.1 Particle Effects

The specific details on how a particular particle system behaves are implemented in the effect file. That is, we will have a different (but similar) effect file for each particle system (e.g., rain, fire, smoke, etc.). The details of how particles are emitted, destroyed, and drawn are all scripted in the corresponding effect file since they vary from system to system. Examples:

■ We might destroy a rain particle when it hits the ground, whereas a fire particle would be destroyed after a few seconds.

■ A smoke particle may fade with time, whereas a rain particle would not. Likewise, the size of a smoke particle may expand with time, whereas a rain particle would not.

■ Line primitives generally work well for modeling rain, whereas a billboard quad would be used for fire/smoke particles. By using different effects for different particle systems, we can have the geometry shader expand points to lines for rain, and points to quads for fire/smoke.

■ The initial positions and velocities of rain and smoke particles would clearly be different.

To reiterate, these particle system-specific details can be implemented in the effect files because in our system the shader code handles the creating, destroying, and updating of particles. This design is quite convenient because to add a new particle system, we just need to script a new effect file describing its behavior.

17.6.2 The Particle System Class

The class shown below handles the C++-related code for creating, updating, and drawing a particle system. This code is general and will apply to all the particle systems we create.

```
class PSystem
{
public:

    PSystem();
    ~PSystem();

    // Time elapsed since the system was reset.
    float getAge()const;
```

```
                void setEyePos(const D3DXVECTOR3& eyePosW);
                void setEmitPos(const D3DXVECTOR3& emitPosW);
                void setEmitDir(const D3DXVECTOR3& emitDirW);

                void init(ID3D10Device* device, ID3D10Effect* FX,
                ID3D10ShaderResourceView* texArrayRV, UINT maxParticles);

                void reset();
                void update(float dt, float gameTime);
                void draw();

        private:
                void buildVB();

                PSystem(const PSystem& rhs);
                PSystem& operator=(const PSystem& rhs);

        private:

                UINT mMaxParticles;
                bool mFirstRun;

                float mGameTime;
                float mTimeStep;
                float mAge;

                D3DXVECTOR4 mEyePosW;
                D3DXVECTOR4 mEmitPosW;
                D3DXVECTOR4 mEmitDirW;

                ID3D10Device* md3dDevice;
                ID3D10Buffer* mInitVB;
                ID3D10Buffer* mDrawVB;
                ID3D10Buffer* mStreamOutVB;

                ID3D10ShaderResourceView* mTexArrayRV;
                ID3D10ShaderResourceView* mRandomTexRV;

                ID3D10EffectTechnique* mStreamOutTech;
                ID3D10EffectTechnique* mDrawTech;
                ID3D10EffectMatrixVariable* mfxViewProjVar;
                ID3D10EffectScalarVariable* mfxGameTimeVar;
                ID3D10EffectScalarVariable* mfxTimeStepVar;
                ID3D10EffectVectorVariable* mfxEyePosVar;
                ID3D10EffectVectorVariable* mfxEmitPosVar;
                ID3D10EffectVectorVariable* mfxEmitDirVar;
                ID3D10EffectShaderResourceVariable* mfxTexArrayVar;
                ID3D10EffectShaderResourceVariable* mfxRandomTexVar;
        };
```

Except for the draw method, the implementations to the particle system class methods are quite routine by now (getting effect handles, creating vertex buffers, etc.); therefore, we do not show them in the book (see the corresponding chapter source code).

Note: The particle system uses a texture array for texturing the particles. The idea is that we might not want all the particles to look exactly the same. For example, to implement a smoke particle system, we might want to use several smoke textures to add some variety; the primitive ID could be used in the pixel shader to alternate between the smoke textures in the texture array.

17.6.3 **Emitter Particles**

Because the geometry shader is responsible for creating/destroying particles, we need to have special emitter particles. Emitter particles may or may not be drawn. For example, if you want your emitter particles to be invisible, then you just need the particle drawing geometry shader to not output them. Emitter particles behave differently than other particles in the system in that they can spawn other particles. For example, an emitter particle may keep track of how much time has passed, and when that time reaches a certain point, it emits a new particle. In this way, new particles are spawned over time. We use the `type` member of the `ParticleVertex` structure to indicate an emitter particle. Moreover, by restricting which particles are allowed to emit other particles, it gives us some control over how particles are emitted. For example, by having only one emitter particle, it is easy to control how many particles will get created per frame. The stream-only geometry shader should always output at least one emitter particle, for if the particle system loses all of its emitters, it effectively dies; however, for some particle systems this may be the desired result.

The particle system we demo in this book only uses one emitter particle for the life of the particle system. However, the particle system framework could be extended to use more if needed. Moreover, other particles can also emit particles. For example, the SDK's ParticlesGS demo has a launcher particle (an invisible particle that spawns shell particles) and shell particles (unexploded fireworks that explode into new ember particles after some time, and some of these embers also explode into new secondary ember particles to create secondary explosions). In this sense, the emitter particle can emit other emitter particles. Exercise 1 asks you to explore this.

17.6.4 **The Initialization Vertex Buffer**

In our particle system, we have a special initialization vertex buffer. This vertex buffer contains only a single emitter particle. We draw this vertex buffer first to kick off the particle system. This emitter particle will then start spawning other particles in subsequent frames. Note that the initialization vertex buffer is drawn only once (except when the system is reset).

After the particle system has been initialized with a single emitter particle, we use the two stream output vertex buffers in a ping-pong fashion.

The initialization vertex buffer is also useful if we need to restart the system from the beginning. We can use this code to restart the particle system:

```
void PSystem::reset()
{
    mFirstRun = true;
    mAge      = 0.0f;
}
```

Setting mFirstRun to true instructs the particle system to draw the initialization vertex buffer on the next draw call, thereby restarting the particle system with a single emitter particle.

17.6.5 The Update/Draw Method

Recall that we need two techniques for rendering our particle systems on the GPU:

- A stream output-only technique used to update the particle system.
- A rendering technique used to draw the particle system.

The following code does this, in addition to handling the ping-pong scheme of the two vertex buffers:

```
void PSystem::draw(const D3DXMATRIX& viewProj)
{
    D3DXMATRIX V = GetCamera().view();
    D3DXMATRIX P = GetCamera().proj();

    //
    // Set constants.
    //
    mfxViewProjVar->SetMatrix((float*)&viewProj);
    mfxGameTimeVar->SetFloat(mGameTime);
    mfxTimeStepVar->SetFloat(mTimeStep);
    mfxEyePosVar->SetFloatVector((float*)&mEyePosW);
    mfxEmitPosVar->SetFloatVector((float*)&mEmitPosW);
    mfxEmitDirVar->SetFloatVector((float*)&mEmitDirW);
    mfxTexArrayVar->SetResource(mTexArrayRV);
    mfxRandomTexVar->SetResource(mRandomTexRV);
    //
    // Set IA stage.
    //
    md3dDevice->IASetInputLayout(mVertexLayout);
    md3dDevice->IASetPrimitiveTopology
                (D3D10_PRIMITIVE_TOPOLOGY_POINTLIST);

    UINT stride = sizeof(Particle);
    UINT offset = 0;
```

```
    // On the first pass, use the initialization VB. Otherwise, use
    // the VB that contains the current particle list.
    if( mFirstRun )
    md3dDevice->IASetVertexBuffers(0, 1, &mInitVB, &stride, &offset);
    else
    md3dDevice->IASetVertexBuffers(0, 1, &mDrawVB, &stride, &offset);


    //
    // Draw the current particle list using stream output only to update
    // them. The updated vertices are streamed out to the target VB.
    //
    md3dDevice->SOSetTargets(1, &mStreamOutVB, &offset);


    D3D10_TECHNIQUE_DESC techDesc;
    mStreamOutTech->GetDesc( &techDesc );
    for(UINT p = 0; p < techDesc.Passes; ++p)
    {
        mStreamOutTech->GetPassByIndex( p )->Apply(0);

        if( mFirstRun )
        {
            md3dDevice->Draw(1, 0);
            mFirstRun = false;
        }
        else
        {
            md3dDevice->DrawAuto();
        }
    }

    // done streaming out--unbind the vertex buffer
    ID3D10Buffer* bufferArray[1] = {0};
    md3dDevice->SOSetTargets(1, bufferArray, &offset);

    // ping-pong the vertex buffers
    std::swap(mDrawVB, mStreamOutVB);


    //
    // Draw the updated particle system we just streamed out.
    //
    md3dDevice->IASetVertexBuffers(0, 1, &mDrawVB, &stride, &offset);

    mDrawTech->GetDesc( &techDesc );
    for(UINT p = 0; p < techDesc.Passes; ++p)
    {
        mDrawTech->GetPassByIndex( p )->Apply(0);

        md3dDevice->DrawAuto();
    }
}
```

17.7 **Fire**

Below is the effect file (*fire.fx*) for rendering a fire particle system. It consists of two techniques:

- A stream output-only technique used to update the particle system.
- A rendering technique used to draw the particle system.

The logic programmed into these two techniques will generally vary from particle system to particle system, as the destroy/spawn/rendering rules will be different. The fire particles are emitted at the emit position, but are given random initial velocities to spread the flames out to create a fireball.

```
//***************************************************
// GLOBALS                                         *
//***************************************************

cbuffer cbPerFrame
{
    float4 gEyePosW;

    // for when the emit position/direction is varying
    float4 gEmitPosW;
    float4 gEmitDirW;

    float gGameTime;
    float gTimeStep;
    float4x4 gViewProj;
};

cbuffer cbFixed
{
    // Net constant used to accelerate the particles.
    float3 gAccelW = {0.0f, 7.8f, 0.0f};

    // Texture coordinates used to stretch texture over quad
    // when we expand point particle into a quad.
    float2 gQuadTexC[4] =
    {
        float2(0.0f, 1.0f),
        float2(1.0f, 1.0f),
        float2(0.0f, 0.0f),
        float2(1.0f, 0.0f)
    };
};

// Array of textures for texturing the particles.
Texture2DArray gTexArray;

// Random texture used to generate random numbers in shaders.
Texture1D gRandomTex;
```

```
SamplerState gTriLinearSam
{
    Filter = MIN_MAG_MIP_LINEAR;
    AddressU = WRAP;
    AddressV = WRAP;
};

DepthStencilState DisableDepth
{
    DepthEnable = FALSE;
    DepthWriteMask = ZERO;
};

DepthStencilState NoDepthWrites
{
    DepthEnable = TRUE;
    DepthWriteMask = ZERO;
};

BlendState AdditiveBlending
{
    AlphaToCoverageEnable = FALSE;
    BlendEnable[0] = TRUE;
    SrcBlend = SRC_ALPHA;
    DestBlend = ONE;
    BlendOp = ADD;
    SrcBlendAlpha = ZERO;
    DestBlendAlpha = ZERO;
    BlendOpAlpha = ADD;
    RenderTargetWriteMask[0] = 0x0F;
};

//***********************************************
// HELPER FUNCTIONS                             *
//***********************************************
float3 RandUnitVec3(float offset)
{
        // Use game time plus offset to sample random texture.
        float u = (gGameTime + offset);

        // coordinates in [-1,1]
        float3 v = gRandomTex.SampleLevel(gTriLinearSam, u, 0);

        // project onto unit sphere
        return normalize(v);
}


//***********************************************
// STREAM OUTPUT TECH                           *
//***********************************************

#define PT_EMITTER 0
#define PT_FLARE 1
```

```
struct Particle
{
    float3 initialPosW : POSITION;
    float3 initialVelW : VELOCITY;
    float2 sizeW       : SIZE;
    float age          : AGE;
    uint type          : TYPE;
};

Particle StreamOutVS(Particle vIn)
{
    return vIn;
}

// The stream output GS is just responsible for emitting
// new particles and destroying old particles. The logic
// programmed here will generally vary from particle system
// to particle system, as the destroy/spawn rules will be
// different.
[maxvertexcount(2)]
void StreamOutGS(point Particle gIn[1],
                 inout PointStream<Particle> ptStream)
{
    gIn[0].age += gTimeStep;

    if( gIn[0].type == PT_EMITTER )
    {
        // time to emit a new particle?
        if( gIn[0].age > 0.005f )
        {
            float3 vRandom = RandUnitVec3(0.0f);
            vRandom.x *= 0.5f;
            vRandom.z *= 0.5f;

            Particle p;
            p.initialPosW = gEmitPosW.xyz;
            p.initialVelW = 4.0f*vRandom;
            p.sizeW       = float2(3.0f, 3.0f);
            p.age         = 0.0f;
            p.type        = PT_FLARE;

            ptStream.Append(p);

            // reset the time to emit
            gIn[0].age = 0.0f;
        }

        // always keep emitters
        ptStream.Append(gIn[0]);
    }
    else
    {
```

```
            // Specify conditions to keep particle; this may vary
            // from system to system.
            if( gIn[0].age <= 1.0f )
                ptStream.Append(gIn[0]);
        }
    }

GeometryShader gsStreamOut = ConstructGSWithSO(
    CompileShader( gs_4_0, StreamOutGS() ),
    "POSITION.xyz; VELOCITY.xyz; SIZE.xy; AGE.x; TYPE.x" );

technique10 StreamOutTech
{
    pass P0
    {
        SetVertexShader( CompileShader( vs_4_0, StreamOutVS() ) );
        SetGeometryShader( gsStreamOut );

        // disable pixel shader for stream output-only
        SetPixelShader(NULL);

        // we must also disable the depth buffer for stream output-only
        SetDepthStencilState( DisableDepth, 0 );
    }
}

//************************************************
// DRAW TECH                                     *
//************************************************

struct VS_OUT
{
    float3 posW  : POSITION;
    float2 sizeW : SIZE;
    float4 color : COLOR;
    uint   type  : TYPE;
};

VS_OUT DrawVS(Particle vIn)
{
    VS_OUT vOut;

    float t = vIn.age;

    // constant acceleration equation
    vOut.posW = 0.5f*t*t*gAccelW + t*vIn.initialVelW + vIn.initialPosW;

    // fade color with time
    float opacity = 1.0f - smoothstep(0.0f, 1.0f, t/1.0f);
    vOut.color = float4(1.0f, 1.0f, 1.0f, opacity);

    vOut.sizeW = vIn.sizeW;
    vOut.type  = vIn.type;
```

```
    return vOut;
}

struct GS_OUT
{
    float4 posH  : SV_Position;
    float4 color : COLOR;
    float2 texC  : TEXCOORD;
};

// The draw GS just expands points into camera facing quads.
[maxvertexcount(4)]
void DrawGS(point VS_OUT gIn[1],
           inout TriangleStream<GS_OUT> triStream)
{
    // do not draw emitter particles.
    if( gIn[0].type != PT_EMITTER )
    {
        //
        // Compute world matrix so that billboard faces the camera.
        //
        float3 look  = normalize(gEyePosW.xyz - gIn[0].posW);
        float3 right = normalize(cross(float3(0,1,0), look));
        float3 up    = cross(look, right);

        float4x4 W;
        W[0] = float4(right,        0.0f);
        W[1] = float4(up,           0.0f);
        W[2] = float4(look,         0.0f);
        W[3] = float4(gIn[0].posW, 1.0f);

        float4x4 WVP = mul(W, gViewProj);

        //
        // Compute 4 triangle strip vertices (quad) in local space.
        // The quad faces down the +z-axis in local space.
        //
        float halfWidth  = 0.5f*gIn[0].sizeW.x;
        float halfHeight = 0.5f*gIn[0].sizeW.y;

        float4 v[4];
        v[0] = float4(-halfWidth, -halfHeight, 0.0f, 1.0f);
        v[1] = float4(+halfWidth, -halfHeight, 0.0f, 1.0f);
        v[2] = float4(-halfWidth, +halfHeight, 0.0f, 1.0f);
        v[3] = float4(+halfWidth, +halfHeight, 0.0f, 1.0f);

        //
        // Transform quad vertices to world space and output
        // them as a triangle strip.
        //
        GS_OUT gOut;
        [unroll]
```

```
        for(int i = 0; i < 4; ++i)
        {
            gOut.posH  = mul(v[i], WVP);
            gOut.texC  = gQuadTexC[i];
            gOut.color = gIn[0].color;
            triStream.Append(gOut);
        }
    }
}


float4 DrawPS(GS_OUT pIn) : SV_TARGET
{
    return gTexArray.Sample(gTriLinearSam, float3(pIn.texC, 0))*pIn.color;
}


technique10 DrawTech
{
    pass P0
    {
        SetVertexShader(   CompileShader( vs_4_0, DrawVS() ) );
        SetGeometryShader( CompileShader( gs_4_0, DrawGS() ) );
        SetPixelShader(    CompileShader( ps_4_0, DrawPS() ) );

        SetBlendState(AdditiveBlending, float4(0.0f, 0.0f, 0.0f, 0.0f),
                      0xffffffff);
        SetDepthStencilState( NoDepthWrites, 0 );
    }
}
```

17.8 **Rain**

We also implement a rain particle system. The behavior of the rain particle system is specified by the rain effect file (*rain.fx*). It follows a similar pattern to *fire.fx*, but the destroy/spawn/rendering rules are different. For example, our raindrops accelerate downward at a slight angle, whereas the fire particles accelerated upward. Moreover, the rain particles are expanded into lines instead of quads (see Figure 17.5). The rain particles are emitted at random positions above the camera; the rain always "follows" the camera so that we do not have to emit rain particles all over the world. That is, just emitting rain particles near the camera is enough to give the illusion it is raining. Note that the rain system does not use any blending.

```
//*********************************************
// GLOBALS                                   *
//*********************************************

cbuffer cbPerFrame
{
    float4 gEyePosW;

    // for when the emit position/direction is varying
```

```
    float4 gEmitPosW;
    float4 gEmitDirW;

    float gGameTime;
    float gTimeStep;
    float4x4 gViewProj;
};

cbuffer cbFixed
{
    // Net constant used to accelerate the particles.
    float3 gAccelW = {-1.0f, -9.8f, 0.0f};

    // Texture coordinates used to stretch texture over quad
    // when we expand point particle into a quad.
    float2 gQuadTexC[4] =
    {
        float2(0.0f, 1.0f),
        float2(1.0f, 1.0f),
        float2(0.0f, 0.0f),
        float2(1.0f, 0.0f)
    };
};

// Array of textures for texturing the particles.
Texture2DArray gTexArray;

// Random texture used to generate random numbers in shaders.
Texture1D gRandomTex;

SamplerState gTriLinearSam
{
    Filter = MIN_MAG_MIP_LINEAR;
    AddressU = WRAP;
    AddressV = WRAP;
};

DepthStencilState DisableDepth
{
    DepthEnable = FALSE;
    DepthWriteMask = ZERO;
};

DepthStencilState NoDepthWrites
{
    DepthEnable = TRUE;
    DepthWriteMask = ZERO;
};


//*********************************************
// HELPER FUNCTIONS                           *
//*********************************************
```

```
float3 RandUnitVec3(float offset)
{
    // Use game time plus offset to sample random texture.
    float u = (gGameTime + offset);

    // coordinates in [-1,1]
    float3 v = gRandomTex.SampleLevel(gTriLinearSam, u, 0);

    // project onto unit sphere
    return normalize(v);
}

float3 RandVec3(float offset)
{
    // Use game time plus offset to sample random texture.
    float u = (gGameTime + offset);

    // coordinates in [-1,1]
    float3 v = gRandomTex.SampleLevel(gTriLinearSam, u, 0);

    return v;
}

//***********************************************
// STREAM OUTPUT TECH                           *
//***********************************************

#define PT_EMITTER 0
#define PT_FLARE 1

struct Particle
{
    float3 initialPosW : POSITION;
    float3 initialVelW : VELOCITY;
    float2 sizeW       : SIZE;
    float age          : AGE;
    uint type          : TYPE;
};

Particle StreamOutVS(Particle vIn)
{
    return vIn;
}

// The stream output GS is just responsible for emitting
// new particles and destroying old particles. The logic
// programmed here will generally vary from particle system
// to particle system, as the destroy/spawn rules will be
// different.
[maxvertexcount(6)]
void StreamOutGS(point Particle gIn[1],
                 inout PointStream<Particle> ptStream)
{
```

```
        gIn[0].age += gTimeStep;

    if( gIn[0].type == PT_EMITTER )
    {
        // time to emit a new particle?
        if( gIn[0].age > 0.001f )
        {
            for(int i = 0; i < 5; ++i)
            {
                // Spread raindrops out above the camera.
                float3 vRandom = 35.0f*RandVec3((float)i/5.0f);
                vRandom.y = 20.0f;

                Particle p;
                p.initialPosW = gEmitPosW.xyz + vRandom;
                p.initialVelW = float3(0.0f, 0.0f, 0.0f);
                p.sizeW       = float2(1.0f, 1.0f);
                p.age         = 0.0f;
                p.type        = PT_FLARE;

                ptStream.Append(p);
            }

            // reset the time to emit
            gIn[0].age = 0.0f;
        }

        // always keep emitters
        ptStream.Append(gIn[0]);
    }
    else
    {
        // Specify conditions to keep particle; this may vary from
        // system to system.
        if( gIn[0].age <= 4.0f )
            ptStream.Append(gIn[0]);
    }
}

GeometryShader gsStreamOut = ConstructGSWithSO(
    CompileShader( gs_4_0, StreamOutGS() ),
    "POSITION.xyz; VELOCITY.xyz; SIZE.xy; AGE.x; TYPE.x" );

technique10 StreamOutTech
{
    pass P0
    {
        SetVertexShader( CompileShader( vs_4_0, StreamOutVS() ) );
        SetGeometryShader( gsStreamOut );

        // disable pixel shader for stream output-only
        SetPixelShader(NULL);
```

```
            // we must also disable the depth buffer for stream output-only
            SetDepthStencilState( DisableDepth, 0 );
        }
    }

    //************************************************
    // DRAW TECH                                     *
    //************************************************

    struct VS_OUT
    {
        float3 posW  : POSITION;
        uint   type  : TYPE;
    };

    VS_OUT DrawVS(Particle vIn)
    {
        VS_OUT vOut;

        float t = vIn.age;

        // constant acceleration equation
        vOut.posW = 0.5f*t*t*gAccelW + t*vIn.initialVelW + vIn.initialPosW;

        vOut.type  = vIn.type;

        return vOut;
    }

    struct GS_OUT
    {
        float4 posH  : SV_Position;
        float2 texC  : TEXCOORD;
    };

    // The draw GS just expands points into lines.
    [maxvertexcount(2)]
    void DrawGS(point VS_OUT gIn[1],
                inout LineStream<GS_OUT> lineStream)
    {
        // do not draw emitter particles.
        if( gIn[0].type != PT_EMITTER )
        {
            // Slant line in acceleration direction.
            float3 p0 = gIn[0].posW;
            float3 p1 = gIn[0].posW + 0.07f*gAccelW;

            GS_OUT v0;
            v0.posH = mul(float4(p0, 1.0f), gViewProj);
            v0.texC = float2(0.0f, 0.0f);
            lineStream.Append(v0);

            GS_OUT v1;
```

```
            v1.posH = mul(float4(p1, 1.0f), gViewProj);
            v1.texC = float2(1.0f, 1.0f);
            lineStream.Append(v1);
        }
    }

    float4 DrawPS(GS_OUT pIn) : SV_TARGET
    {
        return gTexArray.Sample(gTriLinearSam, float3(pIn.texC, 0));
    }

    technique10 DrawTech
    {
        pass P0
        {
            SetVertexShader(   CompileShader( vs_4_0, DrawVS() ) );
            SetGeometryShader( CompileShader( gs_4_0, DrawGS() ) );
            SetPixelShader(    CompileShader( ps_4_0, DrawPS() ) );

            SetDepthStencilState( NoDepthWrites, 0 );
        }
    }
```

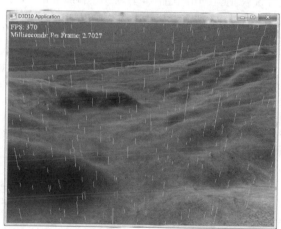

Figure 17.5: Screenshot of Particle System demo showing rain.

17.9 **Summary**

■ A particle system is a collection of particles (usually small) that all behave in a similar, yet somewhat random, manner. Particle systems can be utilized to simulate a wide range of phenomena such as fire, rain, smoke, explosions, droplets from sprinklers, and magic spell effects.

■ We model our particles by points, but then expand them into quads that face the camera in the geometry shader prior to rendering. This means that we get the efficiency of working with a point — a smaller memory footprint — and we only have to apply physics to one point vertex instead of four quad vertices, but furthermore, by later expanding the point into a quad we also get the ability to have different sized particles and to map textures onto them. Note that it is not necessary to expand a point into a quad. For example, lines can be used to model raindrops fairly well; we can use a different geometry to expand points to lines.

■ The trajectory of a particle undergoing constant acceleration is given by $\mathbf{p}(t) = \frac{1}{2}t^2\mathbf{a} + t\mathbf{v}_0 + \mathbf{p}_0$, where $\mathbf{a}$ is the constant acceleration vector, $\mathbf{v}_0$ is the initial velocity of the particle (i.e., the velocity at time $t = 0$), and $\mathbf{p}_0$ is the initial position of the particle (i.e., the position at time $t = 0$). With this equation, we can get the position of the particle at any time $t \geq 0$ by evaluating the function at t.

■ Use additive blending when you want the intensity of a particle system to be proportional with the particle density. Use transparency blending for transparent particles. Not sorting a transparent particle system in back-to-front order may or may not be a problem (i.e., the problems may or may not be noticeable). Commonly for particle systems, depth writes are disabled so that particles do not obscure each other. The depth test, however, is still enabled so that non-particle objects do obscure particles.

■ The stream output (SO) stage allows the GPU to write geometry (in the form of a vertex list) to a vertex buffer V bound to the SO stage of the pipeline. Specifically, the vertices output from the geometry shader are written (or streamed out) to V. The geometry in V can then be drawn later. We use this stream output feature to implement a particle system that runs completely on the GPU. To do this, we use two techniques:

  ■ A stream output-only technique used to update the particle system. In this rendering pass, the geometry shader spawns/destroys/updates particles based on various conditions that vary from particle system to particle system. The living particles are then streamed out to a vertex buffer.

  ■ A rendering technique used to draw the particle system. In this rendering pass, we draw the living particles that were streamed out.

17.10 **Exercises**

1. Implement an explosion particle system where the emitter emits n shell particles in random directions. After a brief time, each shell particle should then explode into m particles. Each shell need not explode at the exact same time — to add some variety you can give them different countdown times. Experiment with different n and m until you get good results. After the emitter spawns the shell particles, destroy it so that no more shells are emitted.

2. Implement a fountain particle system. The particles should originate from a source point and emit randomly through a cone into the air. Eventually gravity should make them fall back to the ground. Note: Give the particles a high enough initial velocity magnitude to initially overcome gravity.

Appendix A

Introduction to Windows Programming

To use the Direct3D API (application programming interface), it is necessary to create a Windows (Win32) application with a main window, upon which we will render our 3D scenes. This appendix serves as an introduction to writing Windows applications using the native Win32 API. Loosely, the Win32 API is a set of low-level functions and structures exposed to us in the C programming language that enables us to create Windows applications. For example, to define a window class, we fill out an instance of the Win32 API WNDCLASS structure; to create a window, we use the Win32 API CreateWindow function; to notify Windows to show a particular window, we use the Win32 API function ShowWindow.

Windows programming is a huge subject, and this appendix introduces only the amount necessary for us to use Direct3D. For readers interested in learning more about Windows programming with the Win32 API, the book *Programming Windows* by Charles Petzold, now in its fifth edition, is the standard text on the subject. Another invaluable resource when working with Microsoft technologies is the MSDN library, which is usually included with Microsoft's Visual Studio but can also be read online at www.msdn.microsoft.com. In general, if you come upon a Win32 function or structure that you would like to know more about, go to MSDN and search for that function or structure to see its full documentation. If we mention a Win32 function or structure in this appendix and do not elaborate on it, it is an implicit suggestion that the reader look up the function in MSDN.

Objectives:

- To learn and understand the event-driven programming model used in Windows programming.
- To learn the minimal code necessary to create a Windows application that is necessary to use Direct3D.

Note: To avoid confusion we will use a capital "W" to refer to Windows the OS, and we will use a lowercase "w" to refer to a particular window running in Windows.

A.1 Overview

As the name suggests, one of the primary themes of Windows programming is programming windows. Many of the components of a Windows application are windows, such as the main application window, menus, toolbars, scroll bars, buttons, and other dialog controls. Therefore, a Windows application typically consists of several windows. The next subsections provide a concise overview of Windows programming concepts we should be familiar with before beginning a more complete discussion.

A.1.1 Resources

In Windows, several applications can run concurrently. Therefore, hardware resources such as CPU cycles, memory, and even the monitor screen must be shared among multiple applications. In order to prevent chaos from ensuing due to several applications accessing/modifying resources without any organization, Windows applications do not have direct access to hardware. One of the main jobs of Windows is to manage the presently instantiated applications and handle the distribution of resources among them. Thus, in order for our application to do something that might affect another running application, it must go through Windows. For example, to display a window you must call the Win32 API function ShowWindow; you cannot write to video memory directly.

A.1.2 Events, the Message Queue, Messages, and the Message Loop

A Windows application follows an _event-driven programming model_. Typically a Windows application sits and waits[1] for something to happen — an _event_. An event can be generated in a number of ways; some common examples are keypresses, mouse clicks, and when a window is created, resized, moved, closed, minimized, maximized, or becomes visible.

When an event occurs, Windows sends a _message_ to the application the event occurred for, and adds the message to the application's _message queue_, which is simply a priority queue that stores messages for an application. The application constantly checks the message queue for messages in a _message loop_ and, when it receives one, it dispatches the message to the _window procedure_ of the particular window the message is for. (Remember, an application can contain several windows.) Every window has with it an associated function called a window procedure[2]. Window procedures are functions we implement that contain code to be executed in response to specific messages. For instance, we may want to destroy a window when the Escape key is pressed. In our window procedure we would write:

```
case WM_KEYDOWN:
    if( wParam == VK_ESCAPE )
        DestroyWindow(ghMainWnd);
    return 0;
```

The messages a window does not handle should be forwarded to the default window procedure, which then handles the message. The Win32 API supplies the default window procedure, which is called DefWindowProc.

To summarize, the user or an application does something to generate an event. The OS finds the application the event was targeted toward, and it sends that application a message in response. The message is then added to the application's message queue. The application is constantly checking its message queue for messages. When it receives a message, the application dispatches it to the window procedure associated with the window the message is targeted for. Finally, the window procedure executes instructions in response to the message.

---

1 We note that an application can perform idle processing; that is, perform a certain task when no events are occurring.
2 Every window has a window procedure, but several windows can share the same window procedure; therefore, we do not necessarily have to write a unique window procedure for each window. Two different windows would have different window procedures if we wanted them to respond to messages differently.

Figure A.1 summarizes the event-driven programming model.

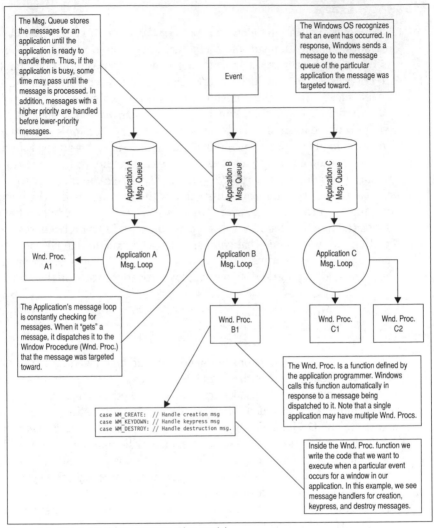

The Msg. Queue stores the messages for an application until the application is ready to handle them. Thus, if the application is busy, some time may pass until the message is processed. In addition, messages with a higher priority are handled before lower-priority messages.

The Windows OS recognizes that an event has occurred. In response, Windows sends a message to the message queue of the particular application the message was targeted toward.

Event

Application A Msg. Queue

Application B Msg. Queue

Application C Msg. Queue

Wnd. Proc. A1

Application A Msg. Loop

Application B Msg. Loop

Application C Msg. Loop

The Application's message loop is constantly checking for messages. When it "gets" a message, it dispatches it to the Window Procedure (Wnd. Proc.) that the message was targeted toward.

Wnd. Proc. B1

Wnd. Proc. C1

Wnd. Proc. C2

The Wnd. Proc. Is a function defined by the application programmer. Windows calls this function automatically in response to a message being dispatched to it. Note that a single application may have multiple Wnd. Procs.

```
case WM_CREATE:   // Handle creation msg
case WM_KEYDOWN:  // Handle keypress msg
case WM_DESTROY:  // Handle destruction msg.
```

Inside the Wnd. Proc. function we write the code that we want to execute when a particular event occurs for a window in our application. In this example, we see message handlers for creation, keypress, and destroy messages.

Figure A.1: The event-driven programming model.

A.1.3 **GUI**

Most Windows programs present a GUI (graphical user interface) that users can work from. A typical Windows application has one main window, a menu, toolbar, and perhaps some other controls. Figure A.2 shows and identifies some common GUI elements. For Direct3D game programming, we do not need a fancy GUI. In fact, all we need is a main window where the client area will be used to render our 3D worlds.

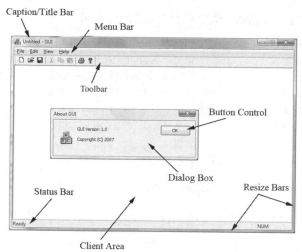

Caption/Title Bar

Menu Bar

Toolbar

About GUI

GUI Version 1.0

Copyright (C) 2007

OK

Button Control

Dialog Box

Resize Bars

Status Bar

Ready

NUM

Client Area

Figure A.2: A typical Windows application GUI. The client area is the entire large white rectangular space of the application. Typically, this area is where the user views most of the program output. When we program our Direct3D applications, we render our 3D scenes into the client area of a window.

A.1.4 **Unicode**

Essentially, Unicode (http://unicode.org/) uses 16-bit values to represent a character. This allows us to represent a larger character set to support international characters and other symbols. For Unicode in C++, we use the *wide-characters* type wchar_t. In 32- and 64-bit Windows, a wchar_t is 16 bits. When using wide characters, we must prefix a string literal with a capital L. For example:

```
const wchar_t* wcstrPtr = L"Hello, World!";
```

The L tells the compiler to treat the string literal as a string of wide characters (i.e., as wchar_t instead of char). The other important issue is that we need to use the wide-character versions of the string functions. For example, to get the length of a string we need to use wcslen instead of strlen, to copy a string we need to use wcscpy instead of strcpy, and to compare two strings we need to use wcscmp instead of strcmp. The wide-character versions of these functions work with wchar_t pointers instead of char pointers. The C++ standard library also provides a wide-character version of its string class: std::wstring. The Windows header file *WinNT.h* also defines:

```
typedef wchar_t WCHAR;    // wc, 16-bit UNICODE character
```

A.2 **Basic Windows Application**

Below is the code for a fully functional, yet simple, Windows program. Follow the code as best you can, and read the explanatory comments. The next section will explain the code a bit at a time. It is recommended that you create a project with your development tool, type the code in by hand, compile it, and execute it as an exercise. Note that for Visual C++, you must create a Win32 application project, *not* a Win32 console application project.

```cpp
//=======================================================================
// Win32Basic.cpp by Frank Luna (C) 2008 All Rights Reserved.
//
// Illustrates the minimal amount of the Win32 code needed for
// Direct3D programming.
//=======================================================================

// Include the Windows header file; this has all the Win32 API
// structures, types, and function declarations we need to program
// Windows.
#include <windows.h>

// The main window handle; this is used to identify a
// created window.
HWND ghMainWnd = 0;

// Wraps the code necessary to initialize a Windows
// application. Function returns true if initialization
// was successful; otherwise, it returns false.
bool InitWindowsApp(HINSTANCE instanceHandle, int show);

// Wraps the message loop code.
int  Run();

// The window procedure handles events our window receives.
LRESULT CALLBACK
WndProc(HWND hWnd, UINT msg, WPARAM wParam, LPARAM lParam);

// Windows equivalant to main()
int WINAPI
WinMain(HINSTANCE hInstance, HINSTANCE hPrevInstance,
    PSTR pCmdLine, int nShowCmd)
{
    // First call our wrapper function (InitWindowsApp) to create
    // and initialize the main application window, passing in the
    // hInstance and nShowCmd values as arguments.
    if(!InitWindowsApp(hInstance, nShowCmd))
    return 0;


    // Once our application has been created and initialized, we
    // enter the message loop. We stay in the message loop until
    // a WM_QUIT message is received, indicating the application
```

```
        // should be terminated.
        return Run();
}

bool InitWindowsApp(HINSTANCE instanceHandle, int show)
{
        // The first task to creating a window is to describe some of its
        // characteristics by filling out a WNDCLASS structure.
        WNDCLASS wc;

        wc.style         = CS_HREDRAW | CS_VREDRAW;
        wc.lpfnWndProc   = WndProc;
        wc.cbClsExtra    = 0;
        wc.cbWndExtra    = 0;
        wc.hInstance     = instanceHandle;
        wc.hIcon         = LoadIcon(0, IDI_APPLICATION);
        wc.hCursor       = LoadCursor(0, IDC_ARROW);
        wc.hbrBackground = (HBRUSH)GetStockObject(WHITE_BRUSH);
        wc.lpszMenuName  = 0;
        wc.lpszClassName = L"BasicWndClass";


        // Next, we register this WNDCLASS instance with Windows so
        // that we can create a window based on it.
        if(!RegisterClass(&wc))
        {
                MessageBox(0, L"RegisterClass FAILED", 0, 0);
                return false;
        }

        // With our WNDCLASS instance registered, we can create a
        // window with the CreateWindow function. This function
        // returns a handle to the window it creates (an HWND).
        // If the creation failed, the handle will have the value
        // of zero. A window handle is a way to refer to the window,
        // which is internally managed by Windows. Many of the Win32 API
        // functions that operate on windows require an HWND so that
        // they know what window to act on.

        ghMainWnd = CreateWindow(
                L"BasicWndClass",    // Registered WNDCLASS instance to use.
                L"Win32Basic",       // window title
                WS_OVERLAPPEDWINDOW, // style flags
                CW_USEDEFAULT,       // x-coordinate
                CW_USEDEFAULT,       // y-coordinate
                CW_USEDEFAULT,       // width
                CW_USEDEFAULT,       // height
                0,                   // parent window
                0,                   // menu handle
                instanceHandle,      // app instance
                0);                  // extra creation parameters

        if(ghMainWnd == 0)
```

```
    {
        MessageBox(0, L"CreateWindow FAILED", 0, 0);
        return false;
    }

    // Even though we just created a window, it is not initially
    // shown. Therefore, the final step is to show and update the
    // window we just created, which can be done with the following
    // two function calls. Observe that we pass the handle to the
    // window we want to show and update so that these functions know
    // which window to show and update.
    ShowWindow(ghMainWnd, show);
    UpdateWindow(ghMainWnd);

    return true;
}

int Run()
{
    MSG msg = {0};

    // Loop until we get a WM_QUIT message. The function
    // GetMessage will only return 0 (false) when a WM_QUIT message
    // is received, which effectively exits the loop. The function
    // returns -1 if there is an error. Also, note that GetMessage
    // puts the application thread to sleep until there is a
    // message.
    BOOL bRet = 1;
    while( (bRet = GetMessage(&msg, 0, 0, 0)) != 0 )
    {
        if(bRet == -1)
        {
            MessageBox(0, L"GetMessage FAILED", L"Error", MB_OK);
            break;
        }
        else
        {
            TranslateMessage(&msg);
            DispatchMessage(&msg);
        }
    }

    return (int)msg.wParam;
}

LRESULT CALLBACK
WndProc(HWND hWnd, UINT msg, WPARAM wParam, LPARAM lParam)
{
    // Handle some specific messages. Note that if we handle a
    // message, we should return 0.
    switch( msg )
    {
        // In the case the left mouse button was pressed,
```

```
            // then display a message box.
    case WM_LBUTTONDOWN:
        MessageBox(0, L"Hello, World", L"Hello", MB_OK);
        return 0;

        // In the case the Escape key was pressed, then
        // destroy the main application window.
    case WM_KEYDOWN:
        if( wParam == VK_ESCAPE )
            DestroyWindow(ghMainWnd);
        return 0;

        // In the case of a destroy message, then send a
        // quit message, which will terminate the message loop.
    case WM_DESTROY:
        PostQuitMessage(0);
        return 0;
    }

    // Forward any other messages we did not handle above to the
    // default window procedure. Note that our window procedure
    // must return the return value of DefWindowProc.
    return DefWindowProc(hWnd, msg, wParam, lParam);
}
```

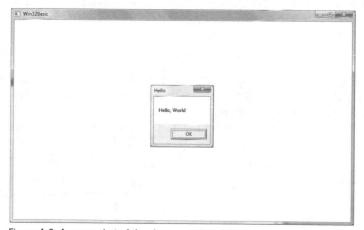

Figure A.3: A screenshot of the above program. Note that the message box appears when you press the left mouse button in the window's client area. Also try exiting the program by pressing the Escape key.

A.3 **Explaining the Basic Windows Application**

We will examine the code from top to bottom, stepping into any function that gets called along the way. Refer back to the code listing above throughout the following subsections.

A.3.1 **Includes, Global Variables, and Prototypes**

The first thing we do is include the *windows.h* header file. By including the *windows.h* file we obtain the structures, types, and function declarations needed for using the basic elements of the Win32 API.

```
#include <windows.h>
```

The second statement is an instantiation of a global variable of type HWND. This stands for "handle to a window" or "window handle." In Windows programming, we often use handles to refer to objects maintained internally by Windows. In this sample, we will use an HWND to refer to our main application window maintained by Windows. We need to hold onto the handles of our windows because many calls to the API require that we pass in the handle of the window we want the API call to act on. For example, the call UpdateWindow takes one argument that is of type HWND that is used to specify the window to update. If we did not pass in a handle to it, the function would not know which window to update.

```
HWND ghMainWnd = 0;
```

The next three lines are function declarations. Briefly, InitWindowsApp creates and initializes our main application window, Run encapsulates the message loop for our application, and WndProc is our main window's window procedure. We will examine these functions in more detail when we come to the point where they are called.

```
bool InitWindowsApp(HINSTANCE instanceHandle, int show);
int  Run();
LRESULT CALLBACK
WndProc(HWND hWnd, UINT msg, WPARAM wParam, LPARAM lParam);
```

A.3.2 **WinMain**

WinMain is the Windows equivalent to the main function in normal C++ programming. WinMain is prototyped as follows:

```
int WINAPI
WinMain(HINSTANCE hInstance, HINSTANCE hPrevInstance,
    PSTR pCmdLine, int nShowCmd)
```

■ hInstance: Handle to the current application instance. It serves as a way of identifying and referring to this application. Remember that there may be several Windows applications running concurrently, so it is useful to be able to refer to each one.

- `hPrevInstance`: Not used in Win32 programming and is 0.
- `pCmdLine`: The command line argument string used to run the program.
- `nShowCmd`: Specifies how the application should be displayed. Some common commands that show the window in its current size and position, maximized, and minimized, respectively, are `SW_SHOW`, `SW_SHOWMAXIMIZED`, and `SW_SHOWMINIMIZED`. See the MSDN library for a complete list of show commands.

If `WinMain` succeeds, it should return the `wParam` member of the `WM_QUIT` message. If the function exits without entering the message loop, it should return 0. The `WINAPI` identifier is defined as:

```
#define WINAPI    __stdcall
```

This specifies the calling convention of the function, which means how the function arguments get placed on the stack.

A.3.3 WNDCLASS and Registration

Inside `WinMain` we call the function `InitWindowsApp`. As you can guess, this function does all the initialization of our program. Let's take a closer look at this function and its implementation. `InitWindowsApp` returns either `true` or `false` — `true` if the initialization was a success and `false` otherwise. In the `WinMain` definition, we pass as arguments a copy of our application instance and the show command variable into `InitWindowsApp`. Both are obtained from the `WinMain` parameter list.

```
if(!InitWindowsApp(hInstance, nShowCmd))
```

The first task at hand in initialization of a window is to describe some basic properties of the window by filling out a `WNDCLASS` (window class) structure. Its definition is:

```
typedef struct _WNDCLASS {
    UINT     style;
    WNDPROC  lpfnWndProc;
    int      cbClsExtra;
    int      cbWndExtra;
    HANDLE   hInstance;
    HICON    hIcon;
    HCURSOR  hCursor;
    HBRUSH   hbrBackground;
    LPCTSTR  lpszMenuName;
    LPCTSTR  lpszClassName;
} WNDCLASS;
```

- `style`: Specifies the class style. In our example we use `CS_HREDRAW` combined with `CS_VREDRAW`. These two-bit flags indicate that the window is to be repainted when either the horizontal or vertical window size is changed. For the complete list and description of the various styles, see the MSDN library.

```
wc.style = CS_HREDRAW | CS_VREDRAW;
```

■ lpfnWndProc: Pointer to the window procedure function to associate with this WNDCLASS instance. Windows that are created based on this WNDCLASS instance will use this window procedure. Thus, to create two windows with the same window procedure, you just create the two windows based on the same WNDCLASS instance. If you want to create two windows with different window procedures, you will need to fill out a different WNDCLASS instance for each of the two windows. The window procedure function is explained in §A.3.6.

```
wc.lpfnWndProc = WndProc;
```

■ cbClsExtra and cbWndExtra: These are extra memory slots you can use for your own purpose. Our program does not require any extra space and therefore sets both of these to 0.

```
wc.cbClsExtra = 0;
wc.cbWndExtra = 0;
```

■ hInstance: This field is a handle to the application instance. Recall the application instance handle is originally passed in through WinMain.

```
wc.hInstance = instanceHandle;
```

■ hIcon: Here you specify a handle to an icon to use for the windows created using this window class. You can use your own icon design, but there are several built-in icons to choose from; see the MSDN library for details. The following uses the default application icon:

```
wc.hIcon = LoadIcon(0, IDI_APPLICATION);
```

■ hCursor: Similar to hIcon, here you specify a handle to a cursor to use when the cursor is over the window's client area. Again, there are several built-in cursors; see the MSDN library for details. The following code uses the standard "arrow" cursor.

```
wc.hCursor = LoadCursor(0, IDC_ARROW);
```

■ hbrBackground: This field is used to specify a handle to a brush, which specifies the background color for the client area of the window. In our sample code we call the Win32 function GetStockObject, which returns a handle to a prebuilt white colored brush; see the MSDN library for other types of built-in brushes.

```
wc.hbrBackground = (HBRUSH)GetStockObject(WHITE_BRUSH);
```

■ lpszMenuName: Specifies the window's menu. Since we have no menu in our application, we set this to 0.

```
wc.lpszMenuName  = 0;
```

- `lpszClassName`: Specifies the name of the window class structure we are creating. This can be anything you want. In our application, we named it BasicWndClass. The name is simply used to identify the class structure so that we can reference it later by its name.

```
wc.lpszClassName = L"BasicWndClass";
```

Once we have filled out a `WNDCLASS` instance, we need to register it with Windows so that we can create windows based on it. This is done with the `RegisterClass` function, which takes a pointer to a `WNDCLASS` structure. This function returns 0 upon failure.

```
if(!RegisterClass(&wc))
{
    MessageBox(0, L"RegisterClass FAILED", 0, 0);
    return false;
}
```

A.3.4 Creating and Displaying the Window

After we have registered a `WNDCLASS` variable with Windows we can create a window based on that class description. We can refer to a registered `WNDCLASS` instance via the class name we gave it (`lpszClassName`). The function we use to create a window is the `CreateWindow` function, which is declared as follows:

```
HWND CreateWindow(
    LPCTSTR lpClassName,
    LPCTSTR lpWindowName,
    DWORD dwStyle,
    int x,
    int y,
    int nWidth,
    int nHeight,
    HWND hWndParent,
    HMENU hMenu,
    HANDLE hInstance,
    LPVOID lpParam
);
```

- `lpClassName`: The name of the registered `WNDCLASS` structure that describes some of the properties of the window we want to create.

- `lpWindowName`: The name we want to give our window; this is also the name that appears in the window's caption bar.

- `dwStyle`: Defines the style of the window. `WS_OVERLAPPEDWINDOW` is a combination of several flags: `WS_OVERLAPPED`, `WS_CAPTION`, `WS_SYSMENU`, `WS_THICKFRAME`, `WS_MINIMIZEBOX`, and `WS_MAXIMIZEBOX`. The names of these flags describe the characteristics of the window they produce. See the MSDN library for the complete list of styles.

- **x**: The *x* position at the top-left corner of the window relative to the screen. You can specify `CW_USEDEFAULT` for this parameter, and Windows will choose an appropriate default.

- **y**: The *y* position at the top-left corner of the window relative to the screen. You can specify `CW_USEDEFAULT` for this parameter, and Windows will choose an appropriate default.

- **nWidth**: The width of the window in pixels. You can specify `CW_USEDEFAULT` for this parameter, and Windows will choose an appropriate default.

- **nHeight**: The height of the window in pixels. You can specify `CW_USEDEFAULT` for this parameter, and Windows will choose an appropriate default.

- **hWndParent**: Handle to a window that is to be the parent of this window. Our window has no relationship with any other windows, and therefore we set this value to 0.

- **hMenu**: A handle to a menu. Our program does not use a menu, so we specify 0 for this field.

- **hInstance**: Handle to the application the window will be associated with.

- **lpParam**: A pointer to user-defined data that you want to be available to a `WM_CREATE` message handler. The `WM_CREATE` message is sent to a window when it is being created, but before `CreateWindow` returns. A window handles the `WM_CREATE` message if it wants to do something when it is created (e.g., initialization).

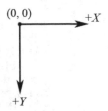

Note: When we specify the *x*- and *y*-coordinates of the window's position, they are relative to the upper-left corner of the screen. Also, the positive *x*-axis runs to the right as usual but the positive *y*-axis runs downward. Figure A.4 shows this coordinate system, which is called *screen coordinates*, or *screen space*.

Figure A.4: Screen space.

`CreateWindow` returns a handle to the window it creates (an `HWND`). If the creation failed, the handle will have the value of 0 (null handle). Remember that the handle is a way to refer to the window, which is managed by Windows. Many of the API calls require a `HWND` so that it knows what window to act on.

```
ghMainWnd = CreateWindow(L"BasicWndClass", L"Win32Basic",
    WS_OVERLAPPEDWINDOW,
    CW_USEDEFAULT, CW_USEDEFAULT,
    CW_USEDEFAULT, CW_USEDEFAULT,
    0, 0, instanceHandle, 0);
if(ghMainWnd == 0)
{
    MessageBox(0, L"CreateWindow FAILED", 0, 0);
```

```
    return false;
}
```

The last two function calls in the InitWindowsApp function have to do with displaying the window. First we call ShowWindow and pass in the handle of our newly created window so that Windows knows which window to show. We also pass in an integer value that defines how the window is to be initially shown (e.g., minimized, maximized, etc.). This value should be nShowCmd, which is a parameter of WinMain. After showing the window, we should refresh it. UpdateWindow does this; it takes one argument that is a handle to the window we wish to update.

```
ShowWindow(ghMainWnd, show);
UpdateWindow(ghMainWnd);
```

If we made it this far in InitWindowsApp, then the initialization is complete; we return true to indicate everything went successfully.

A.3.5 The Message Loop

Having successfully completed initialization we can begin the heart of the program — the message loop. In our Basic Windows Application example, we have wrapped the message loop in a function called Run.

```
int Run()
{
    MSG msg = {0};

    BOOL bRet = 1;
    while( (bRet = GetMessage(&msg, 0, 0, 0)) != 0 )
    {
        if(bRet == -1)
        {
            MessageBox(0, L"GetMessage FAILED", L"Error", MB_OK);
            break;
        }
        else
        {
            TranslateMessage(&msg);
            DispatchMessage(&msg);
        }
    }

    return (int)msg.wParam;
}
```

The first thing done in Run is an instantiation of a variable called msg of type MSG, which is the structure that represents a Windows message. Its definition is as follows:

```
typedef struct tagMSG {
    HWND    hwnd;
    UINT    message;
```

```
    WPARAM  wParam;
    LPARAM  lParam;
    DWORD   time;
    POINT   pt;
} MSG;
```

- hwnd: The handle to the window whose window procedure is to receive the message.

- message: A predefined constant value identifying the message (e.g., WM_QUIT).

- wParam: Extra information about the message. This is dependent upon the specific message.

- lParam: Extra information about the message. This is dependent upon the specific message.

- time: The time the message was posted.

- pt: The x- and y-coordinates of the mouse cursor, in screen coordinates, when the message was posted.

Next, we enter the message loop. The GetMessage function retrieves a message from the message queue, and fills out the msg argument with the details of the message. The second, third, and fourth parameters of GetMessage may be set to 0 for our purposes. If an error occurs in GetMessage, then GetMessage returns −1. If a WM_QUIT message is received, then GetMessage returns 0, thereby terminating the message loop. If GetMessage returns any other value, then two more functions get called: TranslateMessage and DispatchMessage. TranslateMessage has Windows perform some keyboard translations; specifically, virtual key to character messages. DispatchMessage finally dispatches the message to the appropriate window procedure.

If the application successfully exits via a WM_QUIT message, then the WinMain function should return the wParam of the WM_QUIT message (exit code).

A.3.6 The Window Procedure

We mentioned previously that the window procedure is where we write the code that we want to execute in response to a message our window receives. In the Basic Windows Application program, we name the window procedure WndProc and it is prototyped as:

```
LRESULT CALLBACK
WndProc(HWND hWnd, UINT msg, WPARAM wParam, LPARAM lParam);
```

This function returns a value of type LRESULT (defined as an integer), which indicates the success or failure of the function. The CALLBACK identifier specifies that the function is a *callback* function, which means that Windows will be calling this function outside of the code space of the program. As you can see from the Basic Windows Application source code, we never explicitly call the window procedure ourselves — Windows calls it for us when the window needs to process a message.

The window procedure has four parameters in its signature:

- hWnd: The handle to the window receiving the message.
- msg: A predefined value that identifies the particular message. For example, a quit message is defined as WM_QUIT. The prefix WM stands for "window message." There are over a hundred predefined window messages; see the MSDN library for details.
- wParam: Extra information about the message, which is dependent upon the specific message.
- lParam: Extra information about the message, which is dependent upon the specific message.

Our window procedure handles three messages: WM_LBUTTONDOWN, WM_KEYDOWN, and WM_DESTROY. A WM_LBUTTONDOWN message is sent when the user clicks the left mouse button on the window's client area. A WM_KEYDOWN message is sent to a window in focus when a key is pressed. A WM_DESTROY message is sent when a window is being destroyed.

Our code is quite simple; when we receive a WM_LBUTTONDOWN message, we display a message box that prints out "Hello, World":

```
case WM_LBUTTONDOWN:
    MessageBox(0, L"Hello, World", L"Hello", MB_OK);
    return 0;
```

When our window gets a WM_KEYDOWN message, we test if the Escape key was pressed, and if it was, we destroy the main application window using the DestroyWindow function. The wParam passed into the window procedure specifies the _virtual key code_ of the specific key that was pressed. Think of a virtual key code as an identifier for a particular key. The Windows header files have a list of virtual key code constants we can use to then test for a particular key; for example, to test if the Escape key was pressed, we use the virtual key code constant VK_ESCAPE.

```
case WM_KEYDOWN:
    if( wParam == VK_ESCAPE )
        DestroyWindow(ghMainWnd);
    return 0;
```

Remember that the wParam and lParam parameters are used to specify extra information about a particular message. For the WM_KEYDOWN message, wParam specifies the _virtual key code_ of the specific key that was pressed. The MSDN library will specify the information the wParam and lParam parameters carry for each Windows message.

When our window gets destroyed, we post a WM_QUIT message with the PostQuitMessage function (which terminates the message loop):

```
case WM_DESTROY:
    PostQuitMessage(0);
    return 0;
```

At the end of our window procedure, we call another function named DefWindowProc. This function is the default window procedure. In our Basic Windows Application program, we only handle three messages; we use the default behavior specified in DefWindowProc for all the other messages we receive but do not necessarily need to handle ourselves. For example, the Basic Windows Application program can be minimized, maximized, resized, and closed. This functionality is provided to us through the default window procedure, as we did not handle the messages to perform this functionality.

A.3.7 The MessageBox Function

There is one last API function we have not yet covered, and that is the MessageBox function. This function is a very handy way to provide the user with information and to get some quick input. The declaration to the MessageBox function looks like this:

```
int MessageBox(
    HWND hWnd,             // Handle of owner window, may specify null.
    LPCTSTR lpText,        // Text to put in the message box.
    LPCTSTR lpCaption,     // Text for the title of the message box.
    UINT uType             // Style of the message box.
);
```

The return value for the MessageBox function depends on the type of message box. See the MSDN library for a list of possible return values and styles; one possible style is a Yes/No message box, as shown in Figure A.5.

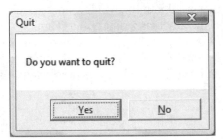

Figure A.5: Yes/No message box.

A.4 A Better Message Loop

Games are very different applications from traditional Windows applications such as office type applications and web browsers. Typically, games do not sit around waiting for a message, but are constantly being updated. This presents a problem, because if there are no messages in the message queue, the function GetMessage puts the thread to sleep and waits for a message. For a game, we do not want this behavior; if there are no Windows messages to be processed, then we want to run our own game code. The fix is to use the PeekMessage function instead of GetMessage. The PeekMessage function returns immediately if there are no messages. Our new message loop is as follows:

```
int Run()
{
    MSG msg = {0};

    while(msg.message != WM_QUIT)
    {
        // If there are Window messages then process them.
        if(PeekMessage( &msg, 0, 0, 0, PM_REMOVE ))
        {
            TranslateMessage( &msg );
            DispatchMessage( &msg );
        }
        // Otherwise, do animation/game stuff.
        else
        {

        }
    }
    return (int)msg.wParam;
}
```

After we instantiate msg we enter into an endless loop. We first call the API function PeekMessage, which checks the message queue for a message. See the MSDN library for the parameter descriptions. If there is a message, it returns true and we handle the message. If there are no messages, PeekMessage returns false, and we execute our own specific game code.

A.5 **Summary**

- To use Direct3D we must create a Windows application that has a main window onto which we can render our 3D scenes. Furthermore, for games we create a special message loop that checks for messages. If there are messages, it processes them; otherwise, it executes our game logic.

- Several Windows applications can be running concurrently, and therefore Windows must manage resources between them and direct messages to the applications for which they were intended. Messages are sent to an application's message queue when an event (keypress, mouse click, timer, etc.) has occurred for that application.

- Every Windows application has a message queue in which messages an application receives are stored. The application's message loop constantly checks the queue for messages and dispatches them to their intended window procedure. Note that a single application can have several windows within it.

- The window procedure is a special callback function we implement that Windows calls when a window in our application receives a message. In the window procedure we write the code we want to be executed when a window in our application receives a particular message. Messages we do not specifically handle are forwarded to a default window procedure for default handling.

A.6 **Exercises**

1. Modify the program in §A.2 to use a different icon, cursor, and background color. (*Hint*: Look up the LoadIcon, LoadCursor, and GetStockObject functions in the MSDN library.)

2. Modify the program in §A.2 by handling the WM_CLOSE message. This message is sent to a window or application indicating that the window or application should close. Use the MessageBox function to ask the users if they really want to exit by displaying a Yes/No styled message box. If the user chooses "Yes," then destroy the window; otherwise, do not destroy the window. You could also use this technique to ask the users if they want to save their work before closing.

3. Modify the program in §A.2 by handling the WM_CREATE message. This message is sent to a window when it is being created, but before CreateWindow returns. Output a message, via the MessageBox function, indicating that the window has been created.

4. Look up the Sleep function in the MSDN library and summarize, in your own words, what the function does.

5. Look up the messages WM_SIZE and WM_ACTIVATE in the MSDN library and summarize, in your own words, when the messages are sent.

Appendix B

High-Level Shading Language Reference

B.1 **Variable Types**

B.1.1 **Scalar Types**

- bool: True or false value. Note that the HLSL provides the true and false keywords like in C++.
- int: 32-bit signed integer.
- half: 16-bit floating-point number.
- float: 32-bit floating-point number.
- double: 64-bit floating-point number.

Note: Some platforms might not support int, half, and double. If this is the case these types will be emulated using float.

B.1.2 **Vector Types**

- float2: 2D vector, where the components are of type float.
- float3: 3D vector, where the components are of type float.
- float4: 4D vector, where the components are of type float.

Note: You can create vectors where the components are of a type other than float, such as int2, half3, and bool4.

We can initialize a vector using array-like syntax or constructor-like syntax:

```
float3 v = {1.0f, 2.0f, 3.0f};
float2 w = float2(x, y);
float4 u = float4(w, 3.0f, 4.0f); // u = (w.x, w.y, 3.0f, 4.0f)
```

We can access a component of a vector using an array subscript syntax. For example, to set the ith component of a vector vec, we would write:

```
vec[i] = 2.0f;
```

In addition, we can access the components of a vector vec, as we would access the members of a structure, using the defined component names x, y, z, w, r, g, b, and a.

```
vec.x = vec.r = 1.0f;
vec.y = vec.g = 2.0f;
vec.z = vec.b = 3.0f;
vec.w = vec.a = 4.0f;
```

The names r, g, b, and a refer to the exact same component as the names x, y, z, and w, respectively. When using vectors to represent colors, the RGBA notation is more desirable since it reinforces the fact that the vector is representing a color.

B.1.2.1 Swizzles

Consider the vector $\mathbf{u} = (u_x, u_y, u_z, u_w)$ and suppose we want to copy the components of $\mathbf{u}$ to a vector $\mathbf{v}$ such that $\mathbf{v} = (u_w, u_y, u_y, u_x)$. The most immediate solution would be to individually copy each component of $\mathbf{u}$ over to $\mathbf{v}$ as necessary. However, the HLSL provides a special syntax for doing these kinds of out-of-order copies called *swizzles*:

```
float4 u = {1.0f, 2.0f, 3.0f, 4.0f};
float4 v = {0.0f, 0.0f, 5.0f, 6.0f};

v = u.wyyx; // v = {4.0f, 2.0f, 2.0f, 1.0f}
```

Another example:

```
float4 u = {1.0f, 2.0f, 3.0f, 4.0f};
float4 v = {0.0f, 0.0f, 5.0f, 6.0f};

v = u.wzyx; // v = {4.0f, 3.0f, 2.0f, 1.0f}
```

When copying vectors, we do not have to copy every component. For example, we can copy only the x- and y-components, as this code snippet illustrates:

```
float4 u = {1.0f, 2.0f, 3.0f, 4.0f};
float4 v = {0.0f, 0.0f, 5.0f, 6.0f};

v.xy = u; // v = {1.0f, 2.0f, 5.0f, 6.0f}
```

B.1.3 **Matrix Types**

We can define an $m \times n$ matrix, where m and n are from 1 to 4, using the following syntax:

```
floatmxn matmxn;
```

Examples:

- float2x2: 2×2 matrix, where the entries are of type float.
- float3x3: 3×3 matrix, where the entries are of type float.
- float4x4: 4×4 matrix, where the entries are of type float.
- float3x4: 3×4 matrix, where the entries are of type float.

Note: You can create matrices where the components are of a type other than float, such as int2x2, half3x3, and bool4x4.

We can access an entry in a matrix using a double array subscript syntax. For example, to set the *ij*th entry of a matrix M we would write:

```
M[i][j] = value;
```

In addition, we can refer to the entries of a matrix M as we would access the members of a structure. The following entry names are defined:

One-based indexing:

```
M._11 = M._12 = M._13 = M._14 = 0.0f;
M._21 = M._22 = M._23 = M._24 = 0.0f;
M._31 = M._32 = M._33 = M._34 = 0.0f;
M._41 = M._42 = M._43 = M._44 = 0.0f;
```

Zero-based indexing:

```
M._m00 = M._m01 = M._m02 = M._m03 = 0.0f;
M._m10 = M._m11 = M._m12 = M._m13 = 0.0f;
M._m20 = M._m21 = M._m22 = M._m23 = 0.0f;
M._m30 = M._m31 = M._m32 = M._m33 = 0.0f;
```

Sometimes we want to refer to a particular row vector in a matrix. We can do so using a single array subscript syntax. For example, to extract the *i*th row vector in a 3×3 matrix M, we would write:

```
float3 ithRow = M[i]; // get the ith row vector in M
```

In this next example, we insert three vectors into the first, second, and third rows of a matrix:

```
float3 N = normalize(pIn.normalW);
float3 T = normalize(pIn.tangentW - dot(pIn.tangentW, N)*N);
float3 B = cross(N,T);
float3x3 TBN;
TBN[0] = T;  // sets row 1
TBN[1] = B;  // sets row 2
TBN[2] = N;  // sets row 3
```

We can also construct a matrix from vectors:

```
float3 N = normalize(pIn.normalW);
float3 T = normalize(pIn.tangentW - dot(pIn.tangentW, N)*N);
float3 B = cross(N,T);

float3x3 TBN = float3x3(T, B, N);
```

Note: Instead of using `float4` and `float4x4` to represent 4D vectors and matrices, you can equivalently use the `vector` and `matrix` type:

```
vector u = {1.0f, 2.0f, 3.0f, 4.0f};
matrix M; // 4x4 matrix
```

B.1.4 **Arrays**

We can declare an array of a particular type using familiar C++ syntax, for example:

```
float   M[4][4];
half    p[4];
float3  v[12]; // 12 3D vectors
```

B.1.5 **Structures**

Structures are defined exactly as they are in C++. However, structures in the HLSL cannot have member functions. Here is an example of a structure in the HLSL:

```
struct SurfaceInfo
{
float3 pos;
    float3 normal;
    float4 diffuse;
    float4 spec;
};

SurfaceInfo v;
litColor += v.diffuse;
dot(lightVec, v.normal);
float specPower  = max(v.spec.a, 1.0f);
```

B.1.6 **The typedef Keyword**

The HLSL `typedef` keyword functions exactly the same as it does in C++. For example, we can give the name `point` to the type `vector<float, 3>` using the following syntax:

```
typedef float3 point;
```

Then instead of writing:

```
float3 myPoint;
```

We can just write:

```
point myPoint;
```

Here is another example showing how to use the `typedef` keyword with the HLSL `const` keyword (which works the same in C++):

```
typedef const float CFLOAT;
```

B.1.7 **Variable Prefixes**

The following keywords can prefix a variable declaration.

- `static`: Essentially the opposite of `extern`; this means that the shader variable will not be exposed to the C++ application.

  ```
  static float3 v = {1.0f, 2.0f, 3.0f};
  ```

- `uniform`: This means that the variable does not change per vertex/pixel — it is constant for all vertices/pixels until we change it at the C++ application level. Uniform variables are initialized from outside the shader program (e.g., by the C++ application).

- `extern`: This means that the C++ application can see the variable (i.e., the variable can be accessed outside the shader file by the C++ application code). Global variables in a shader program are, by default, `uniform` and `extern`.

- `shared`: This is for sharing variables across multiple effect (.fx) files.

- `volatile`: Hints to the effect framework that the variable will be modified often. Only global variables can be prefixed with the `volatile` keyword.

- `const`: The `const` keyword in the HLSL has the same meaning it has in C++. That is, if a variable is prefixed with the `const` keyword, then that variable is constant and cannot be changed.

  ```
  const float pi = 3.14f;
  ```

B.1.8 **Casting**

The HLSL supports a very flexible casting scheme. The casting syntax in the HLSL is the same as in the C programming language. For example, to cast a `float` to a `matrix` we write:

```
float f = 5.0f;
float4x4 m = (float4x4)f; // copy f into each entry of m.
```

What this scalar-matrix cast does is copy the scalar into each entry of the matrix.

Consider the following example:

```
float3 n = float3(...);
float3 v = 2.0f*n - 1.0f;
```

The 2.0f*n is just scalar-vector multiplication, which is well defined. However, to make this a vector equation, the scalar 1.0f is augmented to the vector (1.0f, 1.0f, 1.0f). So the above statement is like:

```
float3 v = 2.0f*n - float3(1.0f, 1.0f, 1.0f);
```

For the examples in this book, you will be able to deduce the meaning of the cast from the syntax. For a complete list of casting rules, search the SDK documentation index for "Casting and Conversion."

B.2 **Keywords and Operators**

B.2.1 **Keywords**

For reference, here is a list of the keywords the HLSL defines:

asm	bool	compile	const	decl	do
double	else	extern	false	float	for
half	if	in	inline	inout	int
matrix	out	pass	pixelshader	return	sampler
shared	static	string	struct	technique	texture
true	typedef	uniform	vector	vertexshader	void
volatile	while				

This next set of keywords displays identifiers that are reserved and unused, but may become keywords in the future:

auto	break	case	catch	char	class
const_cast	continue	default	delete	dynamic_cast	enum
explicit	friend	goto	long	mutable	namespace
new	operator	private	protected	public	register
reinterpret_cast	short	signed	sizeof	static_cast	switch
template	this	throw	try	typename	union
unsigned	using	virtual			

B.2.2 **Operators**

HLSL supports many familiar C++ operators. With a few exceptions noted below, they are used exactly the same way as they are in C++. These are the HLSL operators:

[]	.	>	<	<=	>=
!=	==	!	&&	||	? :
+	+=	−	-=	*	*=
/	/=	%	%=	++	− −
=	()	,			

Although the operators' behavior is very similar to C++, there are some differences. First of all, the modulus operator (%) works on both integer and floating-point types. And, in order to use the modulus operator, both the left-hand-side value and right-hand-side value must have the same sign (e.g., both sides must be positive or both sides must be negative).

Secondly, observe that many of the HLSL operations work on a per-component basis. This is due to the fact that vectors and matrices are built into the language and these types consist of several components. By having the operations work on a component level, operations such as vector-matrix addition, vector-matrix subtraction, and vector/matrix equality tests can be done using the same operators we use for scalar types. See the following examples.

Note: The operators behave as expected for scalars, that is, in the usual C++ way.

```
float4 u = {1.0f, 0.0f, -3.0f, 1.0f};
float4 v = {-4.0f, 2.0f, 1.0f, 0.0f};


// adds corresponding components
float4 sum = u + v; // sum = (-3.0f, 2.0f, -2.0f, 1.0f)
```

Incremonting a vector increments each component:

```
// before increment: sum = (-3.0f, 2.0f, -2.0f, 1.0f)


sum++; // after increment: sum = (-2.0f, 3.0f, -1.0f, 2.0f)
```

Multiplying vectors componentwise:

```
float4 u = {1.0f, 0.0f, -3.0f, 1.0f};
float4 v = {-4.0f, 2.0f, 1.0f, 0.0f};


// multiply corresponding components
float4 product = u * v; // product = (-4.0f, 0.0f, -3.0f, 0.0f)
```

Warning: If you have two matrices:

```
float4x4 A;
float4x4 B;
```

The syntax A*B does componentwise multiplication, not matrix multiplication. You need to use the mul function for matrix multiplication.

Comparison operators are also done per component and return a vector or matrix where each component is of type bool. The resulting "bool" vector contains the results of each compared component. For example:

```
float4 u = { 1.0f, 0.0f, -3.0f, 1.0f};
float4 v = {-4.0f, 0.0f,  1.0f, 1.0f};


float4 b = (u == v); // b = (false, true, false, true)
```

Finally, we conclude by discussing variable promotions with binary operations:

- For binary operations, if the left-hand side and right-hand side differ in dimension, then the side with the smaller dimension is promoted (cast) to have the same dimension as the side with the larger dimension. For example, if x is of type `float` and y is of type `float3`, in the expression (x + y), the variable x is promoted to `float3` and the expression evaluates to a value of type `float3`. The promotion is done using the defined cast. In this case we are casting scalar-to-vector; therefore, after x is promoted to `float3`, x = (x, x, x) as the scalar-to-vector cast defines. Note that the promotion is not defined if the cast is not defined. For example, we can't promote `float2` to `float3` because there exists no such defined cast.

- For binary operations, if the left-hand side and right-hand side differ in type, then the side with the lower type resolution is promoted (cast) to have the same type as the side with the higher type resolution. For example, if x is of type `int` and y is of type `half`, in the expression (x + y), the variable x is promoted to a `half` and the expression evaluates to a value of type `half`.

B.3 **Program Flow**

The HLSL supports many familiar C++ statements for selection, repetition, and general program flow. The syntax of these statements is exactly like C++.

The return statement:

```
return (expression);
```

The if and if...else statements:

```
if( condition )
{
    statement(s);
}
if( condition )
{
    statement(s);
}
else
{
    statement(s);
}
```

The for statement:

```
for(initial; condition; increment)
{
    statement(s);
}
```

The while statement:

```
while( condition )
{
    statement(s);
}
```

The do...while statement:

```
do
{
    statement(s);
}
while( condition );
```

B.4 **Functions**

B.4.1 **User-Defined Functions**

Functions in the HLSL have the following properties:

- Functions use a familiar C++ syntax.
- Parameters are always passed by value.
- Recursion is not supported.
- Functions are always inlined.

Furthermore, the HLSL adds some extra keywords that can be used with functions. For example, consider the following function written in the HLSL:

```
bool foo(in const bool b, // input bool
         out int r1,       // output int
         inout float r2)   // input/output float
{
    if( b ) // test input value
    {
        r1 = 5; // output a value through r1
    }
    else
    {
        r1 = 1; // output a value through r1
    }

    // since r2 is inout we can use it as an input
    // value and also output a value through it
    r2 = r2 * r2 * r2;
```

```
    return true;
}
```

The function is almost identical to a C++ function except for the in, out, and inout keywords.

■ in: Specifies that the *argument* (particular variable we pass into a parameter) should be copied to the parameter before the function begins. It is not necessary to explicitly specify a parameter as in because a parameter is in by default. For example, the following are equivalent:

```
float square(in float x)
{
    return x * x;
}
```

And without explicitly specifying in:

```
float square(float x)
{
    return x * x;
}
```

■ out: Specifies that the parameter should be copied to the argument when the function returns. This is useful for returning values through parameters. The out keyword is necessary because the HLSL doesn't allow us to pass by reference or to pass a pointer. We note that if a parameter is marked as out the argument is not copied to the parameter before the function begins. In other words, an out parameter can only be used to output data — it can't be used for input.

```
void square(in float x, out float y)
{
    y = x * x;
}
```

Here we input the number to be squared through x and return the square of x through the parameter y.

■ inout: Shortcut that denotes a parameter as both in and out. Specify inout if you wish to use a parameter for both input and output.

```
void square(inout float x)
{
    x = x * x;
}
```

Here we input the number to be squared through x and also return the square of x through x.

B.4.2 **Built-in Functions**

The HLSL has a rich set of built in functions that are useful for 3D graphics. The following is an abridged list:

- `abs(x)` — Returns $|x|$.
- `ceil(x)` — Returns the smallest integer $\geq x$.
- `clamp(x, a, b)` — Clamps x to the range $[a, b]$ and returns the result.
- `clip(x)` — This function can only be called in a pixel shader; it discards the current pixel from further processing if $x < 0$.
- `cos(x)` — Returns the cosine of x, where x is in radians.
- `cross(u, v)` — Returns $u \times v$.
- `degrees(x)` — Converts x from radians to degrees.
- `determinant(M)` — Returns the determinant of a matrix.
- `distance(u, v)` — Returns the distance $\|v - u\|$ between the points u and v.
- `dot(u, v)` — Returns $u \cdot v$.
- `floor(x)` — Returns the greatest integer $\leq x$.
- `frac(x)` — This function returns the fractional part of a floating-point number (i.e., the mantissa). For example, if $x = (235.52, 696.32)$, then `frac(x)` = $(0.52, 0.32)$.
- `length(v)` — Returns $\|v\|$.
- `lerp(u, v, t)` — Linearly interpolates between u and v based on the parameter $t \in [0,1]$.
- `log(x)` — Returns $\ln(x)$.
- `log10(x)` — Returns $\log_{10}(x)$.
- `log2(x)` — Returns $\log_2(x)$.
- `max(x, y)` — Returns x if $x \geq y$, else returns y.
- `min(x, y)` — Returns x if $x \leq y$, else returns y.
- `mul(M, N)` — Returns the matrix product MN. Note that the matrix product MN must be defined. If M is a vector, it is treated as a row vector so that the vector-matrix product is defined. Likewise, if N is a vector, it is treated as a column vector so that the matrix-vector product is defined.
- `normalize(v)` — Returns $v/\|v\|$.
- `pow(b, n)` — Returns b^n.
- `radians(x)` — Converts x from degrees to radians.
- `saturate(x)` — Returns `clamp(x, 0.0, 1.0)`.
- `sin(x)` — Returns the sine of x, where x is in radians.
- `sincos(in x, out s, out c)` — Returns the sine and cosine of x, where x is in radians.

- `sqrt(x)` — Returns $\sqrt{x}$.
- `reflect(v, n)` — Computes the reflection vector given the incident vector *v* and the surface normal *n*.
- `refract(v, n, eta)` — Computes the refraction vector given the incident vector *v*, the surface normal *n*, and the ratio of the two indices of refraction of the two materials *eta*. Look up Snell's law in a physics book or on the Internet for information on refraction.
- `rsqrt(x)` — Returns $1/\sqrt{x}$.
- `tan(x)` — Returns the tangent of *x*, where *x* is in radians.
- `transpose(M)` — Returns the transpose M^T.
- `Texture2D::Sample(S, texC)` — Returns a color from a 2D texture map based on the `SamplerState` object *S* (recall a sampler state specifies texture filters and texture address modes), and 2D texture coordinates *texC*.
- `Texture2D::SampleLevel(S, texC, LOD)` — Returns a color from a 2D texture map based on the `SamplerState` object *S* (recall a sampler state specifies texture filters and texture address modes), and 2D texture coordinates *texC*. This function differs from `Texture2D::Sample` in that the third parameter specifies the mipmap level to use. For example, we would specify 0 to access the topmost mipmap LOD. Use this function to manually specify the mipmap level you want to sample.
- `TextureCube::Sample(S, v)` — Returns a color from a cube map based on the `SamplerState` object *S* (recall a sampler specifies texture filters and texture address modes) and 3D lookup vector *v*.

Note: Most of the functions are overloaded to work with all the built-in types for which the function makes sense. For instance, abs makes sense for all scalar types and so is overloaded for all of them. As another example, the cross product cross only makes sense for 3D vectors, so it is only overloaded for 3D vectors of any type (e.g., 3D vectors of ints, floats, doubles, etc.). On the other hand, linear interpolation, lerp, makes sense for scalars, 2D, 3D, and 4D vectors, and therefore is overloaded for all types.

Note: If you pass in a non-scalar type into a "scalar" function, that is, a function that traditionally operates on scalars (e.g., cos(x)), the function will act per component. For example, if you write:

```
float3 v = float3(0.0f, 0.0f, 0.0f);

v = cos(v);
```

Then the function will act per component: $\mathbf{v} = (\cos(x), \cos(y), \cos(z))$.

Note: For further reference, the complete list of the built-in HLSL functions can be found in the DirectX documentation. Search the index for "HLSL Intrinsic Functions."

Appendix C

Some Analytic Geometry

In this appendix, we use vectors and points as building blocks for more complicated geometry. These topics are used in the book, but not as frequently as vectors, matrices, and transformations; hence, we have put them in an appendix rather than in the main text.

C.1 Rays, Lines, and Segments

A line can be described by a point $\mathbf{p}_0$ on the line and a vector $\mathbf{u}$ that aims parallel to the line (see Figure C.1). The vector line equation is:

$$\mathbf{p}(t) = \mathbf{p}_0 + t\mathbf{u} \quad \text{for} \quad t \in \mathbb{R}$$

By plugging in different values for t (t can be any real number) we obtain different points on the line.

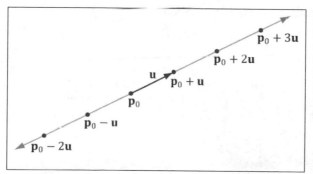

Figure C.1: A line described by a point $\mathbf{p}_0$ on the line and a vector $\mathbf{u}$ that aims parallel to the line. We can generate points on the line by plugging in any real number t.

If we restrict t to nonnegative numbers, then the graph of the vector line equation is a ray with origin $\mathbf{p}_0$ and direction $\mathbf{u}$ (see Figure C.2).

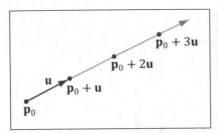

Figure C.2: A ray described by an origin $\mathbf{p}_0$ and direction $\mathbf{u}$. We can generate points on the ray by plugging in scalars for t that are greater than or equal to 0.

Now suppose we wish to define a line segment by the endpoints $\mathbf{p}_0$ and $\mathbf{p}_1$. We first construct the vector $\mathbf{u} = \mathbf{p}_1 - \mathbf{p}_0$ from $\mathbf{p}_0$ to $\mathbf{p}_1$ (see Figure C.3). Then, for $t \in [0,1]$, the graph of the equation $\mathbf{p}(t) = \mathbf{p}_0 + t\mathbf{u} = \mathbf{p}_0 + t(\mathbf{p}_1 - \mathbf{p}_0)$ is the line segment defined by $\mathbf{p}_0$ and $\mathbf{p}_1$. Note that if you go outside the range $t \in [0,1]$, then you get a point on the line that coincides with the segment, but is not on the segment.

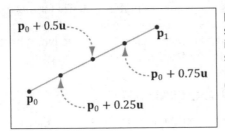

Figure C.3: We generate points on the line segment by plugging in different values for t in [0, 1]. For example, the midpoint of the line segment is given at $t = 0.5$. Also note that if $t = 0$, we get the endpoint $\mathbf{p}_0$ and if $t = 1$, we get the endpoint $\mathbf{p}_1$.

C.2 **Parallelograms**

Let $\mathbf{q}$ be a point, and $\mathbf{u}$ and $\mathbf{v}$ be two vectors that are not scalar multiples of one another (i.e., $\mathbf{u} \neq k\mathbf{v}$ for any scalar k). Then the graph of the following function is a parallelogram (see Figure C.4):

$$\mathbf{p}(s,t) = \mathbf{q} + s\mathbf{u} + t\mathbf{v} \quad \text{for} \quad s,t \in [0,1]$$

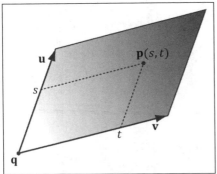

Figure C.4: Parallelogram. By plugging in different $s,t \in [0,1]$ we generate different points on the parallelogram.

Let's explore the reason for the "$\mathbf{u} \neq k\mathbf{v}$ for any scalar k" requirement: If $\mathbf{u} = k\mathbf{v}$, then we could write:

$$\mathbf{p}(s,t) = \mathbf{q} + s\mathbf{u} + t\mathbf{v}$$
$$= \mathbf{q} + sk\mathbf{v} + t\mathbf{v}$$
$$= \mathbf{q} + (sk + t)\mathbf{v}$$
$$= \mathbf{q} + \bar{t}\mathbf{v}$$

which is just the equation of a line. In other words, we only have one degree of freedom. To get a 2D shape like a parallelogram, we need two degrees of freedom, so the vectors $\mathbf{u}$ and $\mathbf{v}$ must not be scalar multiples of each another.

C.3 **Triangles**

The vector equation of a triangle is similar to that of the parallelogram equation, except that we restrict the domain of the parameters further:

$$\mathbf{p}(s,t) = \mathbf{q} + s\mathbf{u} + t\mathbf{v} \quad \text{for} \quad s \geq 0, t \geq 0, s + t \leq 1$$

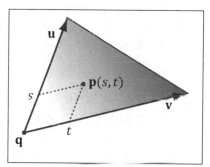

Figure C.5: Triangle. By plugging in different s, t such that $s \geq 0, t \geq 0, s + t \leq 1$, we generate different points on the triangle.

Observe from Figure C.5 that if any of the conditions on s and t do not hold, then $\mathbf{p}(s, t)$ will be a point "outside" the triangle, but on the plane of the triangle.

C.4 **Planes**

A *plane* can be viewed as an infinitely thin, infinitely wide, and infinitely long sheet of paper. A plane can be specified with a vector $\mathbf{n}$ and a point $\mathbf{p}_0$ on the plane. The vector $\mathbf{n}$, not necessarily unit length, is called the plane's *normal vector* and is perpendicular to the plane (see Figure C.6). A plane divides space into a *positive half-space* and a *negative half-space*. The positive half-space is the space in front of the plane, where the *front* of the plane is the side the normal vector emanates from. The negative half-space is the space behind the plane.

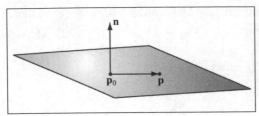

Figure C.6: A plane defined by a normal vector **n** and a point $\mathbf{p}_0$ on the plane. If $\mathbf{p}_0$ is a point on the plane, then the point **p** is also on the plane if and only if the vector $\mathbf{p} - \mathbf{p}_0$ is orthogonal to the plane's normal vector.

By Figure C.6, we see that the graph of a plane is all the points **p** that satisfy the *plane equation*:

$$\mathbf{n} \cdot (\mathbf{p} - \mathbf{p}_0) = 0$$

When describing a particular plane, the normal **n** and a known point $\mathbf{p}_0$ on the plane are fixed, so it is typical to rewrite the plane equation as:

$$\mathbf{n} \cdot (\mathbf{p} - \mathbf{p}_0) = \mathbf{n} \cdot \mathbf{p} - \mathbf{n} \cdot \mathbf{p}_0 = \mathbf{n} \cdot \mathbf{p} + d = 0$$

where $d = -\mathbf{n} \cdot \mathbf{p}_0$. If $\mathbf{n} = (a, b, c)$ and $\mathbf{p} = (x, y, z)$, then the plane equation can be written as:

$$ax + by + cz + d = 0$$

If the plane's normal vector **n** is of unit length, then $d = -\mathbf{n} \cdot \mathbf{p}_0$ gives the shortest *signed* distance from the origin to the plane (see Figure C.7).

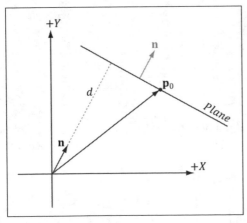

Figure C.7: Shortest distance from a plane to the origin.

Note: To make the figures easier to draw, we sometimes draw in 2D and use a line to represent a plane. A line, with a perpendicular normal, can be thought of as a 2D plane since the line divides the 2D space into a positive half-space and negative half-space.

C.4.1 **D3DXPlane**

When representing a plane in code, it suffices to store only the normal vector **n** and the constant d. It is useful to think of this as a 4D vector, which we denote as $(\mathbf{n}, d) = (a, b, c, d)$. The D3DX library uses the following structure for a plane:

```
typedef struct D3DXPLANE
{
#ifdef __cplusplus
public:
    D3DXPLANE() {}
    D3DXPLANE( CONST FLOAT* );
    D3DXPLANE( CONST D3DXFLOAT16* );
    D3DXPLANE( FLOAT a, FLOAT b, FLOAT c, FLOAT d );

    // casting
    operator FLOAT* ();
    operator CONST FLOAT* () const;

    // assignment operators
    D3DXPLANE& operator *= ( FLOAT );
    D3DXPLANE& operator /= ( FLOAT );

    // unary operators
    D3DXPLANE operator + () const;
    D3DXPLANE operator - () const;

    // binary operators
    D3DXPLANE operator * ( FLOAT ) const;
    D3DXPLANE operator / ( FLOAT ) const;

    friend D3DXPLANE operator * ( FLOAT, CONST D3DXPLANE& );

    BOOL operator == ( CONST D3DXPLANE& ) const;
    BOOL operator != ( CONST D3DXPLANE& ) const;

#endif //__cplusplus
    FLOAT a, b, c, d;
} D3DXPLANE, *LPD3DXPLANE;
```

C.4.2 **Point/Plane Spatial Relation**

Given any point **p**, observe from Figure C.6 and Figure C.8 that

- If $\mathbf{n} \cdot (\mathbf{p} - \mathbf{p}_0) = \mathbf{n} \cdot \mathbf{p} + d > 0$, then **p** is in front of the plane.

- If $\mathbf{n} \cdot (\mathbf{p} - \mathbf{p}_0) = \mathbf{n} \cdot \mathbf{p} + d < 0$, then **p** is behind the plane.

- If $\mathbf{n} \cdot (\mathbf{p} - \mathbf{p}_0) = \mathbf{n} \cdot \mathbf{p} + d = 0$, then **p** is on the plane.

These tests are useful for testing the spatial location of points relative to a plane.

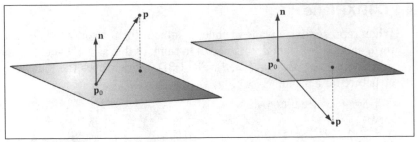

Figure C.8: Point/plane spatial relation.

The following D3DX function evaluates $\mathbf{n} \cdot \mathbf{p} + d$ for a particular plane and point:

```
FLOAT D3DXPlaneDotCoord(
    CONST D3DXPLANE *pP,    // plane.
    CONST D3DXVECTOR3 *pV   // point.
);

// Test the locality of a point relative to a plane.
D3DXPLANE p(0.0f, 1.0f, 0.0f, 0.0f);

D3DXVECTOR3 v(3.0f, 5.0f, 2.0f);

float x = D3DXPlaneDotCoord( &p, &v );

if( x approximately equals 0.0f ) // v is coplanar to the plane.
if( x > 0 )     // v is in positive half-space.
if( x < 0 )     // v is in negative half-space.
```

Note: We say "approximately equals" due to floating-point imprecision.

Note: Methods similar to `D3DXPlaneDotCoord` are `D3DXPlaneDot` and `D3DXPlaneDotNormal`. See the DirectX documentation for details.

C.4.3 Construction

Besides directly specifying the plane coefficients $(\mathbf{n}, d) = (a, b, c, d)$ we can calculate these coefficients in two other ways. Given the normal $\mathbf{n}$ and a known point on the plane $\mathbf{p}_0$, we can solve for the d component:

$$\mathbf{n} \cdot \mathbf{p}_0 + d = 0 \Rightarrow d = -\mathbf{n} \cdot \mathbf{p}_0$$

The D3DX library provides the following function to construct a plane from a point and normal in this way:

```
D3DXPLANE *D3DXPlaneFromPointNormal(
    D3DXPLANE* pOut,           // Result.
```

```
    CONST D3DXVECTOR3* pPoint, // Point on the plane.
    CONST D3DXVECTOR3* pNormal // The normal of the plane.
);
```

The second way we can construct a plane is by specifying three distinct points on the plane.

Given the points $\mathbf{p}_0$, $\mathbf{p}_1$, $\mathbf{p}_2$, we can form two vectors on the plane:

$$\mathbf{u} = \mathbf{p}_1 - \mathbf{p}_0$$
$$\mathbf{v} = \mathbf{p}_2 - \mathbf{p}_0$$

From that we can compute the normal of the plane by taking the cross product of the two vectors on the plane. (Remember the left-hand-thumb rule.)

$$\mathbf{n} = \mathbf{u} \times \mathbf{v}$$

Then, we compute $d = -\mathbf{n} \cdot \mathbf{p}_0$.

The D3DX library provides the following function to compute a plane given three points on the plane:

```
D3DXPLANE *D3DXPlaneFromPoints(
    D3DXPLANE* pOut,         // Result.
    CONST D3DXVECTOR3* pV1,  // Point 1 on the plane.
    CONST D3DXVECTOR3* pV2,  // Point 2 on the plane.
    CONST D3DXVECTOR3* pV3   // Point 3 on the plane.
);
```

C.4.4 Normalizing a Plane

Sometimes we might have a plane and would like to normalize the normal vector. At first thought, it would seem that we could just normalize the normal vector as we would any other vector. But recall that the d component also depends on the normal vector: $d = -\mathbf{n} \cdot \mathbf{p}_0$. Therefore, if we normalize the normal vector, we must also recalculate d. This is done as follows:

$$d' = \frac{d}{\|\mathbf{n}\|} = -\frac{\mathbf{n}}{\|\mathbf{n}\|} \cdot \mathbf{p}_0$$

Thus, we have the following formula to normalize the normal vector of the plane $(\mathbf{n}, d)$:

$$\frac{1}{\|\mathbf{n}\|}(\mathbf{n}, d) = \left(\frac{\mathbf{n}}{\|\mathbf{n}\|}, \frac{d}{\|\mathbf{n}\|} \right)$$

We can use the following D3DX function to normalize a plane's normal vector:

```
D3DXPLANE *D3DXPlaneNormalize(
    D3DXPLANE *pOut,        // Resulting normalized plane.
    CONST D3DXPLANE *pP     // Input plane.
);
```

C.4.5 **Transforming a Plane**

[Lengyel02] shows that we can transform a plane $(\mathbf{n}, d)$ by treating it as a 4D vector and multiplying it by the inverse-transpose of the desired transformation matrix. Note that the plane's normal vector must be normalized first.

We use the following D3DX function to do this:

```
D3DXPLANE *D3DXPlaneTransform(
    D3DXPLANE *pOut,        // Result
    CONST D3DXPLANE *pP,    // Input plane.
    CONST D3DXMATRIX *pM    // Transformation matrix.
);
```

Sample code:

```
D3DXMATRIX T(...);  // Initialize T to a desired transformation.
D3DXMATRIX inverseOfT;
D3DXMATRIX inverseTransposeOfT;

D3DXMatrixInverse( &inverseOfT, 0, &T );
D3DXMatrixTranspose( &inverseTransposeOfT, &inverseOfT );

D3DXPLANE p(...);  // Initialize plane.
D3DXPlaneNormalize( &p, &p ); // make sure normal is normalized.

D3DXPlaneTransform( &p, &p, &inverseTransposeOfT );
```

C.4.6 **Finding the Nearest Point on a Plane to a Given Point**

Suppose we have a point $\mathbf{p}$ in space and we would like to find the point $\mathbf{q}$ on the plane $(\mathbf{n}, d)$ that is closest to $\mathbf{p}$. From Figure C.9, we see that

$$\mathbf{q} = \mathbf{p} - \text{proj}_{\mathbf{n}}(\mathbf{p} - \mathbf{p}_0)$$

Assuming $\|\mathbf{n}\| = 1$ so that $\text{proj}_{\mathbf{n}}(\mathbf{p} - \mathbf{p}_0) = [(\mathbf{p} - \mathbf{p}_0) \cdot \mathbf{n}]\mathbf{n}$, we can rewrite this as:

$$\mathbf{q} = \mathbf{p} - [(\mathbf{p} - \mathbf{p}_0) \cdot \mathbf{n}]\mathbf{n}$$
$$= \mathbf{p} - (\mathbf{p} \cdot \mathbf{n} - \mathbf{p}_0 \cdot \mathbf{n})\mathbf{n}$$
$$= \mathbf{p} - (\mathbf{p} \cdot \mathbf{n} + d)\mathbf{n}$$

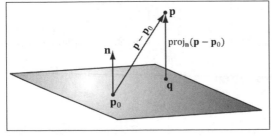

Figure C.9: The nearest point on a plane to a point $\mathbf{p}$. The point $\mathbf{p}_0$ is a point on the plane.

C.4.7 **Ray/Plane Intersection**

Given a ray $\mathbf{p}(t) = \mathbf{p}_0 + t\mathbf{u}$ and the equation of a plane $\mathbf{n} \cdot \mathbf{p} + d = 0$, we would like to know if the ray intersects the plane and also the point of intersection. To do this, we plug the ray into the plane equation and solve for the parameter t that satisfies the plane equation, thereby giving us the parameter that yields the intersection point:

$\mathbf{n} \cdot \mathbf{p}(t) + d = 0$	Plug ray into plane equation
$\mathbf{n} \cdot (\mathbf{p}_0 + t\mathbf{u}) + d = 0$	Substitute
$\mathbf{n} \cdot \mathbf{p}_0 + t\mathbf{n} \cdot \mathbf{u} + d = 0$	Distributive property
$t\mathbf{n} \cdot \mathbf{u} = -\mathbf{n} \cdot \mathbf{p}_0 - d$	Add $-\mathbf{n} \cdot \mathbf{p}_0 - d$ to both sides
$t = \dfrac{-\mathbf{n} \cdot \mathbf{p}_0 - d}{\mathbf{n} \cdot \mathbf{u}}$	Solve for t

If $\mathbf{n} \cdot \mathbf{u} = 0$, then the ray is parallel to the plane and there are either no solutions or infinite many solutions (infinite if the ray coincides with the plane). If t is not in the interval $[0, \infty)$, the ray does not intersect the plane, but the line coincident with the ray does. If t is in the interval $[0, \infty)$, then the ray does intersect the plane and the intersection point is found by evaluating the ray equation at $t_0 = \frac{-\mathbf{n} \cdot \mathbf{p}_0 - d}{\mathbf{n} \cdot \mathbf{u}}$.

C.4.8 **Reflecting Vectors**

Given a vector $\mathbf{I}$ we wish to reflect it about a plane with normal $\mathbf{n}$. Because vectors do not have positions, only the plane normal is involved when reflecting a vector. Figure C.10 shows the geometric situation, from which we conclude the reflection vector is given by:

$$\mathbf{r} = \mathbf{I} - 2(\mathbf{n} \cdot \mathbf{I})\mathbf{n}$$

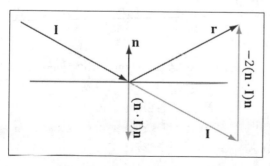

Figure C.10: Geometry of vector reflection.

C.4.9 **Reflecting Points**

Points reflect differently from vectors since points have position. Figure C.11 shows that the reflected point $\mathbf{q}$ is given by:

$$\mathbf{q} = \mathbf{p} - 2\mathrm{proj}_{\mathbf{n}}(\mathbf{p} - \mathbf{p}_0)$$

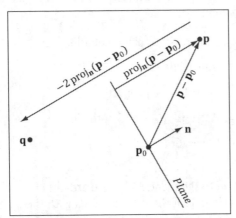

Figure C.11: Geometry of point reflection.

C.4.10 **Reflection Matrix**

Let $(\mathbf{n}, d) = (n_x, n_y, n_z, d)$ be the coefficients of a plane, where $d = -\mathbf{n} \cdot \mathbf{p}_0$. Then, using homogeneous coordinates, we can reflect both points and vectors about this plane using a single 4×4 reflection matrix:

$$\mathbf{R} = \begin{bmatrix} 1 - 2n_x n_x & -2n_x n_y & -2n_x n_z & 0 \\ -2n_x n_y & 1 - 2n_y n_y & -2n_y n_z & 0 \\ -2n_x n_z & -2n_y n_z & 1 - 2n_z n_z & 0 \\ -2dn_x & -2dn_y & -2dn_z & 1 \end{bmatrix}$$

This matrix assumes the plane is normalized so that

$$
\begin{aligned}
\mathit{proj}_{\mathbf{n}}(\mathbf{p} - \mathbf{p}_0) &= [\mathbf{n} \cdot (\mathbf{p} - \mathbf{p}_0)]\mathbf{n} \\
&= [\mathbf{n} \cdot \mathbf{p} - \mathbf{n} \cdot \mathbf{p}_0]\mathbf{n} \\
&= [\mathbf{n} \cdot \mathbf{p} + d]\mathbf{n}
\end{aligned}
$$

If we multiply a point by this matrix, we get the point reflection formula:

$$[p_x, p_y, p_z, 1] \begin{bmatrix} 1 - 2n_x n_x & -2n_x n_y & -2n_x n_z & 0 \\ -2n_x n_y & 1 - 2n_y n_y & -2n_y n_z & 0 \\ -2n_x n_z & -2n_y n_z & 1 - 2n_z n_z & 0 \\ -2dn_x & -2dn_y & -2dn_z & 1 \end{bmatrix}$$

$$
= \begin{bmatrix} p_x - 2p_x n_x n_x - 2p_y n_x n_y - 2p_z n_x n_z - 2dn_x \\ -2p_x n_x n_y + p_y - 2p_y n_y n_y - 2p_z n_y n_z - 2dn_y \\ -2p_x n_x n_z - 2p_y n_y n_z + p_z - 2p_z n_z n_z - 2dn_z \\ 1 \end{bmatrix}^T
$$

$$
= \begin{bmatrix} p_x \\ p_y \\ p_z \\ 1 \end{bmatrix}^T + \begin{bmatrix} -2n_x(p_x n_x + p_y n_y + p_z n_z + d) \\ -2n_y(p_x n_x + p_y n_y + p_z n_z + d) \\ -2n_z(p_x n_x + p_y n_y + p_z n_z + d) \\ 0 \end{bmatrix}^T
$$

$$
= \begin{bmatrix} p_x \\ p_y \\ p_z \\ 1 \end{bmatrix}^T + \begin{bmatrix} -2n_x(\mathbf{n} \cdot \mathbf{p} + d) \\ -2n_y(\mathbf{n} \cdot \mathbf{p} + d) \\ -2n_z(\mathbf{n} \cdot \mathbf{p} + d) \\ 0 \end{bmatrix}^T
$$

$$
= \mathbf{p} - 2[\mathbf{n} \cdot \mathbf{p} + d]\mathbf{n}
$$

$$
= \mathbf{p} - 2\mathrm{proj}_{\mathbf{n}}(\mathbf{p} - \mathbf{p}_0)
$$

Note: We take the transpose to turn row vectors into column vectors. This is just to make the presentation neater; otherwise, we would get very long row vectors.

And similarly, if we multiply a vector by this matrix, we get the vector reflection formula:

$$
[v_x, v_y, v_z, 0] \begin{bmatrix} 1 - 2n_x n_x & -2n_x n_y & -2n_x n_z & 0 \\ -2n_x n_y & 1 - 2n_y n_y & -2n_y n_z & 0 \\ -2n_x n_z & -2n_y n_z & 1 - 2n_z n_z & 0 \\ -2dn_x & -2dn_y & -2dn_z & 1 \end{bmatrix}
$$

$$
= \mathbf{v} - 2(\mathbf{n} \cdot \mathbf{v})\mathbf{n}
$$

The following D3DX matrix can be used to construct the above reflection matrix given a plane:

```
D3DXMATRIX * D3DXMatrixReflect(
    D3DXMATRIX *pOut,
    CONST D3DXPLANE *pPlane
);
```

C.5 **Exercises**

1. Let $\mathbf{p}(t) = (1, 1) + t(2, 1)$ be a ray relative to some coordinate system. Plot the points on the ray at $t = 0.0, 0.5, 1.0, 2.0,$ and 5.0.

2. Let $\mathbf{p}_0$ and $\mathbf{p}_1$ define the endpoints of a line segment. Show that the equation for a line segment can also be written as $\mathbf{p}(t) = (1-t)\mathbf{p}_0 + t\mathbf{p}_1$ for $t \in [0, 1]$.

3. Let $\mathbf{p}_0 = (0, 1, 0)$, $\mathbf{p}_1 = (-1, 3, 6)$, and $\mathbf{p}_2 = (8, 5, 3)$ be three points. Find the plane these points define.

4. Let $\left(\frac{1}{\sqrt{3}}, \frac{1}{\sqrt{3}}, \frac{1}{\sqrt{3}}, -5\right)$ be a plane. Define the locality of the following points relative to the plane: $\left(3\sqrt{3}, 5\sqrt{3}, 0\right)$, $\left(2\sqrt{3}, \sqrt{3}, 2\sqrt{3}\right)$, and $\left(\sqrt{3}, -\sqrt{3}, 0\right)$.

5. Let $\left(\frac{1}{\sqrt{3}}, \frac{1}{\sqrt{3}}, \frac{1}{\sqrt{3}}, -5\right)$ be a plane. Find the point on the plane nearest to the point $\left(2\sqrt{3}, 6\sqrt{3}, \sqrt{3}\right)$.

6. Let $\left(\frac{1}{\sqrt{3}}, \frac{1}{\sqrt{3}}, \frac{1}{\sqrt{3}}, -5\right)$ be a plane. Find the reflection of the point $\left(2\sqrt{3}, 6\sqrt{3}, \sqrt{3}\right)$ about the plane.

7. Let $\left(\frac{1}{\sqrt{3}}, \frac{1}{\sqrt{3}}, \frac{1}{\sqrt{3}}, -5\right)$ be a plane, and let $\mathbf{r}(t) = (-1, 1, -1) + t(1, 0, 0)$ be a ray. Find the point at which the ray intersects the plane. Then write a short program using the D3DXPlaneIntersectLine function (see the SDK documentation for the prototype) to verify your answer.

Bibliography and Further Reading

[Angel00] Angel, Edward. *Interactive Computer Graphics: A Top-Down Approach with OpenGL*, Second Edition. Addison-Wesley, 2000.

[Blinn78] Blinn, James F., and Martin E. Newell. "Clipping using Homogeneous Coordinates," *Computer Graphics (SIGGRAPH '78 Proceedings)*, pp 245-251. New York, 1978.

[Blinn96] Blinn, Jim. *Jim Blinn's Corner: A Trip Down the Graphics Pipeline*. Morgan Kaufmann Publishers, Inc., 1996.

[Brennan02] Brennan, Chris. "Accurate Reflections and Refractions by Adjusting for Object Distance," *Direct3D ShaderX: Vertex and Pixel Shader Tips and Tricks*. Wordware Publishing, Inc., 2002.

[Burg00] Burg, John van der. "Building an Advanced Particle System," *Gamasutra*, June 2000 (http://www.gamasutra.com/features/20000623/vanderburg_01.htm).

[De berg00] de Berg, M., M. van Kreveld, M. Overmars, and O. Schwarzkopf. *Computational Geometry: Algorithms and Applications Second Edition*. Springer-Verlag Berlin Heidelberg, 2000.

[Dietrich] Dietrich, Sim. "Texture Space Bump Maps" (http://developer.nvidia.com/object/texture_space_bump_mapping.html).

[Dunlop03] Dunlop, Robert. "FPS versus Frame Time," 2003 (http://www.mvps.org/directx/articles/fps_versus_frame_time.htm).

[DXSDK07] Microsoft DirectX November 2007 SDK Documentation, Microsoft Corporation, 2007.

[Eberly01] Eberly, David H. *3D Game Engine Design*. Morgan Kaufmann Publishers, Inc., 2001.

[Engel02] Engel, Wolfgang (Editor). *Direct3D ShaderX: Vertex and Pixel Shader Tips and Tricks*. Wordware Publishing, Inc., 2002.

[Engel04] Engel, Wolfgang (Editor). *ShaderX²: Shader Programming Tips & Tricks with DirectX 9*. Wordware Publishing, Inc., 2004.

[Engel06] Engel, Wolfgang (Editor). *ShaderX⁵: Advanced Rendering Techniques*. Charles River Media, Inc., 2006.

[Farin98] Farin, Gerald, and Dianne Hansford. *The Geometry Toolbox: For Graphics and Modeling*. AK Peters, Ltd., 1998.

[Fernando03] Fernando, Randima, and Mark J. Kilgard. *The CG Tutorial: The Definitive Guide to Programmable Real-Time Graphics*. Addison-Wesley, 2003.

[Fraleigh95] Fraleigh, John B., and Raymond A. Beauregard. *Linear Algebra 3rd Edition*. Addison-Wesley, 1995.

[Friedberg03] Friedberg, Stephen H., Arnold J. Insel, and Lawrence E. Spence. *Linear Algebra Fourth Edition*. Pearson Education, Inc., 2003.

[Halliday01] Halliday, David, Robert Resnick, and Jearl Walker. *Fundamentals of Physics: Sixth Edition*. John Wiley & Sons, Inc., 2001.

[Hausner98] Hausner, Melvin. *A Vector Space Approach to Geometry*. Dover Publications, Inc. (www.doverpublications.com), 1998.

[Hoffmann75] Hoffmann, Banesh. *About Vectors*. Dover Publications, Inc. (www.doverpublications.com), 1975.

[Kilgard99] Kilgard, Mark J. "Creating Reflections and Shadows Using Stencil Buffers," *Game Developers Conference*, NVIDIA slide presentation, 1999 (http://developer.nvidia.com/docs/IO/1407/ATT/stencil.ppt).

[Kilgard01] Kilgard, Mark J. "Shadow Mapping with Today's OpenGL Hardware," Computer Entertainment Software Association's CEDEC, NVIDIA presentation, 2001 (http://developer.nvidia.com/object/cedec_shadowmap.html).

[Kryachko05] Kryachko, Yuri. "Using Vertex Texture Displacement for Realistic Water Rendering," *GPU Gems 2: Programming Techniques for High-Performance Graphics and General Purpose Computation*. Addison-Wesley, 2005.

[Lengyel02] Lengyel, Eric. *Mathematics for 3D Game Programming and Computer Graphics*. Charles River Media, Inc., 2002.

[Möller02] Möller, Tomas, and Eric Haines. *Real-Time Rendering: Second Edition*. AK Peters, Ltd., 2002.

[Mortenson99] Mortenson, M.E. *Mathematics for Computer Graphics Applications*. Industrial Press, Inc., 1999.

[Parent02] Parent, Rick. *Computer Animation: Algorithms and Techniques*. Morgan Kaufmann Publishers (www.mkp.com), 2002.

[Pelzer04] Pelzer, Kurt. "Rendering Countless Blades of Waving Grass," *GPU Gems: Programming Techniques, Tips, and Tricks for Real-Time Graphics*. Addison-Wesley, 2004.

[Petzold99] Petzold, Charles. *Programming Windows*, Fifth Edition. Microsoft Press, 1999.

[Prosise99] Prosise, Jeff. *Programming Windows with MFC*, Second Edition. Microsoft Press, 1999.

[Santrock03] Santrock, John W. *Psychology 7*. The McGraw-Hill Companies, Inc., 2003.

[Savchenko00] Savchenko, Sergei. *3D Graphics Programming: Games and Beyond*. Sams Publishing, 2000.

[Schneider03] Schneider, Philip J., and David H. Eberly. *Geometric Tools for Computer Graphics*. Morgan Kaufmann Publishers (www.mkp.com), 2003.

[Snook03] Snook, Greg. *Real-Time 3D Terrain Engines using C++ and DirectX9*. Charles River Media, Inc., 2003.

[Sutherland74] Sutherland, I. E., and G. W. Hodgeman. "Reentrant Polygon Clipping," *Communications of the ACM,* 17(1):32-42, 1974.

[Uralsky05] Uralsky, Yuri. "Efficient Soft-Edged Shadows Using Pixel Shader Branching," *GPU Gems 2: Programming Techniques for High-Performance Graphics and General Purpose Computation*. Addison-Wesley, 2005.

[Verth04] Verth, James M. van, and Lars M. Bishop. *Essential Mathematics for Games & Interactive Applications: A Programmer's Guide*. Morgan Kaufmann Publishers (www.mkp.com), 2004.

[Watt92] Watt, Alan, and Mark Watt. *Advanced Animation and Rendering Techniques: Theory and Practice*. Addison-Wesley, 1992.

[Watt00] Watt, Alan. *3D Computer Graphics*, Third Edition. Addison-Wesley, 2000.

[Watt01] Watt, Alan, and Fabio Policarpo. *3D Games: Real-time Rendering and Software Technology*. Addison-Wesley, 2001.

[Weinreich98] Weinreich, Gabriel. *Geometrical Vectors*. The University of Chicago Press, 1998.

[Whatley05] Whatley, David. "Toward Photorealism in Virtual Botany," *GPU Gems 2: Programming Techniques for High-Performance Graphics and General Purpose Computation*. Addison-Wesley, 2005.

Index

Looking for More?

Check out Wordware's market-leading Graphics Applications and Programming Libraries featuring the following titles.

Essential 3ds Max 2008
1-59822-050-0 • $39.95
6 x 9 • 456 pp.

Making a Game Demo: From Concept to Demo Gold
1-55622-048-0 • $44.95
6 x 9 • 424 pp.

Word 2003 Document Automation with VBA, XML, XSLT and Smart Documents
1-55622-086-3 • $36.95
6 x 9 • 464 pp.

Excel 2003 VBA Programming with XML and ASP
1-55622-225-4 • $36.95
6 x 9 • 968 pp.

Advanced SQL Functions in Oracle 10g
1-59822-021-7 • $36.95
6 x 9 • 416 pp.

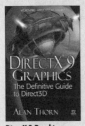

Photoshop CS3 for Screen Printers
1-59822-036-5 • $44.95
6 x 9 • 608 pp.

Web Designer's Guide to Adobe Photoshop
1-59822-001-2 • $29.95
6 x 9 • 272 pp.

Administrator's Guide to Sybase ASE 15
1-55622-360-9 • $44.95
6 x 9 • 488 pp.

LightWave 3D 8 Cartoon Character Creation Vol. 1: Modeling & Texturing
1-55622-253-X • $49.95
6 x 9 • 496 pp.

LightWave 3D 8 Cartoon Character Creation Vol. 2: Rigging & Animation
1-55622-254-8 • $49.95
6 x 9 • 440 pp.

DirectX 9 Graphics The Definitive Guide to Direct3D
1-55622-229-7 • $44.95
6 x 9 • 368 pp.

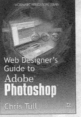

OpenGL Game Development
1-55622-989-5 • $44.95
6 x 9 • 496 pp.

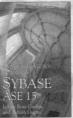

Modeling, UV Mapping, and Texturing 3D Game Weapons
1-55622-870-8 • $39.95
6 x 9 • 368 pp.

Polygonal Modeling: Basic and Advanced Techniques
1-59822-007-1 • $39.95
6 x 9 • 424 pp.

Maya 8.0 Character Modeling
1-59822-020-9 • $44.95
6 x 9 • 504 pp.

The Art of Flash Animation: Creative Cartooning
1-59822-026-8 • $34.95
6 x 9 • 480 pp.

LightWave v9 Texturing
1-59822-029-2 • $44.95
6 x 9 • 648 pp.

LightWave v9 Lighting
1-59822-039-X • $44.95
6 x 9 • 616 pp.

3ds max Lighting
1-55622-401-X • $49.95
6 x 9 • 432 pp.

The Mechanics of Anime and Manga
1-59822-019-5 • $29.95
7.25 x 10.25 • 328 pp.

Visit us online at **www.wordware.com** for more information.
Use the following coupon code for online specials: dx100535